THE UNOFFICIAL

HOLY BIBLE
FOR
MINECRAFTERS

A CHILDREN'S GUIDE TO THE OLD & NEW TESTAMENT

❮ GARRETT ROMINES AND CHRISTOPHER MIKO ❯

SKY PONY PRESS
NEW YORK

This book is not authorized or sponsored by Microsoft Corp., Mojang AB, Notch Development AB or Scholastic Inc., or any other person or entity owning or controlling rights in the Minecraft name, trademark, or copyrights.

Sky Pony Press books may be purchased in bulk at special discounts for sales promotion, corporate gifts, fund-raising, or educational purposes. Special editions can also be created to specifications. For details, contact the Special Sales Department, Sky Pony Press, 307 West 36th Street, 11th Floor, New York, NY 10018 or info@skyhorsepublishing.com.

Visit our website at www.skyponypress.com.

10 9 8 7 6 5

Library of Congress Cataloging-in-Publication Data is available on file.

Print ISBN: 978-1-63220-730-2
Ebook ISBN: 978-1-63220-731-9

Printed in Canada

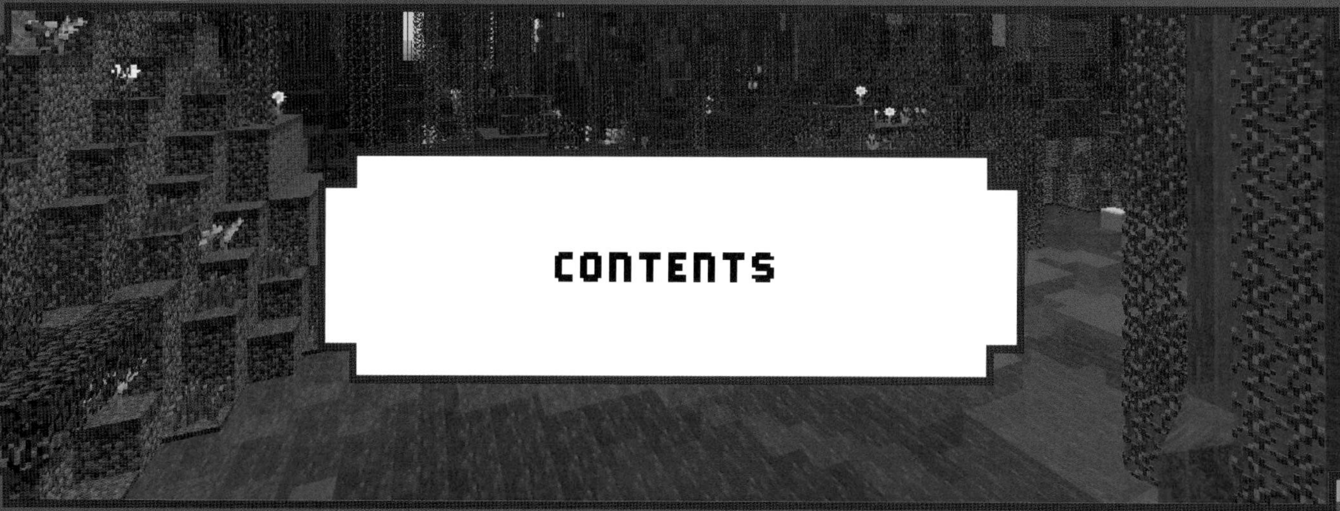

CONTENTS

FOREWORD

WE ARE ALL GOD-SEEKING PEOPLE from the time we are born. The Bible is God's story about Himself and His relationship with human beings. Children who wish to learn more about the Bible and about God are blessed children! Bible stories inspire young people to grow in ways beyond their imagination. They will use these stories to become wonderful human beings.

As parents, it can be difficult to get children to read the Bible. In the *Unofficial Holy Bible for Minecrafters*, children will engage the Bible in a way that they enjoy. God's story—from the creation to the birth of Jesus and beyond—is full of profound life lessons. There are many answers in this book to challenges children may be facing in their own lives. Kids will learn from these stories how to be strong and courageous. Jesus faced bullies and had allies. He experienced peer-pressure and had to become comfortable with his identity as the Son of God. The Bible is an essential part of knowing and learning about our true selves. Scripture provides a blueprint and structure for how to live a wonderful life.

The colorful illustrations in this marvelous work bring biblical characters to life in a way far beyond what I could have ever imagined having available to me as a child. The illustrations were created in the video game Minecraft and provide a unique setting for the stories. This also further teaches parents to embrace the new world of youth and gaming and learn how it can be used as a resource in education overall.

I encourage the Christian community to share this book with their loved ones and to facilitate further discussion about God and the Bible in their homes and communities. This book definitely makes it more fun!

TERRY A. SMITH,
Lead Pastor, The Life Christian Church

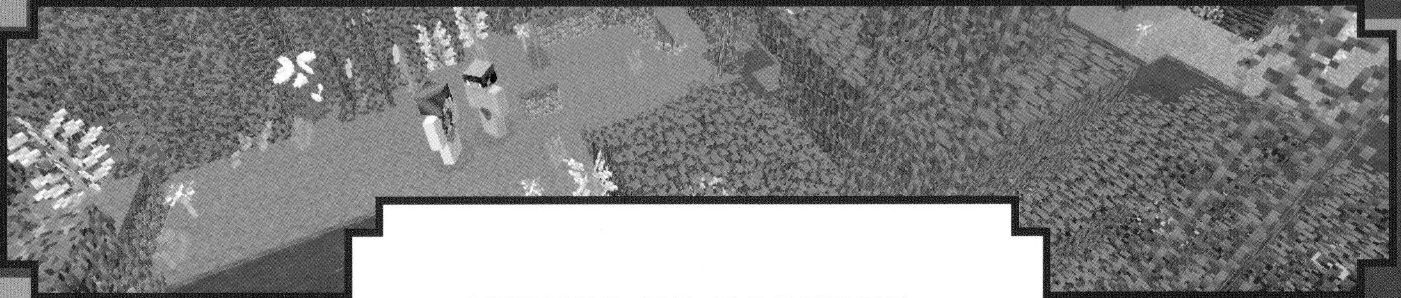

LETTER TO PARENTS

DEAR PARENTS,

If your child is one of the mass millions who enjoys playing Minecraft and you want to encourage your child to learn more and take a stronger interest in reading the Bible, *The Unofficial Holy Bible for Minecrafters: A Children's Guide to the Old & New Testament* provides an excellent opportunity to introduce Bible stories in a fun and exciting way.

This beautifully illustrated book, full of over 450 amazing images and significant stories will enable the child not to just read the Bible stories but to understand them in a way he or she can incorporate the messages into everyday decision-making.

As they read the stories of Moses, David, Mary, and more, they will explore competency, autonomy, and self-identity from a new perspective. The Minecraft game gives players the opportunity to be creative, solve problems, and interact. In many ways, that is what we want children to do with the Bible stories. Bible stories serve to teach our children about how God interacts in the world and how God would want us to interact in the world.

The Unofficial Holy Bible for Minecrafters: A Children's Guide to the Old & New Testament uses the world of Minecraft to capture the imagination of children and is cutting edge. It joins a long line of contemporary methods used to introduce the Bible to children.

Sincerely,
Rev. Dr. Wanda M. Lundry

THE CREATION STORY

Gabriel.

Yes, my Lord.

Do you see the vast blackness that stretches before us?

We shall begin with a big bang!
IN THE BEGINNING, GOD CREATED THE HEAVENS AND EARTH.

THE EARTH WAS WITHOUT FORM AND SHAPE. DARKNESS WAS ON THE FACE OF THE DEEP.

GOD CALLED THE LIGHT "DAY," AND THE DARKNESS "NIGHT," AND THE EVENING AND MORNING OF THE FIRST DAY PASSED.

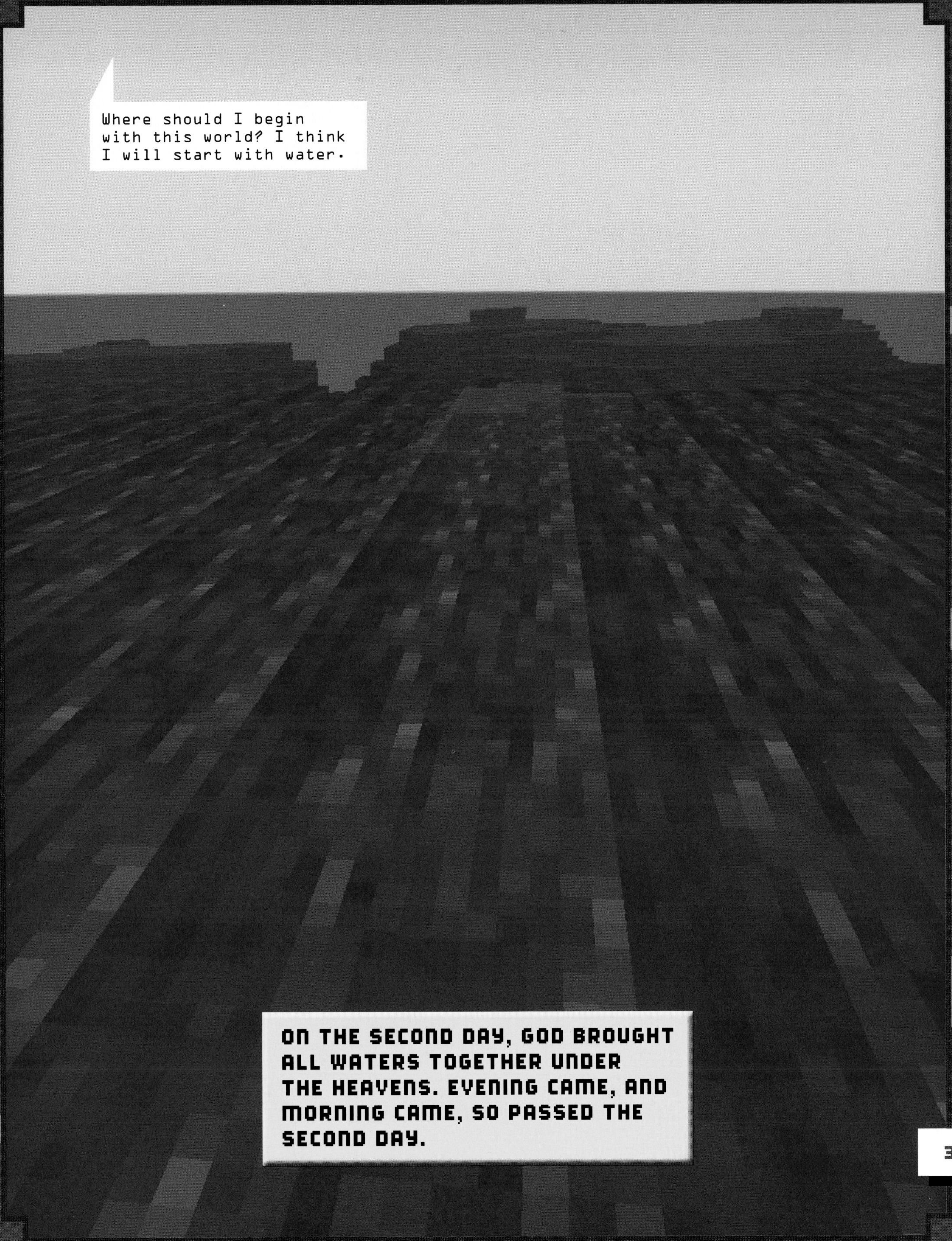
Where should I begin with this world? I think I will start with water.
ON THE SECOND DAY, GOD BROUGHT ALL WATERS TOGETHER UNDER THE HEAVENS. EVENING CAME, AND MORNING CAME, SO PASSED THE SECOND DAY.

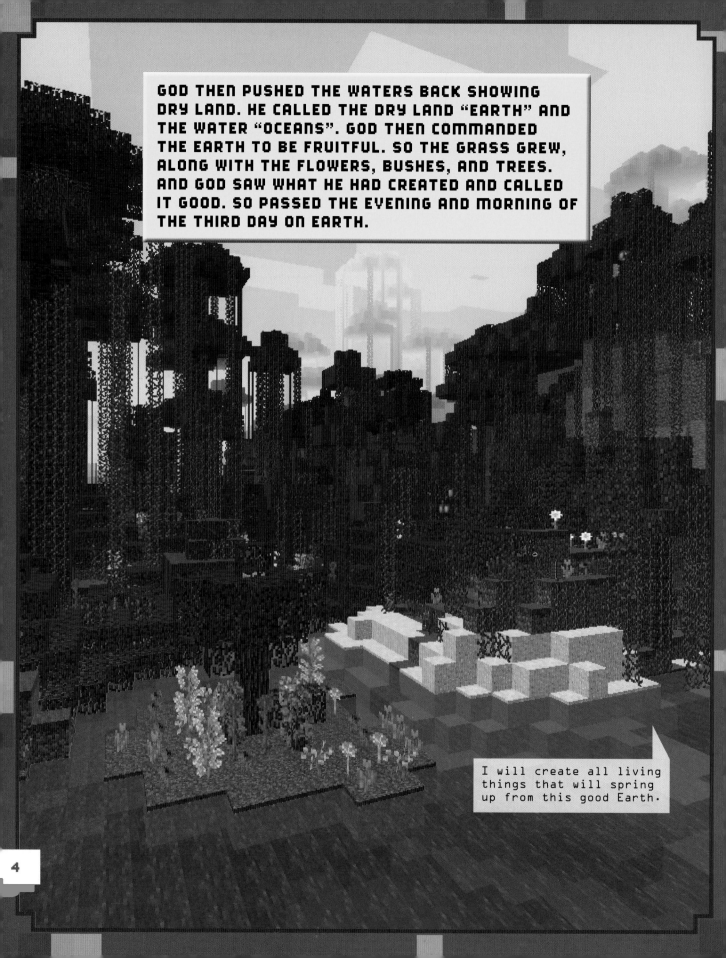

GOD THEN PUSHED THE WATERS BACK SHOWING DRY LAND. HE CALLED THE DRY LAND "EARTH" AND THE WATER "OCEANS". GOD THEN COMMANDED THE EARTH TO BE FRUITFUL. SO THE GRASS GREW, ALONG WITH THE FLOWERS, BUSHES, AND TREES. AND GOD SAW WHAT HE HAD CREATED AND CALLED IT GOOD. SO PASSED THE EVENING AND MORNING OF THE THIRD DAY ON EARTH.

I will create all living things that will spring up from this good Earth.

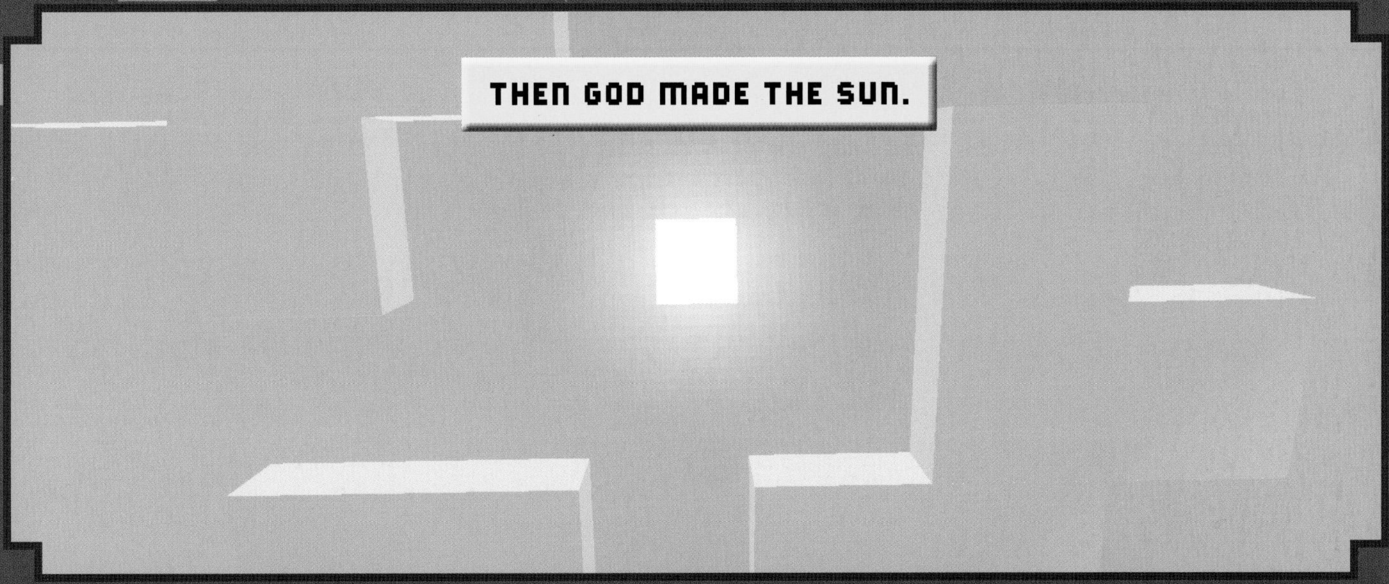
THEN GOD MADE THE SUN.

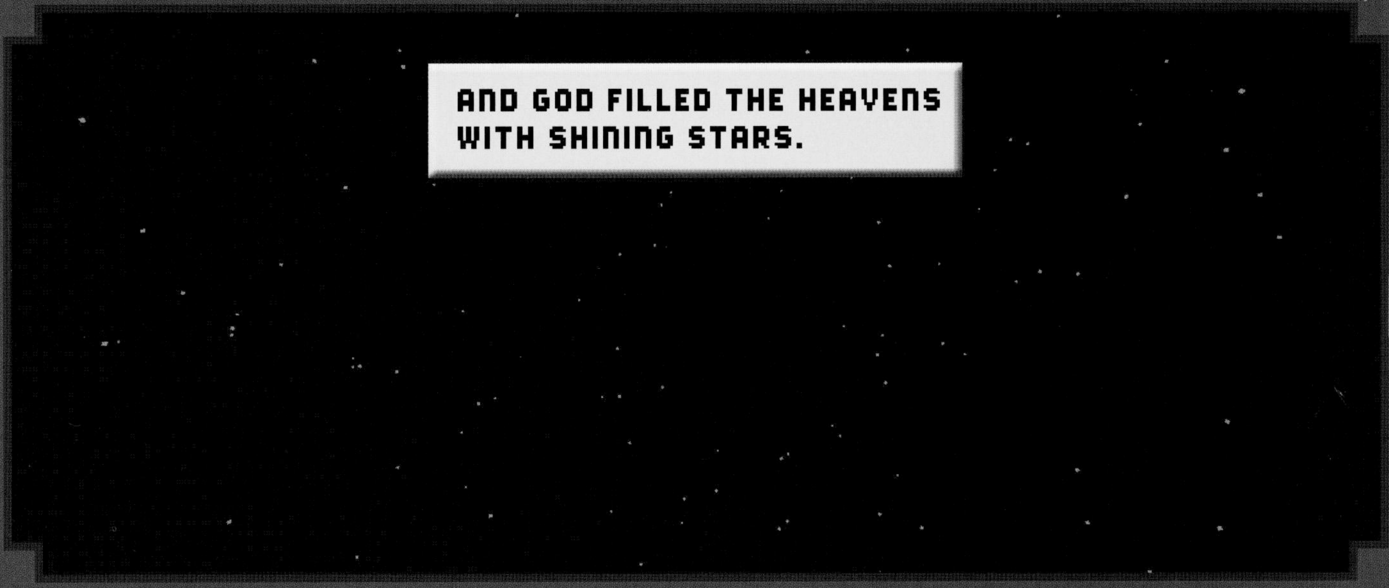
AND GOD FILLED THE HEAVENS WITH SHINING STARS.

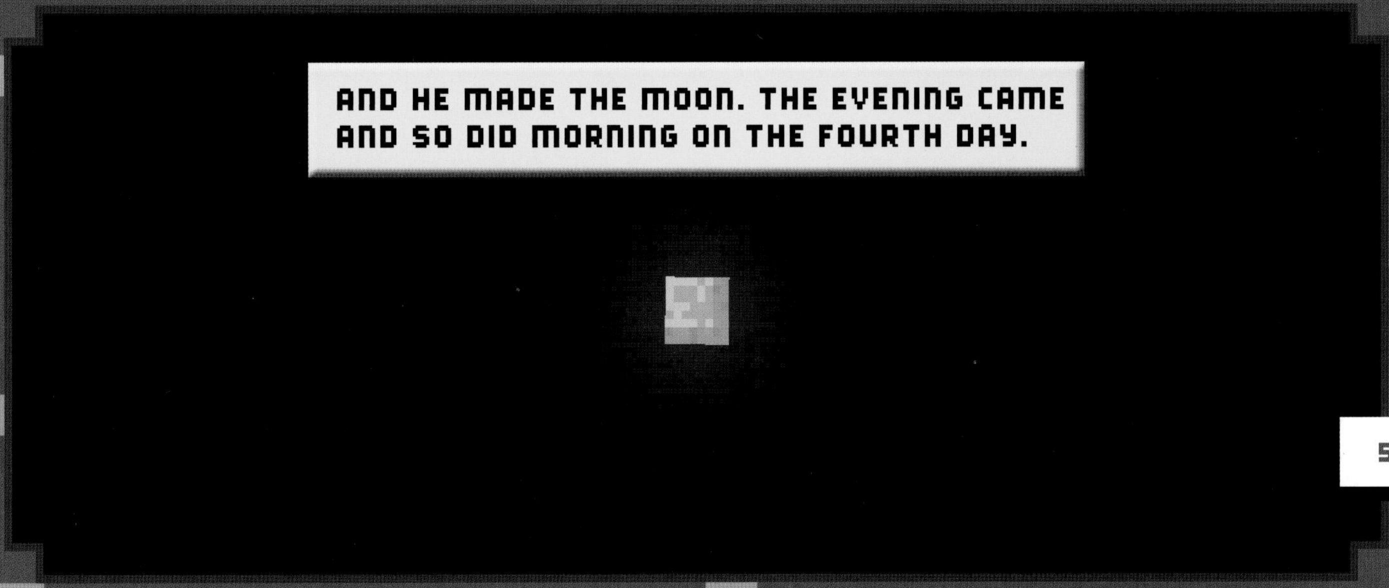
AND HE MADE THE MOON. THE EVENING CAME AND SO DID MORNING ON THE FOURTH DAY.

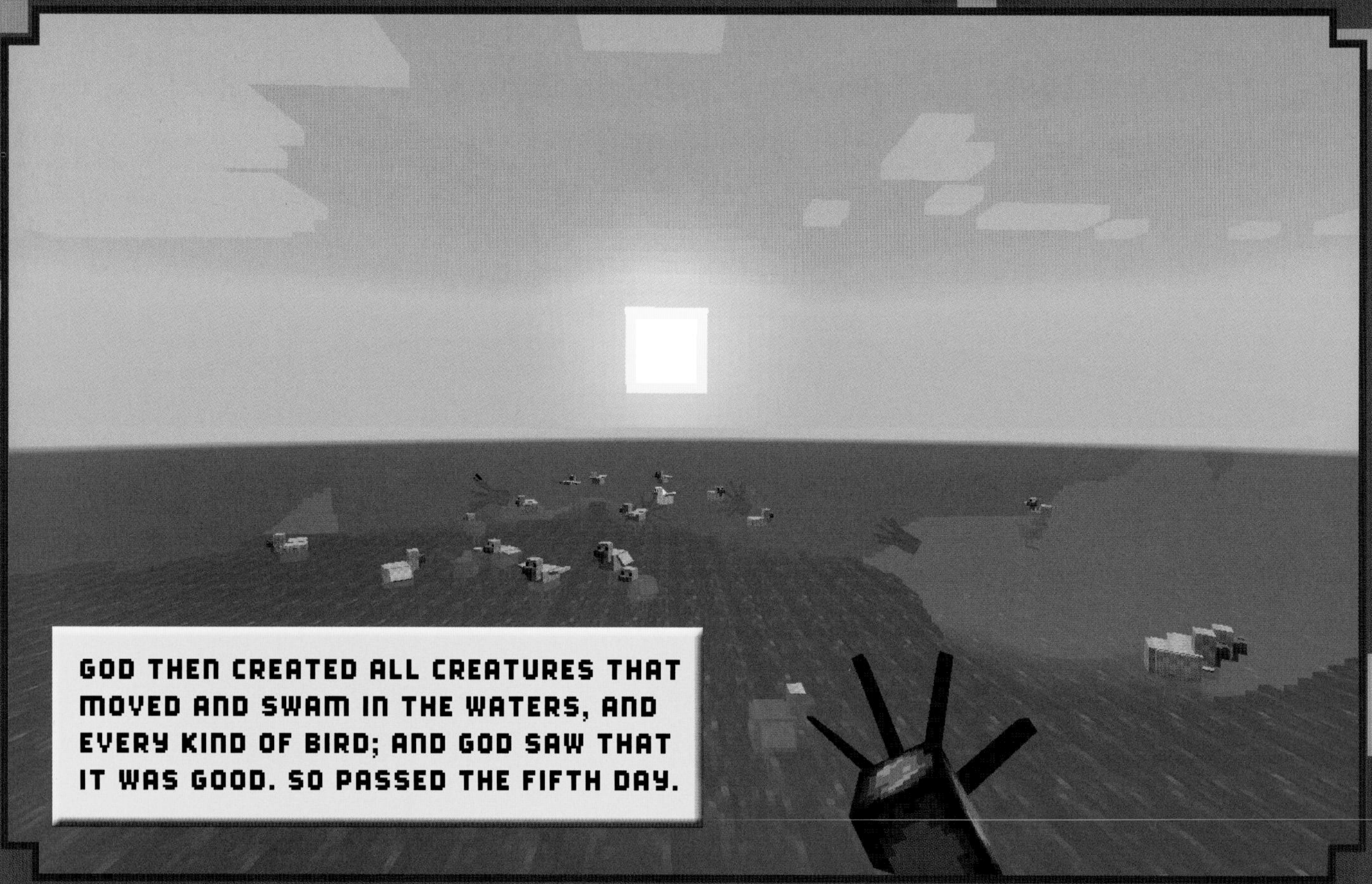
GOD THEN CREATED ALL CREATURES THAT MOVED AND SWAM IN THE WATERS, AND EVERY KIND OF BIRD; AND GOD SAW THAT IT WAS GOOD. SO PASSED THE FIFTH DAY.

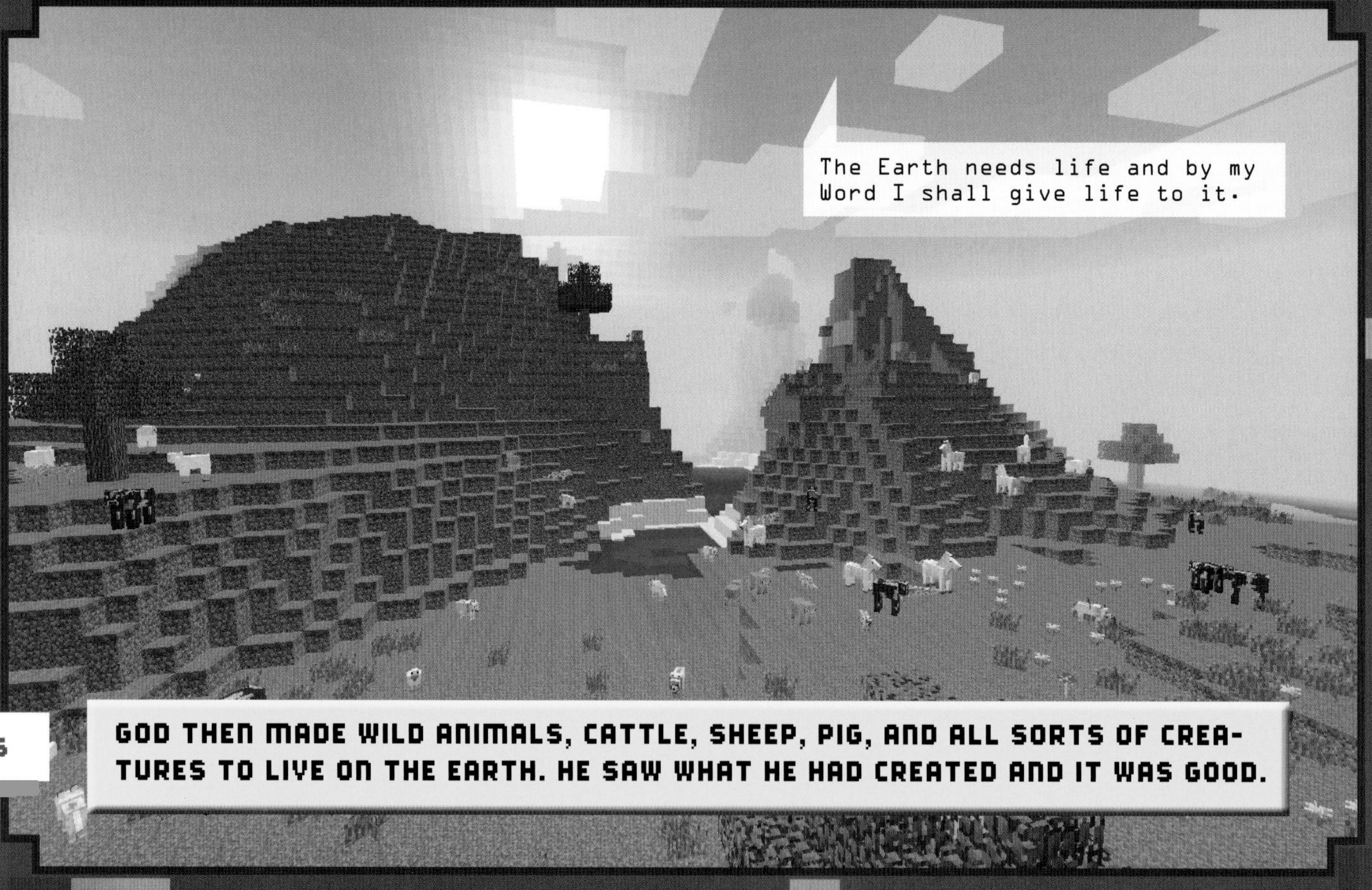
The Earth needs life and by my Word I shall give life to it.
GOD THEN MADE WILD ANIMALS, CATTLE, SHEEP, PIG, AND ALL SORTS OF CREATURES TO LIVE ON THE EARTH. HE SAW WHAT HE HAD CREATED AND IT WAS GOOD.

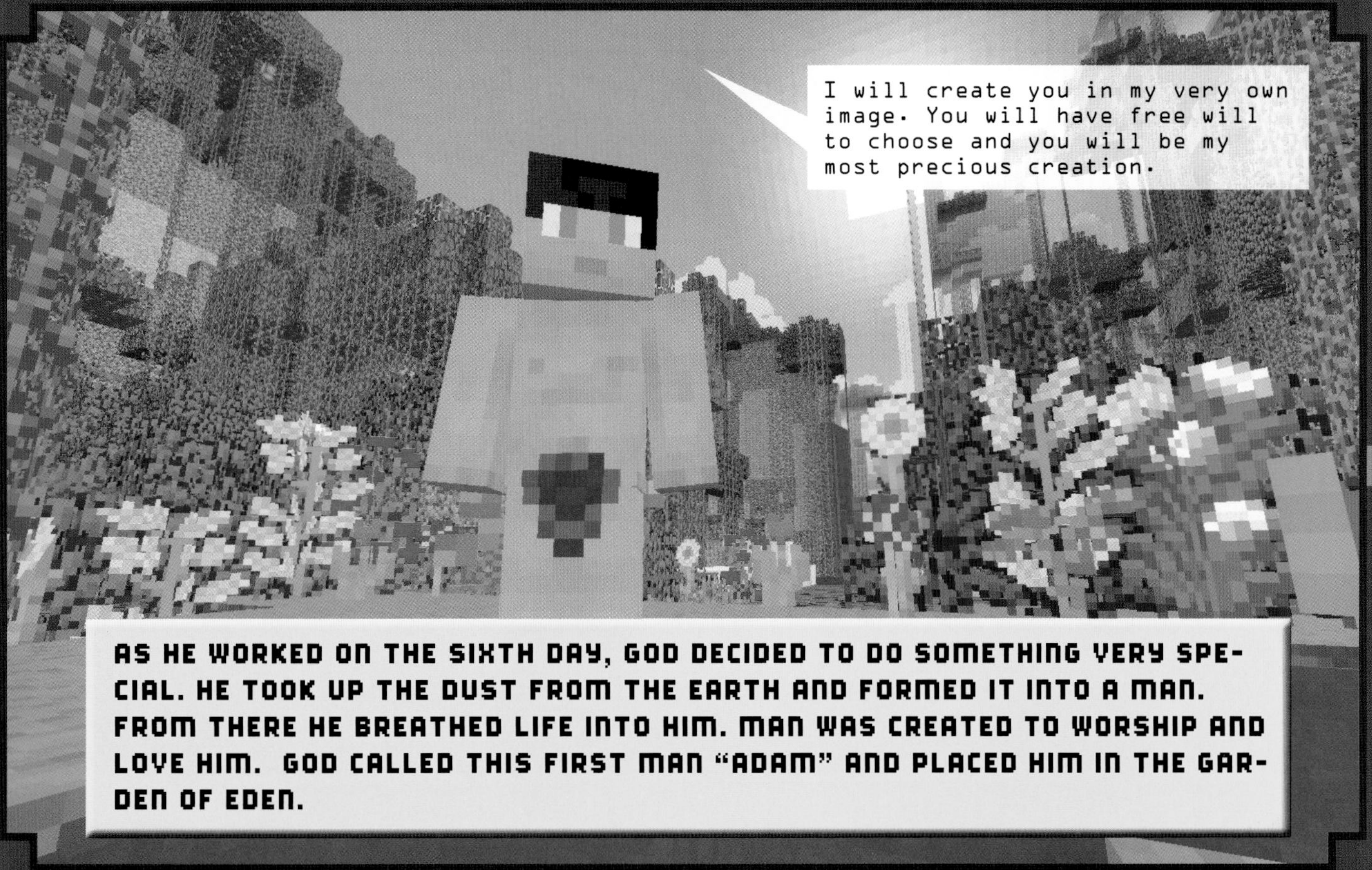
I will create you in my very own image. You will have free will to choose and you will be my most precious creation.
AS HE WORKED ON THE SIXTH DAY, GOD DECIDED TO DO SOMETHING VERY SPECIAL. HE TOOK UP THE DUST FROM THE EARTH AND FORMED IT INTO A MAN. FROM THERE HE BREATHED LIFE INTO HIM. MAN WAS CREATED TO WORSHIP AND LOVE HIM. GOD CALLED THIS FIRST MAN "ADAM" AND PLACED HIM IN THE GARDEN OF EDEN.

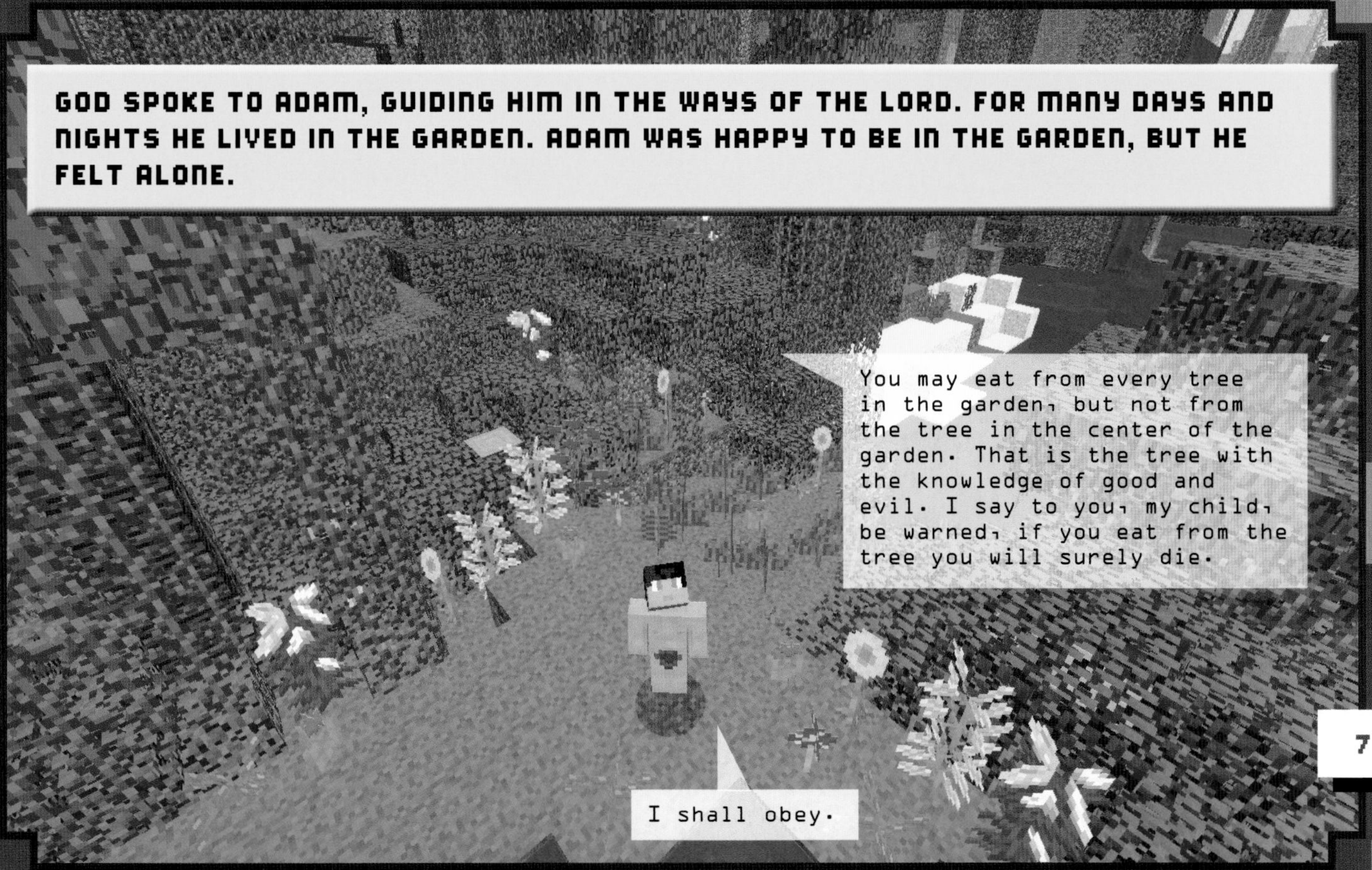
GOD SPOKE TO ADAM, GUIDING HIM IN THE WAYS OF THE LORD. FOR MANY DAYS AND NIGHTS HE LIVED IN THE GARDEN. ADAM WAS HAPPY TO BE IN THE GARDEN, BUT HE FELT ALONE.
You may eat from every tree in the garden, but not from the tree in the center of the garden. That is the tree with the knowledge of good and evil. I say to you, my child, be warned, if you eat from the tree you will surely die.
I shall obey.

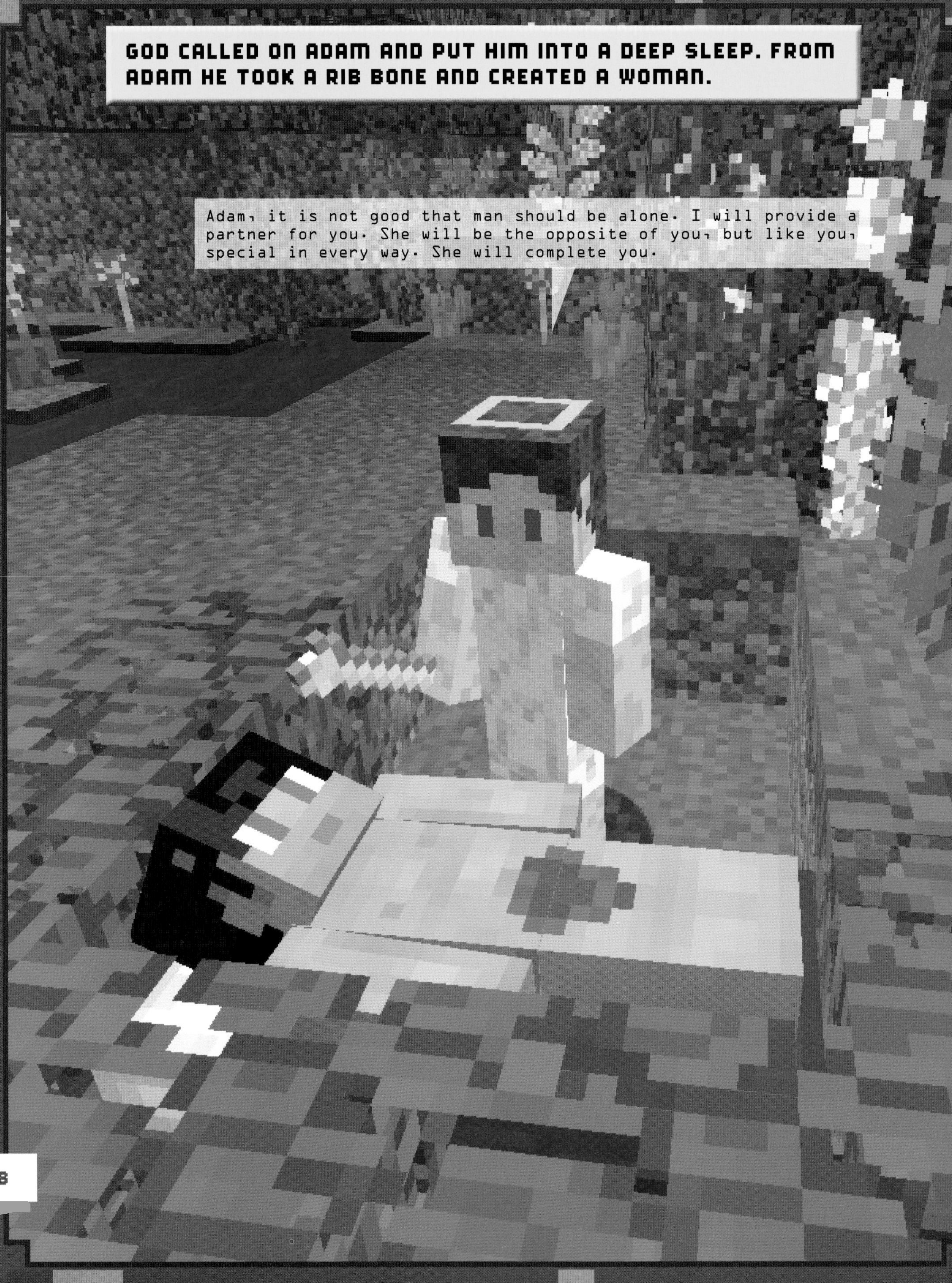
GOD CALLED ON ADAM AND PUT HIM INTO A DEEP SLEEP. FROM ADAM HE TOOK A RIB BONE AND CREATED A WOMAN.
Adam, it is not good that man should be alone. I will provide a partner for you. She will be the opposite of you, but like you, special in every way. She will complete you.

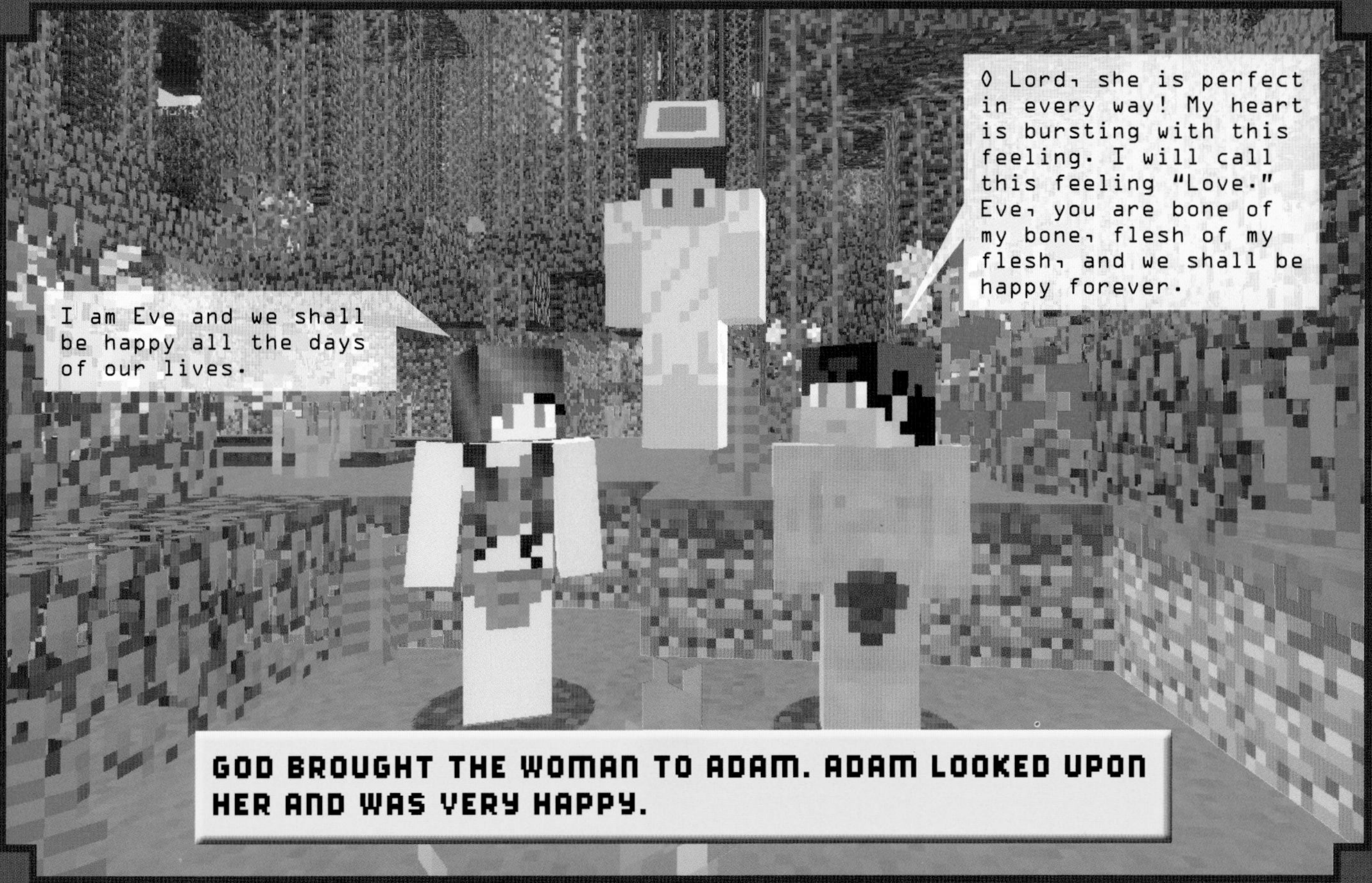

O Lord, she is perfect in every way! My heart is bursting with this feeling. I will call this feeling "Love." Eve, you are bone of my bone, flesh of my flesh, and we shall be happy forever.
I am Eve and we shall be happy all the days of our lives.
GOD BROUGHT THE WOMAN TO ADAM. ADAM LOOKED UPON HER AND WAS VERY HAPPY.

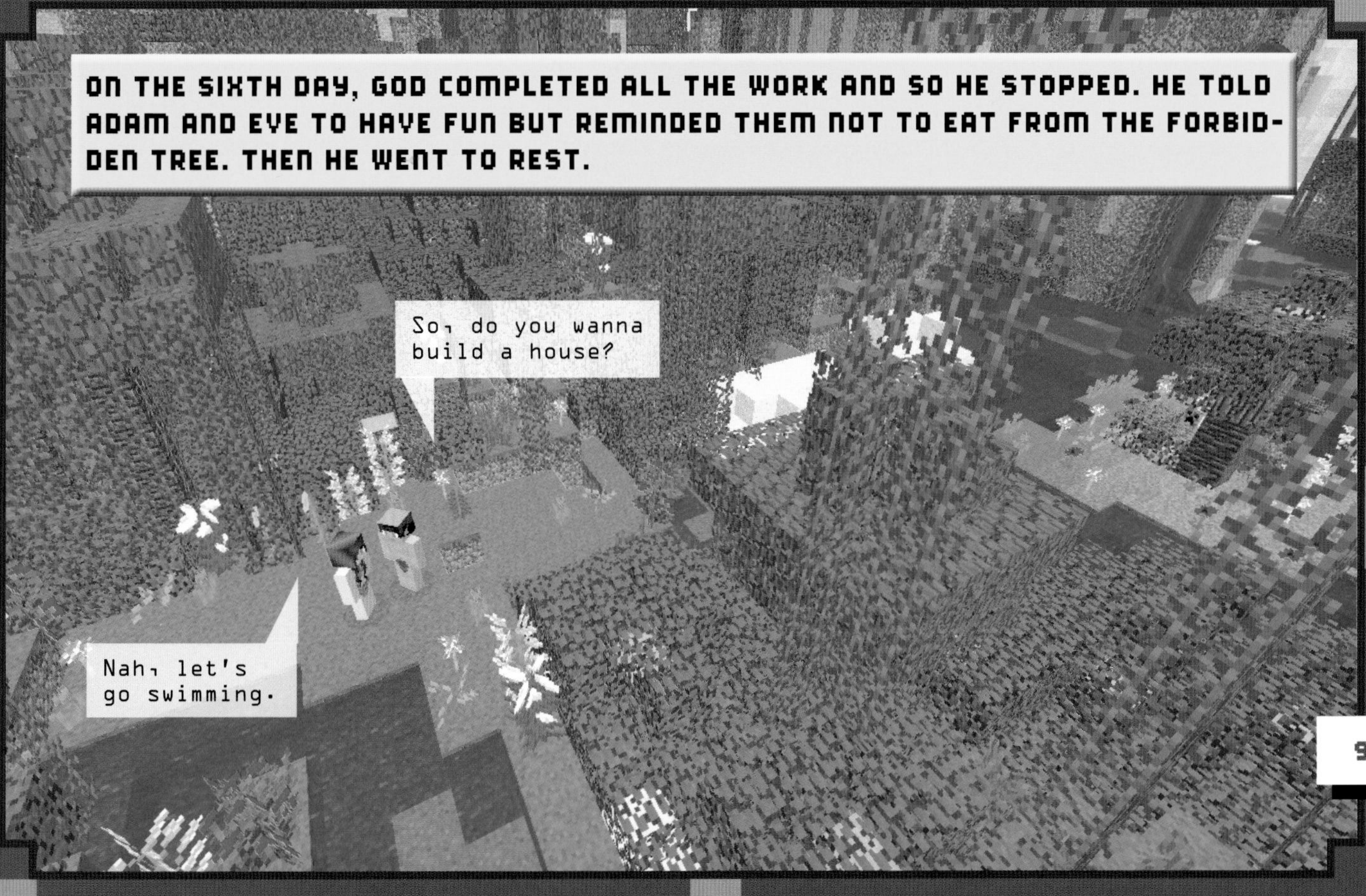

ON THE SIXTH DAY, GOD COMPLETED ALL THE WORK AND SO HE STOPPED. HE TOLD ADAM AND EVE TO HAVE FUN BUT REMINDED THEM NOT TO EAT FROM THE FORBIDDEN TREE. THEN HE WENT TO REST.
So, do you wanna build a house?
Nah, let's go swimming.

MAN'S LOSS OF PARADISE

Now can I cook, or
can't I?

Yes, the Earth is truly beautiful to us angels.

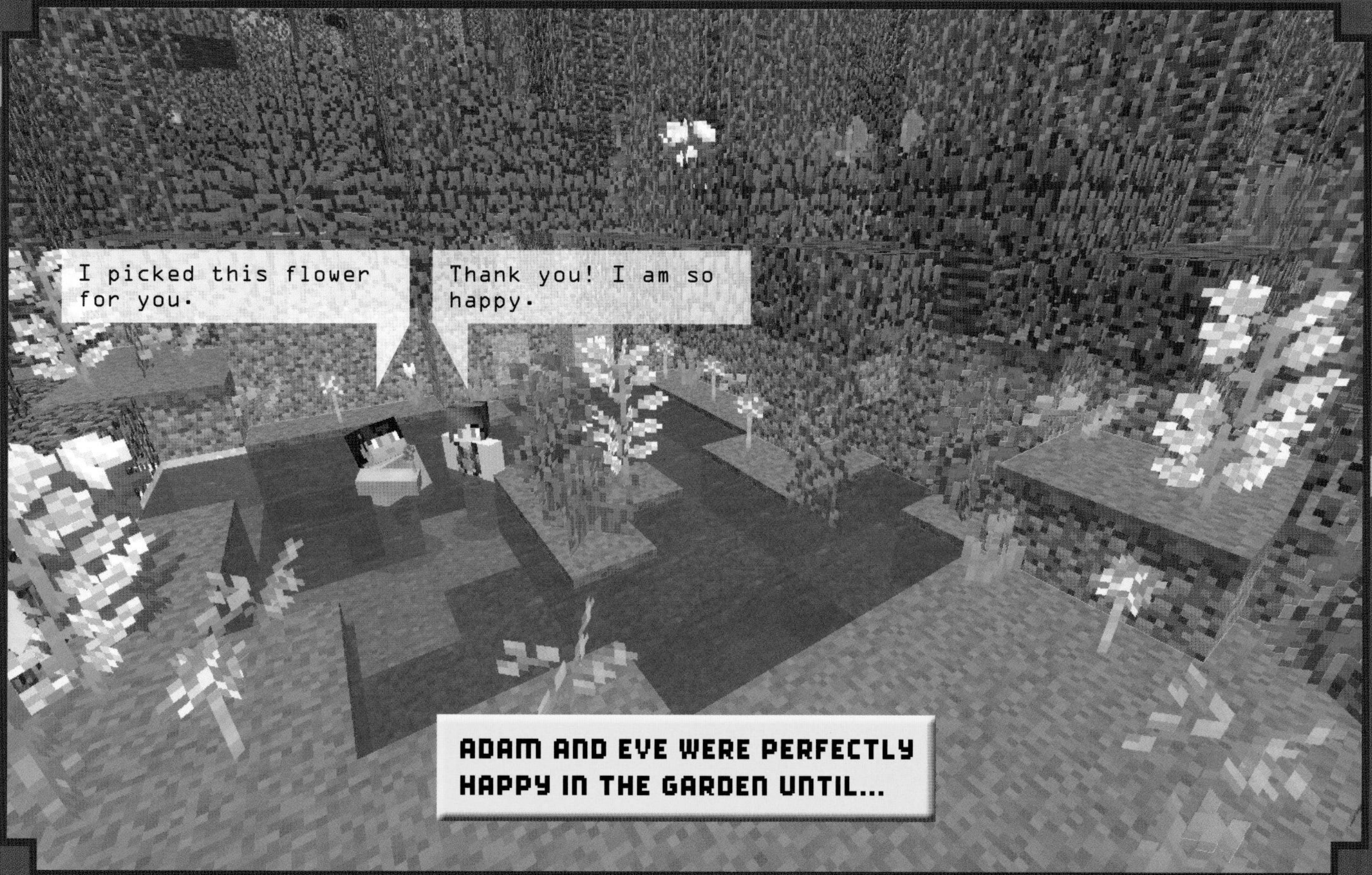
I picked this flower for you.
Thank you! I am so happy.
ADAM AND EVE WERE PERFECTLY HAPPY IN THE GARDEN UNTIL...

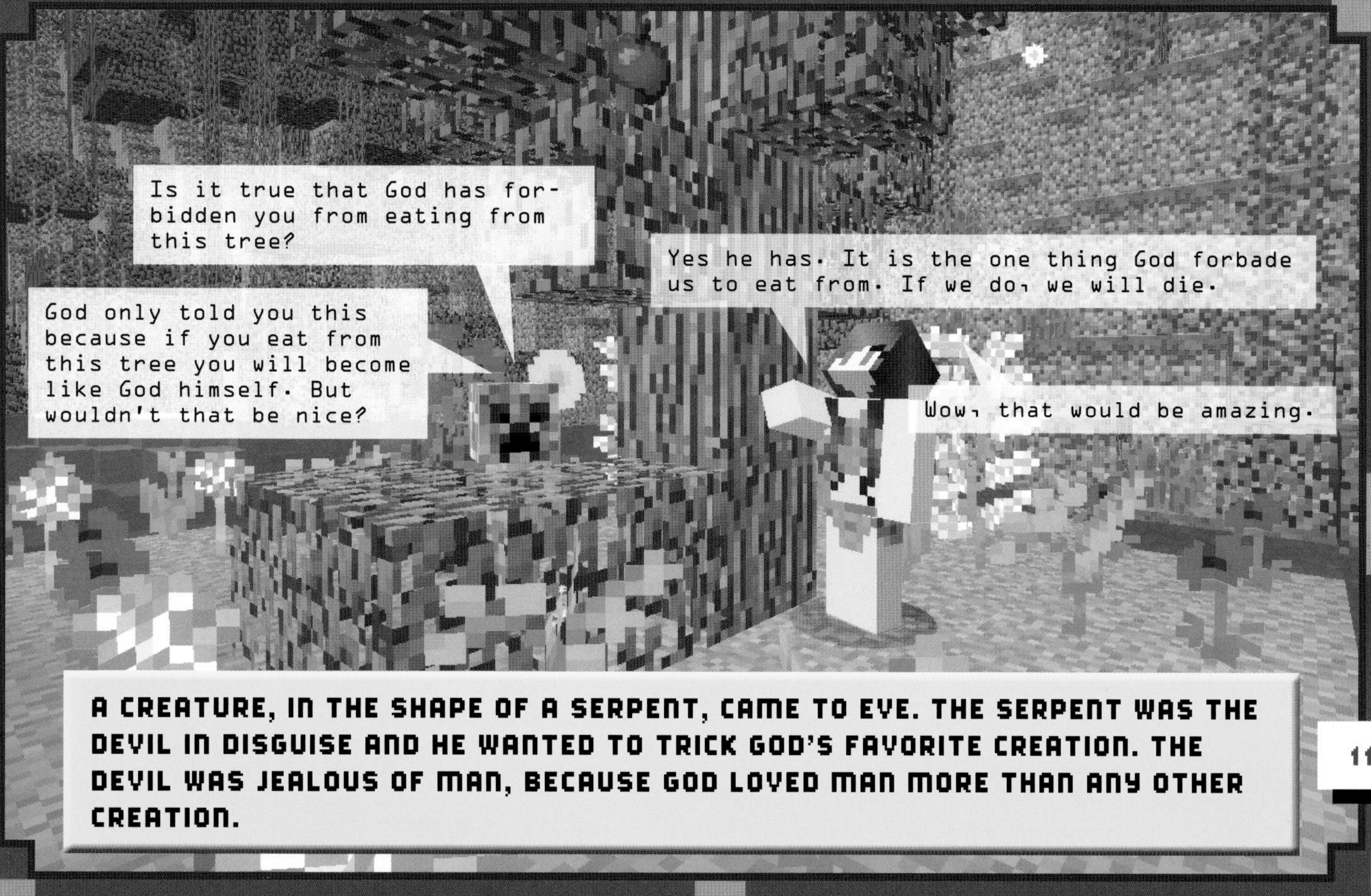
Is it true that God has forbidden you from eating from this tree?
Yes he has. It is the one thing God forbade us to eat from. If we do, we will die.
God only told you this because if you eat from this tree you will become like God himself. But wouldn't that be nice?
Wow, that would be amazing.
A CREATURE, IN THE SHAPE OF A SERPENT, CAME TO EVE. THE SERPENT WAS THE DEVIL IN DISGUISE AND HE WANTED TO TRICK GOD'S FAVORITE CREATION. THE DEVIL WAS JEALOUS OF MAN, BECAUSE GOD LOVED MAN MORE THAN ANY OTHER CREATION.

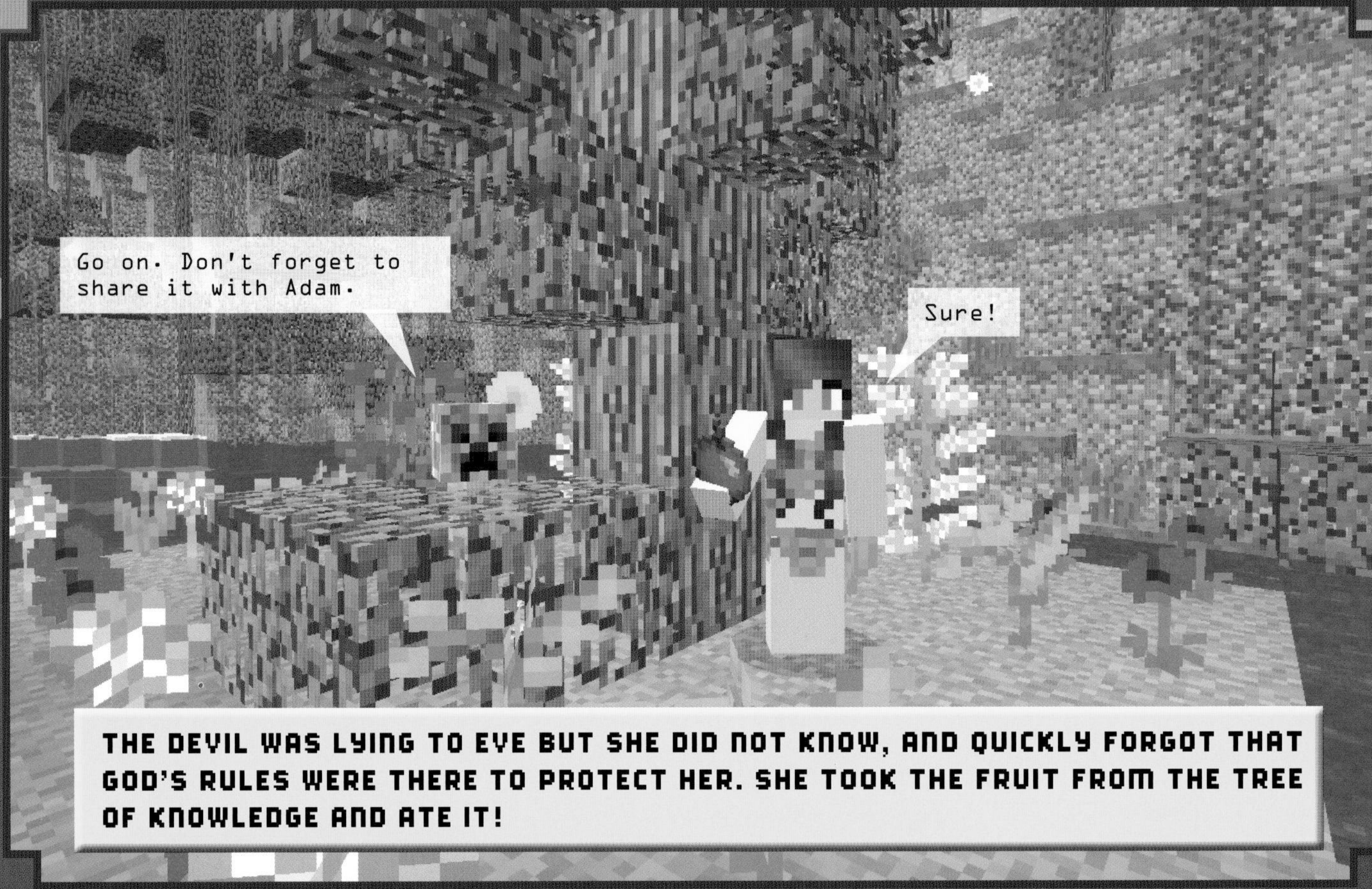
Go on. Don't forget to share it with Adam.
Sure!
THE DEVIL WAS LYING TO EVE BUT SHE DID NOT KNOW, AND QUICKLY FORGOT THAT GOD'S RULES WERE THERE TO PROTECT HER. SHE TOOK THE FRUIT FROM THE TREE OF KNOWLEDGE AND ATE IT!

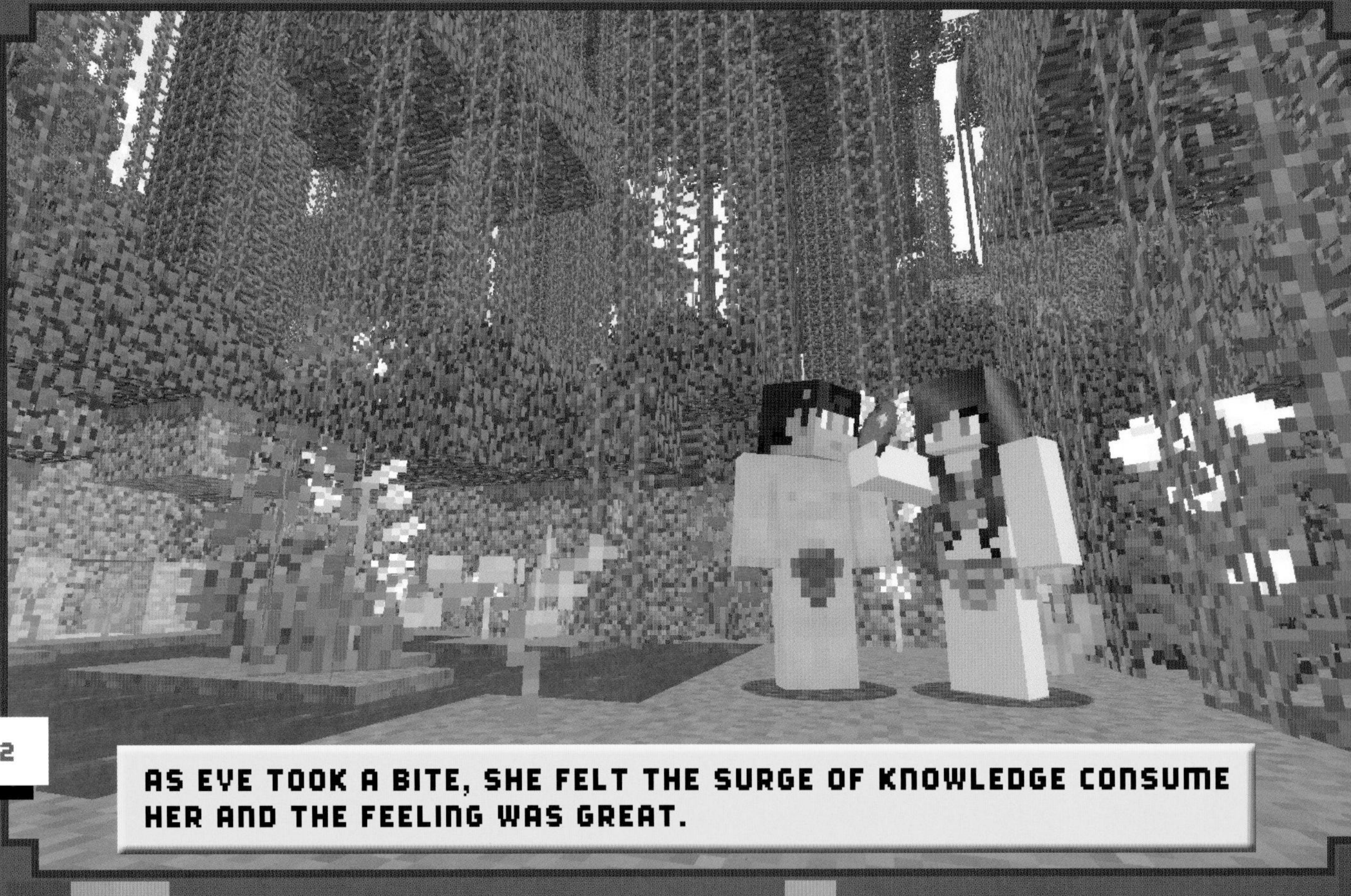
AS EVE TOOK A BITE, SHE FELT THE SURGE OF KNOWLEDGE CONSUME HER AND THE FEELING WAS GREAT.

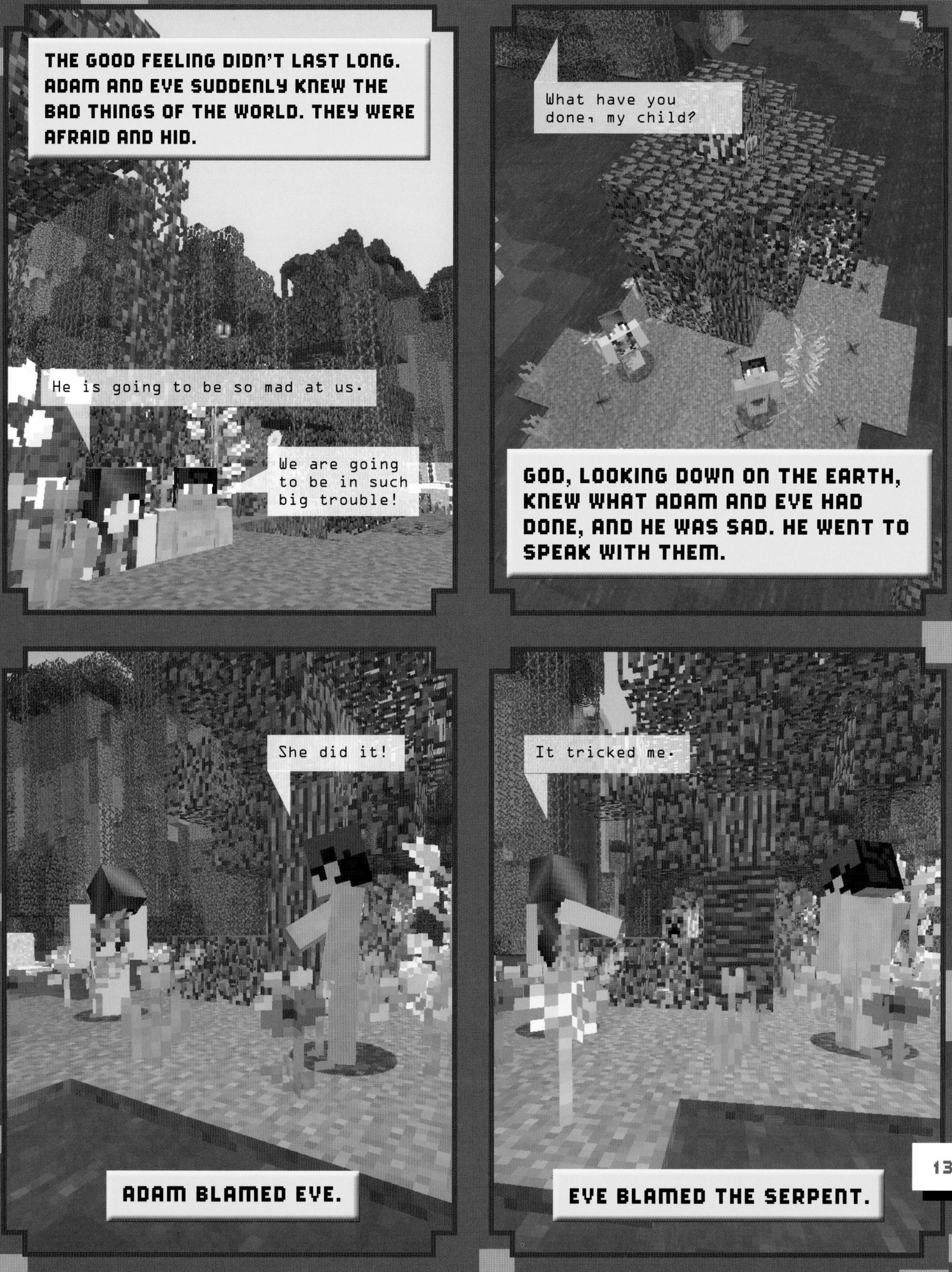
THE GOOD FEELING DIDN'T LAST LONG. ADAM AND EVE SUDDENLY KNEW THE BAD THINGS OF THE WORLD. THEY WERE AFRAID AND HID.
He is going to be so mad at us.
We are going to be in such big trouble!
What have you done, my child?
GOD, LOOKING DOWN ON THE EARTH, KNEW WHAT ADAM AND EVE HAD DONE, AND HE WAS SAD. HE WENT TO SPEAK WITH THEM.
She did it!
ADAM BLAMED EVE.
It tricked me.
EVE BLAMED THE SERPENT.

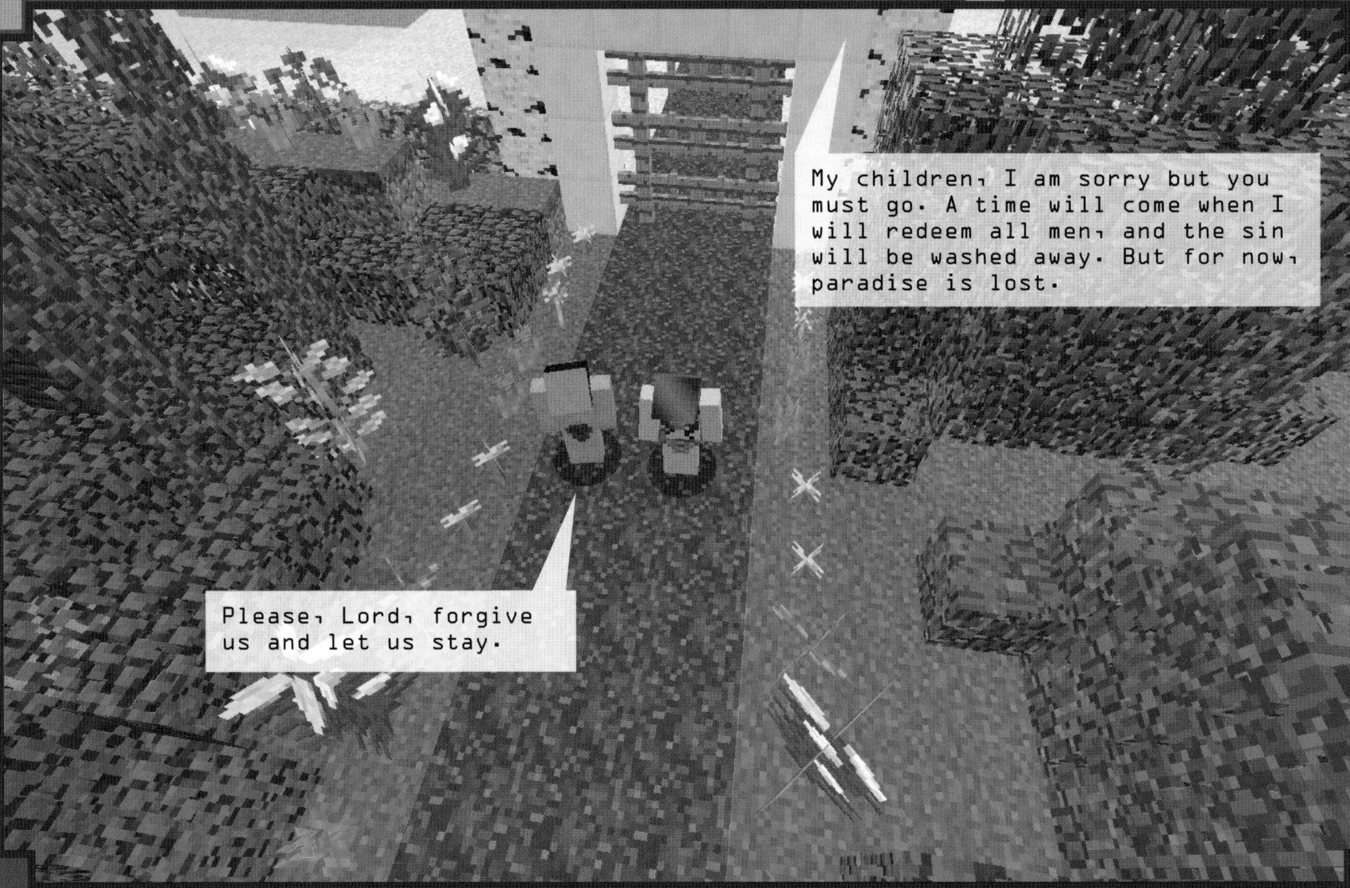
My children, I am sorry but you must go. A time will come when I will redeem all men, and the sin will be washed away. But for now, paradise is lost.
Please, Lord, forgive us and let us stay.

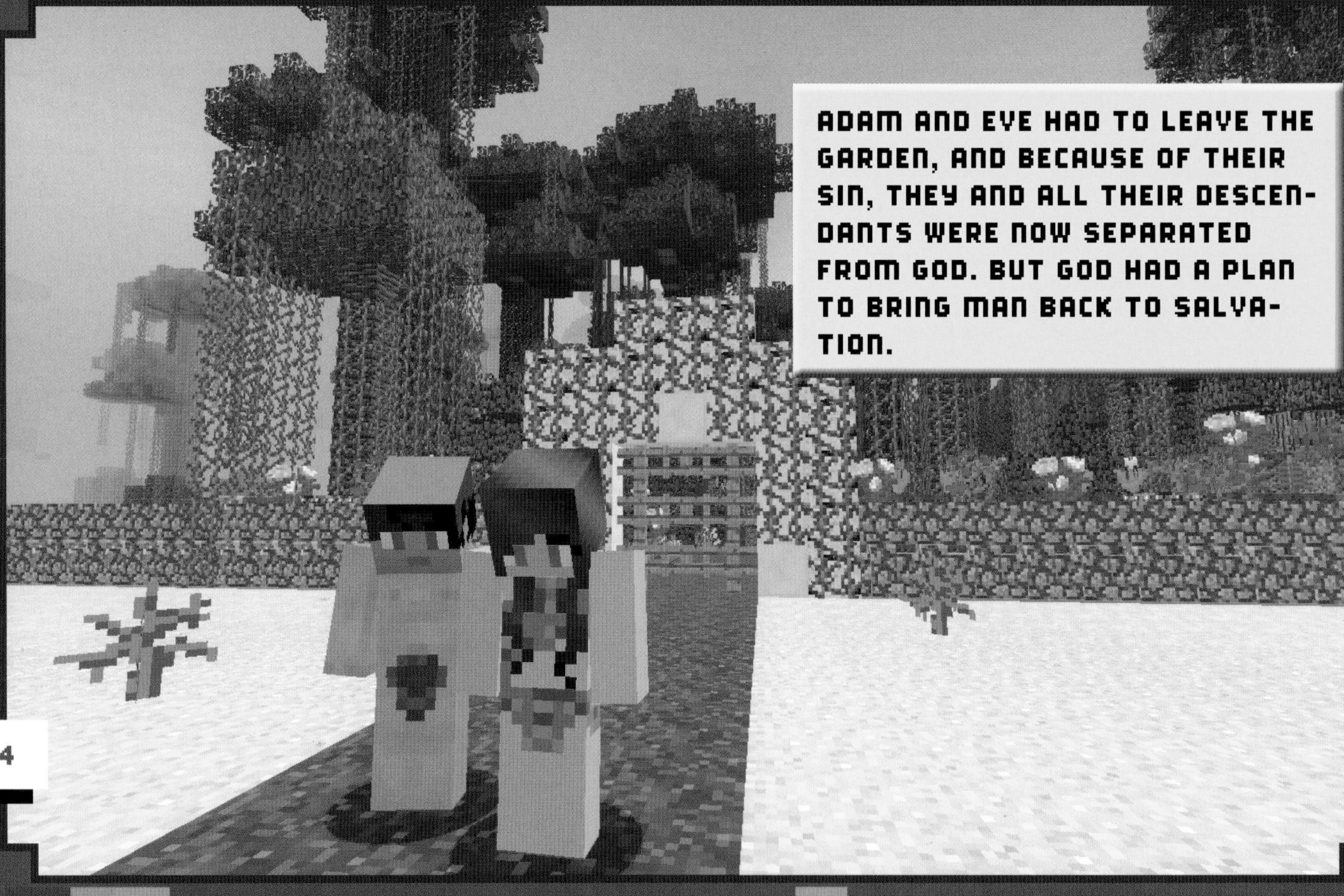
ADAM AND EVE HAD TO LEAVE THE GARDEN, AND BECAUSE OF THEIR SIN, THEY AND ALL THEIR DESCENDANTS WERE NOW SEPARATED FROM GOD. BUT GOD HAD A PLAN TO BRING MAN BACK TO SALVATION.

NOAH AND THE GREAT FLOOD

It looks like things on Earth are now a bit rocky. What happened?

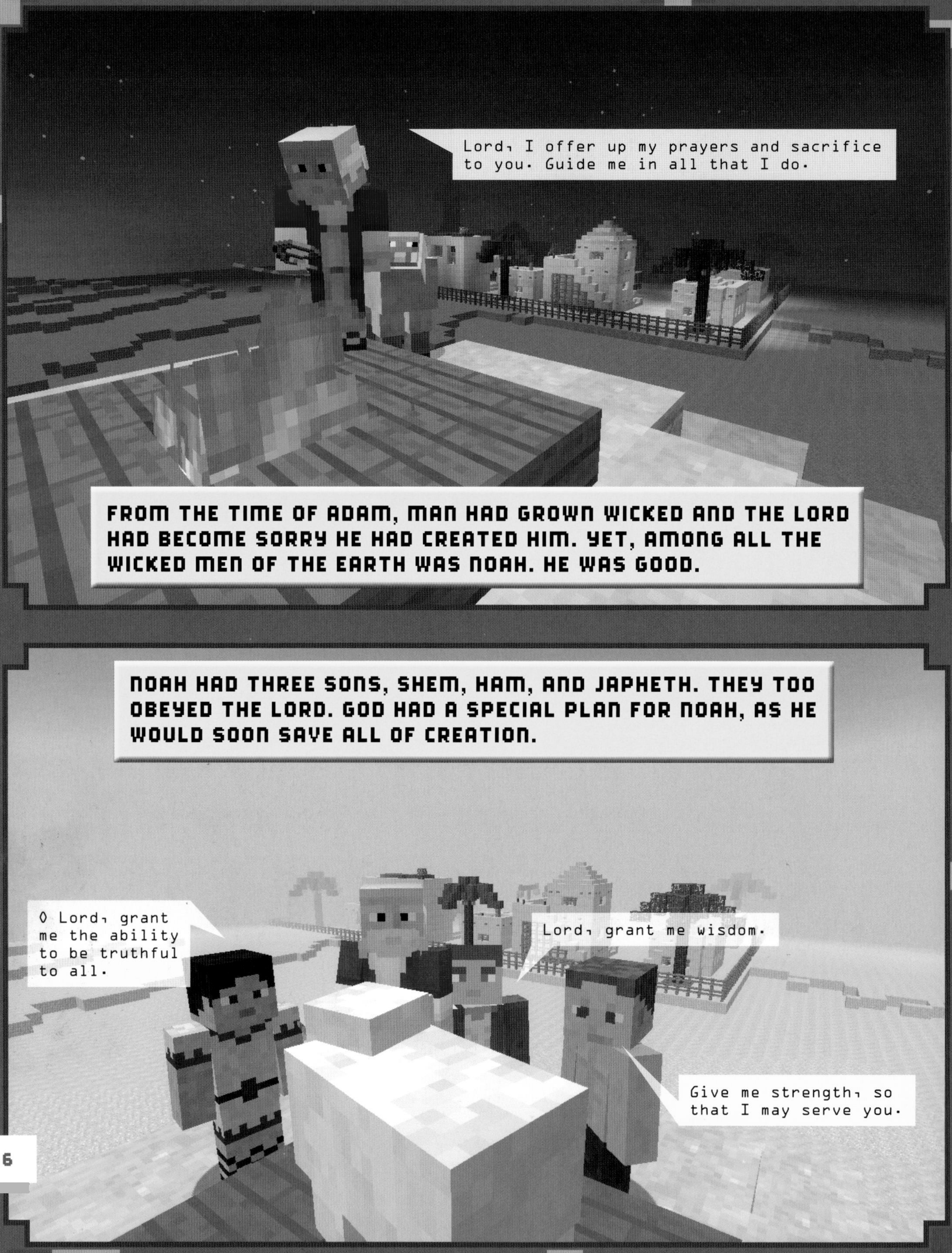
Lord, I offer up my prayers and sacrifice to you. Guide me in all that I do.
FROM THE TIME OF ADAM, MAN HAD GROWN WICKED AND THE LORD HAD BECOME SORRY HE HAD CREATED HIM. YET, AMONG ALL THE WICKED MEN OF THE EARTH WAS NOAH. HE WAS GOOD.
NOAH HAD THREE SONS, SHEM, HAM, AND JAPHETH. THEY TOO OBEYED THE LORD. GOD HAD A SPECIAL PLAN FOR NOAH, AS HE WOULD SOON SAVE ALL OF CREATION.
O Lord, grant me the ability to be truthful to all.
Lord, grant me wisdom.
Give me strength, so that I may serve you.

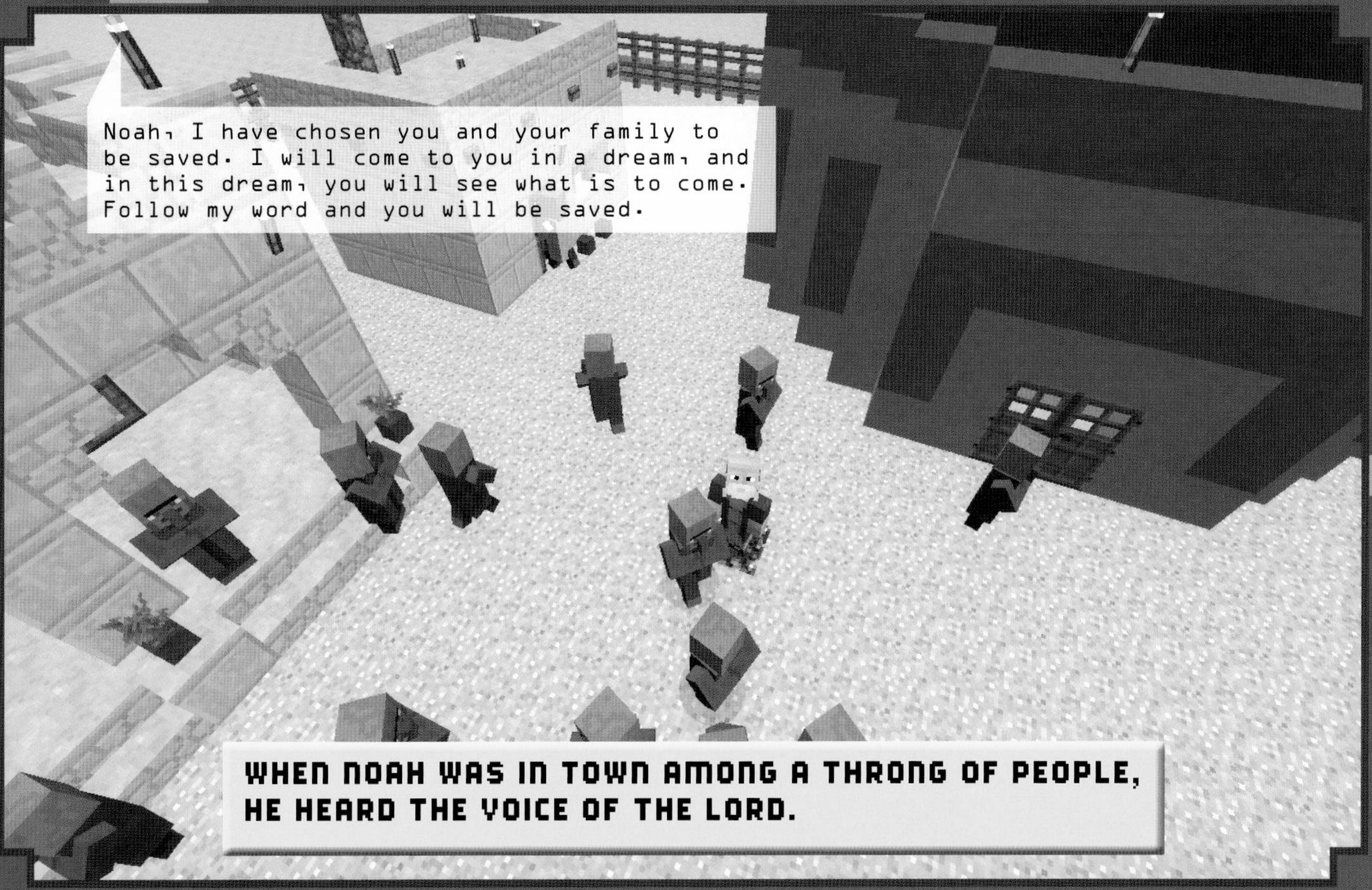
Noah, I have chosen you and your family to be saved. I will come to you in a dream, and in this dream, you will see what is to come. Follow my word and you will be saved.
WHEN NOAH WAS IN TOWN AMONG A THRONG OF PEOPLE, HE HEARD THE VOICE OF THE LORD.

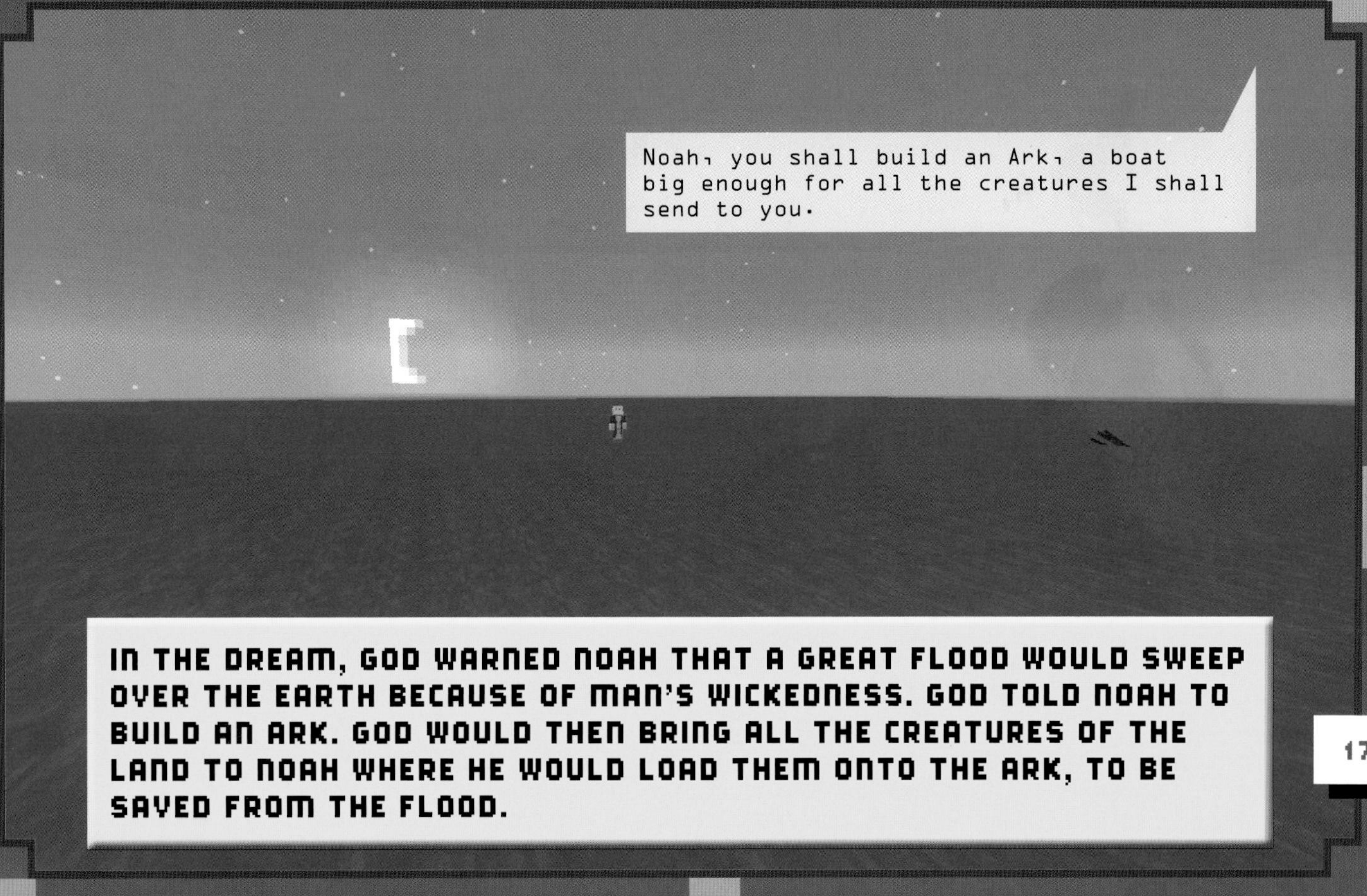
Noah, you shall build an Ark, a boat big enough for all the creatures I shall send to you.
IN THE DREAM, GOD WARNED NOAH THAT A GREAT FLOOD WOULD SWEEP OVER THE EARTH BECAUSE OF MAN'S WICKEDNESS. GOD TOLD NOAH TO BUILD AN ARK. GOD WOULD THEN BRING ALL THE CREATURES OF THE LAND TO NOAH WHERE HE WOULD LOAD THEM ONTO THE ARK, TO BE SAVED FROM THE FLOOD.

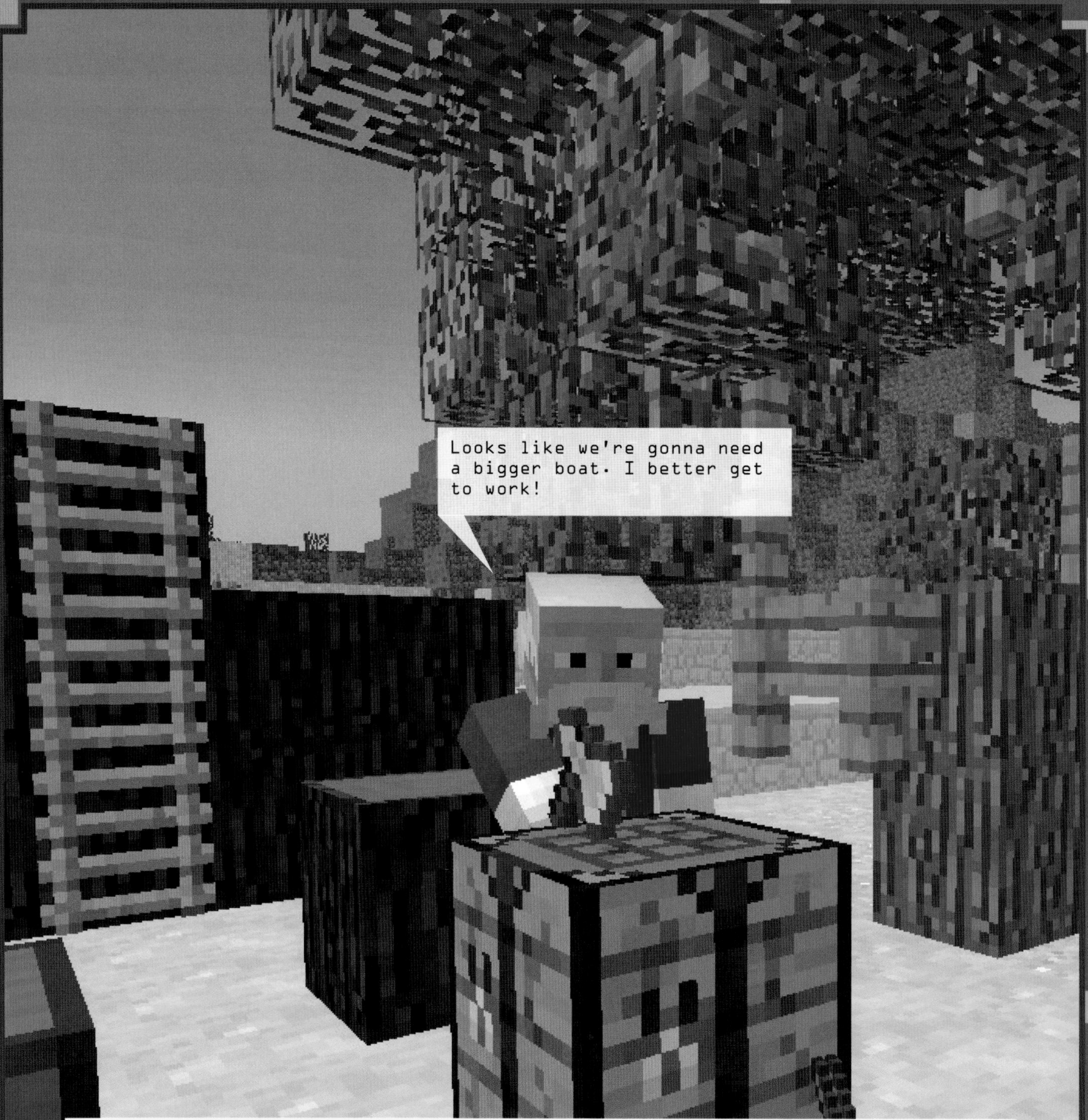
Looks like we're gonna need a bigger boat. I better get to work!

NOAH FOLLOWED GOD'S INSTRUCTIONS FOR HOW TO BUILD THE ARK. GOD SAID, "THE ARK IS TO BE MADE OF CYPRESS WOOD; WITH ROOMS IN IT AND COATED WITH PITCH INSIDE AND OUT. THE ARK IS TO BE 450 FEET LONG, 75 FEET WIDE, AND 45 FEET HIGH. IT IS TO HAVE A DOOR IN THE SIDE, WITH LOWER, MIDDLE, AND UPPER DECKS. TWO OF EVERY KIND OF BIRD, OF EVERY KIND OF ANIMAL, AND OF EVERY KIND OF CREATURE THAT MOVES ALONG THE GROUND WILL COME TO YOU TO BE KEPT ALIVE. YOU ARE TO TAKE EVERY KIND OF FOOD THAT IS TO BE EATEN AND STORE IT AWAY AS FOOD FOR YOU AND FOR THEM."

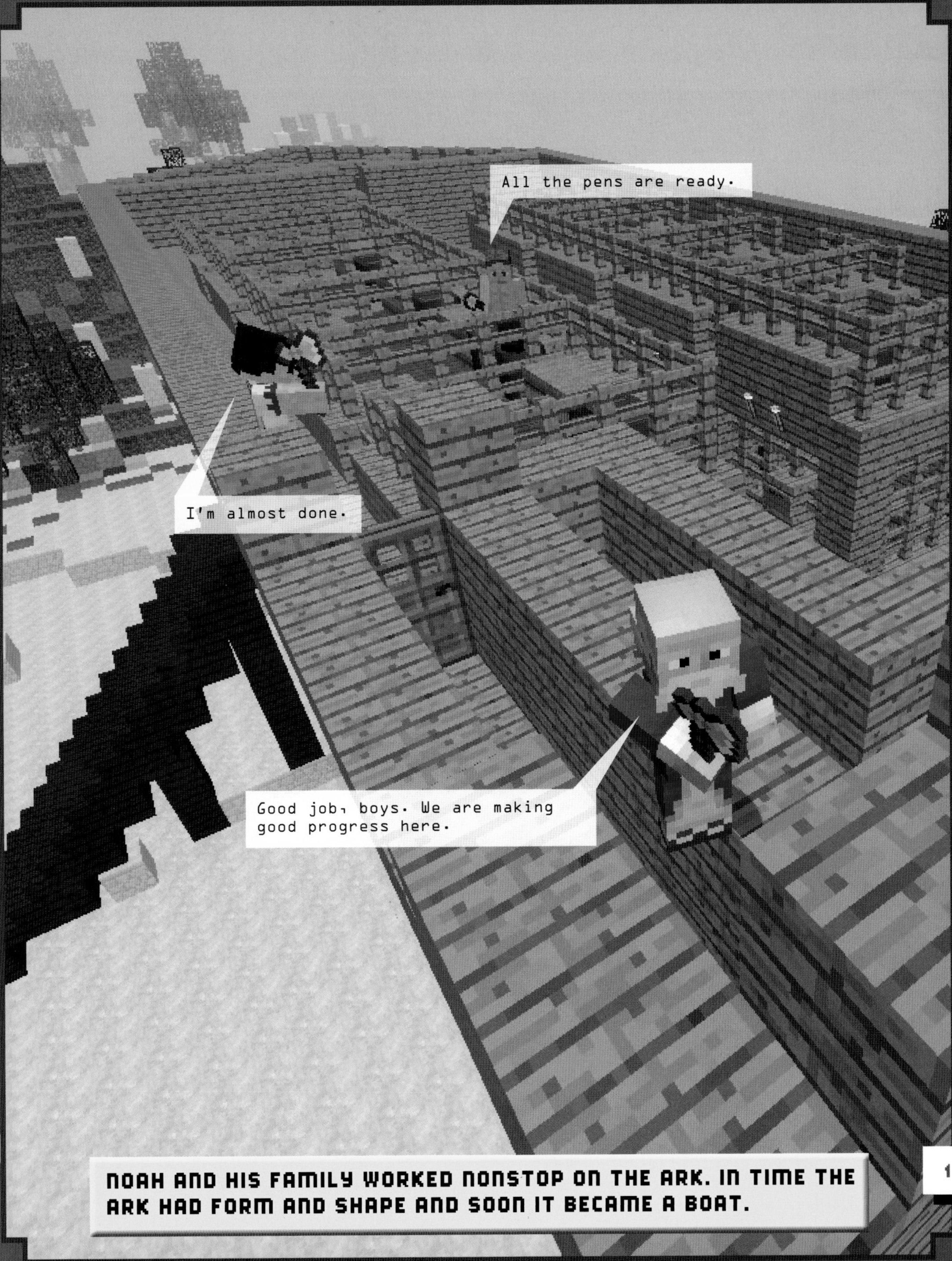
All the pens are ready.
I'm almost done.
Good job, boys. We are making good progress here.

NOAH AND HIS FAMILY WORKED NONSTOP ON THE ARK. IN TIME THE ARK HAD FORM AND SHAPE AND SOON IT BECAME A BOAT.

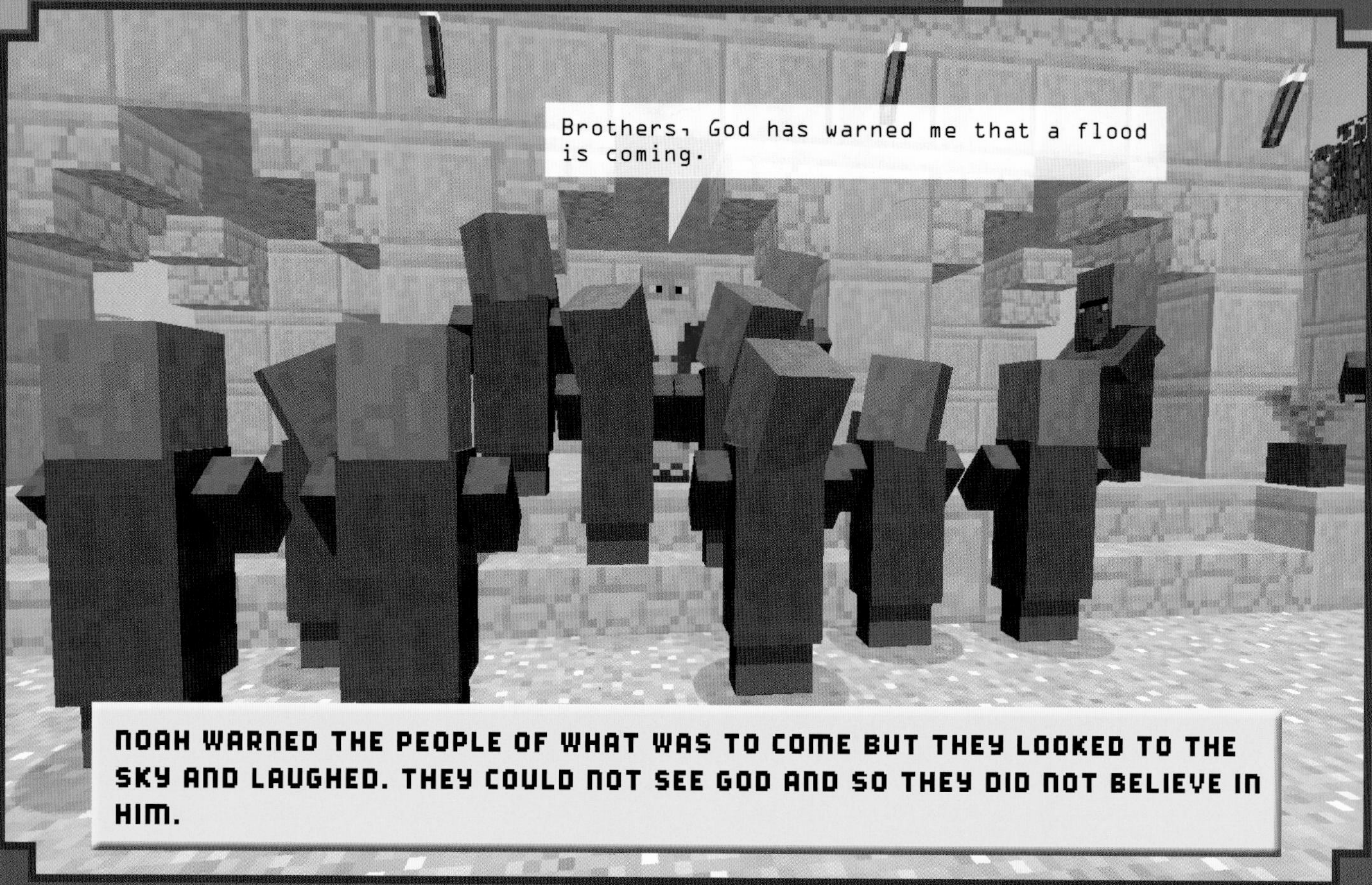
Brothers, God has warned me that a flood is coming.
NOAH WARNED THE PEOPLE OF WHAT WAS TO COME BUT THEY LOOKED TO THE SKY AND LAUGHED. THEY COULD NOT SEE GOD AND SO THEY DID NOT BELIEVE IN HIM.

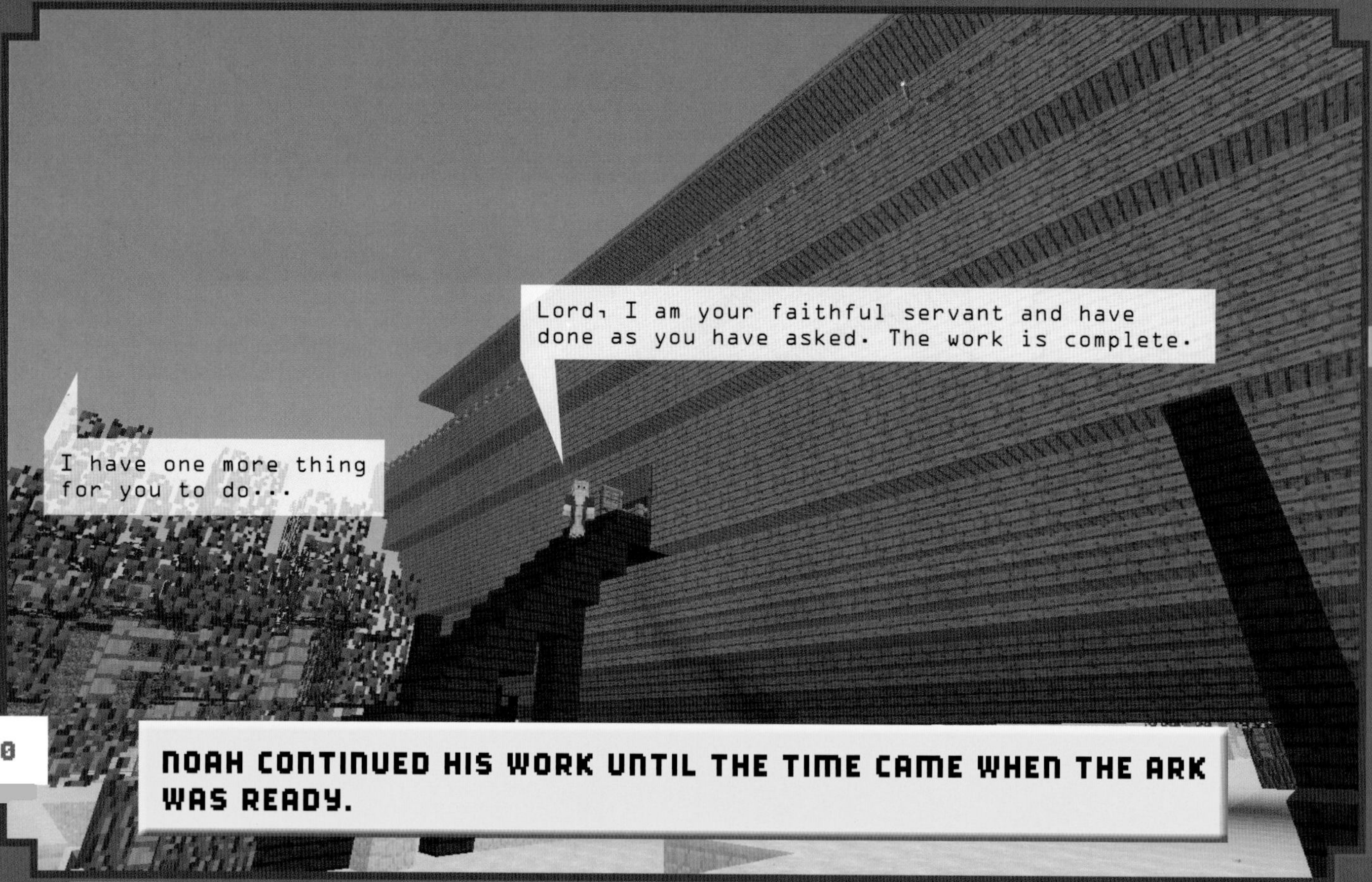
Lord, I am your faithful servant and have done as you have asked. The work is complete.
I have one more thing for you to do...
NOAH CONTINUED HIS WORK UNTIL THE TIME CAME WHEN THE ARK WAS READY.

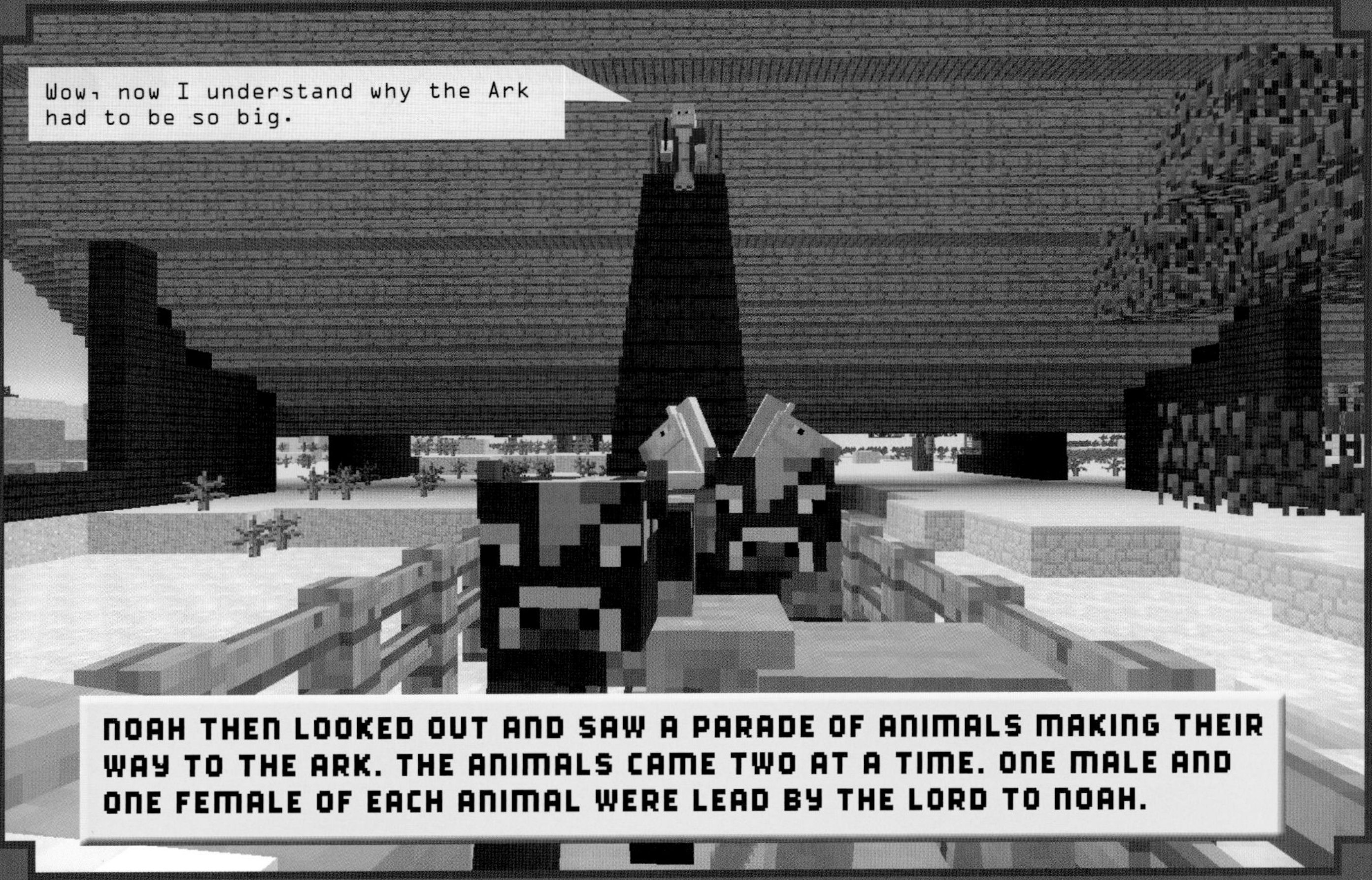
Wow, now I understand why the Ark had to be so big.
NOAH THEN LOOKED OUT AND SAW A PARADE OF ANIMALS MAKING THEIR WAY TO THE ARK. THE ANIMALS CAME TWO AT A TIME. ONE MALE AND ONE FEMALE OF EACH ANIMAL WERE LEAD BY THE LORD TO NOAH.

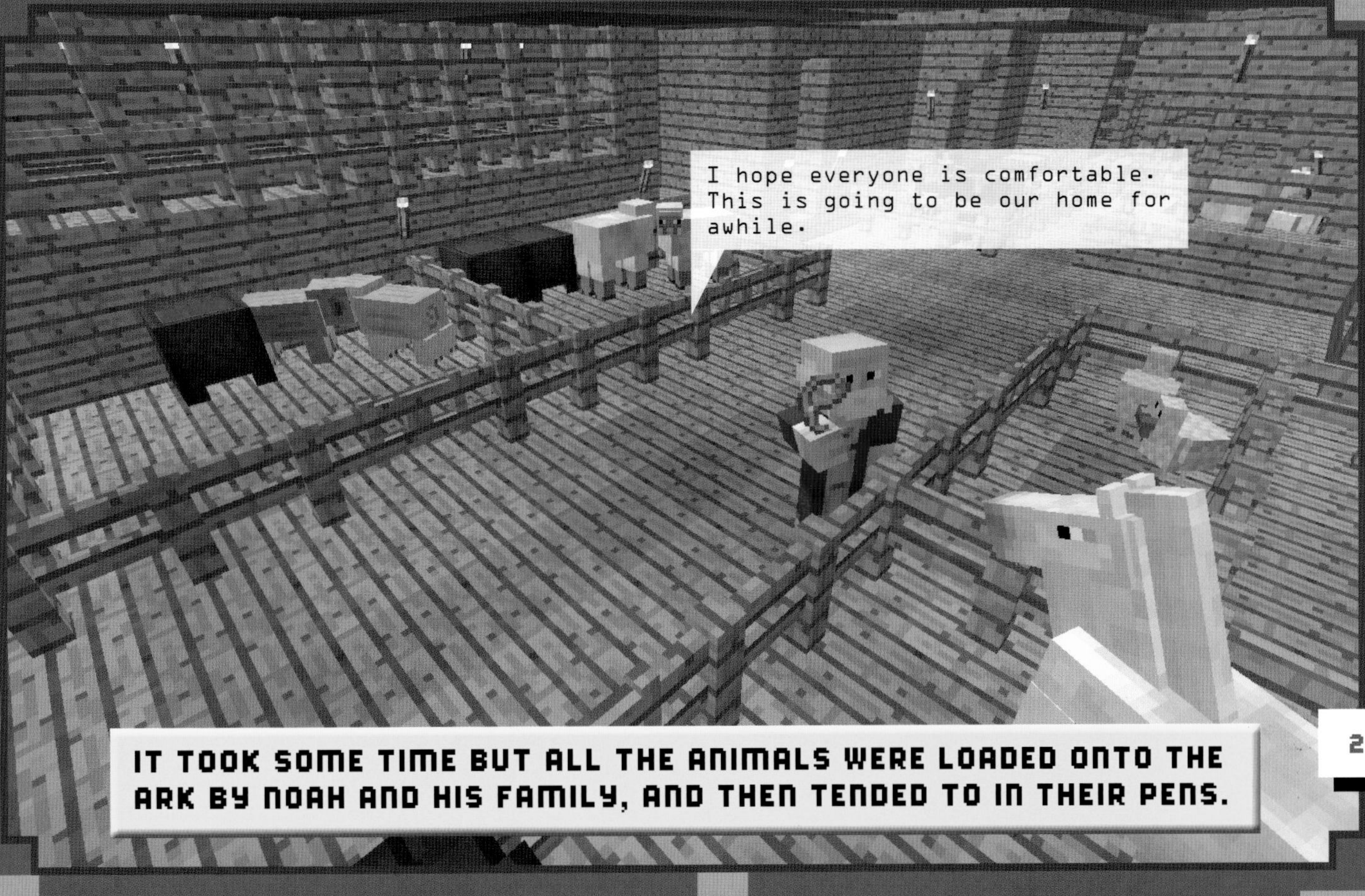
I hope everyone is comfortable. This is going to be our home for awhile.
IT TOOK SOME TIME BUT ALL THE ANIMALS WERE LOADED ONTO THE ARK BY NOAH AND HIS FAMILY, AND THEN TENDED TO IN THEIR PENS.

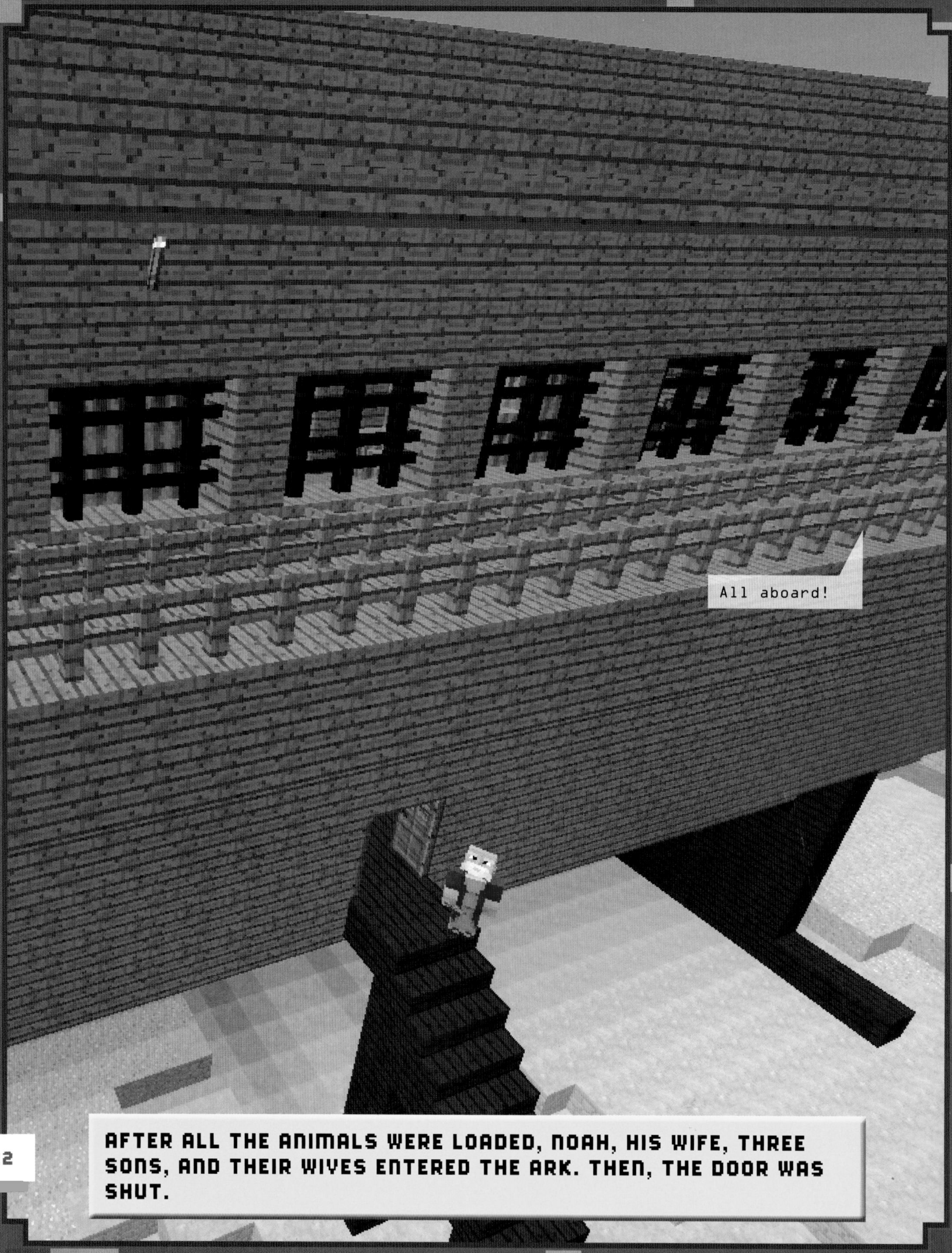
All aboard!
AFTER ALL THE ANIMALS WERE LOADED, NOAH, HIS WIFE, THREE SONS, AND THEIR WIVES ENTERED THE ARK. THEN, THE DOOR WAS SHUT.

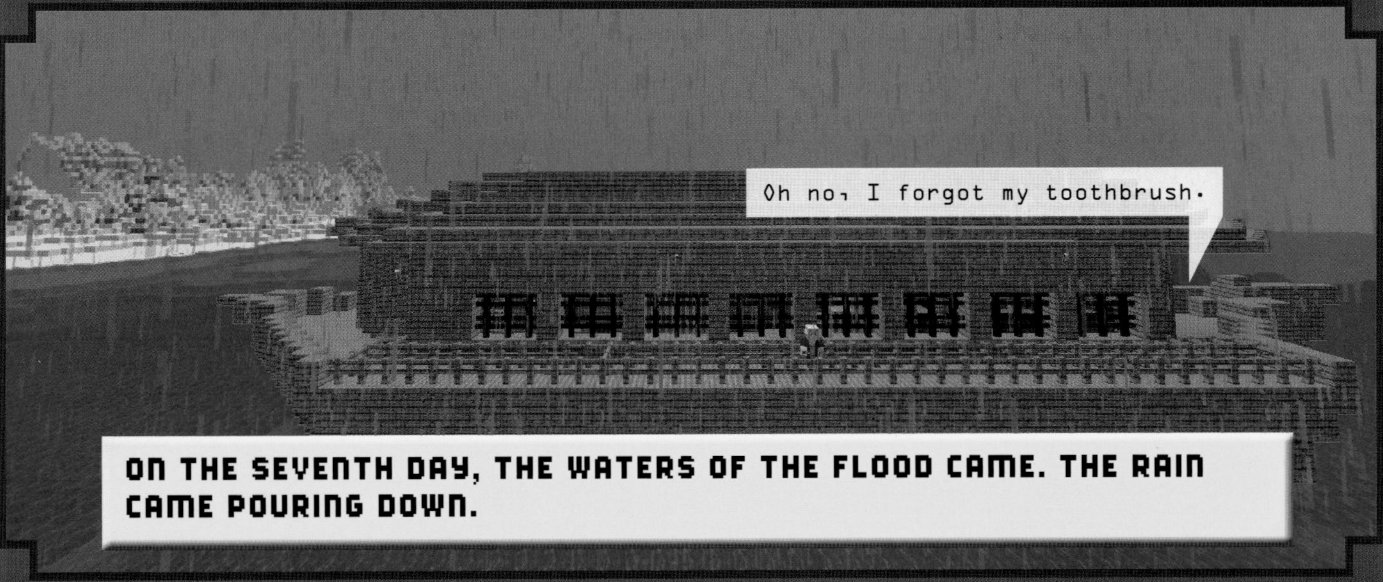
Oh no, I forgot my toothbrush.
ON THE SEVENTH DAY, THE WATERS OF THE FLOOD CAME. THE RAIN CAME POURING DOWN.

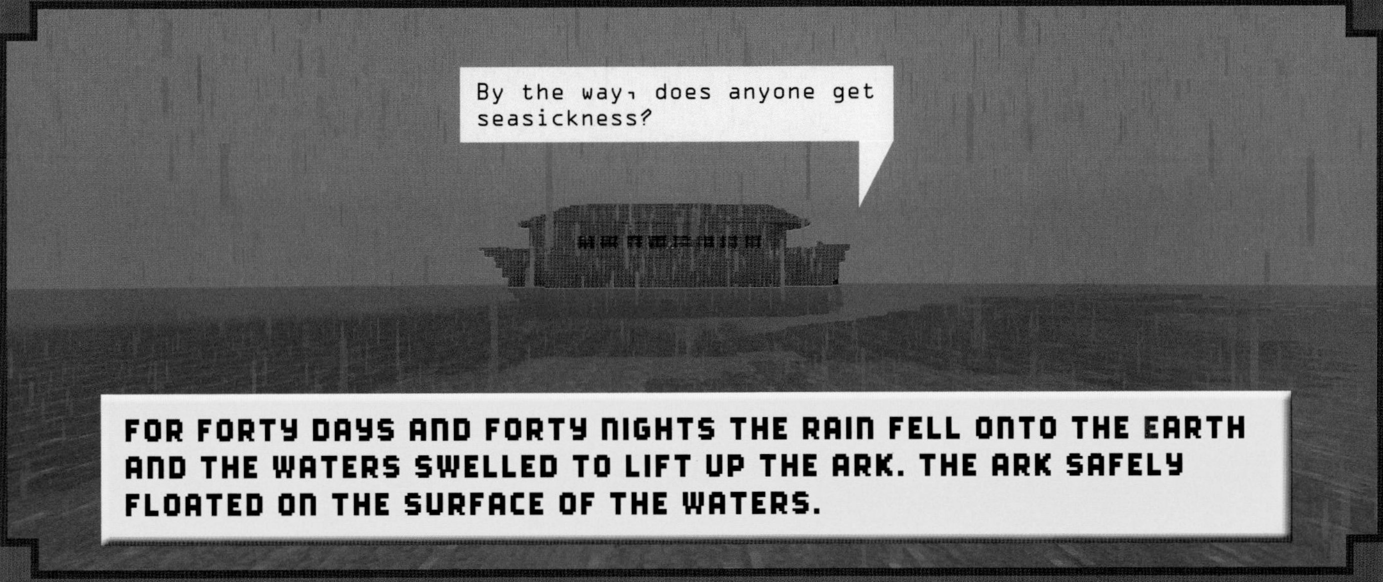
By the way, does anyone get seasickness?
FOR FORTY DAYS AND FORTY NIGHTS THE RAIN FELL ONTO THE EARTH AND THE WATERS SWELLED TO LIFT UP THE ARK. THE ARK SAFELY FLOATED ON THE SURFACE OF THE WATERS.

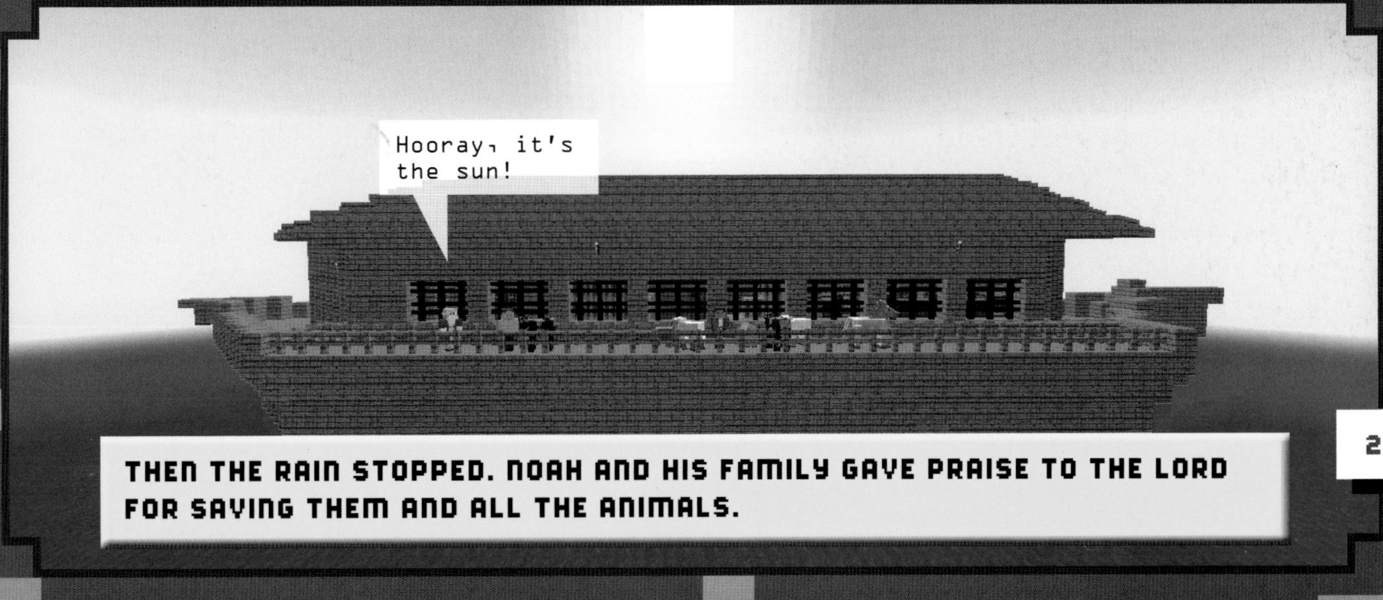
Hooray, it's the sun!
THEN THE RAIN STOPPED. NOAH AND HIS FAMILY GAVE PRAISE TO THE LORD FOR SAVING THEM AND ALL THE ANIMALS.

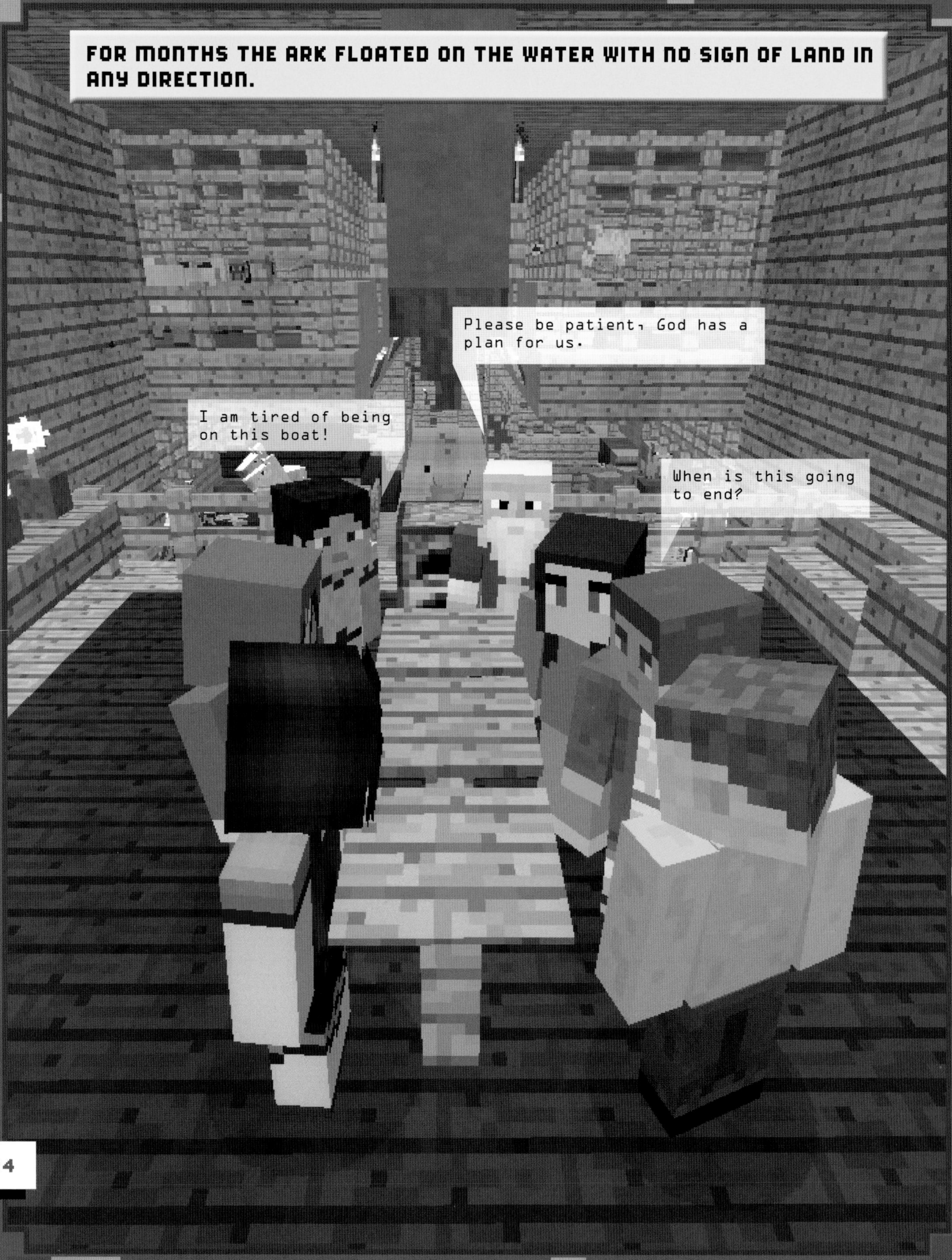
FOR MONTHS THE ARK FLOATED ON THE WATER WITH NO SIGN OF LAND IN ANY DIRECTION.
I am tired of being on this boat!
Please be patient, God has a plan for us.
When is this going to end?

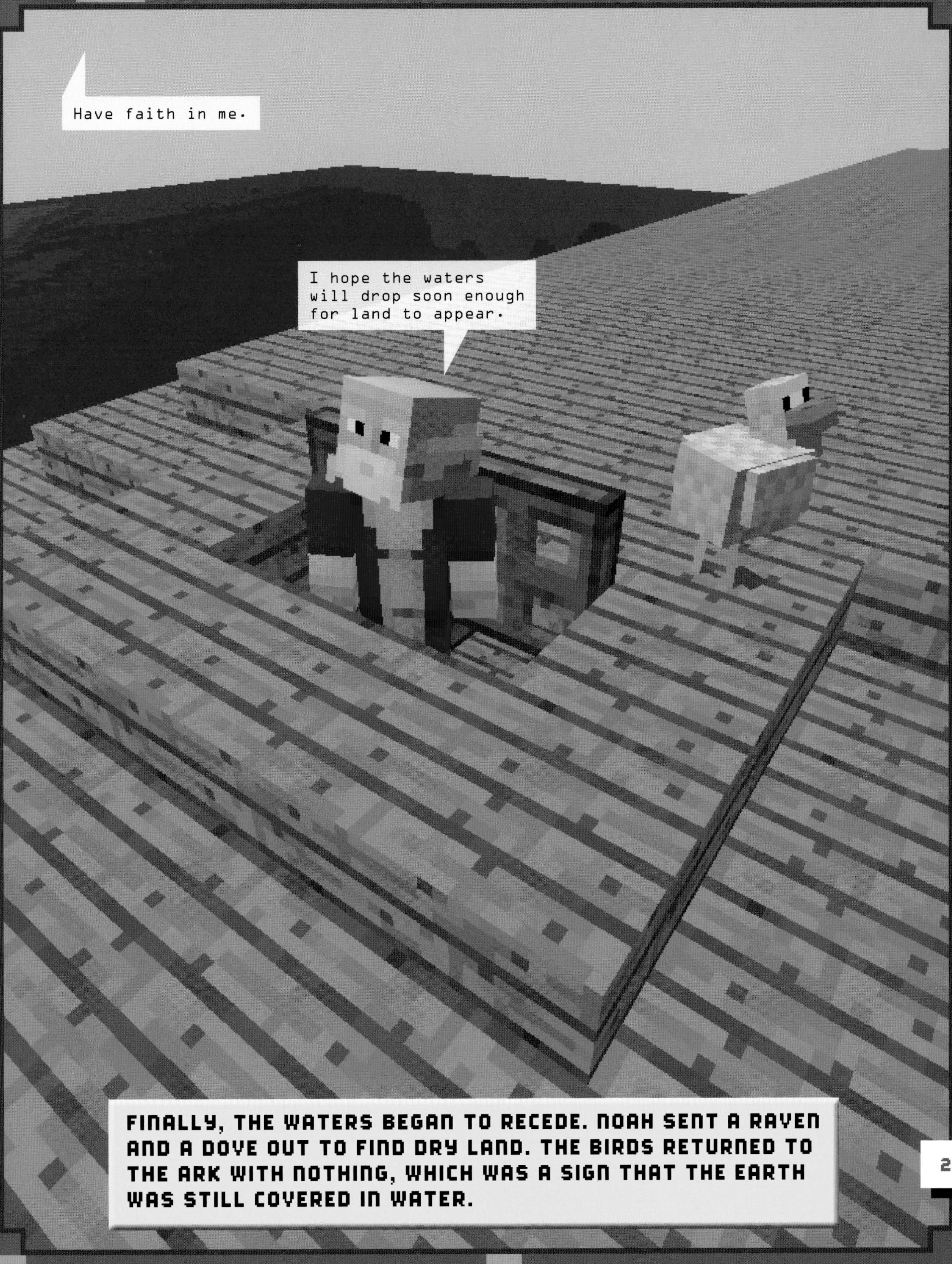
Have faith in me.
I hope the waters will drop soon enough for land to appear.
FINALLY, THE WATERS BEGAN TO RECEDE. NOAH SENT A RAVEN AND A DOVE OUT TO FIND DRY LAND. THE BIRDS RETURNED TO THE ARK WITH NOTHING, WHICH WAS A SIGN THAT THE EARTH WAS STILL COVERED IN WATER.

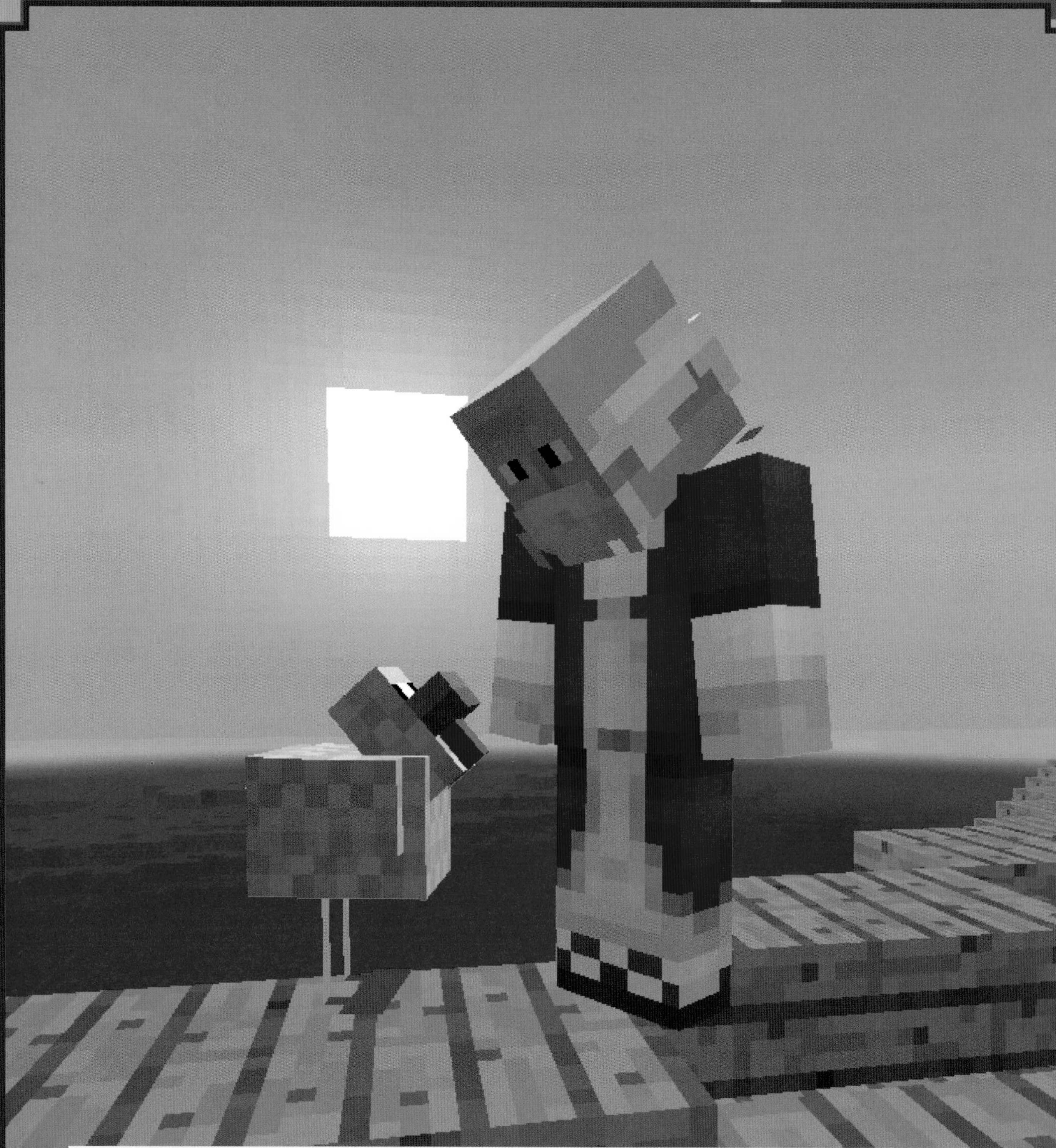

WEEKS PASSED, BUT NOAH AND HIS FAMILY DID NOT LOSE HOPE. NOAH SENT OUT THE BIRDS AGAIN AND AGAIN, BUT EACH TIME THEY WOULD COME BACK WITH NOTHING. FINALLY, NOAH TRIED ONE MORE TIME. HE PRAYED TO THE LORD THAT LAND WOULD BE FOUND. NOAH'S HEART BEGAN TO SINK WHEN HE REALIZED THE DOVE HAD PLUCKED A NEWLY GROWN OLIVE BRANCH AND BROUGHT IT BACK TO HIM. THIS WAS THE SIGN THAT THE EARTH WAS DRY AND LIFE COULD BEGIN AGAIN.

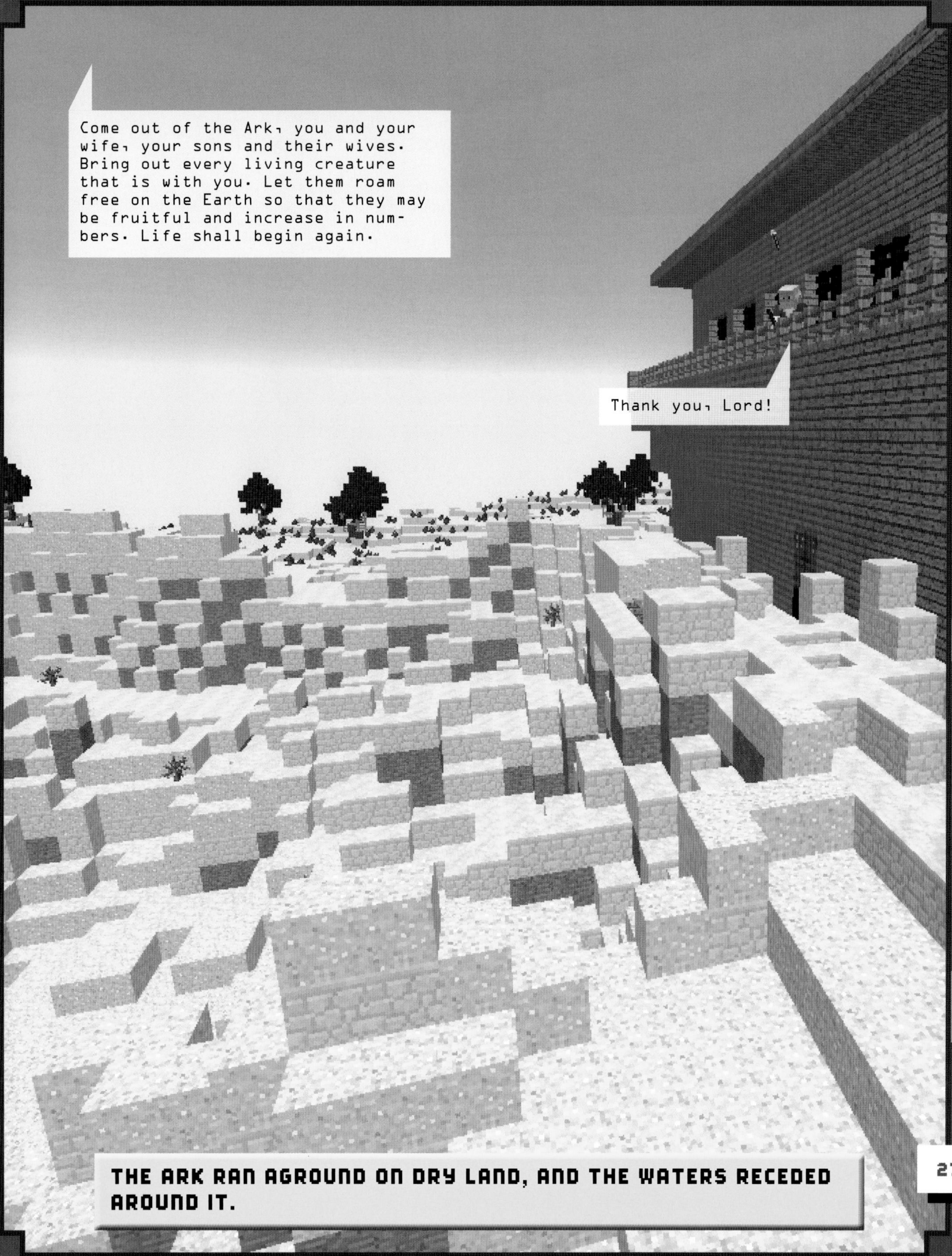
Come out of the Ark, you and your wife, your sons and their wives. Bring out every living creature that is with you. Let them roam free on the Earth so that they may be fruitful and increase in numbers. Life shall begin again.
Thank you, Lord!
THE ARK RAN AGROUND ON DRY LAND, AND THE WATERS RECEDED AROUND IT.

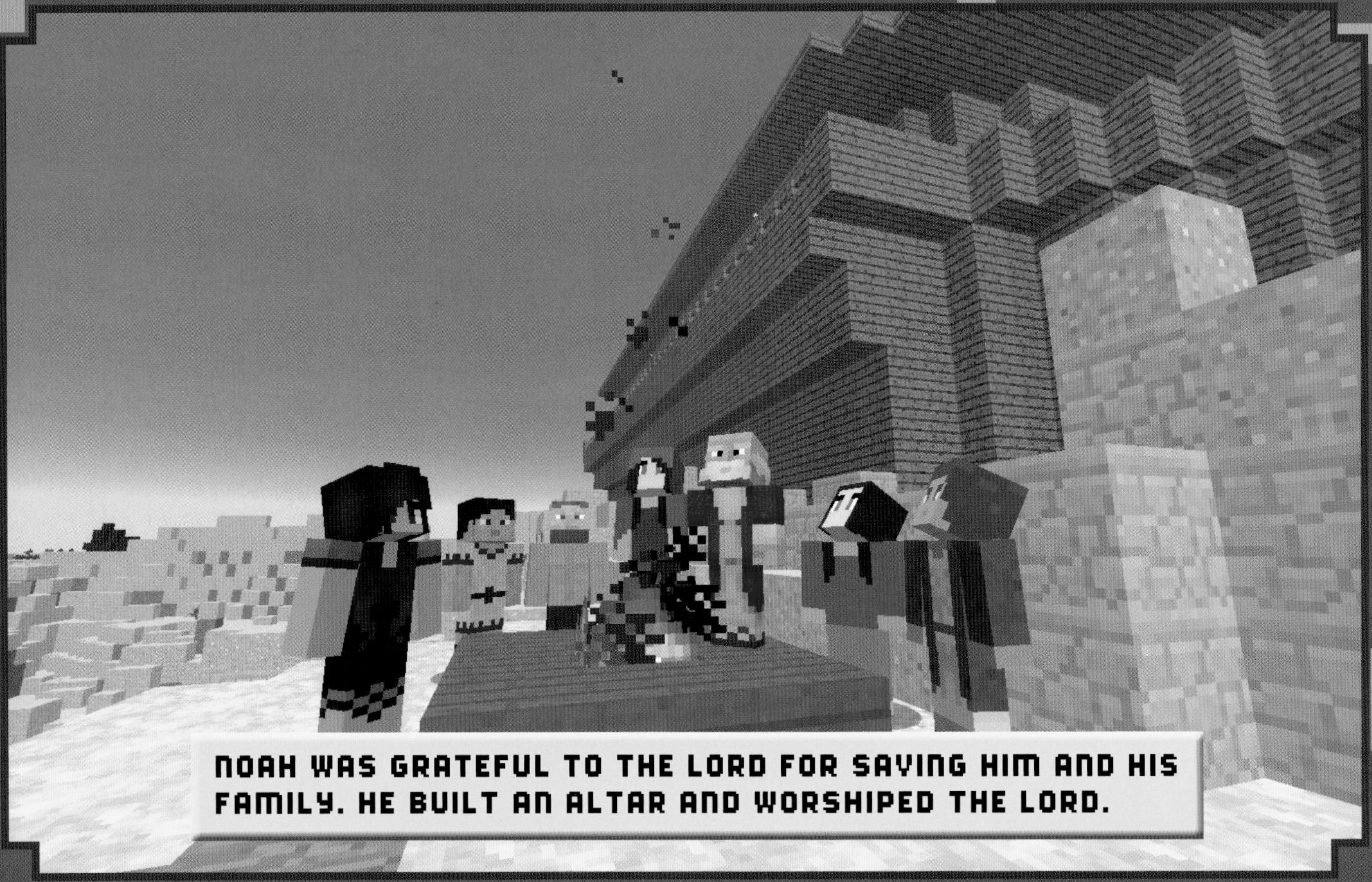
NOAH WAS GRATEFUL TO THE LORD FOR SAVING HIM AND HIS FAMILY. HE BUILT AN ALTAR AND WORSHIPED THE LORD.

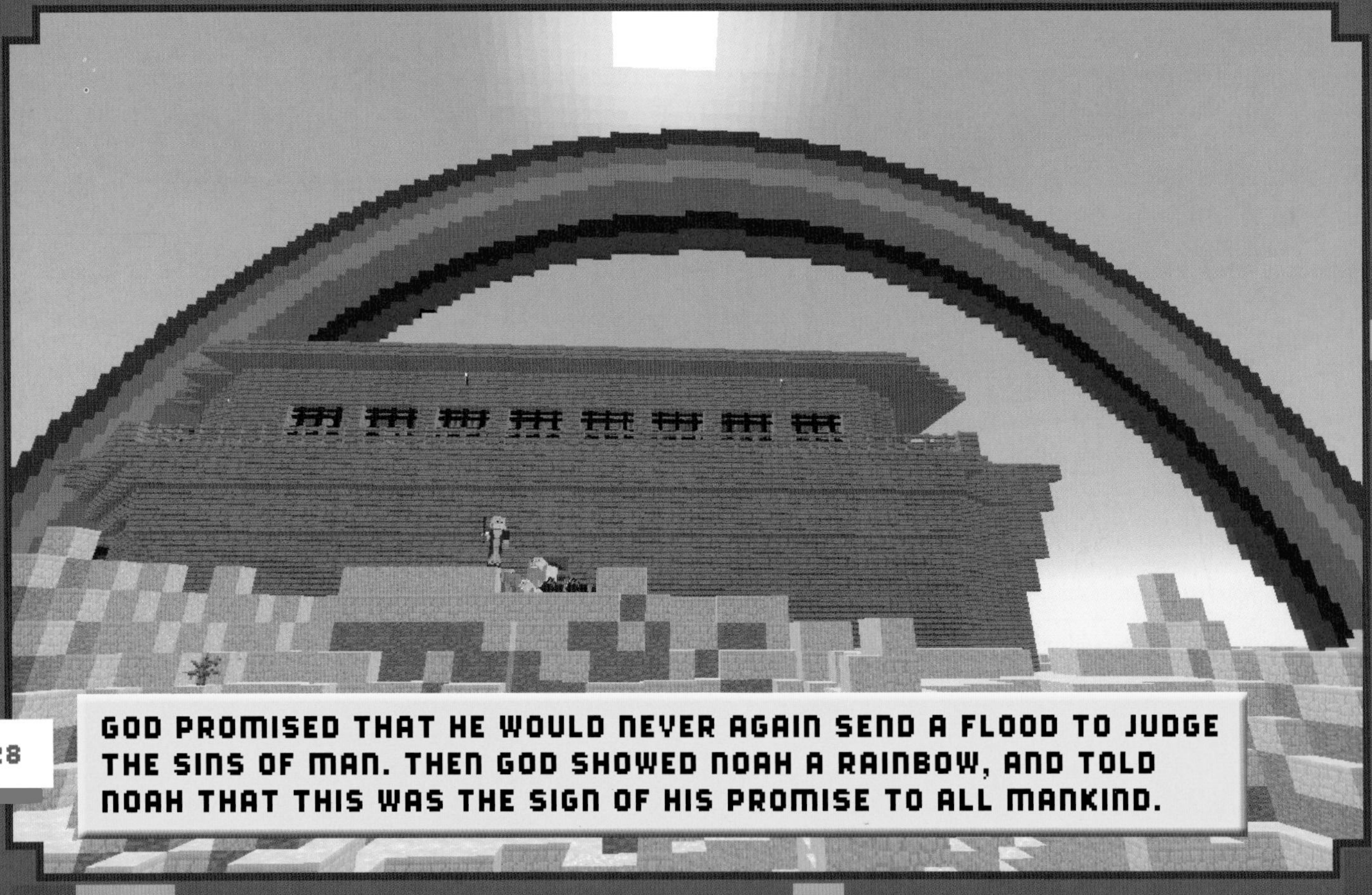
GOD PROMISED THAT HE WOULD NEVER AGAIN SEND A FLOOD TO JUDGE THE SINS OF MAN. THEN GOD SHOWED NOAH A RAINBOW, AND TOLD NOAH THAT THIS WAS THE SIGN OF HIS PROMISE TO ALL MANKIND.

TOWER OF BABEL

They are trying to build physical structures to reach me.

But you are reached by going within one-self.

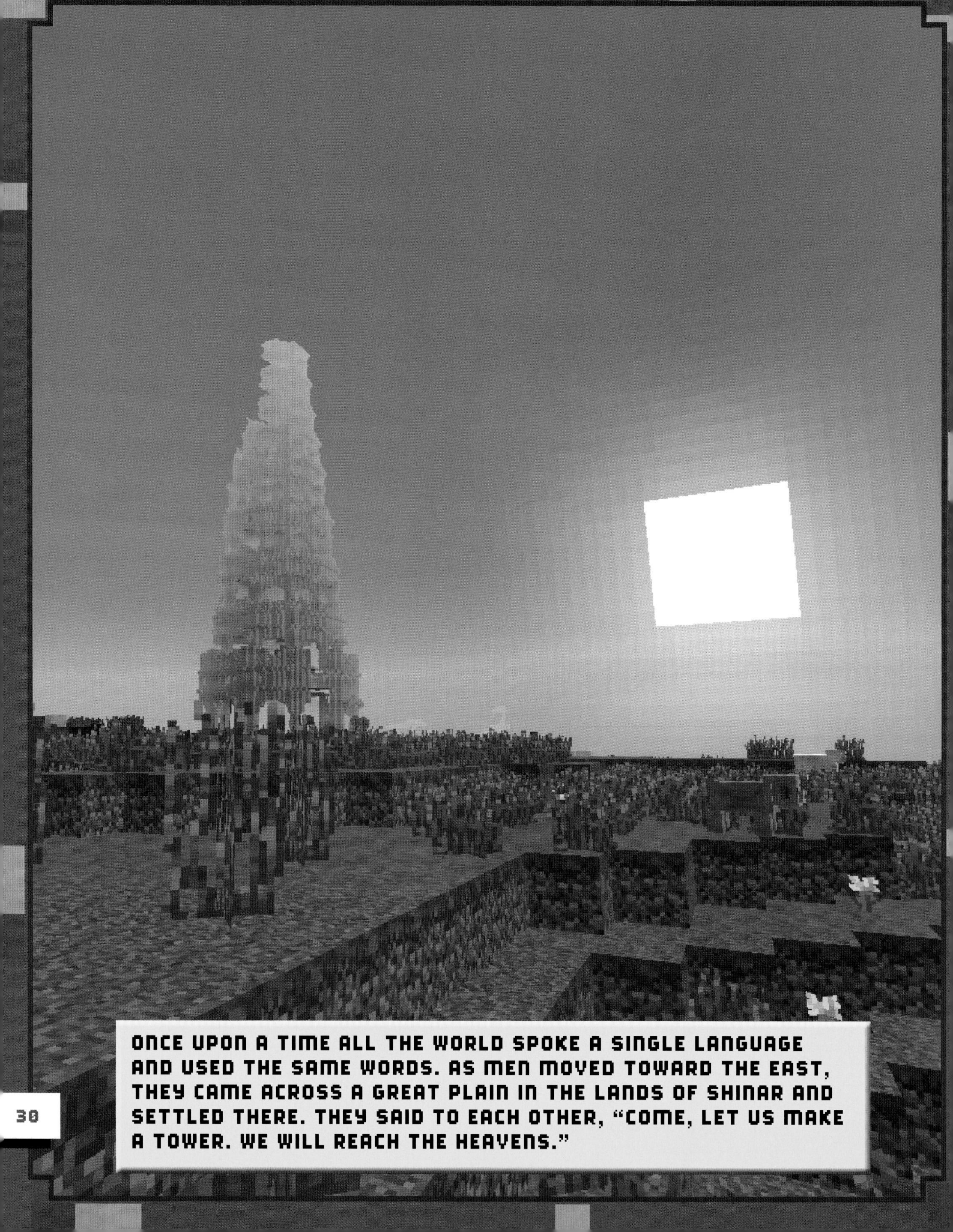

ONCE UPON A TIME ALL THE WORLD SPOKE A SINGLE LANGUAGE AND USED THE SAME WORDS. AS MEN MOVED TOWARD THE EAST, THEY CAME ACROSS A GREAT PLAIN IN THE LANDS OF SHINAR AND SETTLED THERE. THEY SAID TO EACH OTHER, "COME, LET US MAKE A TOWER. WE WILL REACH THE HEAVENS."

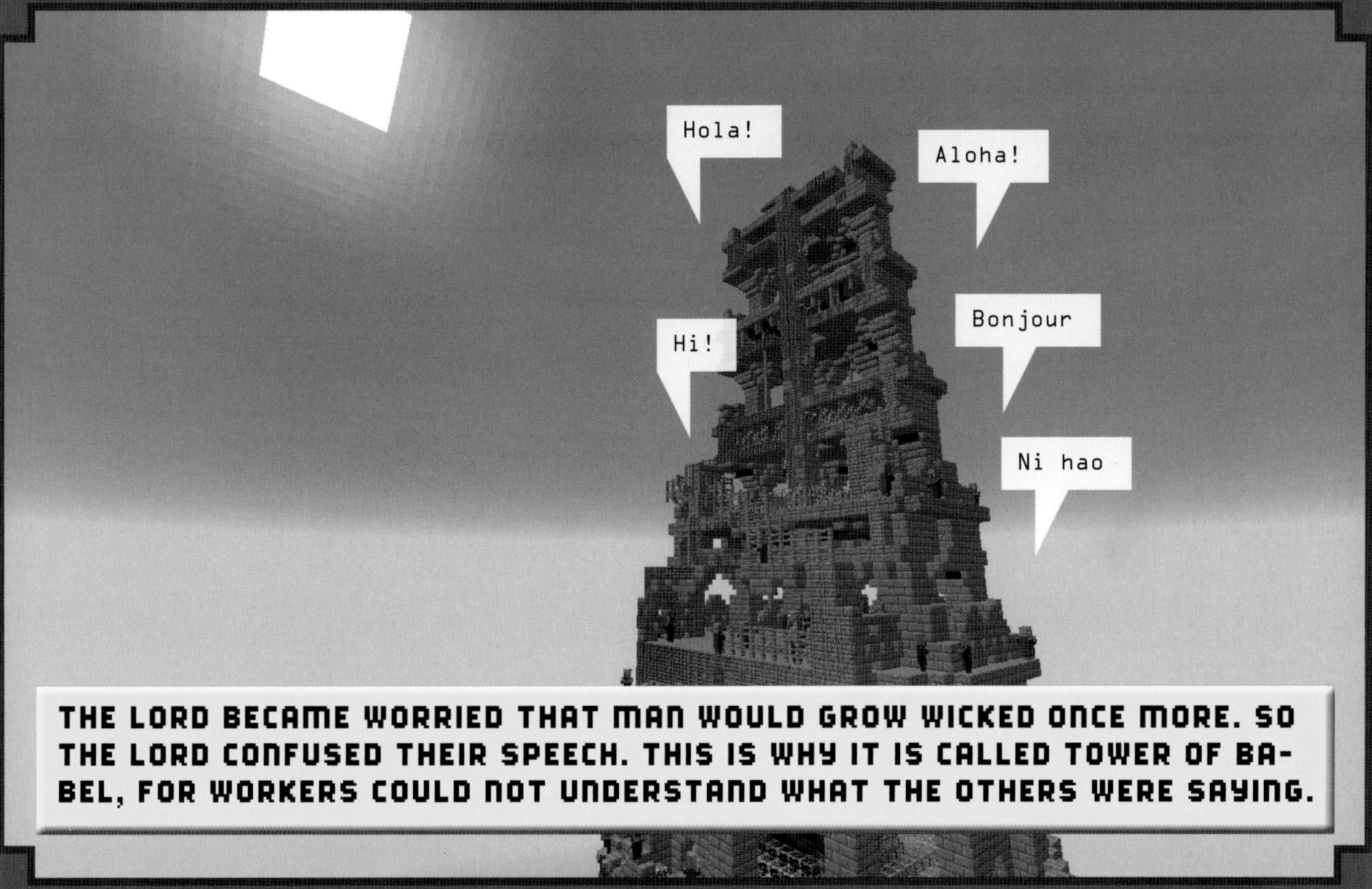
Hola!
Aloha!
Hi!
Bonjour
Ni hao
THE LORD BECAME WORRIED THAT MAN WOULD GROW WICKED ONCE MORE. SO THE LORD CONFUSED THEIR SPEECH. THIS IS WHY IT IS CALLED TOWER OF BABEL, FOR WORKERS COULD NOT UNDERSTAND WHAT THE OTHERS WERE SAYING.

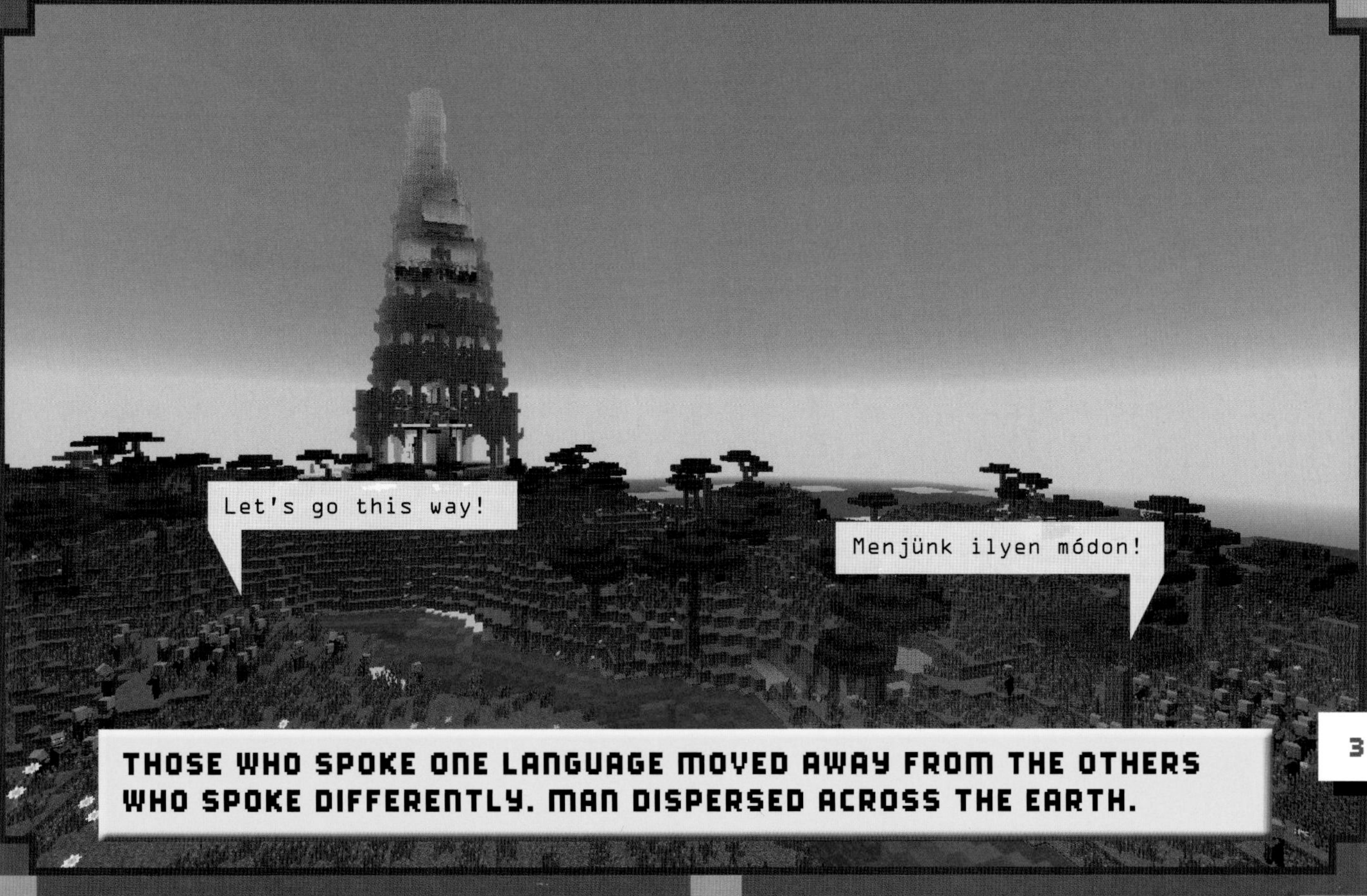
Let's go this way!
Menjünk ilyen módon!
THOSE WHO SPOKE ONE LANGUAGE MOVED AWAY FROM THE OTHERS WHO SPOKE DIFFERENTLY. MAN DISPERSED ACROSS THE EARTH.

GOD CALLS ABRAHAM

I have selected which group will be the Chosen People to carry on with my work on Earth.

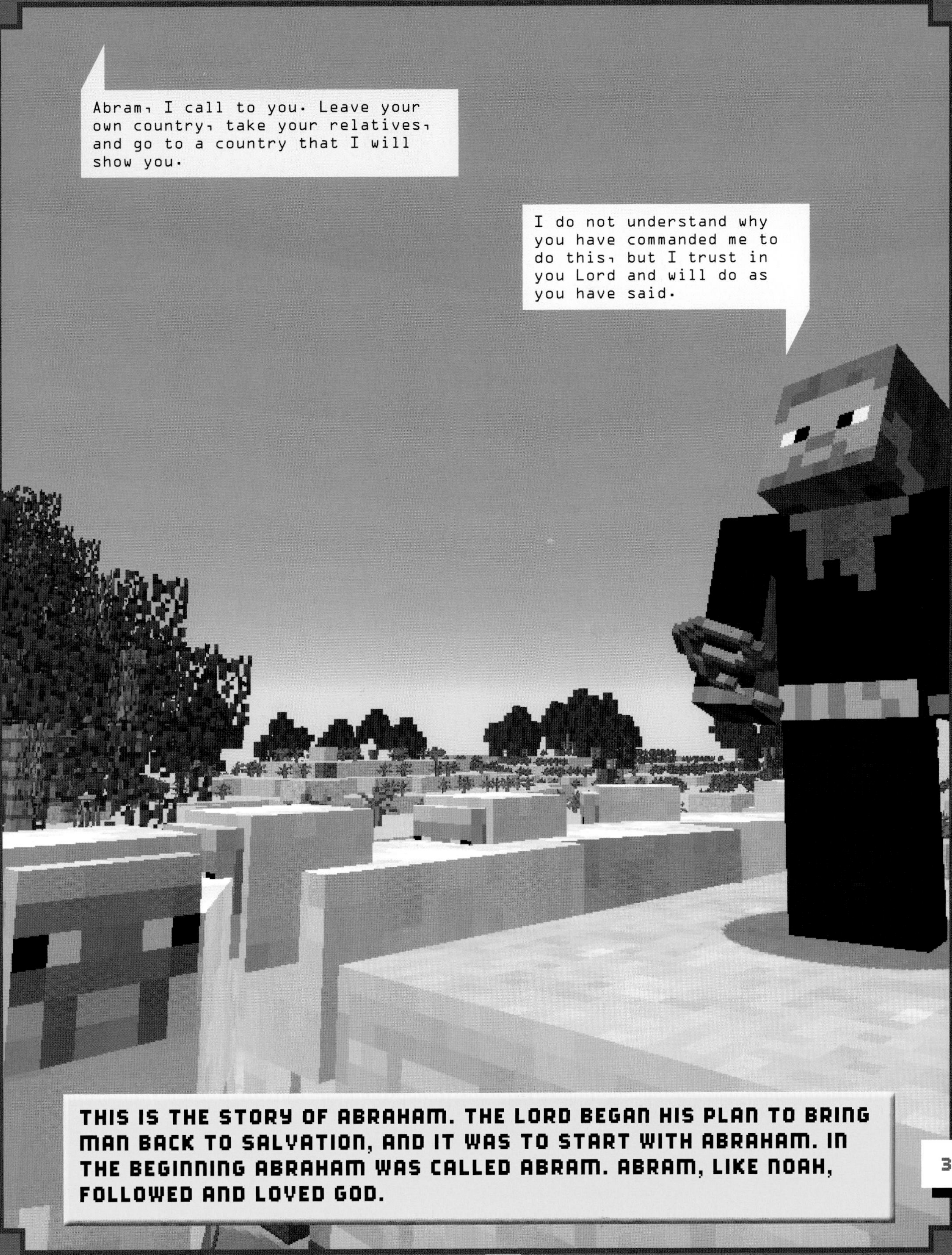
Abram, I call to you. Leave your own country, take your relatives, and go to a country that I will show you.
I do not understand why you have commanded me to do this, but I trust in you Lord and will do as you have said.
THIS IS THE STORY OF ABRAHAM. THE LORD BEGAN HIS PLAN TO BRING MAN BACK TO SALVATION, AND IT WAS TO START WITH ABRAHAM. IN THE BEGINNING ABRAHAM WAS CALLED ABRAM. ABRAM, LIKE NOAH, FOLLOWED AND LOVED GOD.

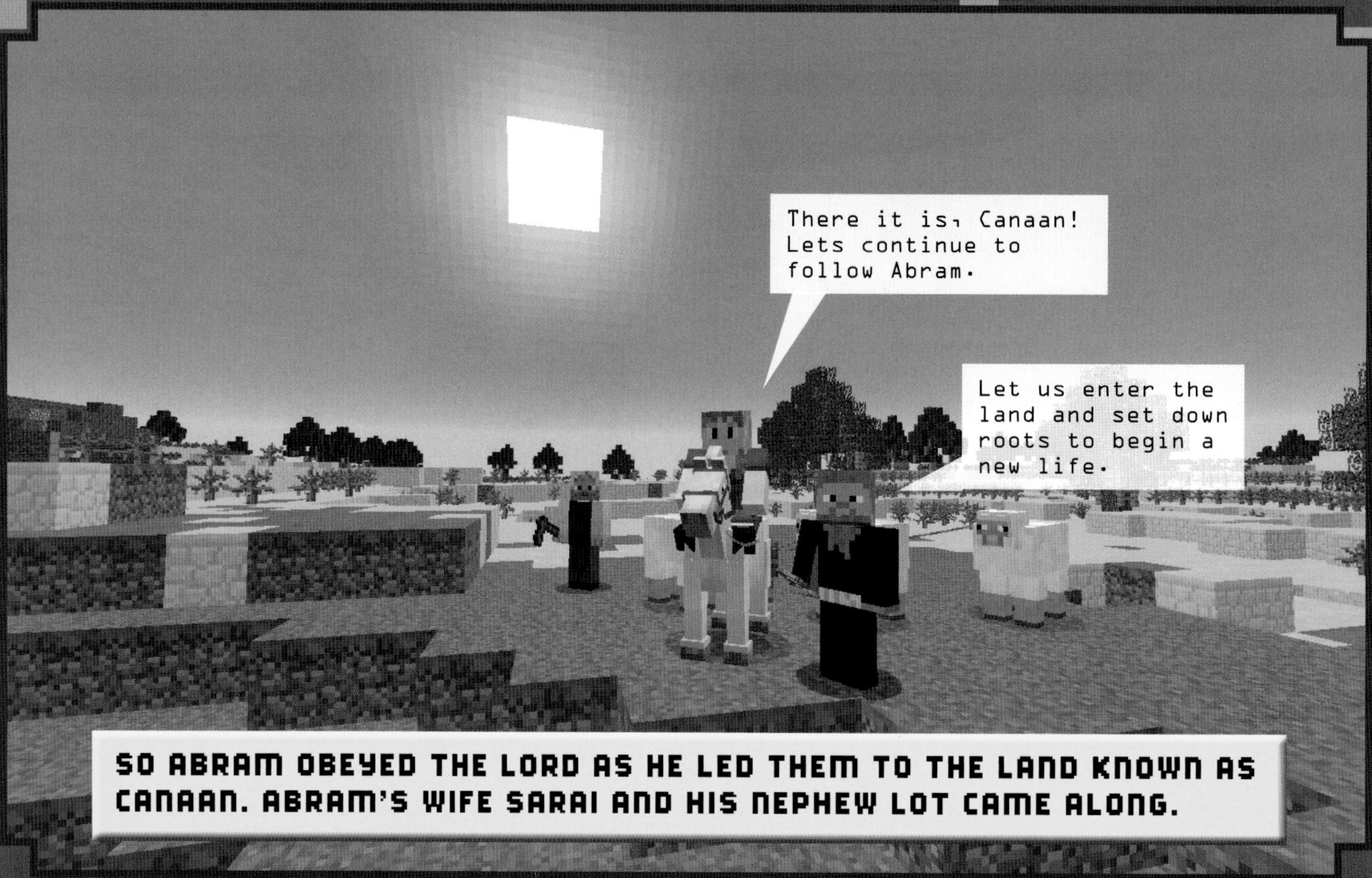
There it is, Canaan! Lets continue to follow Abram.
Let us enter the land and set down roots to begin a new life.
SO ABRAM OBEYED THE LORD AS HE LED THEM TO THE LAND KNOWN AS CANAAN. ABRAM'S WIFE SARAI AND HIS NEPHEW LOT CAME ALONG.

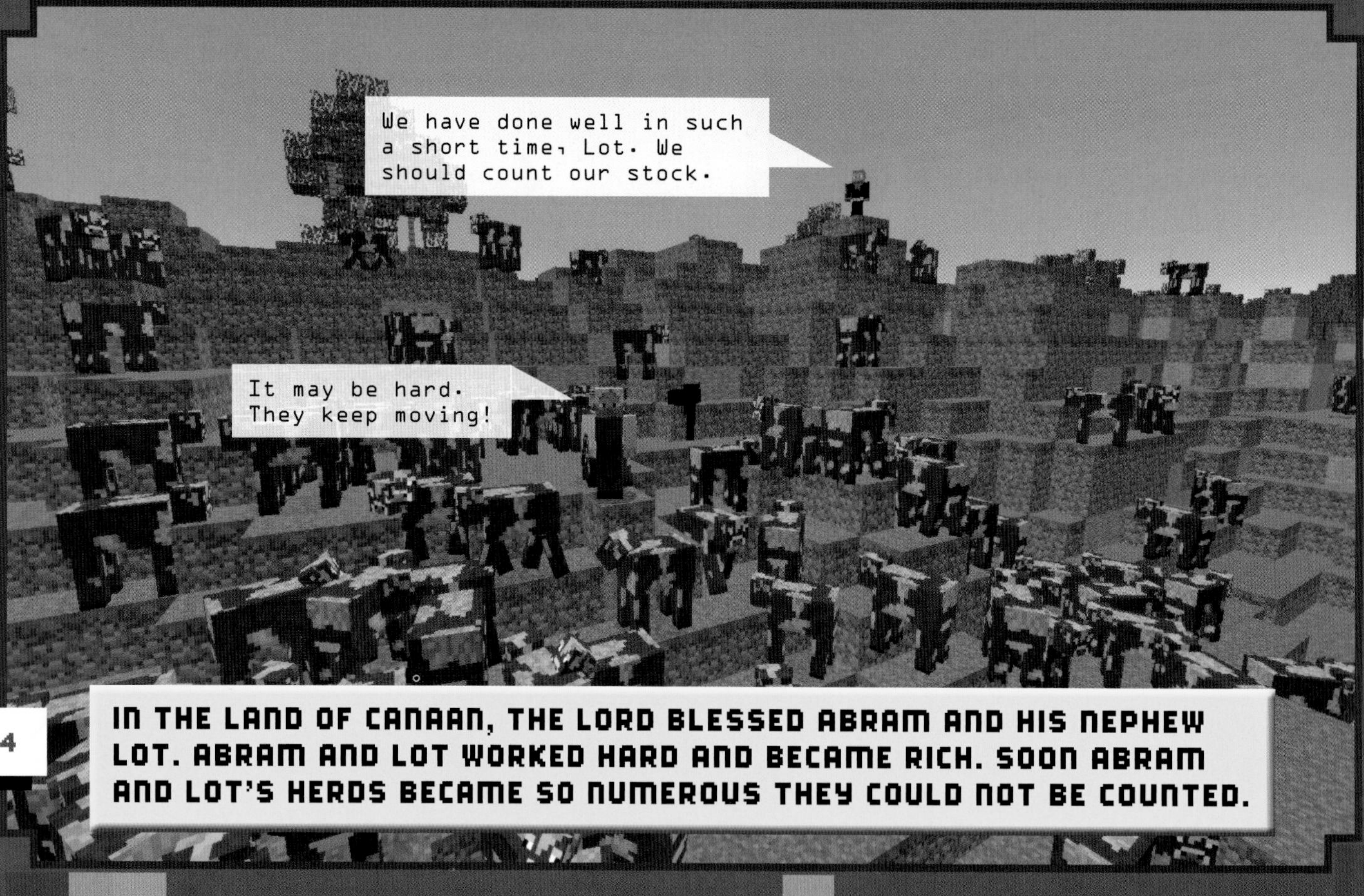
We have done well in such a short time, Lot. We should count our stock.
It may be hard. They keep moving!
IN THE LAND OF CANAAN, THE LORD BLESSED ABRAM AND HIS NEPHEW LOT. ABRAM AND LOT WORKED HARD AND BECAME RICH. SOON ABRAM AND LOT'S HERDS BECAME SO NUMEROUS THEY COULD NOT BE COUNTED.

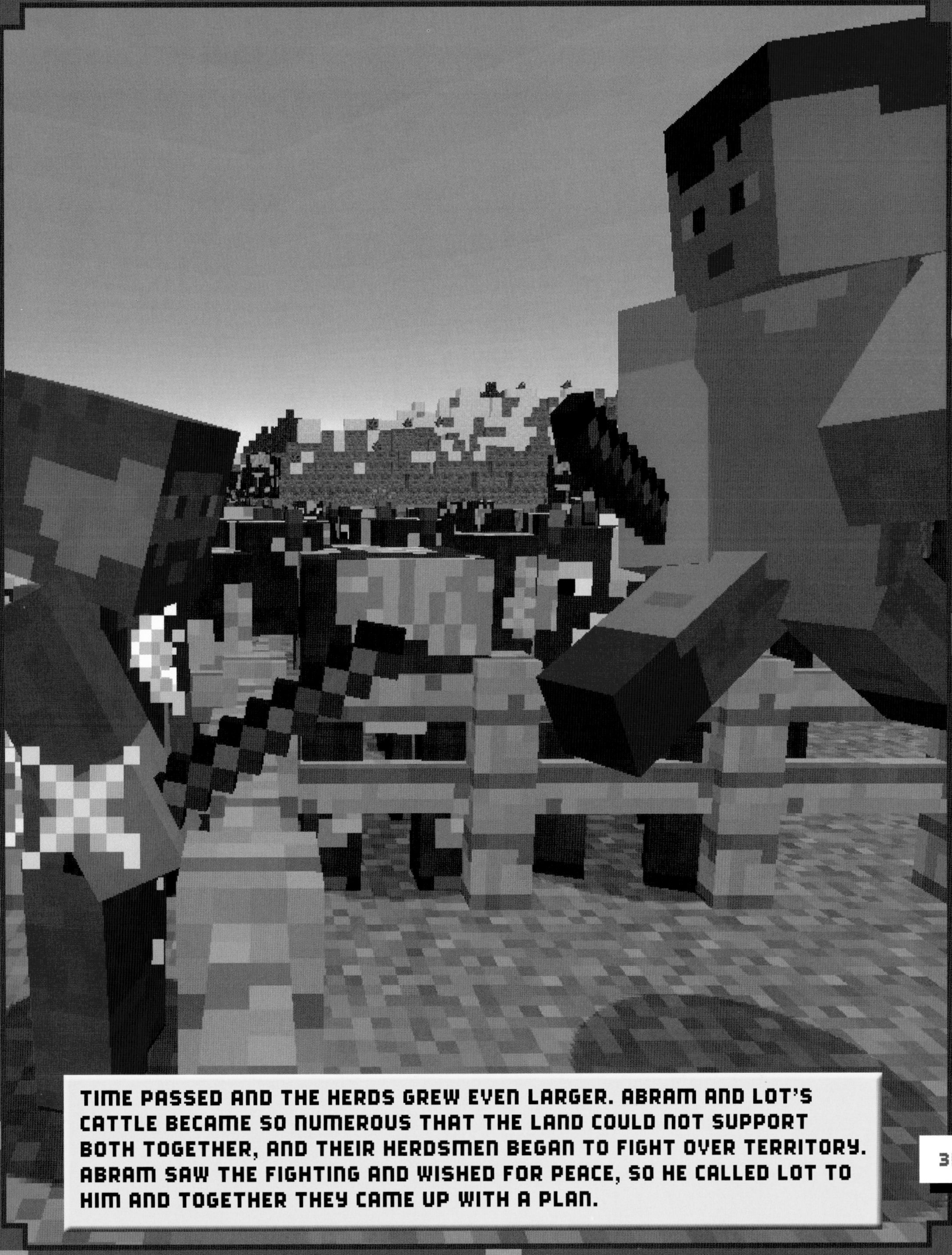
TIME PASSED AND THE HERDS GREW EVEN LARGER. ABRAM AND LOT'S CATTLE BECAME SO NUMEROUS THAT THE LAND COULD NOT SUPPORT BOTH TOGETHER, AND THEIR HERDSMEN BEGAN TO FIGHT OVER TERRITORY. ABRAM SAW THE FIGHTING AND WISHED FOR PEACE, SO HE CALLED LOT TO HIM AND TOGETHER THEY CAME UP WITH A PLAN.

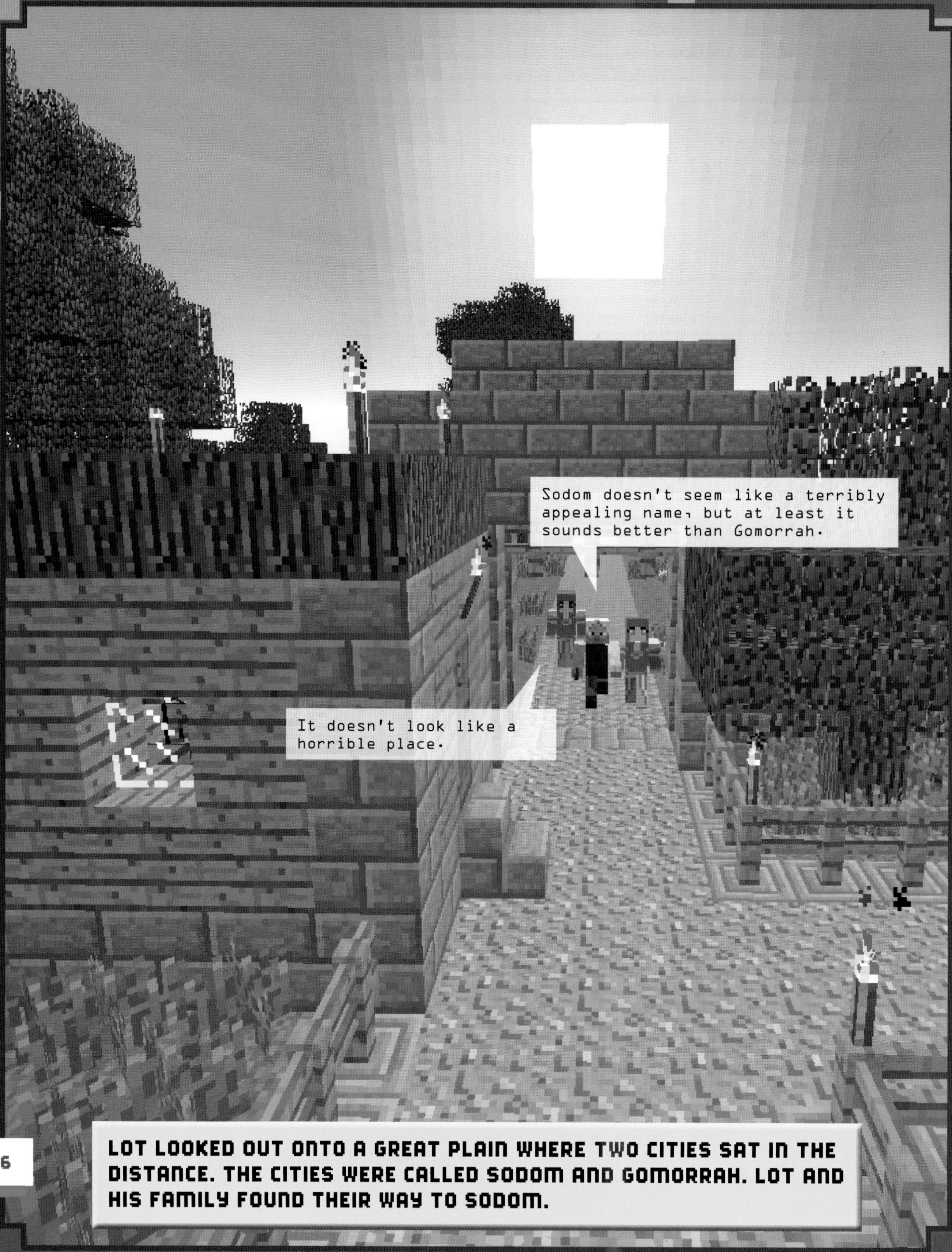
Sodom doesn't seem like a terribly appealing name, but at least it sounds better than Gomorrah.
It doesn't look like a horrible place.
LOT LOOKED OUT ONTO A GREAT PLAIN WHERE TWO CITIES SAT IN THE DISTANCE. THE CITIES WERE CALLED SODOM AND GOMORRAH. LOT AND HIS FAMILY FOUND THEIR WAY TO SODOM.

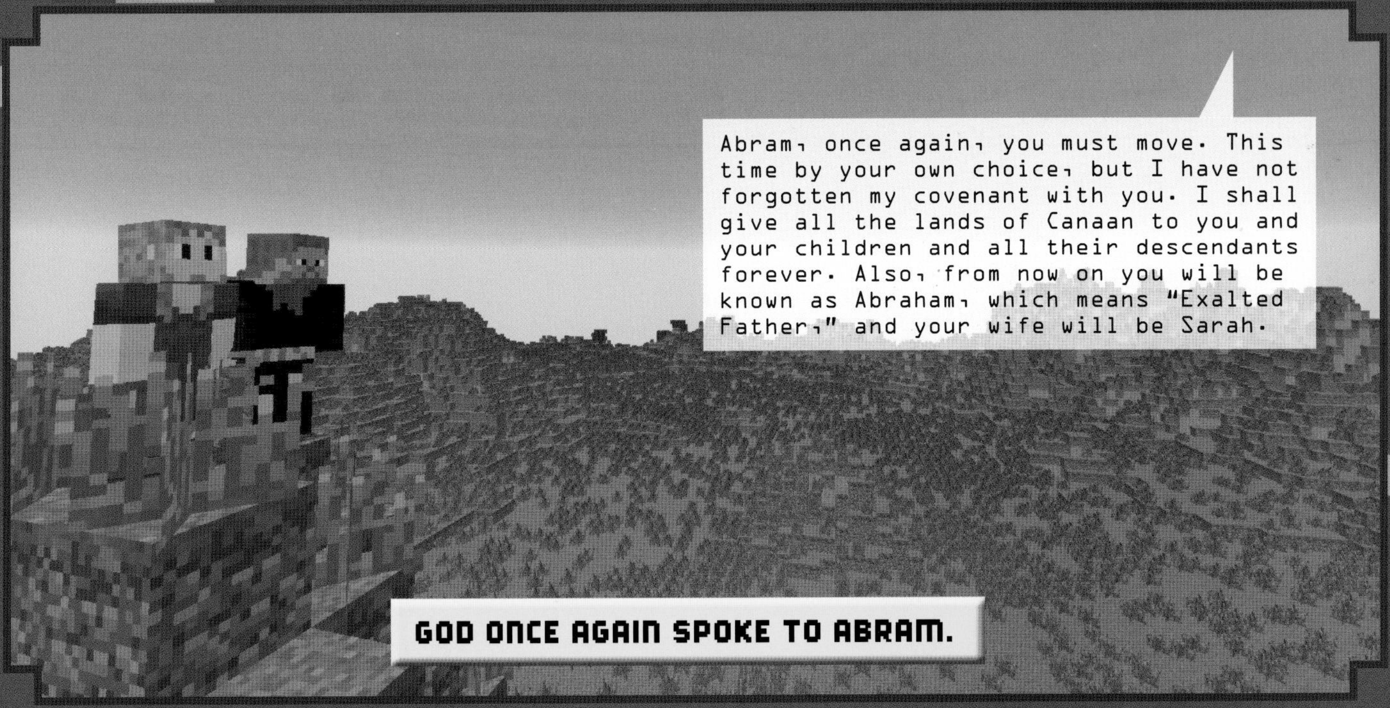
Abram, once again, you must move. This time by your own choice, but I have not forgotten my covenant with you. I shall give all the lands of Canaan to you and your children and all their descendants forever. Also, from now on you will be known as Abraham, which means "Exalted Father," and your wife will be Sarah.
GOD ONCE AGAIN SPOKE TO ABRAM.

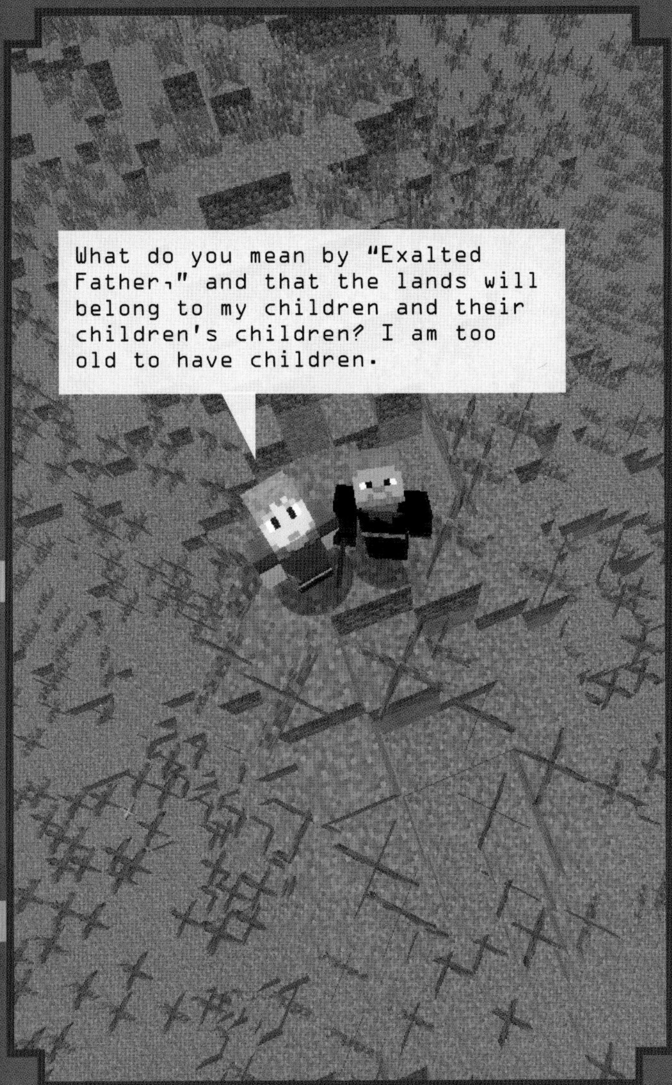
What do you mean by "Exalted Father," and that the lands will belong to my children and their children's children? I am too old to have children.

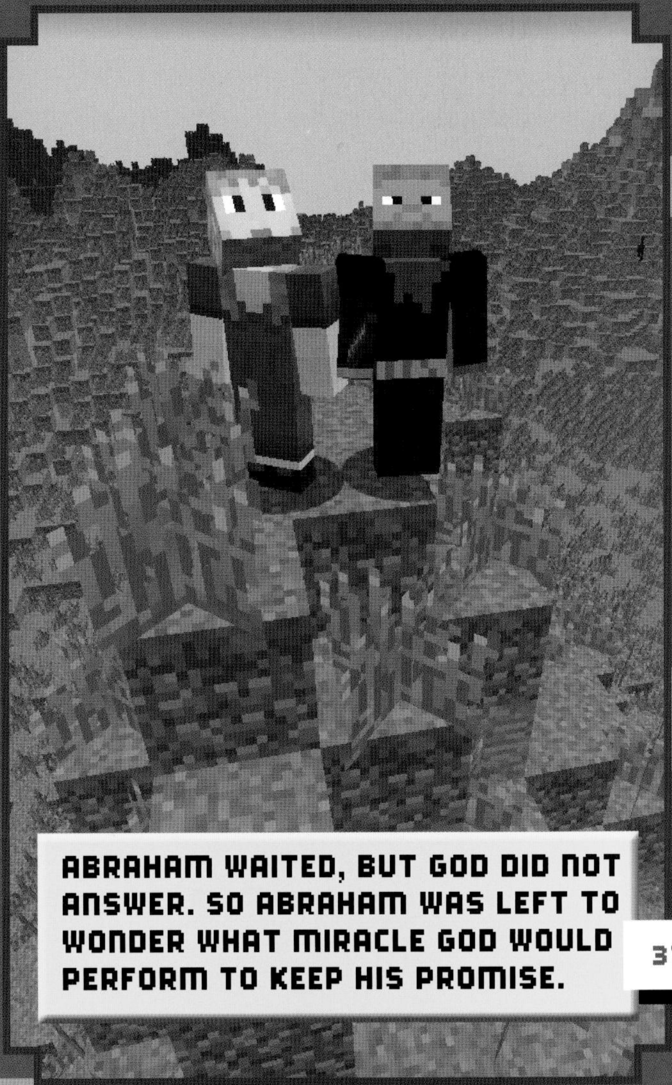
ABRAHAM WAITED, BUT GOD DID NOT ANSWER. SO ABRAHAM WAS LEFT TO WONDER WHAT MIRACLE GOD WOULD PERFORM TO KEEP HIS PROMISE.

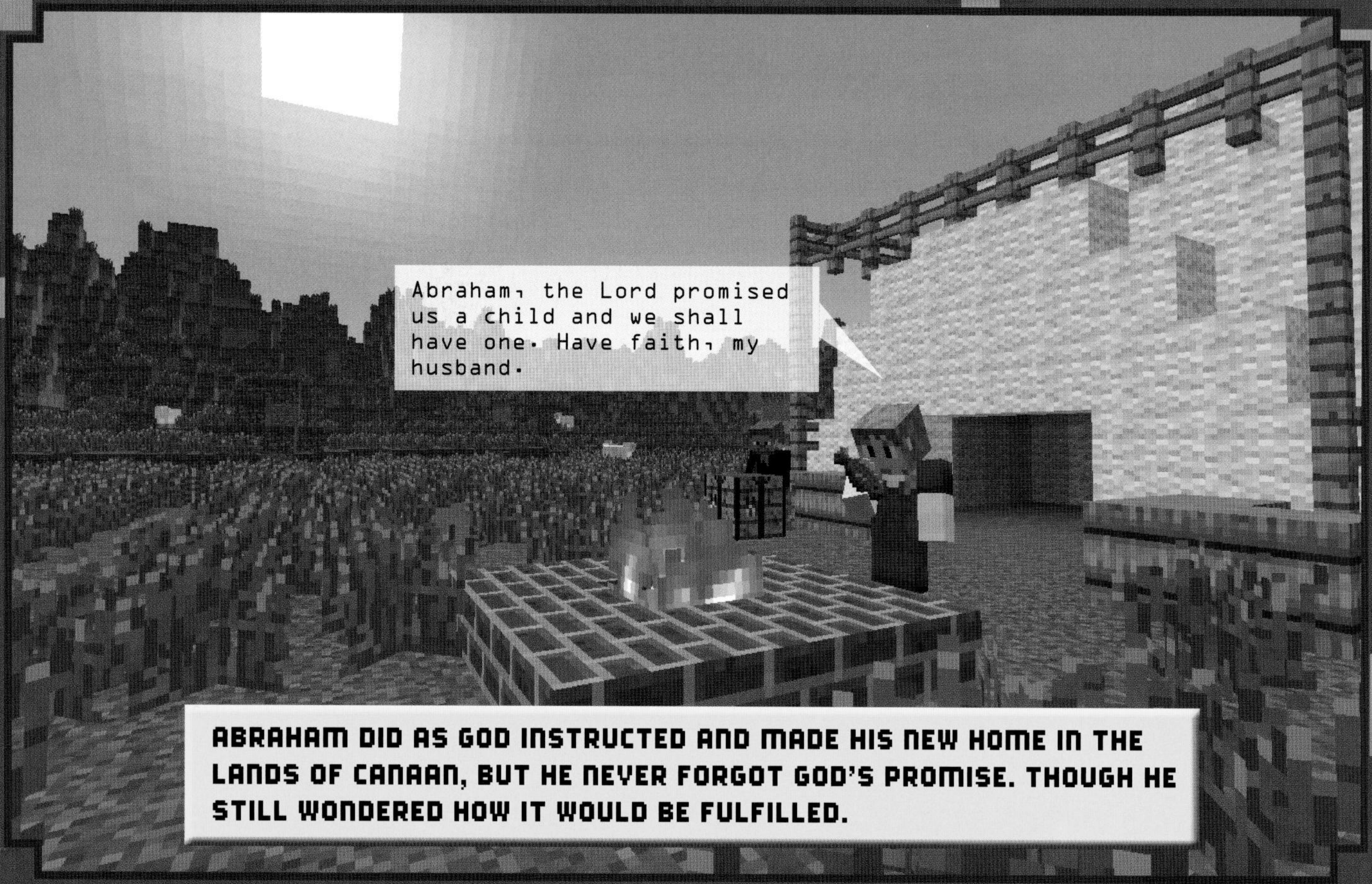
Abraham, the Lord promised us a child and we shall have one. Have faith, my husband.
ABRAHAM DID AS GOD INSTRUCTED AND MADE HIS NEW HOME IN THE LANDS OF CANAAN, BUT HE NEVER FORGOT GOD'S PROMISE. THOUGH HE STILL WONDERED HOW IT WOULD BE FULFILLED.

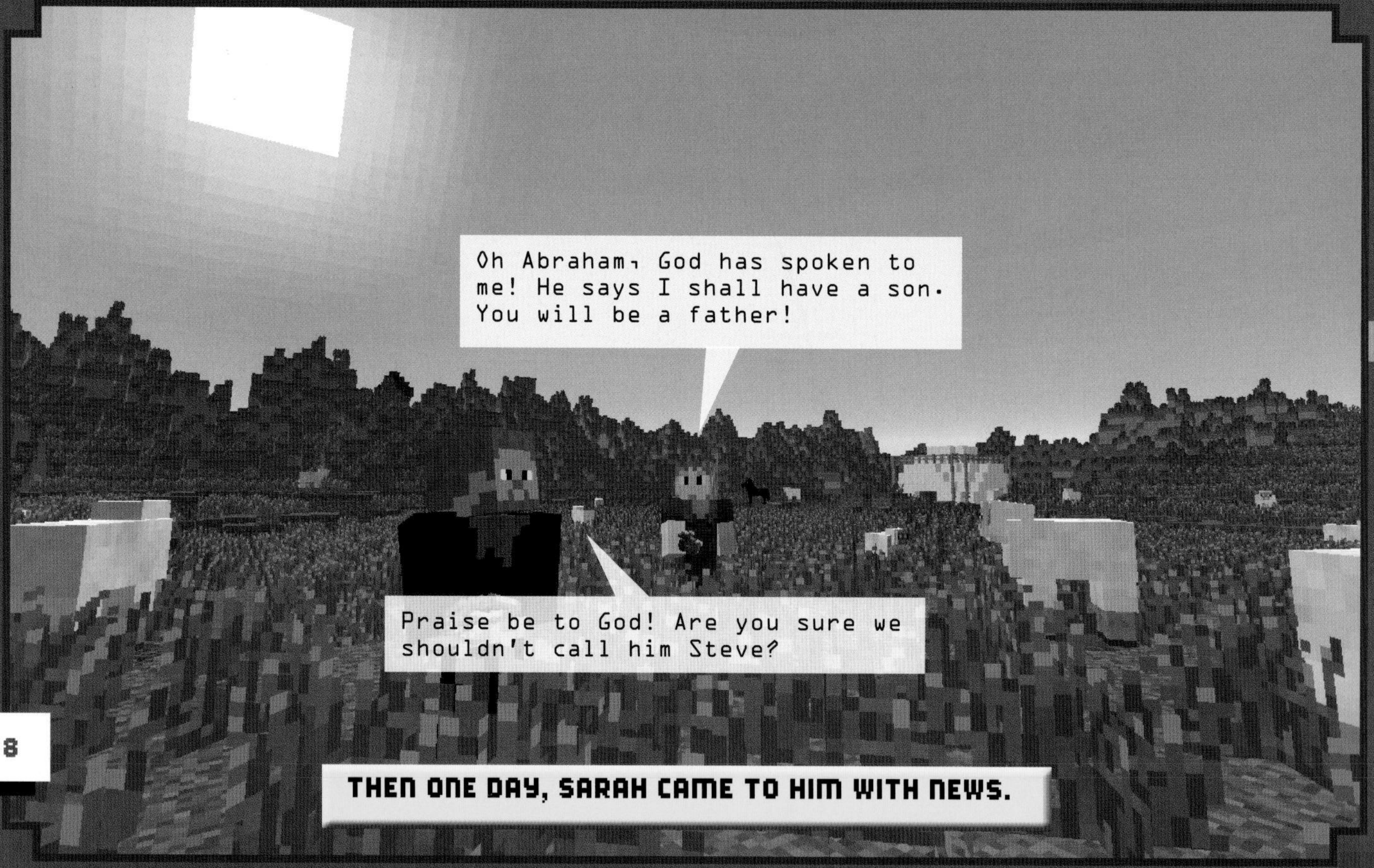
Oh Abraham, God has spoken to me! He says I shall have a son. You will be a father!
Praise be to God! Are you sure we shouldn't call him Steve?
THEN ONE DAY, SARAH CAME TO HIM WITH NEWS.

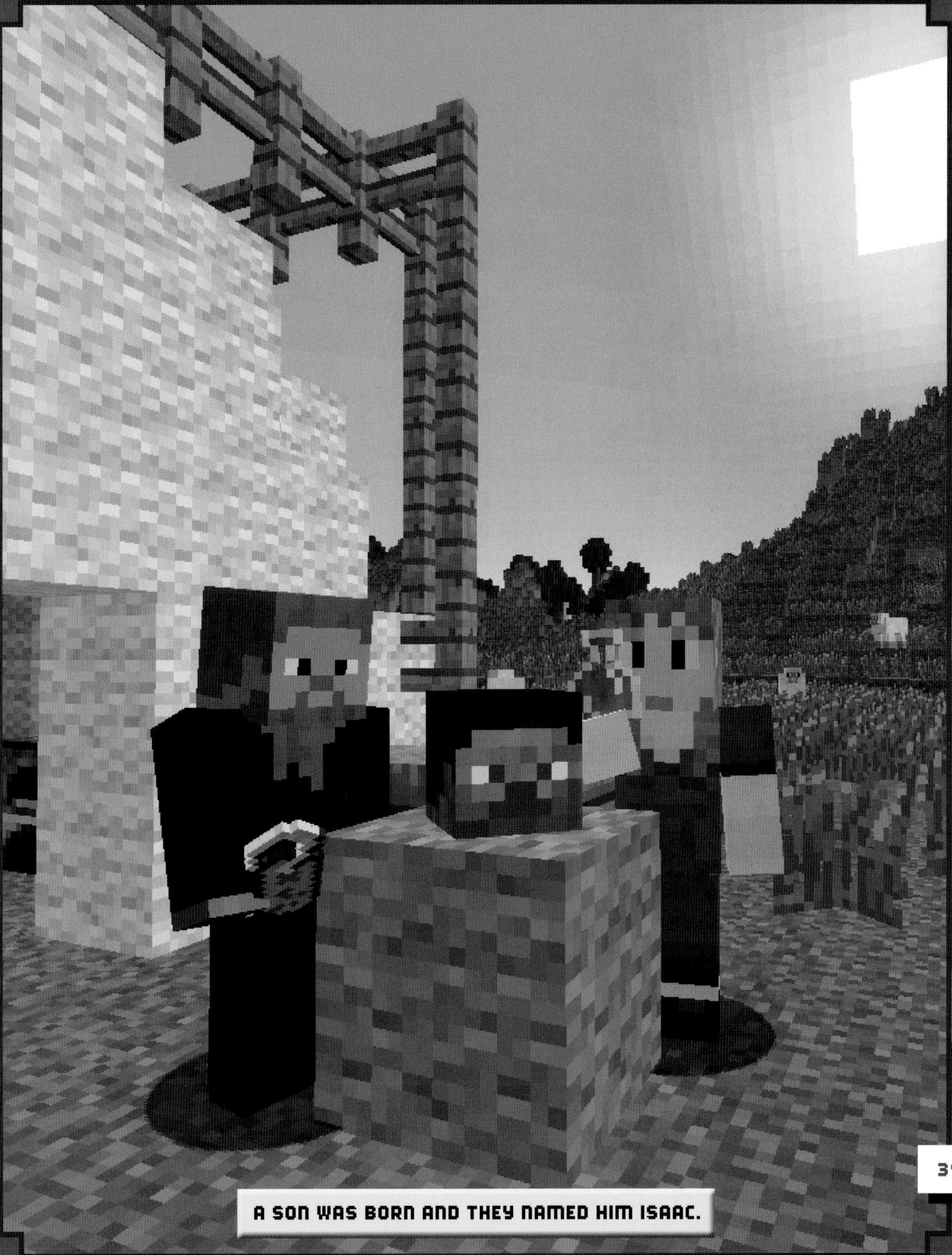

A SON WAS BORN AND THEY NAMED HIM ISAAC.

SODOM AND GOMORRAH

Uh, God?

Yes, Gabriel.

Looks like there's some more cleansing that has to be done.

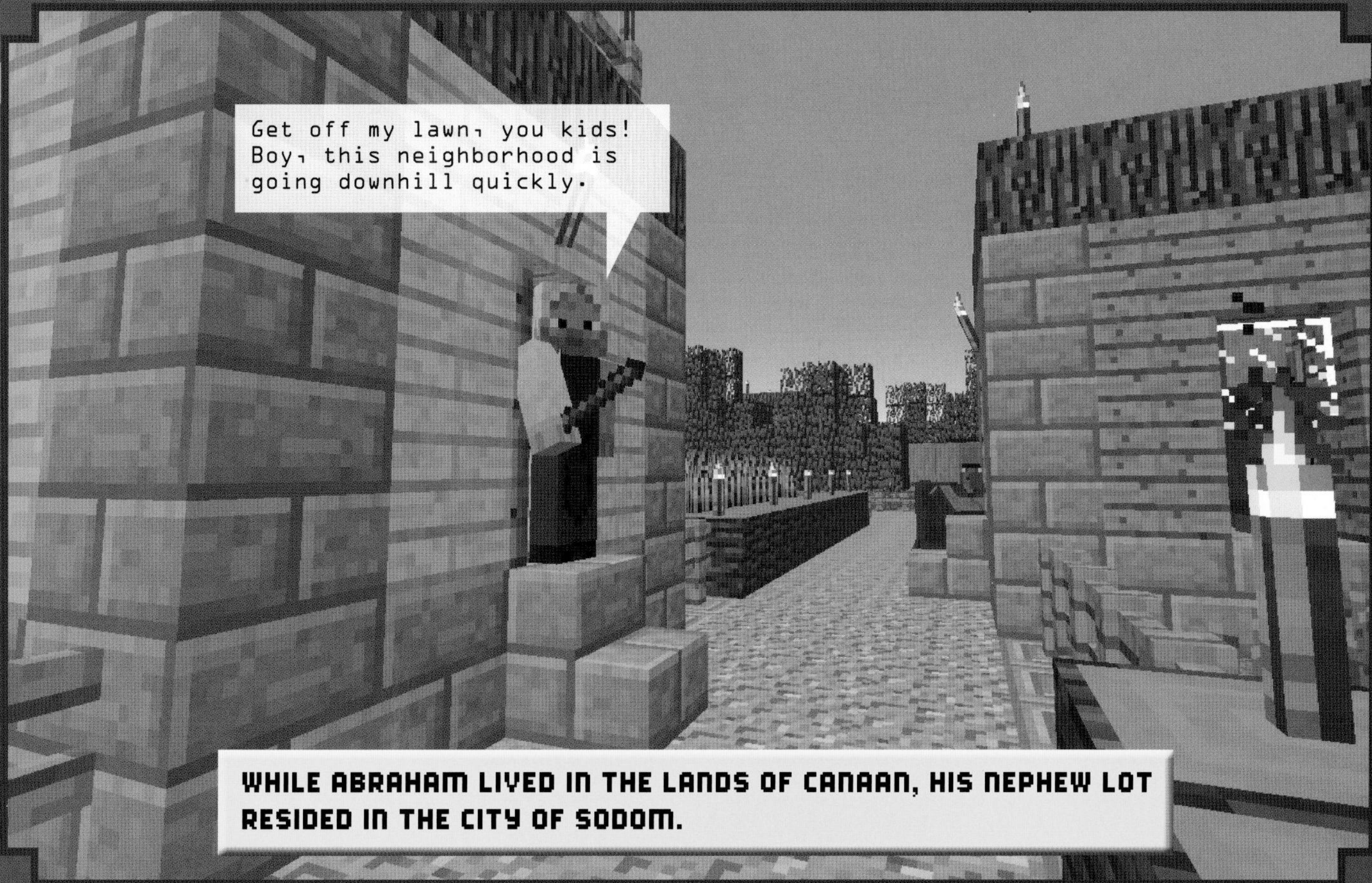
Get off my lawn, you kids! Boy, this neighborhood is going downhill quickly.
WHILE ABRAHAM LIVED IN THE LANDS OF CANAAN, HIS NEPHEW LOT RESIDED IN THE CITY OF SODOM.

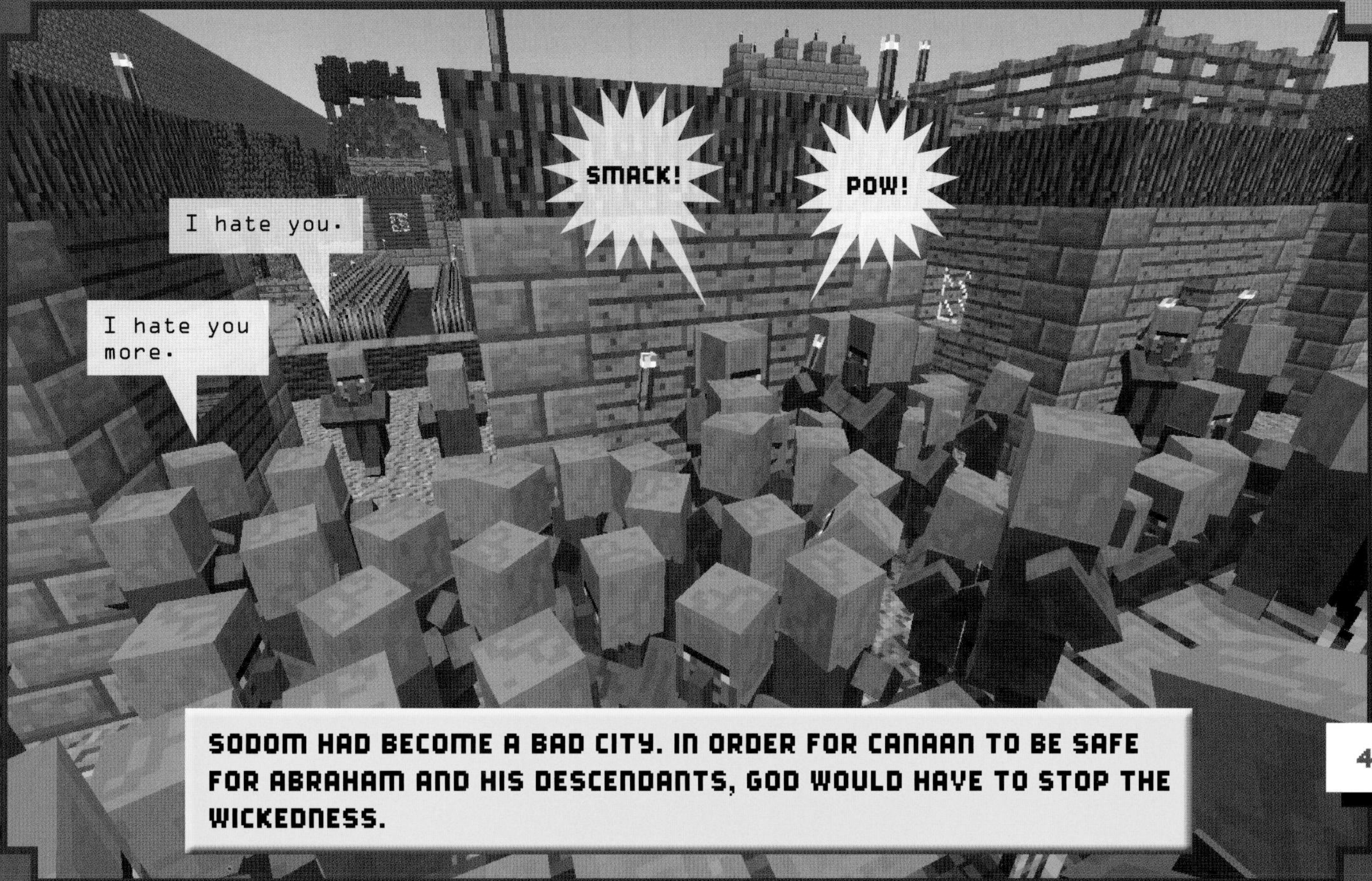
I hate you.
I hate you more.
SMACK!
POW!
SODOM HAD BECOME A BAD CITY. IN ORDER FOR CANAAN TO BE SAFE FOR ABRAHAM AND HIS DESCENDANTS, GOD WOULD HAVE TO STOP THE WICKEDNESS.

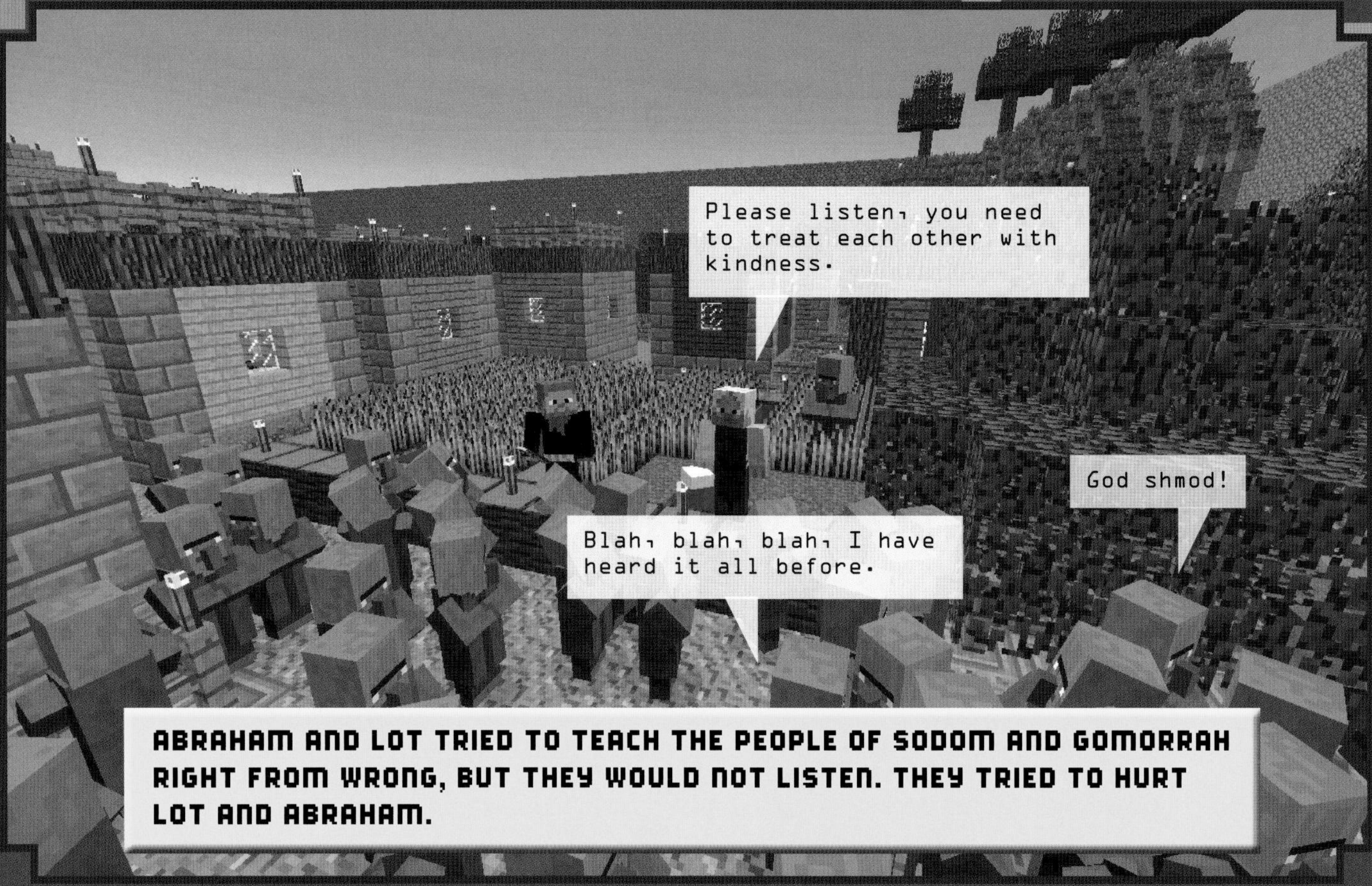
Please listen, you need to treat each other with kindness.
God shmod!
Blah, blah, blah, I have heard it all before.
ABRAHAM AND LOT TRIED TO TEACH THE PEOPLE OF SODOM AND GOMORRAH RIGHT FROM WRONG, BUT THEY WOULD NOT LISTEN. THEY TRIED TO HURT LOT AND ABRAHAM.

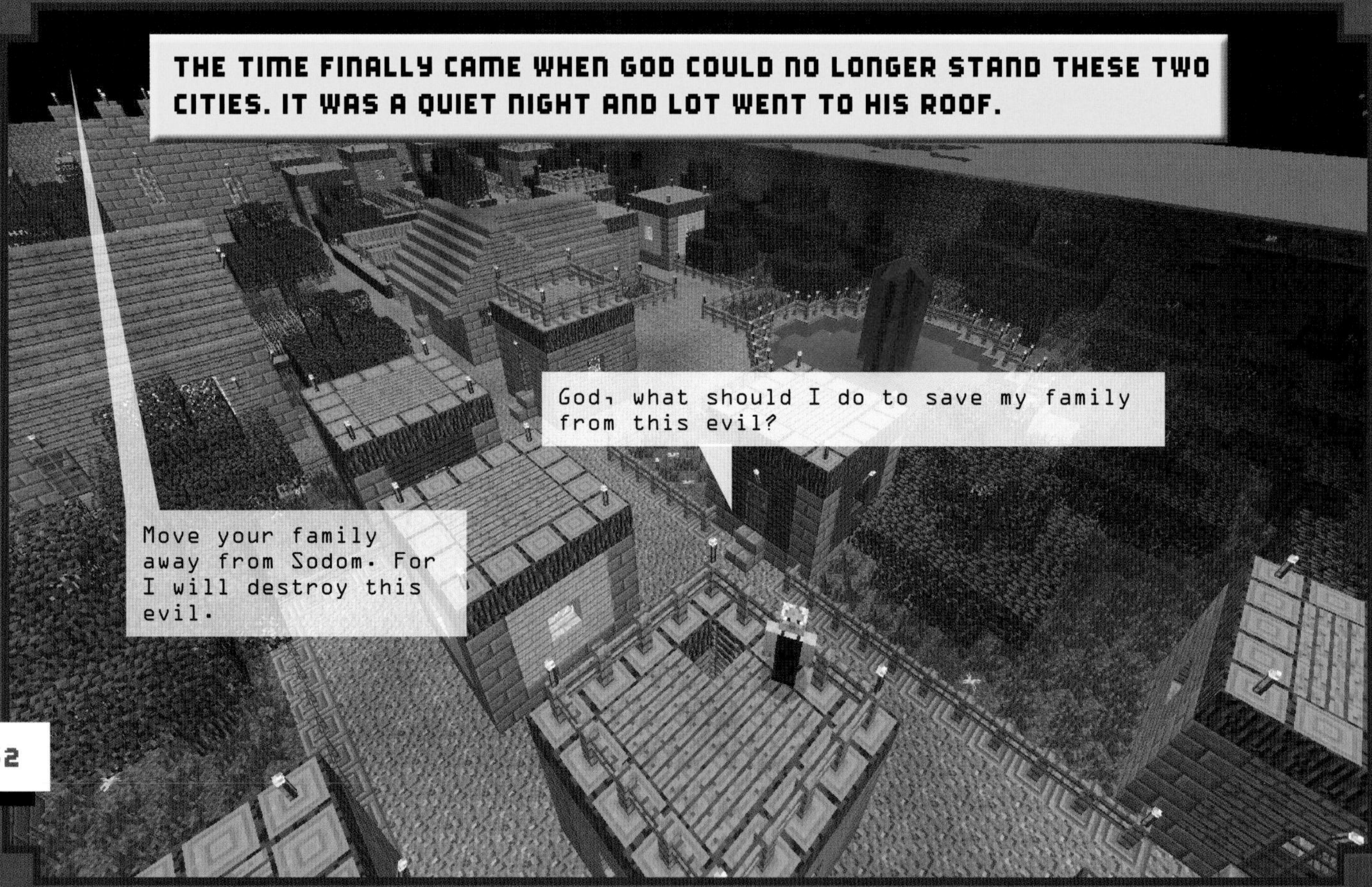
THE TIME FINALLY CAME WHEN GOD COULD NO LONGER STAND THESE TWO CITIES. IT WAS A QUIET NIGHT AND LOT WENT TO HIS ROOF.
God, what should I do to save my family from this evil?
Move your family away from Sodom. For I will destroy this evil.

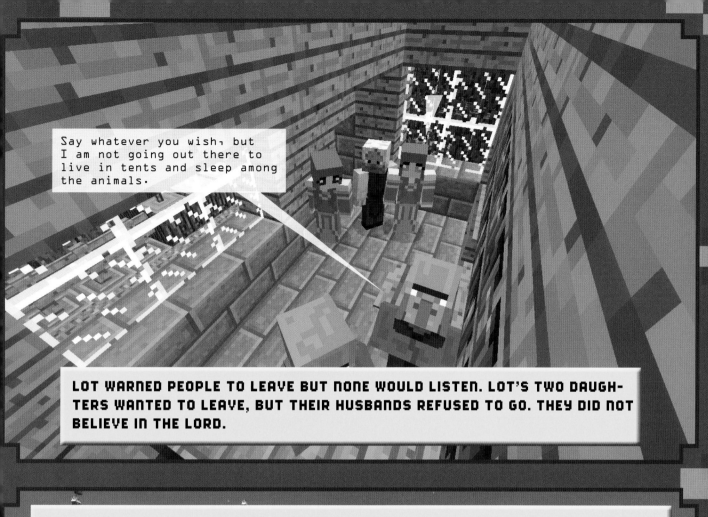

Say whatever you wish, but I am not going out there to live in tents and sleep among the animals.

LOT WARNED PEOPLE TO LEAVE BUT NONE WOULD LISTEN. LOT'S TWO DAUGHTERS WANTED TO LEAVE, BUT THEIR HUSBANDS REFUSED TO GO. THEY DID NOT BELIEVE IN THE LORD.

LOT AND HIS TWO DAUGHTERS WERE THE ONLY ONES TO MAKE IT SAFELY OUT. FOR GOD HAD SENT FIRE AND BRIMSTONE TO DESTROY THE CITIES OF SODOM AND GOMORRAH.

JOSEPH AND HIS DREAMCOAT

Drought and famine are coming. I need to
send someone ahead to make arrangements
from the inside.

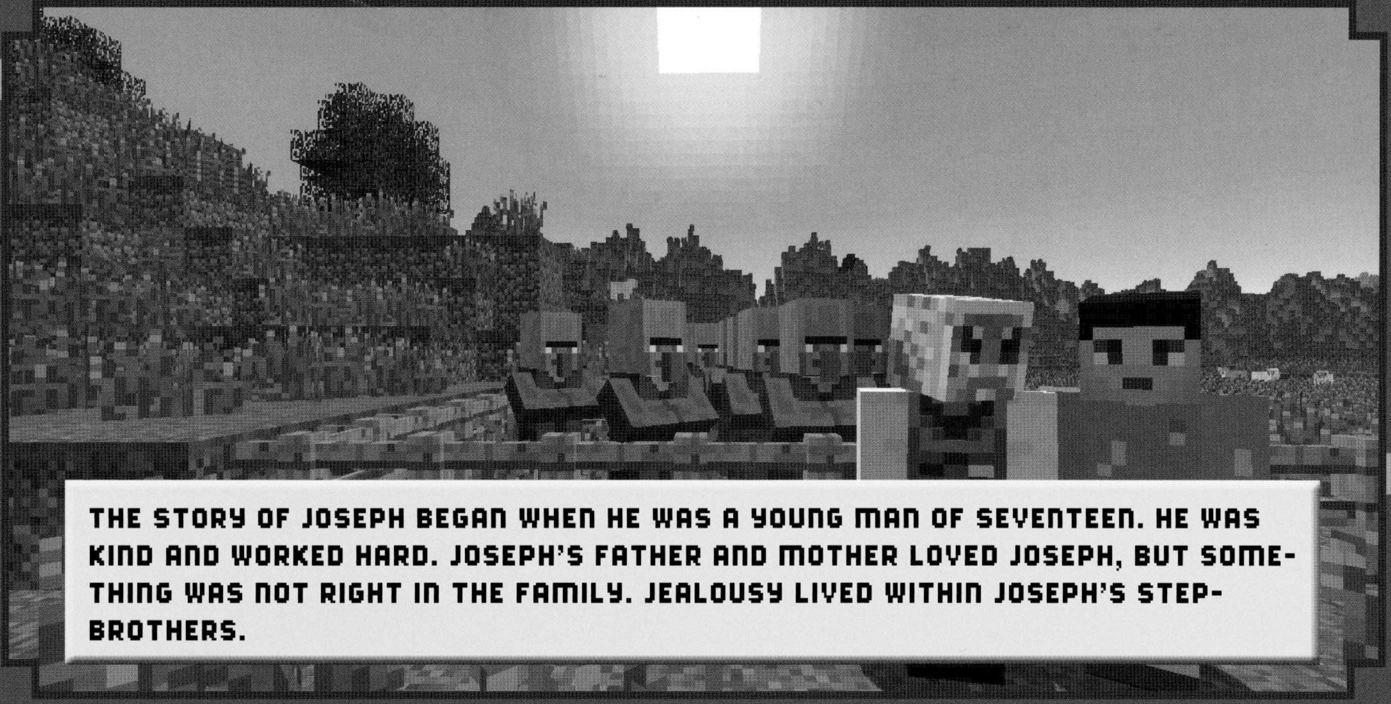
THE STORY OF JOSEPH BEGAN WHEN HE WAS A YOUNG MAN OF SEVENTEEN. HE WAS KIND AND WORKED HARD. JOSEPH'S FATHER AND MOTHER LOVED JOSEPH, BUT SOME-THING WAS NOT RIGHT IN THE FAMILY. JEALOUSY LIVED WITHIN JOSEPH'S STEP-BROTHERS.

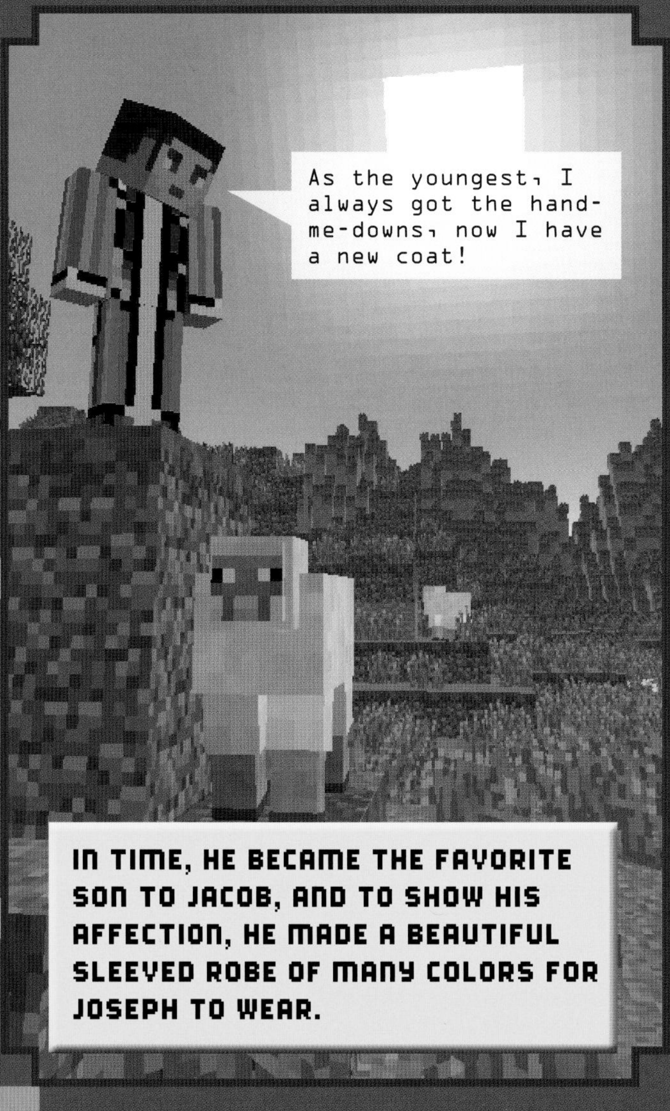
As the youngest, I always got the hand-me-downs, now I have a new coat!
IN TIME, HE BECAME THE FAVORITE SON TO JACOB, AND TO SHOW HIS AFFECTION, HE MADE A BEAUTIFUL SLEEVED ROBE OF MANY COLORS FOR JOSEPH TO WEAR.

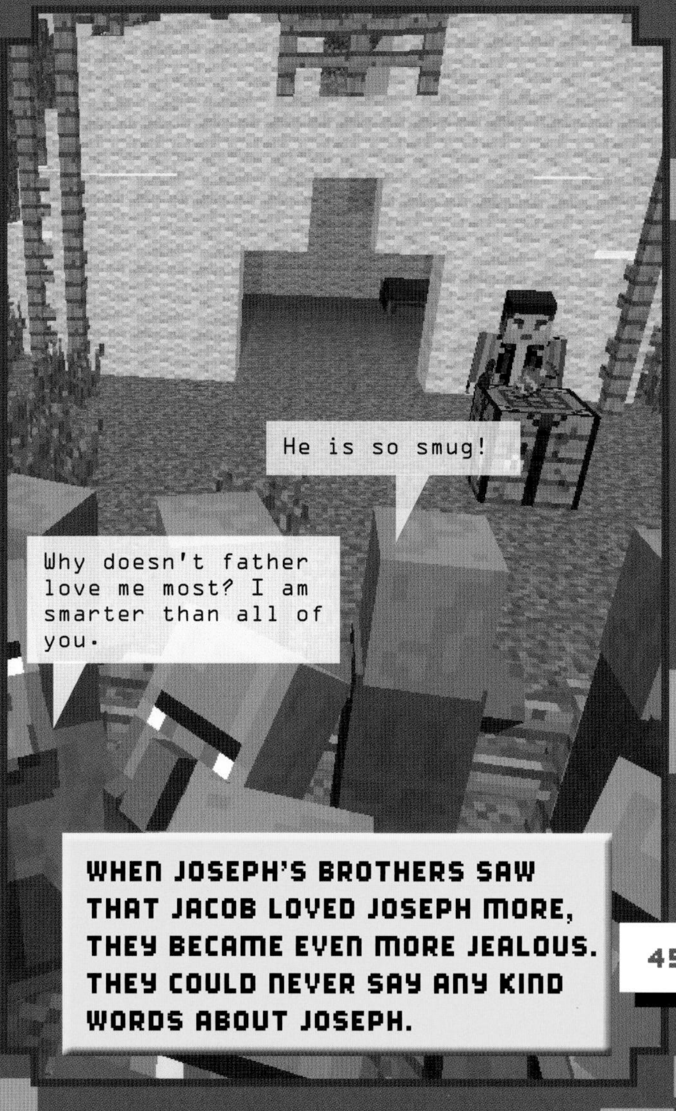
He is so smug!
Why doesn't father love me most? I am smarter than all of you.
WHEN JOSEPH'S BROTHERS SAW THAT JACOB LOVED JOSEPH MORE, THEY BECAME EVEN MORE JEALOUS. THEY COULD NEVER SAY ANY KIND WORDS ABOUT JOSEPH.

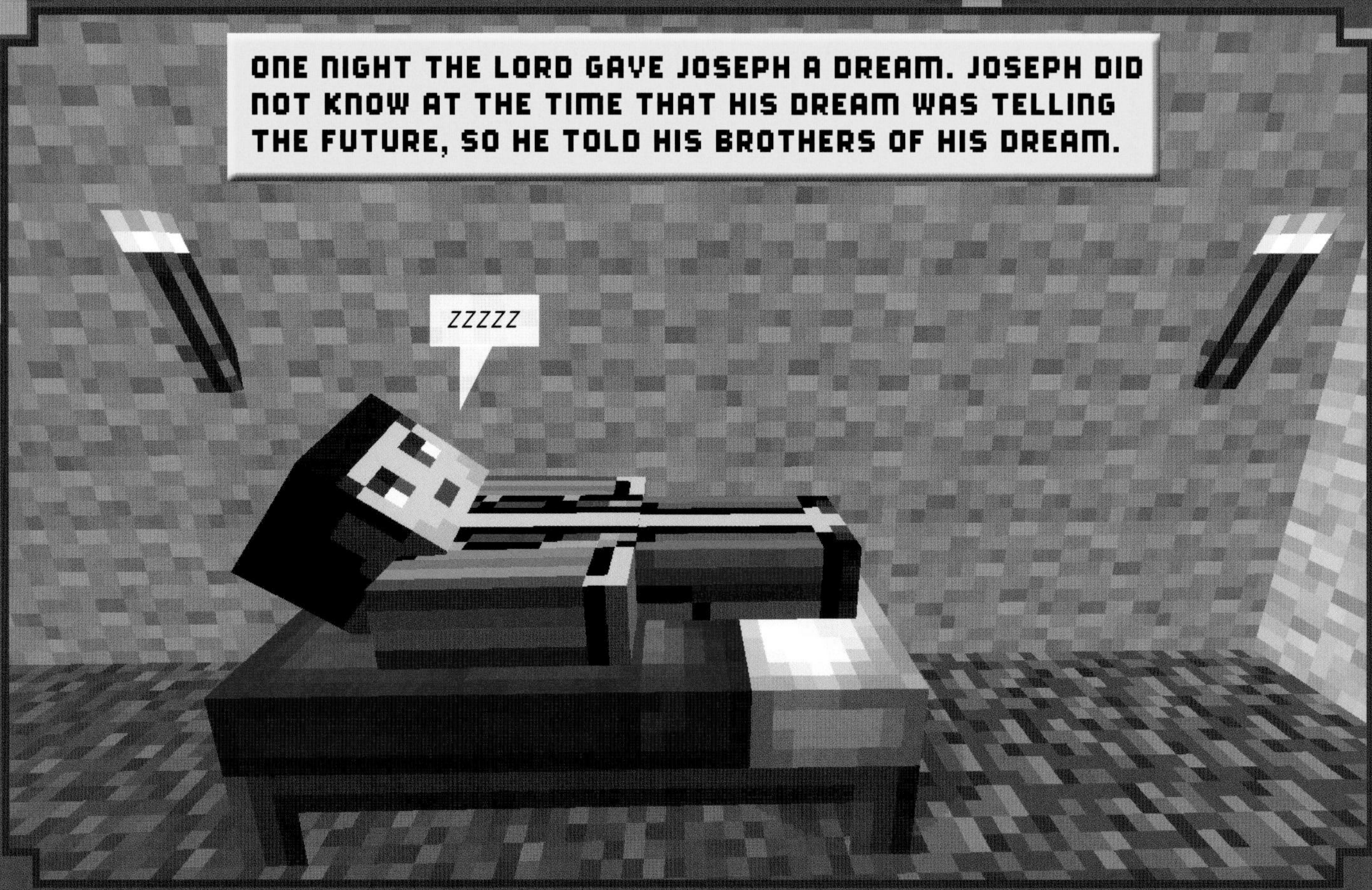
ONE NIGHT THE LORD GAVE JOSEPH A DREAM. JOSEPH DID NOT KNOW AT THE TIME THAT HIS DREAM WAS TELLING THE FUTURE, SO HE TOLD HIS BROTHERS OF HIS DREAM.
ZZZZZ

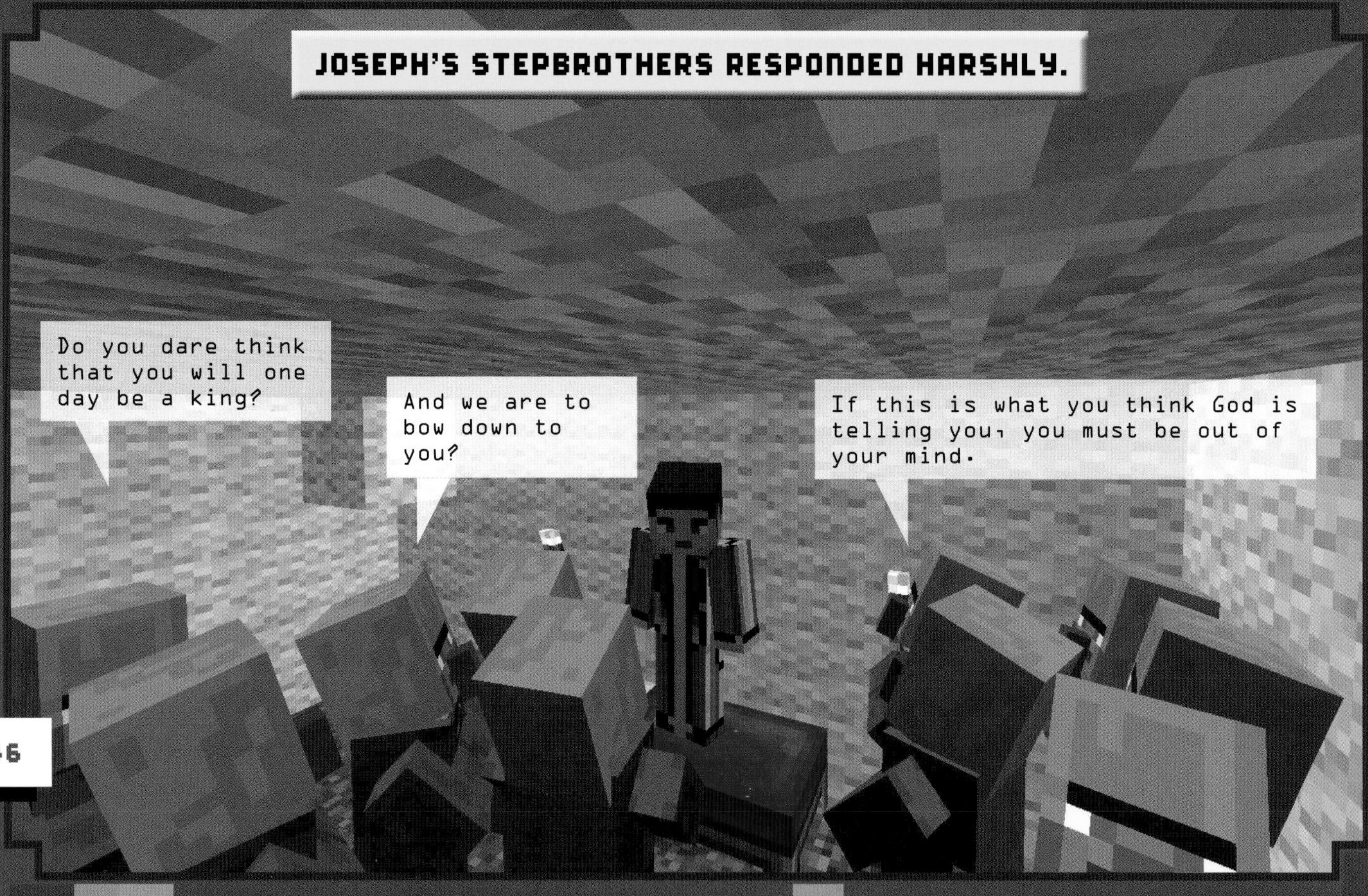
JOSEPH'S STEPBROTHERS RESPONDED HARSHLY.
Do you dare think that you will one day be a king?
And we are to bow down to you?
If this is what you think God is telling you, you must be out of your mind.

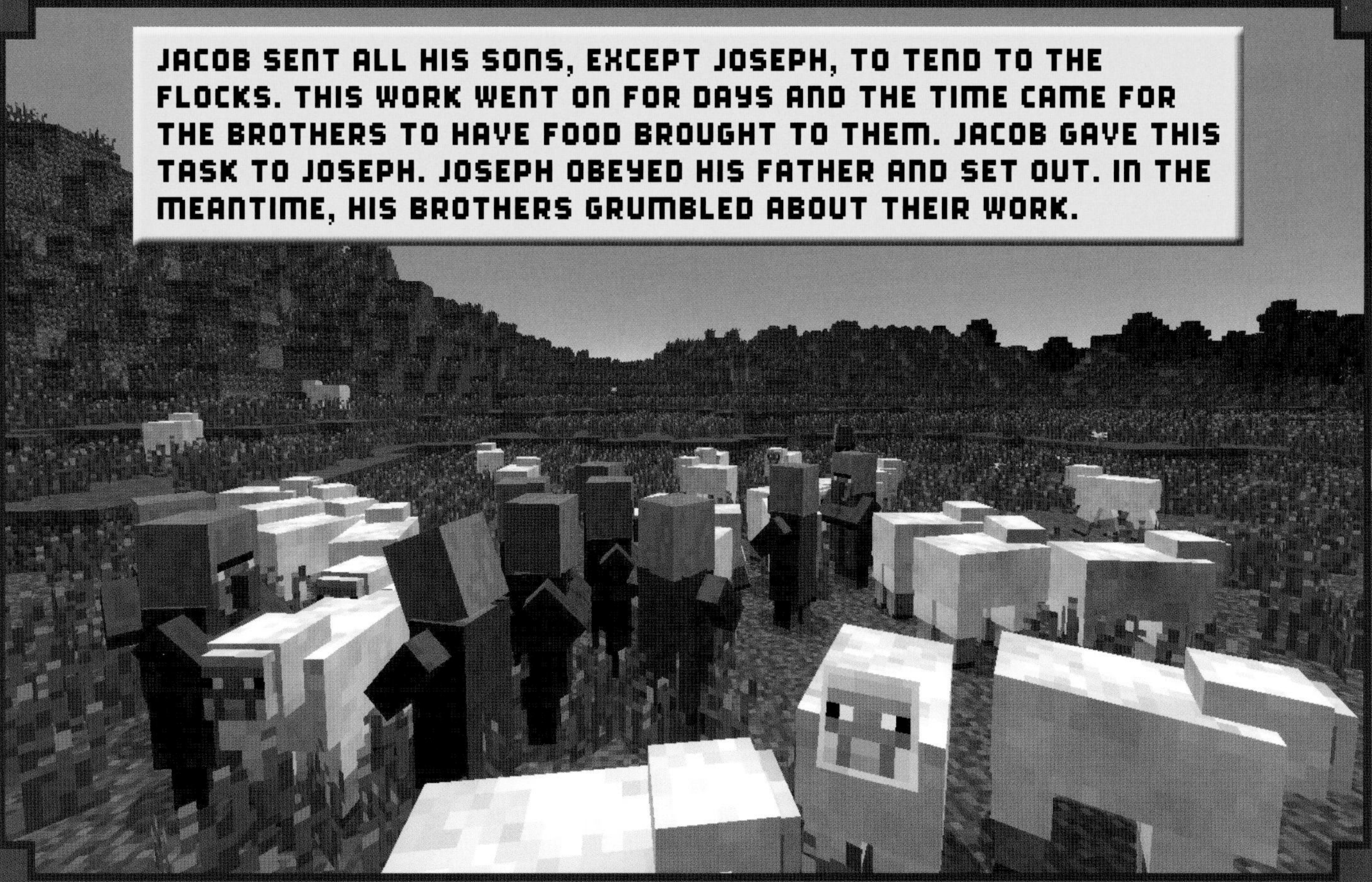
JACOB SENT ALL HIS SONS, EXCEPT JOSEPH, TO TEND TO THE FLOCKS. THIS WORK WENT ON FOR DAYS AND THE TIME CAME FOR THE BROTHERS TO HAVE FOOD BROUGHT TO THEM. JACOB GAVE THIS TASK TO JOSEPH. JOSEPH OBEYED HIS FATHER AND SET OUT. IN THE MEANTIME, HIS BROTHERS GRUMBLED ABOUT THEIR WORK.

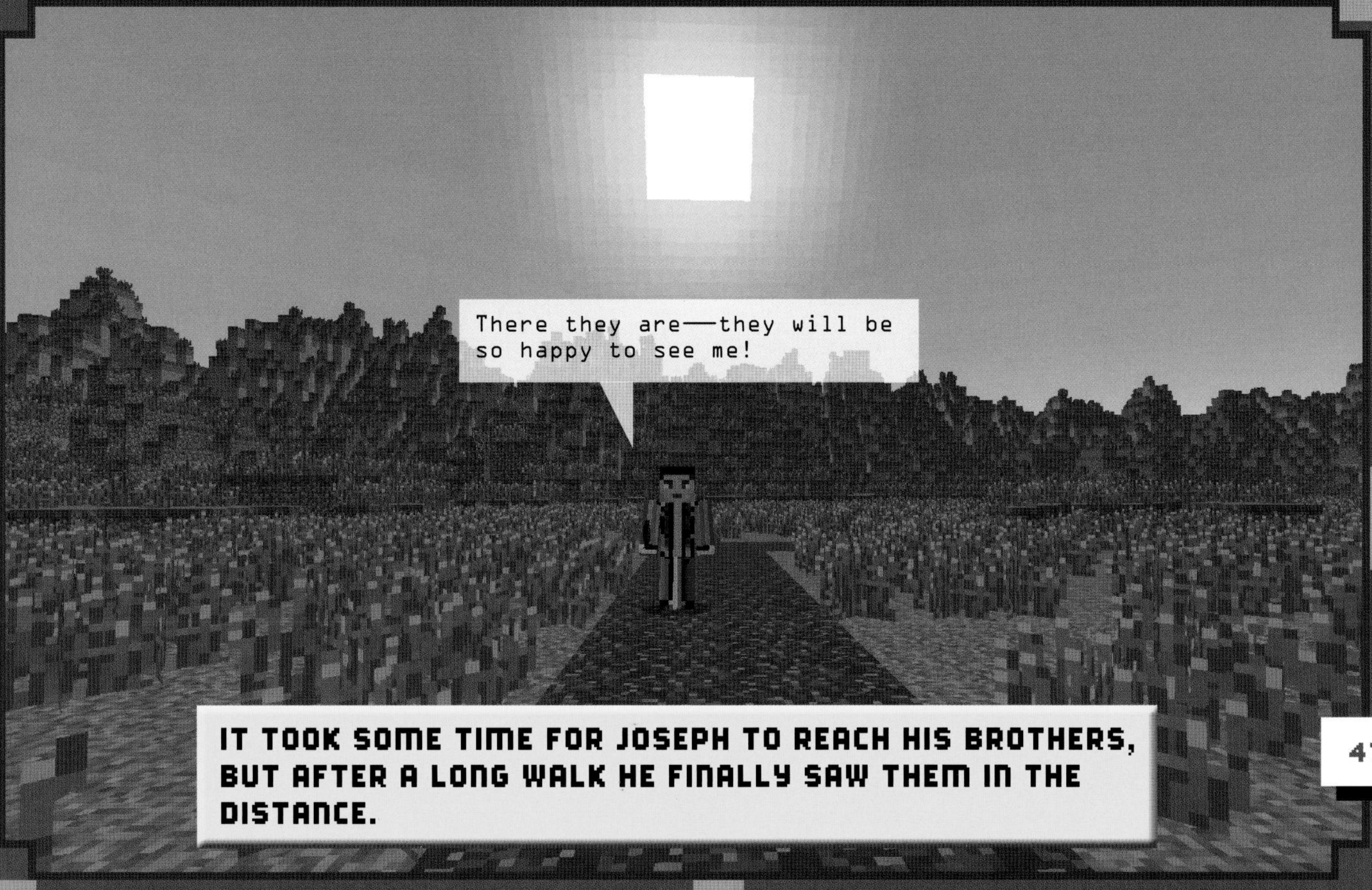
There they are—they will be so happy to see me!
IT TOOK SOME TIME FOR JOSEPH TO REACH HIS BROTHERS, BUT AFTER A LONG WALK HE FINALLY SAW THEM IN THE DISTANCE.

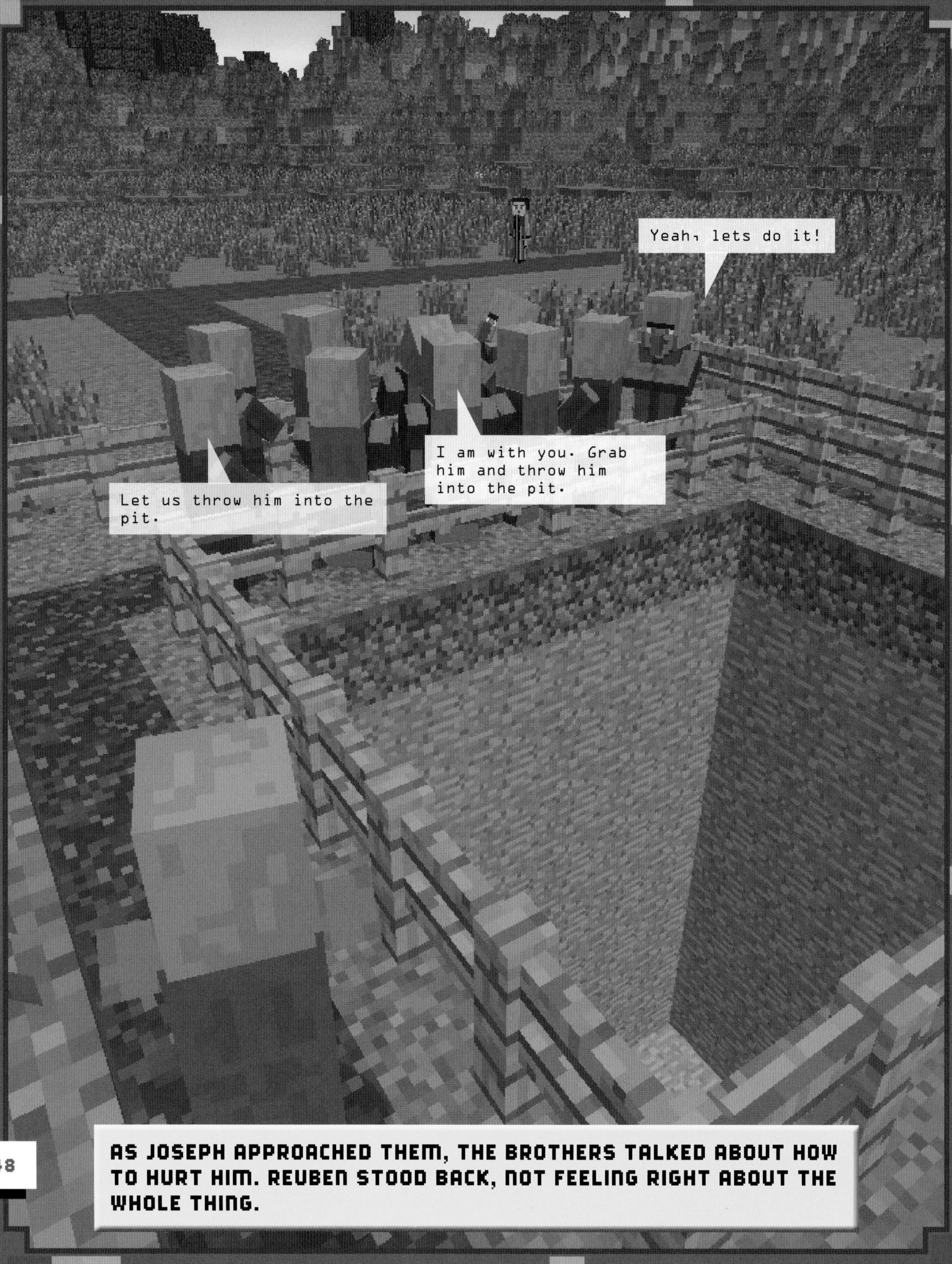
Yeah, lets do it!
I am with you. Grab him and throw him into the pit.
Let us throw him into the pit.
AS JOSEPH APPROACHED THEM, THE BROTHERS TALKED ABOUT HOW TO HURT HIM. REUBEN STOOD BACK, NOT FEELING RIGHT ABOUT THE WHOLE THING.

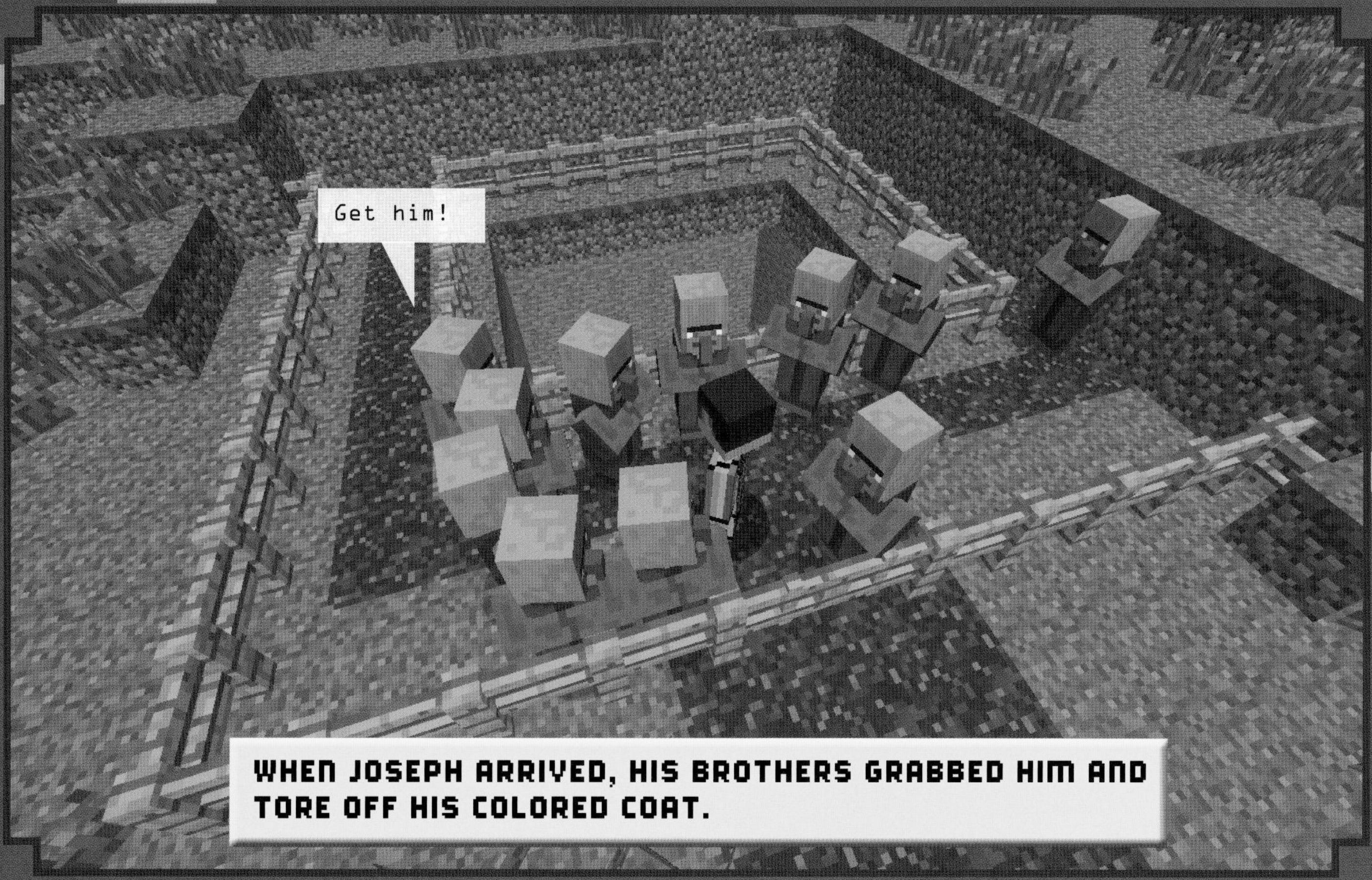
Get him!
WHEN JOSEPH ARRIVED, HIS BROTHERS GRABBED HIM AND TORE OFF HIS COLORED COAT.

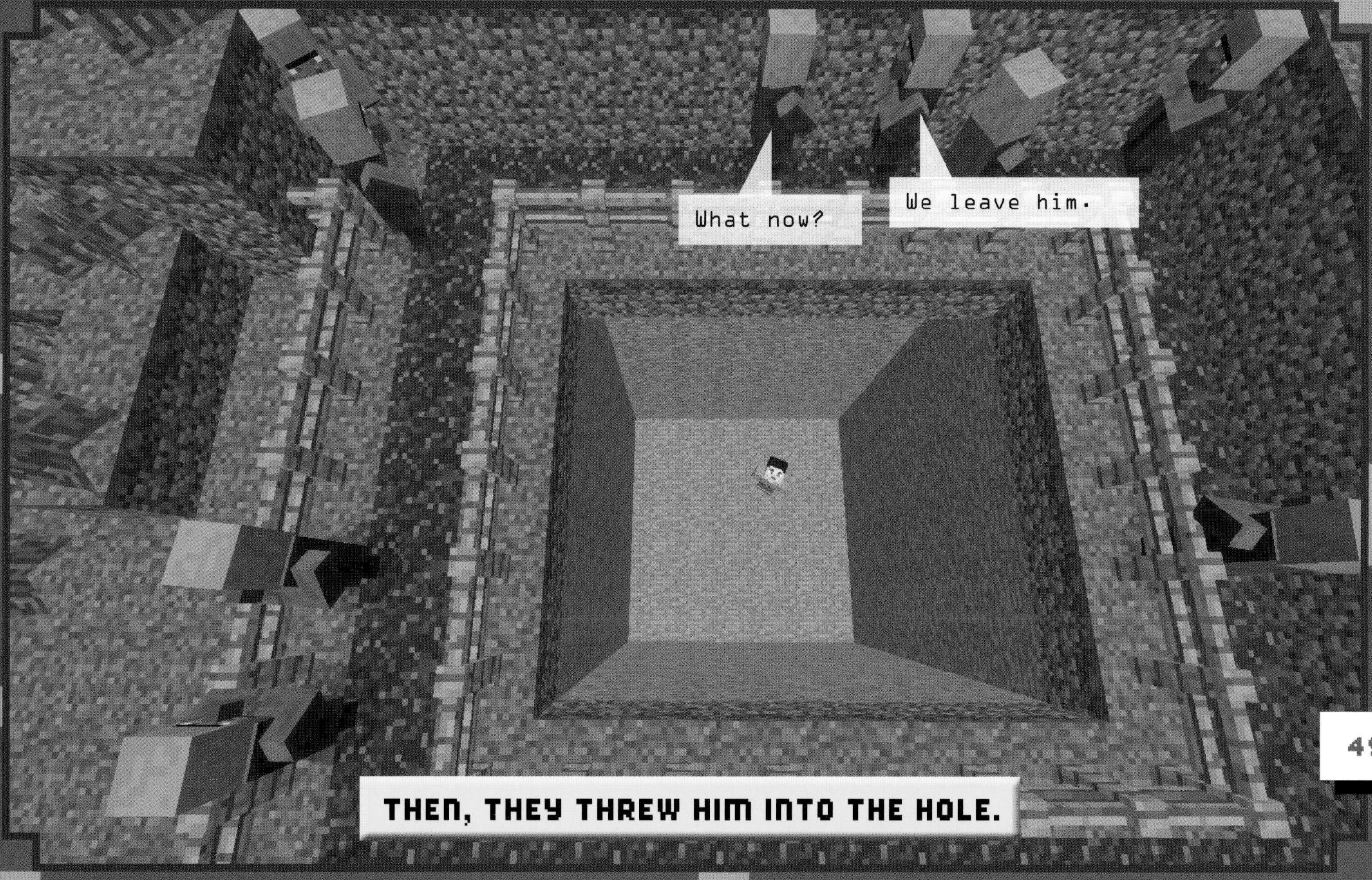
What now?
We leave him.
THEN, THEY THREW HIM INTO THE HOLE.

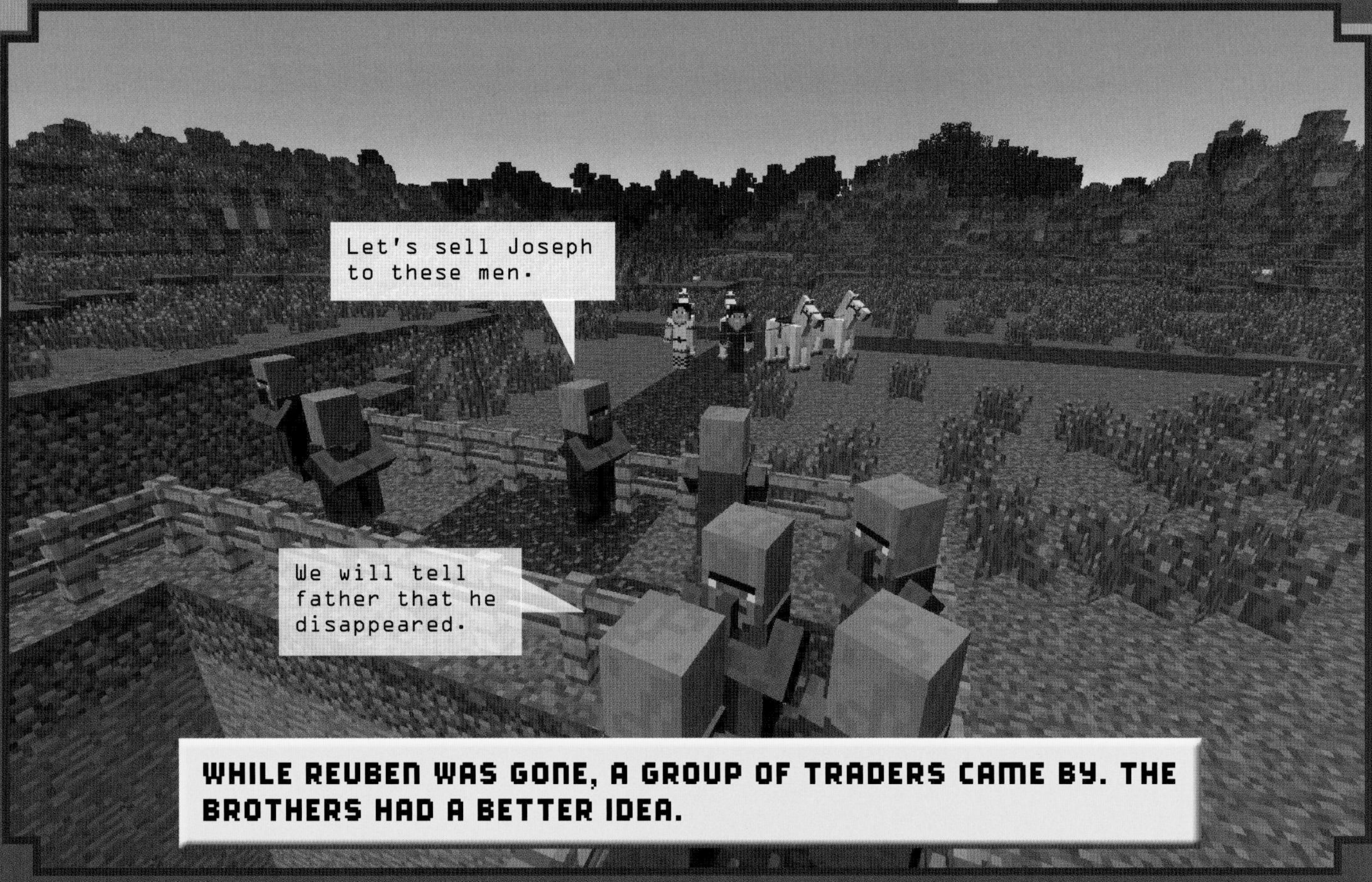
Let's sell Joseph to these men.
We will tell father that he disappeared.
WHILE REUBEN WAS GONE, A GROUP OF TRADERS CAME BY. THE BROTHERS HAD A BETTER IDEA.

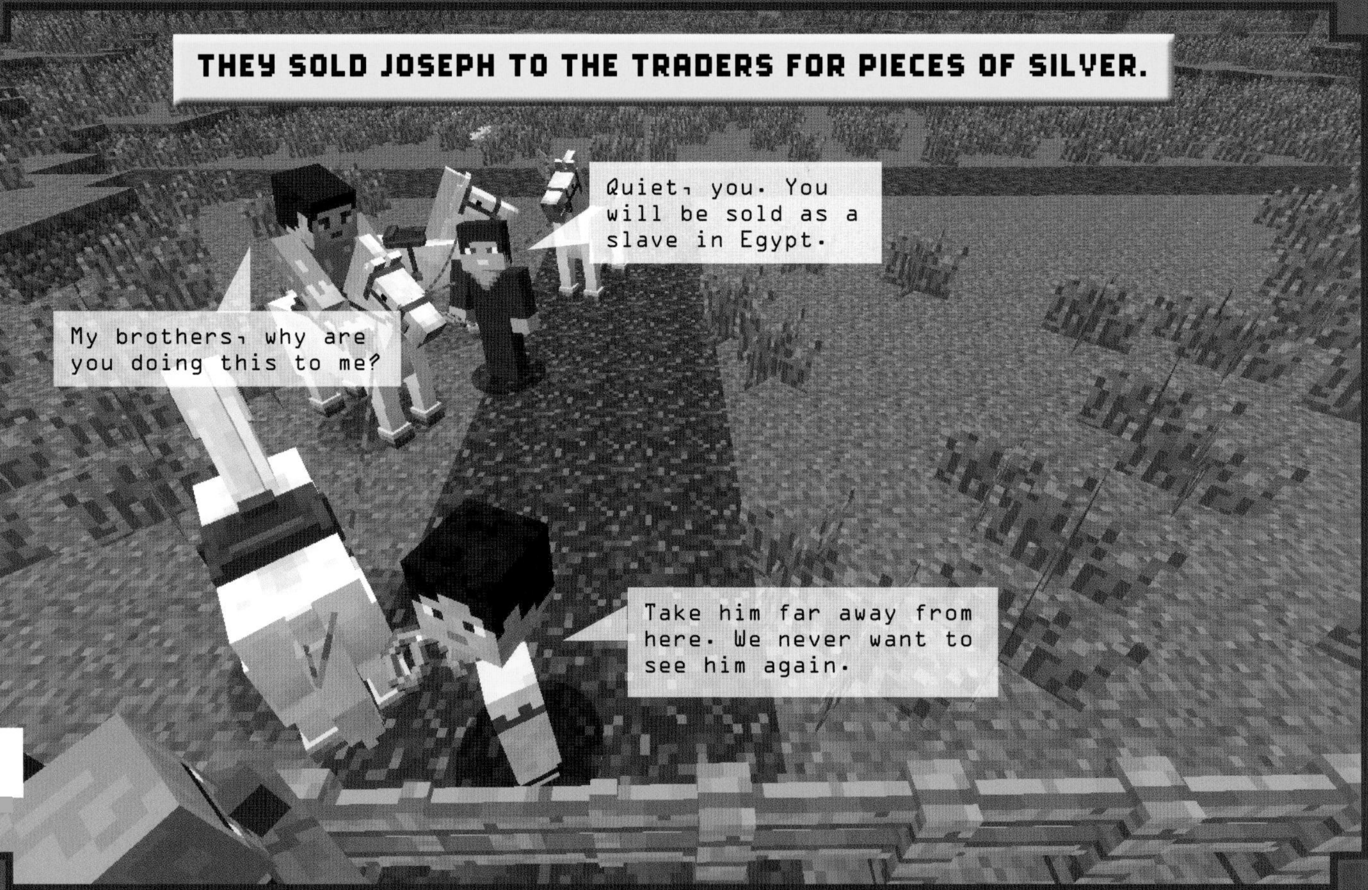
THEY SOLD JOSEPH TO THE TRADERS FOR PIECES OF SILVER.
Quiet, you. You will be sold as a slave in Egypt.
My brothers, why are you doing this to me?
Take him far away from here. We never want to see him again.

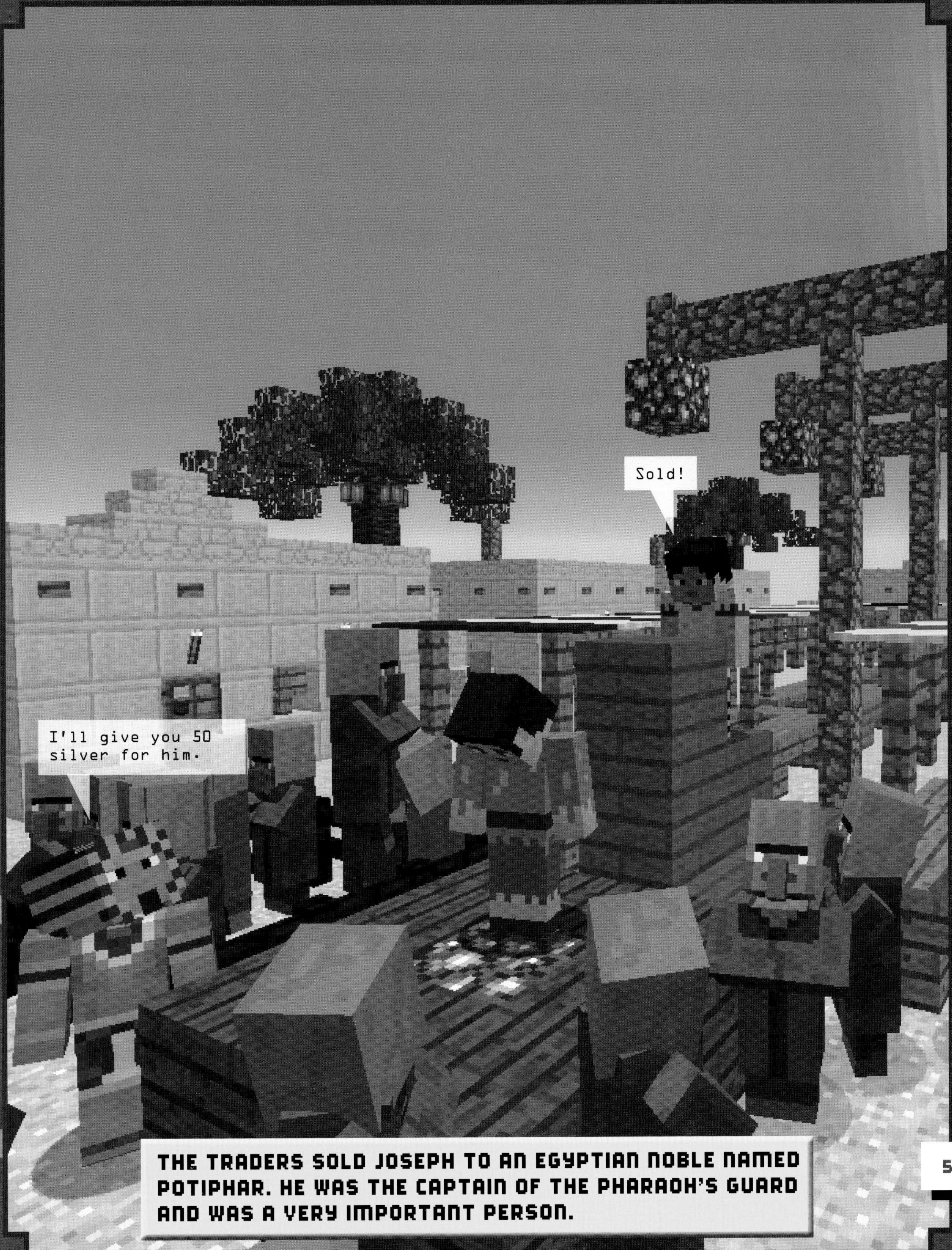
Sold!
I'll give you 50 silver for him.

THE TRADERS SOLD JOSEPH TO AN EGYPTIAN NOBLE NAMED POTIPHAR. HE WAS THE CAPTAIN OF THE PHARAOH'S GUARD AND WAS A VERY IMPORTANT PERSON.

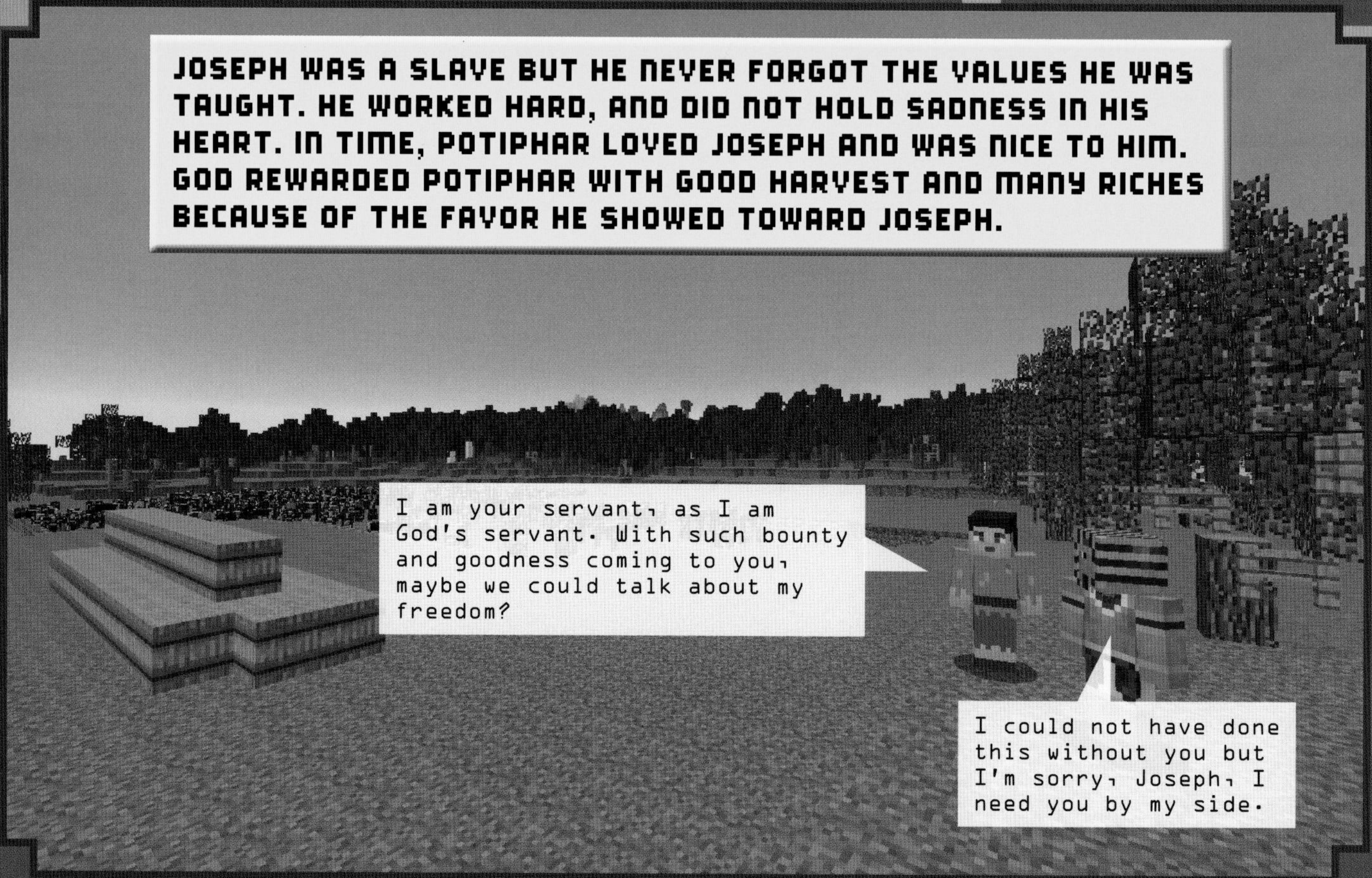
JOSEPH WAS A SLAVE BUT HE NEVER FORGOT THE VALUES HE WAS TAUGHT. HE WORKED HARD, AND DID NOT HOLD SADNESS IN HIS HEART. IN TIME, POTIPHAR LOVED JOSEPH AND WAS NICE TO HIM. GOD REWARDED POTIPHAR WITH GOOD HARVEST AND MANY RICHES BECAUSE OF THE FAVOR HE SHOWED TOWARD JOSEPH.
I am your servant, as I am God's servant. With such bounty and goodness coming to you, maybe we could talk about my freedom?
I could not have done this without you but I'm sorry, Joseph, I need you by my side.

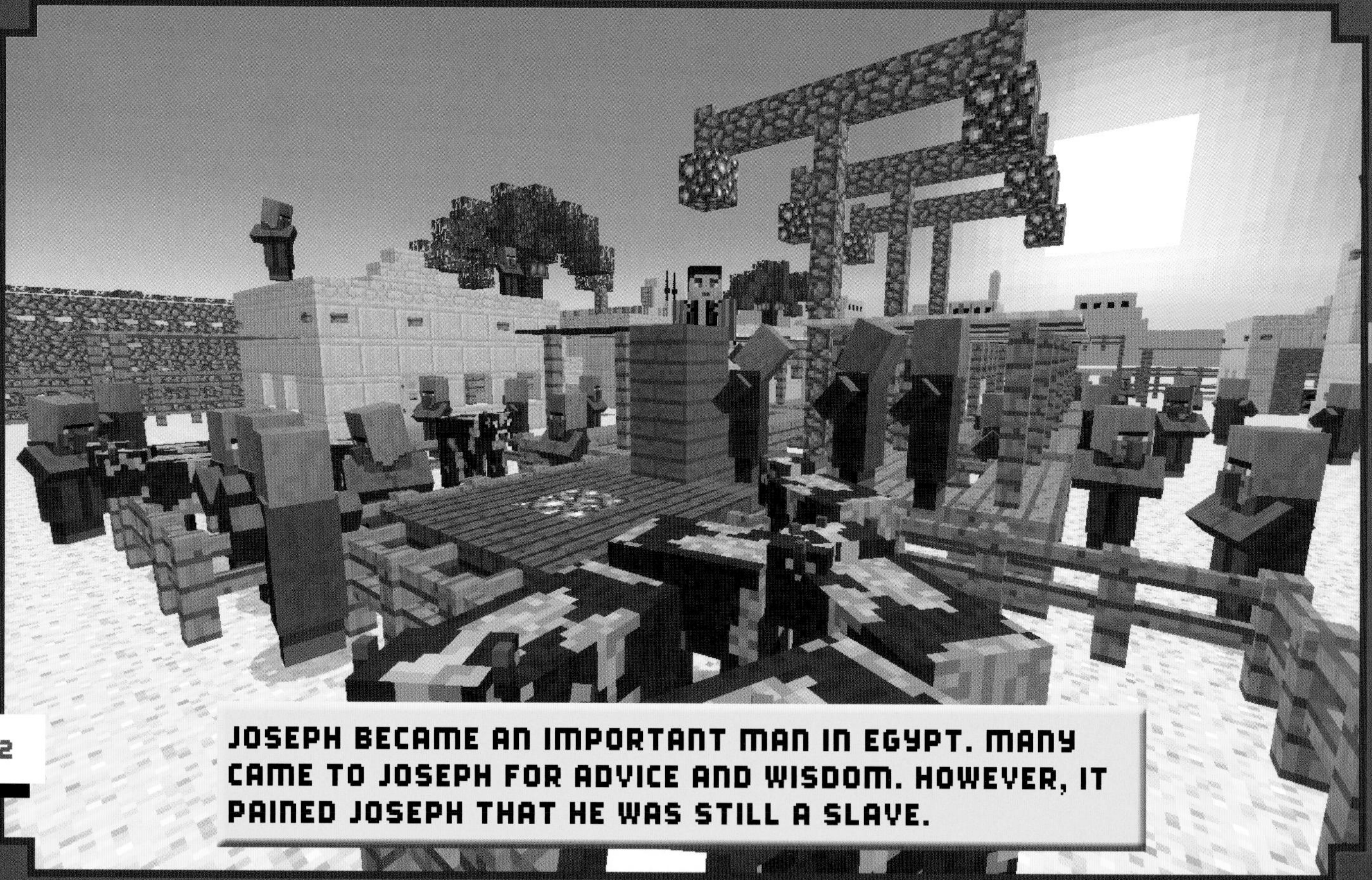
JOSEPH BECAME AN IMPORTANT MAN IN EGYPT. MANY CAME TO JOSEPH FOR ADVICE AND WISDOM. HOWEVER, IT PAINED JOSEPH THAT HE WAS STILL A SLAVE.

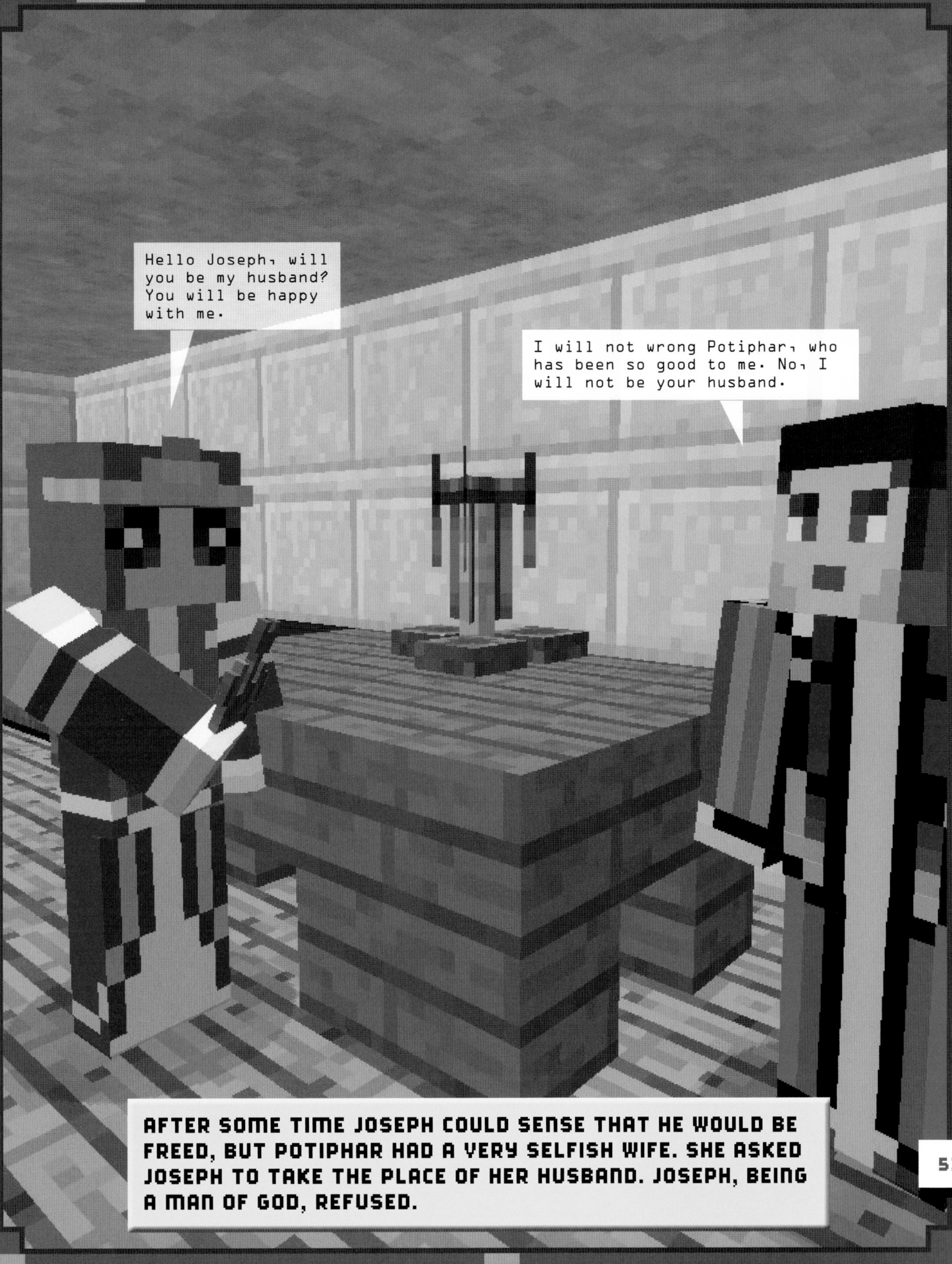
Hello Joseph, will you be my husband? You will be happy with me.
I will not wrong Potiphar, who has been so good to me. No, I will not be your husband.
AFTER SOME TIME JOSEPH COULD SENSE THAT HE WOULD BE FREED, BUT POTIPHAR HAD A VERY SELFISH WIFE. SHE ASKED JOSEPH TO TAKE THE PLACE OF HER HUSBAND. JOSEPH, BEING A MAN OF GOD, REFUSED.

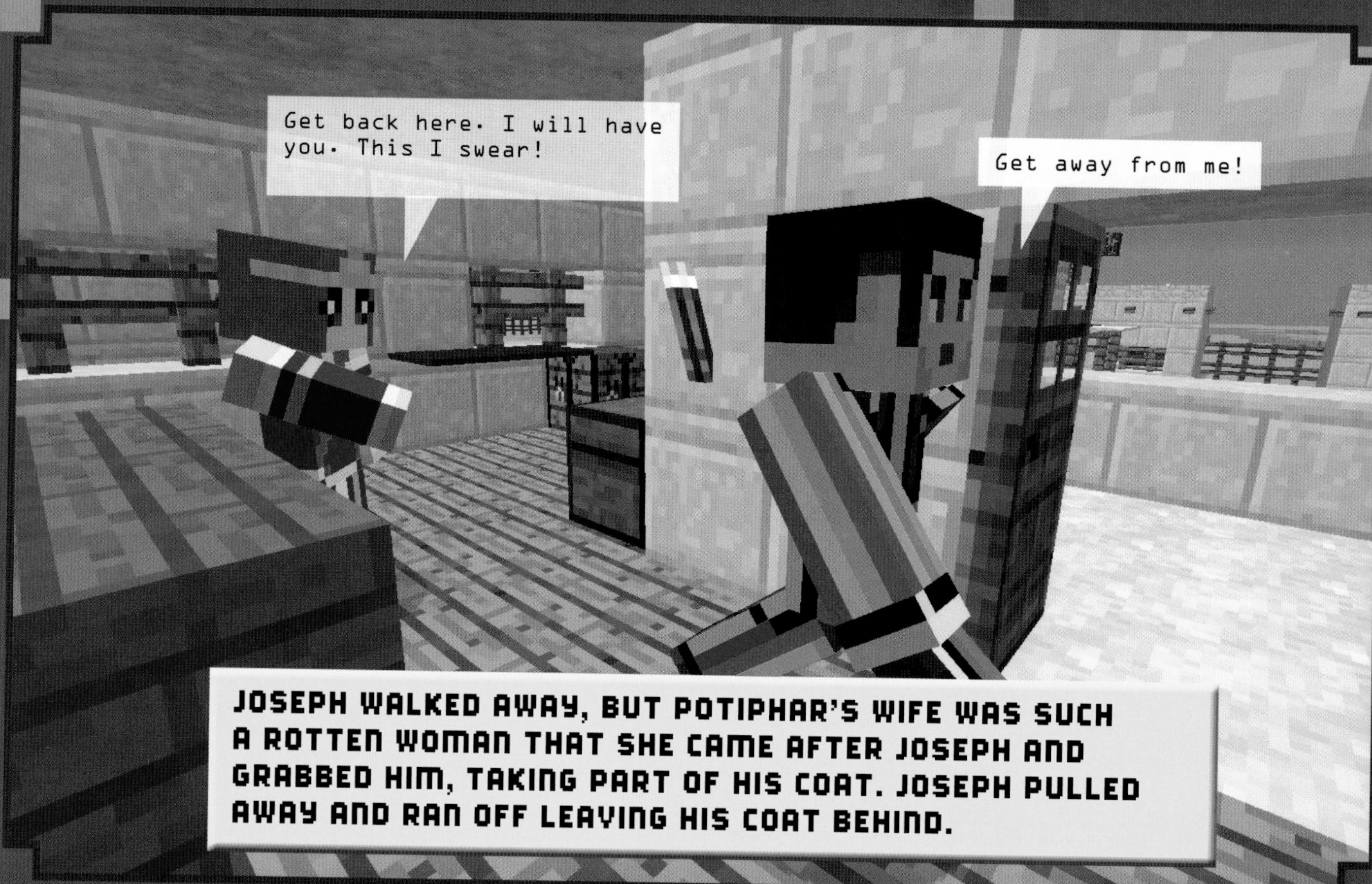
Get back here. I will have you. This I swear!
Get away from me!
JOSEPH WALKED AWAY, BUT POTIPHAR'S WIFE WAS SUCH A ROTTEN WOMAN THAT SHE CAME AFTER JOSEPH AND GRABBED HIM, TAKING PART OF HIS COAT. JOSEPH PULLED AWAY AND RAN OFF LEAVING HIS COAT BEHIND.

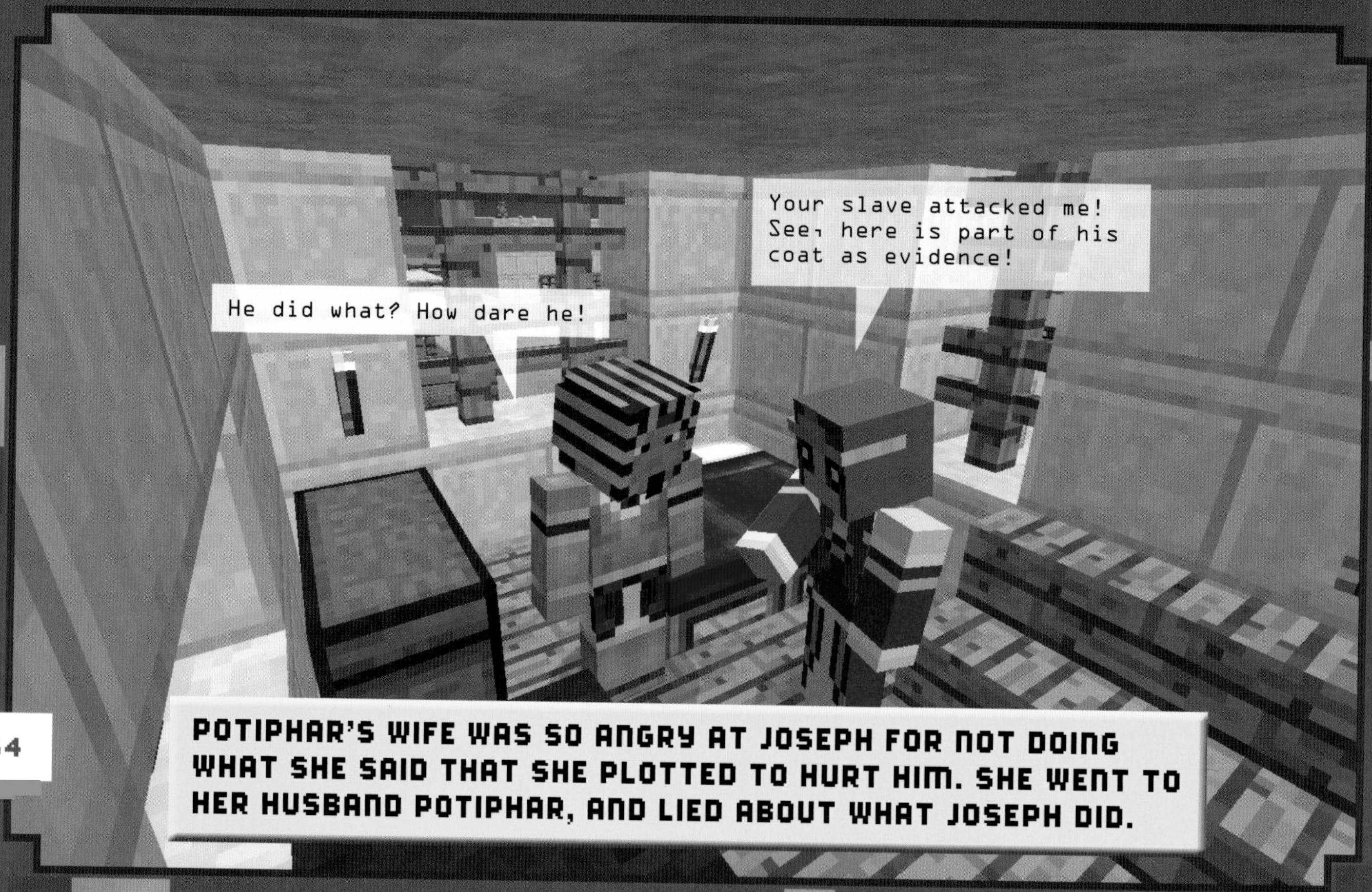
Your slave attacked me! See, here is part of his coat as evidence!
He did what? How dare he!
POTIPHAR'S WIFE WAS SO ANGRY AT JOSEPH FOR NOT DOING WHAT SHE SAID THAT SHE PLOTTED TO HURT HIM. SHE WENT TO HER HUSBAND POTIPHAR, AND LIED ABOUT WHAT JOSEPH DID.

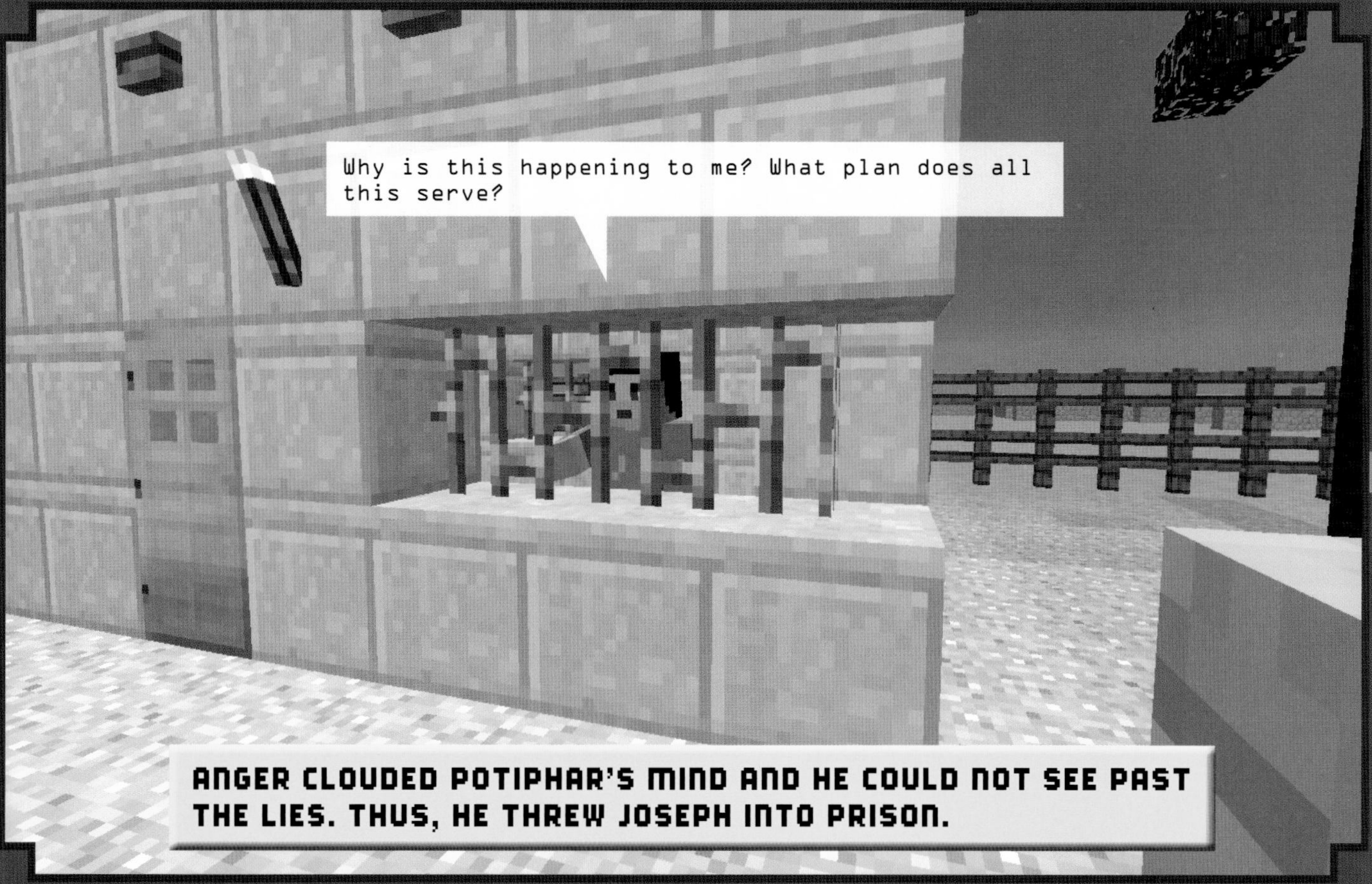
Why is this happening to me? What plan does all this serve?
ANGER CLOUDED POTIPHAR'S MIND AND HE COULD NOT SEE PAST THE LIES. THUS, HE THREW JOSEPH INTO PRISON.

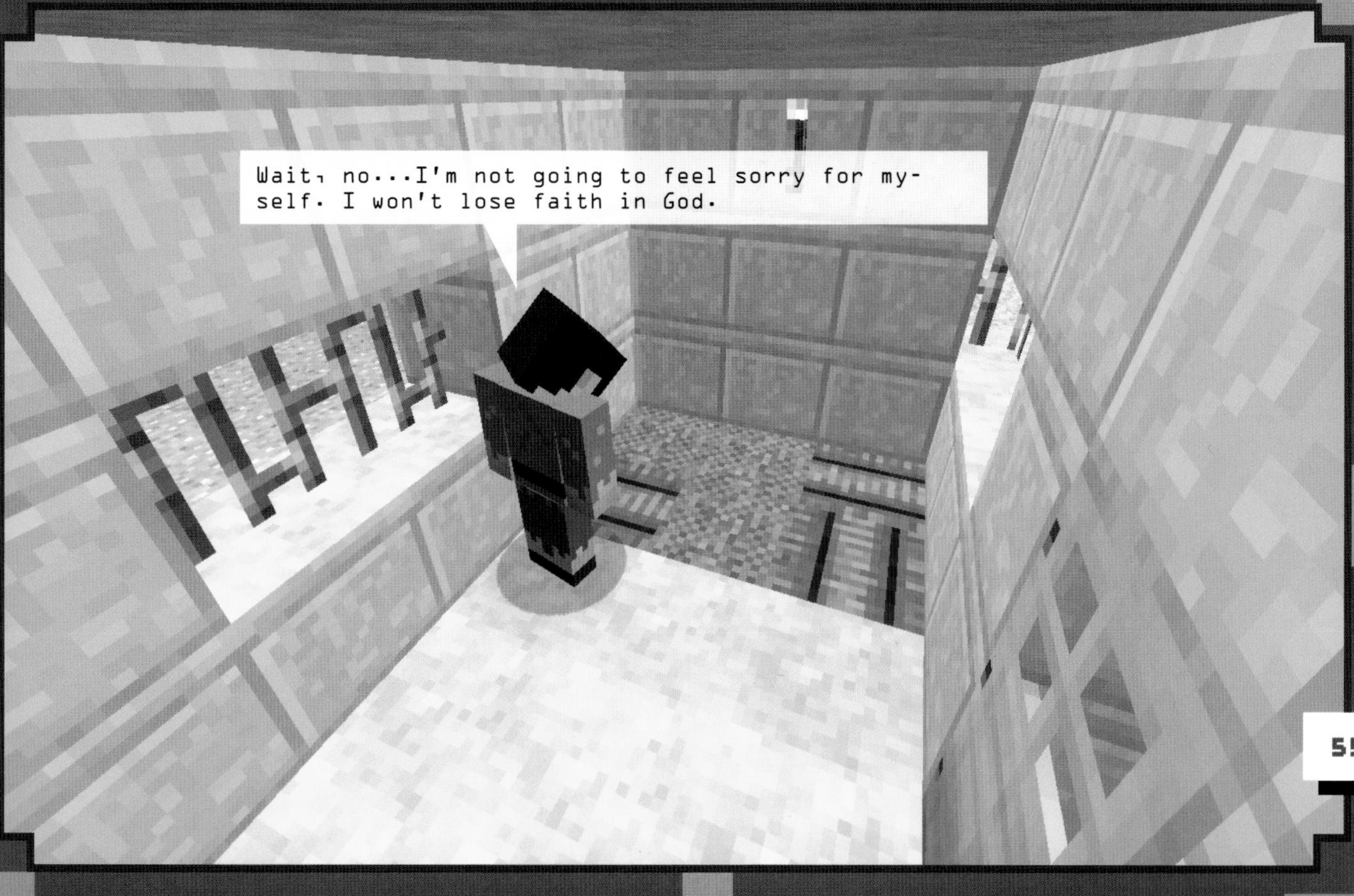
Wait, no...I'm not going to feel sorry for my-self. I won't lose faith in God.

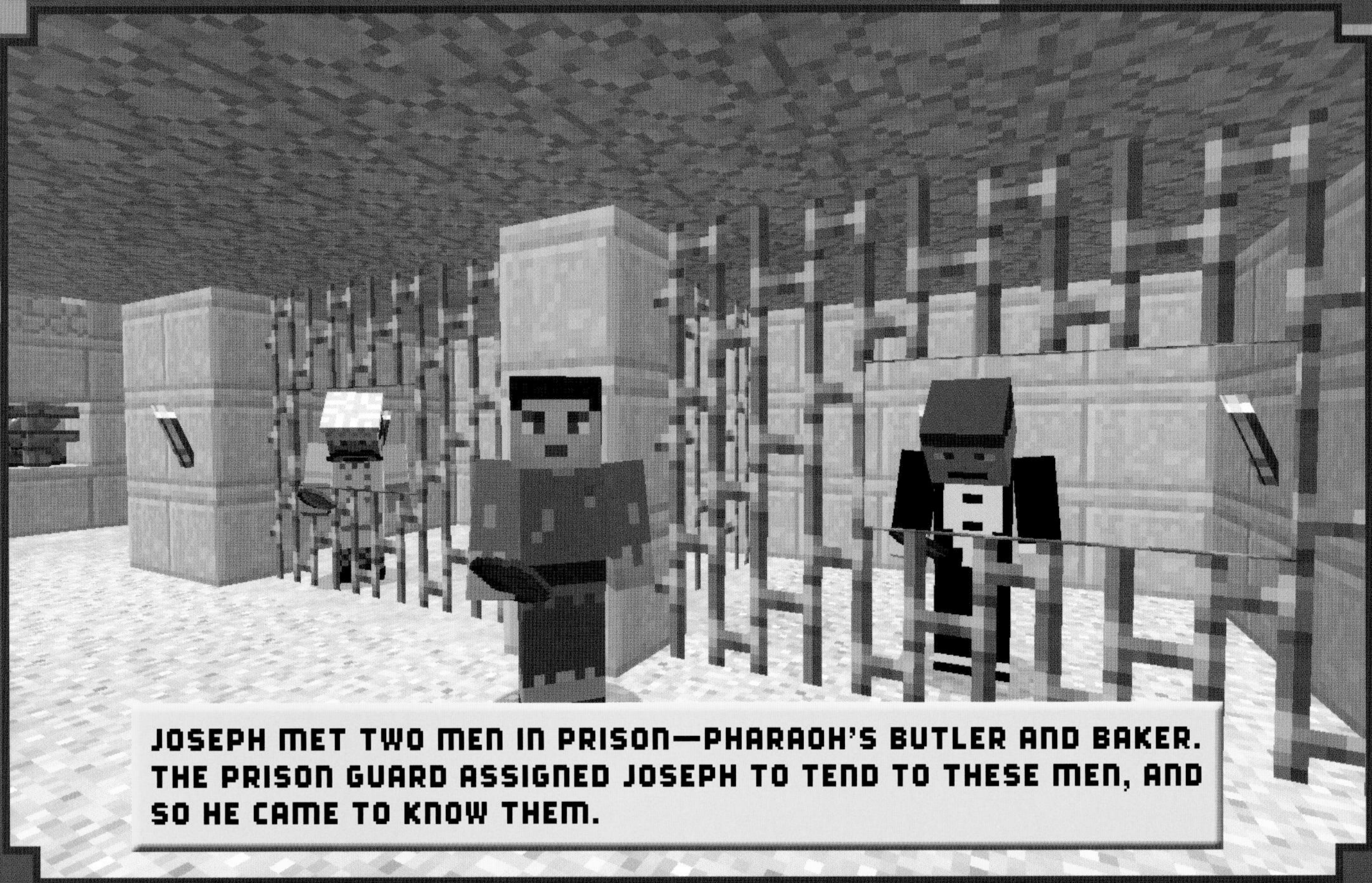
JOSEPH MET TWO MEN IN PRISON—PHARAOH'S BUTLER AND BAKER. THE PRISON GUARD ASSIGNED JOSEPH TO TEND TO THESE MEN, AND SO HE CAME TO KNOW THEM.

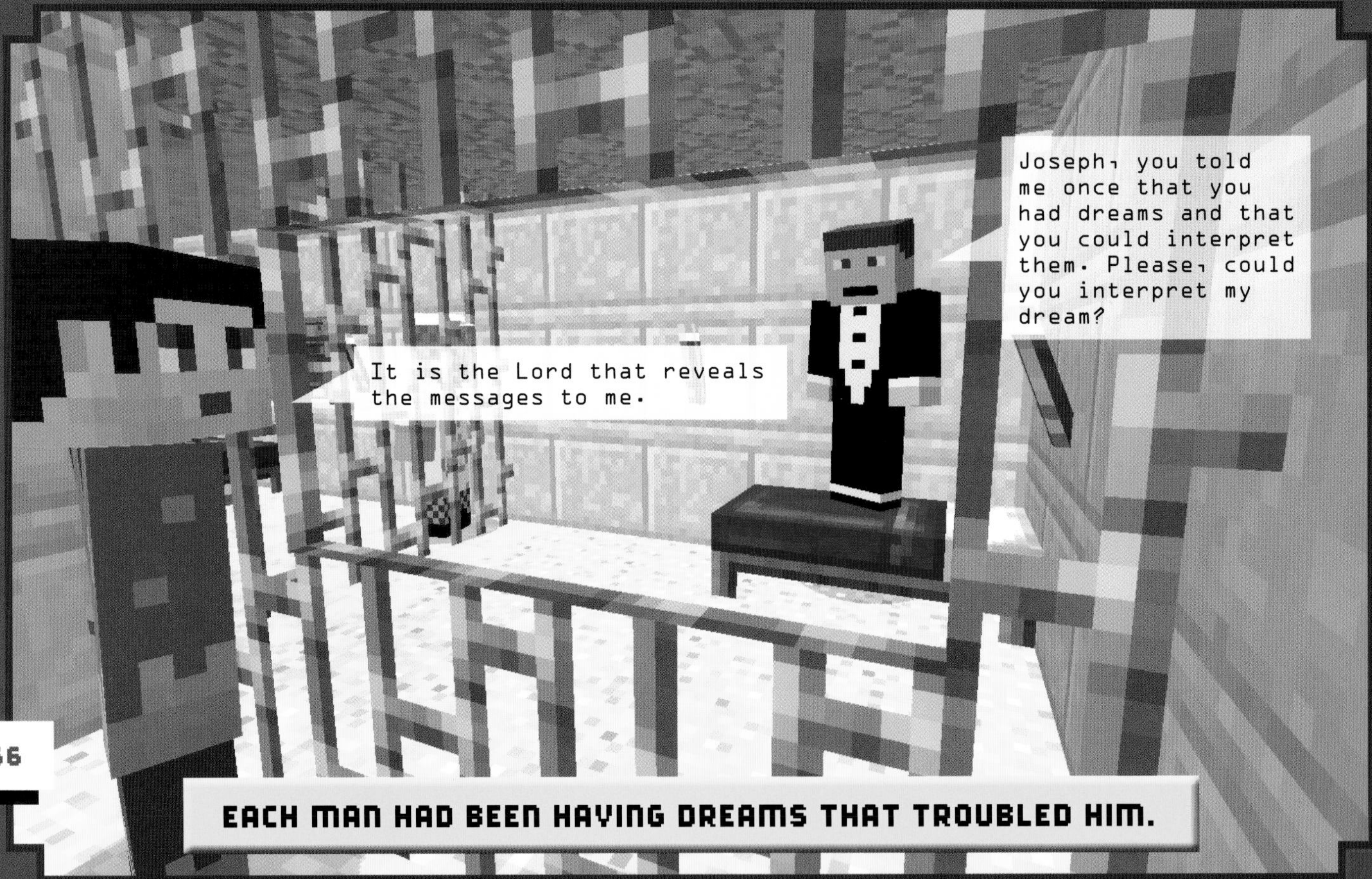
Joseph, you told me once that you had dreams and that you could interpret them. Please, could you interpret my dream?
It is the Lord that reveals the messages to me.
EACH MAN HAD BEEN HAVING DREAMS THAT TROUBLED HIM.

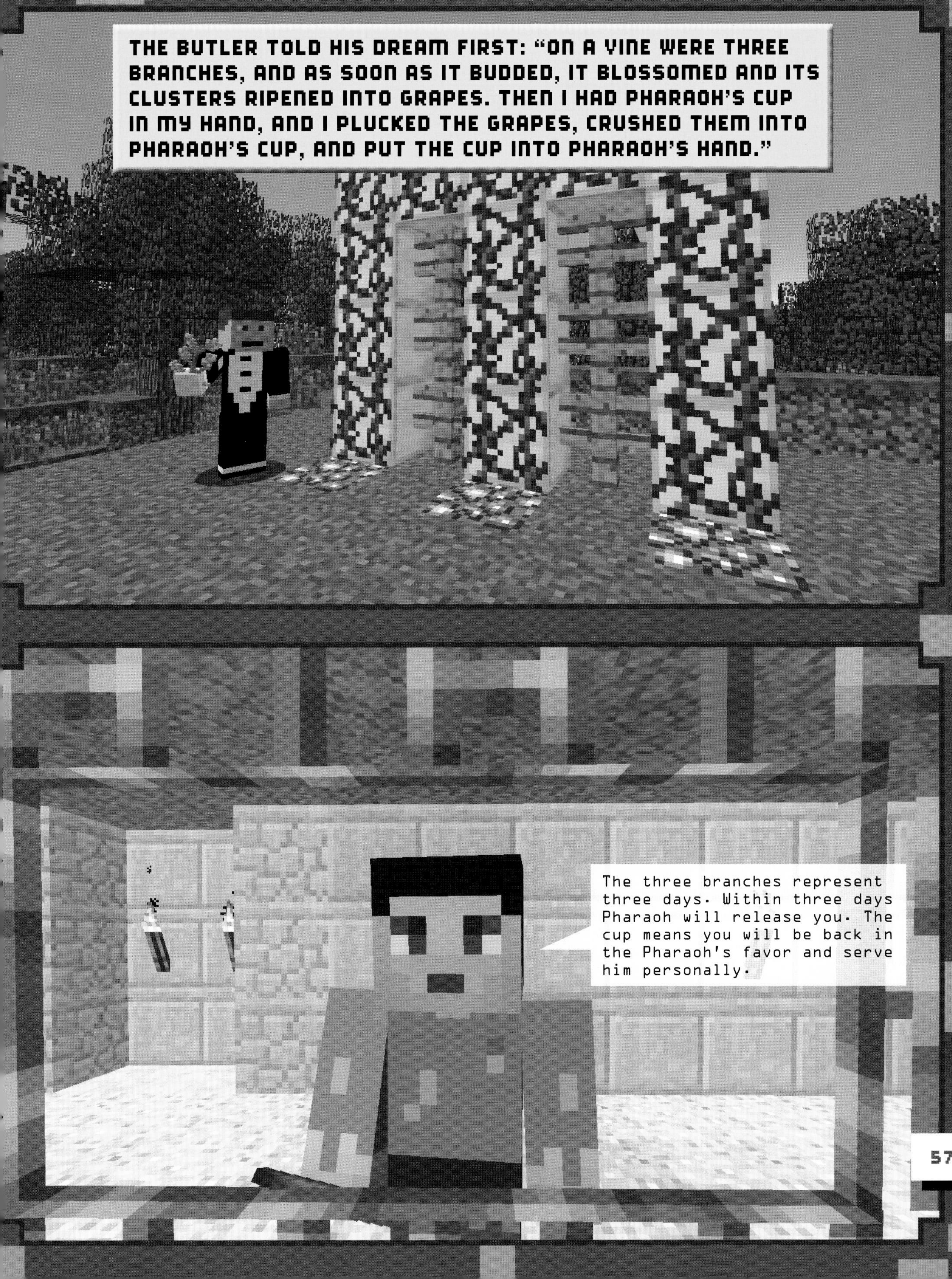
THE BUTLER TOLD HIS DREAM FIRST: "ON A VINE WERE THREE BRANCHES, AND AS SOON AS IT BUDDED, IT BLOSSOMED AND ITS CLUSTERS RIPENED INTO GRAPES. THEN I HAD PHARAOH'S CUP IN MY HAND, AND I PLUCKED THE GRAPES, CRUSHED THEM INTO PHARAOH'S CUP, AND PUT THE CUP INTO PHARAOH'S HAND."
The three branches represent three days. Within three days Pharaoh will release you. The cup means you will be back in the Pharaoh's favor and serve him personally.

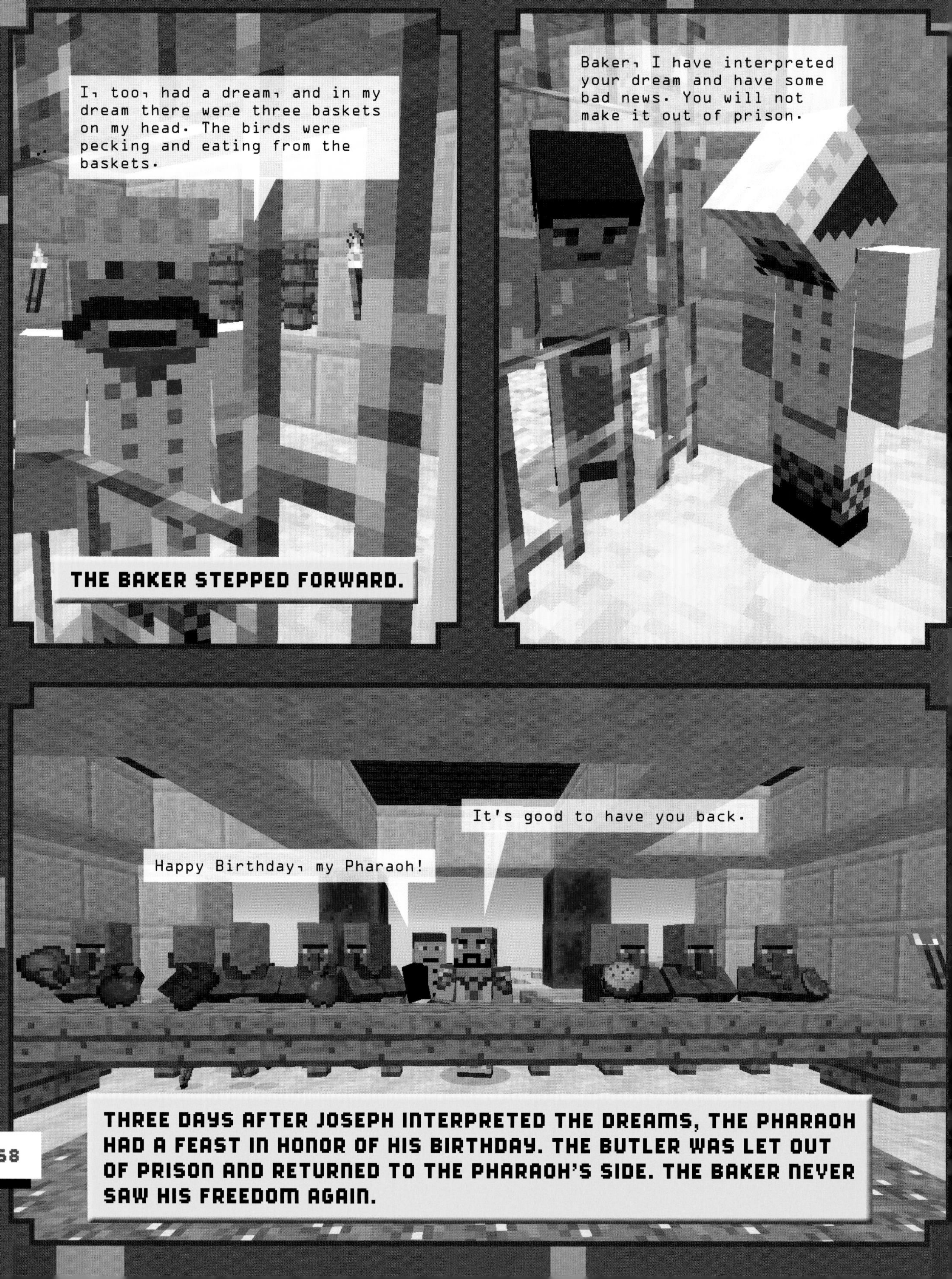

I, too, had a dream, and in my dream there were three baskets on my head. The birds were pecking and eating from the baskets.
THE BAKER STEPPED FORWARD.
Baker, I have interpreted your dream and have some bad news. You will not make it out of prison.
Happy Birthday, my Pharaoh!
It's good to have you back.
THREE DAYS AFTER JOSEPH INTERPRETED THE DREAMS, THE PHARAOH HAD A FEAST IN HONOR OF HIS BIRTHDAY. THE BUTLER WAS LET OUT OF PRISON AND RETURNED TO THE PHARAOH'S SIDE. THE BAKER NEVER SAW HIS FREEDOM AGAIN.

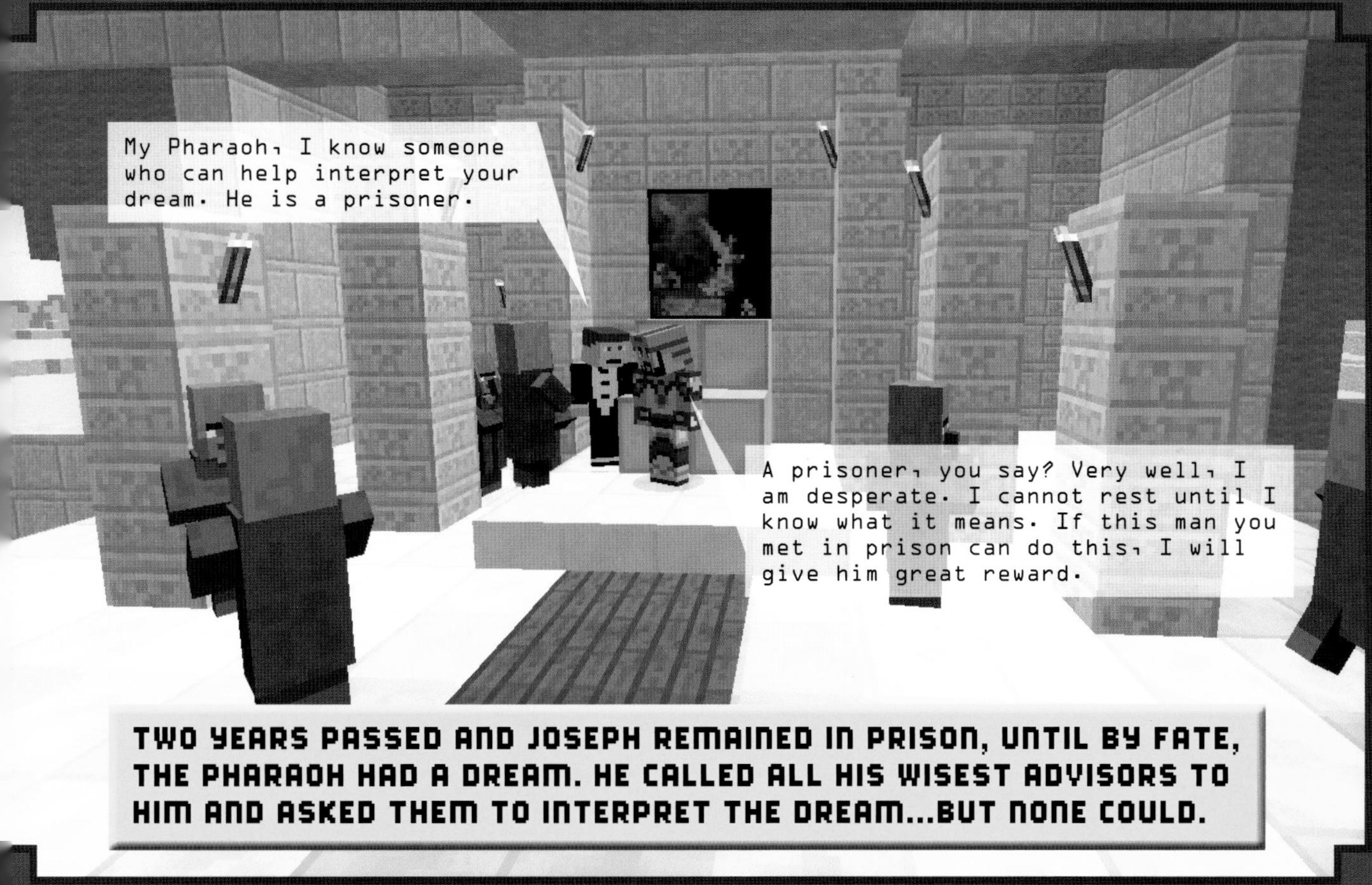
TWO YEARS PASSED AND JOSEPH REMAINED IN PRISON, UNTIL BY FATE, THE PHARAOH HAD A DREAM. HE CALLED ALL HIS WISEST ADVISORS TO HIM AND ASKED THEM TO INTERPRET THE DREAM...BUT NONE COULD.
My Pharaoh, I know someone who can help interpret your dream. He is a prisoner.
A prisoner, you say? Very well, I am desperate. I cannot rest until I know what it means. If this man you met in prison can do this, I will give him great reward.

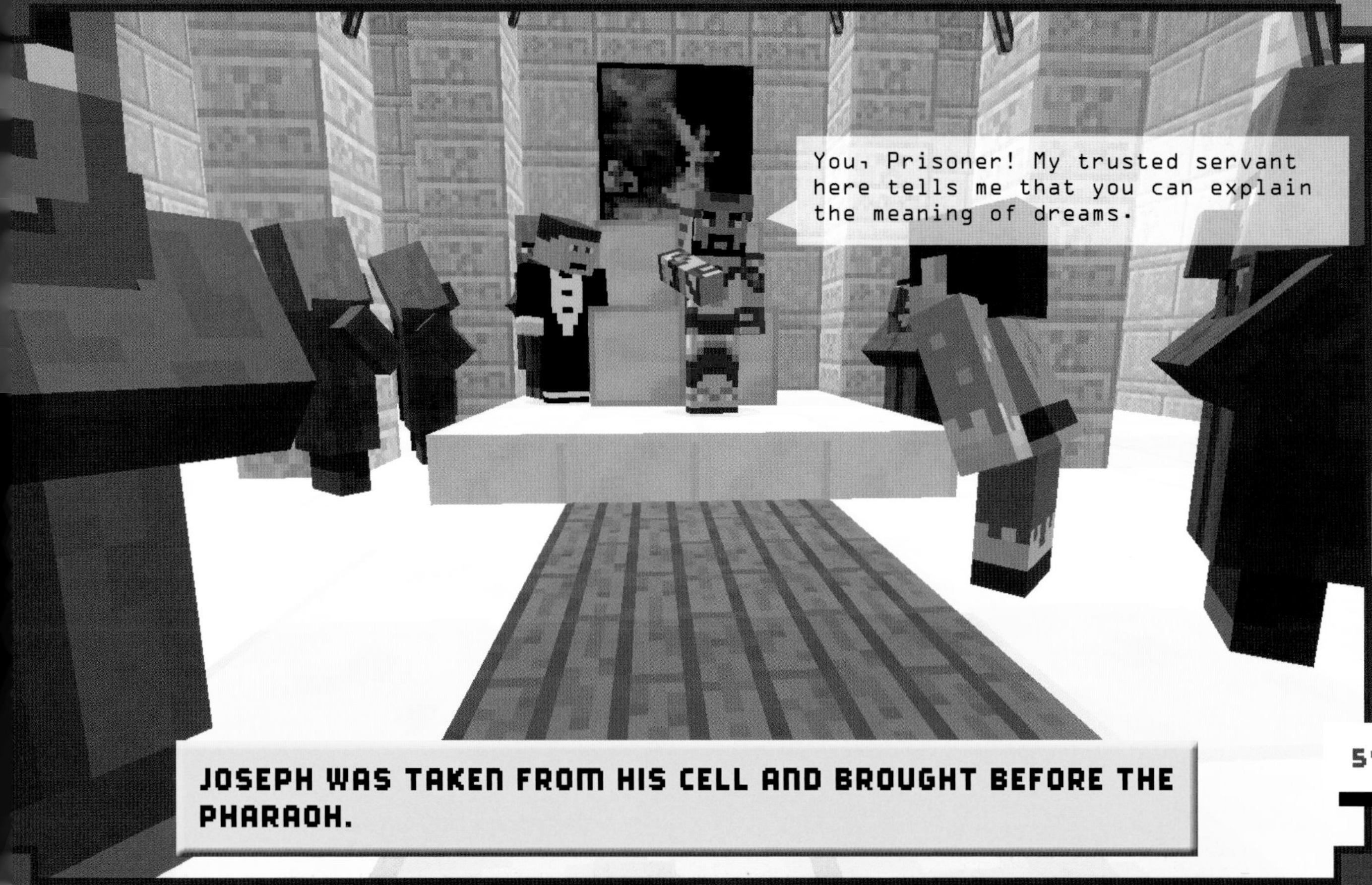
You, Prisoner! My trusted servant here tells me that you can explain the meaning of dreams.
JOSEPH WAS TAKEN FROM HIS CELL AND BROUGHT BEFORE THE PHARAOH.

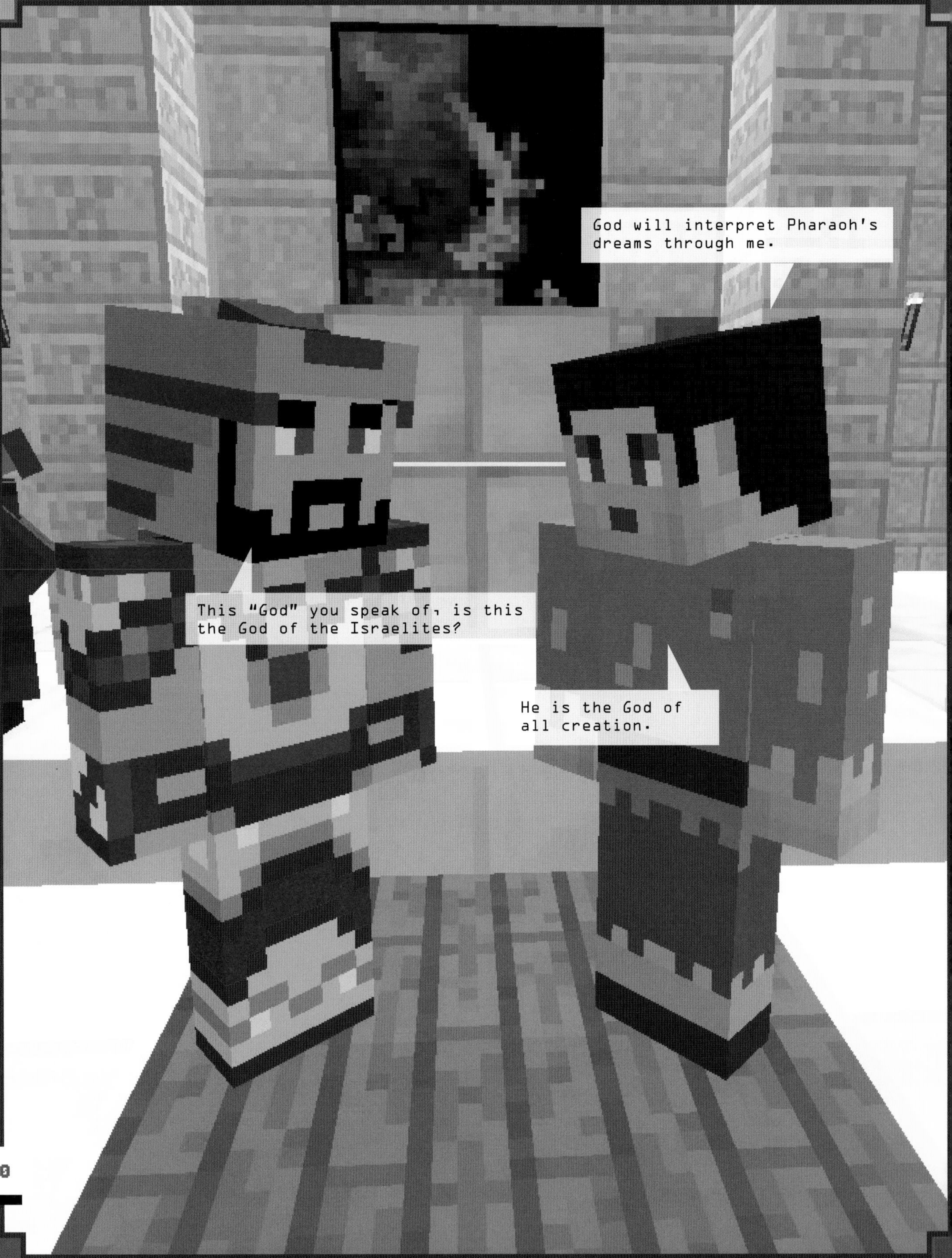
God will interpret Pharaoh's dreams through me.
This "God" you speak of, is this the God of the Israelites?
He is the God of all creation.

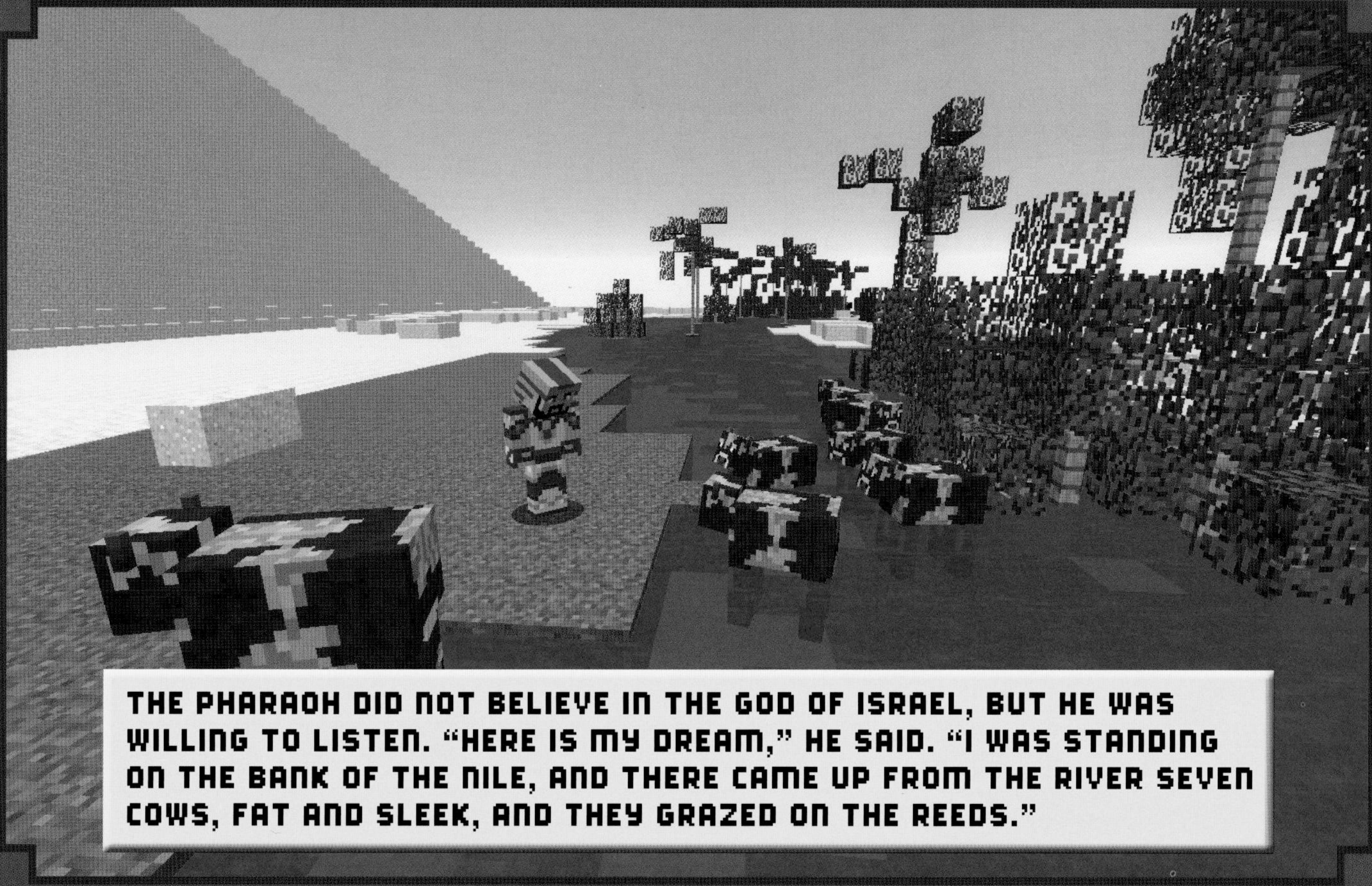
THE PHARAOH DID NOT BELIEVE IN THE GOD OF ISRAEL, BUT HE WAS WILLING TO LISTEN. "HERE IS MY DREAM," HE SAID. "I WAS STANDING ON THE BANK OF THE NILE, AND THERE CAME UP FROM THE RIVER SEVEN COWS, FAT AND SLEEK, AND THEY GRAZED ON THE REEDS."

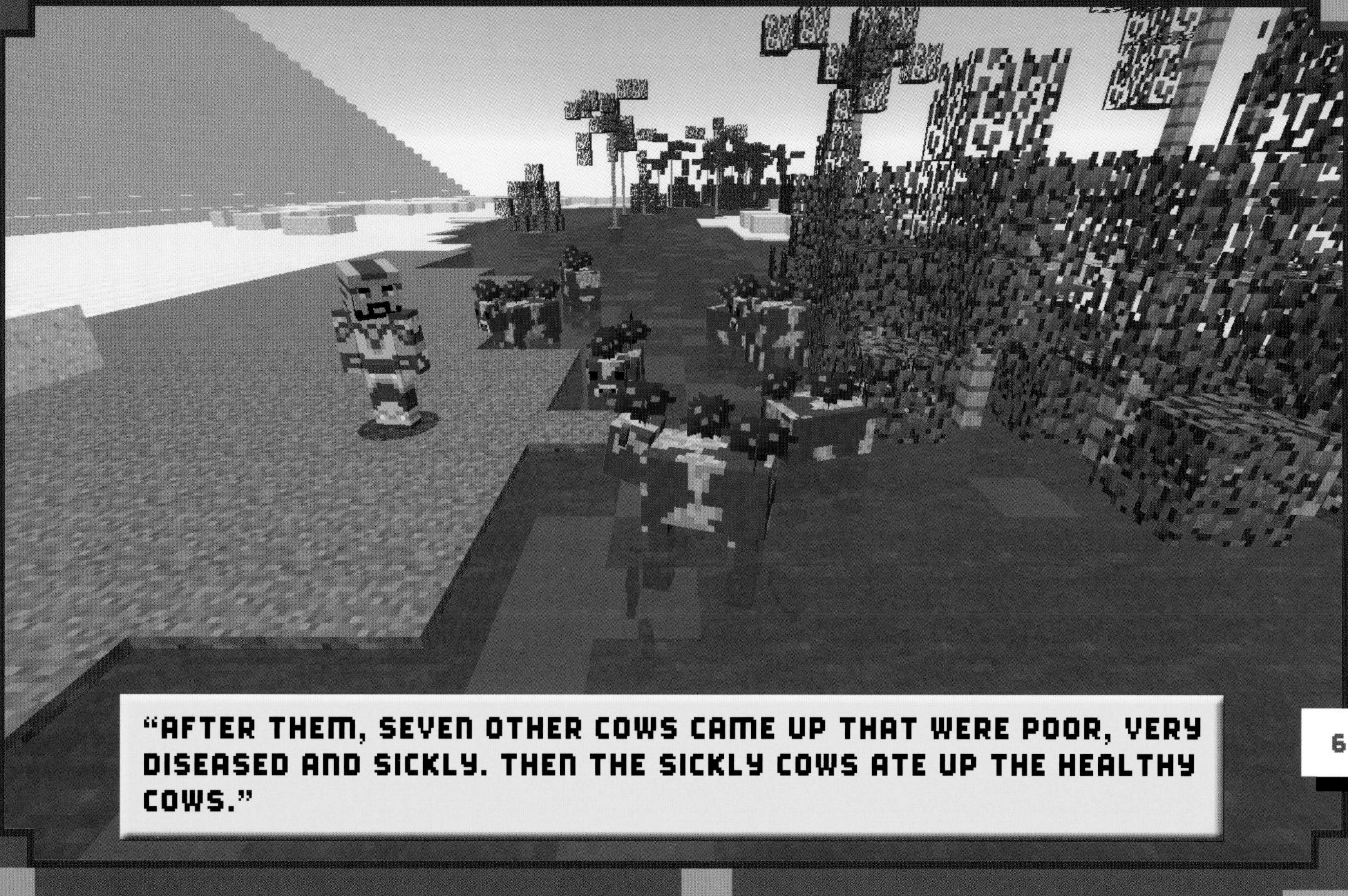
"AFTER THEM, SEVEN OTHER COWS CAME UP THAT WERE POOR, VERY DISEASED AND SICKLY. THEN THE SICKLY COWS ATE UP THE HEALTHY COWS."

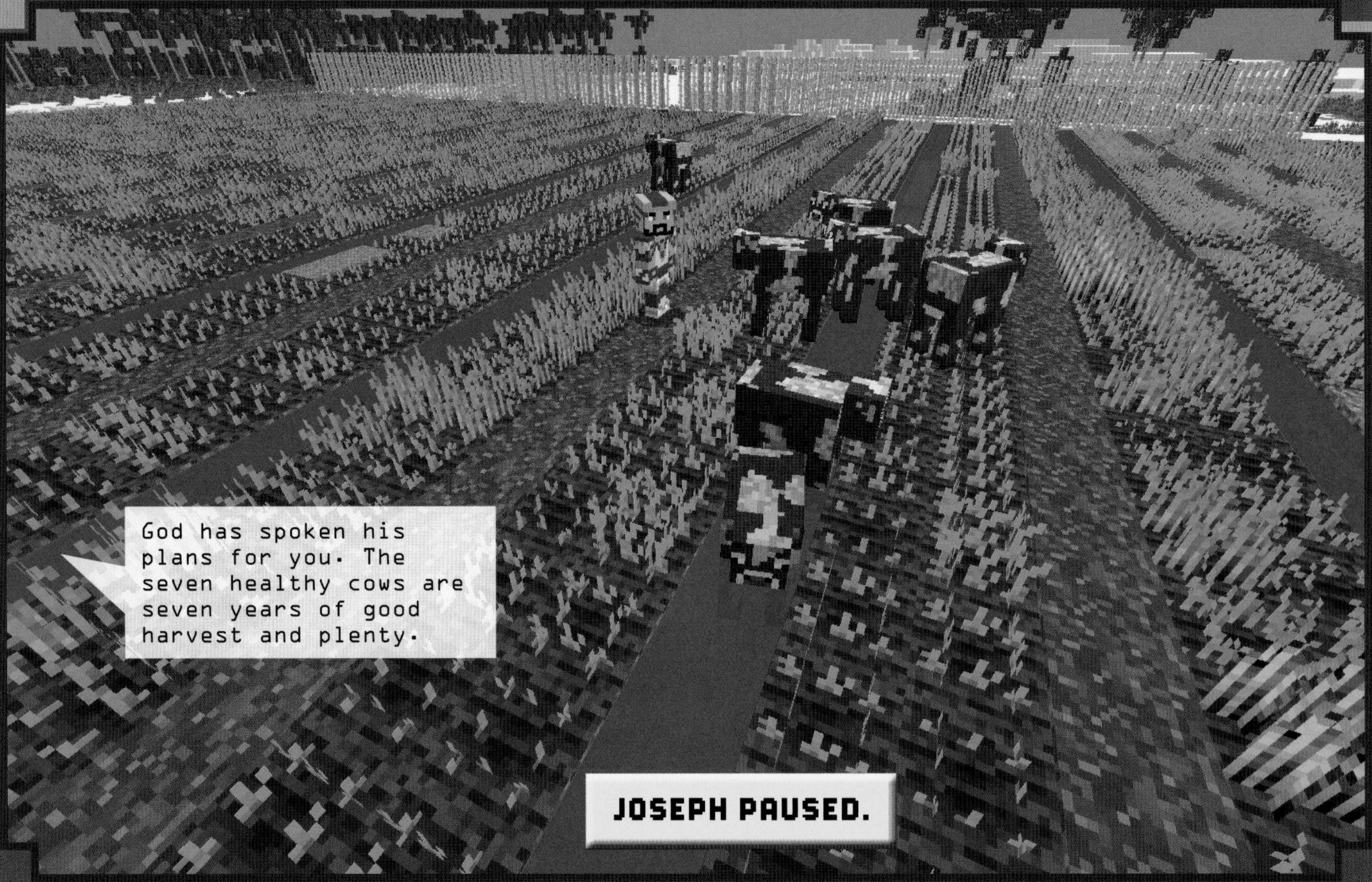
God has spoken his plans for you. The seven healthy cows are seven years of good harvest and plenty.
JOSEPH PAUSED.

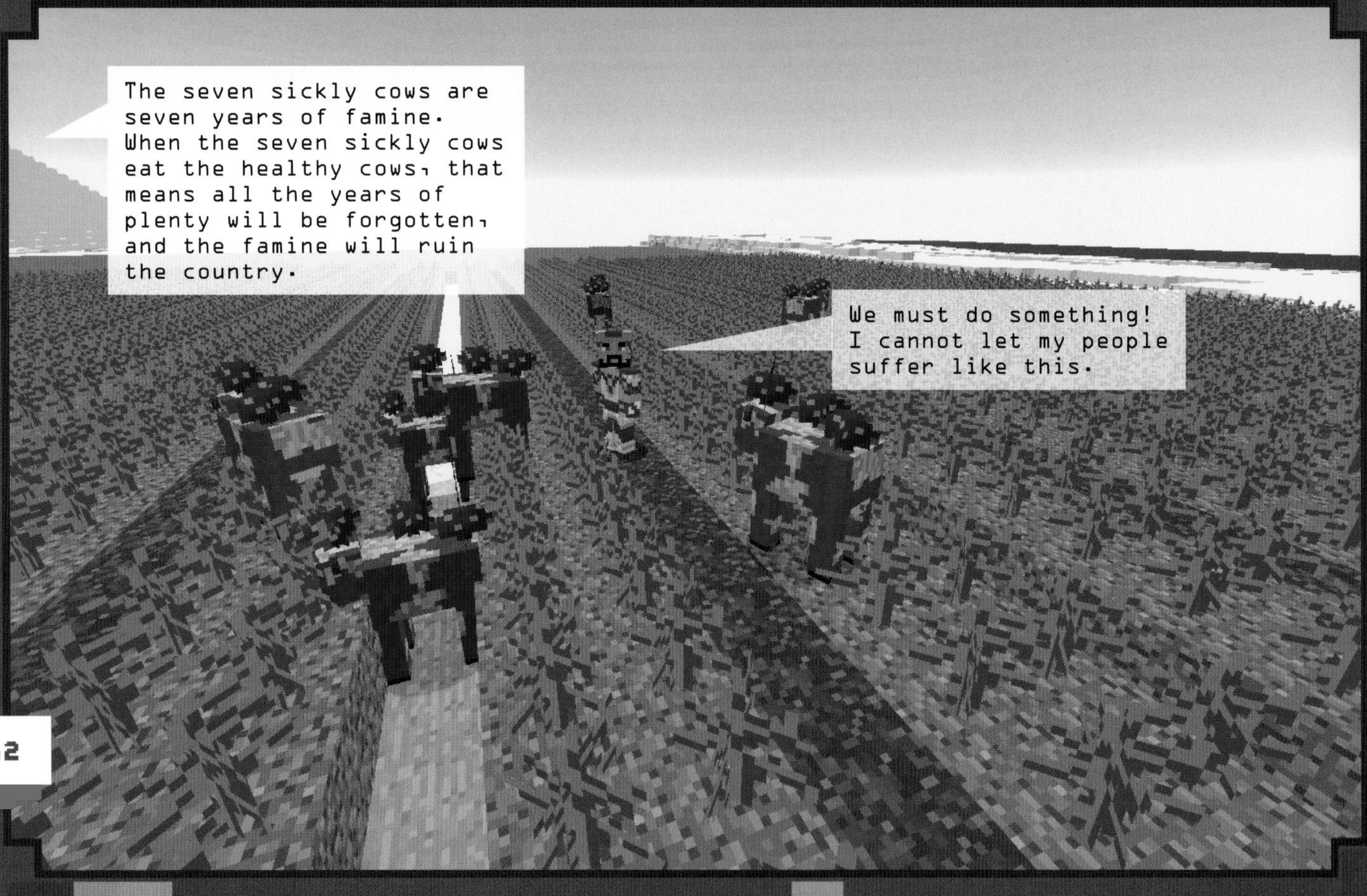
The seven sickly cows are seven years of famine. When the seven sickly cows eat the healthy cows, that means all the years of plenty will be forgotten, and the famine will ruin the country.
We must do something! I cannot let my people suffer like this.

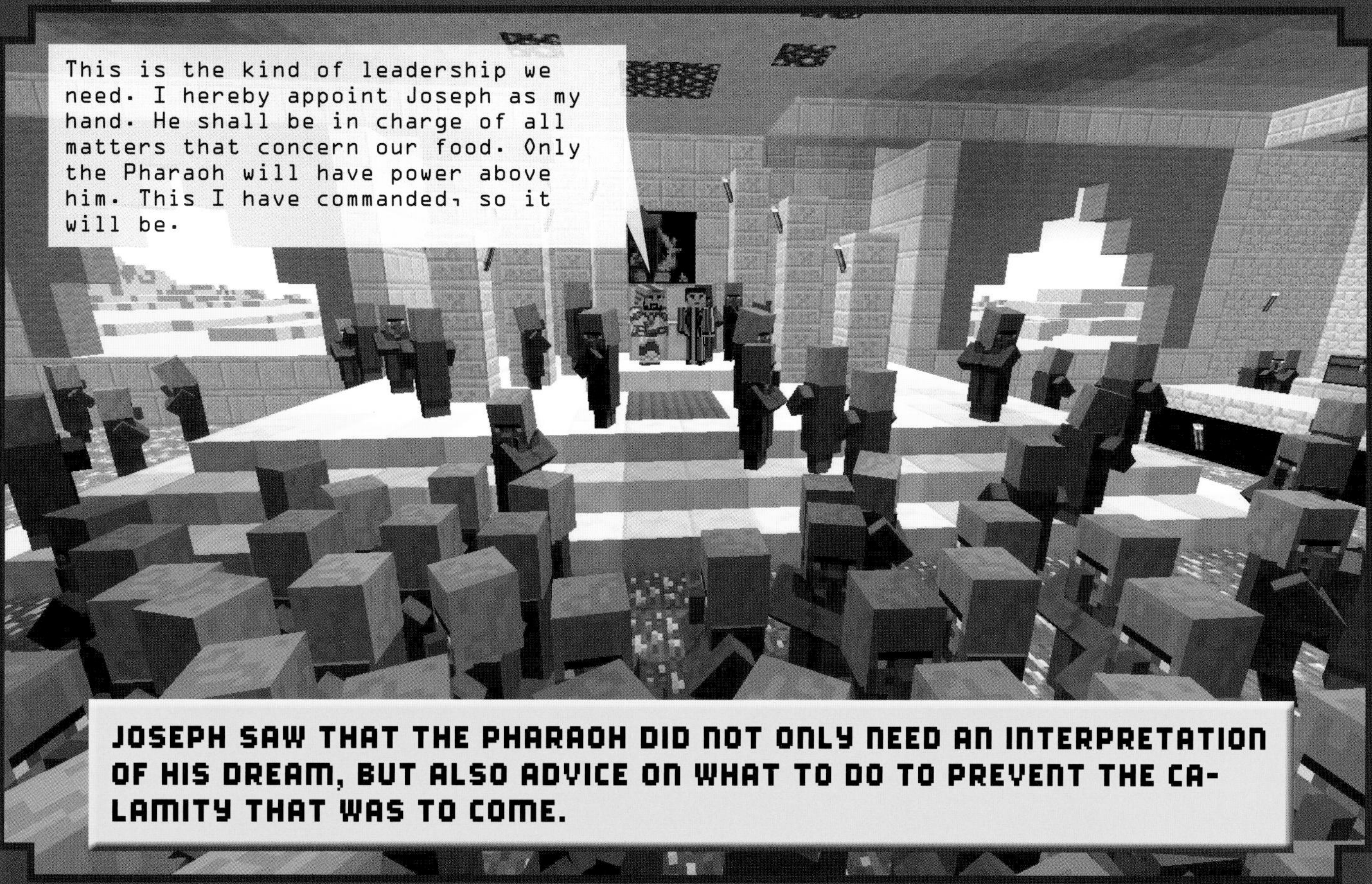
This is the kind of leadership we need. I hereby appoint Joseph as my hand. He shall be in charge of all matters that concern our food. Only the Pharaoh will have power above him. This I have commanded, so it will be.
JOSEPH SAW THAT THE PHARAOH DID NOT ONLY NEED AN INTERPRETATION OF HIS DREAM, BUT ALSO ADVICE ON WHAT TO DO TO PREVENT THE CALAMITY THAT WAS TO COME.

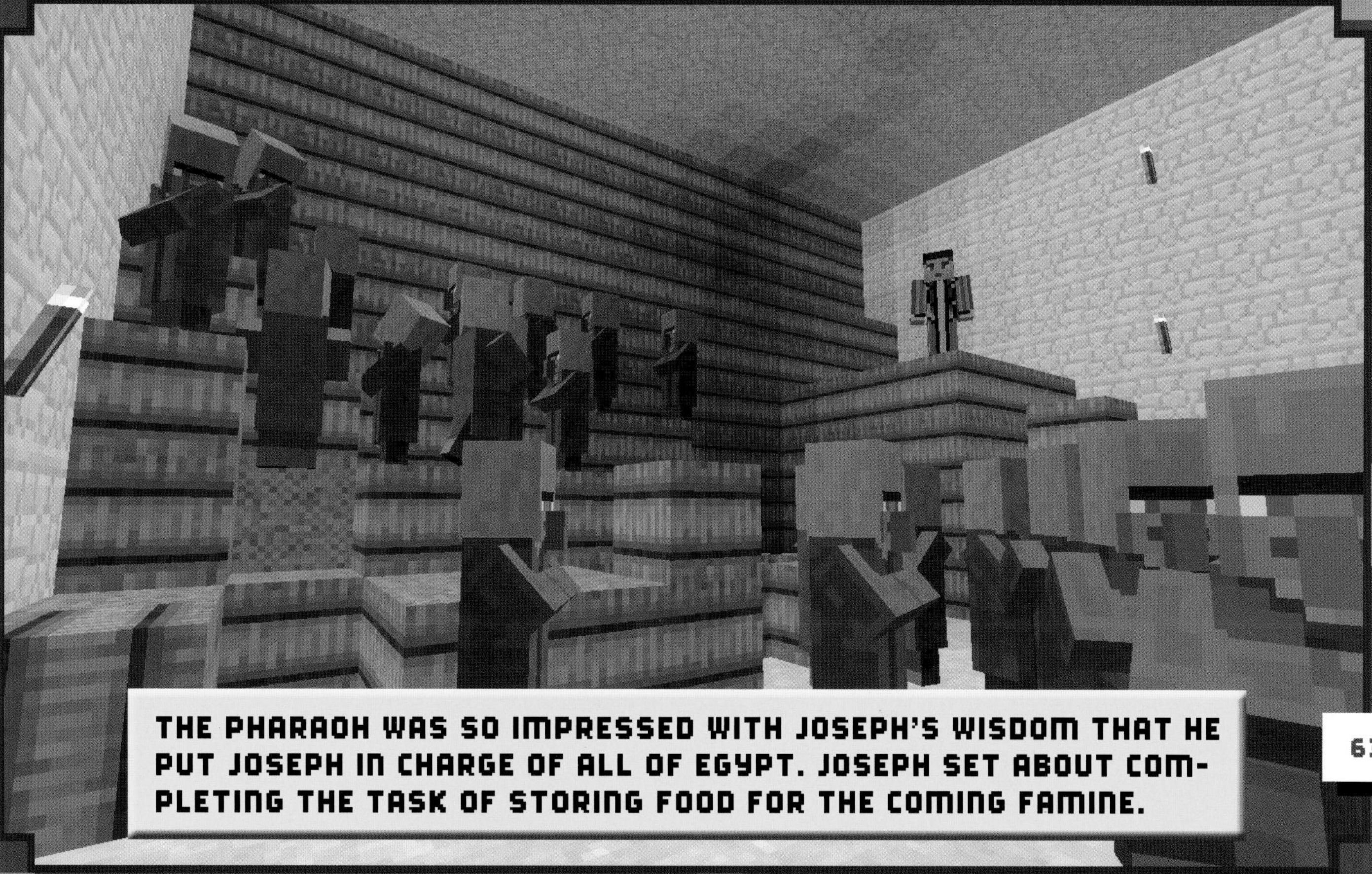
THE PHARAOH WAS SO IMPRESSED WITH JOSEPH'S WISDOM THAT HE PUT JOSEPH IN CHARGE OF ALL OF EGYPT. JOSEPH SET ABOUT COMPLETING THE TASK OF STORING FOOD FOR THE COMING FAMINE.

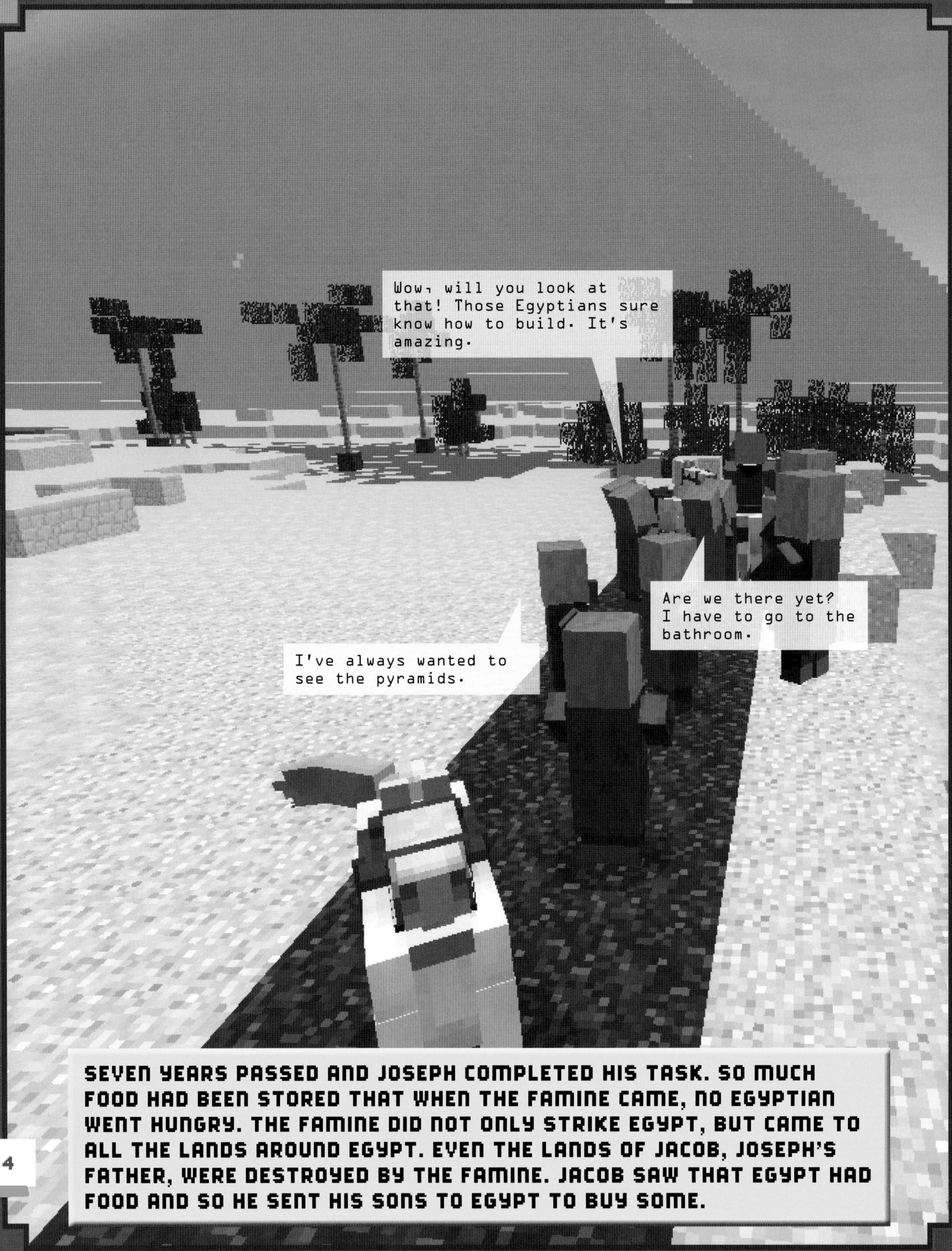
Wow, will you look at that! Those Egyptians sure know how to build. It's amazing.
Are we there yet? I have to go to the bathroom.
I've always wanted to see the pyramids.
SEVEN YEARS PASSED AND JOSEPH COMPLETED HIS TASK. SO MUCH FOOD HAD BEEN STORED THAT WHEN THE FAMINE CAME, NO EGYPTIAN WENT HUNGRY. THE FAMINE DID NOT ONLY STRIKE EGYPT, BUT CAME TO ALL THE LANDS AROUND EGYPT. EVEN THE LANDS OF JACOB, JOSEPH'S FATHER, WERE DESTROYED BY THE FAMINE. JACOB SAW THAT EGYPT HAD FOOD AND SO HE SENT HIS SONS TO EGYPT TO BUY SOME.

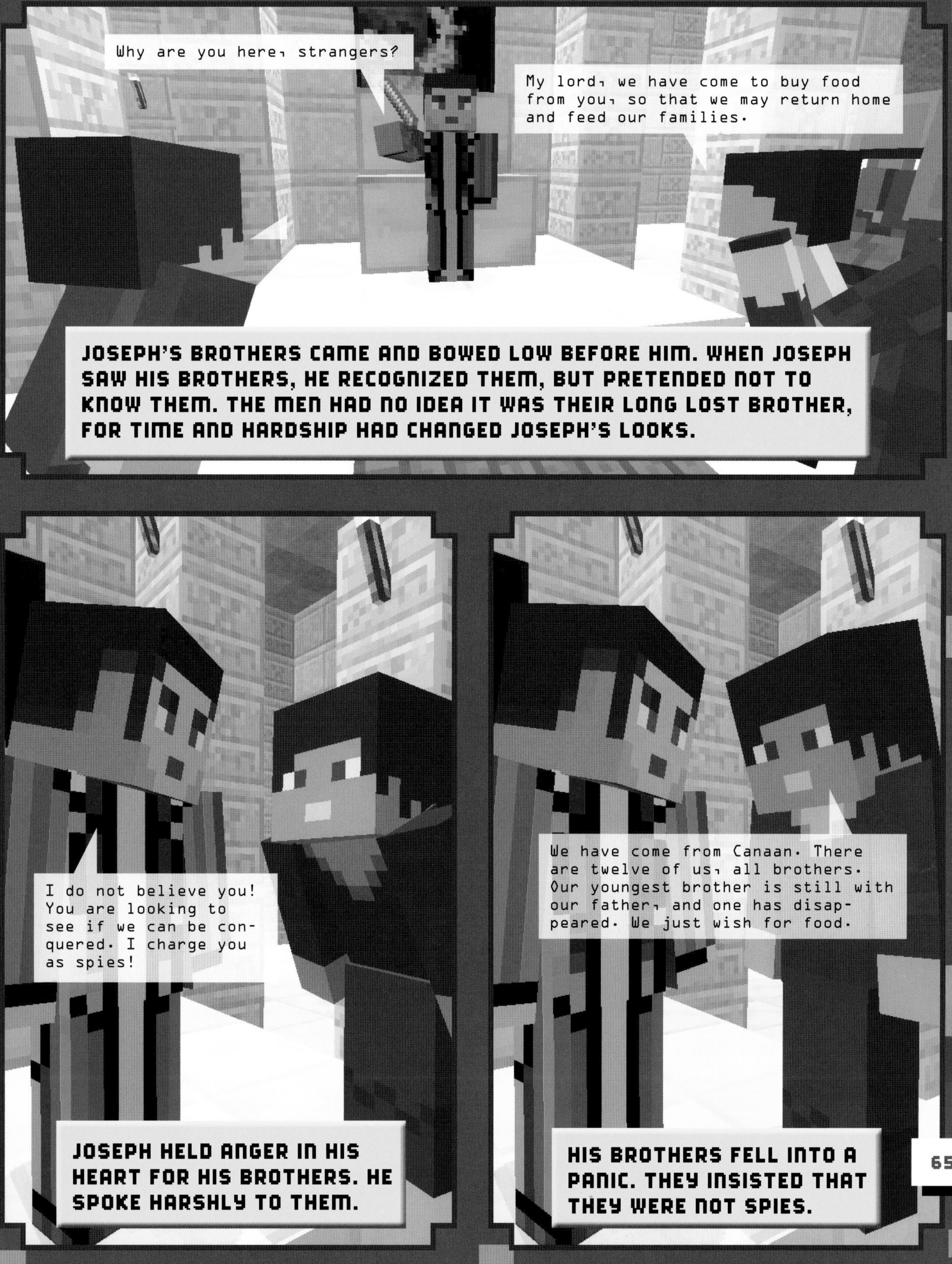
Why are you here, strangers?
My lord, we have come to buy food from you, so that we may return home and feed our families.
JOSEPH'S BROTHERS CAME AND BOWED LOW BEFORE HIM. WHEN JOSEPH SAW HIS BROTHERS, HE RECOGNIZED THEM, BUT PRETENDED NOT TO KNOW THEM. THE MEN HAD NO IDEA IT WAS THEIR LONG LOST BROTHER, FOR TIME AND HARDSHIP HAD CHANGED JOSEPH'S LOOKS.
I do not believe you! You are looking to see if we can be conquered. I charge you as spies!
JOSEPH HELD ANGER IN HIS HEART FOR HIS BROTHERS. HE SPOKE HARSHLY TO THEM.
We have come from Canaan. There are twelve of us, all brothers. Our youngest brother is still with our father, and one has disappeared. We just wish for food.
HIS BROTHERS FELL INTO A PANIC. THEY INSISTED THAT THEY WERE NOT SPIES.

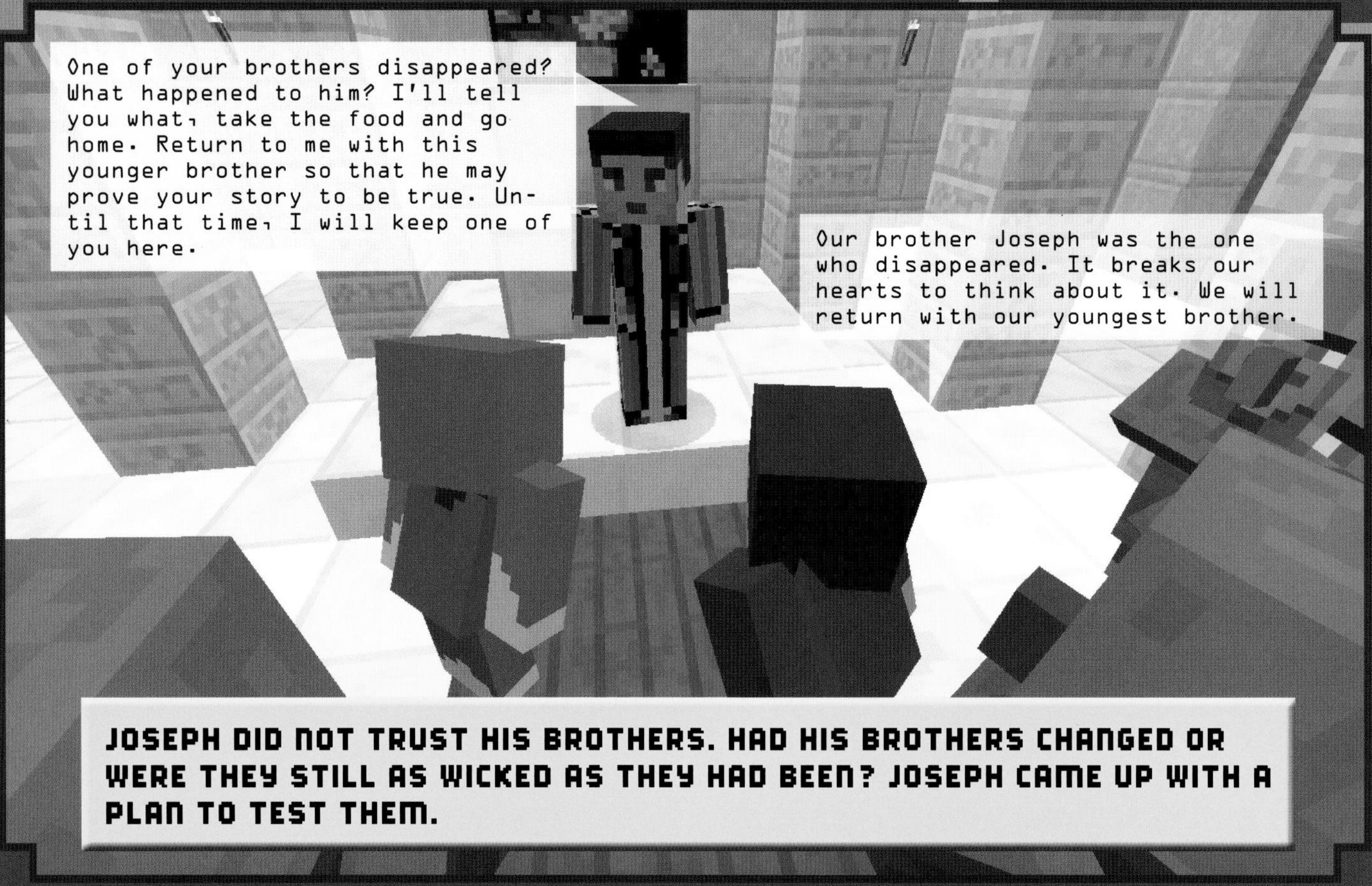
One of your brothers disappeared? What happened to him? I'll tell you what, take the food and go home. Return to me with this younger brother so that he may prove your story to be true. Until that time, I will keep one of you here.
Our brother Joseph was the one who disappeared. It breaks our hearts to think about it. We will return with our youngest brother.
JOSEPH DID NOT TRUST HIS BROTHERS. HAD HIS BROTHERS CHANGED OR WERE THEY STILL AS WICKED AS THEY HAD BEEN? JOSEPH CAME UP WITH A PLAN TO TEST THEM.

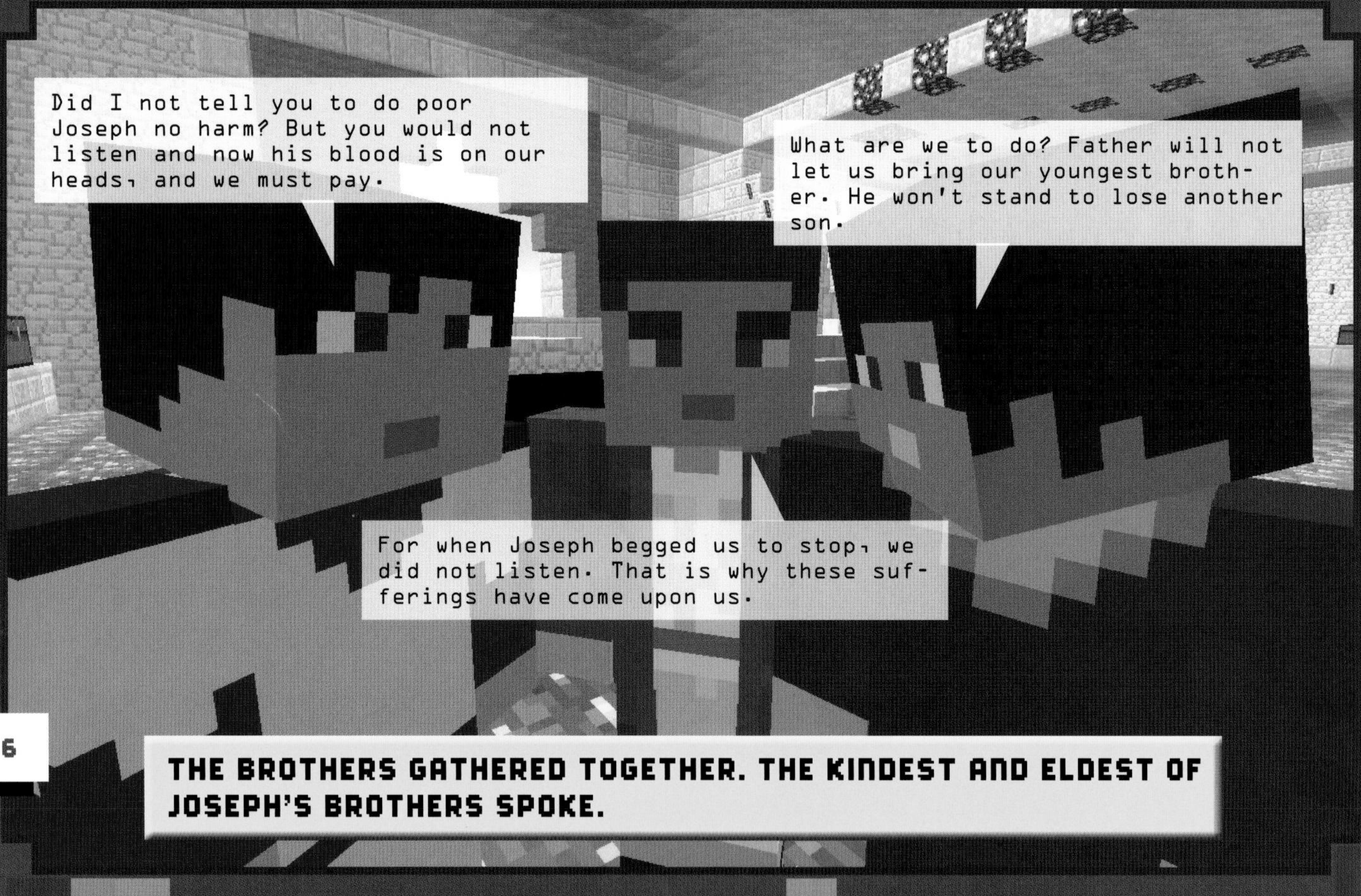
Did I not tell you to do poor Joseph no harm? But you would not listen and now his blood is on our heads, and we must pay.
What are we to do? Father will not let us bring our youngest brother. He won't stand to lose another son.
For when Joseph begged us to stop, we did not listen. That is why these sufferings have come upon us.
THE BROTHERS GATHERED TOGETHER. THE KINDEST AND ELDEST OF JOSEPH'S BROTHERS SPOKE.

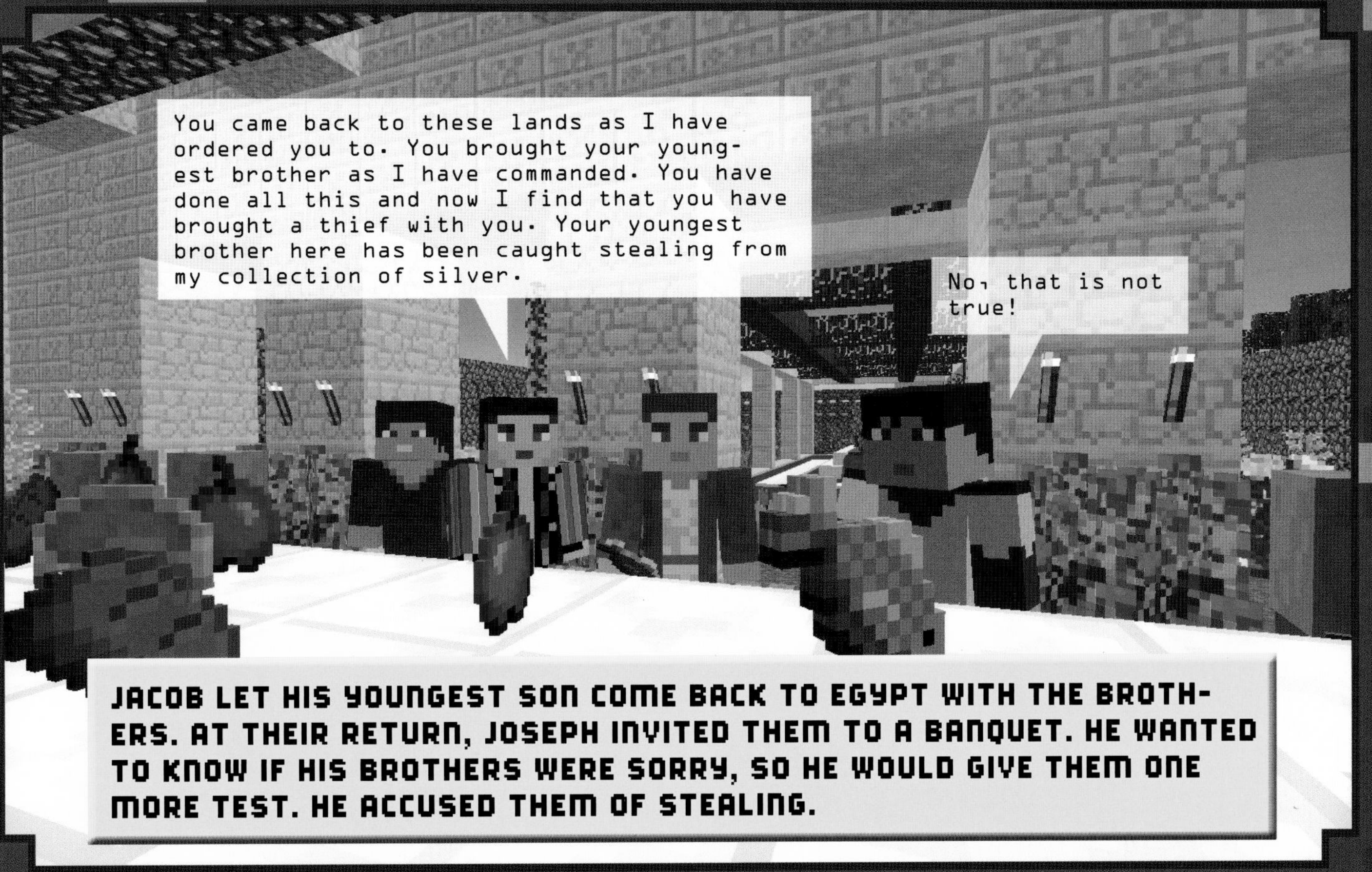
You came back to these lands as I have ordered you to. You brought your youngest brother as I have commanded. You have done all this and now I find that you have brought a thief with you. Your youngest brother here has been caught stealing from my collection of silver.
No, that is not true!
JACOB LET HIS YOUNGEST SON COME BACK TO EGYPT WITH THE BROTHERS. AT THEIR RETURN, JOSEPH INVITED THEM TO A BANQUET. HE WANTED TO KNOW IF HIS BROTHERS WERE SORRY, SO HE WOULD GIVE THEM ONE MORE TEST. HE ACCUSED THEM OF STEALING.

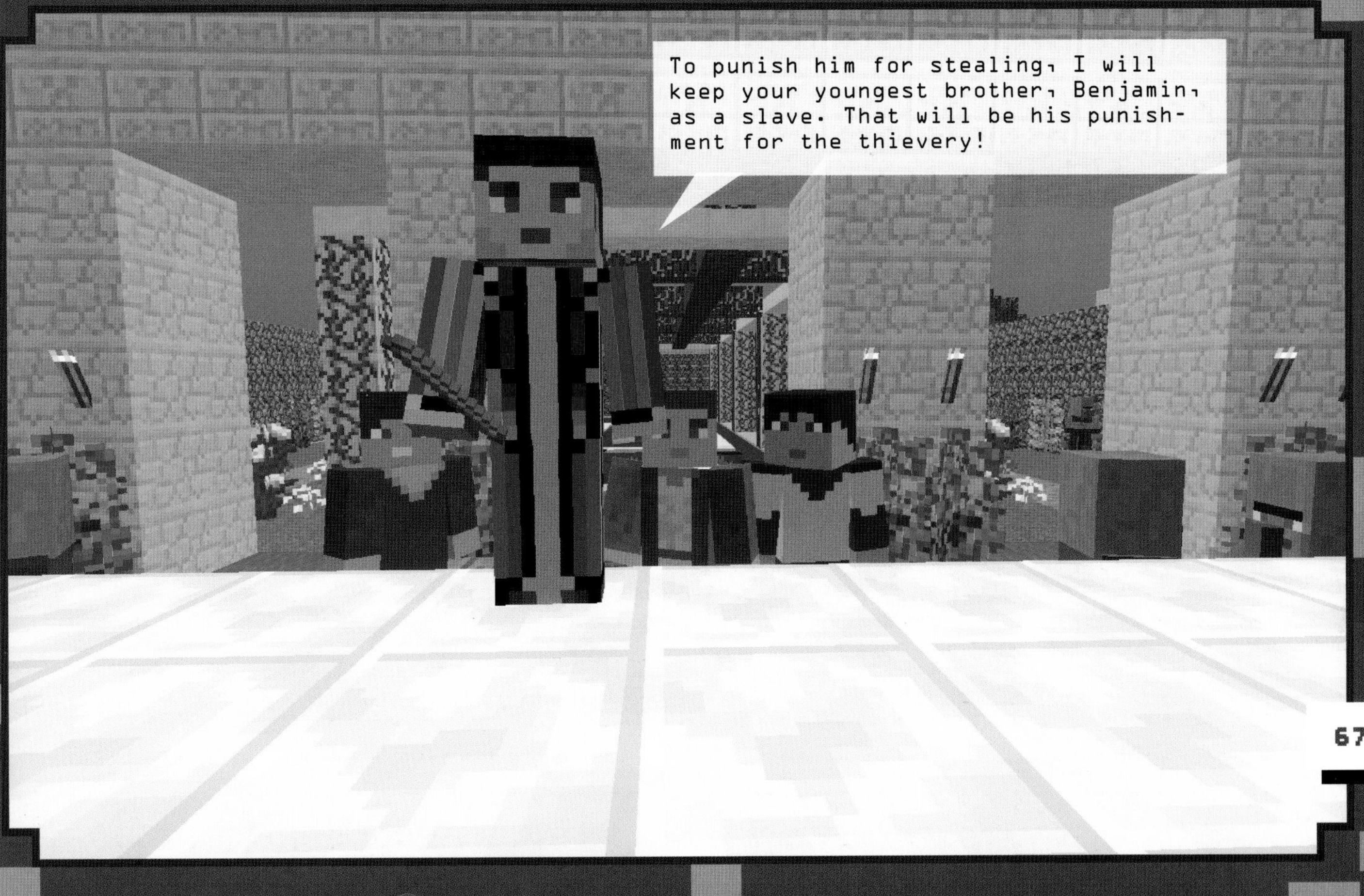
To punish him for stealing, I will keep your youngest brother, Benjamin, as a slave. That will be his punishment for the thievery!

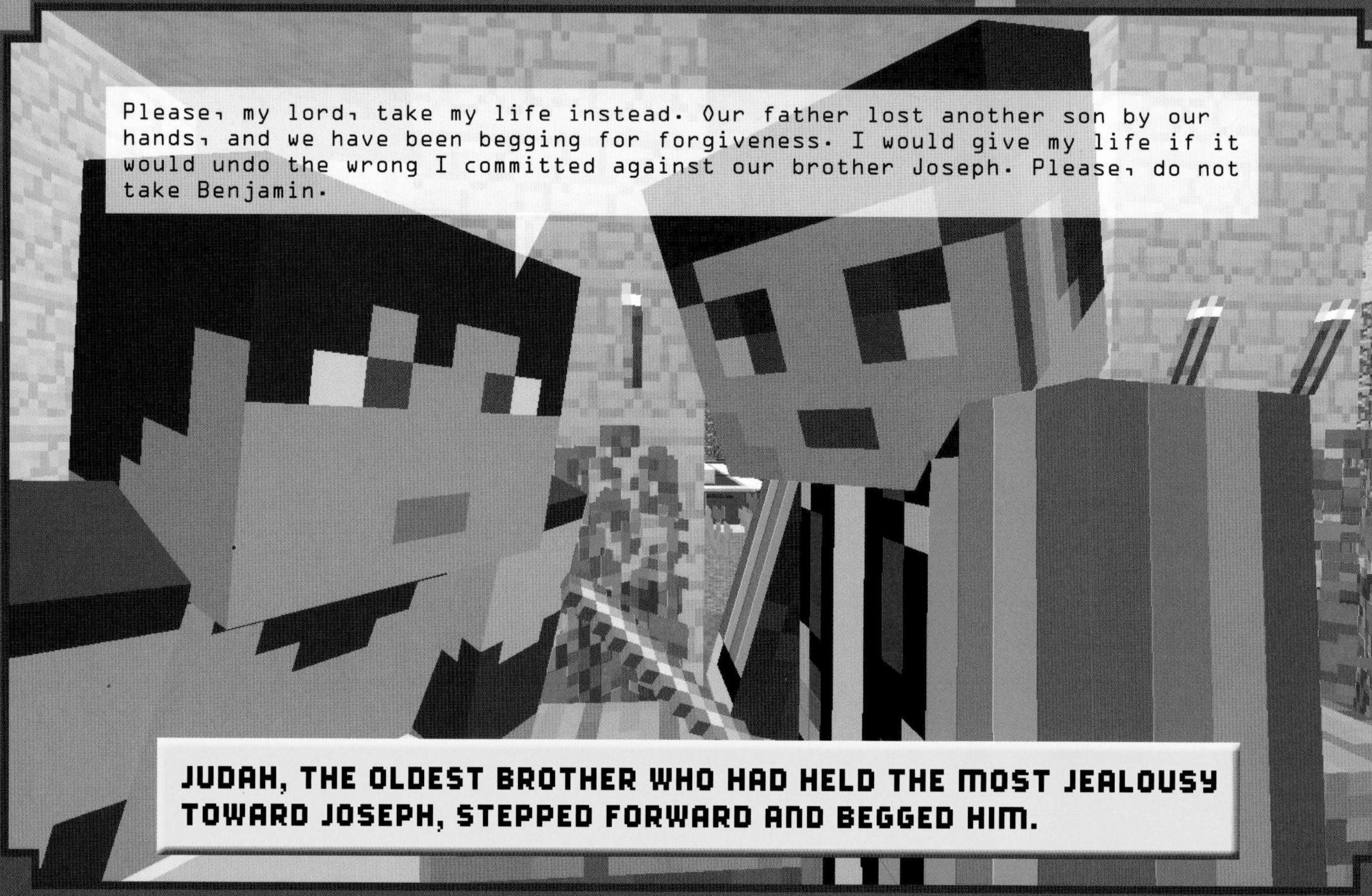
Please, my lord, take my life instead. Our father lost another son by our hands, and we have been begging for forgiveness. I would give my life if it would undo the wrong I committed against our brother Joseph. Please, do not take Benjamin.
JUDAH, THE OLDEST BROTHER WHO HAD HELD THE MOST JEALOUSY TOWARD JOSEPH, STEPPED FORWARD AND BEGGED HIM.

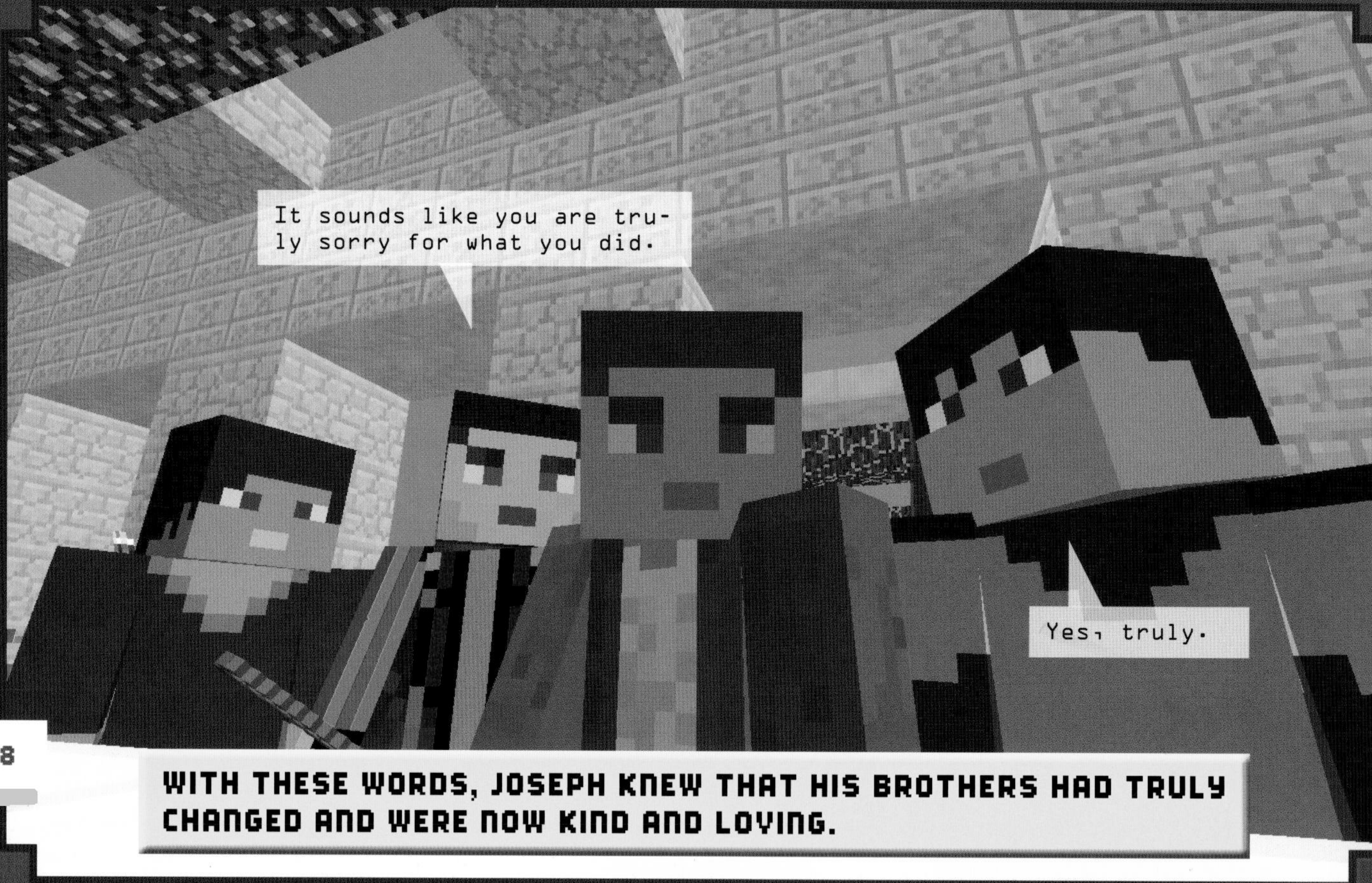
It sounds like you are truly sorry for what you did.
Yes, truly.
WITH THESE WORDS, JOSEPH KNEW THAT HIS BROTHERS HAD TRULY CHANGED AND WERE NOW KIND AND LOVING.

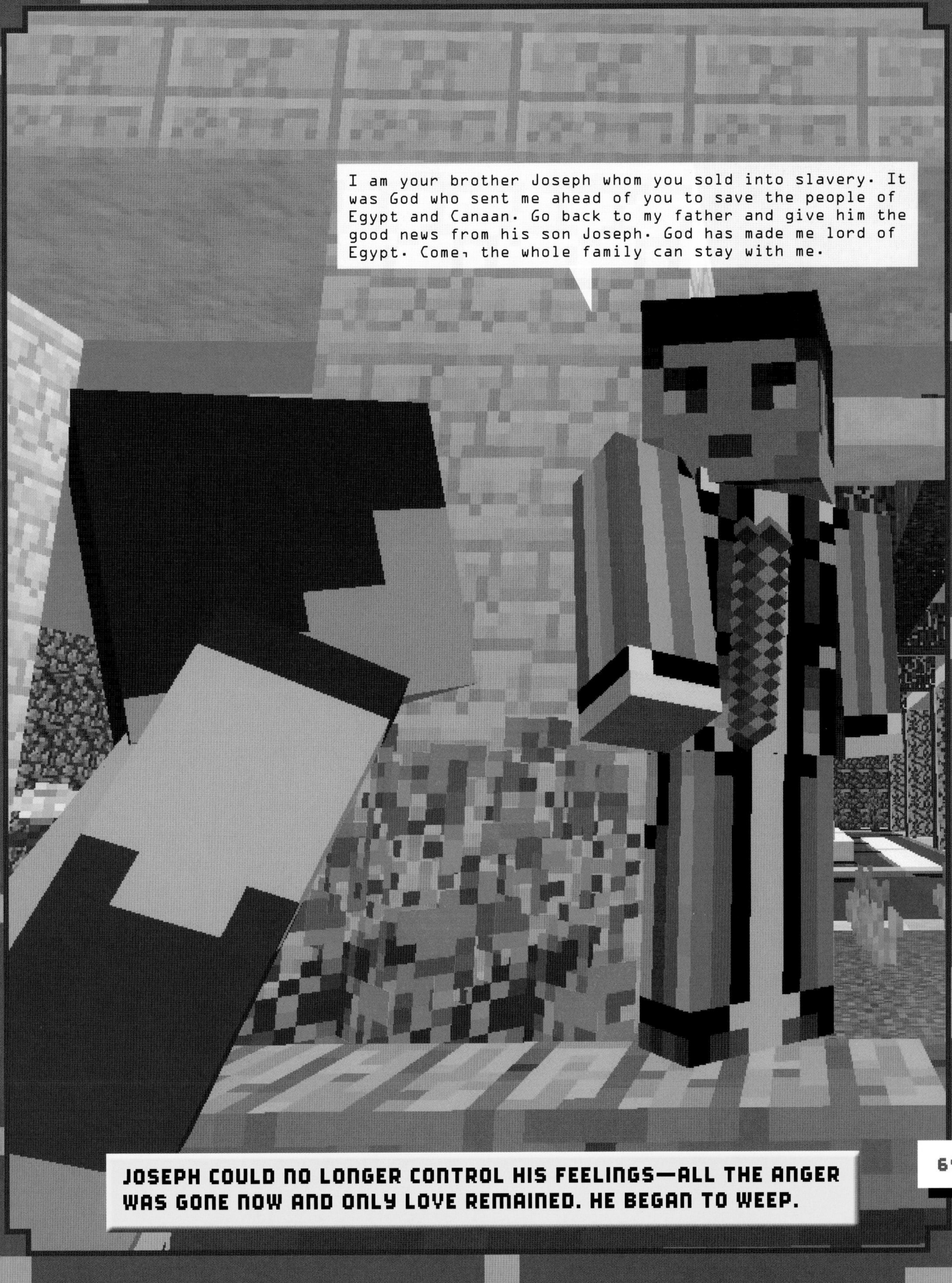
I am your brother Joseph whom you sold into slavery. It was God who sent me ahead of you to save the people of Egypt and Canaan. Go back to my father and give him the good news from his son Joseph. God has made me lord of Egypt. Come, the whole family can stay with me.
JOSEPH COULD NO LONGER CONTROL HIS FEELINGS—ALL THE ANGER WAS GONE NOW AND ONLY LOVE REMAINED. HE BEGAN TO WEEP.

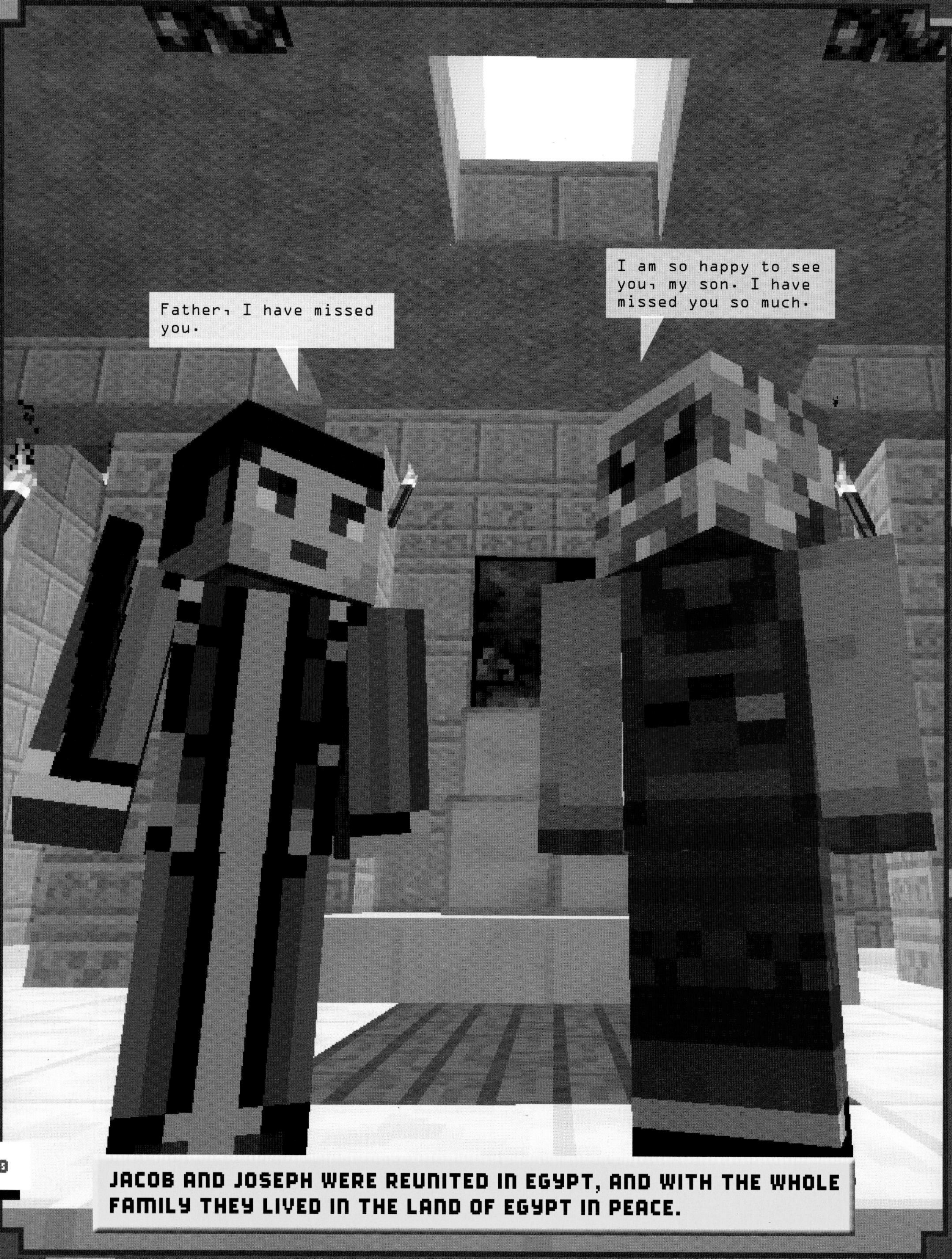
Father, I have missed you.
I am so happy to see you, my son. I have missed you so much.
JACOB AND JOSEPH WERE REUNITED IN EGYPT, AND WITH THE WHOLE FAMILY THEY LIVED IN THE LAND OF EGYPT IN PEACE.

THE STORY OF MOSES

Great plan sending them to Egypt!

Thanks! But once again, Gabriel, my Chosen People are under duress.

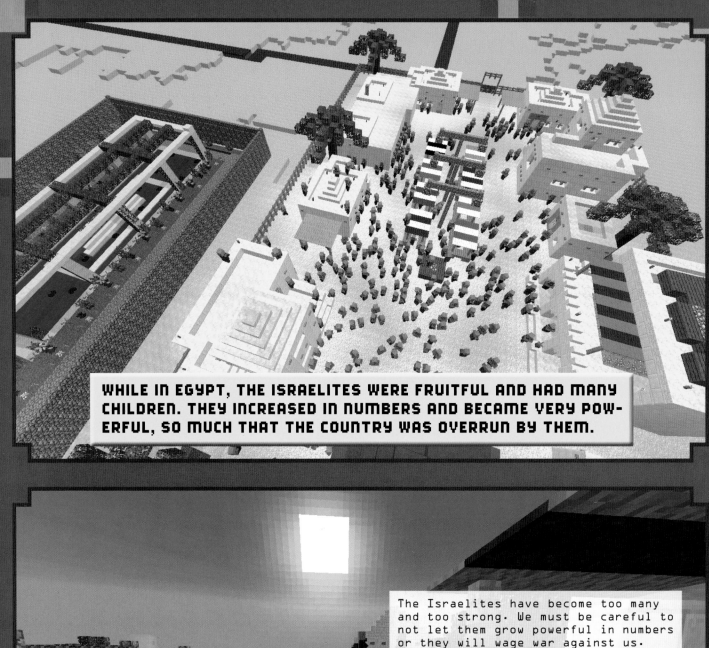

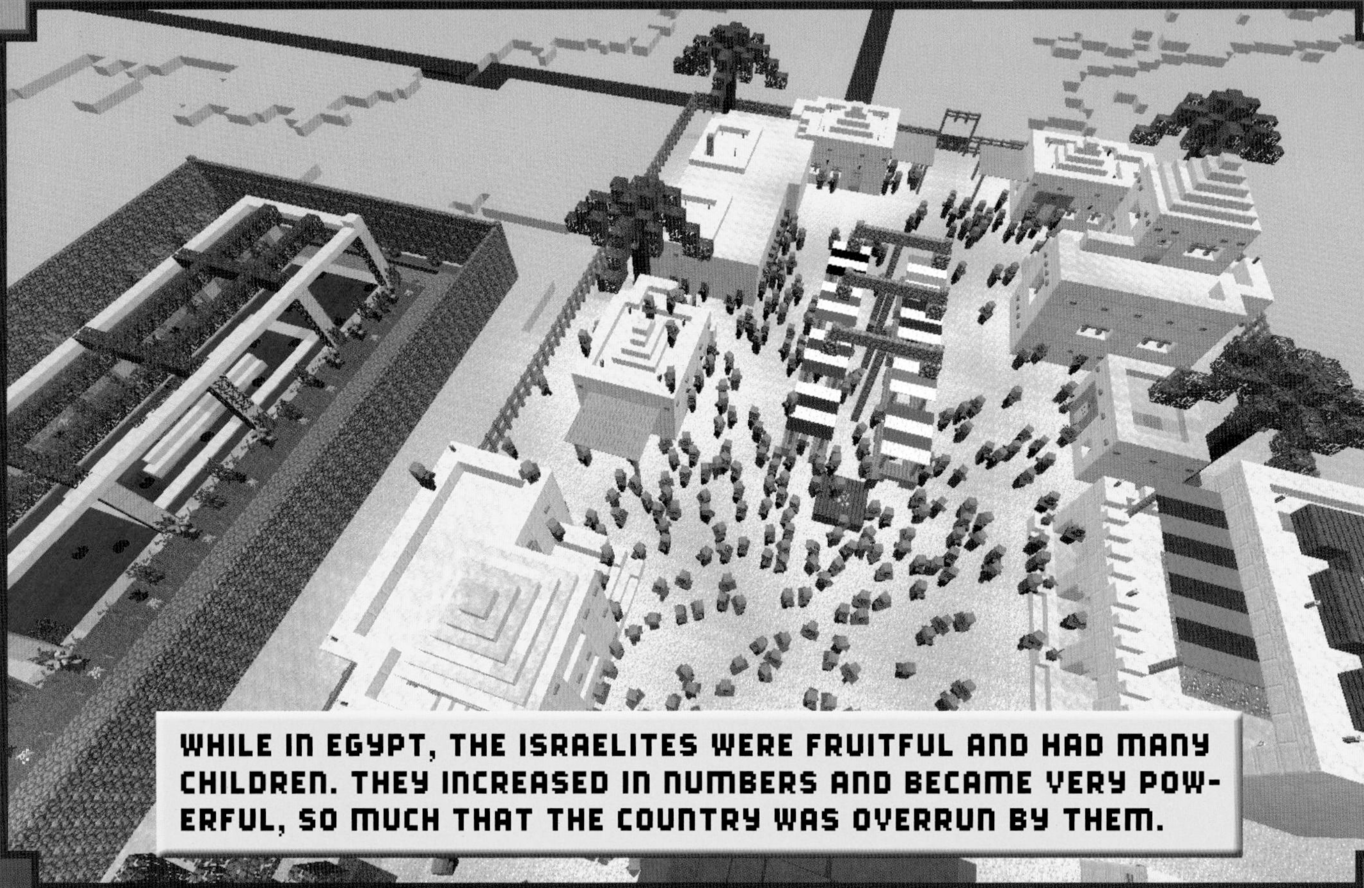
WHILE IN EGYPT, THE ISRAELITES WERE FRUITFUL AND HAD MANY CHILDREN. THEY INCREASED IN NUMBERS AND BECAME VERY POWERFUL, SO MUCH THAT THE COUNTRY WAS OVERRUN BY THEM.

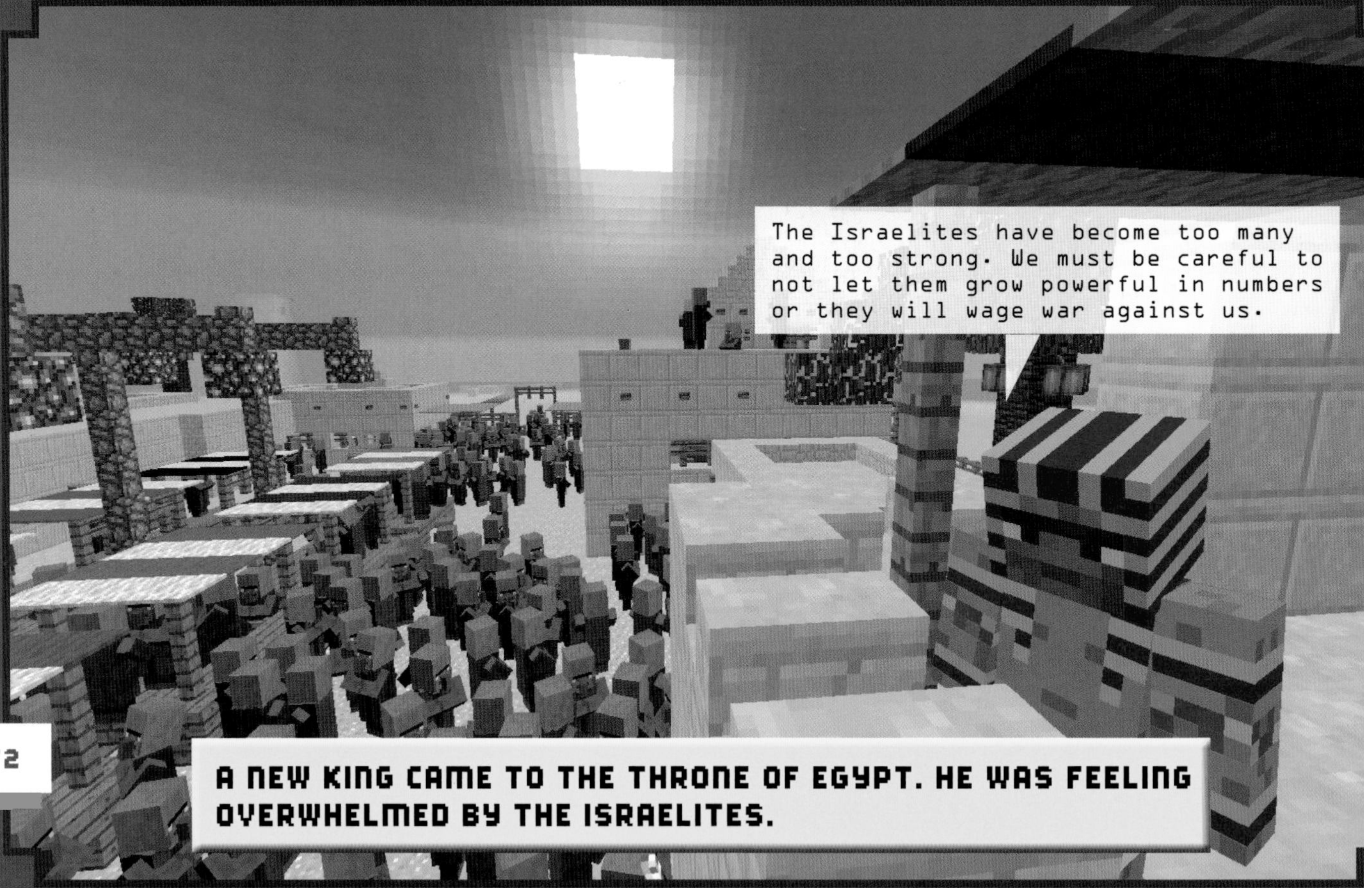
The Israelites have become too many and too strong. We must be careful to not let them grow powerful in numbers or they will wage war against us.
A NEW KING CAME TO THE THRONE OF EGYPT. HE WAS FEELING OVERWHELMED BY THE ISRAELITES.

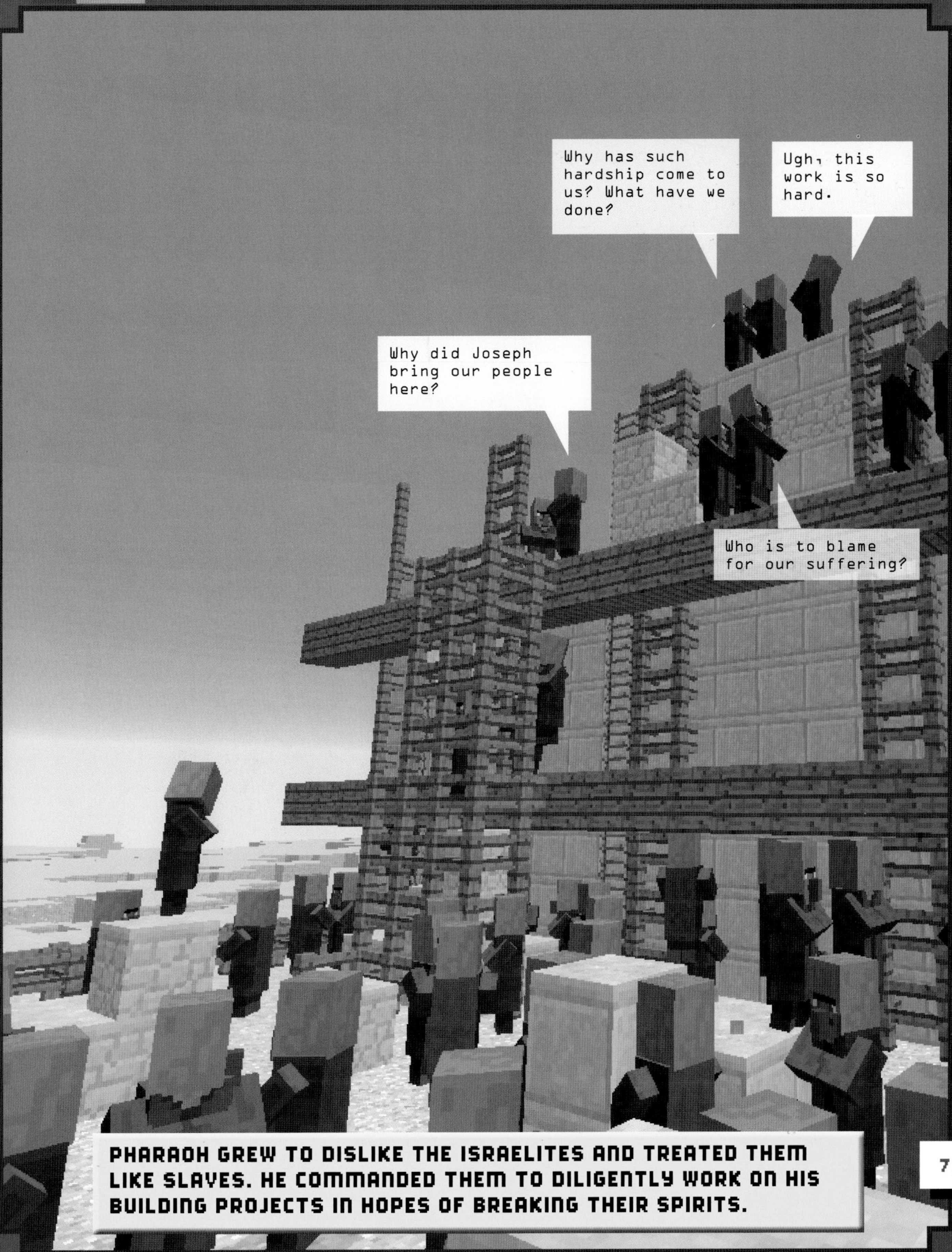
Why has such hardship come to us? What have we done?
Ugh, this work is so hard.
Why did Joseph bring our people here?
Who is to blame for our suffering?
PHARAOH GREW TO DISLIKE THE ISRAELITES AND TREATED THEM LIKE SLAVES. HE COMMANDED THEM TO DILIGENTLY WORK ON HIS BUILDING PROJECTS IN HOPES OF BREAKING THEIR SPIRITS.

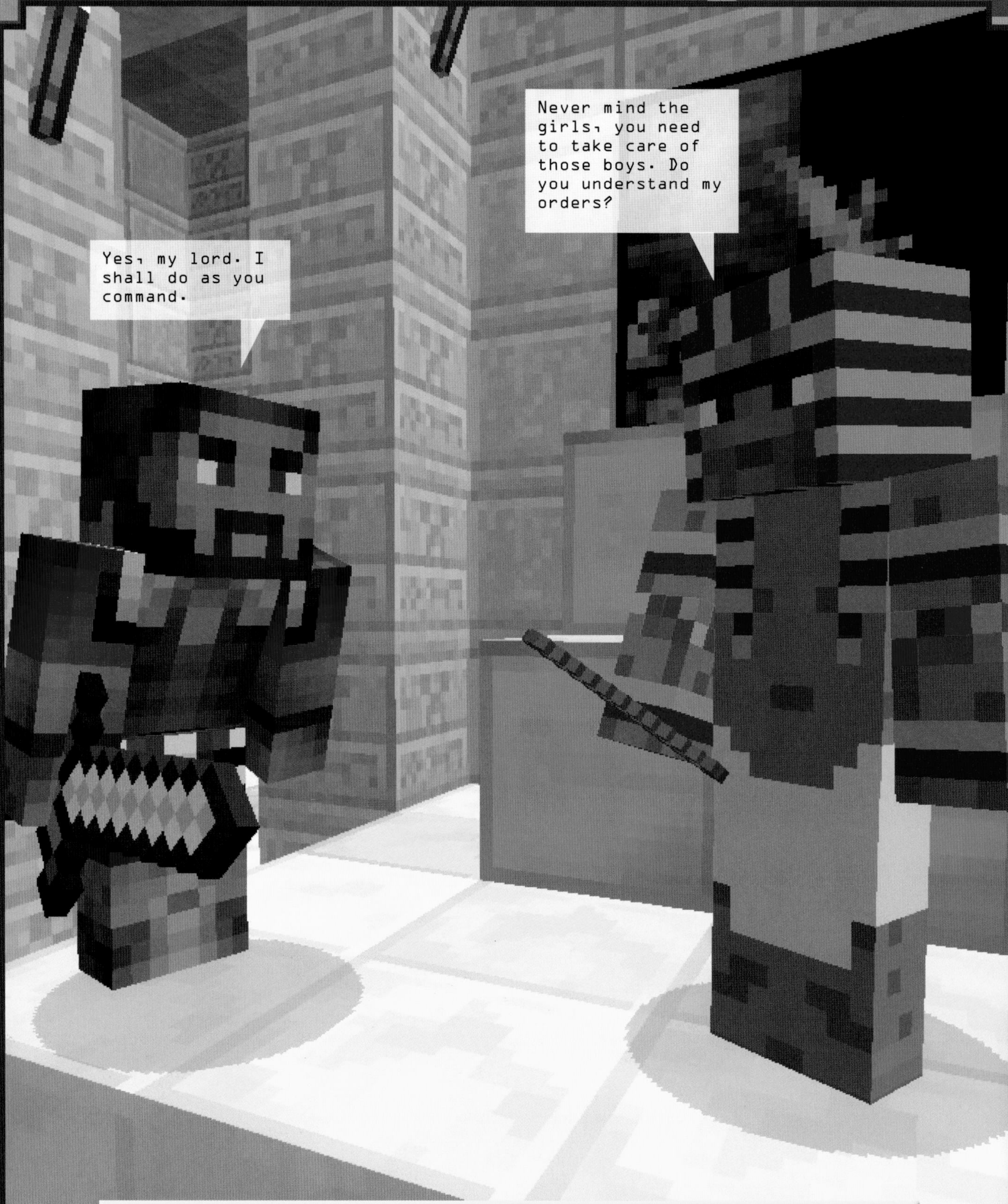
Never mind the girls, you need to take care of those boys. Do you understand my orders?
Yes, my lord. I shall do as you command.

THE PHARAOH ANNOUNCED A DECREE THAT ALL NEWBORN ISRAELITE BOYS BE THROWN INTO THE RIVER NILE. PHARAOH WAS DETERMINED TO REDUCE THE NUMBER OF HEBREWS IN HIS LAND.

ONE DAY, A DESCENDANT OF JOSEPH HAD A BABY BOY. THE FATHER AND MOTHER WERE AFRAID OF WHAT WOULD HAPPEN TO THEIR SON, SO THEY DECIDED TO PLACE HIM IN A BASKET THAT WOULD FLOAT DOWN THE RIVER NILE.

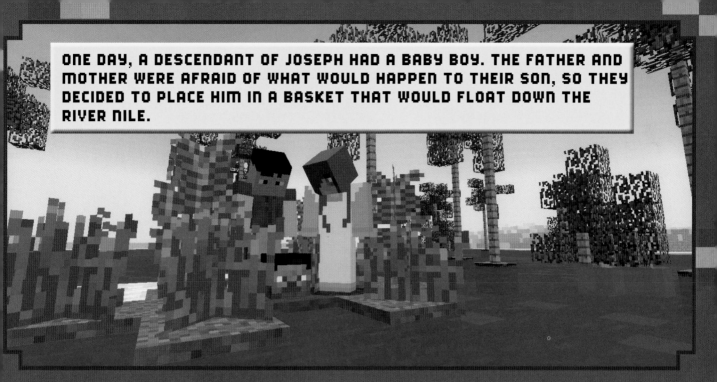

GOD PROTECTED THE CHILD AS IT WENT DOWN THE RIVER. THE BASKET THEN HIT A FLURRY OF WATER THAT PUSHED THE BASKET TOWARD THE SHORE.

AT THAT TIME THE PHARAOH'S DAUGHTER CAME TO BATHE IN THE RIVER NILE. THE DAUGHTER OF PHARAOH COULD NOT HAVE ANY CHILDREN, AND SHE HAD PRAYED FOR YEARS TO HAVE A BABY.

I will name him Moses!

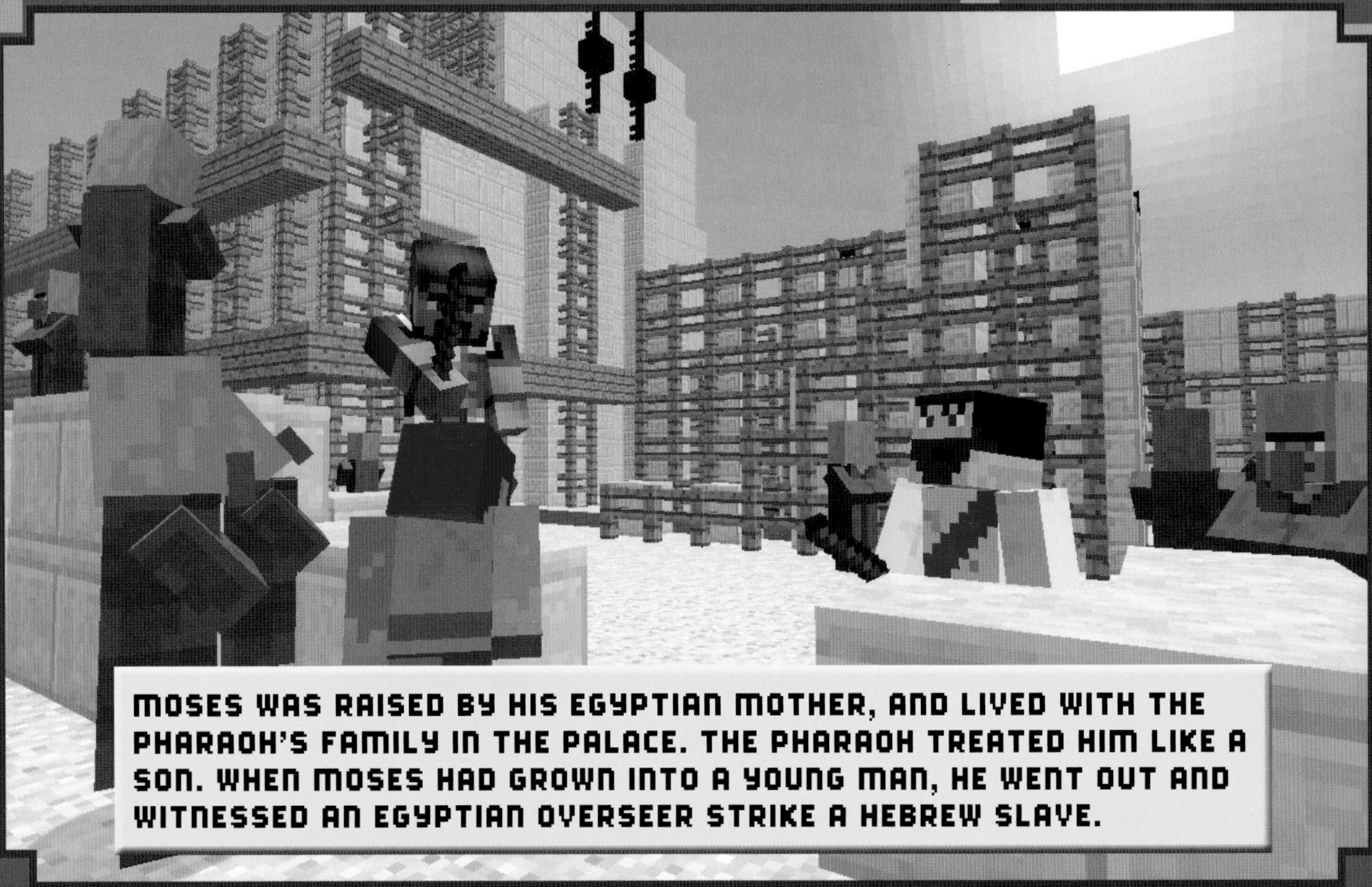
MOSES WAS RAISED BY HIS EGYPTIAN MOTHER, AND LIVED WITH THE PHARAOH'S FAMILY IN THE PALACE. THE PHARAOH TREATED HIM LIKE A SON. WHEN MOSES HAD GROWN INTO A YOUNG MAN, HE WENT OUT AND WITNESSED AN EGYPTIAN OVERSEER STRIKE A HEBREW SLAVE.

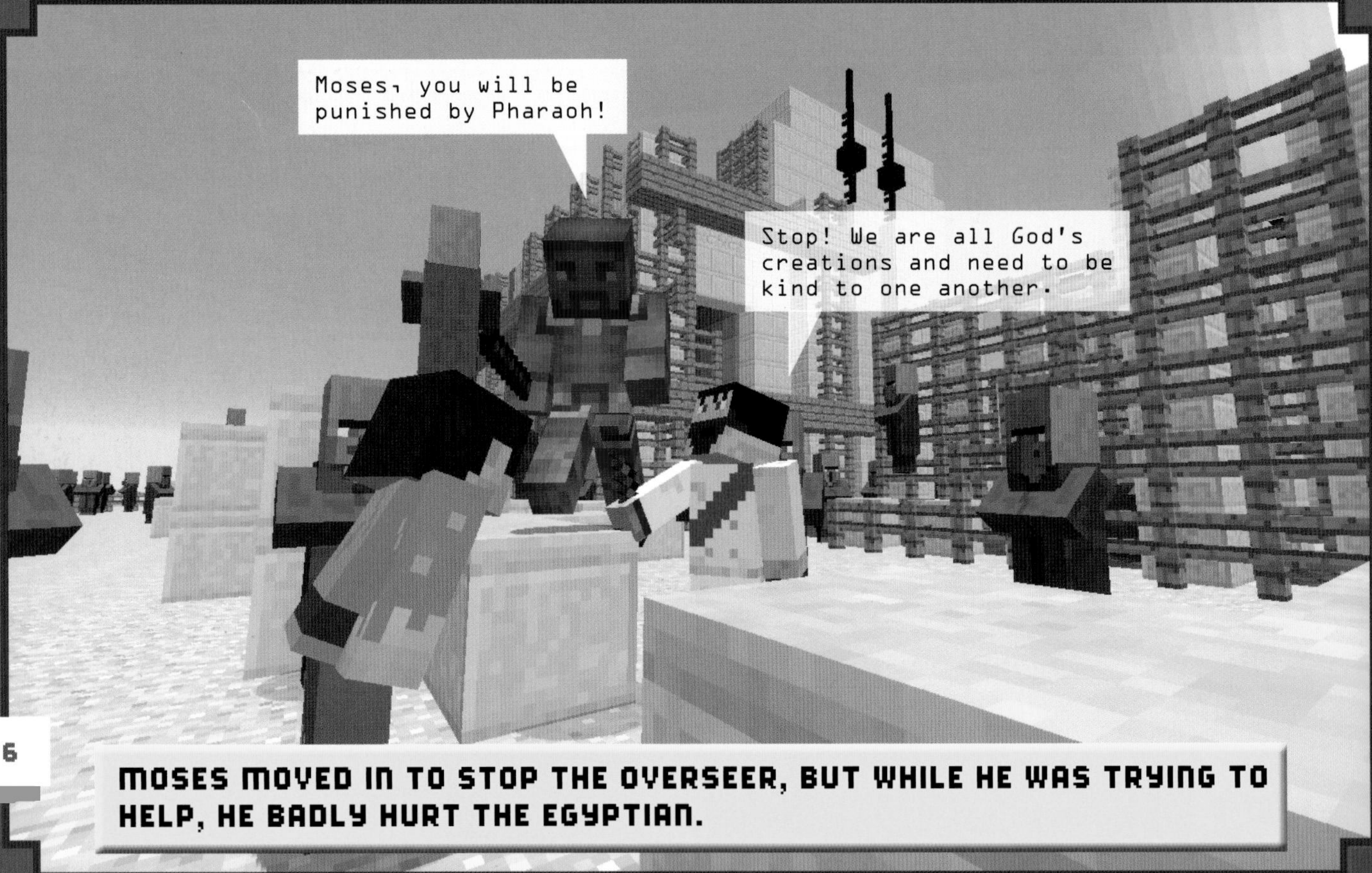
Moses, you will be punished by Pharaoh!
Stop! We are all God's creations and need to be kind to one another.
MOSES MOVED IN TO STOP THE OVERSEER, BUT WHILE HE WAS TRYING TO HELP, HE BADLY HURT THE EGYPTIAN.

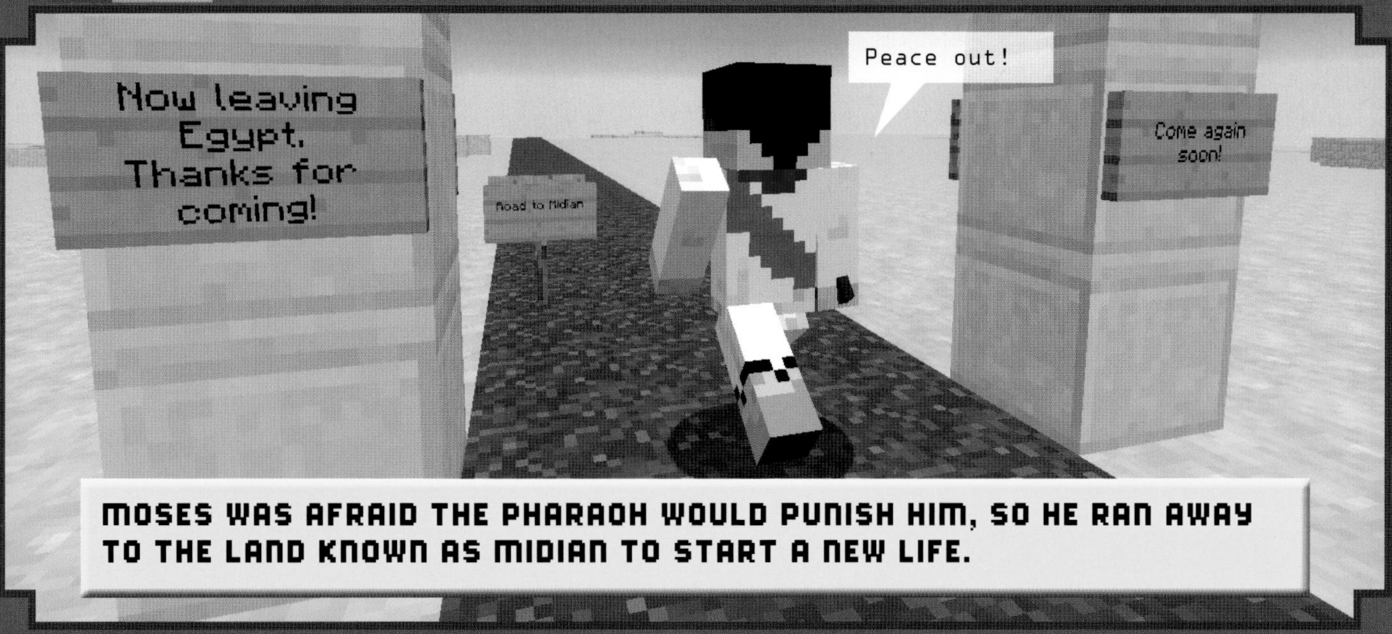
Now leaving Egypt. Thanks for coming!
Road to Midian
Peace out!
Come again soon!
MOSES WAS AFRAID THE PHARAOH WOULD PUNISH HIM, SO HE RAN AWAY TO THE LAND KNOWN AS MIDIAN TO START A NEW LIFE.

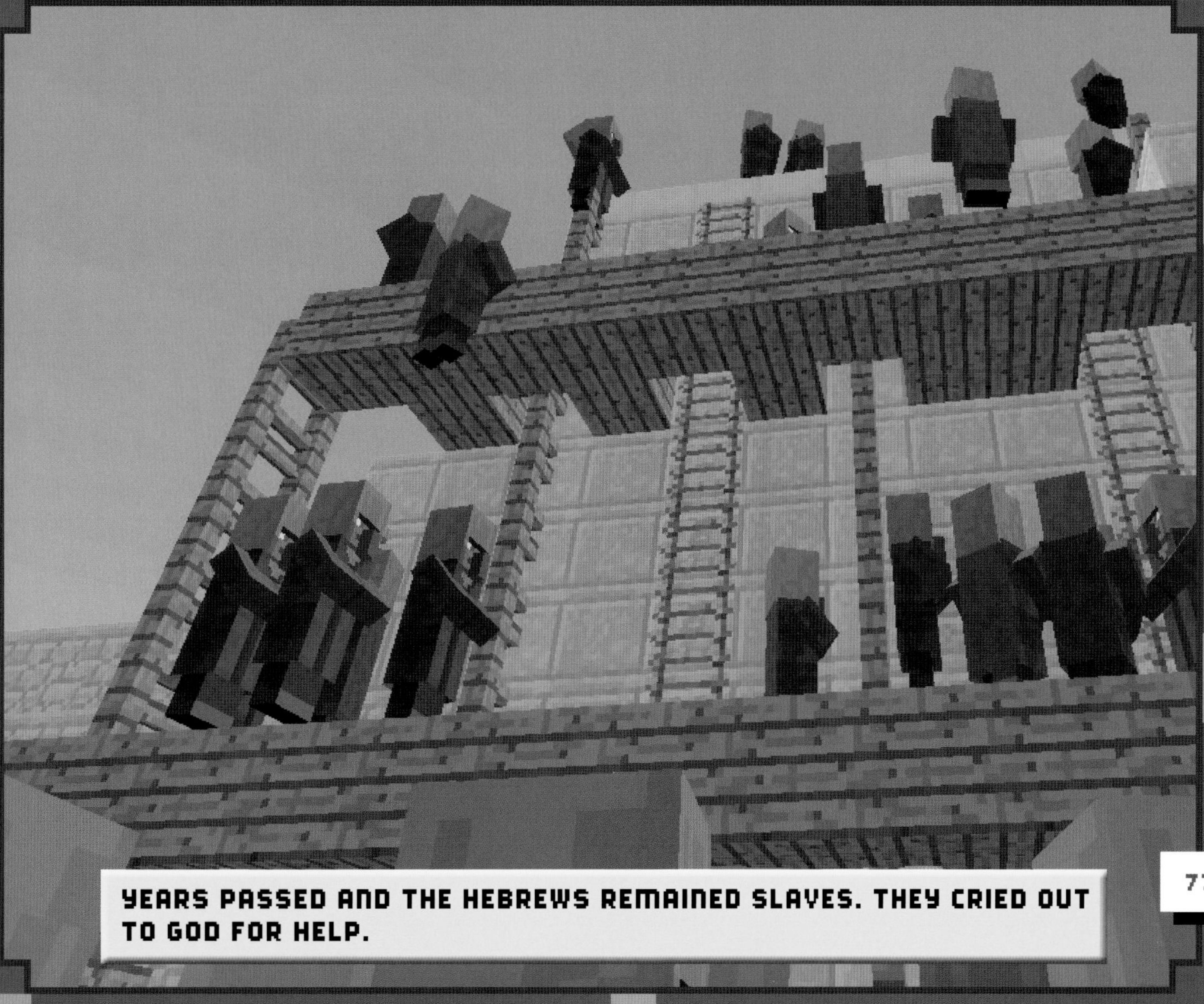
YEARS PASSED AND THE HEBREWS REMAINED SLAVES. THEY CRIED OUT TO GOD FOR HELP.

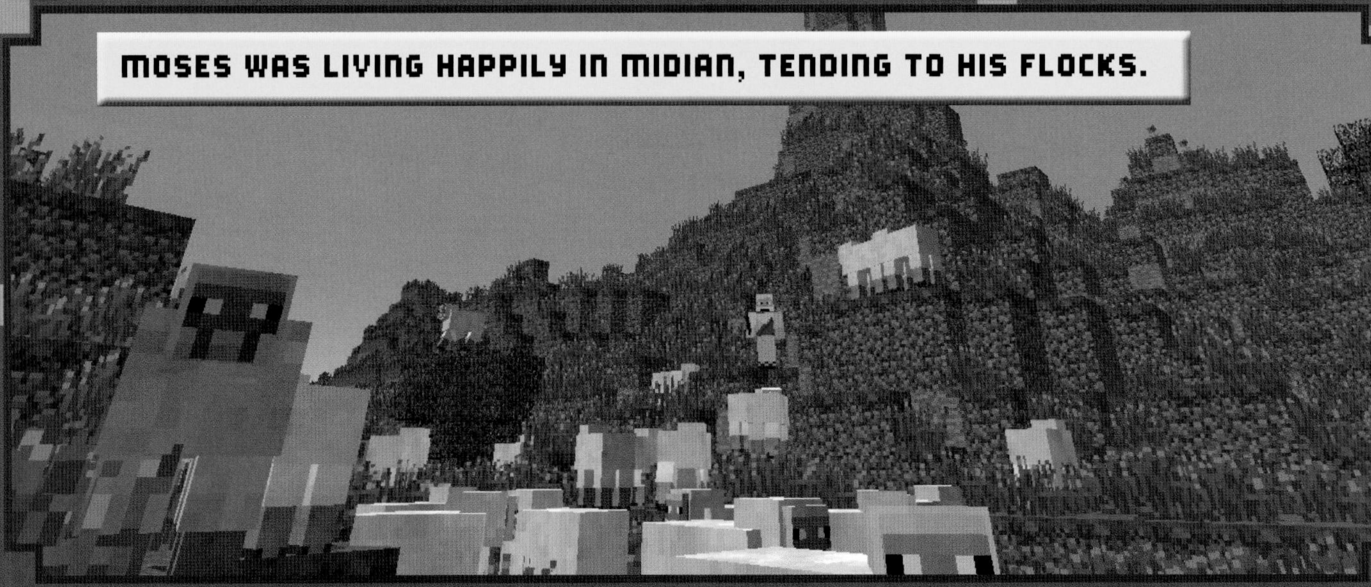
MOSES WAS LIVING HAPPILY IN MIDIAN, TENDING TO HIS FLOCKS.

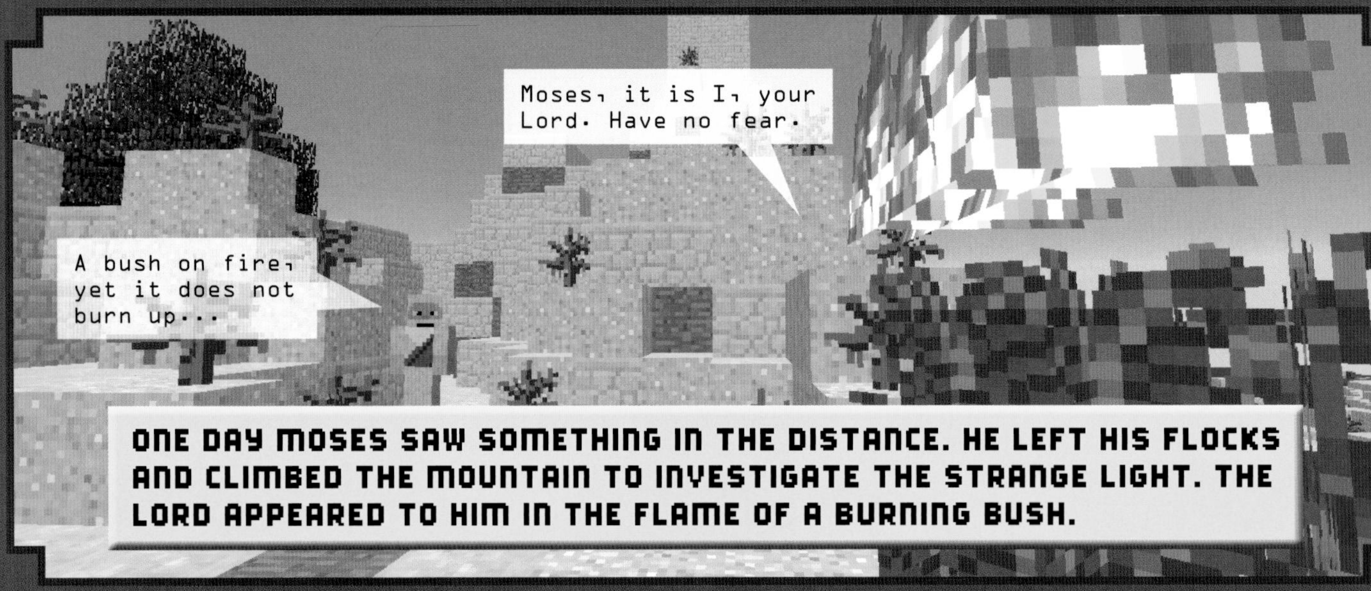
A bush on fire, yet it does not burn up...
Moses, it is I, your Lord. Have no fear.
ONE DAY MOSES SAW SOMETHING IN THE DISTANCE. HE LEFT HIS FLOCKS AND CLIMBED THE MOUNTAIN TO INVESTIGATE THE STRANGE LIGHT. THE LORD APPEARED TO HIM IN THE FLAME OF A BURNING BUSH.

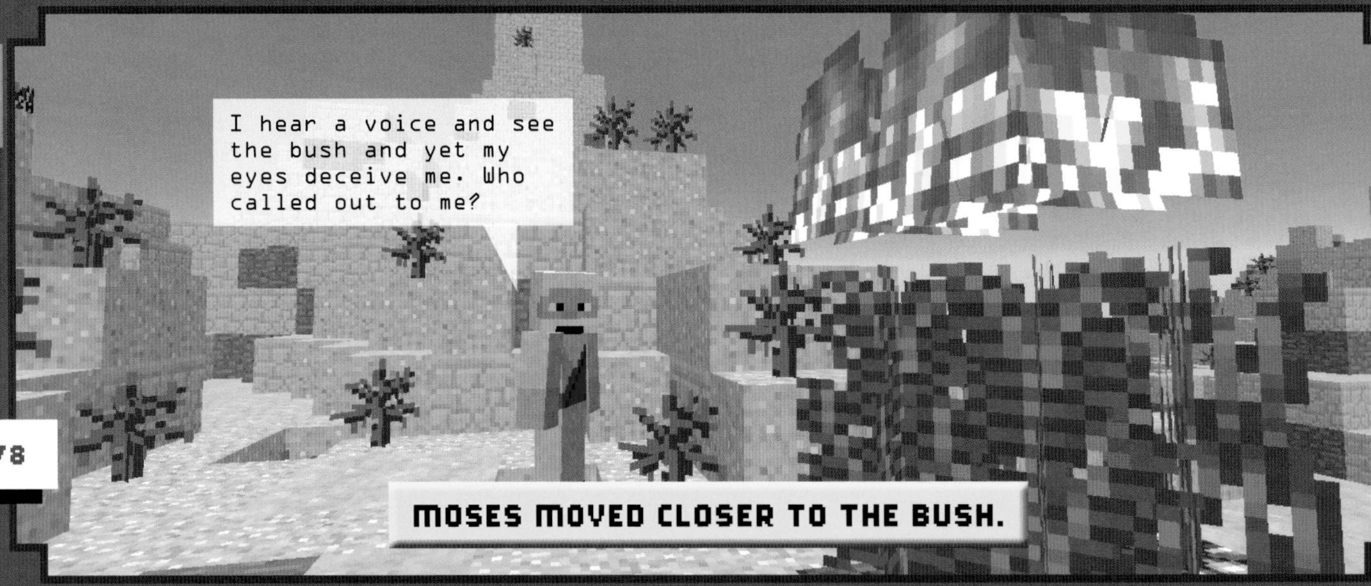
I hear a voice and see the bush and yet my eyes deceive me. Who called out to me?
MOSES MOVED CLOSER TO THE BUSH.

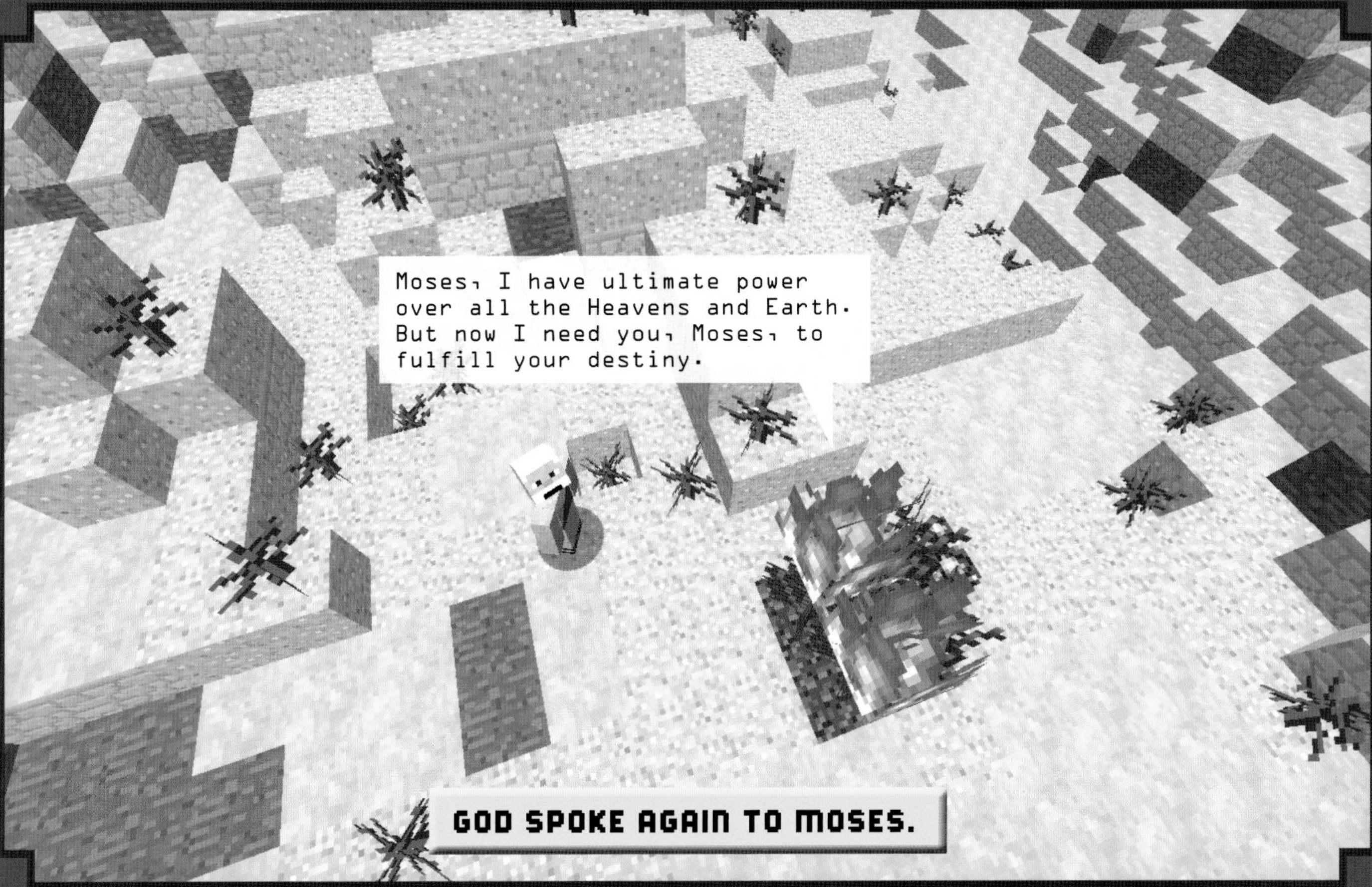
Moses, I have ultimate power over all the Heavens and Earth. But now I need you, Moses, to fulfill your destiny.
GOD SPOKE AGAIN TO MOSES.

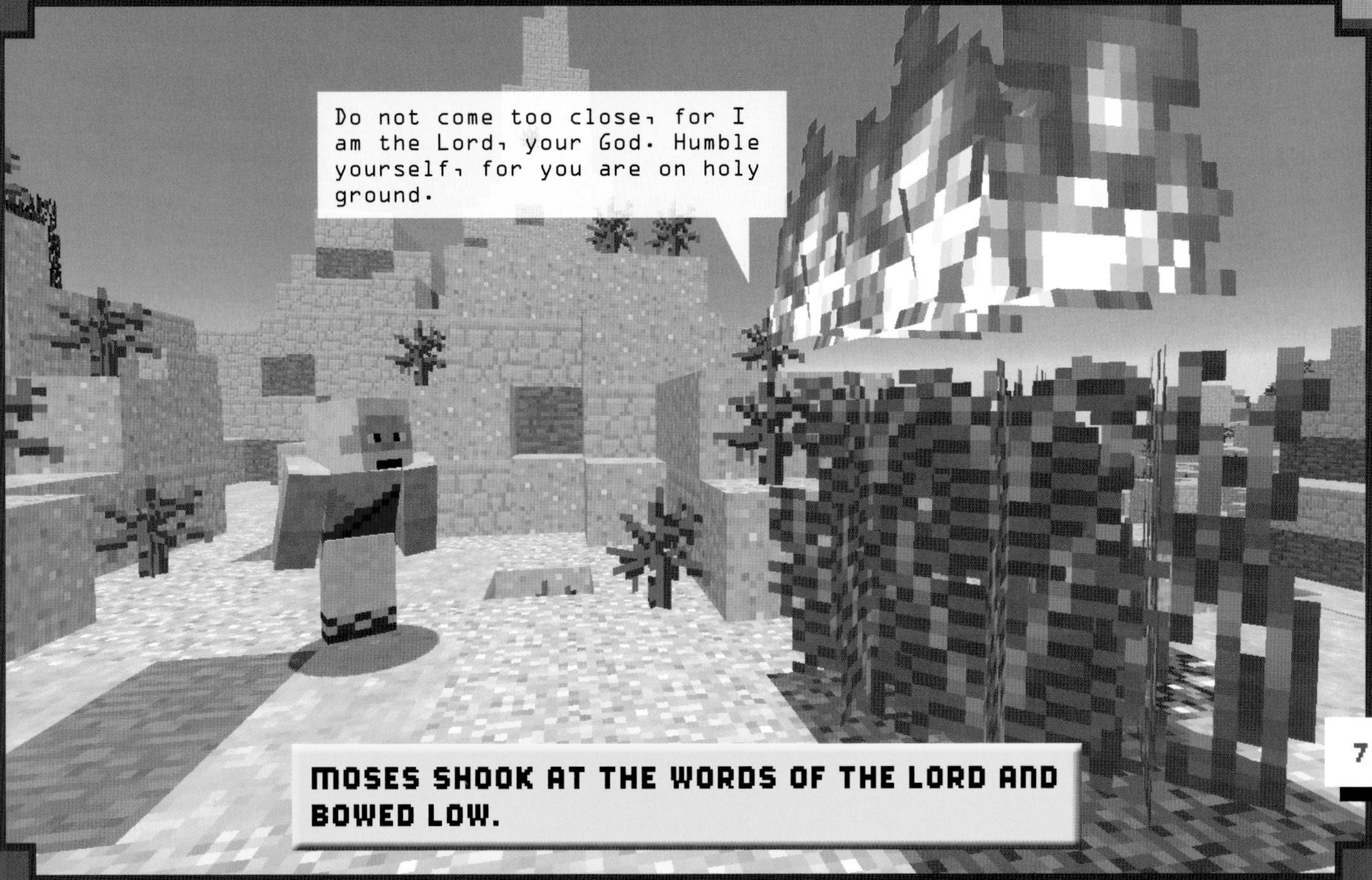
Do not come too close, for I am the Lord, your God. Humble yourself, for you are on holy ground.
MOSES SHOOK AT THE WORDS OF THE LORD AND BOWED LOW.

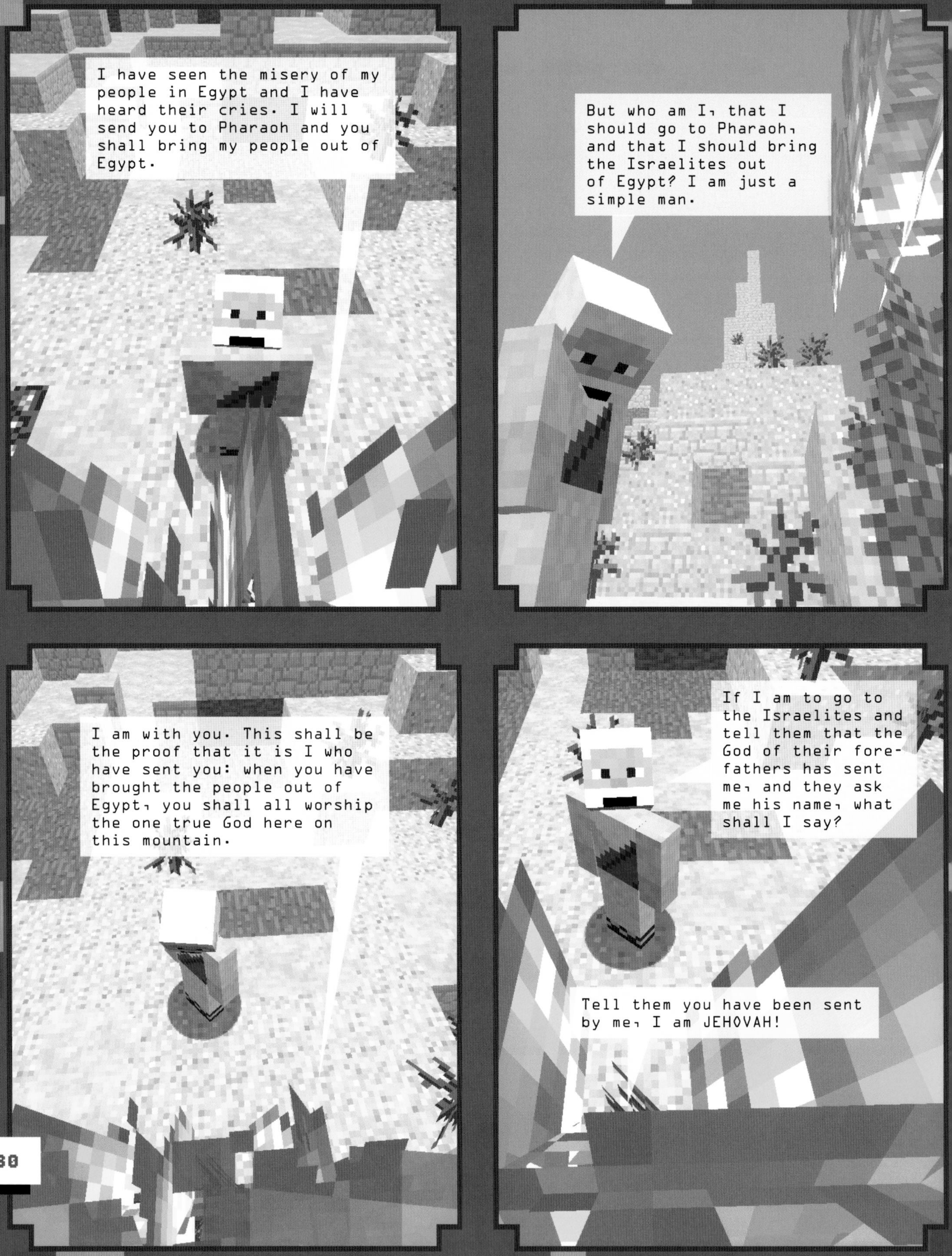
I have seen the misery of my people in Egypt and I have heard their cries. I will send you to Pharaoh and you shall bring my people out of Egypt.
But who am I, that I should go to Pharaoh, and that I should bring the Israelites out of Egypt? I am just a simple man.
I am with you. This shall be the proof that it is I who have sent you: when you have brought the people out of Egypt, you shall all worship the one true God here on this mountain.
If I am to go to the Israelites and tell them that the God of their forefathers has sent me, and they ask me his name, what shall I say?
Tell them you have been sent by me, I am JEHOVAH!

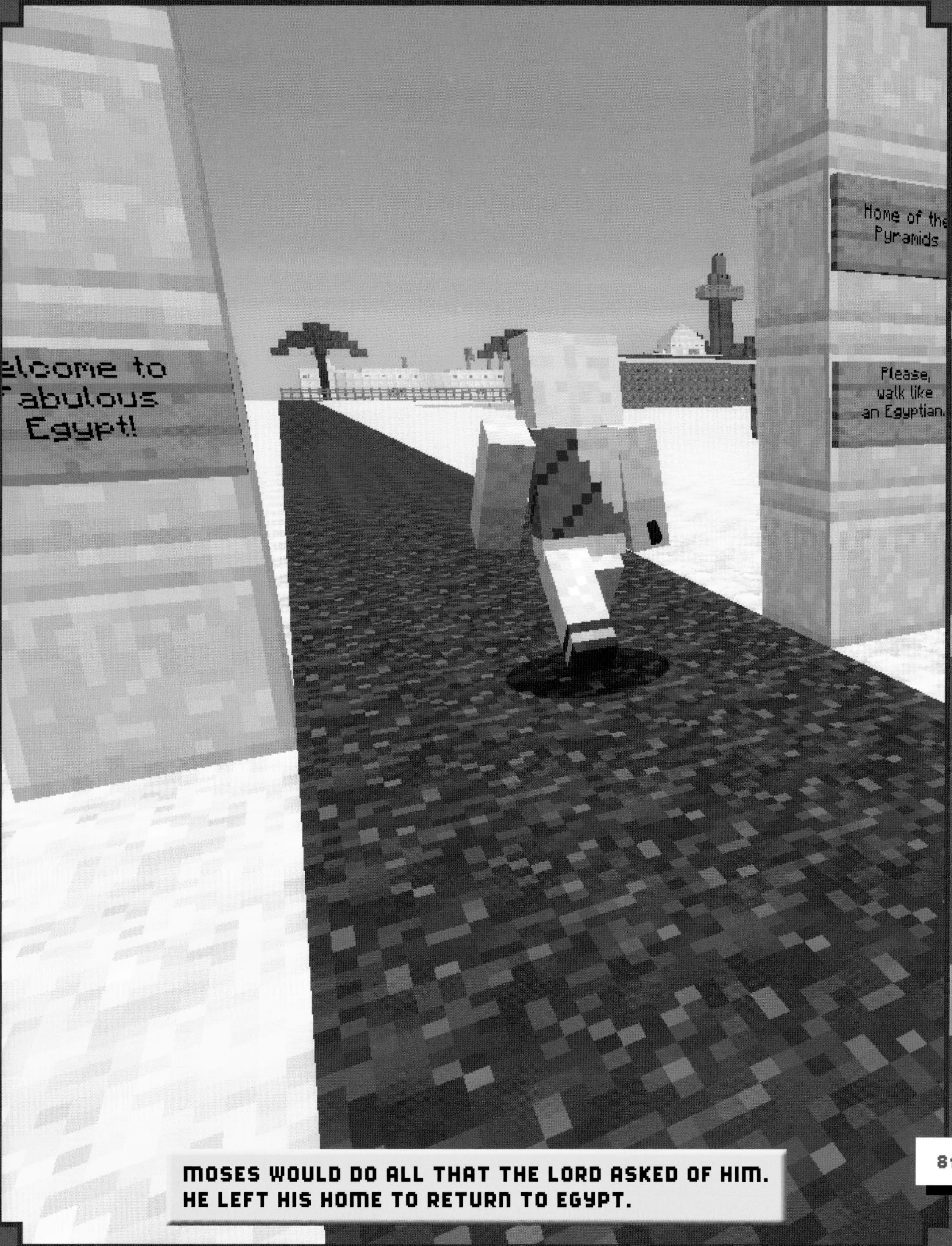
elcome to
'abulous
Egypt!
Home of the
Pyramids
Please,
walk like
an Egyptian.

MOSES WOULD DO ALL THAT THE LORD ASKED OF HIM.
HE LEFT HIS HOME TO RETURN TO EGYPT.

THE STORY OF THE PLAGUES

Somehow, I have a feeling this isn't going to bode well for the Egyptians.

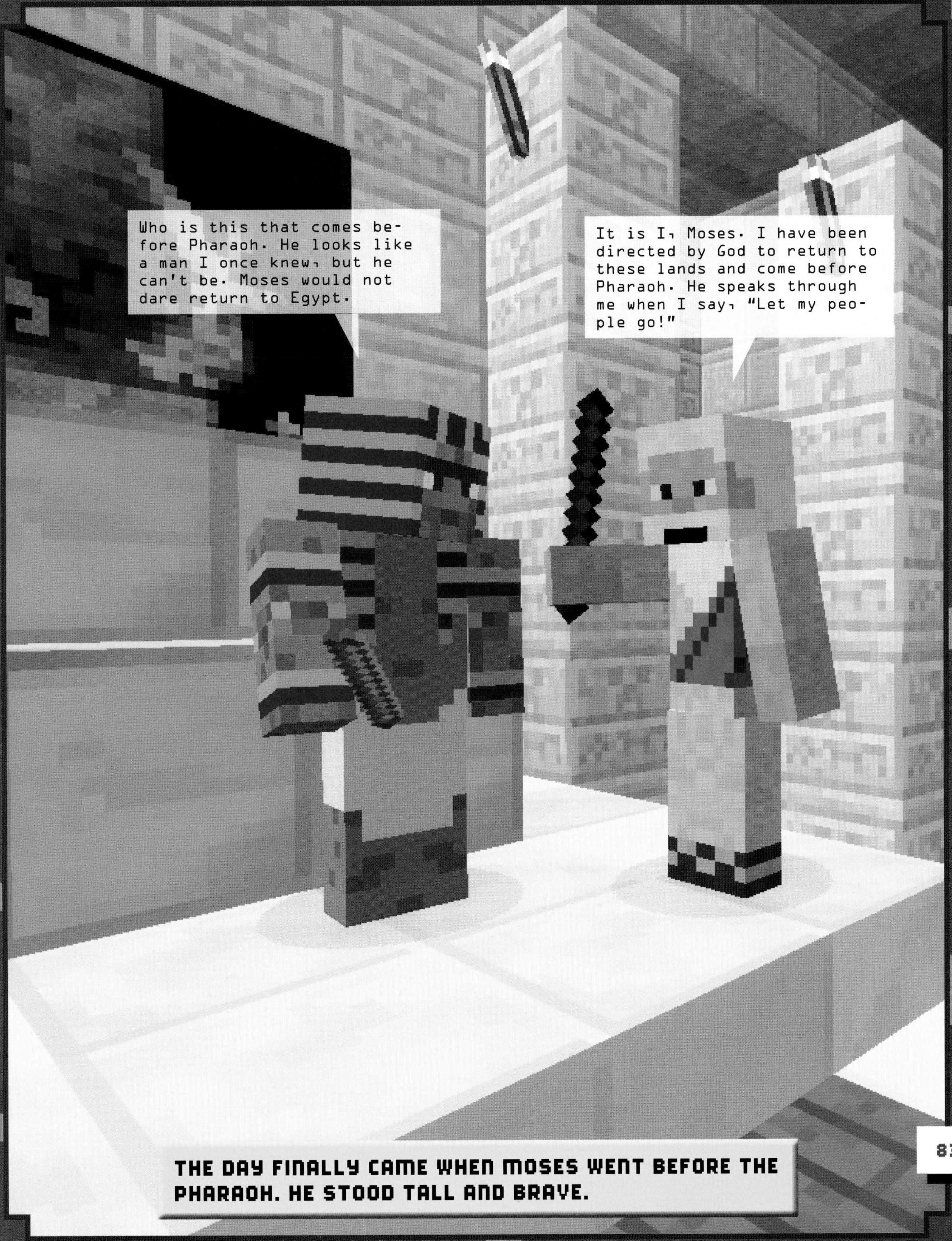
Who is this that comes before Pharaoh. He looks like a man I once knew, but he can't be. Moses would not dare return to Egypt.
It is I, Moses. I have been directed by God to return to these lands and come before Pharaoh. He speaks through me when I say, "Let my people go!"
THE DAY FINALLY CAME WHEN MOSES WENT BEFORE THE PHARAOH. HE STOOD TALL AND BRAVE.

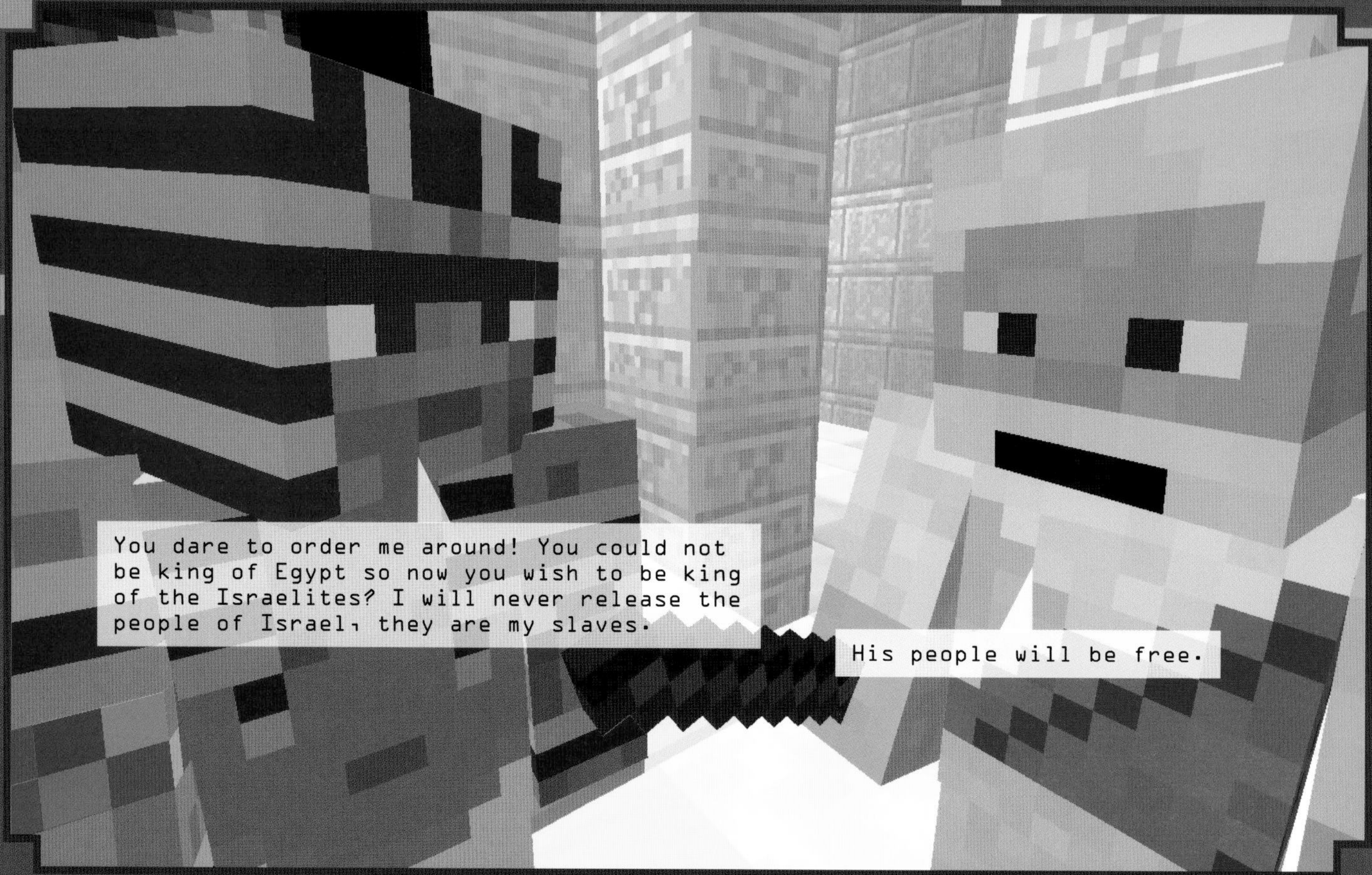

You dare to order me around! You could not be king of Egypt so now you wish to be king of the Israelites? I will never release the people of Israel, they are my slaves.
His people will be free.

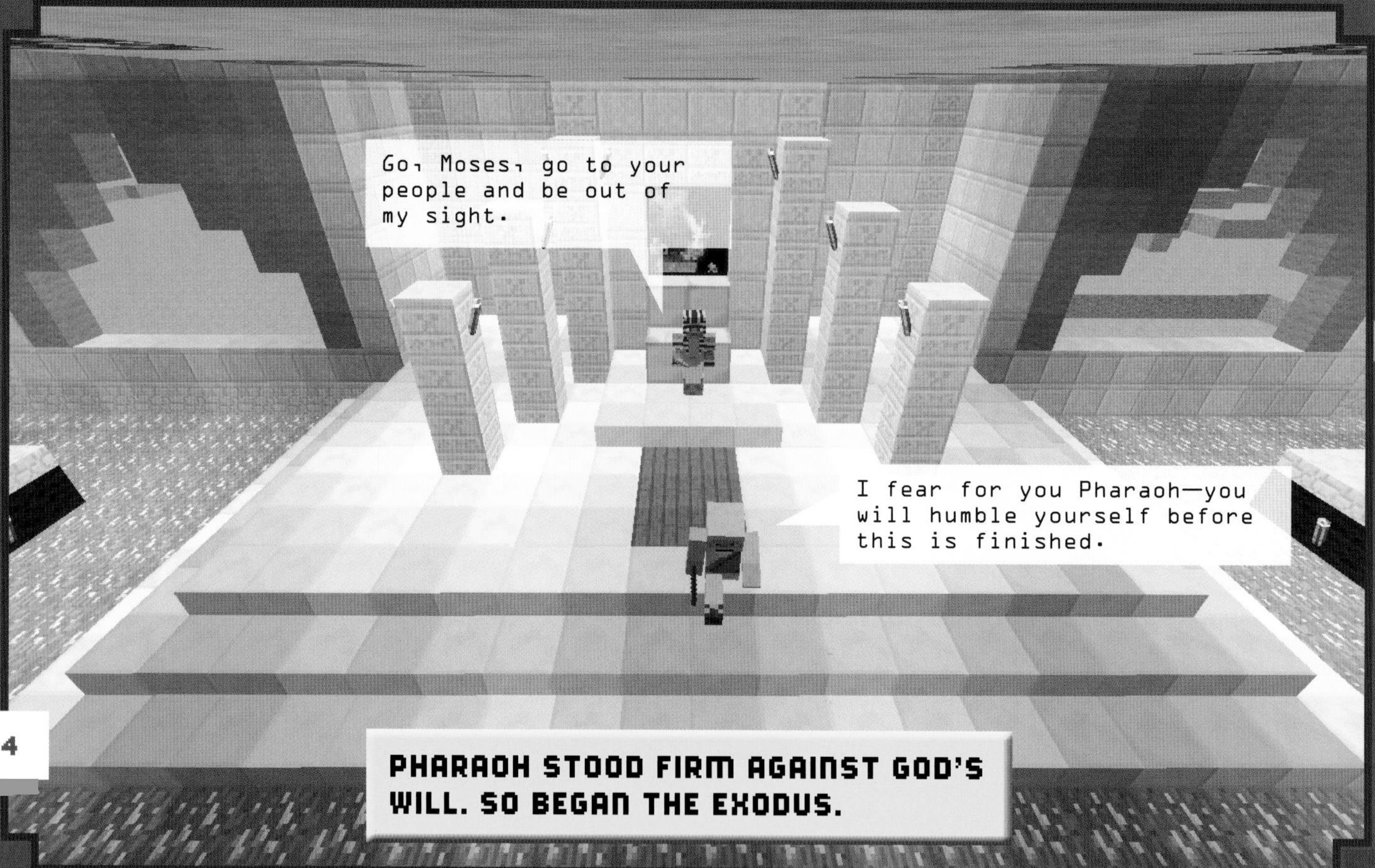

Go, Moses, go to your people and be out of my sight.
I fear for you Pharaoh—you will humble yourself before this is finished.
PHARAOH STOOD FIRM AGAINST GOD'S WILL. SO BEGAN THE EXODUS.

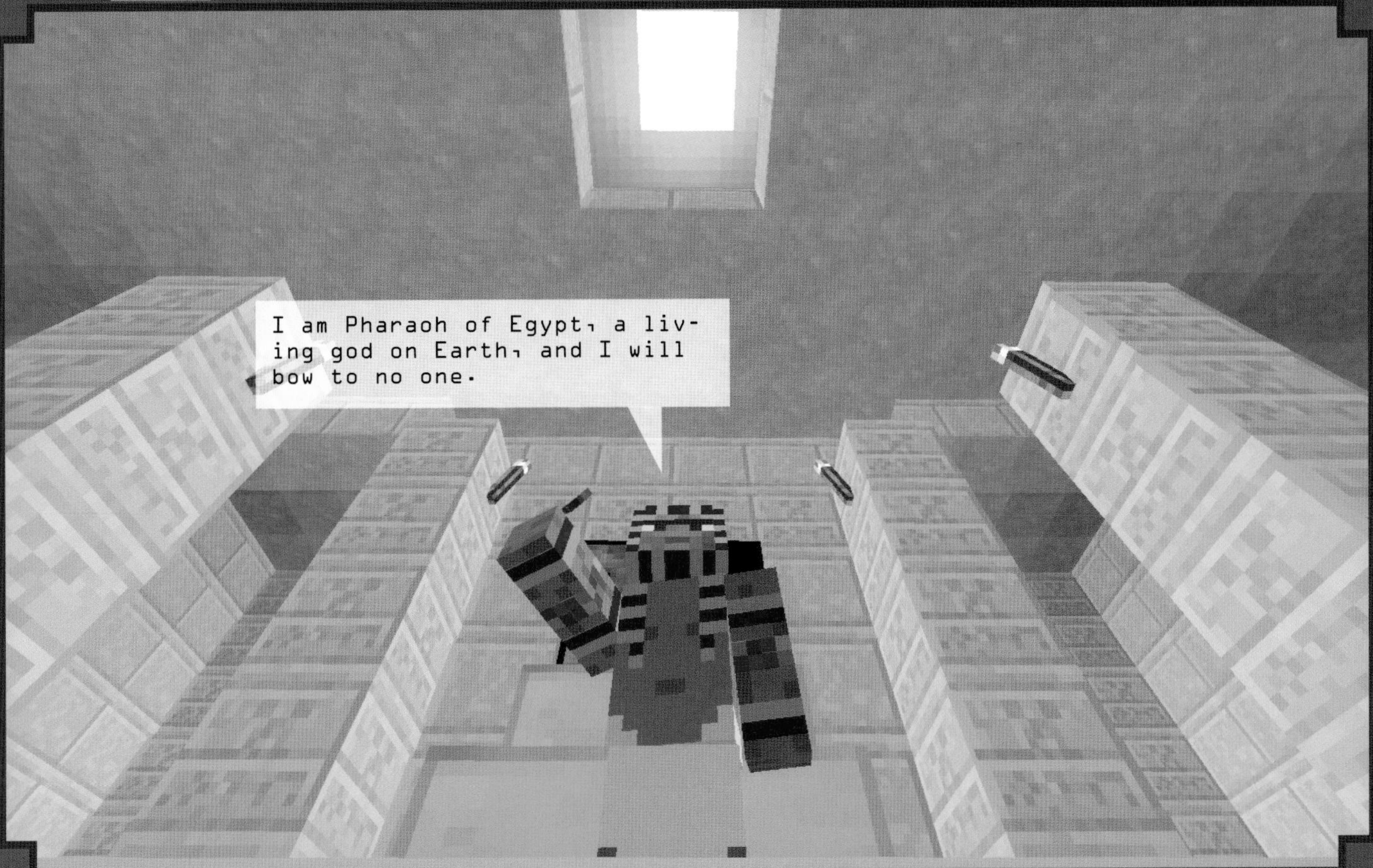
I am Pharaoh of Egypt, a living god on Earth, and I will bow to no one.

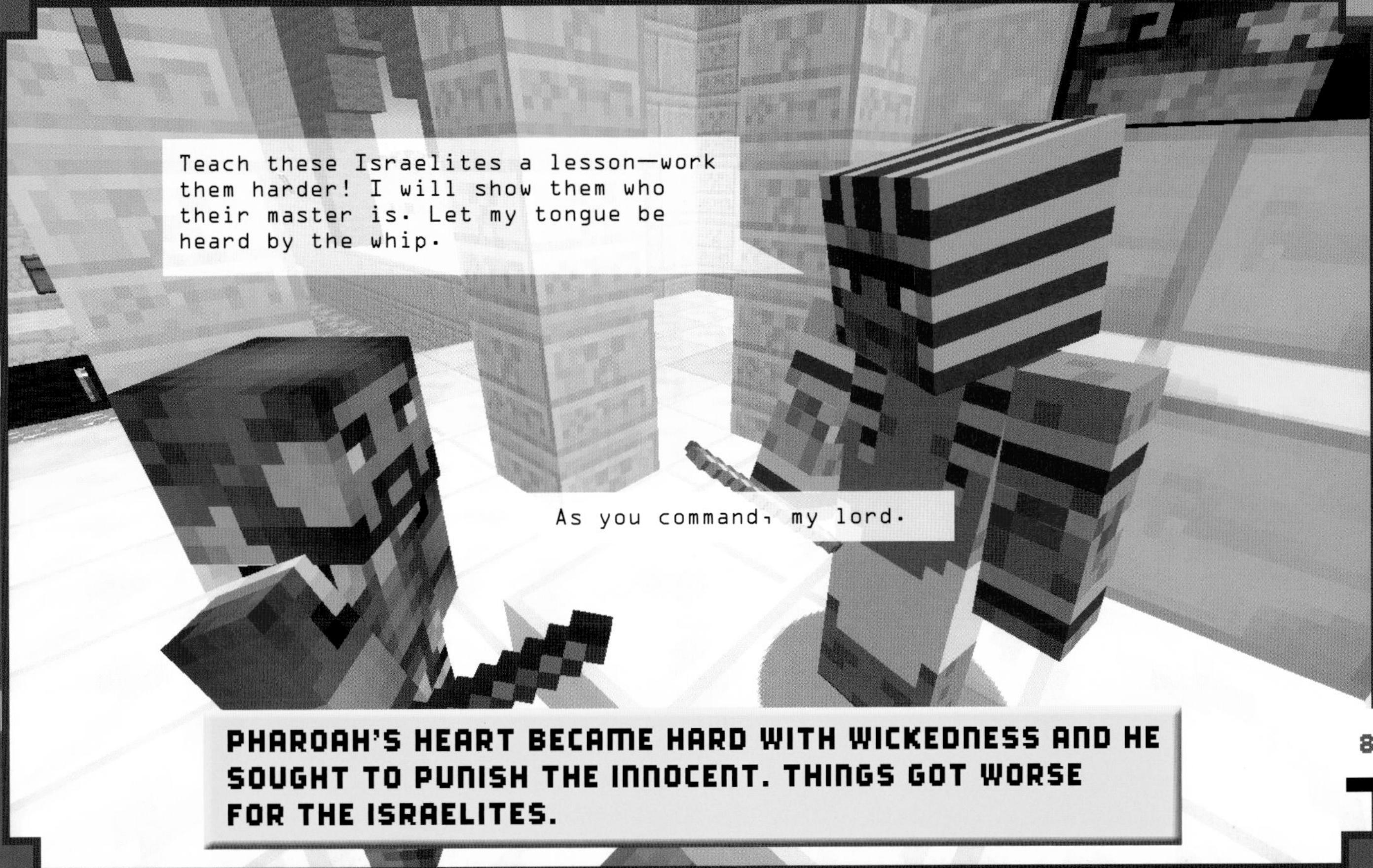
Teach these Israelites a lesson—work them harder! I will show them who their master is. Let my tongue be heard by the whip.
As you command, my lord.
PHAROAH'S HEART BECAME HARD WITH WICKEDNESS AND HE SOUGHT TO PUNISH THE INNOCENT. THINGS GOT WORSE FOR THE ISRAELITES.

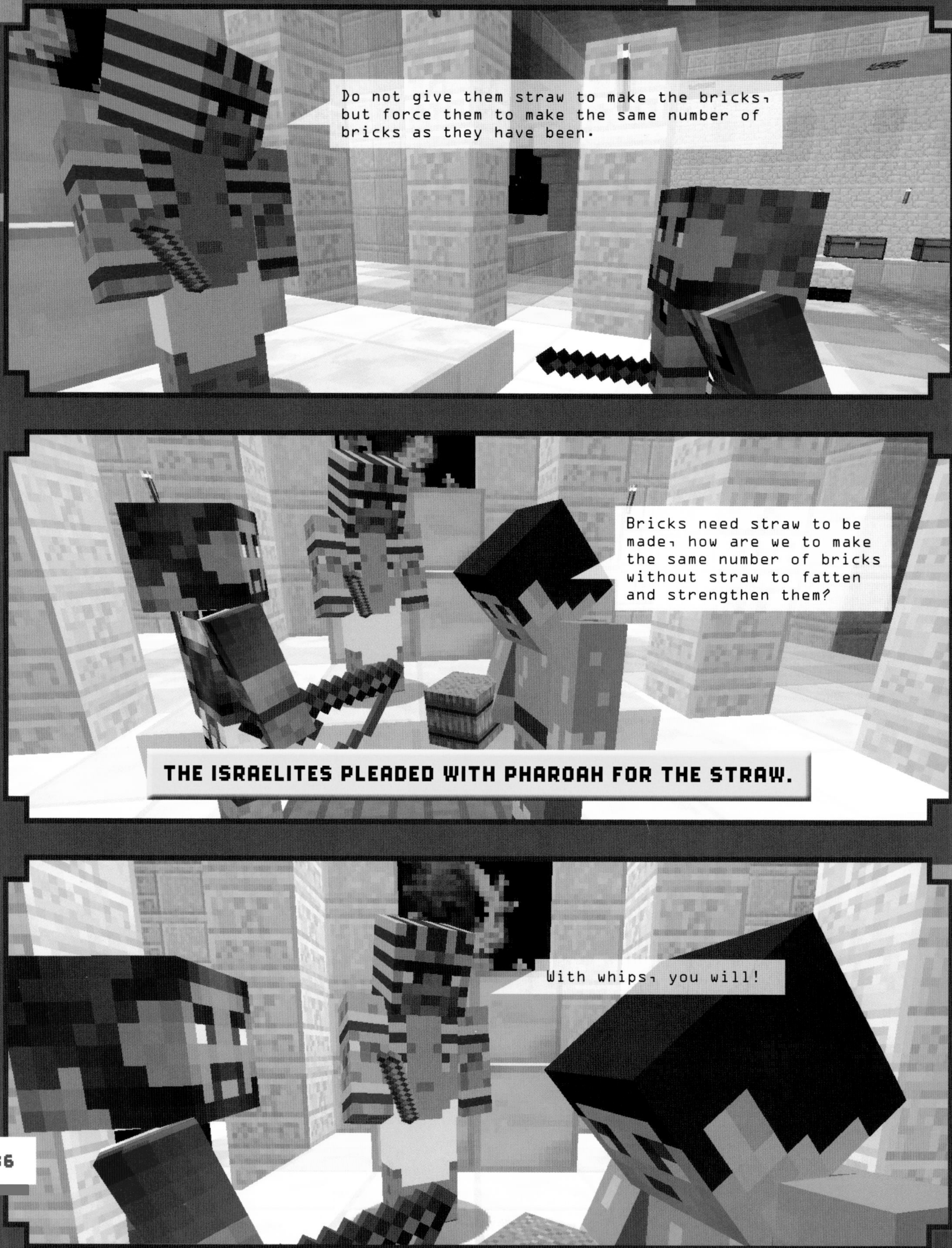
Do not give them straw to make the bricks, but force them to make the same number of bricks as they have been.
Bricks need straw to be made, how are we to make the same number of bricks without straw to fatten and strengthen them?
THE ISRAELITES PLEADED WITH PHAROAH FOR THE STRAW.
With whips, you will!

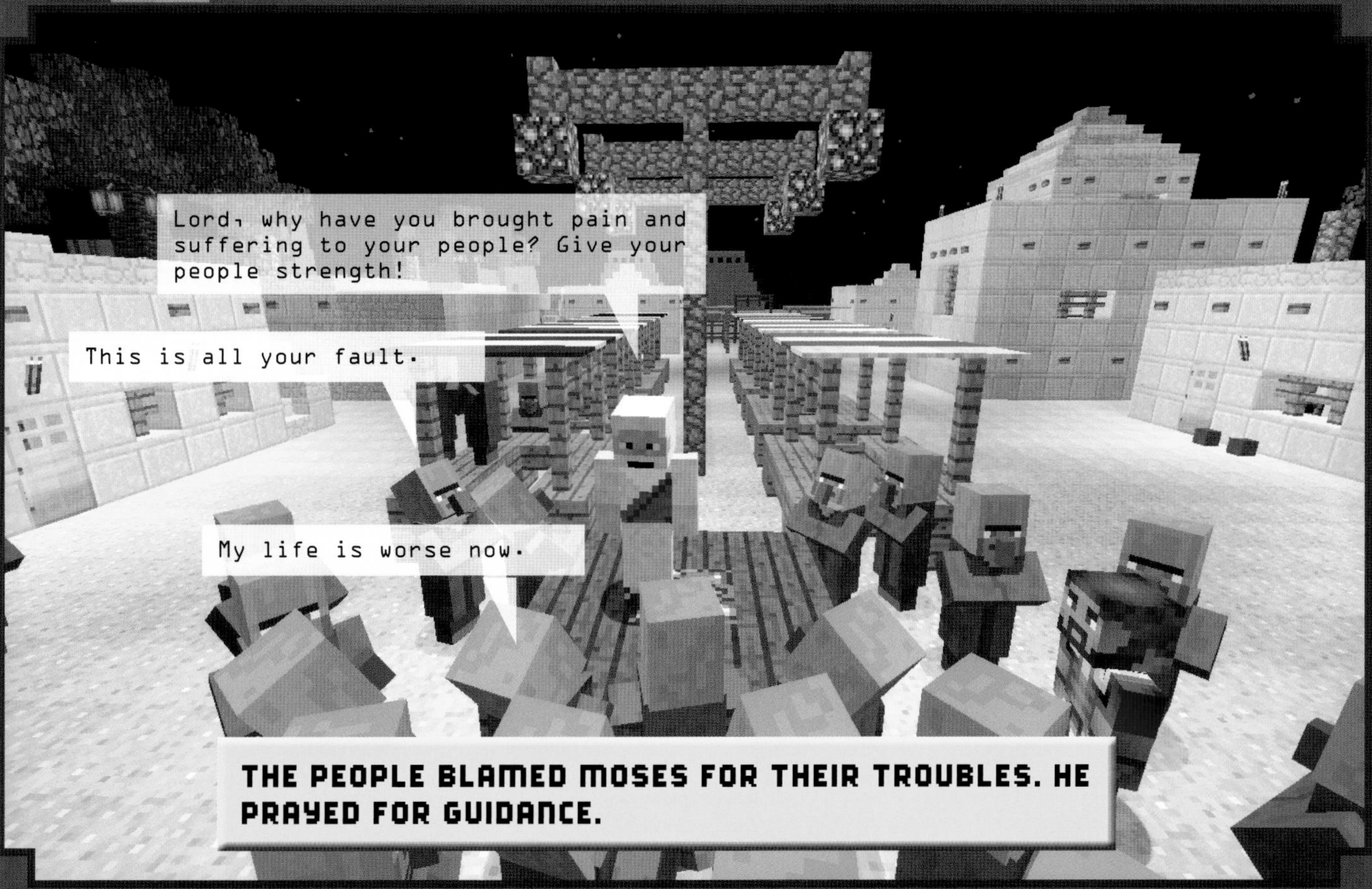
Lord, why have you brought pain and suffering to your people? Give your people strength!
This is all your fault.
My life is worse now.
THE PEOPLE BLAMED MOSES FOR THEIR TROUBLES. HE PRAYED FOR GUIDANCE.

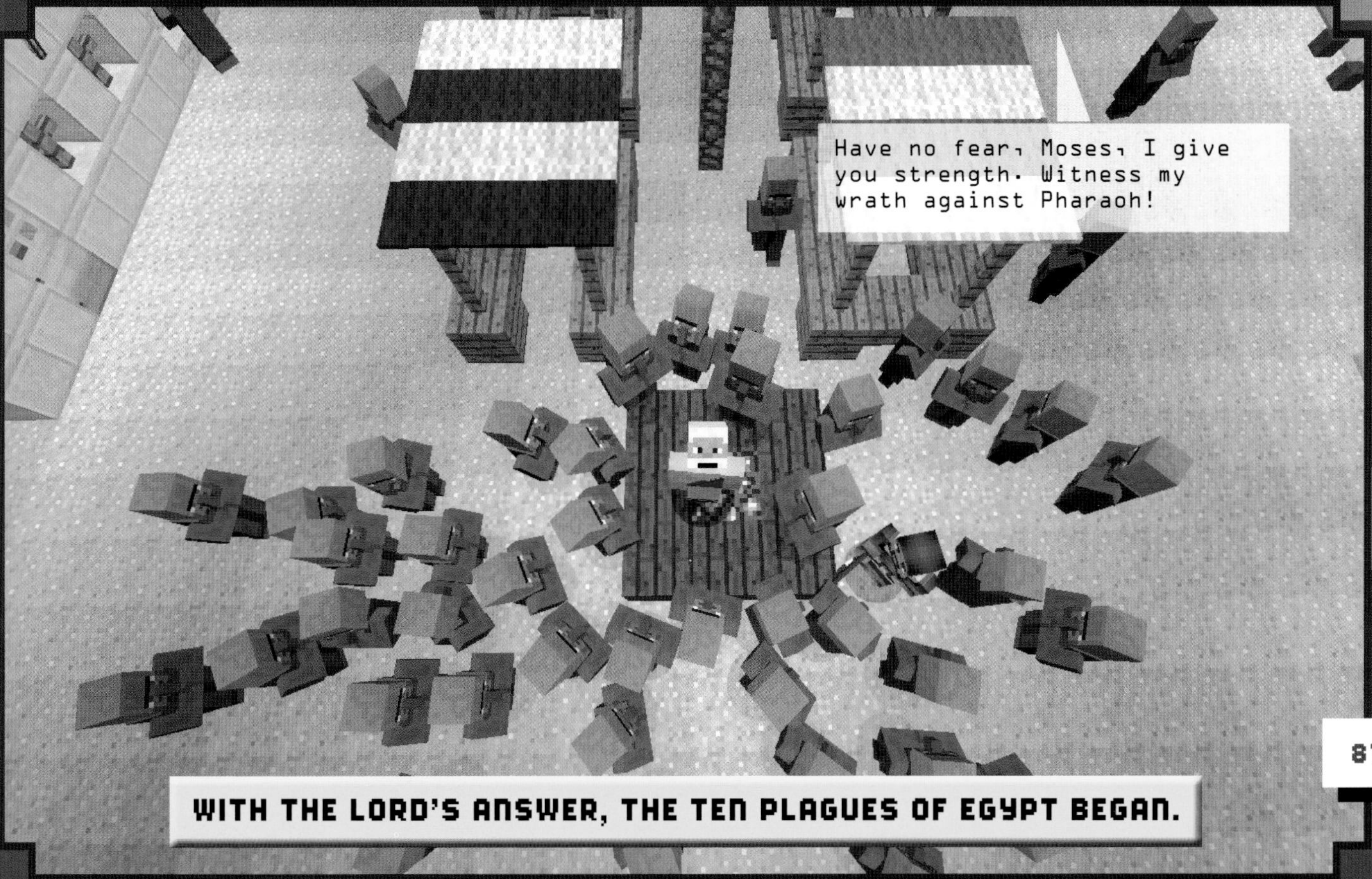
Have no fear, Moses, I give you strength. Witness my wrath against Pharaoh!
WITH THE LORD'S ANSWER, THE TEN PLAGUES OF EGYPT BEGAN.

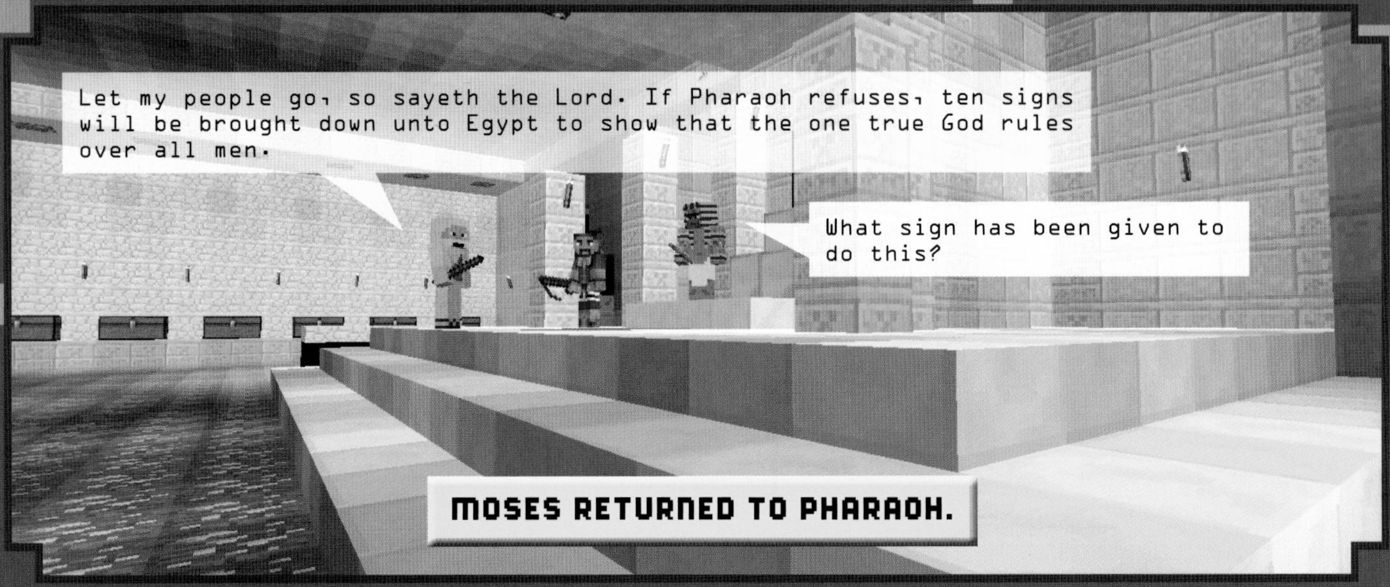
Let my people go, so sayeth the Lord. If Pharaoh refuses, ten signs will be brought down unto Egypt to show that the one true God rules over all men.
What sign has been given to do this?
MOSES RETURNED TO PHARAOH.

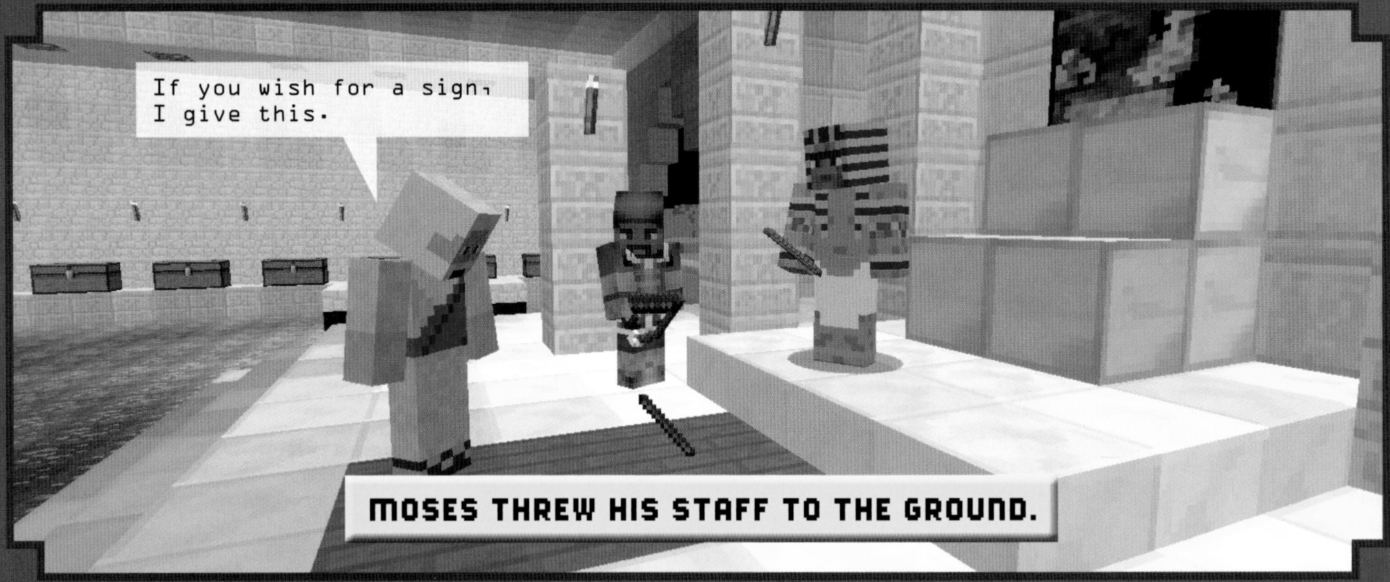
If you wish for a sign, I give this.
MOSES THREW HIS STAFF TO THE GROUND.

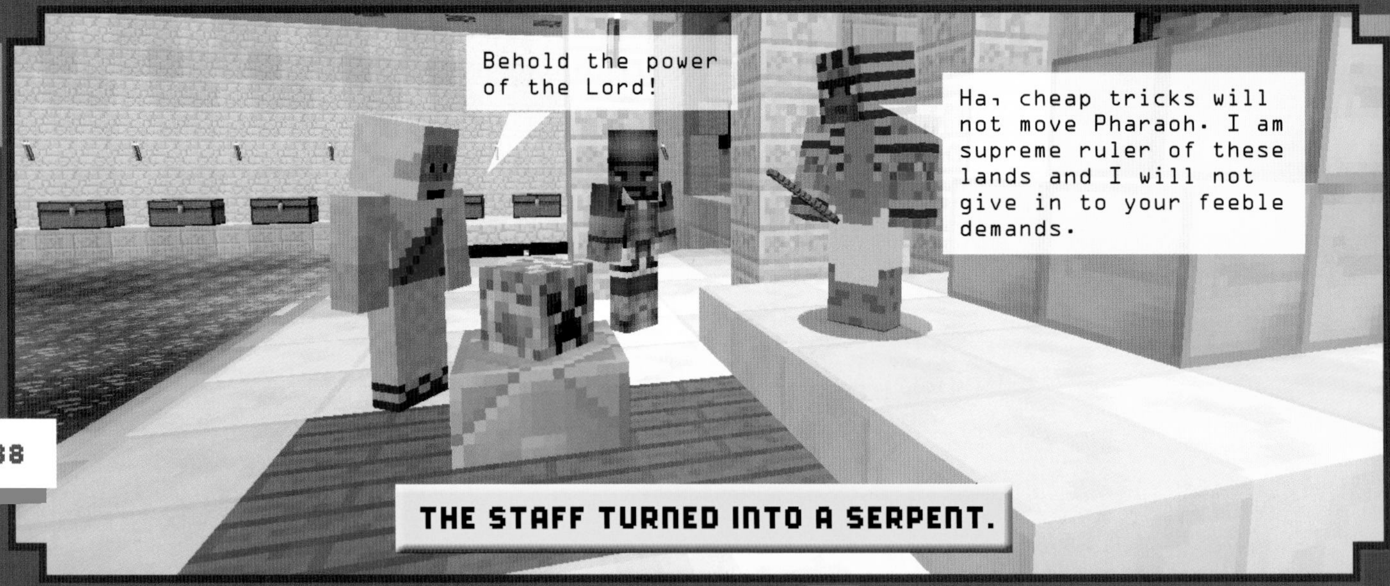
Behold the power of the Lord!
Ha, cheap tricks will not move Pharaoh. I am supreme ruler of these lands and I will not give in to your feeble demands.
THE STAFF TURNED INTO A SERPENT.

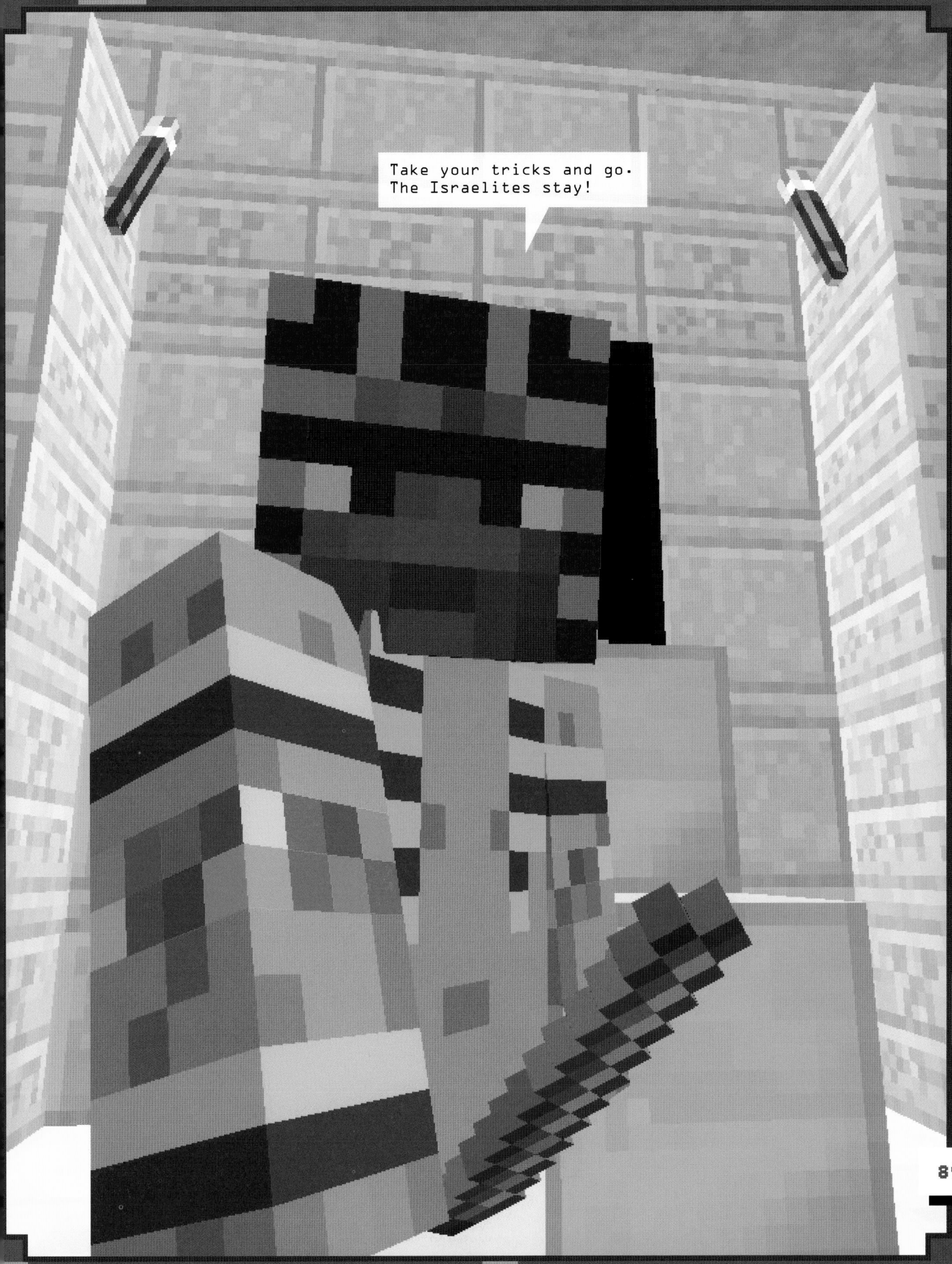
Take your tricks and go.
The Israelites stay!

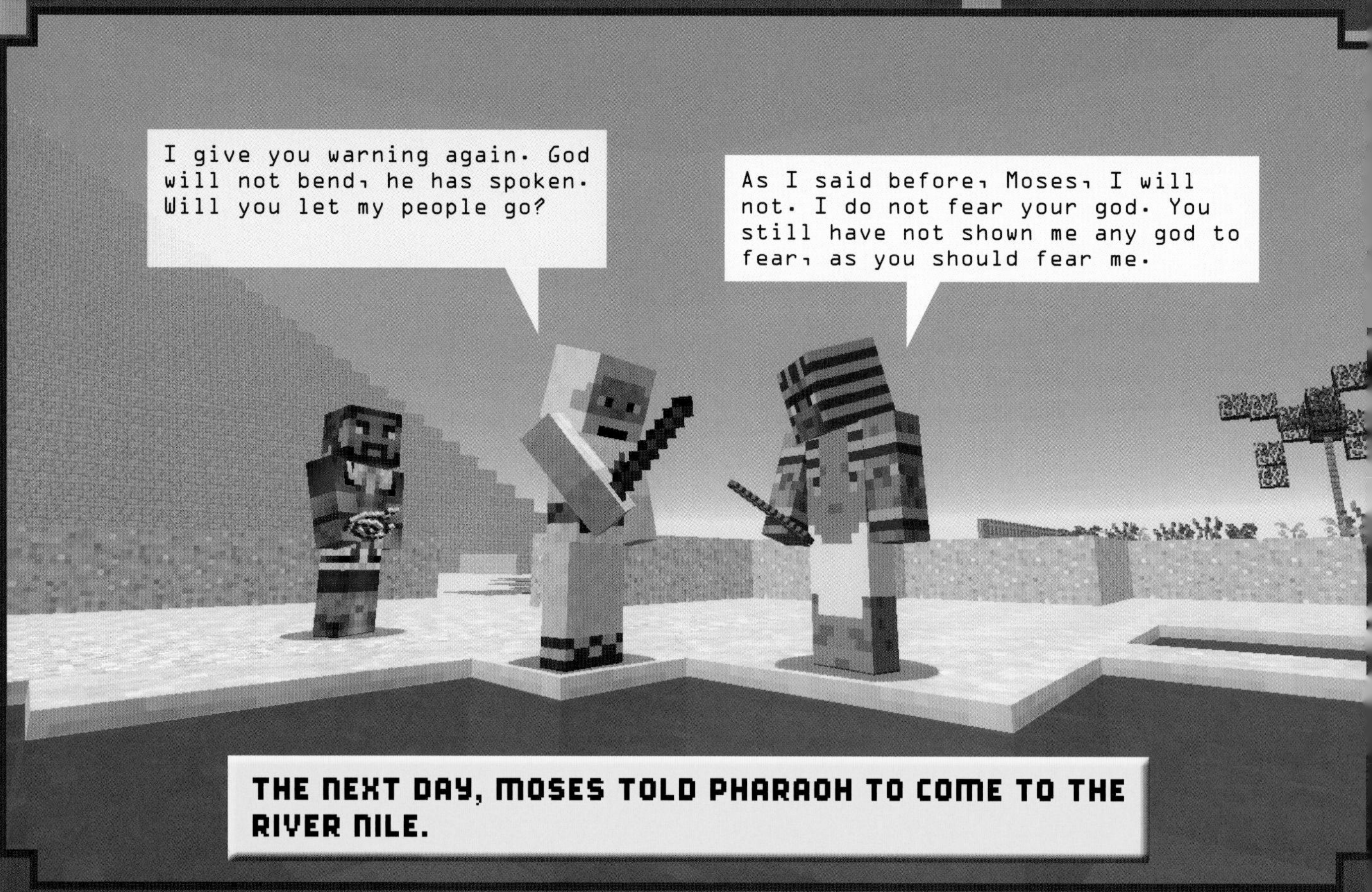
I give you warning again. God will not bend, he has spoken. Will you let my people go?
As I said before, Moses, I will not. I do not fear your god. You still have not shown me any god to fear, as you should fear me.
THE NEXT DAY, MOSES TOLD PHARAOH TO COME TO THE RIVER NILE.

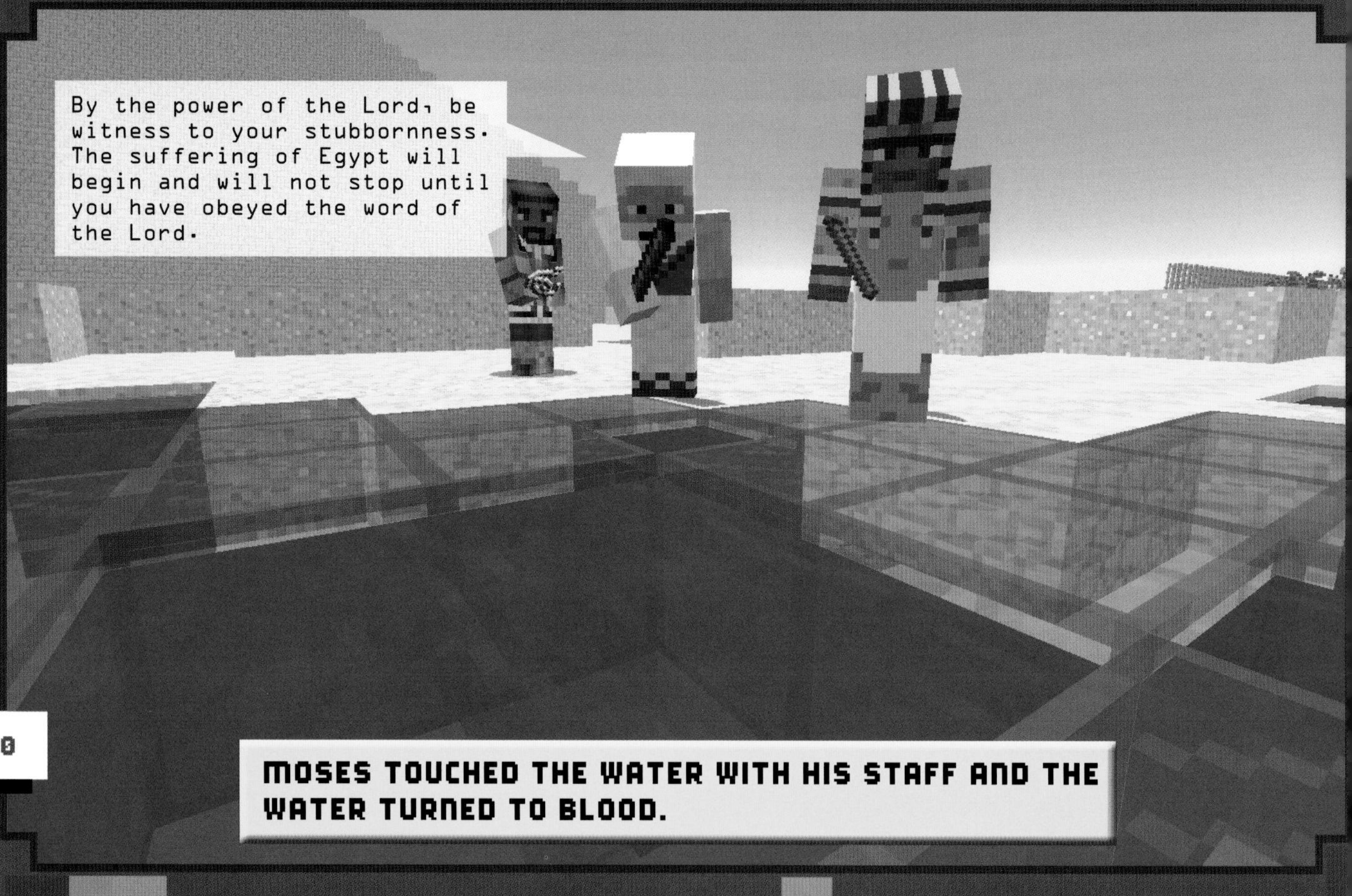
By the power of the Lord, be witness to your stubbornness. The suffering of Egypt will begin and will not stop until you have obeyed the word of the Lord.
MOSES TOUCHED THE WATER WITH HIS STAFF AND THE WATER TURNED TO BLOOD.

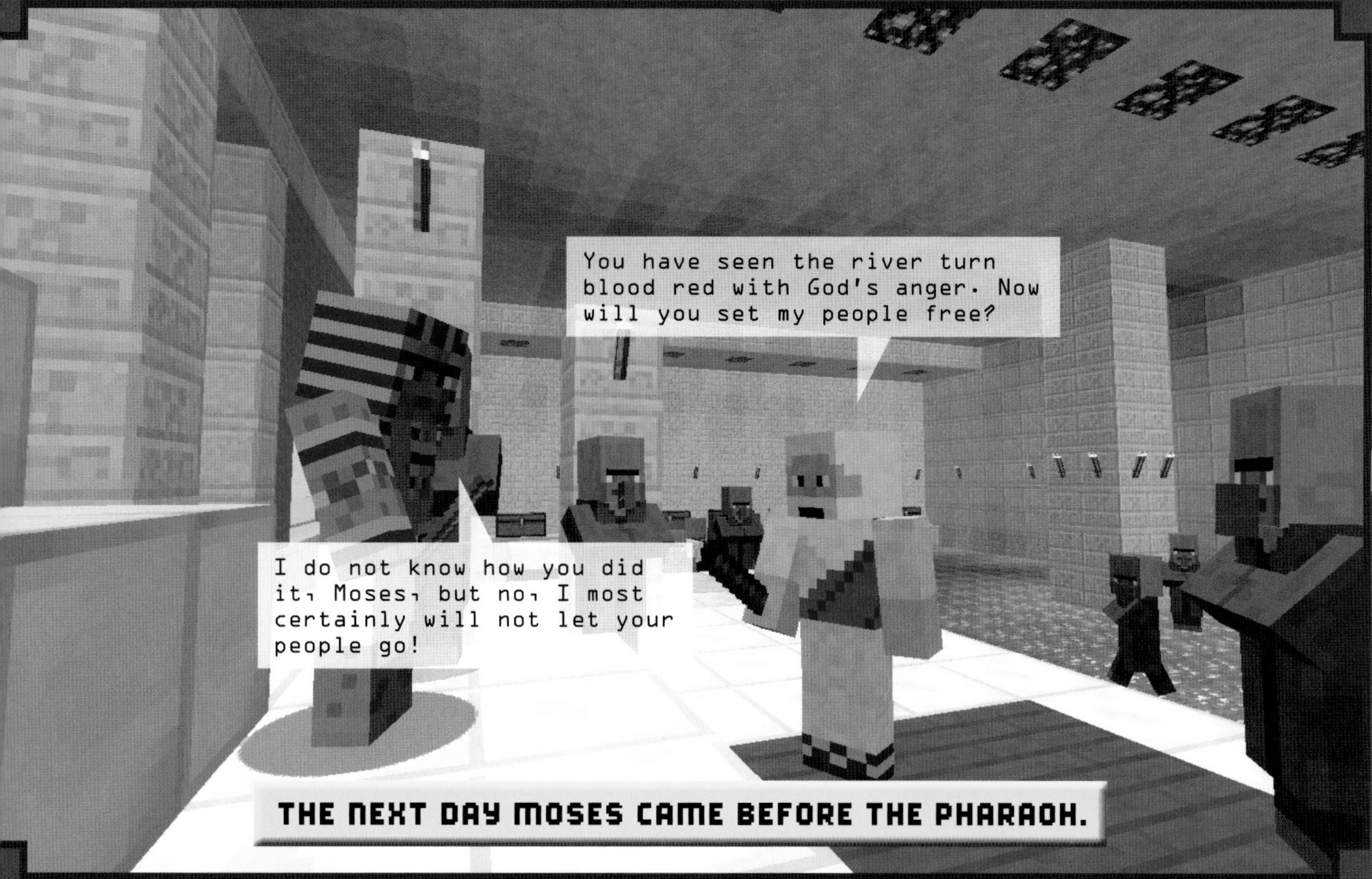
THE NEXT DAY MOSES CAME BEFORE THE PHARAOH.
You have seen the river turn blood red with God's anger. Now will you set my people free?
I do not know how you did it, Moses, but no, I most certainly will not let your people go!

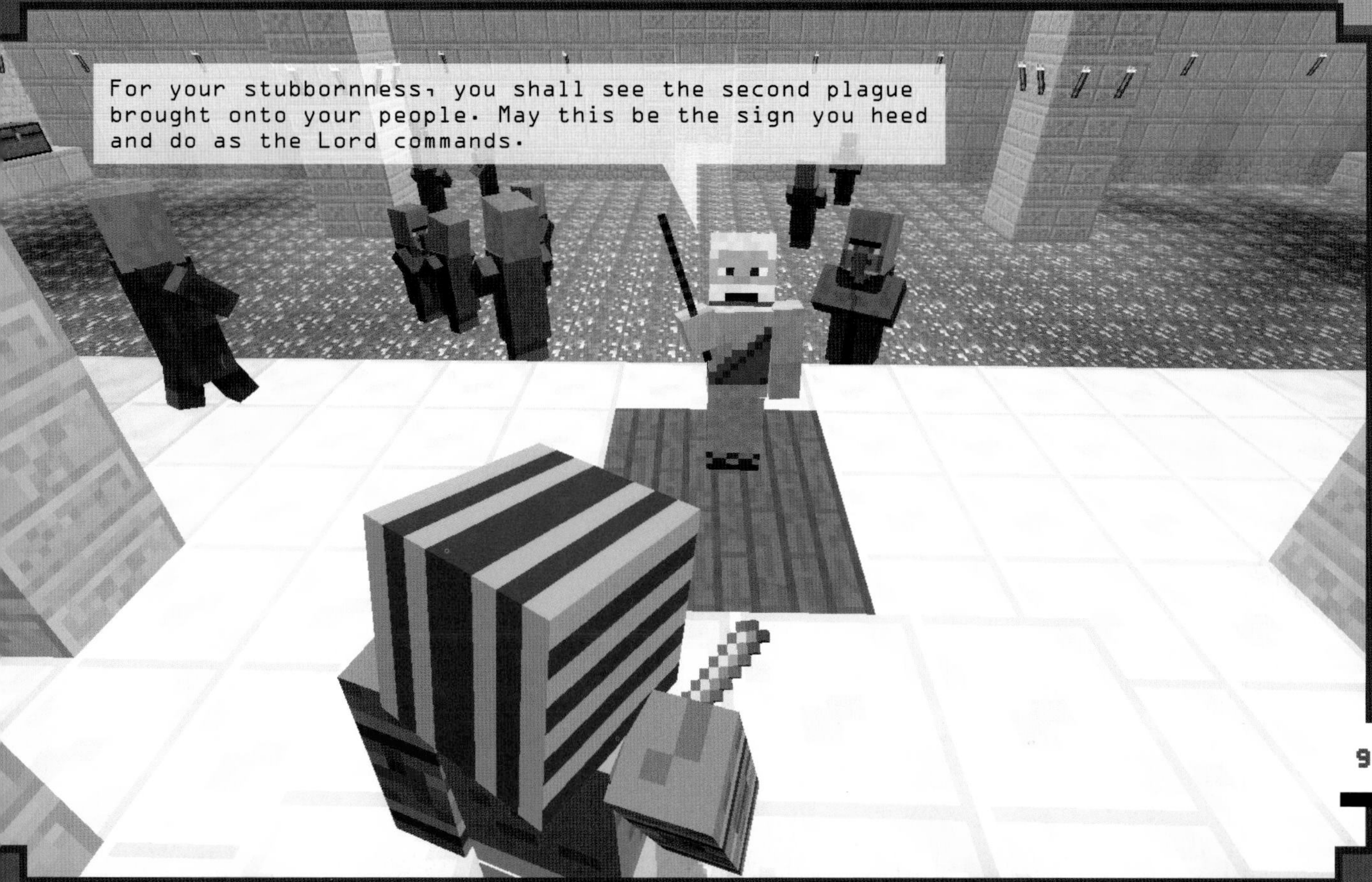
For your stubbornness, you shall see the second plague brought onto your people. May this be the sign you heed and do as the Lord commands.

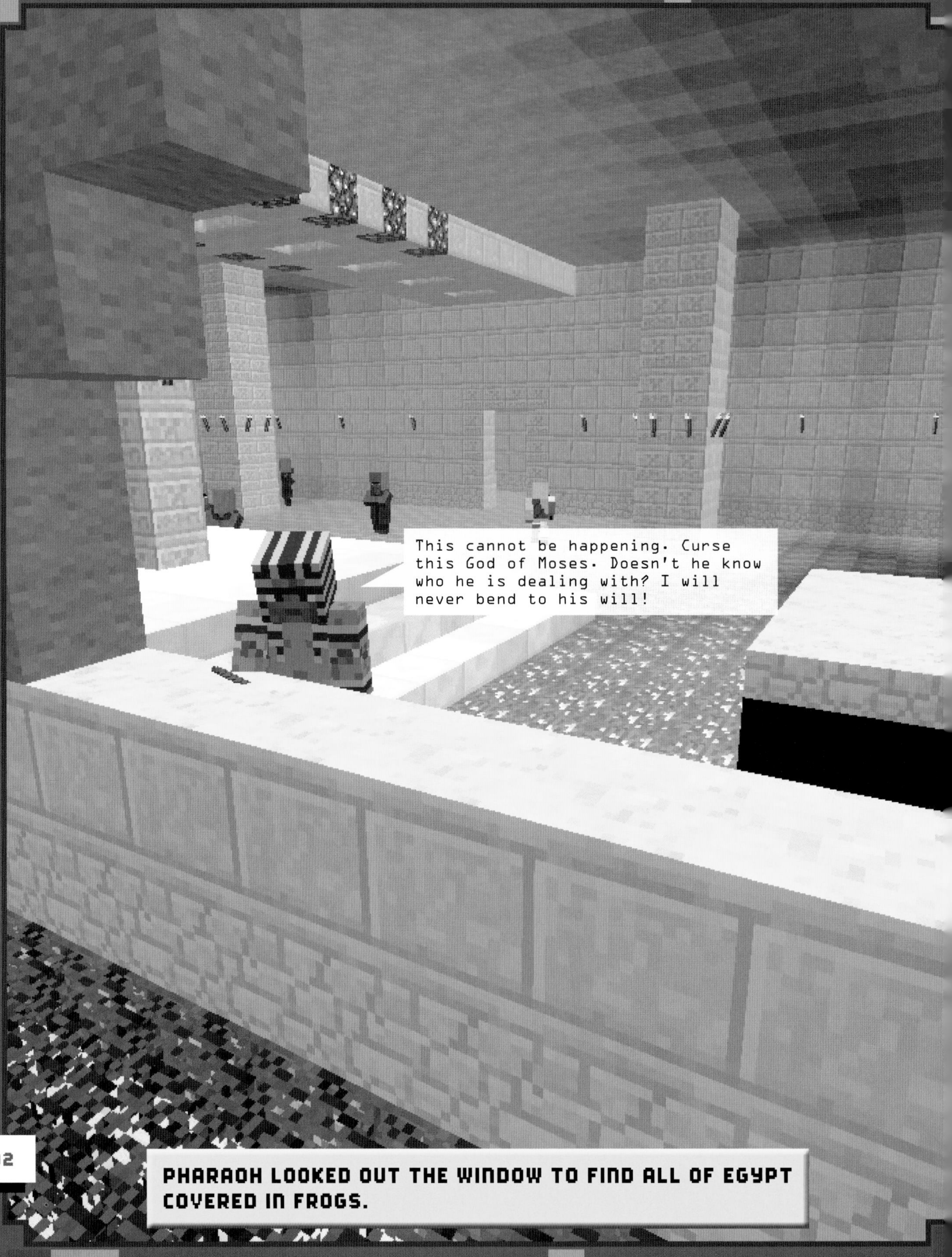
This cannot be happening. Curse this God of Moses. Doesn't he know who he is dealing with? I will never bend to his will!

PHARAOH LOOKED OUT THE WINDOW TO FIND ALL OF EGYPT COVERED IN FROGS.

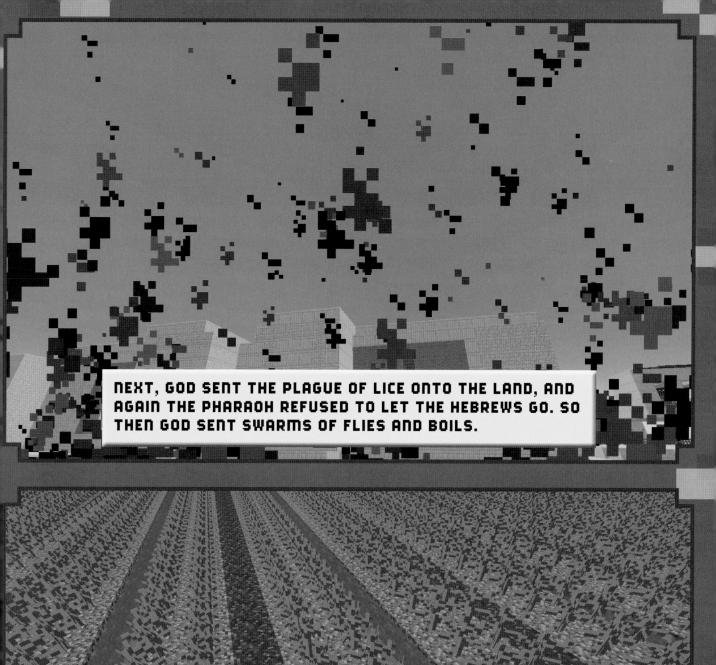

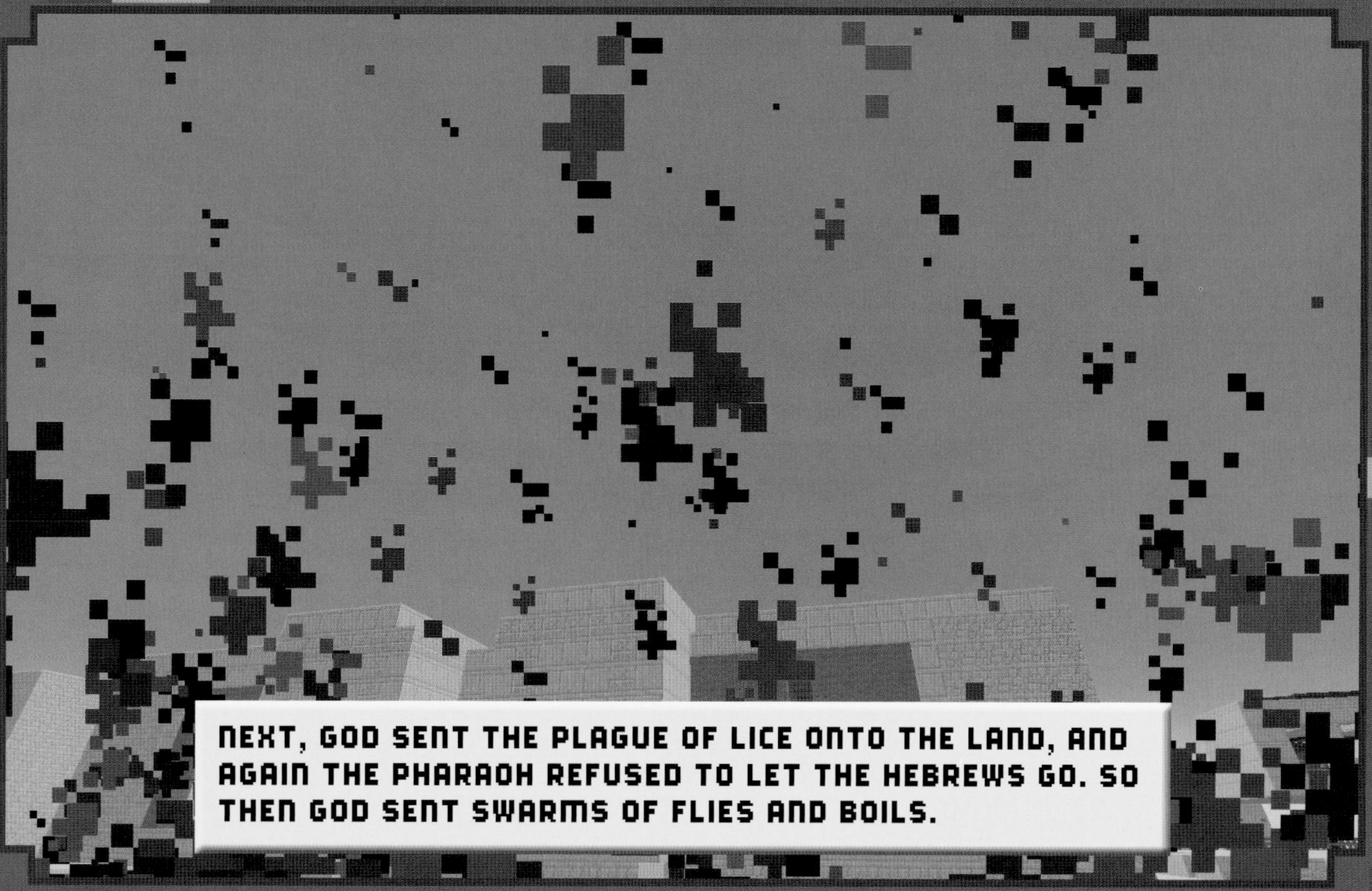
NEXT, GOD SENT THE PLAGUE OF LICE ONTO THE LAND, AND AGAIN THE PHARAOH REFUSED TO LET THE HEBREWS GO. SO THEN GOD SENT SWARMS OF FLIES AND BOILS.

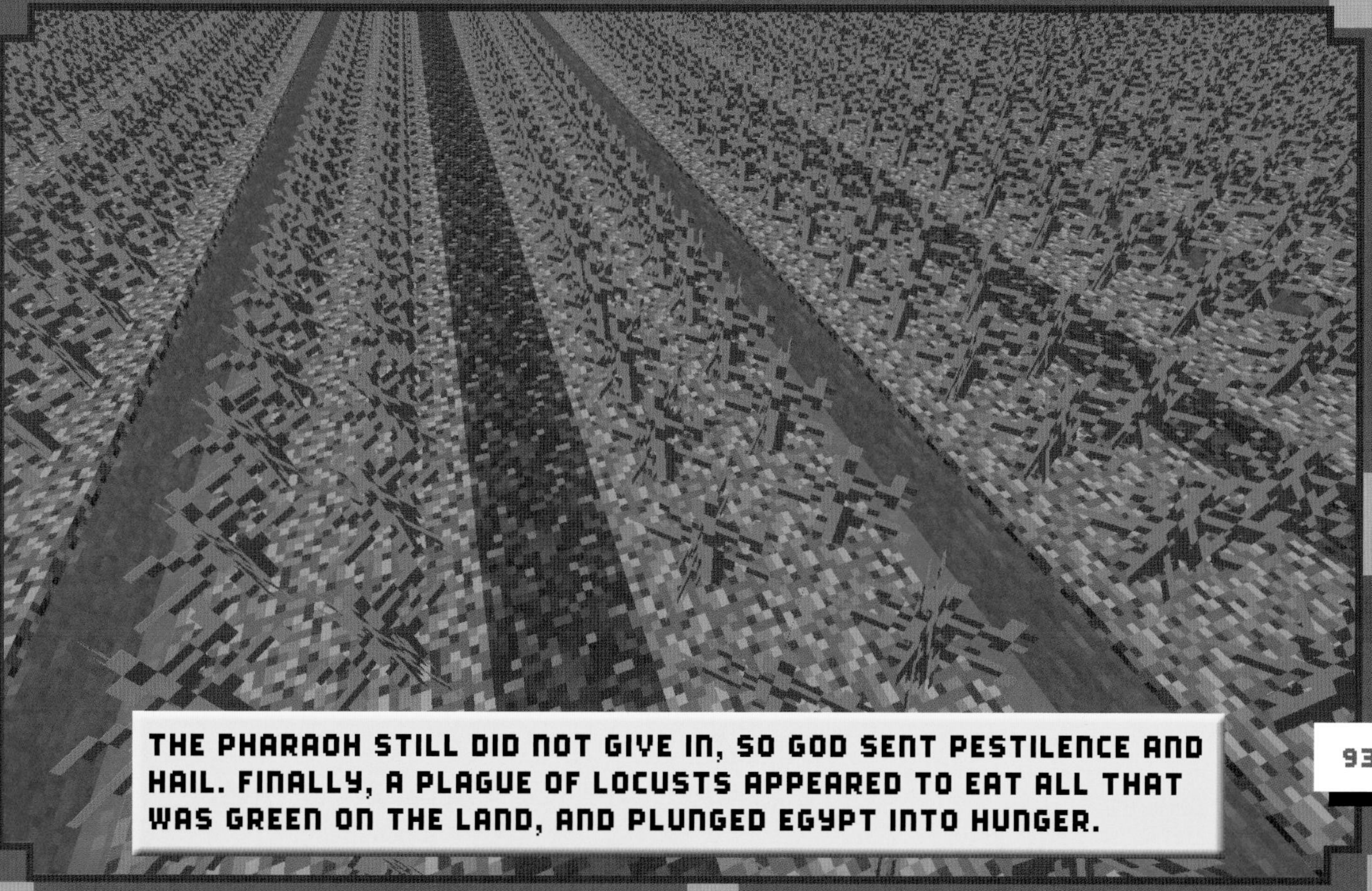
THE PHARAOH STILL DID NOT GIVE IN, SO GOD SENT PESTILENCE AND HAIL. FINALLY, A PLAGUE OF LOCUSTS APPEARED TO EAT ALL THAT WAS GREEN ON THE LAND, AND PLUNGED EGYPT INTO HUNGER.

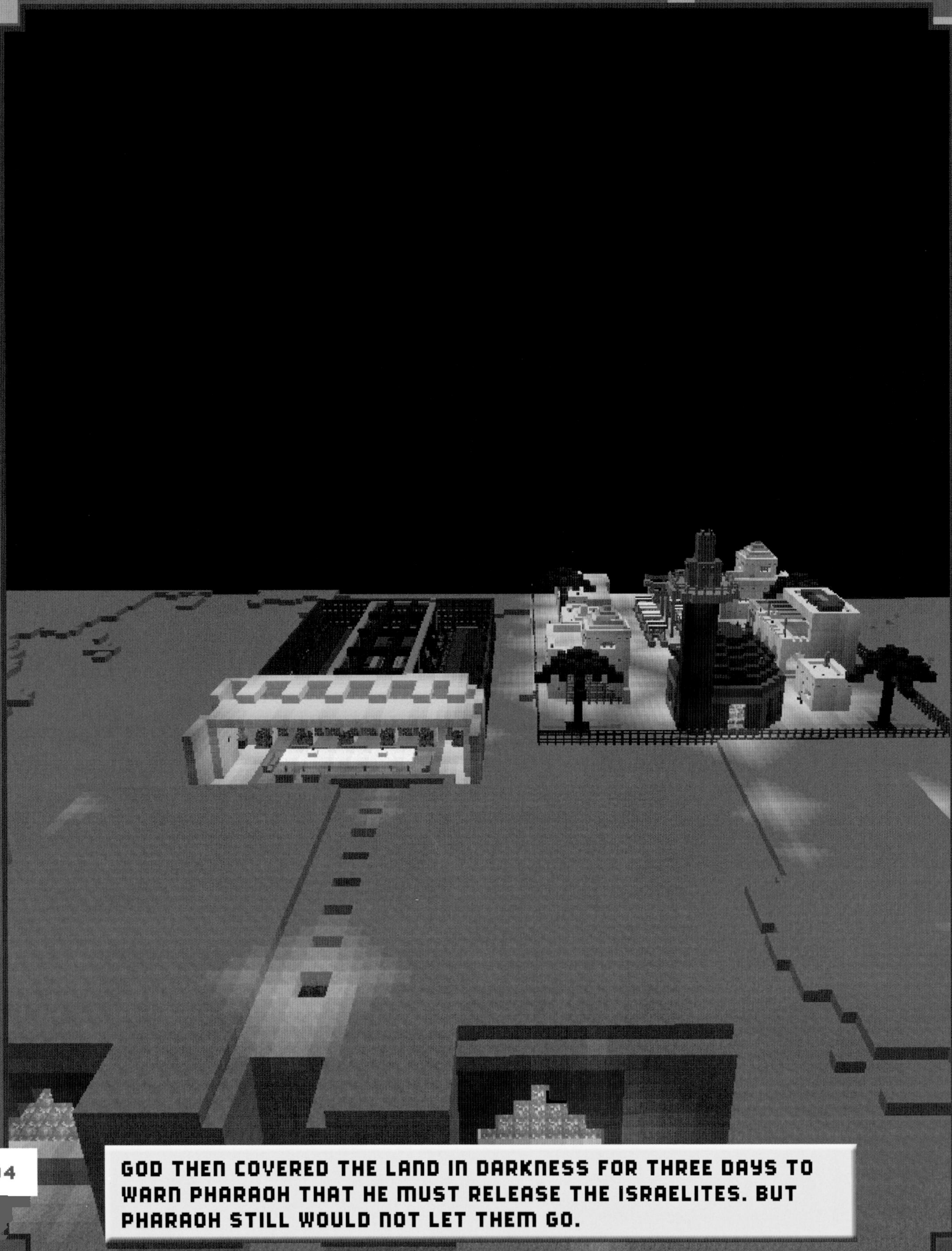

GOD THEN COVERED THE LAND IN DARKNESS FOR THREE DAYS TO WARN PHARAOH THAT HE MUST RELEASE THE ISRAELITES. BUT PHARAOH STILL WOULD NOT LET THEM GO.

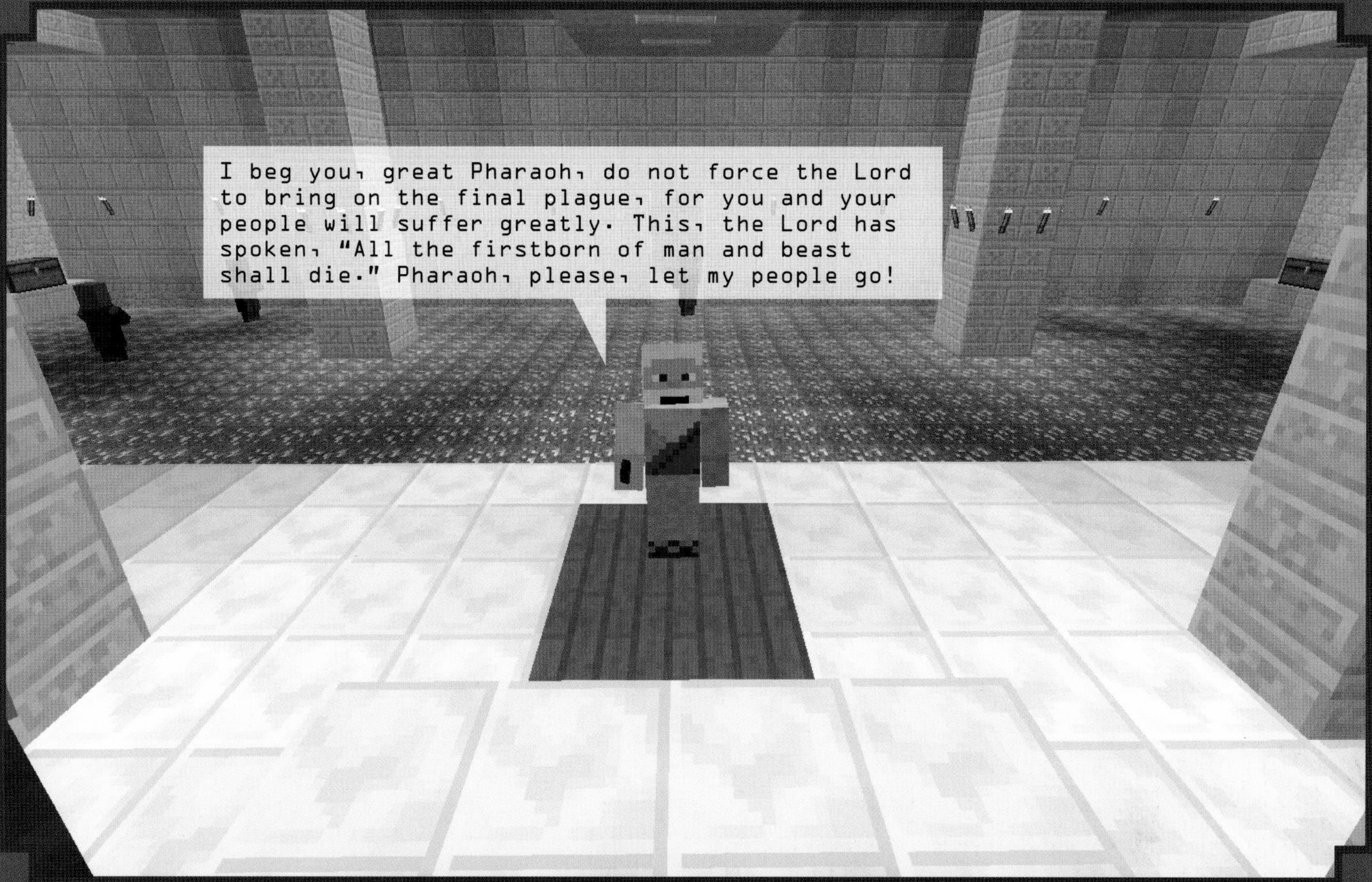
I beg you, great Pharaoh, do not force the Lord to bring on the final plague, for you and your people will suffer greatly. This, the Lord has spoken, "All the firstborn of man and beast shall die." Pharaoh, please, let my people go!

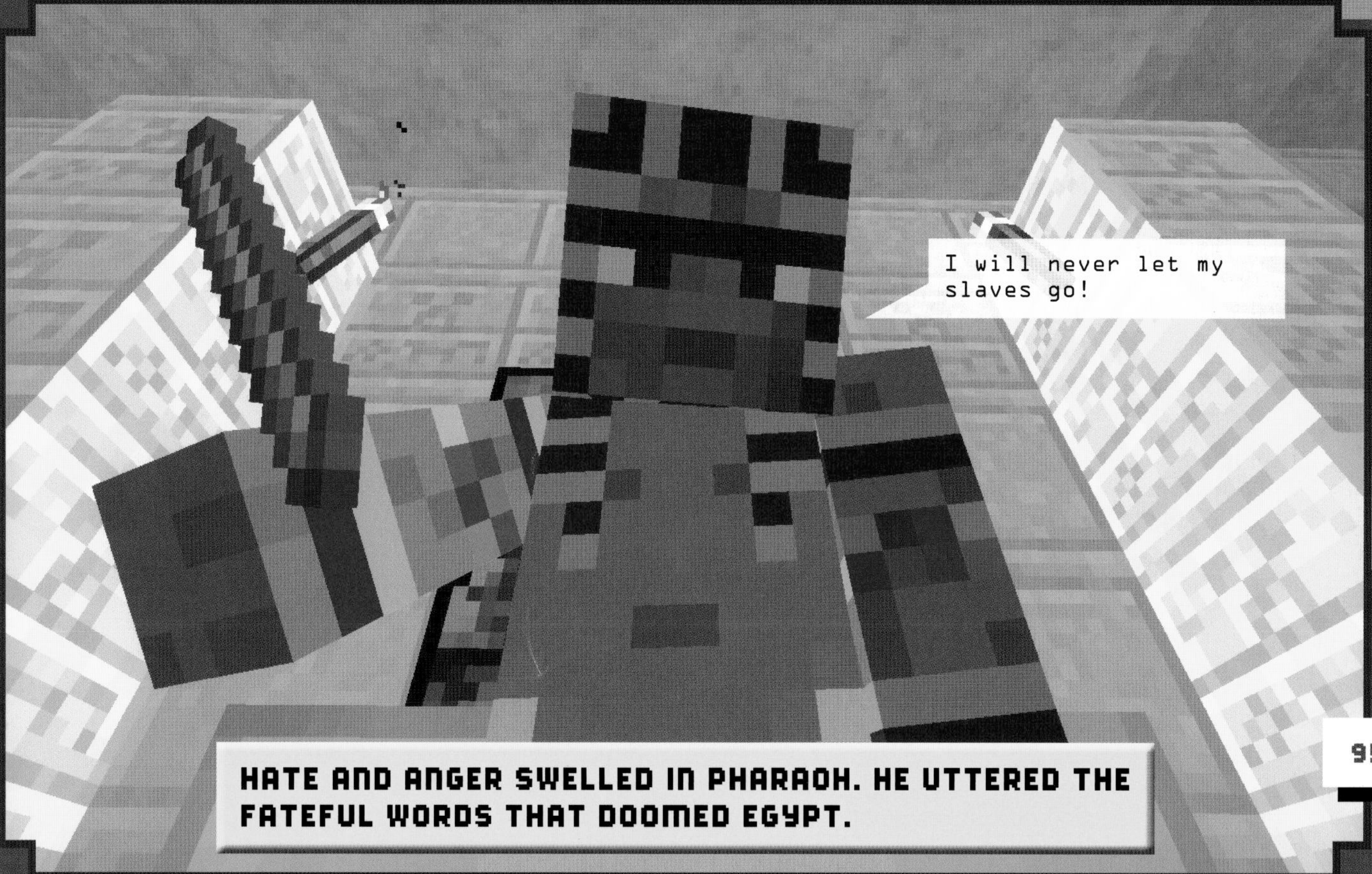
I will never let my slaves go!
HATE AND ANGER SWELLED IN PHARAOH. HE UTTERED THE FATEFUL WORDS THAT DOOMED EGYPT.

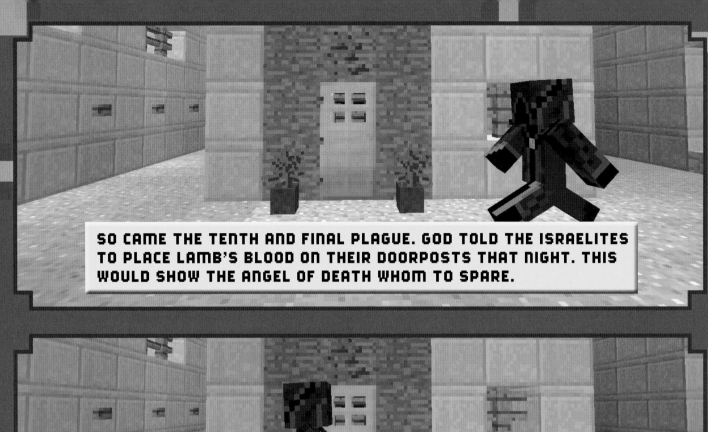

SO CAME THE TENTH AND FINAL PLAGUE. GOD TOLD THE ISRAELITES TO PLACE LAMB'S BLOOD ON THEIR DOORPOSTS THAT NIGHT. THIS WOULD SHOW THE ANGEL OF DEATH WHOM TO SPARE.

AS THE ANGEL OF DEATH PASSED OVER EACH HOUSE THAT HELD THE LAMB'S BLOOD, THIS BECAME KNOWN AS THE PASSOVER.

AND THUS THE ANGEL OF DEATH PASSED BY THE DOORS OF ALL THE HEBREWS, WHILE BRINGING A SILENT DOOM TO THE FIRSTBORN OF ALL THE GENTILE FAMILIES OF EGYPT.

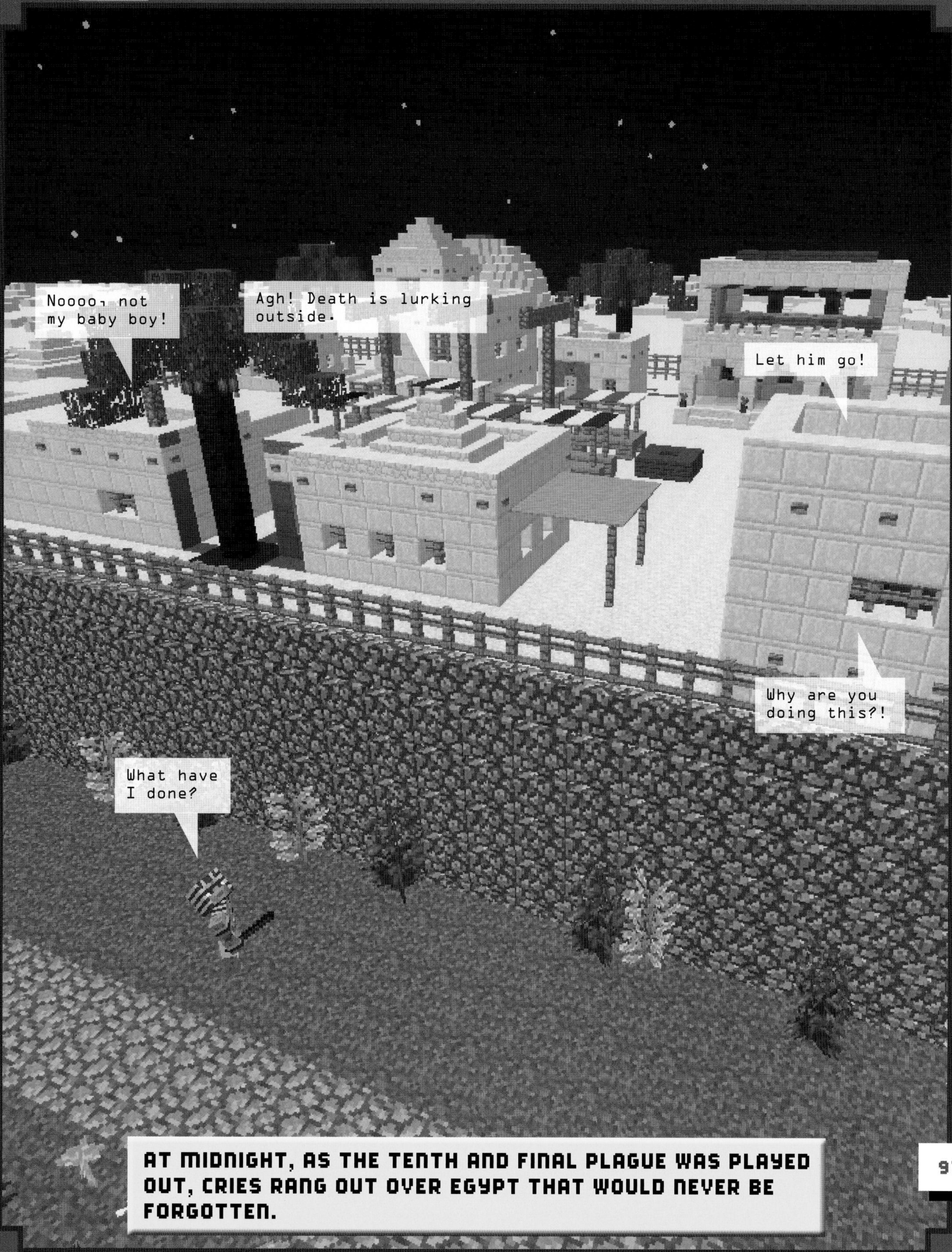
Noooo, not my baby boy!
Agh! Death is lurking outside.
Let him go!
Why are you doing this?!
What have I done?
AT MIDNIGHT, AS THE TENTH AND FINAL PLAGUE WAS PLAYED OUT, CRIES RANG OUT OVER EGYPT THAT WOULD NEVER BE FORGOTTEN.

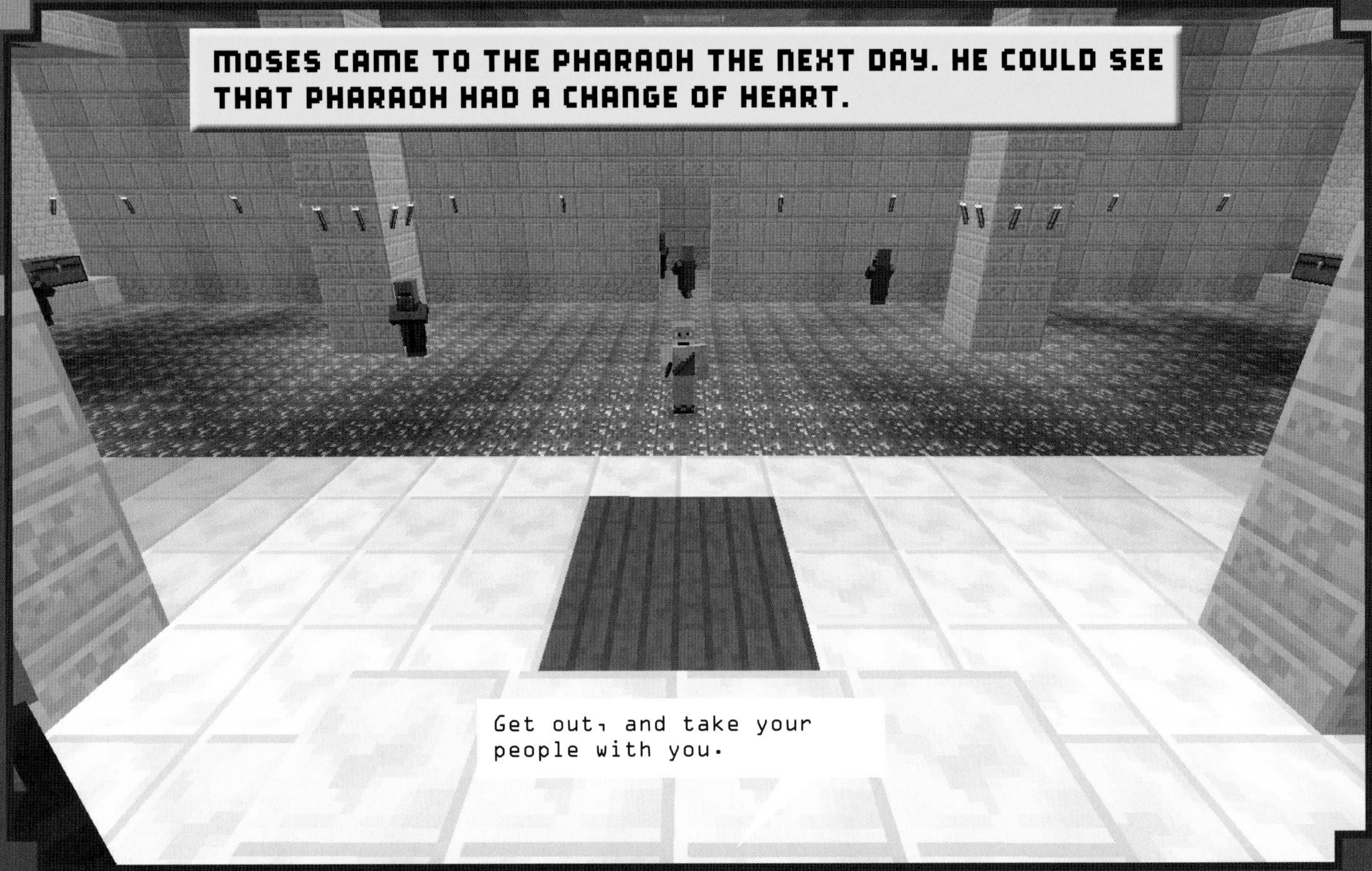
MOSES CAME TO THE PHARAOH THE NEXT DAY. HE COULD SEE THAT PHARAOH HAD A CHANGE OF HEART.
Get out, and take your people with you.

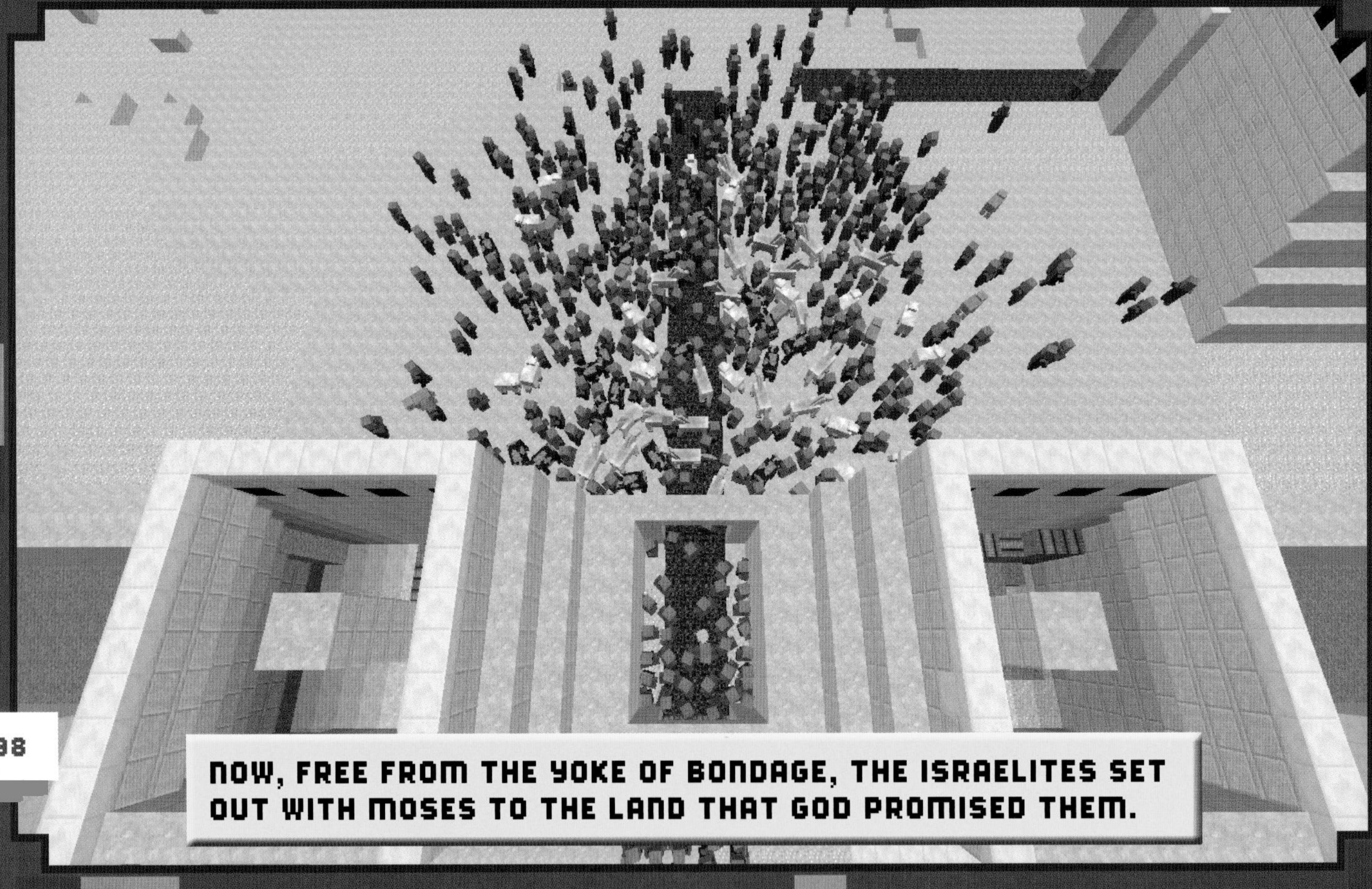
NOW, FREE FROM THE YOKE OF BONDAGE, THE ISRAELITES SET OUT WITH MOSES TO THE LAND THAT GOD PROMISED THEM.

PARTING OF THE RED SEA

Sweet, freedom for the Hebrews!

But they're not out of danger yet.

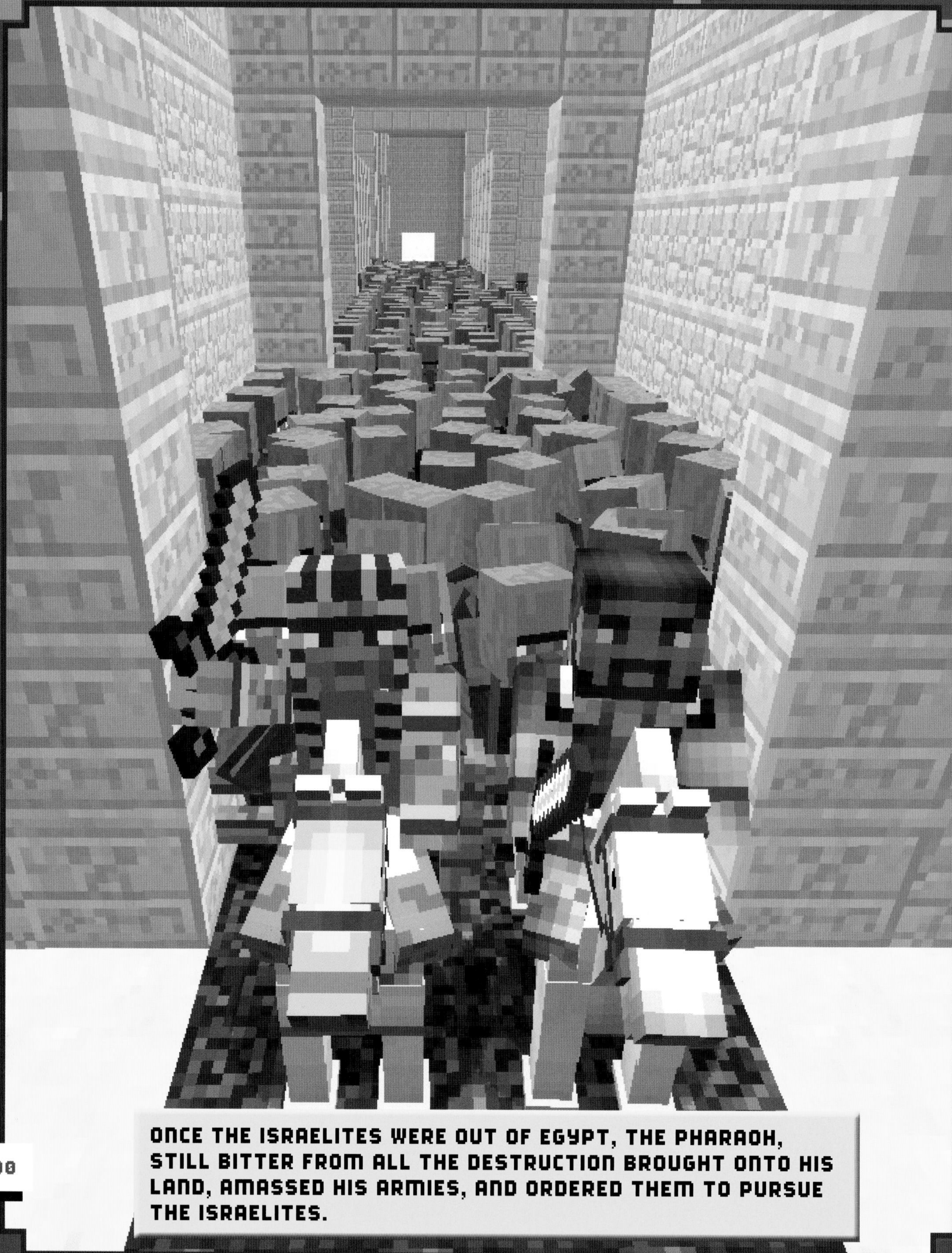

ONCE THE ISRAELITES WERE OUT OF EGYPT, THE PHARAOH, STILL BITTER FROM ALL THE DESTRUCTION BROUGHT ONTO HIS LAND, AMASSED HIS ARMIES, AND ORDERED THEM TO PURSUE THE ISRAELITES.

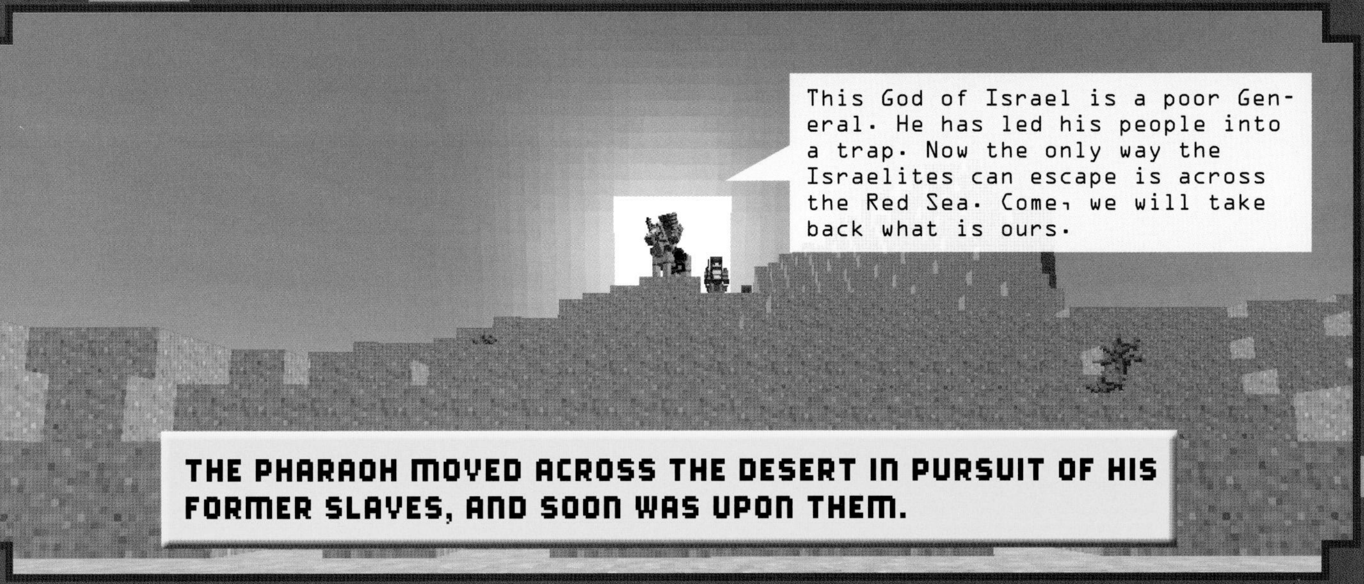
This God of Israel is a poor General. He has led his people into a trap. Now the only way the Israelites can escape is across the Red Sea. Come, we will take back what is ours.
THE PHARAOH MOVED ACROSS THE DESERT IN PURSUIT OF HIS FORMER SLAVES, AND SOON WAS UPON THEM.

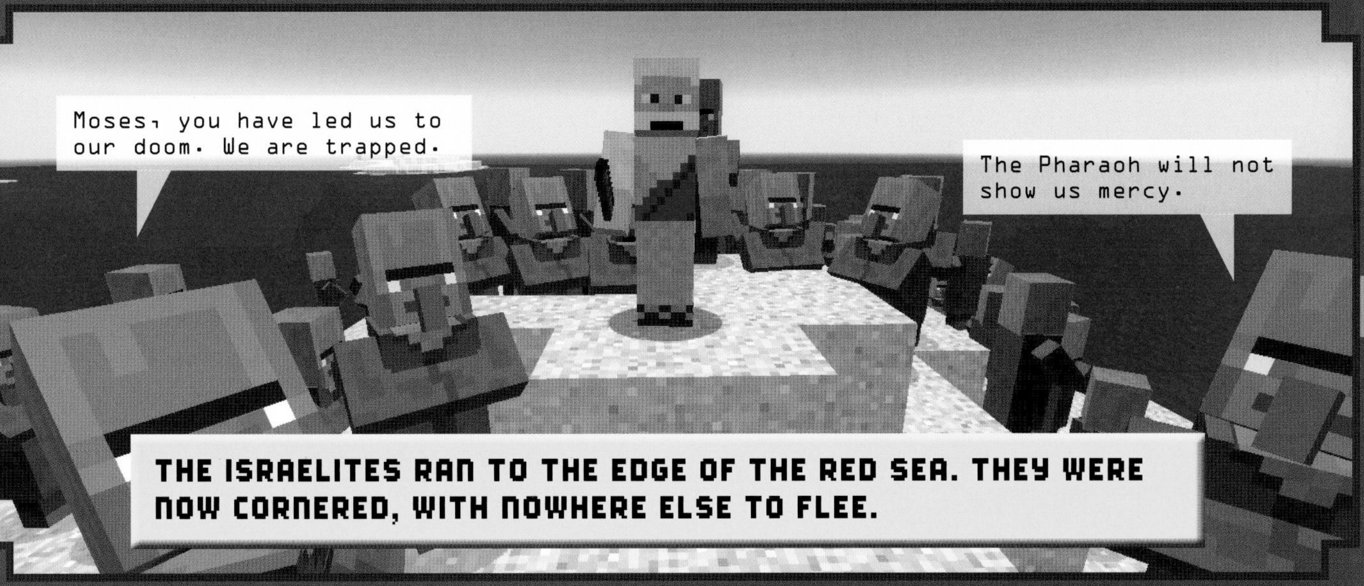
Moses, you have led us to our doom. We are trapped.
The Pharaoh will not show us mercy.
THE ISRAELITES RAN TO THE EDGE OF THE RED SEA. THEY WERE NOW CORNERED, WITH NOWHERE ELSE TO FLEE.

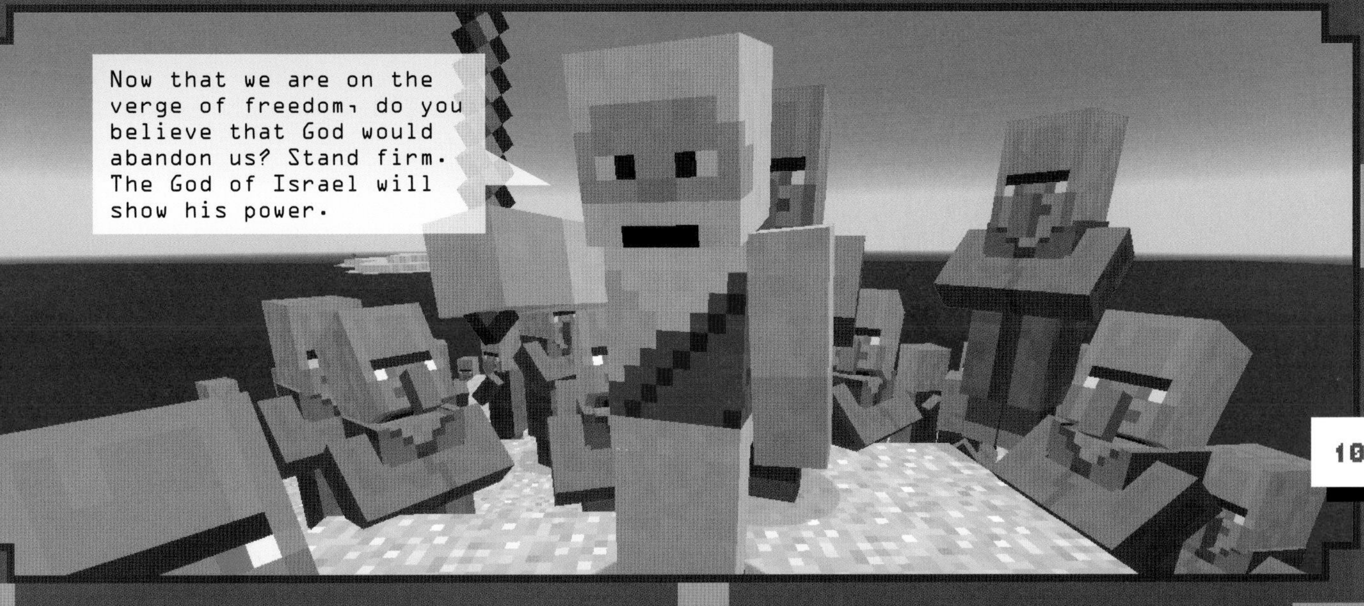
Now that we are on the verge of freedom, do you believe that God would abandon us? Stand firm. The God of Israel will show his power.

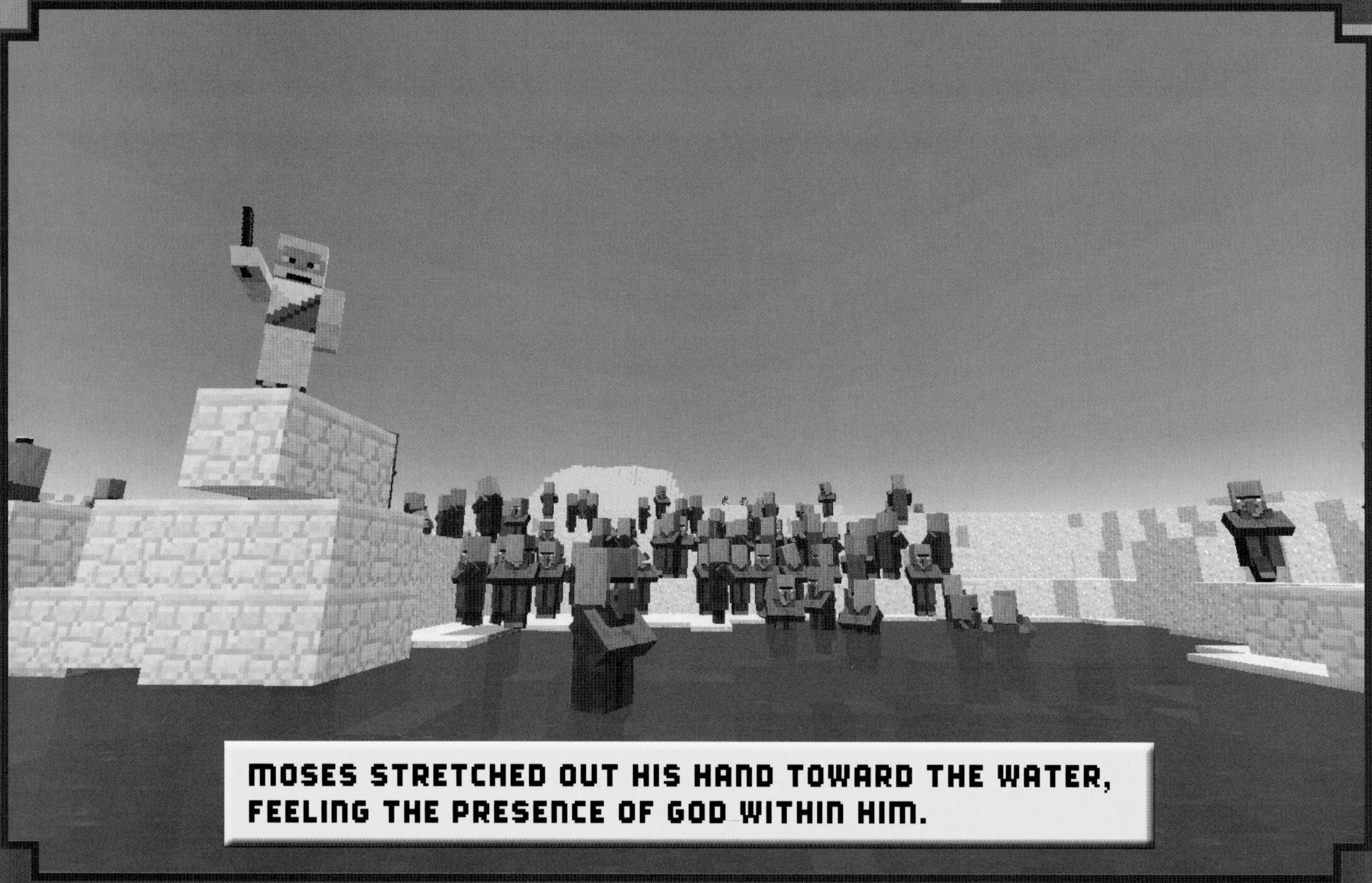
MOSES STRETCHED OUT HIS HAND TOWARD THE WATER, FEELING THE PRESENCE OF GOD WITHIN HIM.

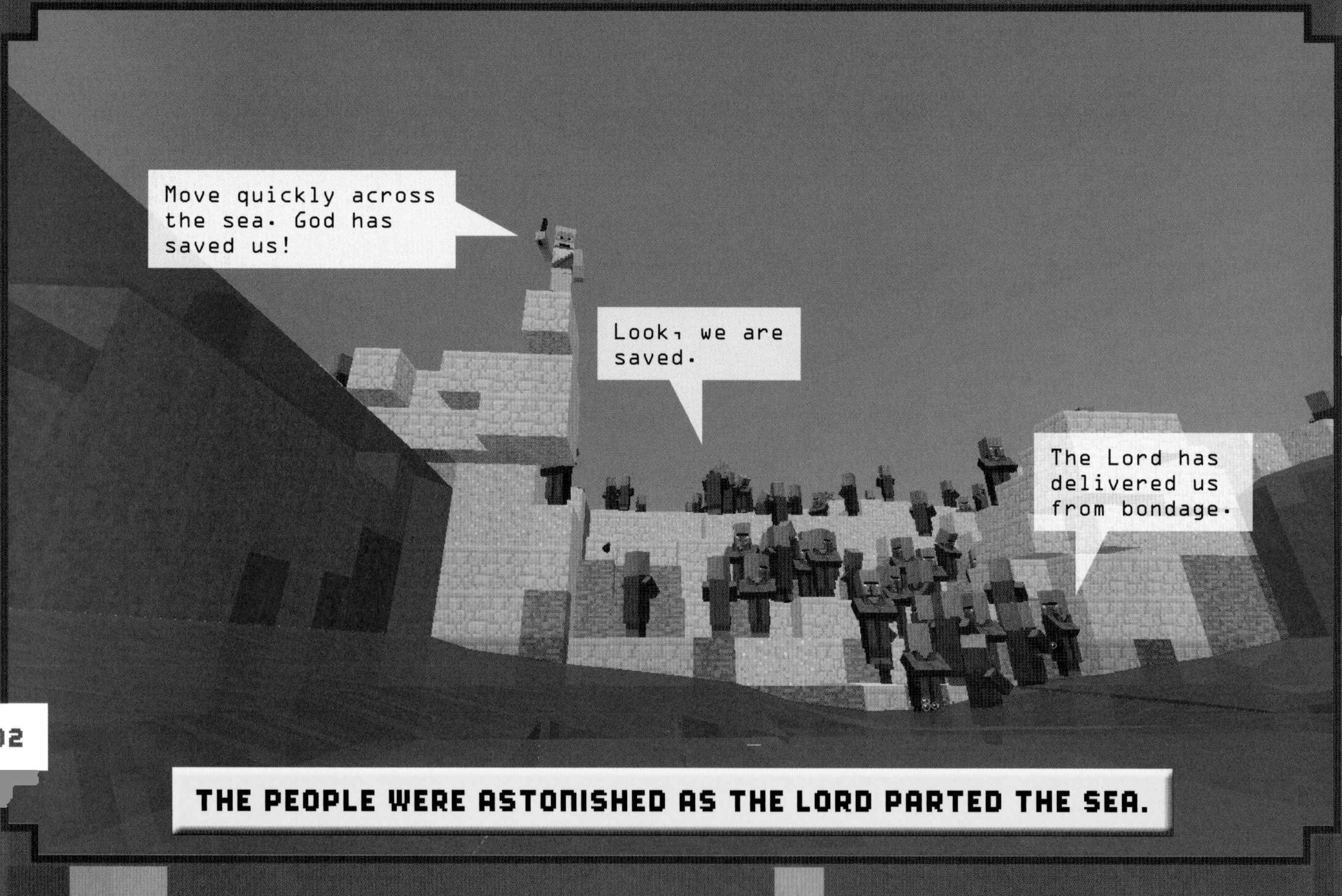
Move quickly across the sea. God has saved us!
Look, we are saved.
The Lord has delivered us from bondage.
THE PEOPLE WERE ASTONISHED AS THE LORD PARTED THE SEA.

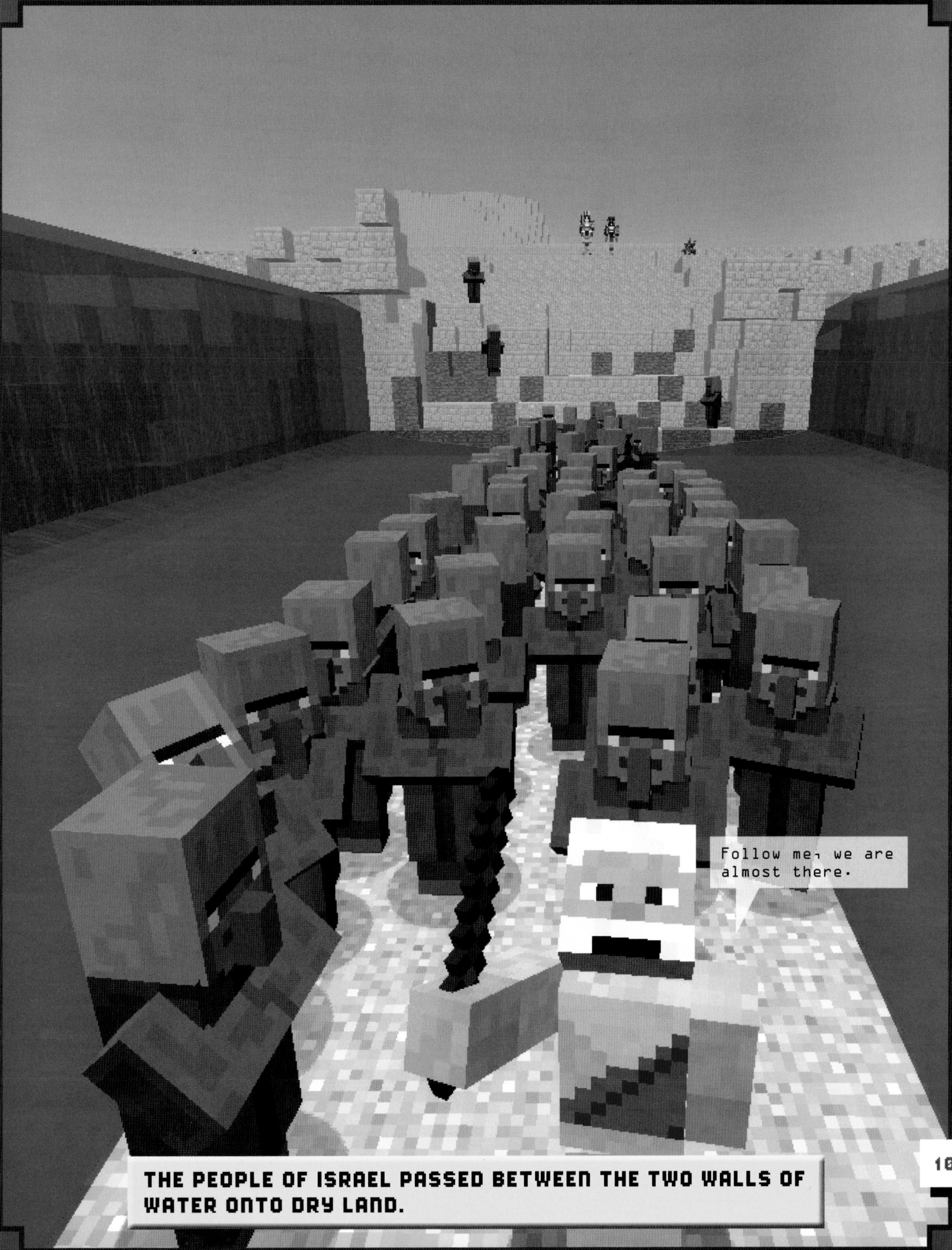
Follow me, we are almost there.

THE PEOPLE OF ISRAEL PASSED BETWEEN THE TWO WALLS OF WATER ONTO DRY LAND.

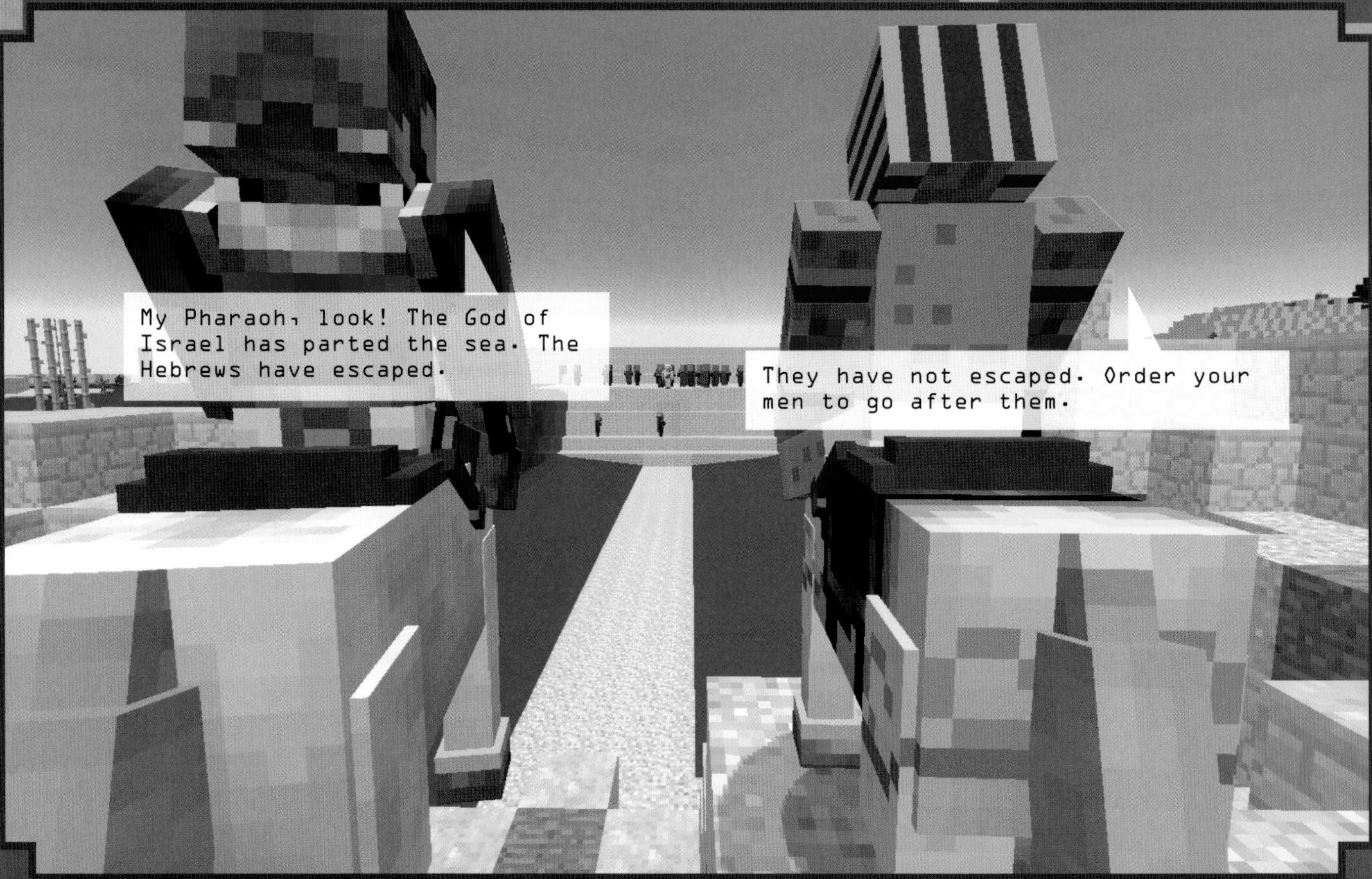
My Pharaoh, look! The God of Israel has parted the sea. The Hebrews have escaped.
They have not escaped. Order your men to go after them.

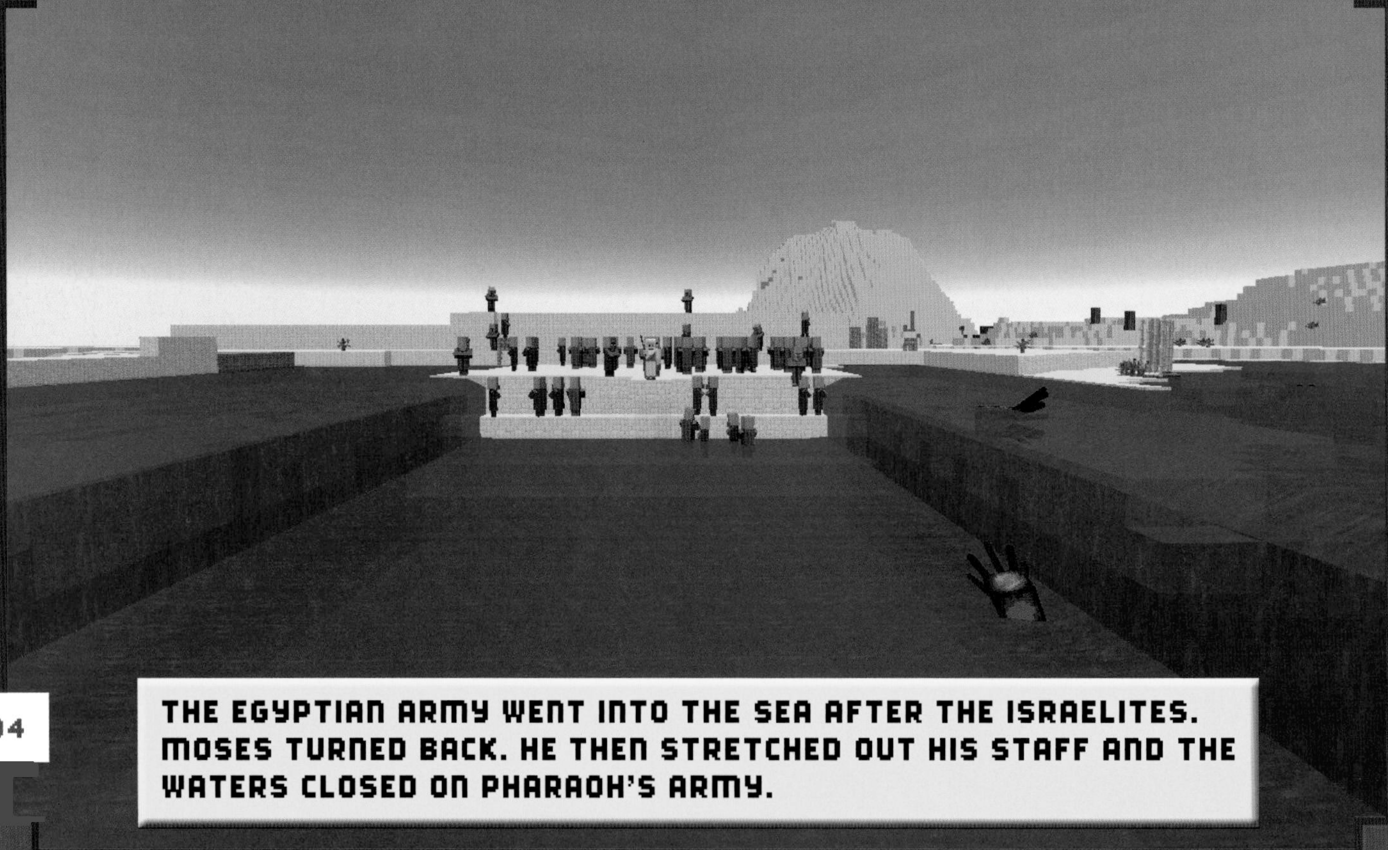
THE EGYPTIAN ARMY WENT INTO THE SEA AFTER THE ISRAELITES. MOSES TURNED BACK. HE THEN STRETCHED OUT HIS STAFF AND THE WATERS CLOSED ON PHARAOH'S ARMY.

THE TEN COMMANDMENTS

It's time I give concrete instructions for a righteous path in life.

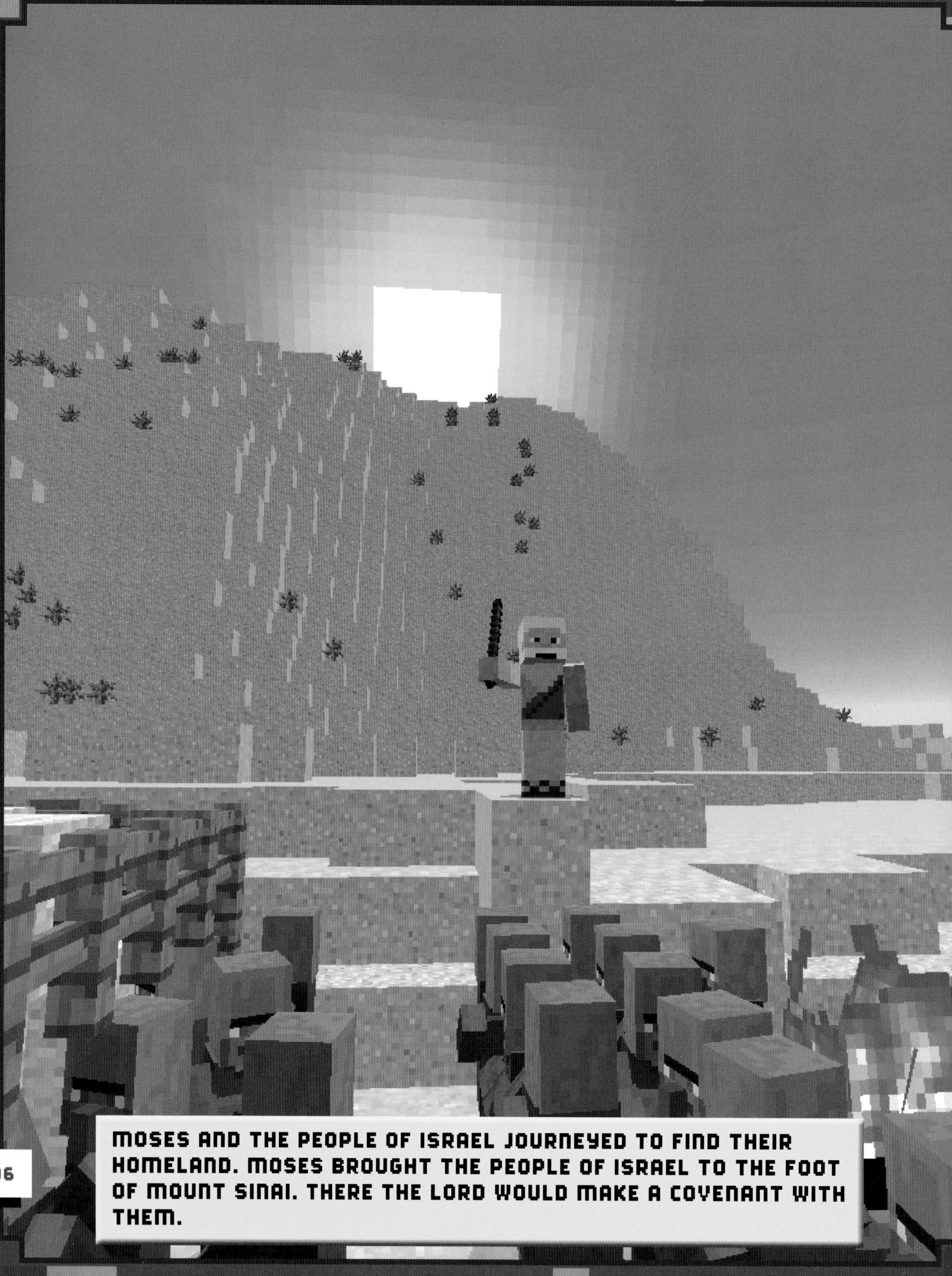

MOSES AND THE PEOPLE OF ISRAEL JOURNEYED TO FIND THEIR HOMELAND. MOSES BROUGHT THE PEOPLE OF ISRAEL TO THE FOOT OF MOUNT SINAI. THERE THE LORD WOULD MAKE A COVENANT WITH THEM.

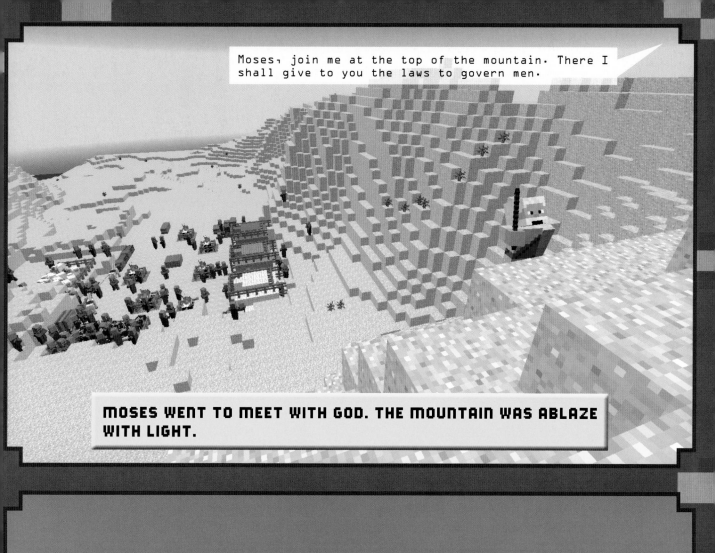

Moses, join me at the top of the mountain. There I shall give to you the laws to govern men.

MOSES WENT TO MEET WITH GOD. THE MOUNTAIN WAS ABLAZE WITH LIGHT.

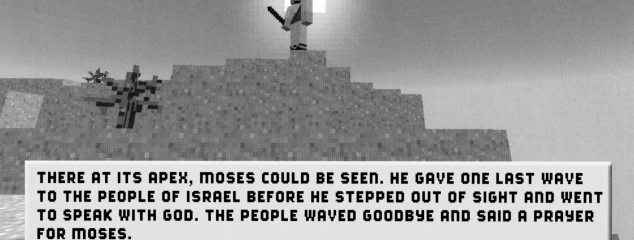

THERE AT ITS APEX, MOSES COULD BE SEEN. HE GAVE ONE LAST WAVE TO THE PEOPLE OF ISRAEL BEFORE HE STEPPED OUT OF SIGHT AND WENT TO SPEAK WITH GOD. THE PEOPLE WAVED GOODBYE AND SAID A PRAYER FOR MOSES.

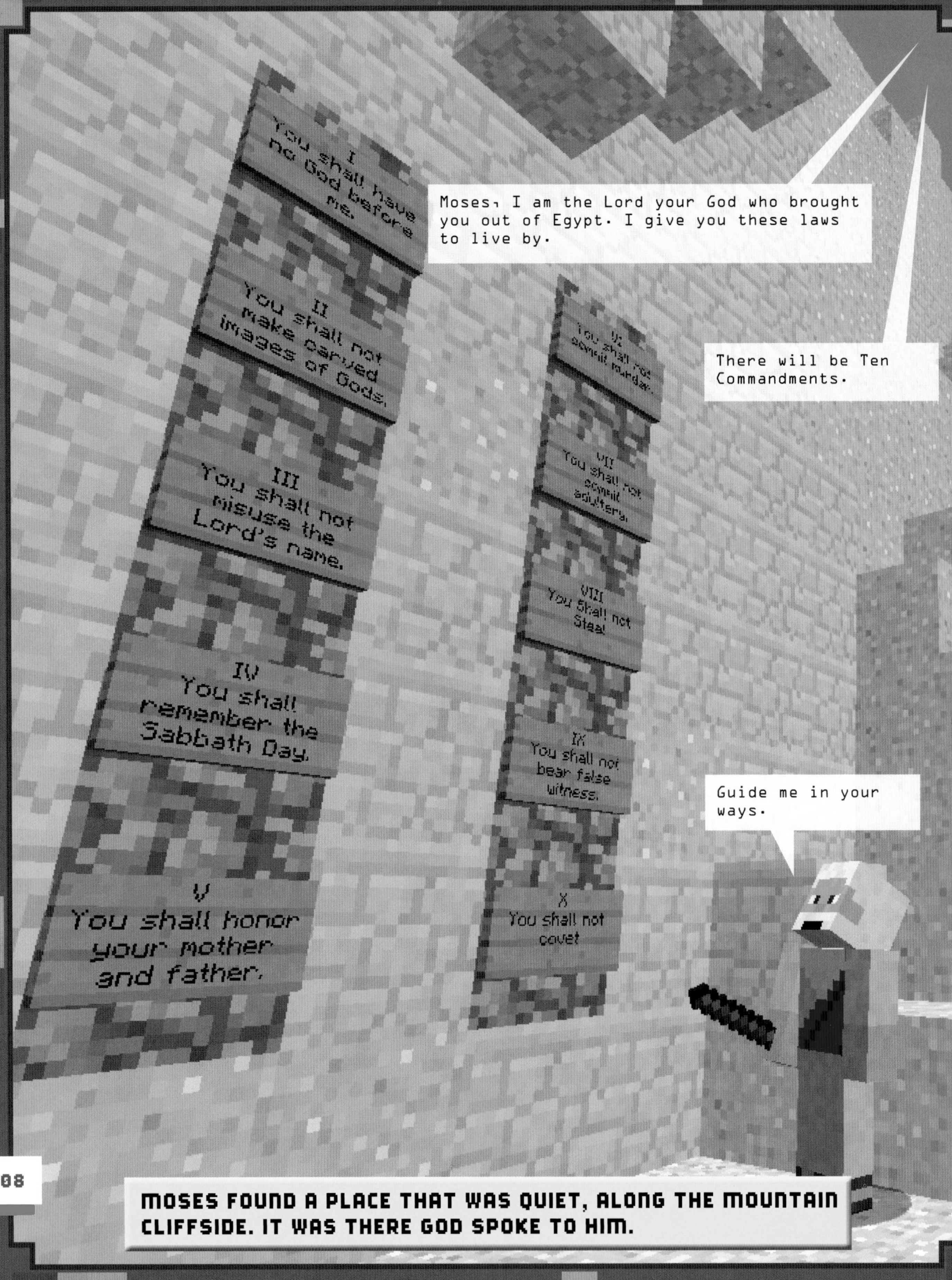

I You shall have no God before me.
II You shall not make carved images of Gods.
III You shall not misuse the Lord's name.
IV You shall remember the Sabbath Day.
V You shall honor your mother and father.
VI You shall not commit murder.
VII You shall not commit adultery.
VIII You Shall not Steal
IX You shall not bear false witness.
X You shall not covet
Moses, I am the Lord your God who brought you out of Egypt. I give you these laws to live by.
There will be Ten Commandments.
Guide me in your ways.
MOSES FOUND A PLACE THAT WAS QUIET, ALONG THE MOUNTAIN CLIFFSIDE. IT WAS THERE GOD SPOKE TO HIM.

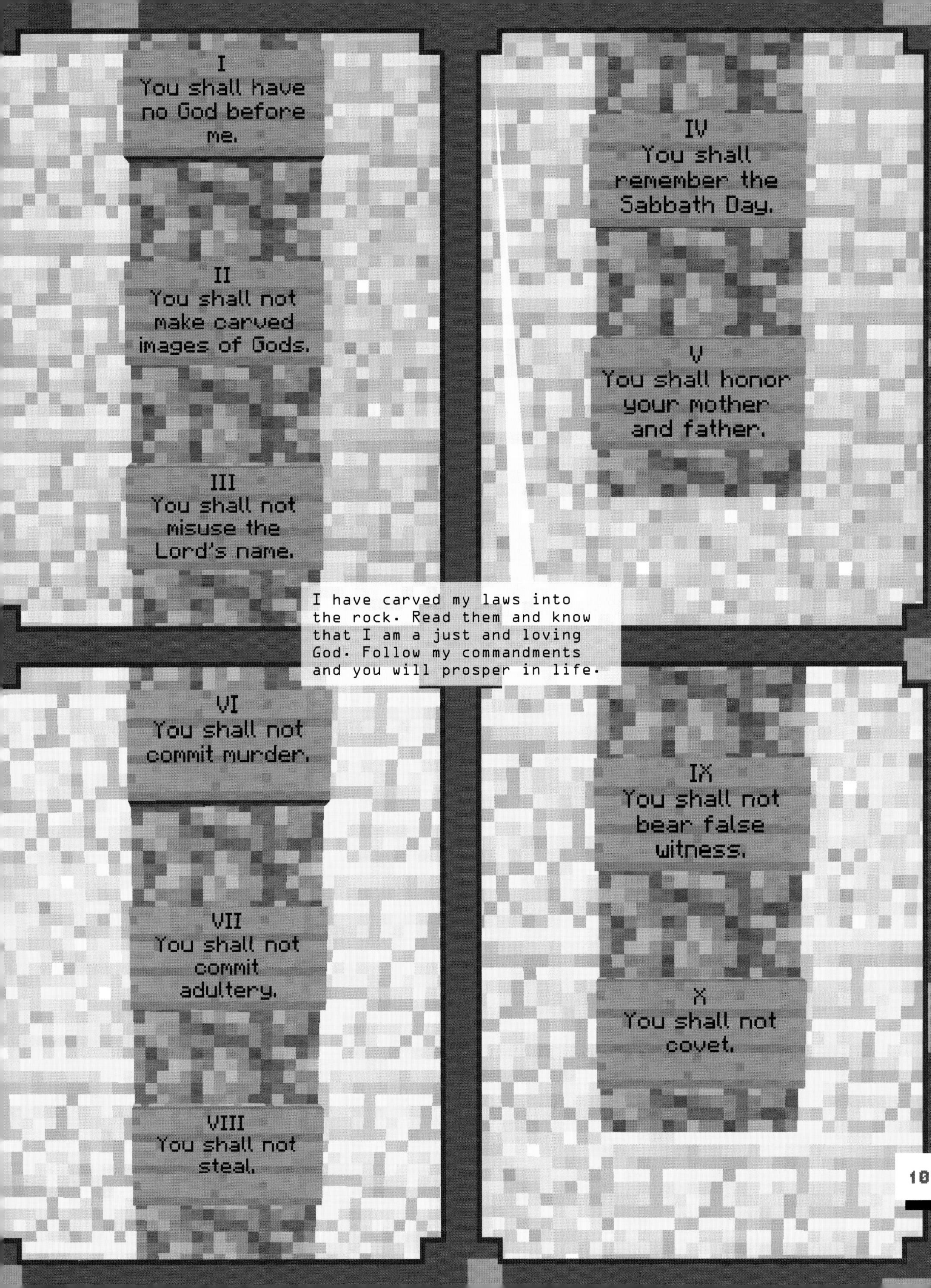

I You shall have no God before me.
II You shall not make carved images of Gods.
III You shall not misuse the Lord's name.
IV You shall remember the Sabbath Day.
V You shall honor your mother and father.
I have carved my laws into the rock. Read them and know that I am a just and loving God. Follow my commandments and you will prosper in life.
VI You shall not commit murder.
VII You shall not commit adultery.
VIII You shall not steal.
IX You shall not bear false witness.
X You shall not covet.

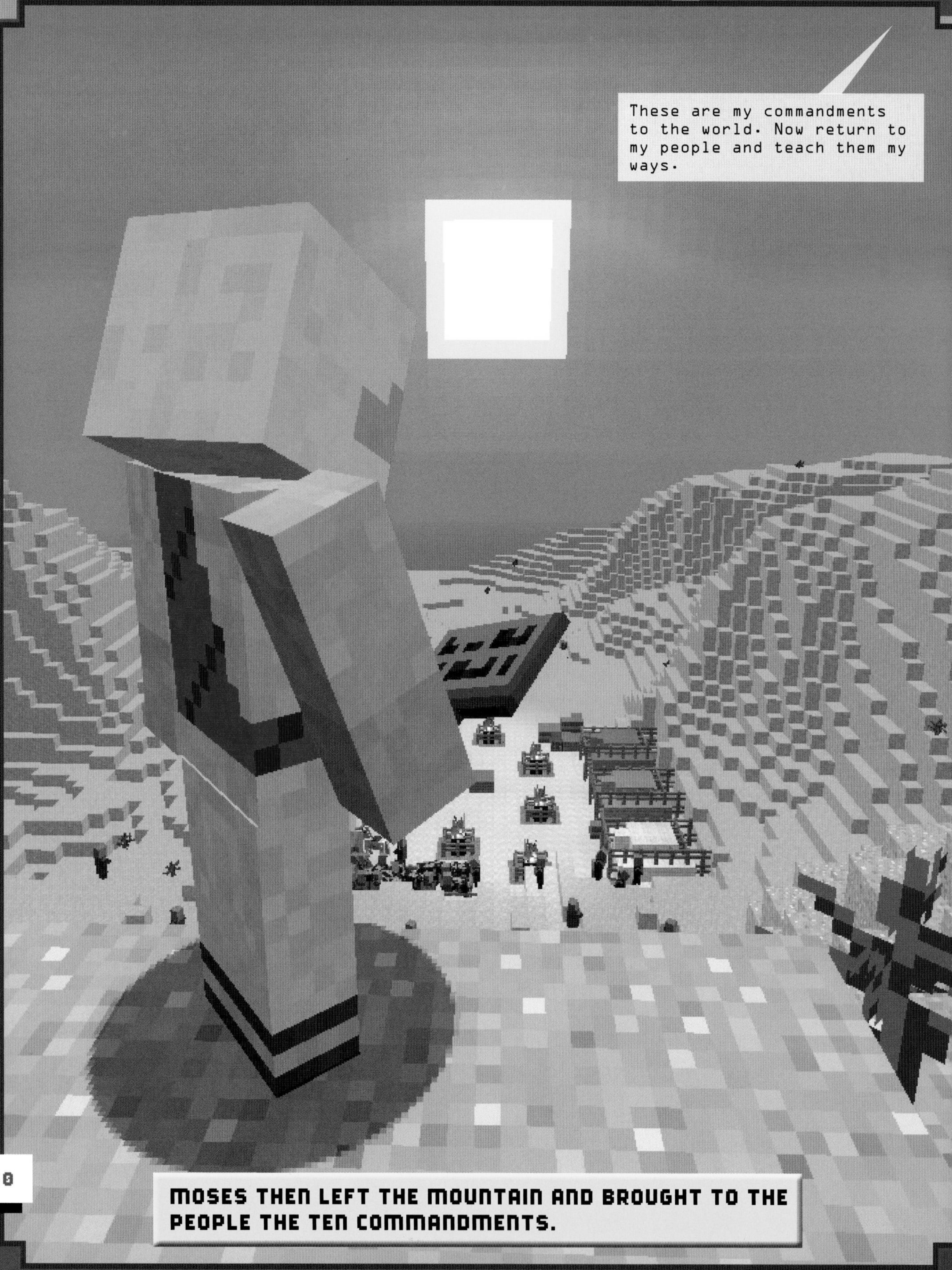
These are my commandments to the world. Now return to my people and teach them my ways.
MOSES THEN LEFT THE MOUNTAIN AND BROUGHT TO THE PEOPLE THE TEN COMMANDMENTS.

THE WALLS OF JERICHO

Nice job on the commandments!

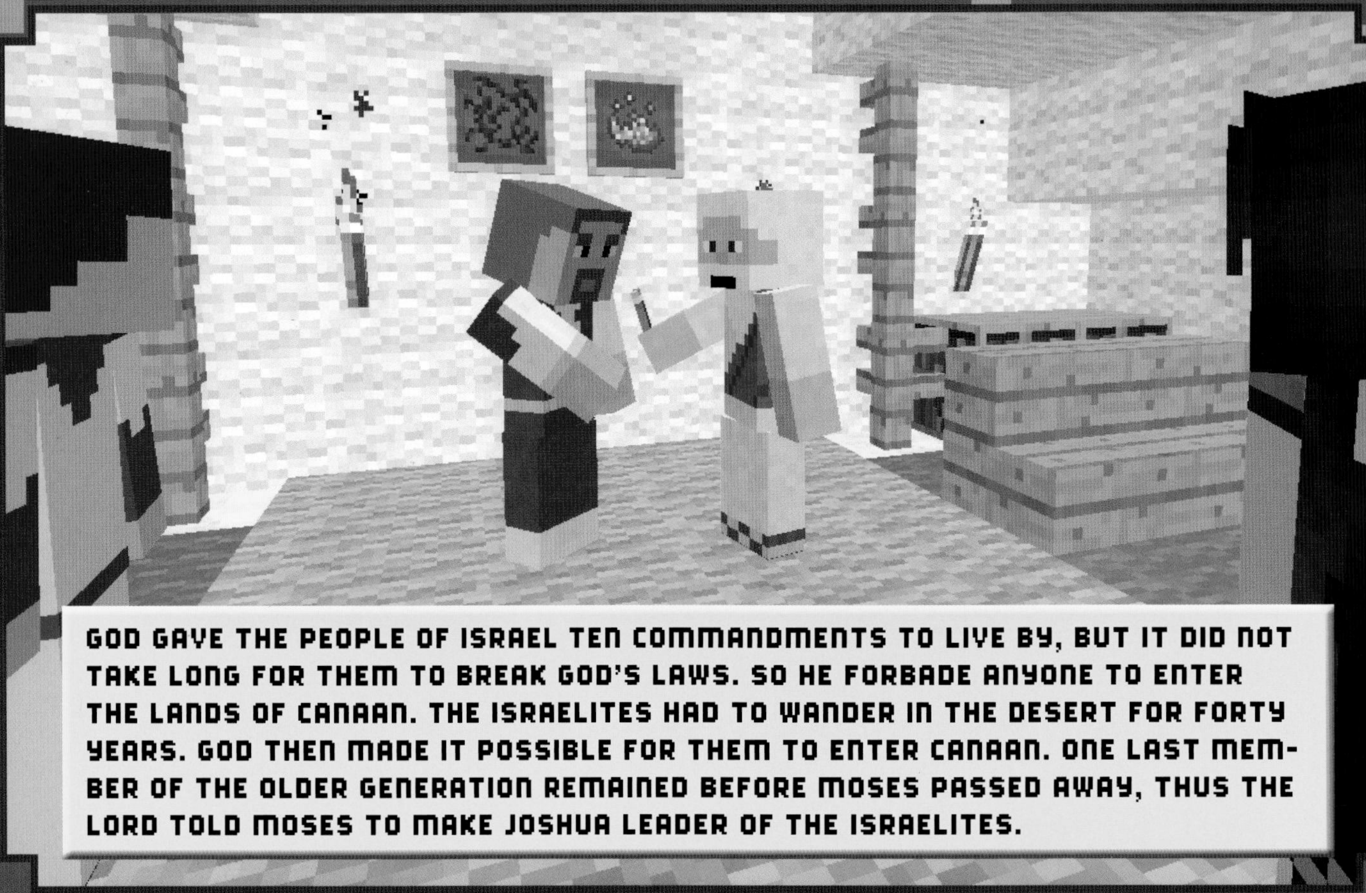
GOD GAVE THE PEOPLE OF ISRAEL TEN COMMANDMENTS TO LIVE BY, BUT IT DID NOT TAKE LONG FOR THEM TO BREAK GOD'S LAWS. SO HE FORBADE ANYONE TO ENTER THE LANDS OF CANAAN. THE ISRAELITES HAD TO WANDER IN THE DESERT FOR FORTY YEARS. GOD THEN MADE IT POSSIBLE FOR THEM TO ENTER CANAAN. ONE LAST MEMBER OF THE OLDER GENERATION REMAINED BEFORE MOSES PASSED AWAY, THUS THE LORD TOLD MOSES TO MAKE JOSHUA LEADER OF THE ISRAELITES.

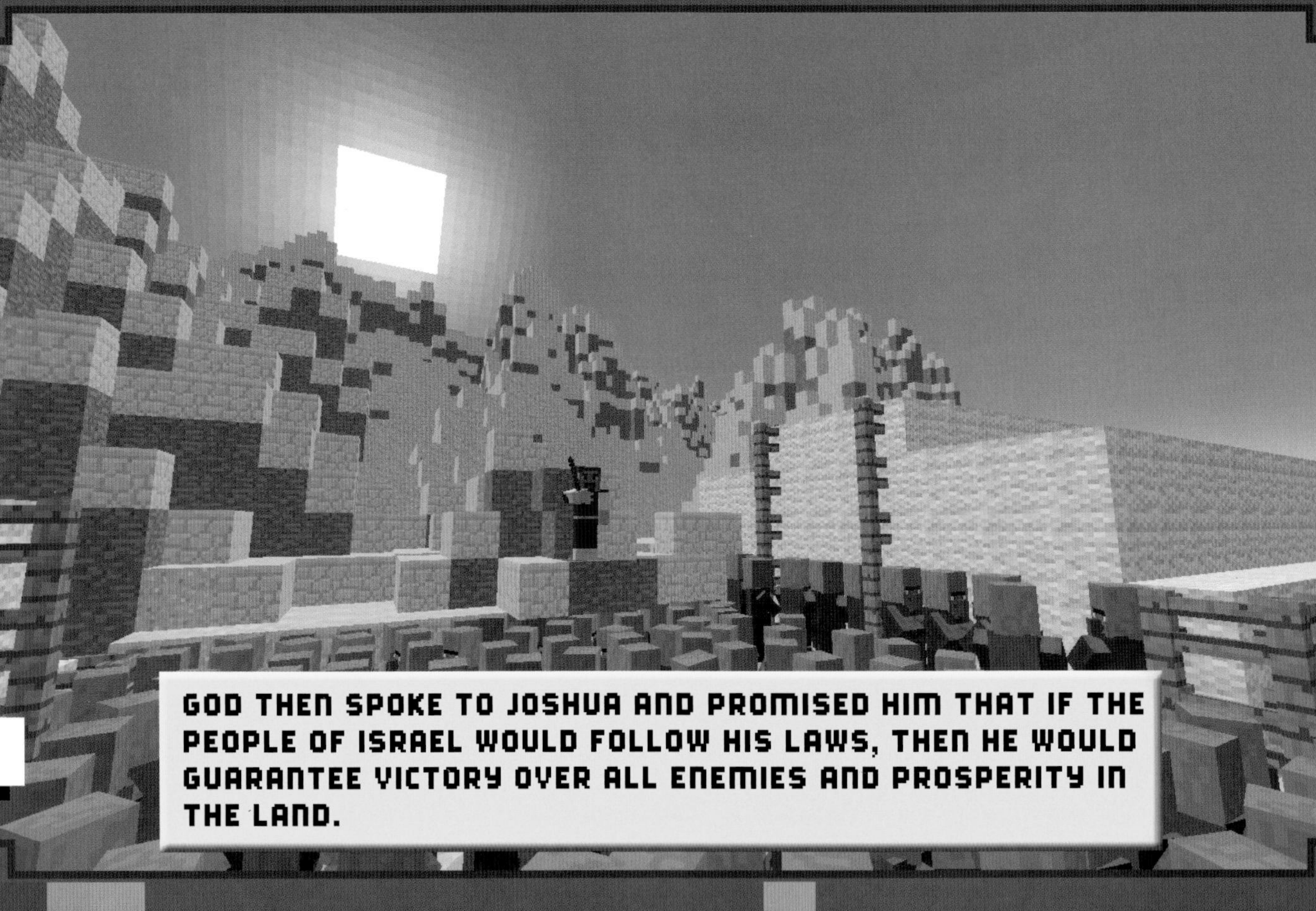
GOD THEN SPOKE TO JOSHUA AND PROMISED HIM THAT IF THE PEOPLE OF ISRAEL WOULD FOLLOW HIS LAWS, THEN HE WOULD GUARANTEE VICTORY OVER ALL ENEMIES AND PROSPERITY IN THE LAND.

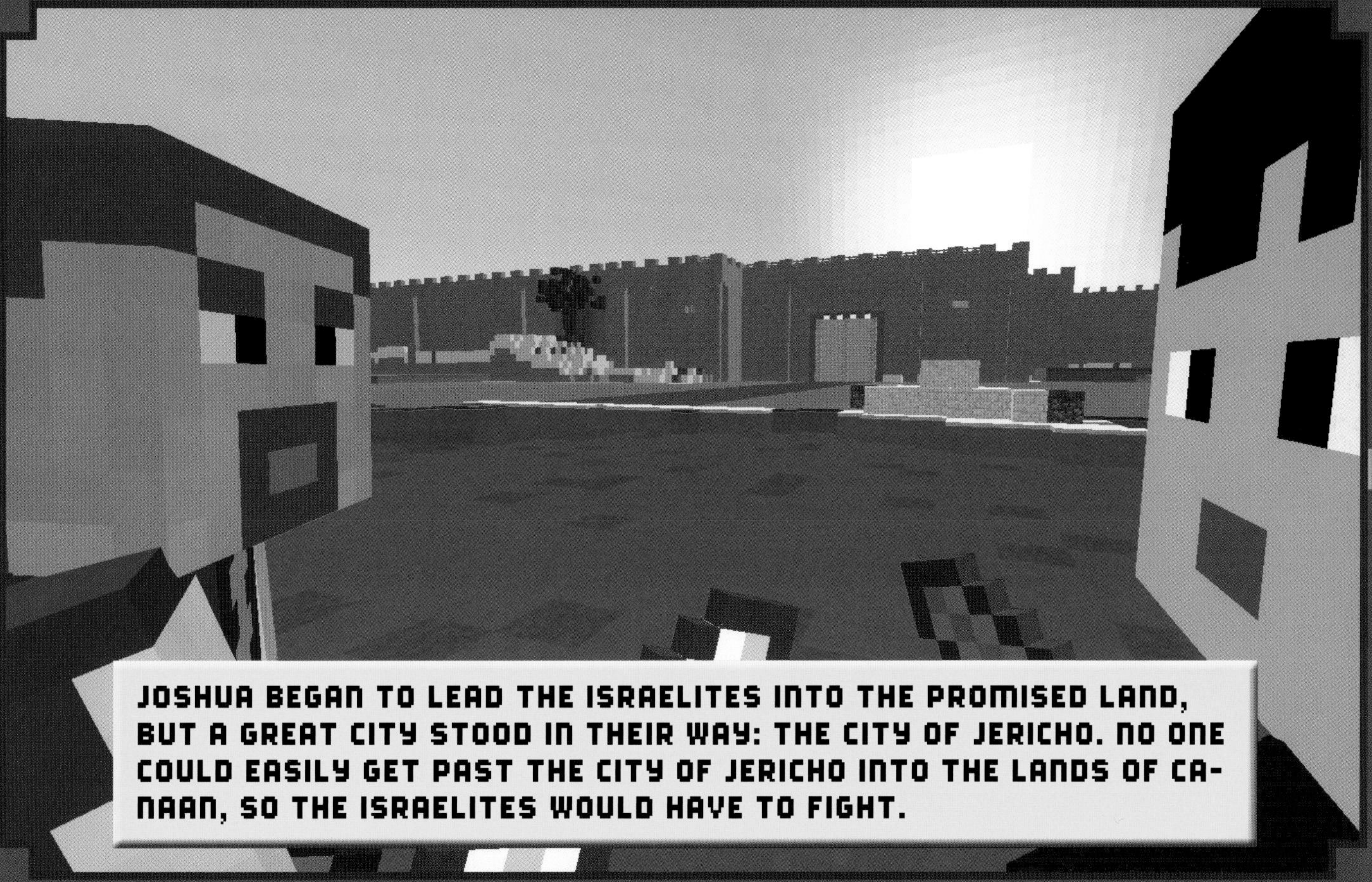
JOSHUA BEGAN TO LEAD THE ISRAELITES INTO THE PROMISED LAND, BUT A GREAT CITY STOOD IN THEIR WAY: THE CITY OF JERICHO. NO ONE COULD EASILY GET PAST THE CITY OF JERICHO INTO THE LANDS OF CANAAN, SO THE ISRAELITES WOULD HAVE TO FIGHT.

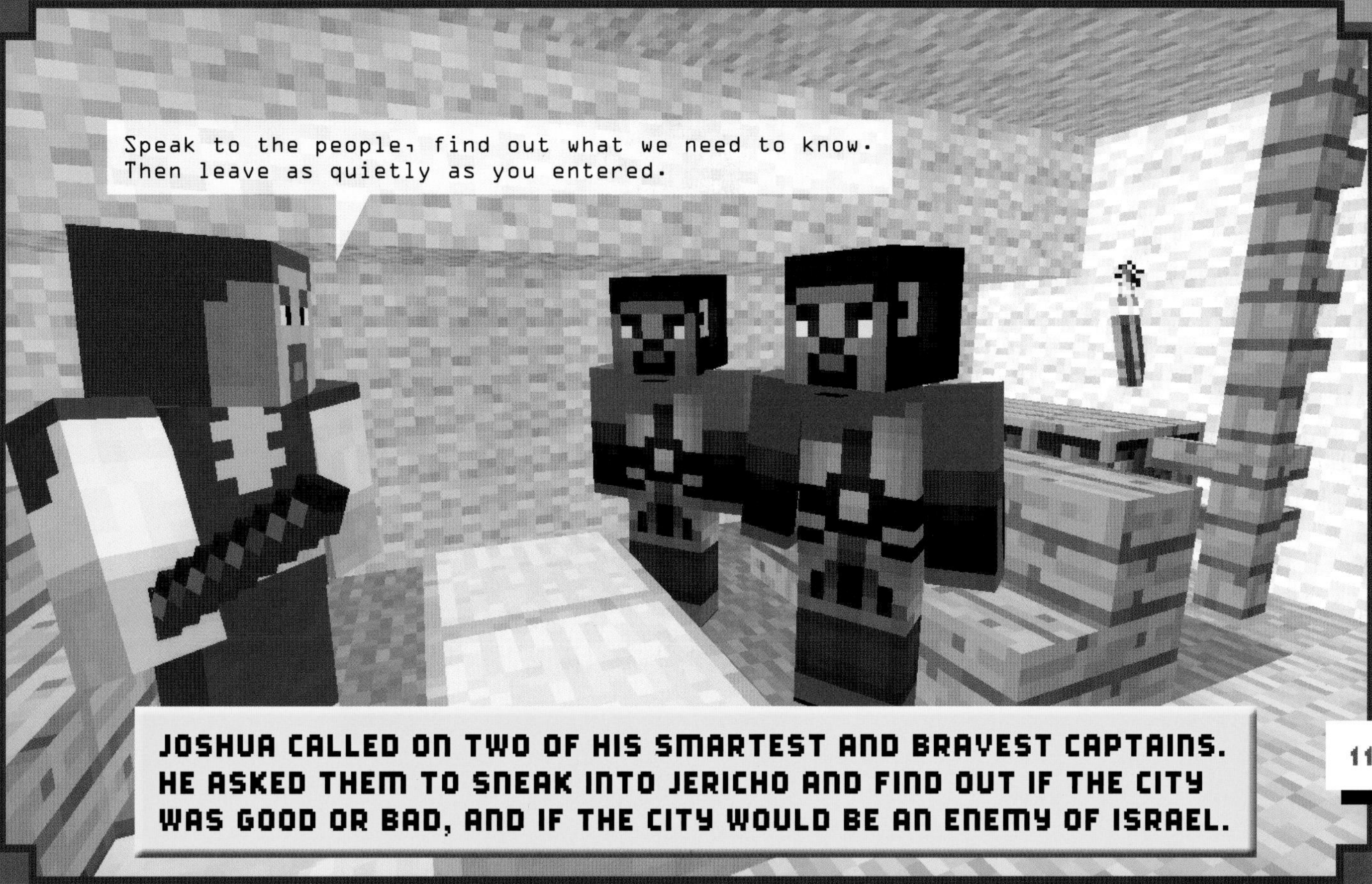
Speak to the people, find out what we need to know. Then leave as quietly as you entered.
JOSHUA CALLED ON TWO OF HIS SMARTEST AND BRAVEST CAPTAINS. HE ASKED THEM TO SNEAK INTO JERICHO AND FIND OUT IF THE CITY WAS GOOD OR BAD, AND IF THE CITY WOULD BE AN ENEMY OF ISRAEL.

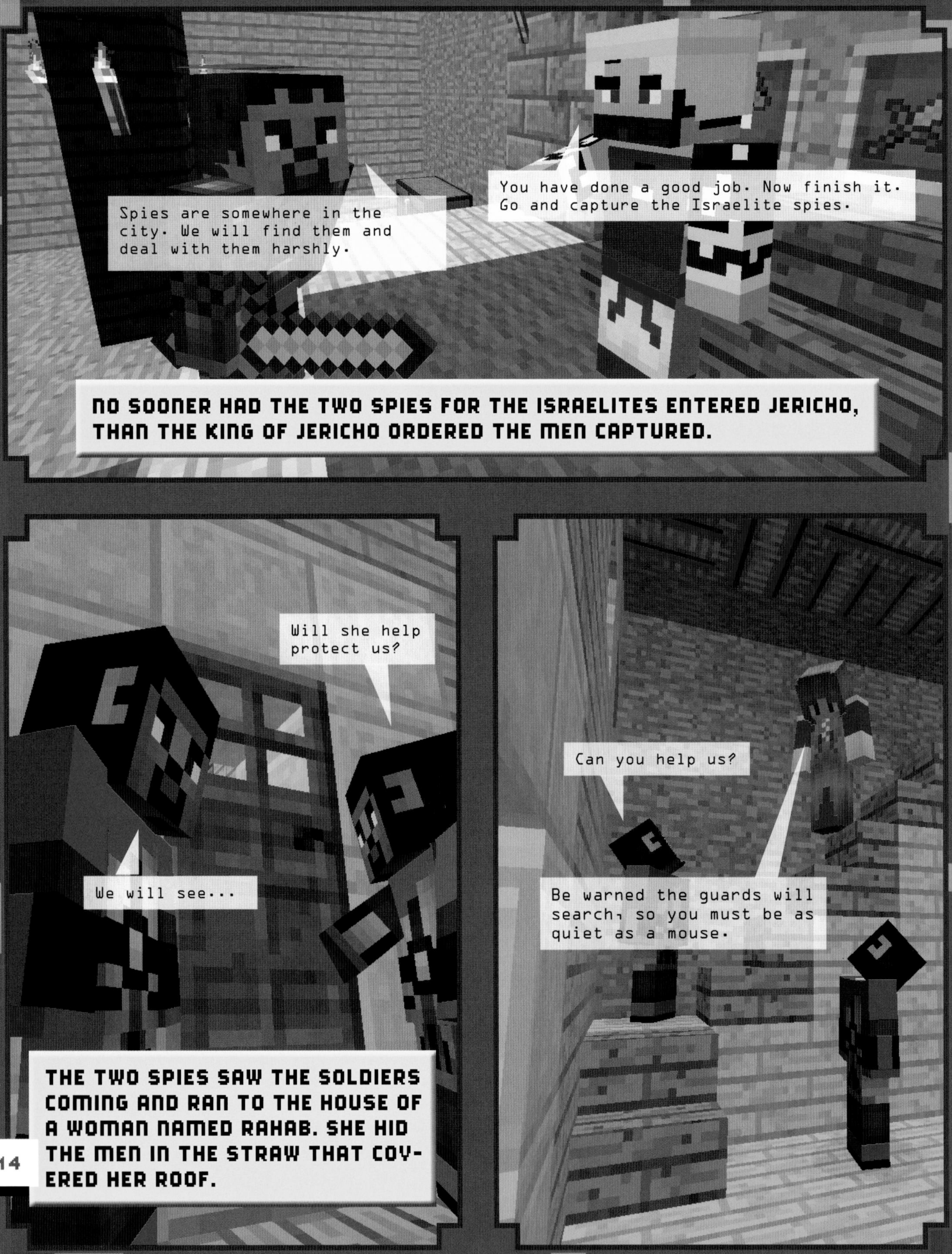
Spies are somewhere in the city. We will find them and deal with them harshly.
You have done a good job. Now finish it. Go and capture the Israelite spies.
NO SOONER HAD THE TWO SPIES FOR THE ISRAELITES ENTERED JERICHO, THAN THE KING OF JERICHO ORDERED THE MEN CAPTURED.
Will she help protect us?
We will see...
THE TWO SPIES SAW THE SOLDIERS COMING AND RAN TO THE HOUSE OF A WOMAN NAMED RAHAB. SHE HID THE MEN IN THE STRAW THAT COV-ERED HER ROOF.
Can you help us?
Be warned the guards will search, so you must be as quiet as a mouse.

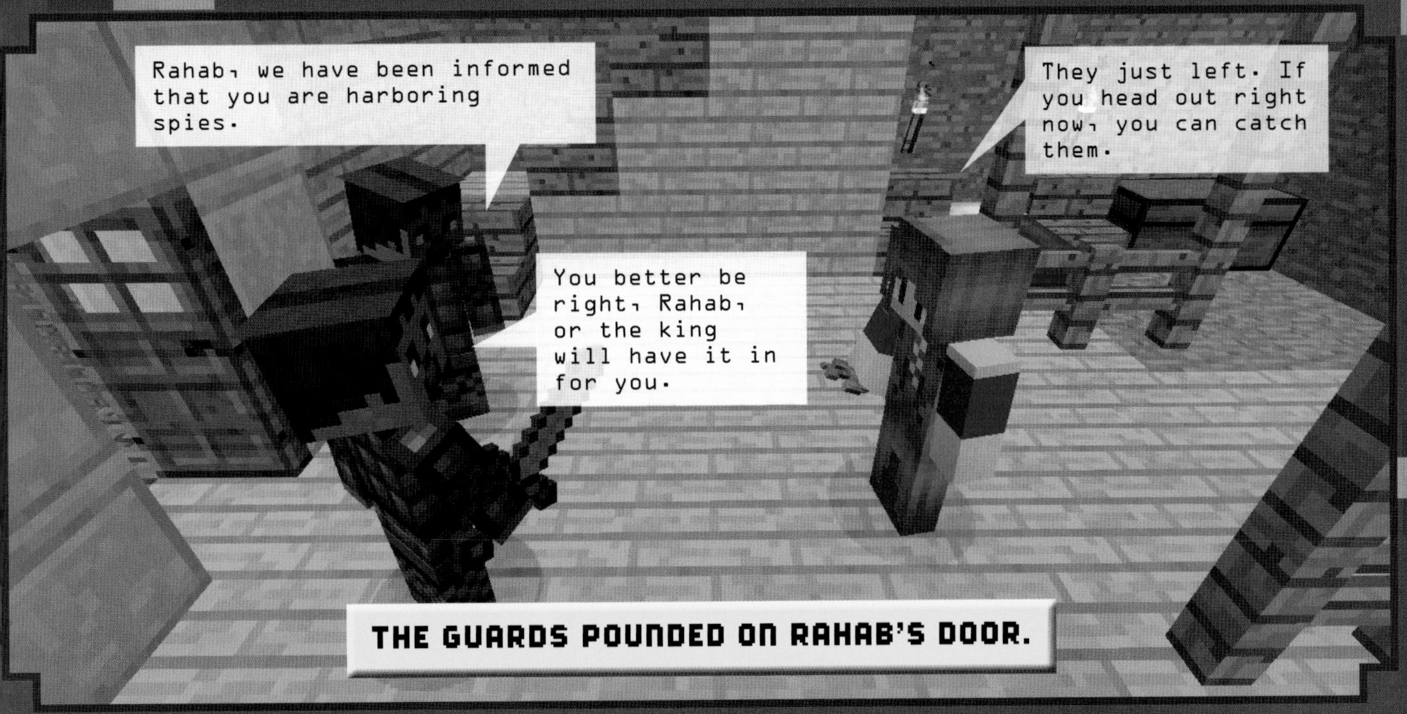
Rahab, we have been informed that you are harboring spies.
They just left. If you head out right now, you can catch them.
You better be right, Rahab, or the king will have it in for you.
THE GUARDS POUNDED ON RAHAB'S DOOR.

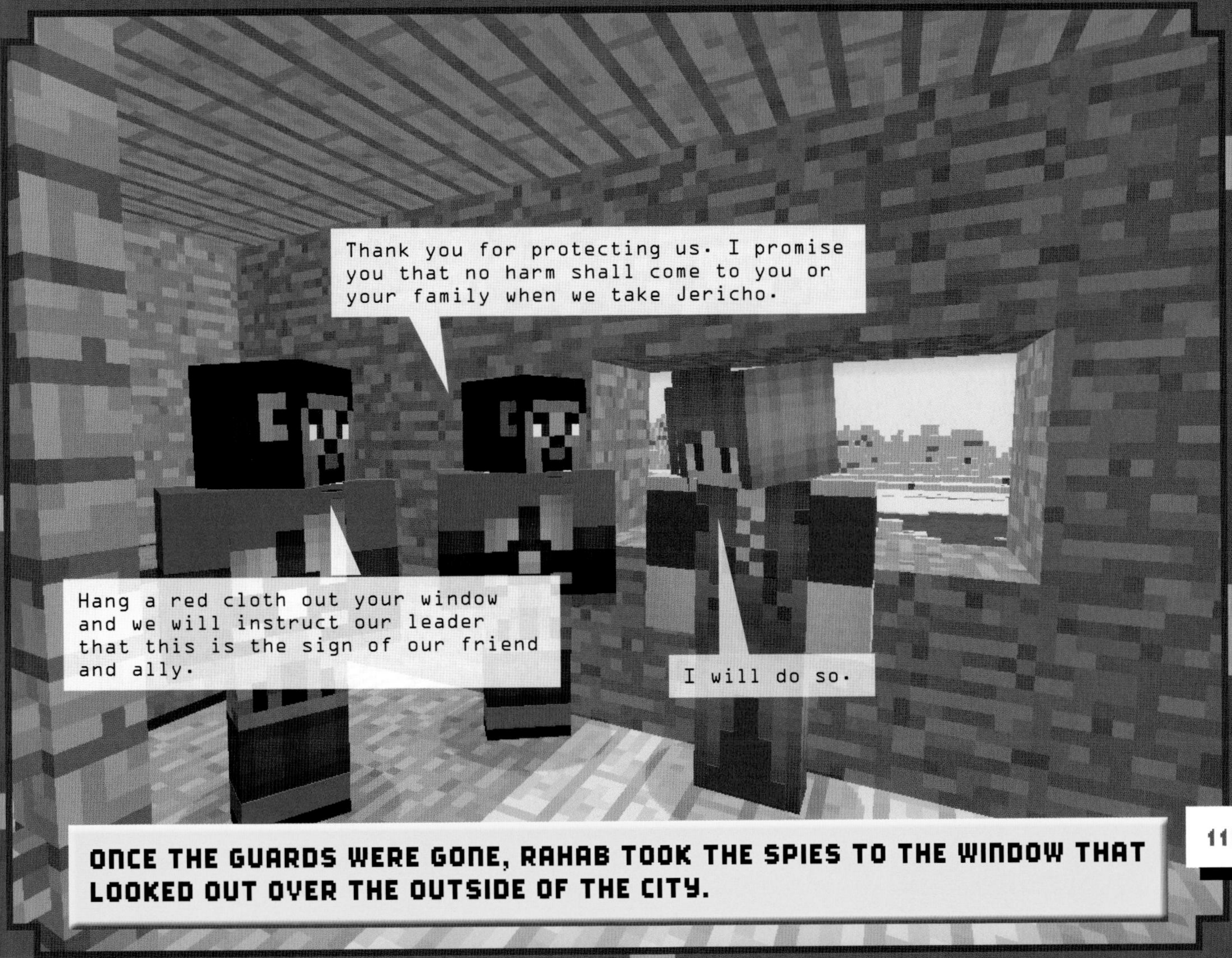
Thank you for protecting us. I promise you that no harm shall come to you or your family when we take Jericho.
Hang a red cloth out your window and we will instruct our leader that this is the sign of our friend and ally.
I will do so.
ONCE THE GUARDS WERE GONE, RAHAB TOOK THE SPIES TO THE WINDOW THAT LOOKED OUT OVER THE OUTSIDE OF THE CITY.

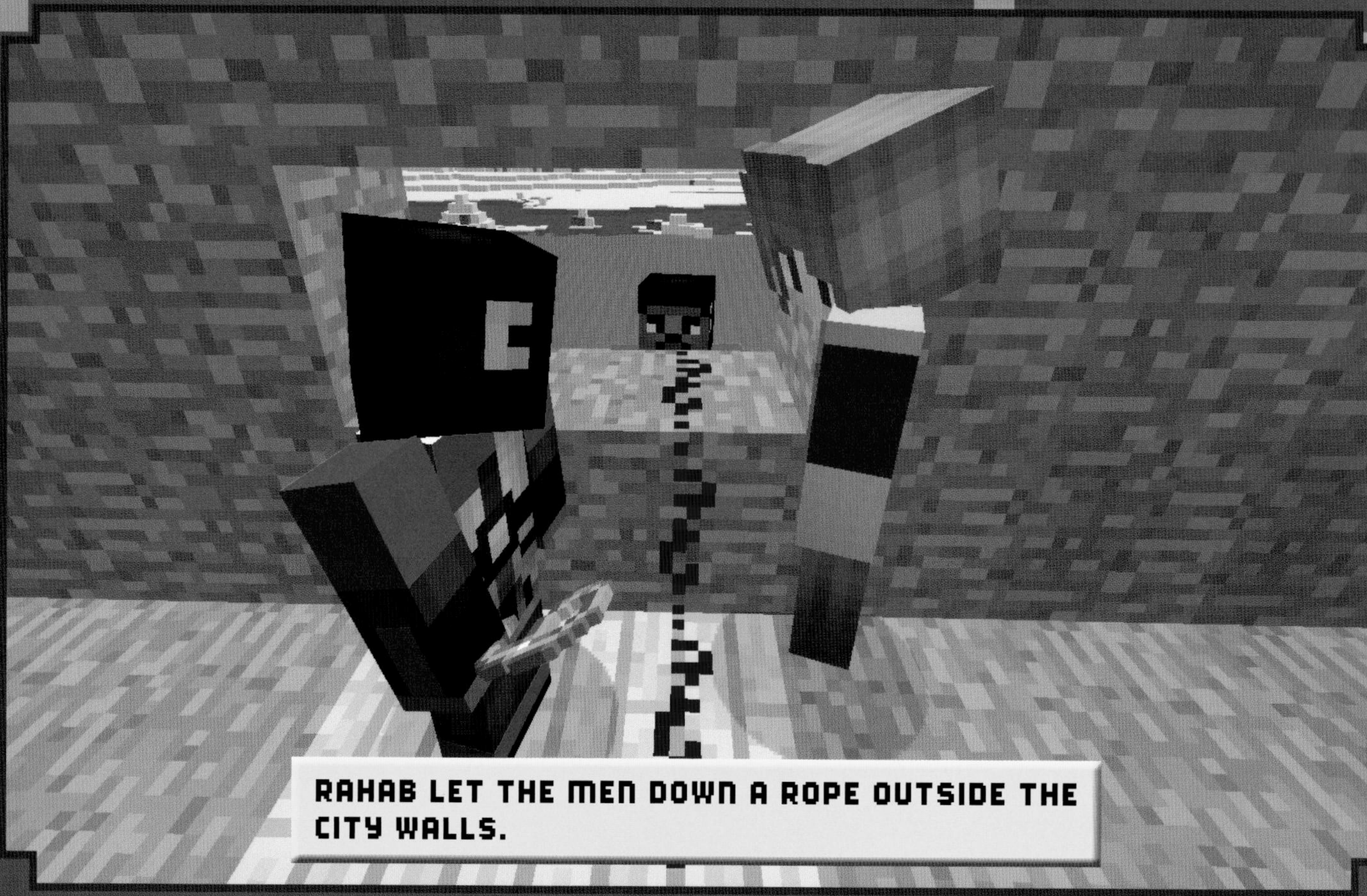
RAHAB LET THE MEN DOWN A ROPE OUTSIDE THE CITY WALLS.

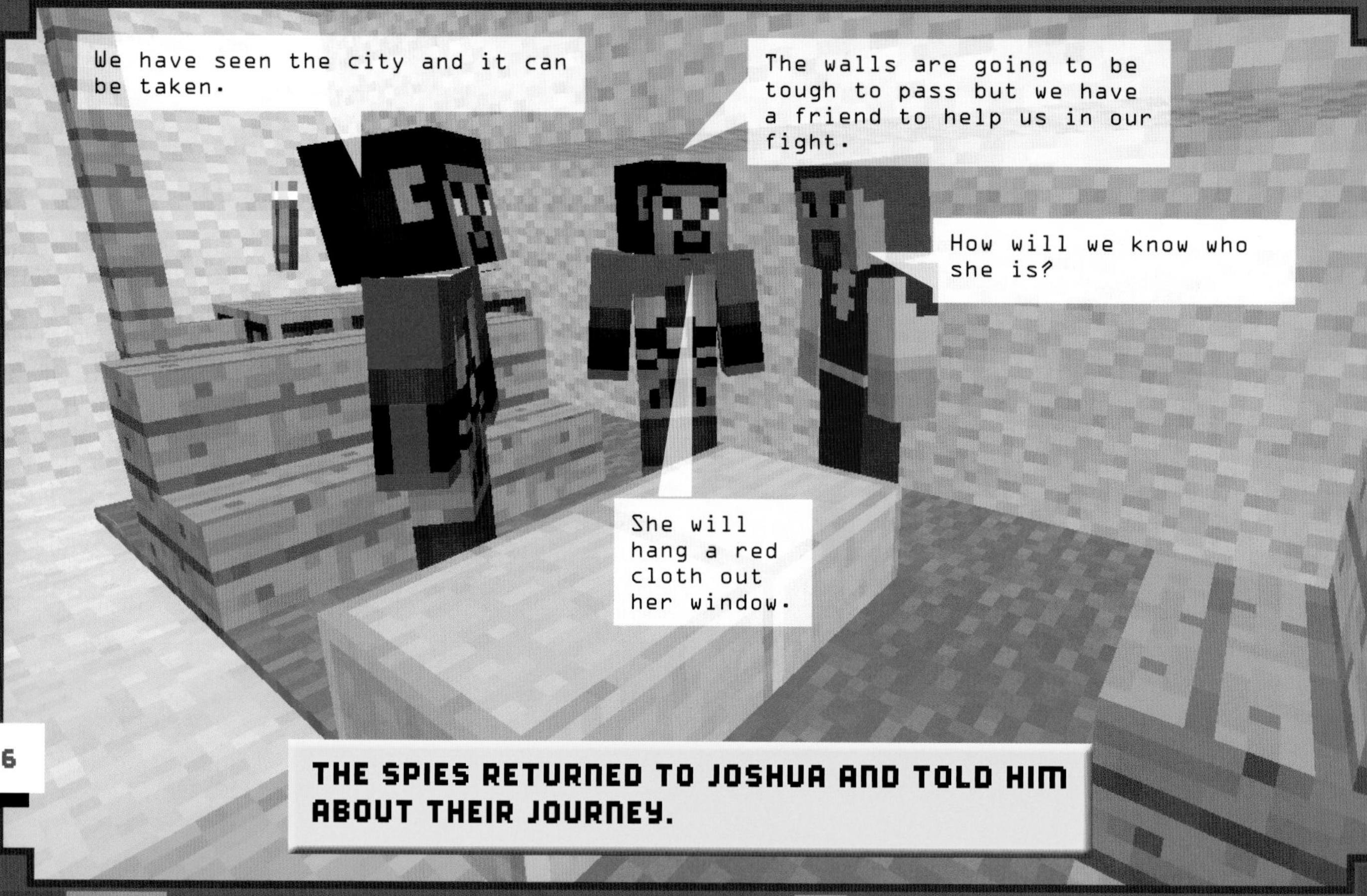
We have seen the city and it can be taken.
The walls are going to be tough to pass but we have a friend to help us in our fight.
How will we know who she is?
She will hang a red cloth out her window.
THE SPIES RETURNED TO JOSHUA AND TOLD HIM ABOUT THEIR JOURNEY.

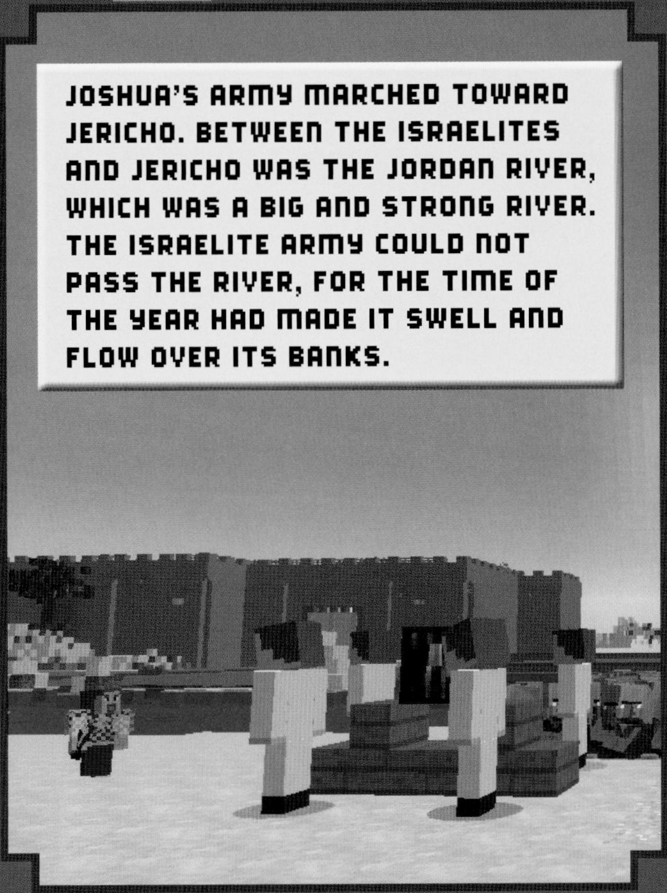
JOSHUA'S ARMY MARCHED TOWARD JERICHO. BETWEEN THE ISRAELITES AND JERICHO WAS THE JORDAN RIVER, WHICH WAS A BIG AND STRONG RIVER. THE ISRAELITE ARMY COULD NOT PASS THE RIVER, FOR THE TIME OF THE YEAR HAD MADE IT SWELL AND FLOW OVER ITS BANKS.

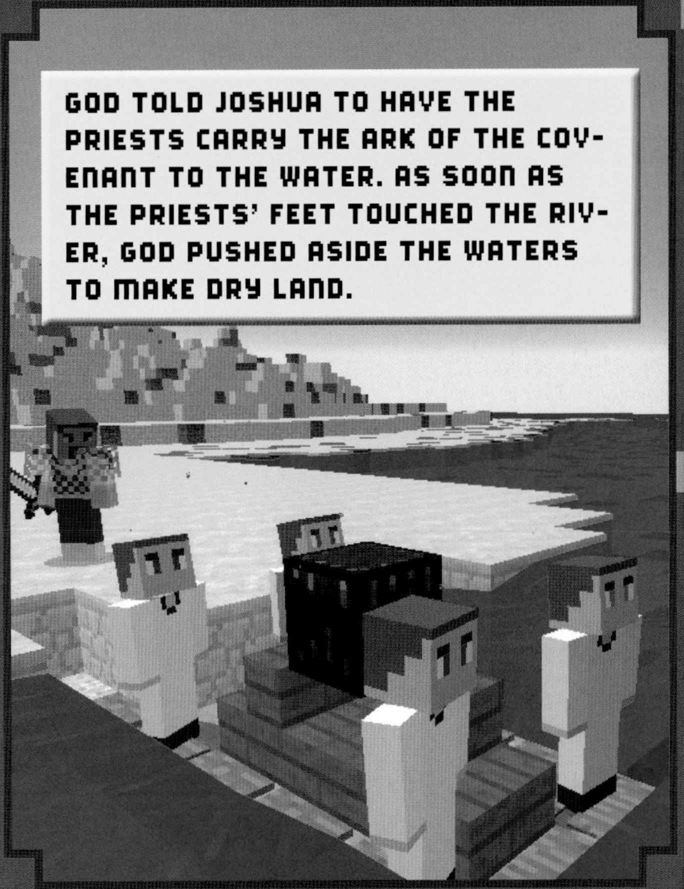
GOD TOLD JOSHUA TO HAVE THE PRIESTS CARRY THE ARK OF THE COVENANT TO THE WATER. AS SOON AS THE PRIESTS' FEET TOUCHED THE RIVER, GOD PUSHED ASIDE THE WATERS TO MAKE DRY LAND.

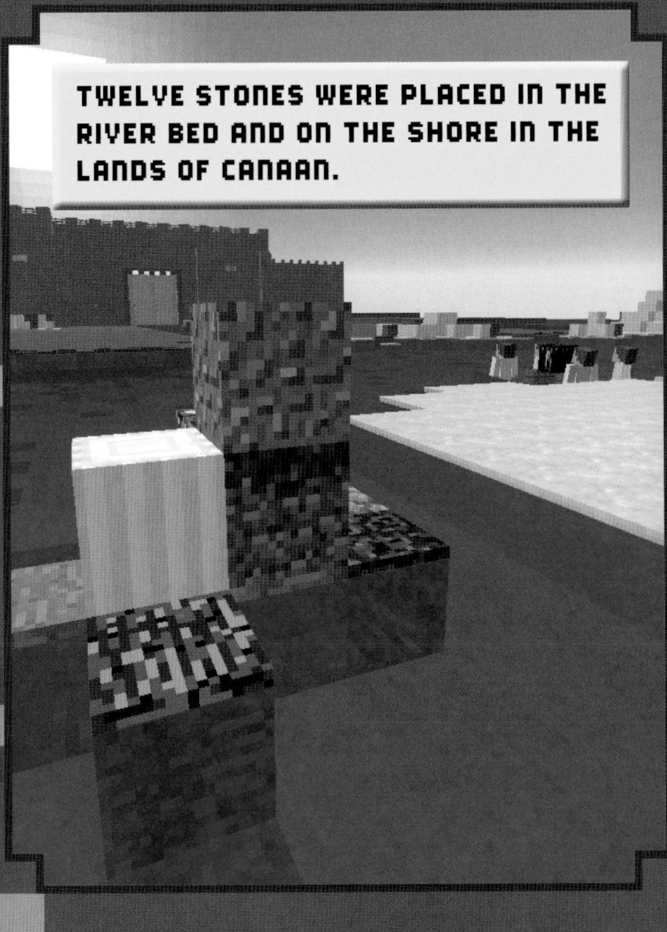
TWELVE STONES WERE PLACED IN THE RIVER BED AND ON THE SHORE IN THE LANDS OF CANAAN.

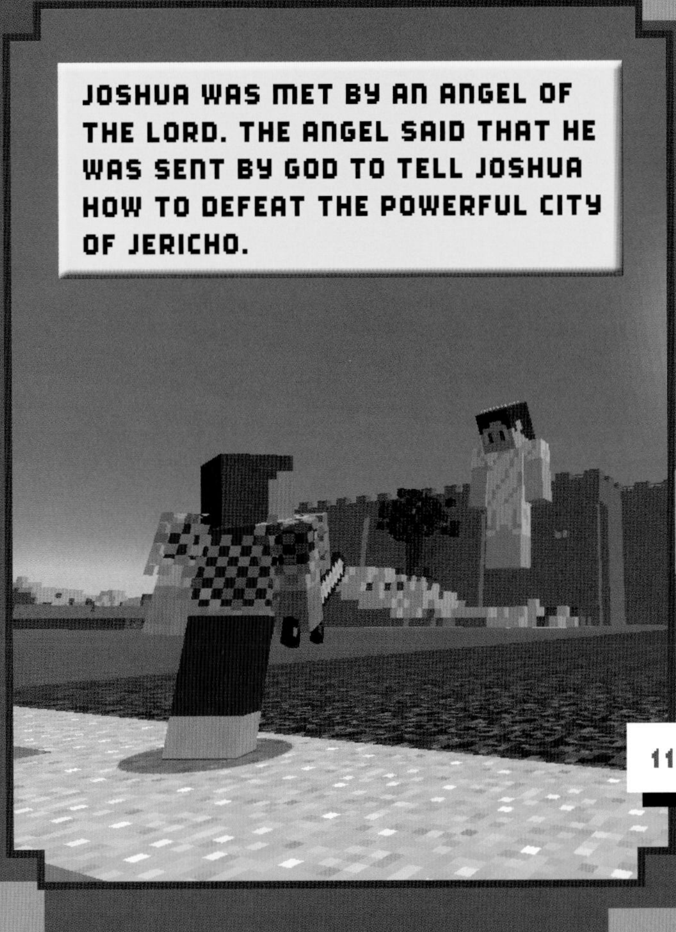
JOSHUA WAS MET BY AN ANGEL OF THE LORD. THE ANGEL SAID THAT HE WAS SENT BY GOD TO TELL JOSHUA HOW TO DEFEAT THE POWERFUL CITY OF JERICHO.

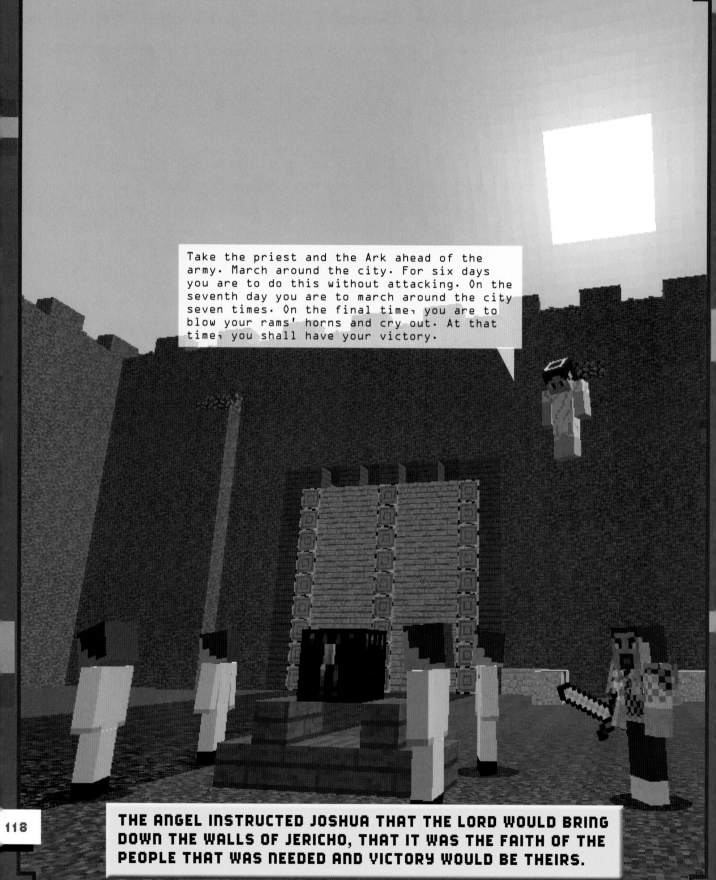

Take the priest and the Ark ahead of the army. March around the city. For six days you are to do this without attacking. On the seventh day you are to march around the city seven times. On the final time, you are to blow your rams' horns and cry out. At that time, you shall have your victory.

THE ANGEL INSTRUCTED JOSHUA THAT THE LORD WOULD BRING DOWN THE WALLS OF JERICHO, THAT IT WAS THE FAITH OF THE PEOPLE THAT WAS NEEDED AND VICTORY WOULD BE THEIRS.

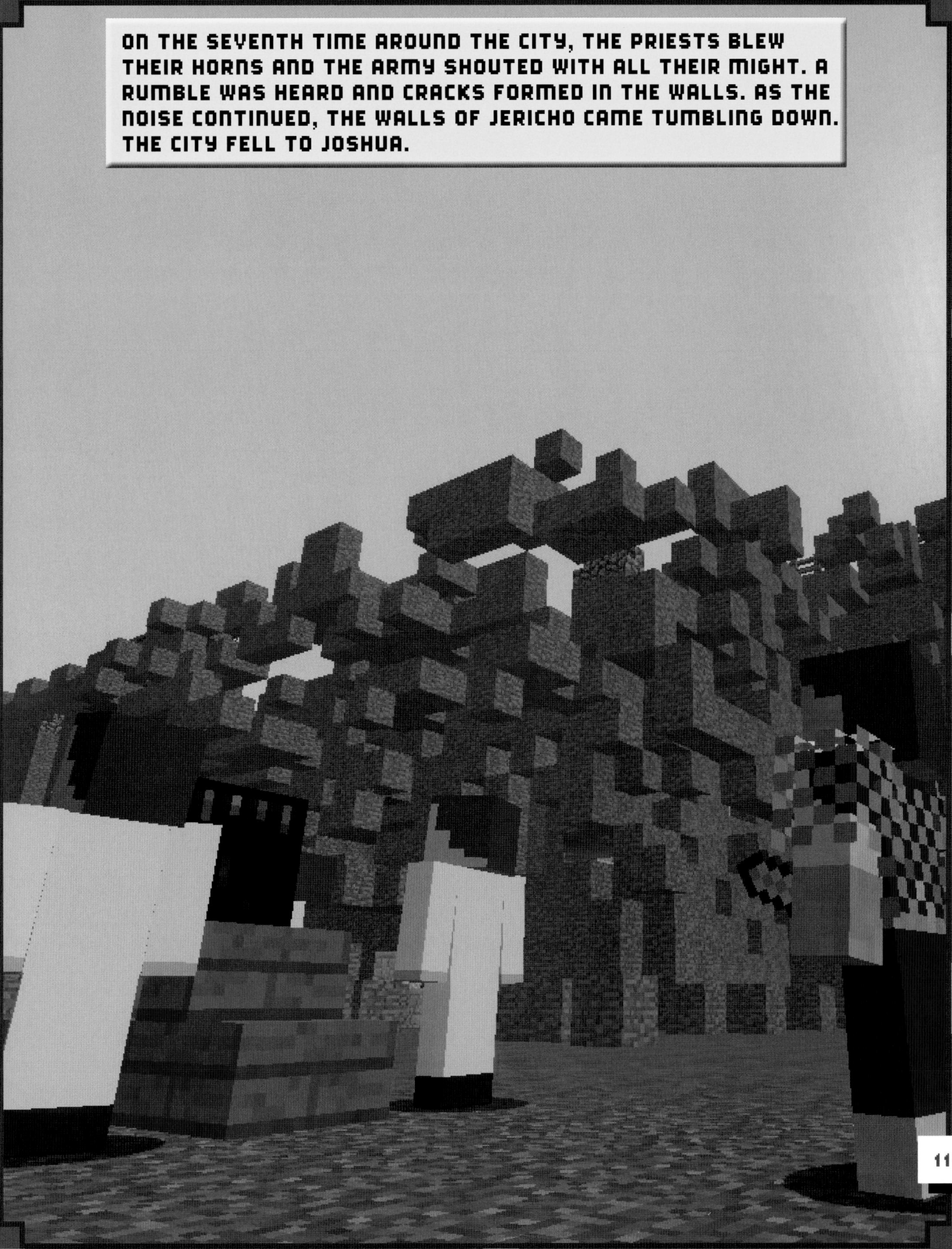
ON THE SEVENTH TIME AROUND THE CITY, THE PRIESTS BLEW THEIR HORNS AND THE ARMY SHOUTED WITH ALL THEIR MIGHT. A RUMBLE WAS HEARD AND CRACKS FORMED IN THE WALLS. AS THE NOISE CONTINUED, THE WALLS OF JERICHO CAME TUMBLING DOWN. THE CITY FELL TO JOSHUA.

RUTH

Eventually Joshua leads the Hebrews back to Canaan, right?

Yes, he does. But it isn't easy.

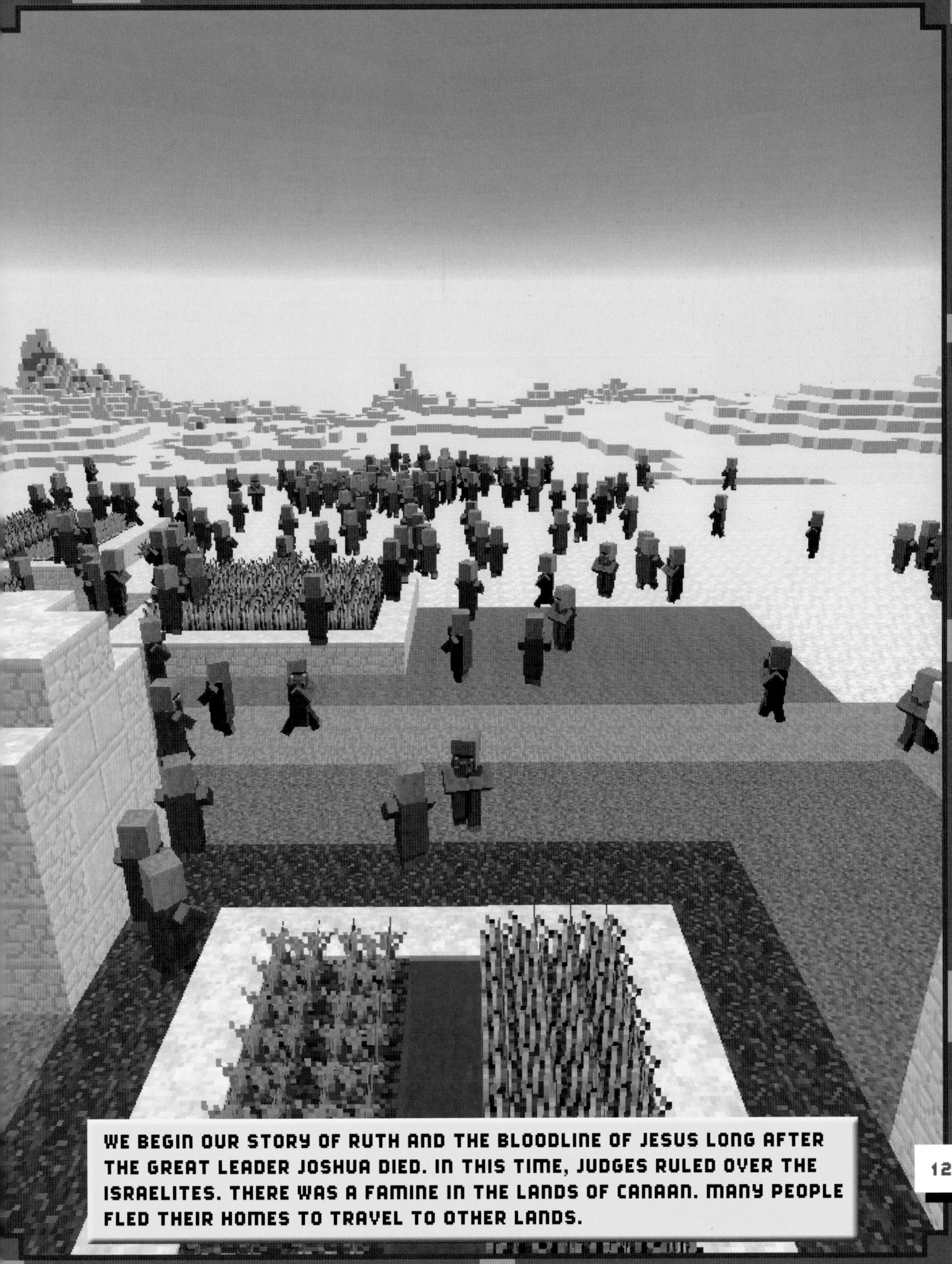
WE BEGIN OUR STORY OF RUTH AND THE BLOODLINE OF JESUS LONG AFTER THE GREAT LEADER JOSHUA DIED. IN THIS TIME, JUDGES RULED OVER THE ISRAELITES. THERE WAS A FAMINE IN THE LANDS OF CANAAN. MANY PEOPLE FLED THEIR HOMES TO TRAVEL TO OTHER LANDS.

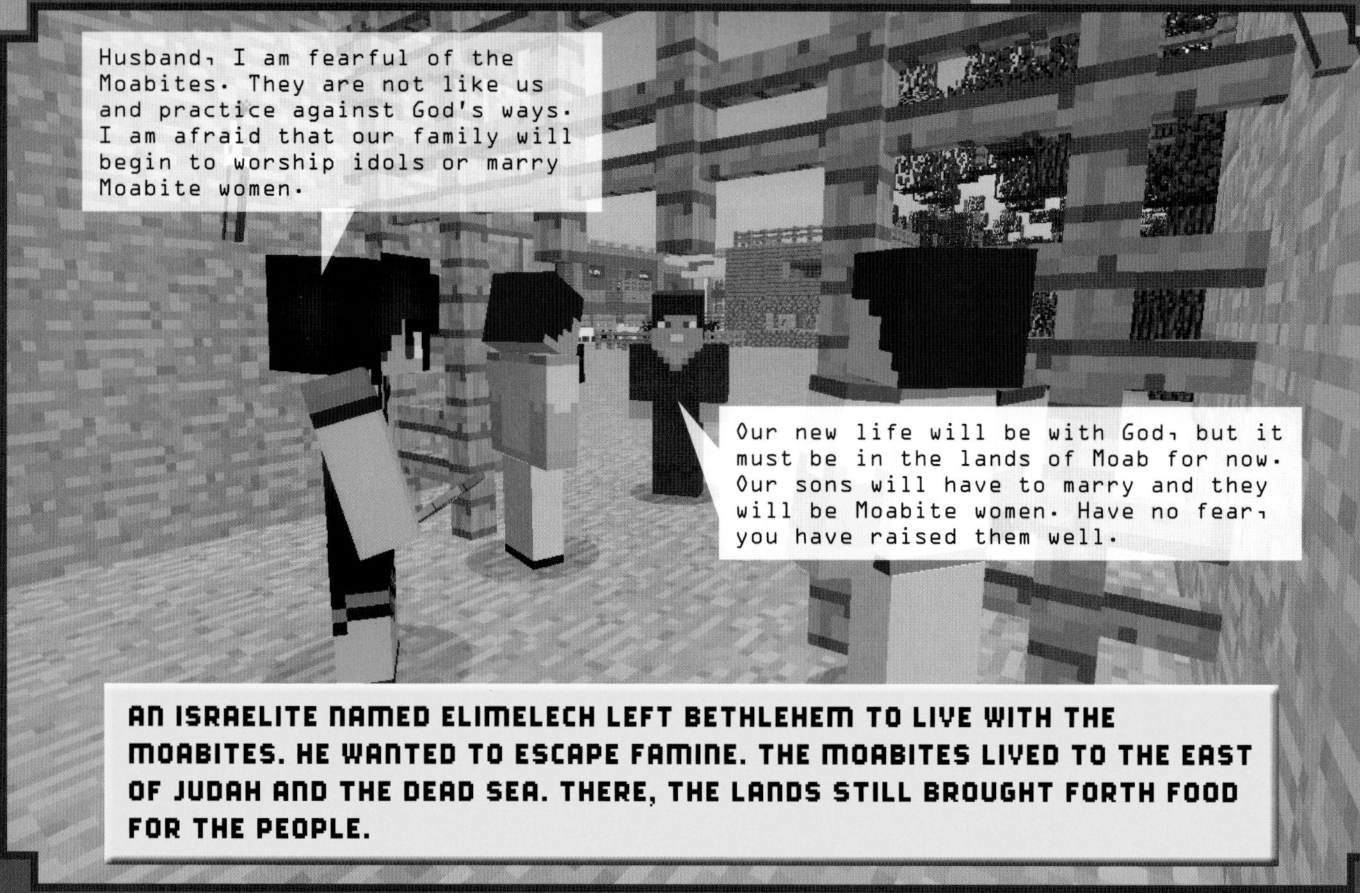
Husband, I am fearful of the Moabites. They are not like us and practice against God's ways. I am afraid that our family will begin to worship idols or marry Moabite women.
Our new life will be with God, but it must be in the lands of Moab for now. Our sons will have to marry and they will be Moabite women. Have no fear, you have raised them well.
AN ISRAELITE NAMED ELIMELECH LEFT BETHLEHEM TO LIVE WITH THE MOABITES. HE WANTED TO ESCAPE FAMINE. THE MOABITES LIVED TO THE EAST OF JUDAH AND THE DEAD SEA. THERE, THE LANDS STILL BROUGHT FORTH FOOD FOR THE PEOPLE.

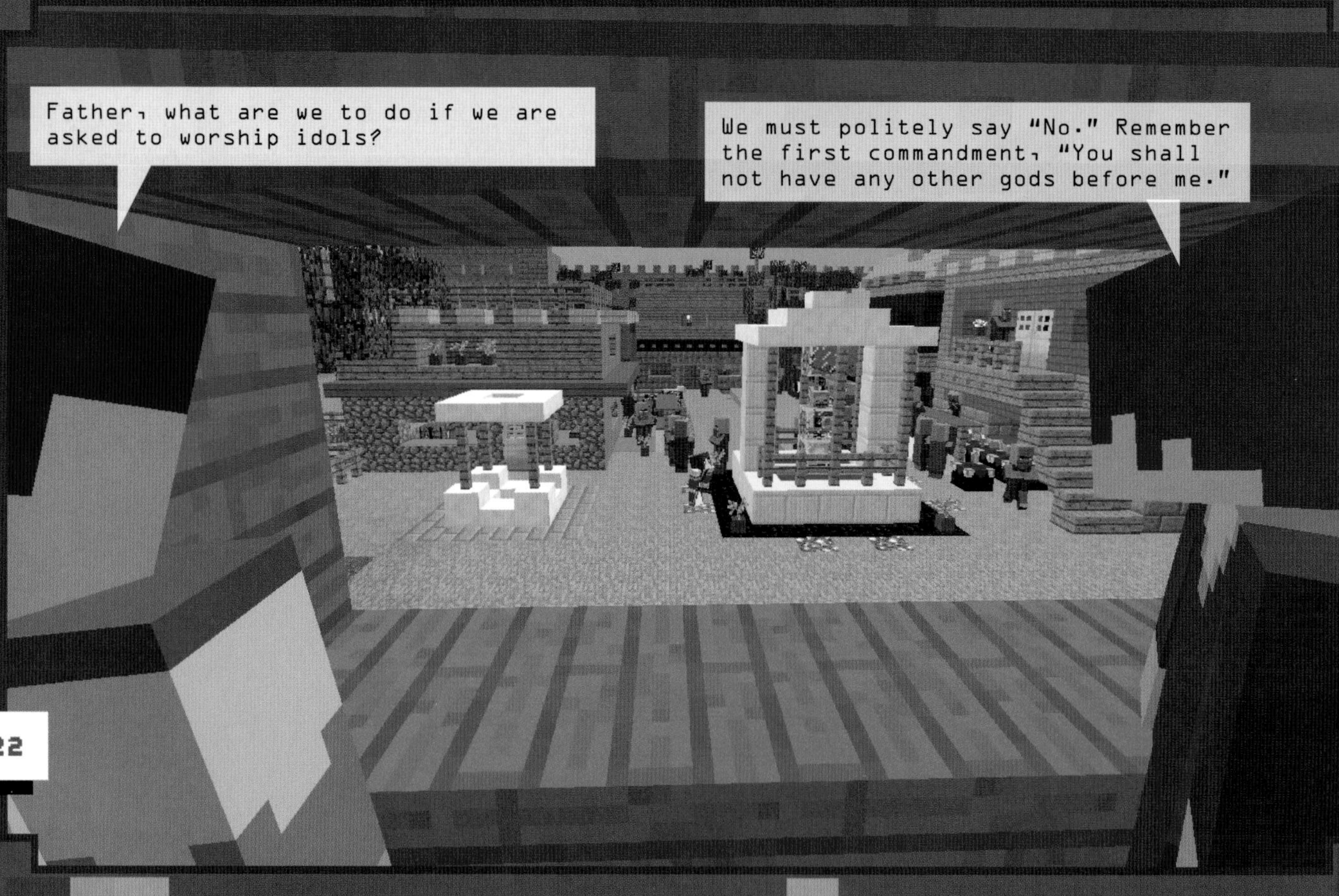
Father, what are we to do if we are asked to worship idols?
We must politely say "No." Remember the first commandment, "You shall not have any other gods before me."

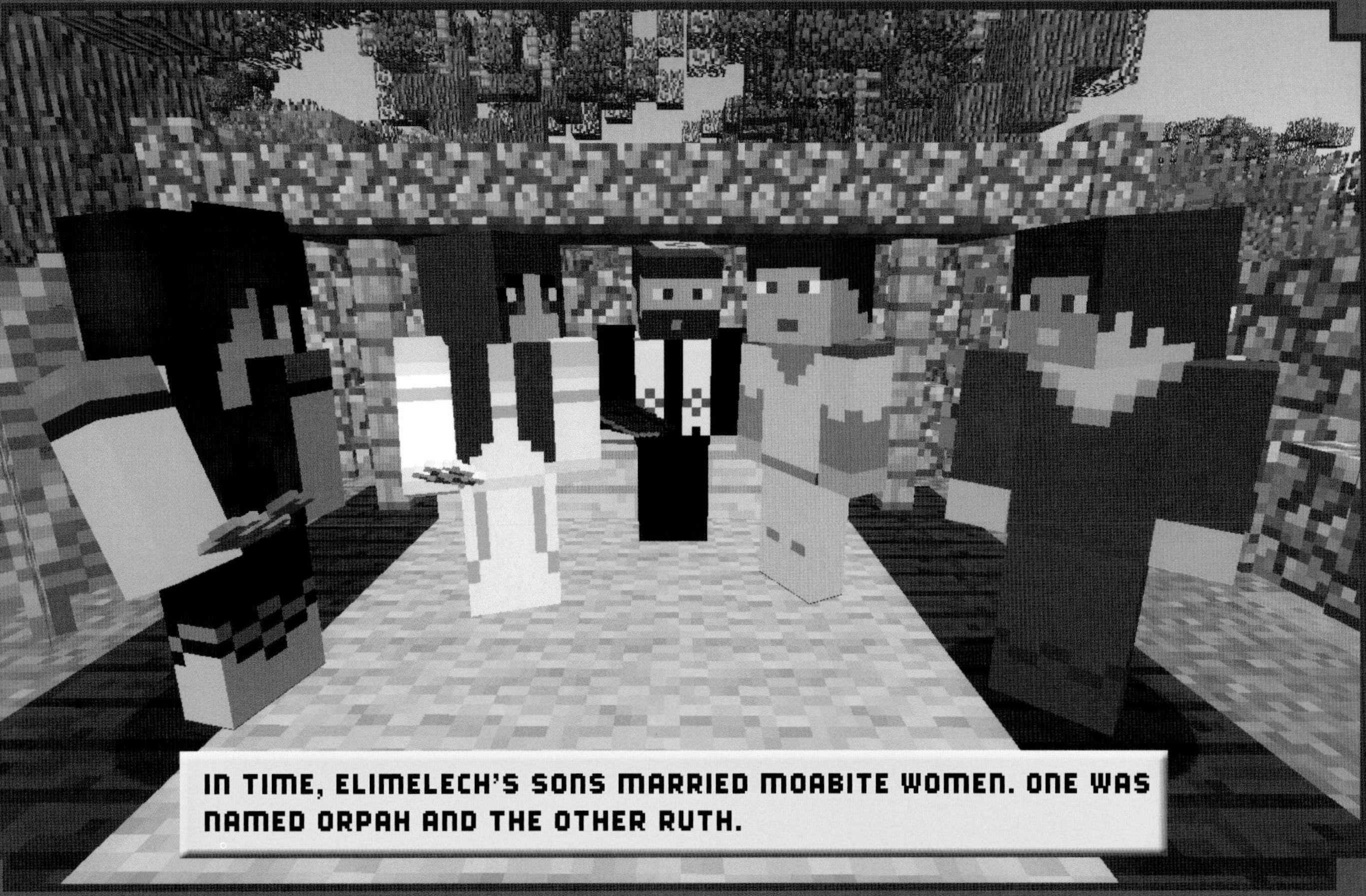
IN TIME, ELIMELECH'S SONS MARRIED MOABITE WOMEN. ONE WAS NAMED ORPAH AND THE OTHER RUTH.

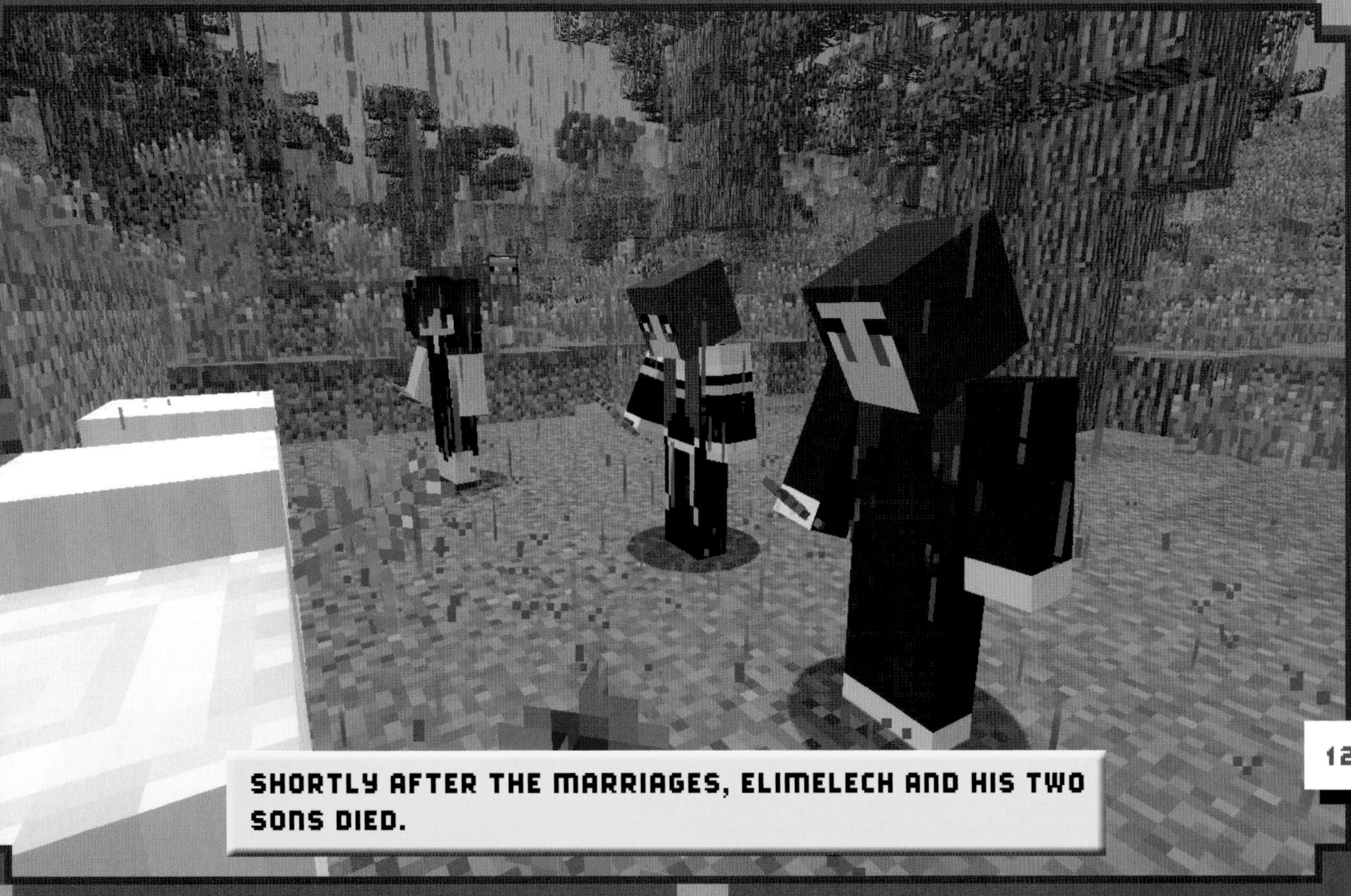
SHORTLY AFTER THE MARRIAGES, ELIMELECH AND HIS TWO SONS DIED.

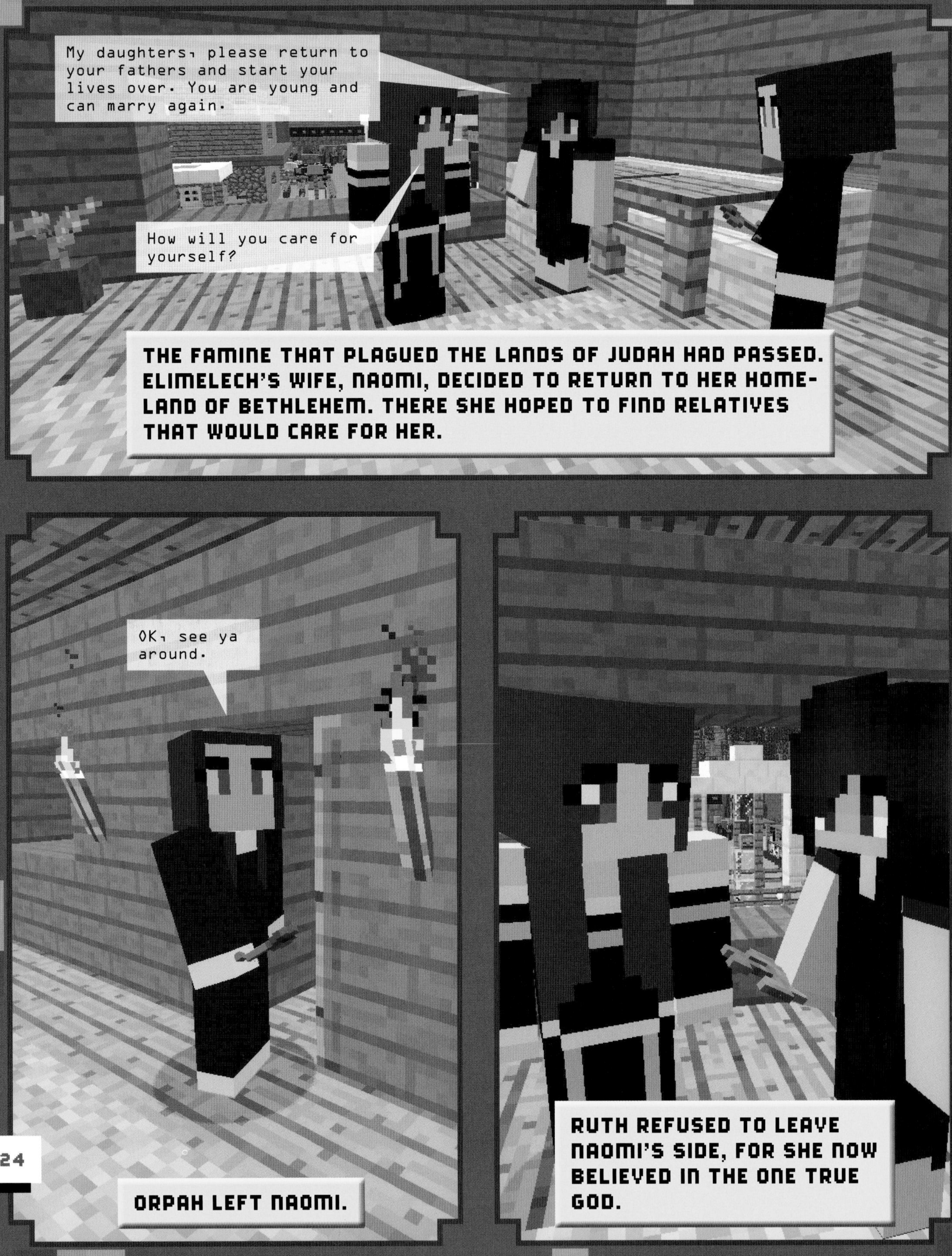
My daughters, please return to your fathers and start your lives over. You are young and can marry again.
How will you care for yourself?
THE FAMINE THAT PLAGUED THE LANDS OF JUDAH HAD PASSED. ELIMELECH'S WIFE, NAOMI, DECIDED TO RETURN TO HER HOMELAND OF BETHLEHEM. THERE SHE HOPED TO FIND RELATIVES THAT WOULD CARE FOR HER.
OK, see ya around.
ORPAH LEFT NAOMI.
RUTH REFUSED TO LEAVE NAOMI'S SIDE, FOR SHE NOW BELIEVED IN THE ONE TRUE GOD.

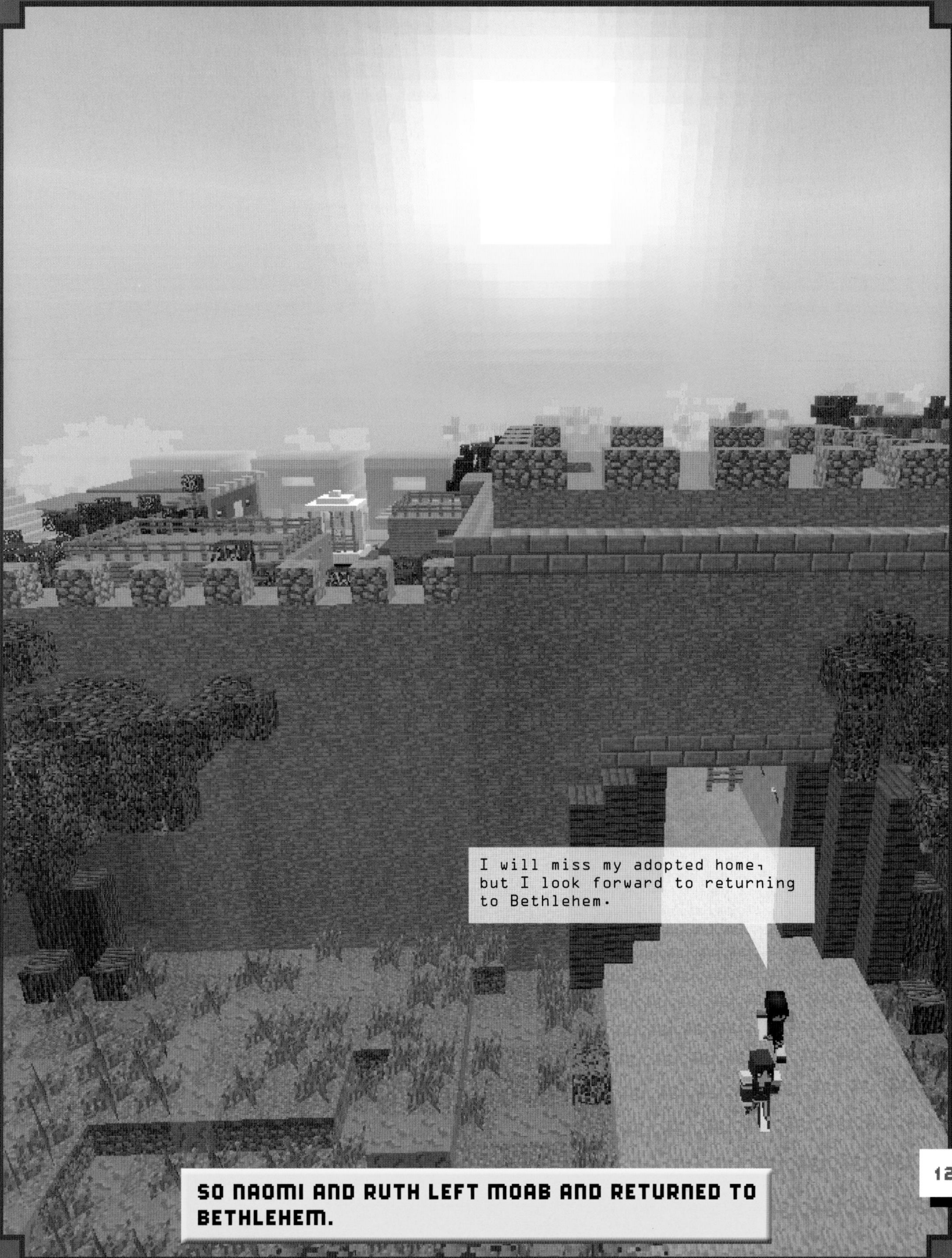
I will miss my adopted home, but I look forward to returning to Bethlehem.
SO NAOMI AND RUTH LEFT MOAB AND RETURNED TO BETHLEHEM.

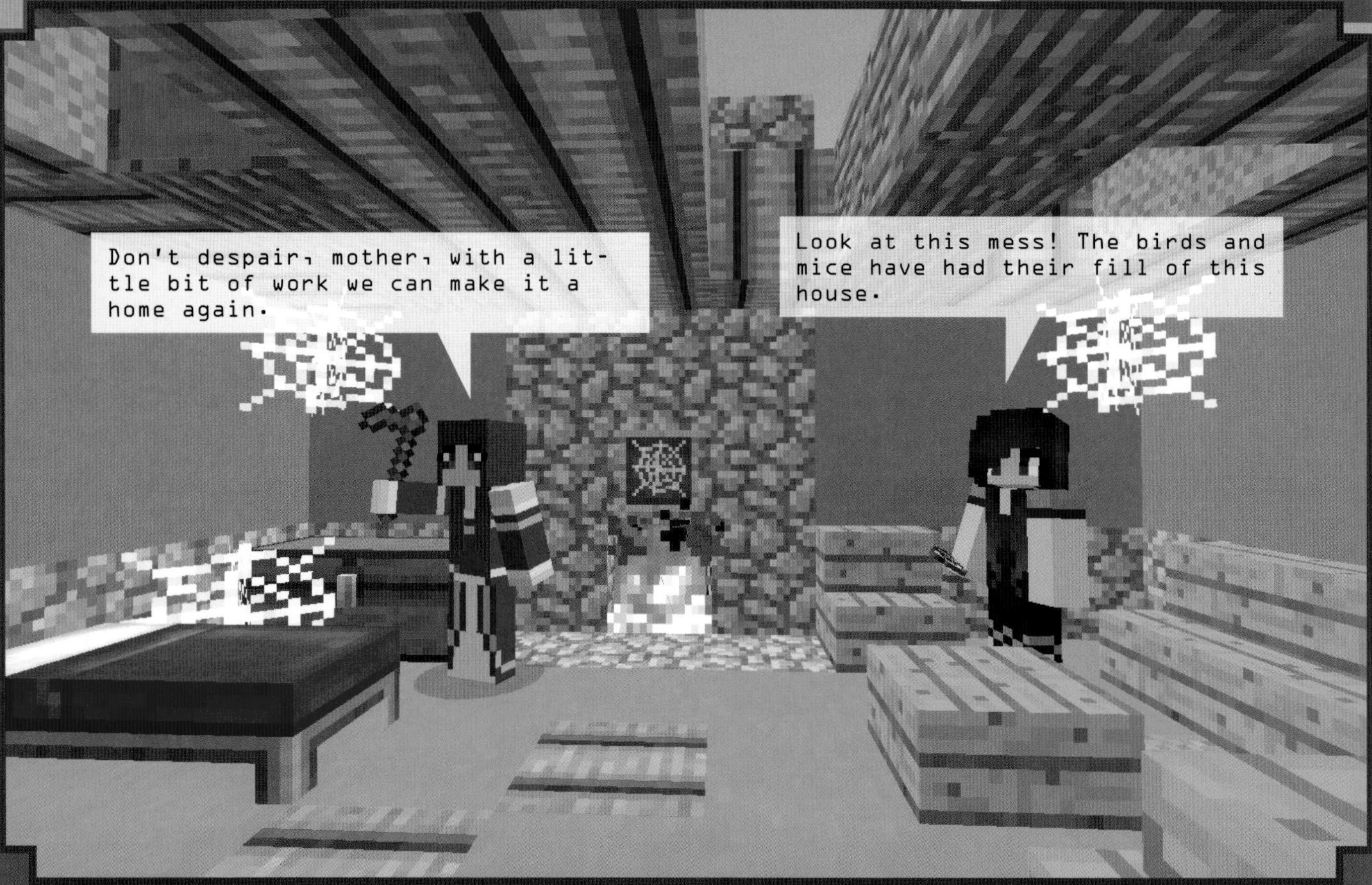
Don't despair, mother, with a little bit of work we can make it a home again.
Look at this mess! The birds and mice have had their fill of this house.

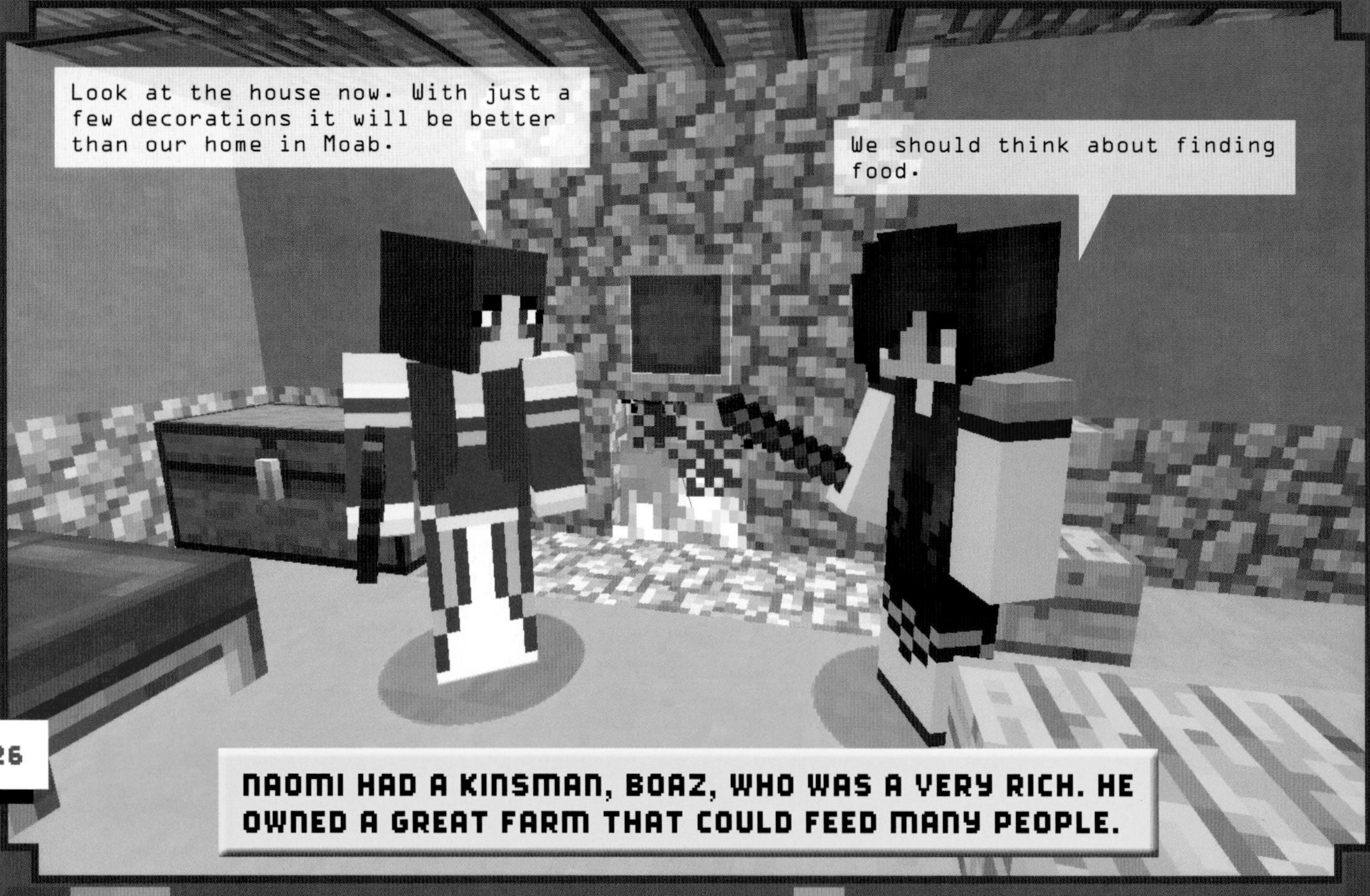
Look at the house now. With just a few decorations it will be better than our home in Moab.
We should think about finding food.
NAOMI HAD A KINSMAN, BOAZ, WHO WAS A VERY RICH. HE OWNED A GREAT FARM THAT COULD FEED MANY PEOPLE.

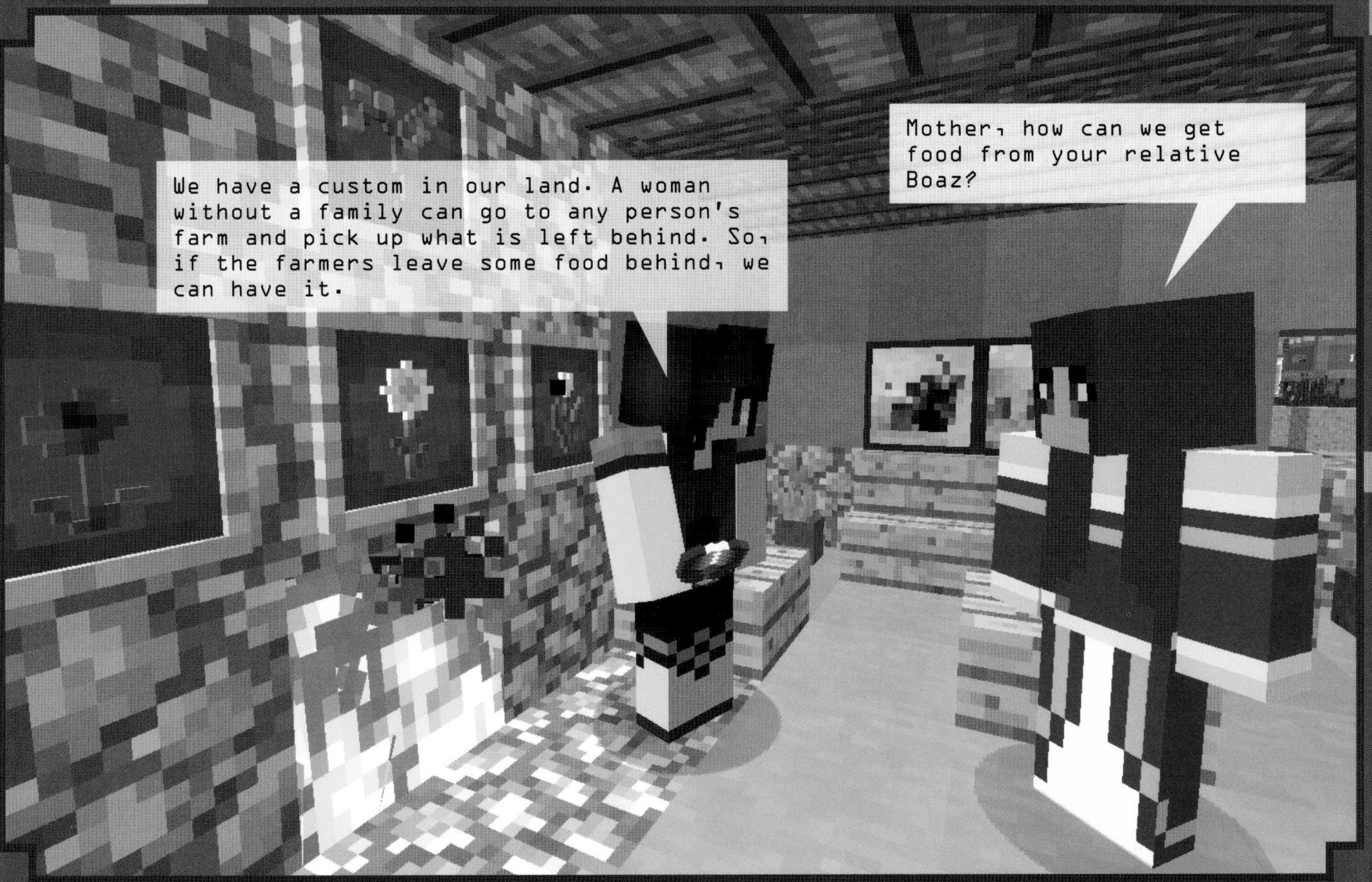
Mother, how can we get food from your relative Boaz?
We have a custom in our land. A woman without a family can go to any person's farm and pick up what is left behind. So, if the farmers leave some food behind, we can have it.

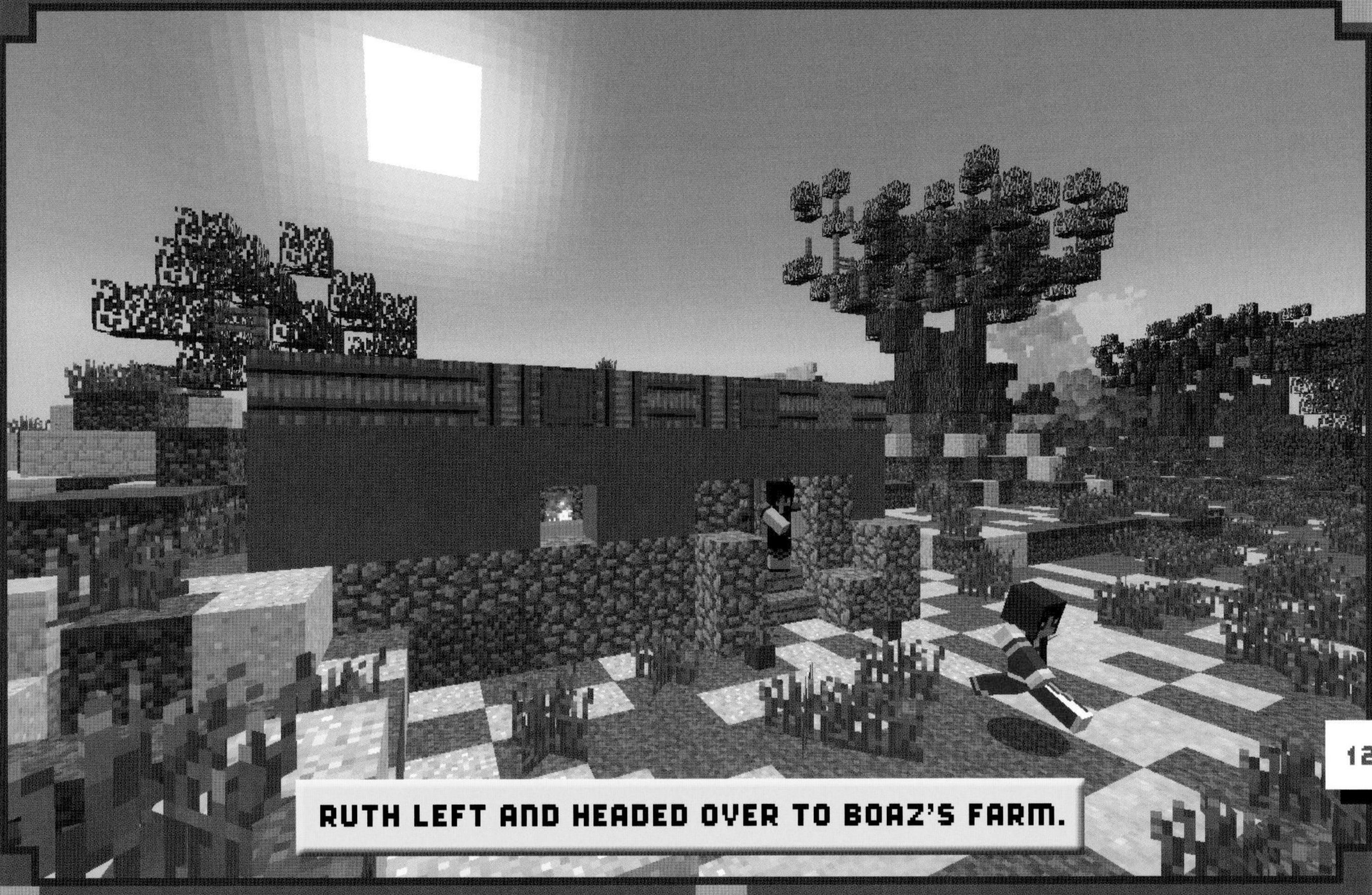
RUTH LEFT AND HEADED OVER TO BOAZ'S FARM.

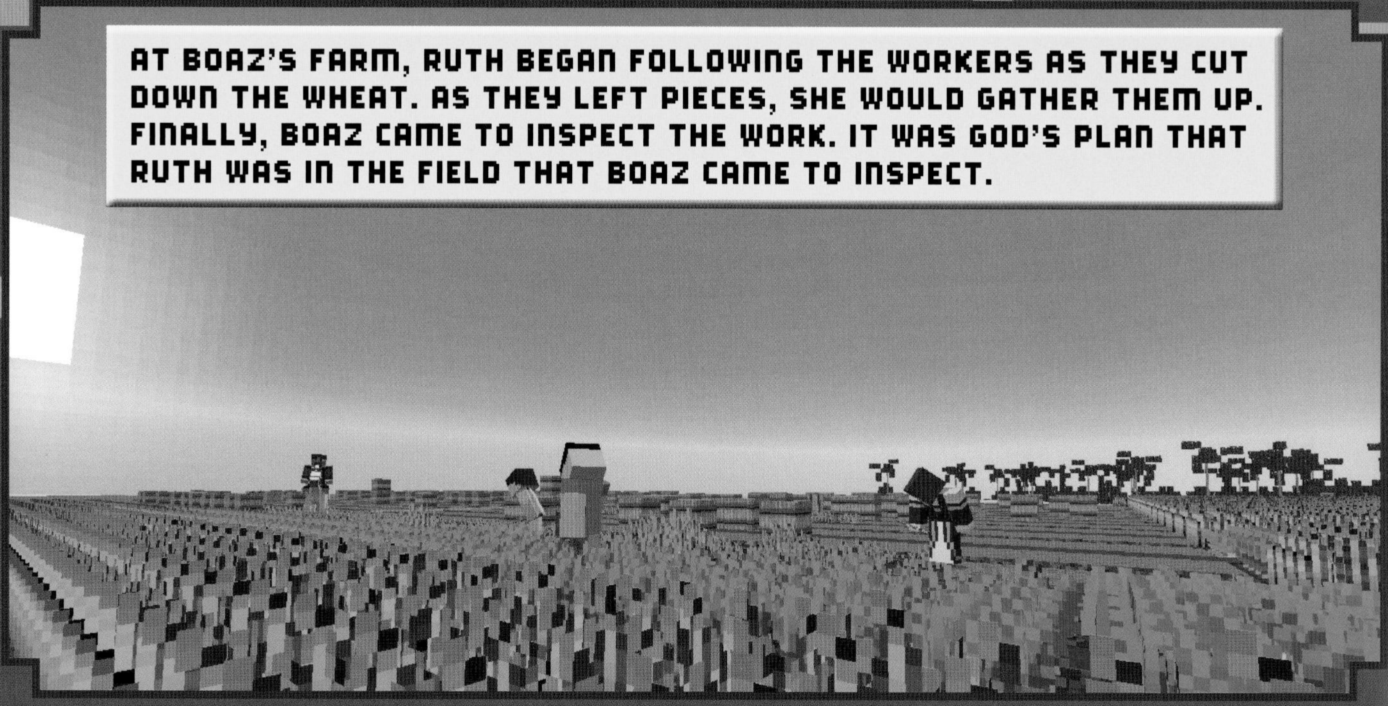
AT BOAZ'S FARM, RUTH BEGAN FOLLOWING THE WORKERS AS THEY CUT DOWN THE WHEAT. AS THEY LEFT PIECES, SHE WOULD GATHER THEM UP. FINALLY, BOAZ CAME TO INSPECT THE WORK. IT WAS GOD'S PLAN THAT RUTH WAS IN THE FIELD THAT BOAZ CAME TO INSPECT.

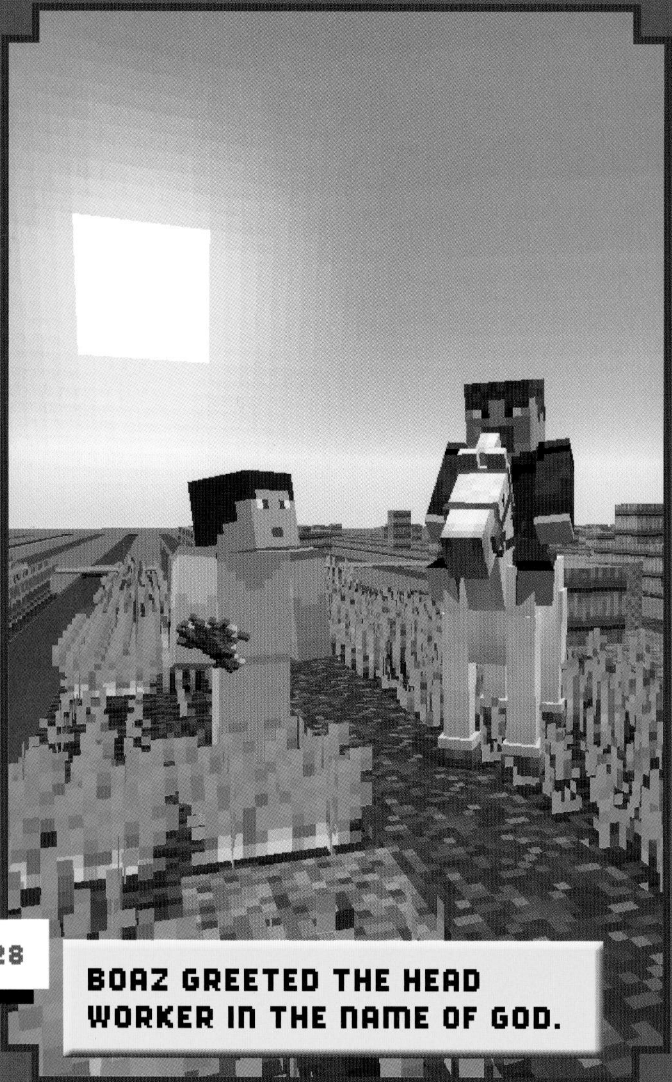
BOAZ GREETED THE HEAD WORKER IN THE NAME OF GOD.

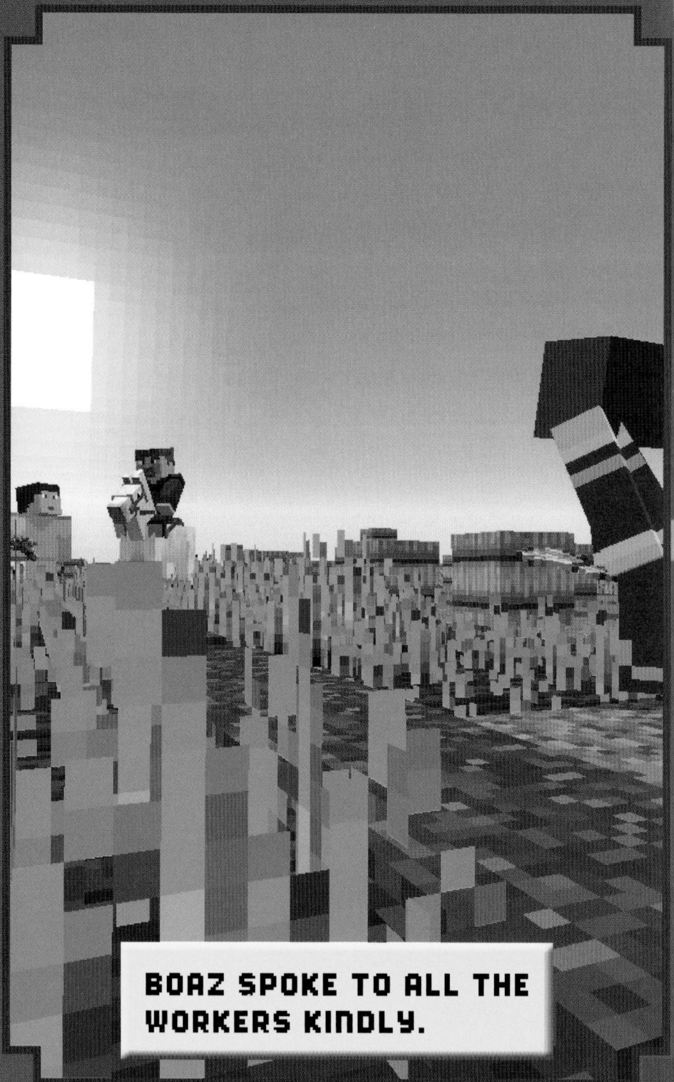
BOAZ SPOKE TO ALL THE WORKERS KINDLY.

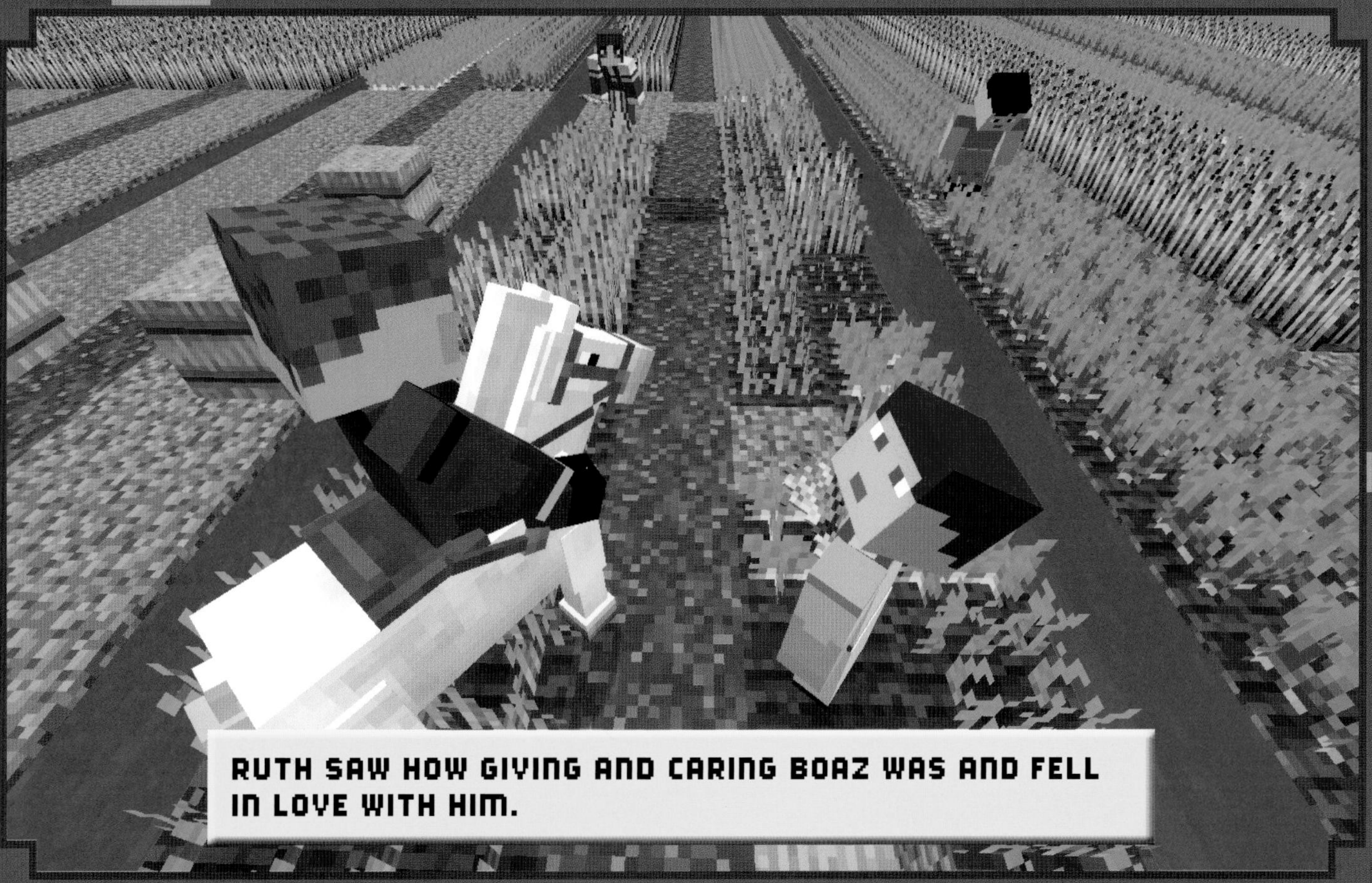
RUTH SAW HOW GIVING AND CARING BOAZ WAS AND FELL IN LOVE WITH HIM.

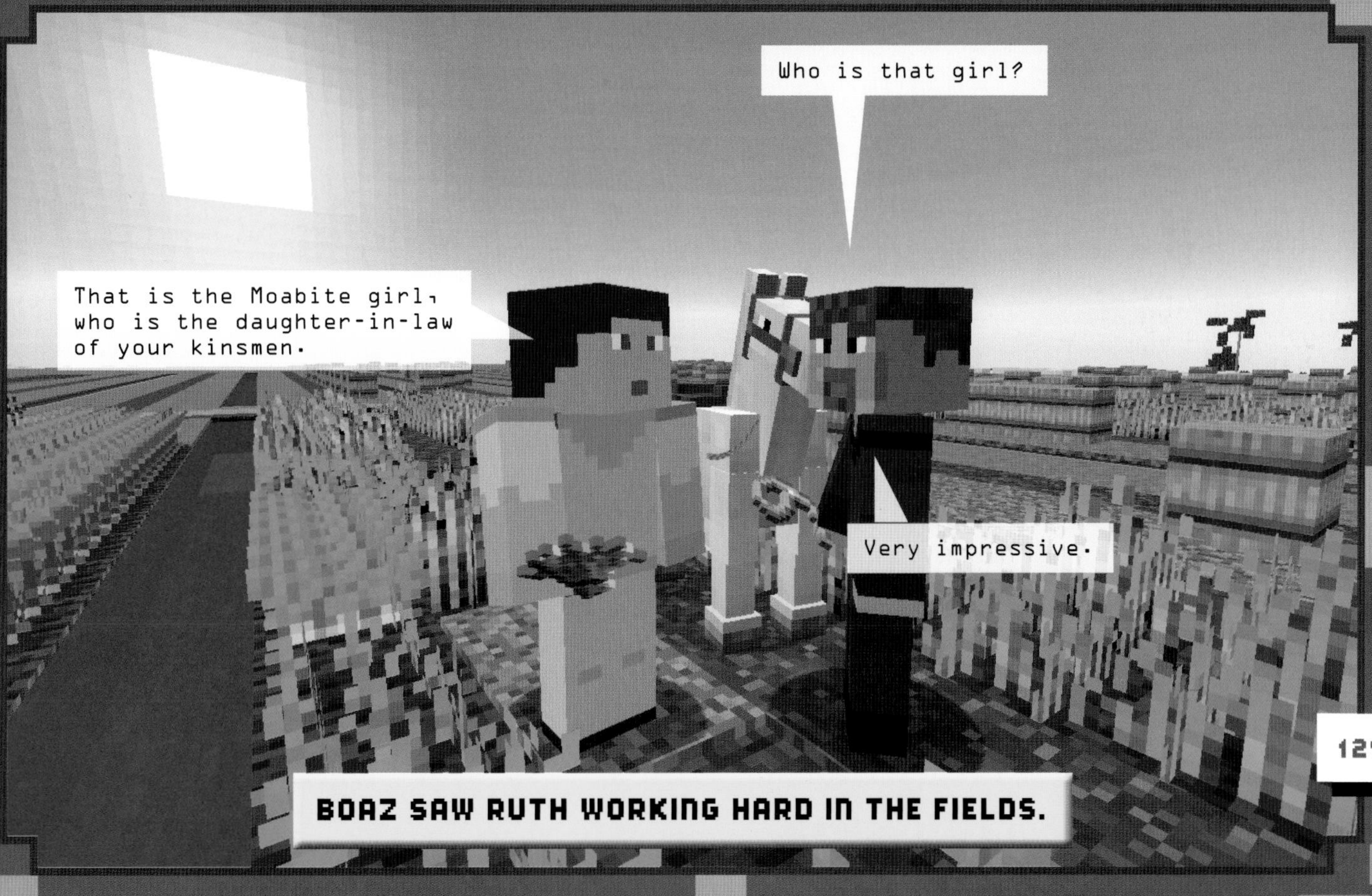
Who is that girl?
That is the Moabite girl, who is the daughter-in-law of your kinsmen.
Very impressive.
BOAZ SAW RUTH WORKING HARD IN THE FIELDS.

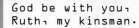

God be with you, Ruth, my kinsman.

And God be with you, my kinsman.

Daughter of Naomi, you may take as much as you want. Your troubles and hardships are over.

BOAZ WALKED OVER TO RUTH.

Why are you so kind as to take notice of me when I am only a foreigner?

RUTH FELL TO HER KNEES.

My men have told me all that you have done for your Mother-in-Law Naomi. It is because of you that these rewards have come, not because of me.

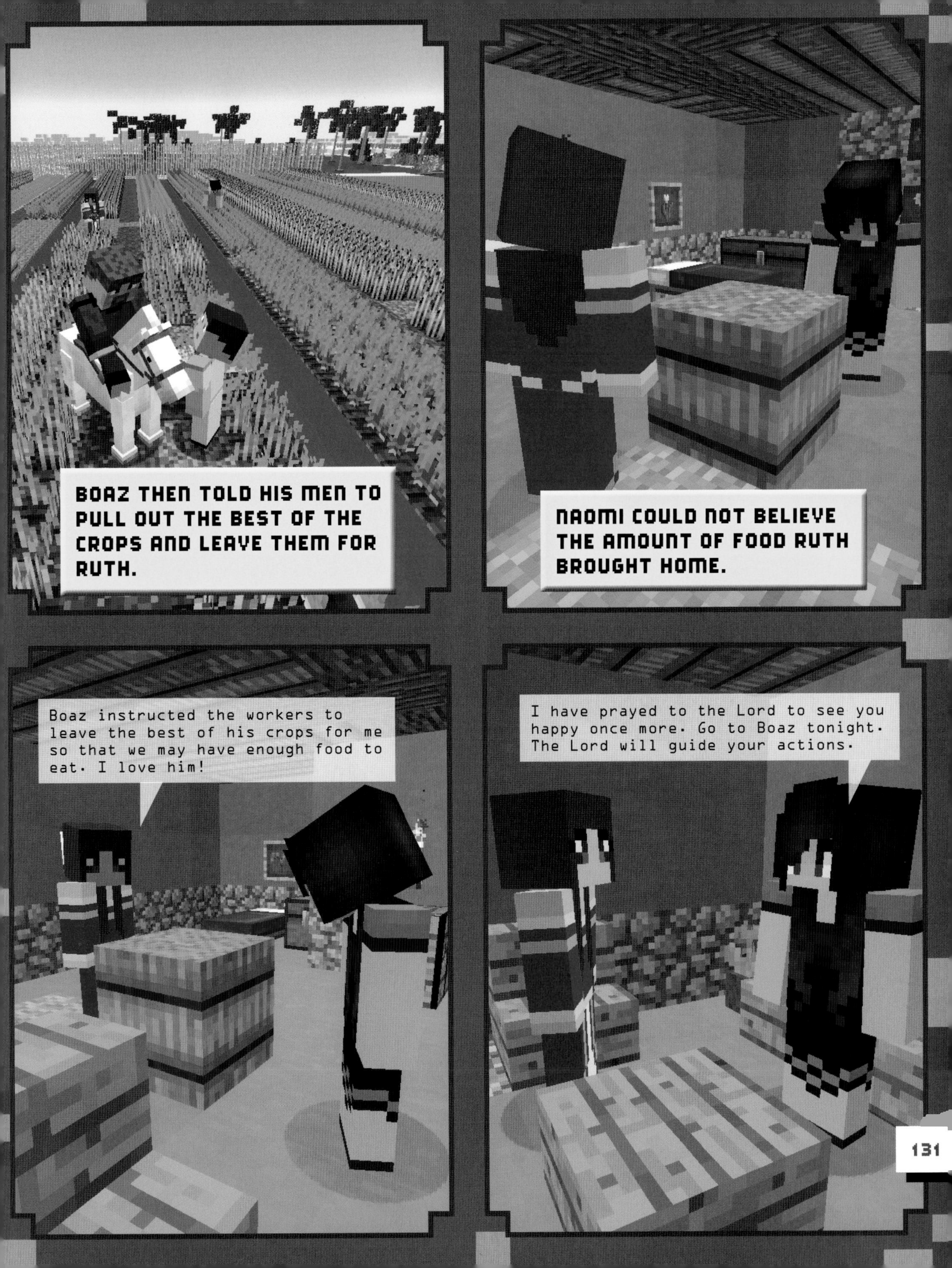
BOAZ THEN TOLD HIS MEN TO PULL OUT THE BEST OF THE CROPS AND LEAVE THEM FOR RUTH.
NAOMI COULD NOT BELIEVE THE AMOUNT OF FOOD RUTH BROUGHT HOME.
Boaz instructed the workers to leave the best of his crops for me so that we may have enough food to eat. I love him!
I have prayed to the Lord to see you happy once more. Go to Boaz tonight. The Lord will guide your actions.

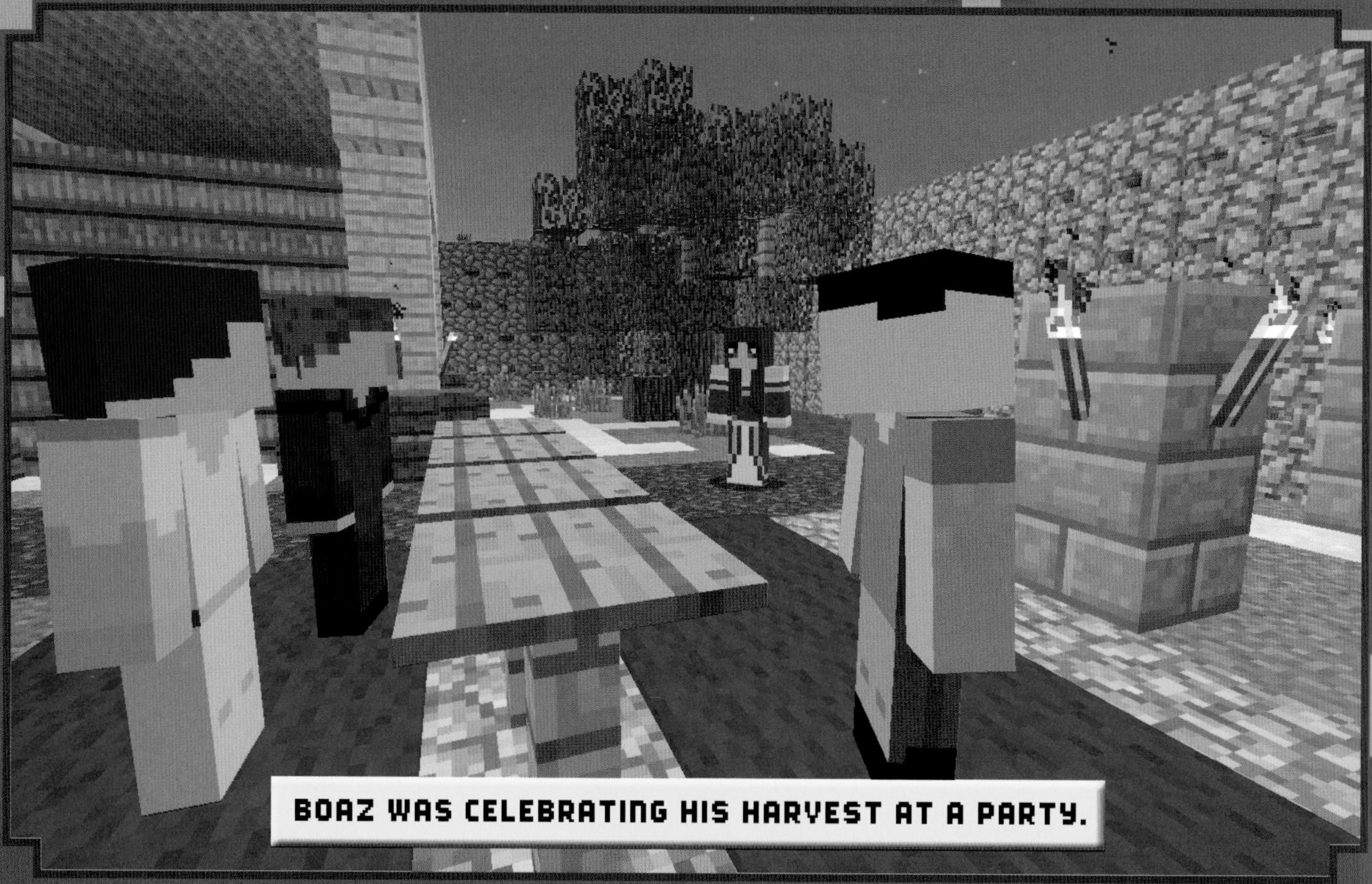
BOAZ WAS CELEBRATING HIS HARVEST AT A PARTY.

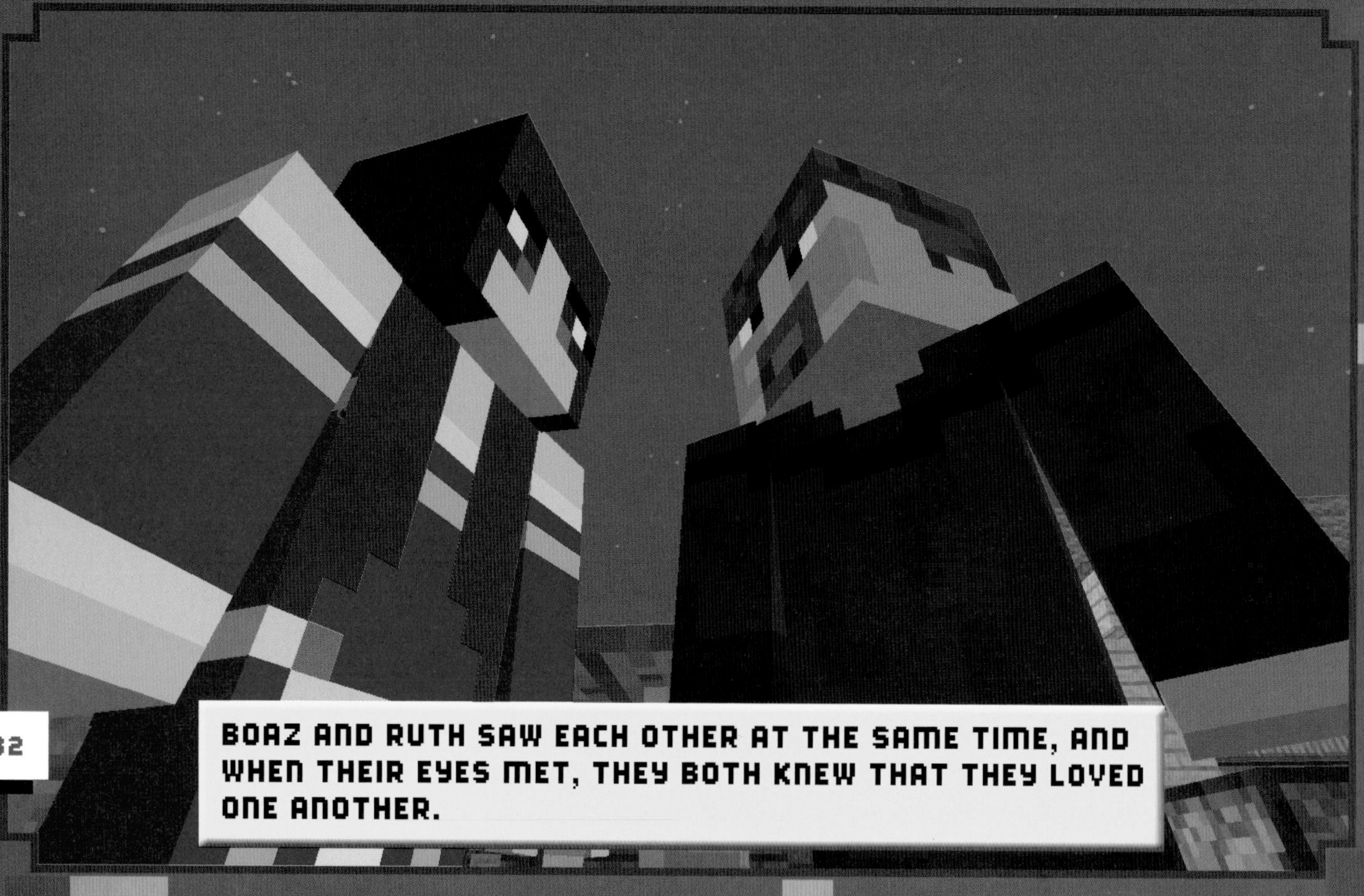
BOAZ AND RUTH SAW EACH OTHER AT THE SAME TIME, AND WHEN THEIR EYES MET, THEY BOTH KNEW THAT THEY LOVED ONE ANOTHER.

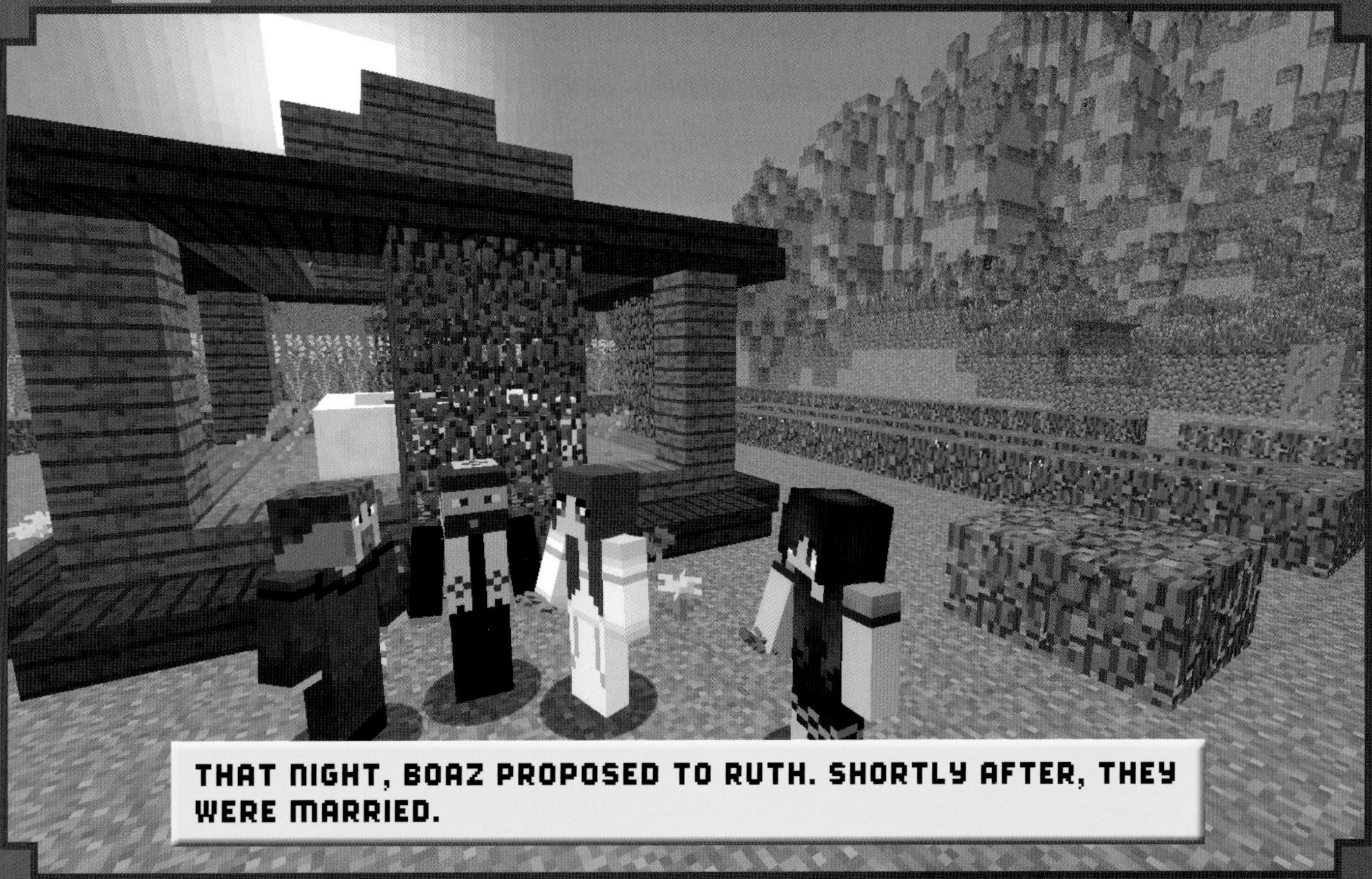
THAT NIGHT, BOAZ PROPOSED TO RUTH. SHORTLY AFTER, THEY WERE MARRIED.

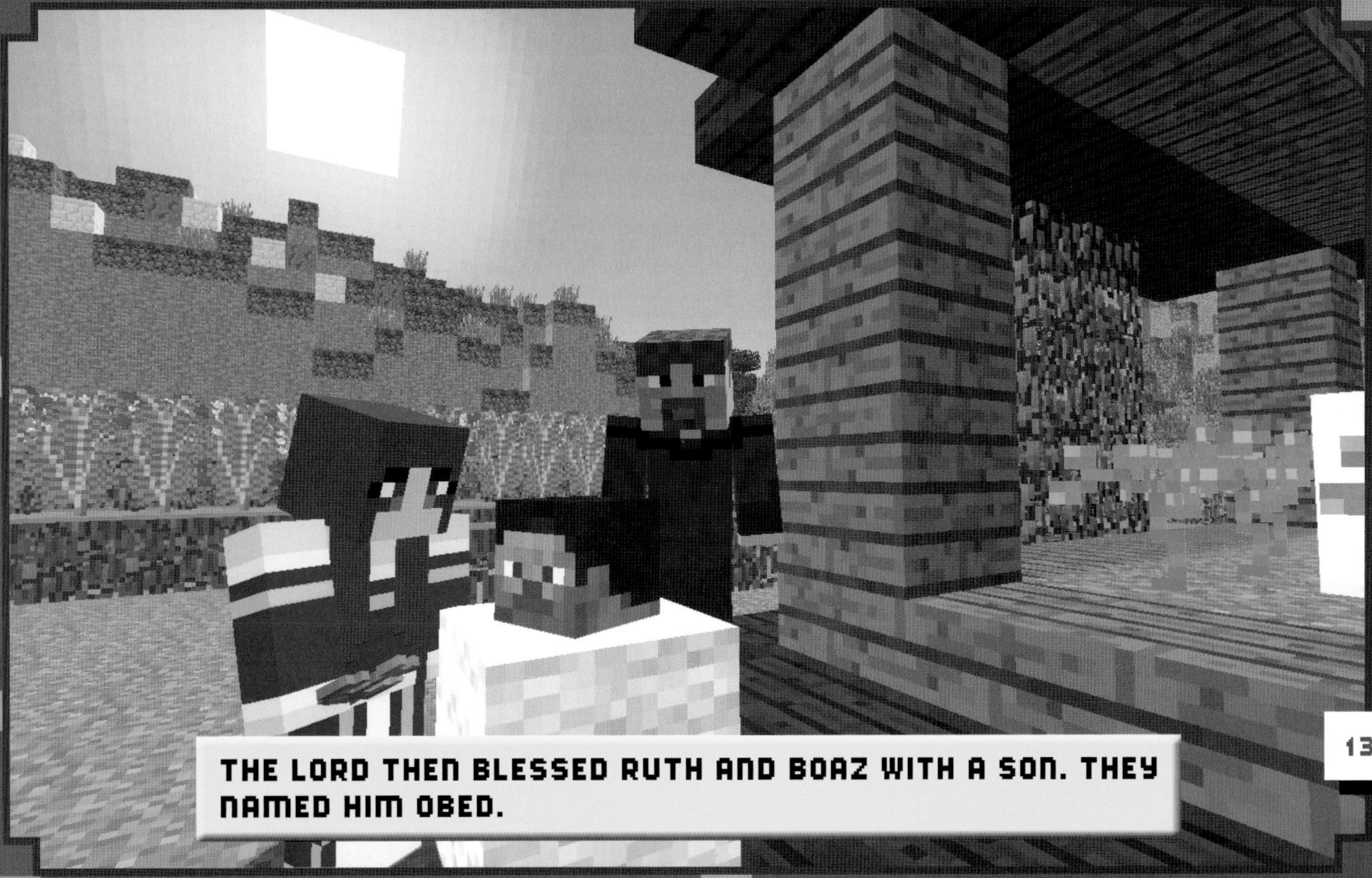
THE LORD THEN BLESSED RUTH AND BOAZ WITH A SON. THEY NAMED HIM OBED.

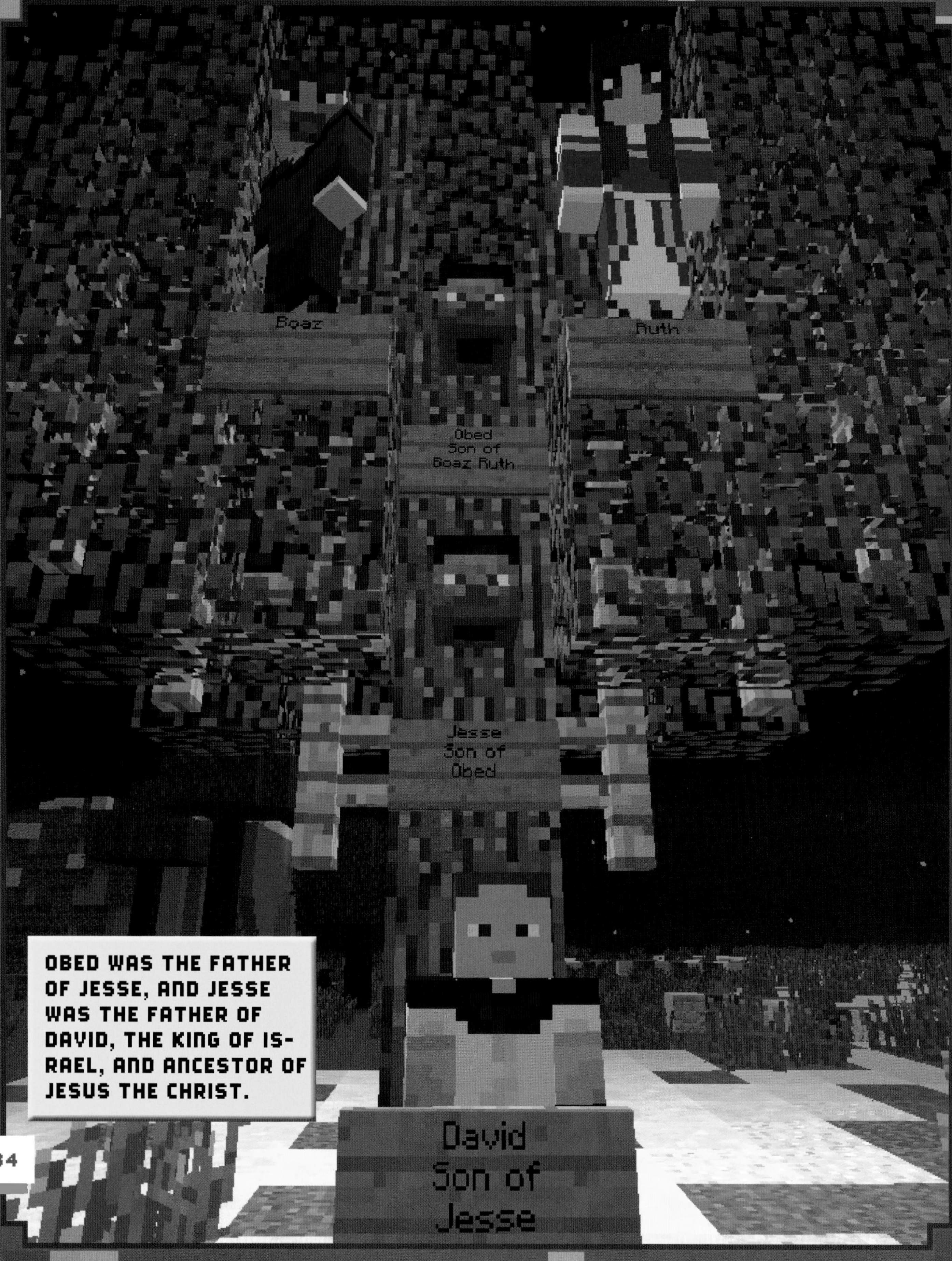
Boaz
Ruth
Obed
Son of
Boaz Ruth
Jesse
Son of
Obed
David
Son of
Jesse

OBED WAS THE FATHER OF JESSE, AND JESSE WAS THE FATHER OF DAVID, THE KING OF ISRAEL, AND ANCESTOR OF JESUS THE CHRIST.

DAVID AND GOLIATH

It's time the Hebrews had a formal leader.

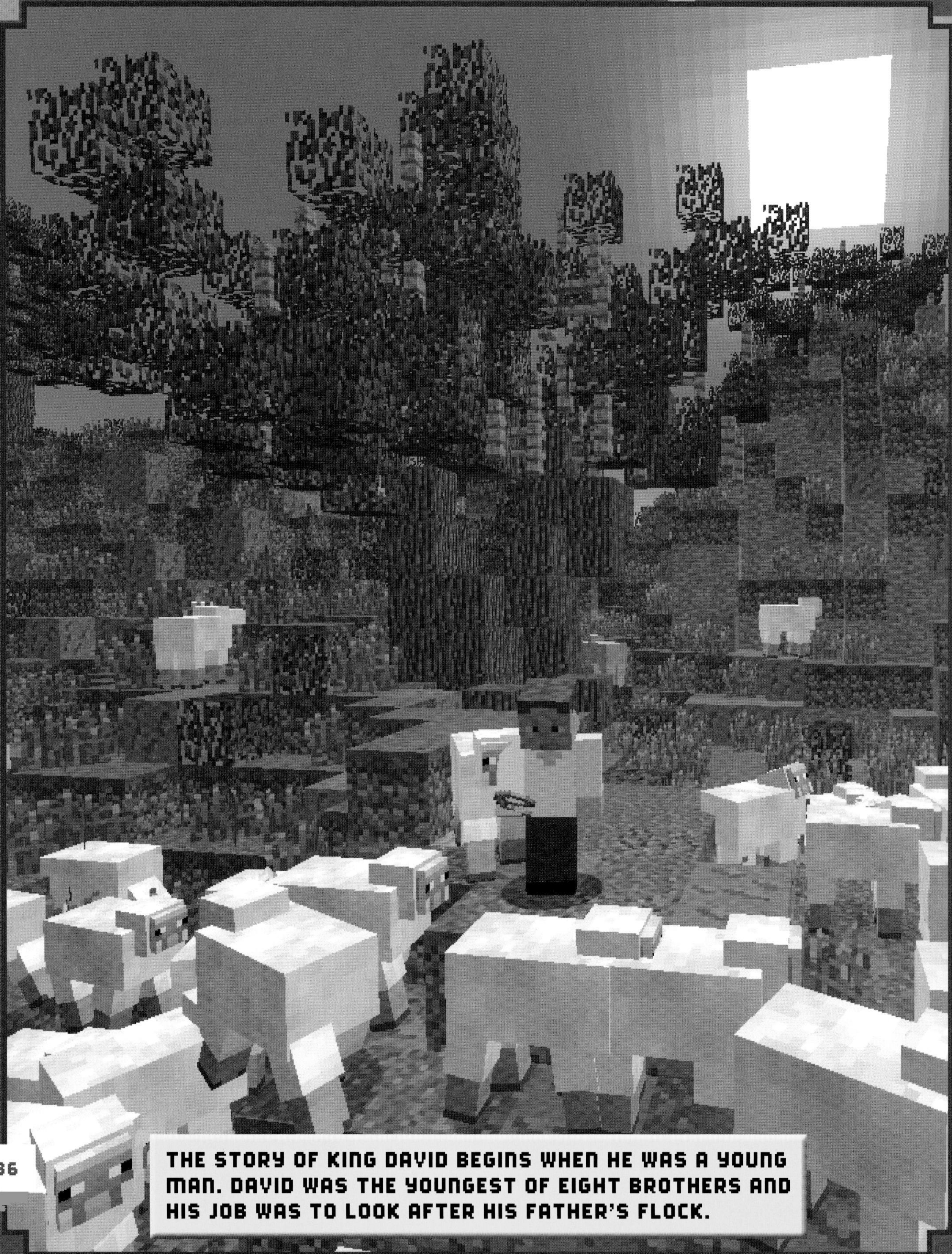

THE STORY OF KING DAVID BEGINS WHEN HE WAS A YOUNG MAN. DAVID WAS THE YOUNGEST OF EIGHT BROTHERS AND HIS JOB WAS TO LOOK AFTER HIS FATHER'S FLOCK.

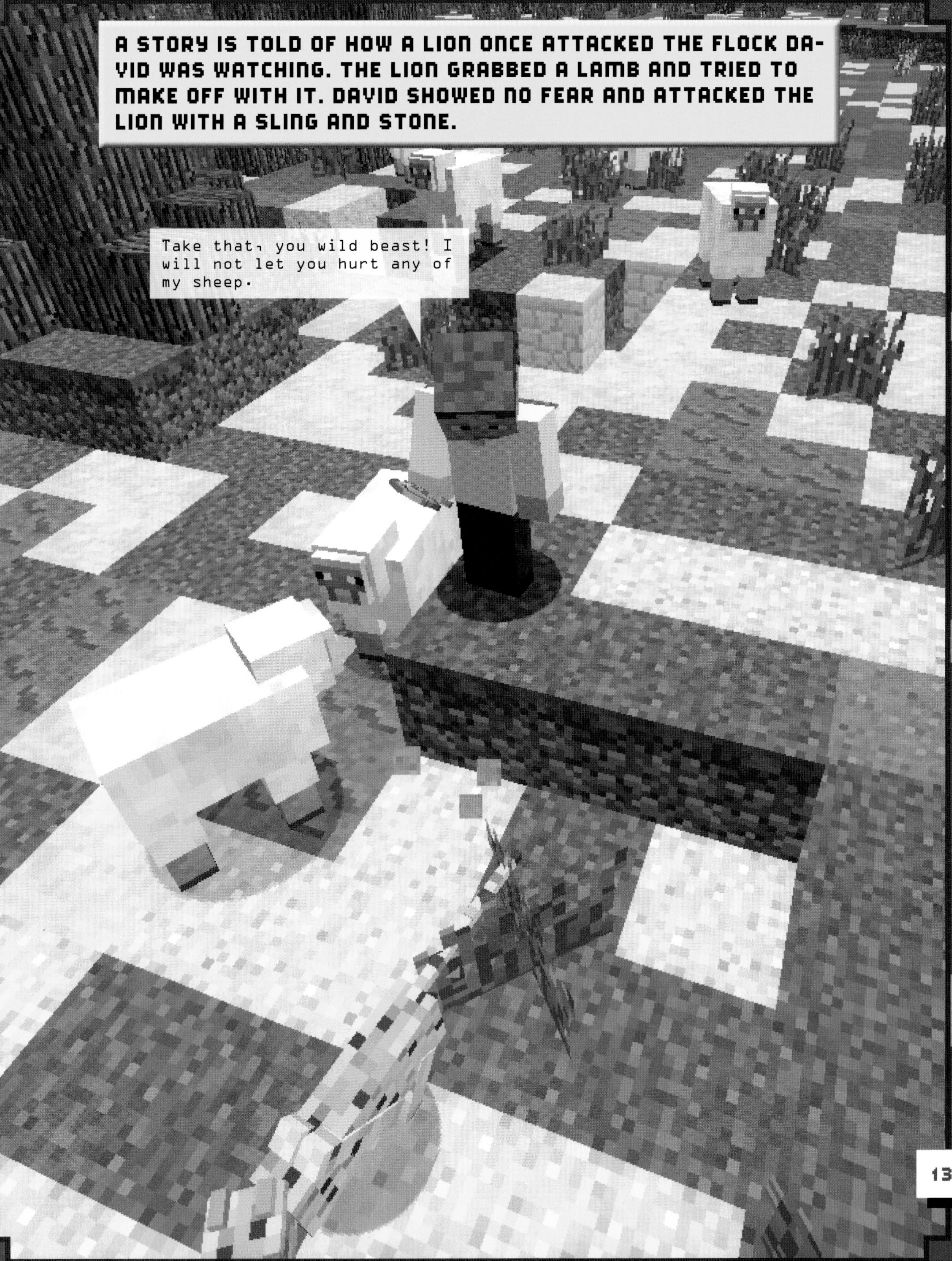
A STORY IS TOLD OF HOW A LION ONCE ATTACKED THE FLOCK DAVID WAS WATCHING. THE LION GRABBED A LAMB AND TRIED TO MAKE OFF WITH IT. DAVID SHOWED NO FEAR AND ATTACKED THE LION WITH A SLING AND STONE.
Take that, you wild beast! I will not let you hurt any of my sheep.

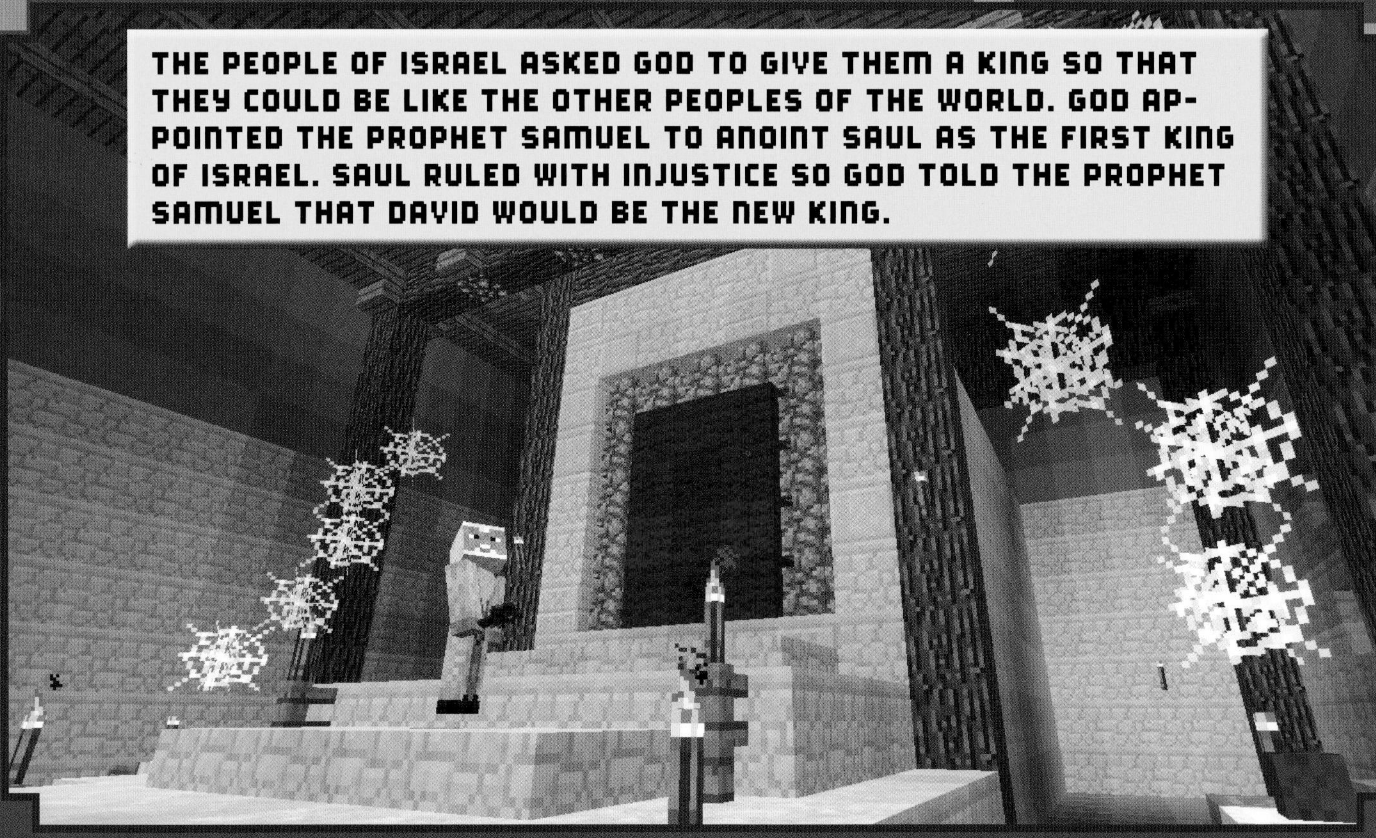
THE PEOPLE OF ISRAEL ASKED GOD TO GIVE THEM A KING SO THAT THEY COULD BE LIKE THE OTHER PEOPLES OF THE WORLD. GOD APPOINTED THE PROPHET SAMUEL TO ANOINT SAUL AS THE FIRST KING OF ISRAEL. SAUL RULED WITH INJUSTICE SO GOD TOLD THE PROPHET SAMUEL THAT DAVID WOULD BE THE NEW KING.

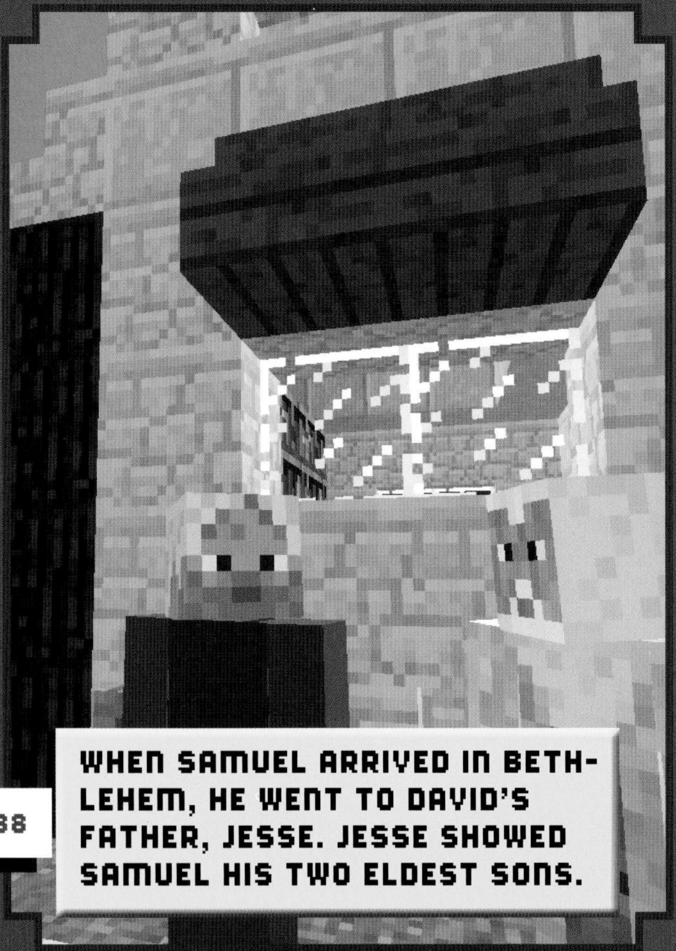
WHEN SAMUEL ARRIVED IN BETHLEHEM, HE WENT TO DAVID'S FATHER, JESSE. JESSE SHOWED SAMUEL HIS TWO ELDEST SONS.

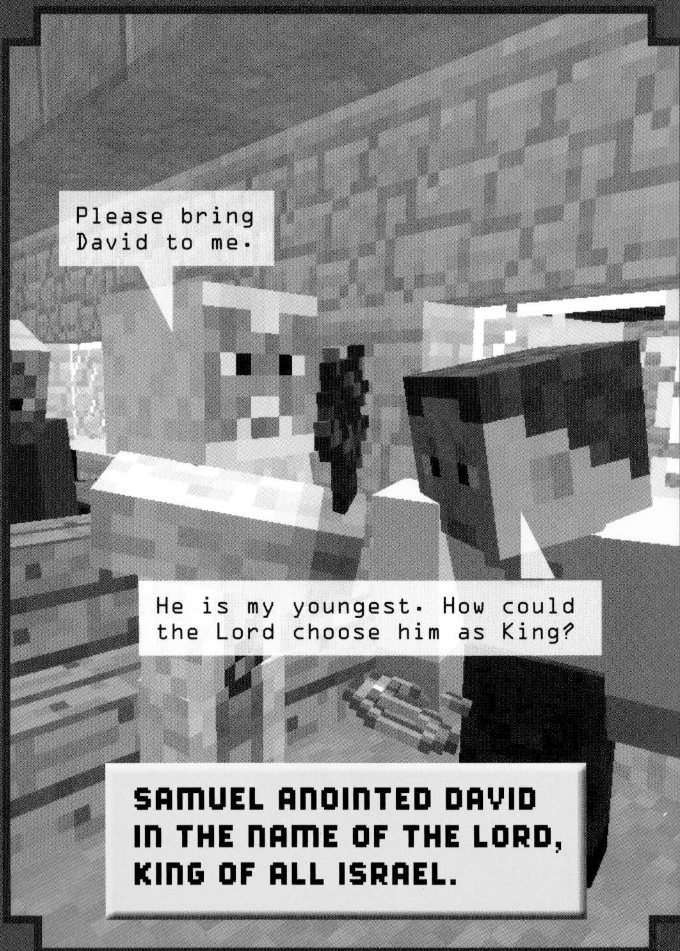
Please bring David to me.
He is my youngest. How could the Lord choose him as King?
SAMUEL ANOINTED DAVID IN THE NAME OF THE LORD, KING OF ALL ISRAEL.

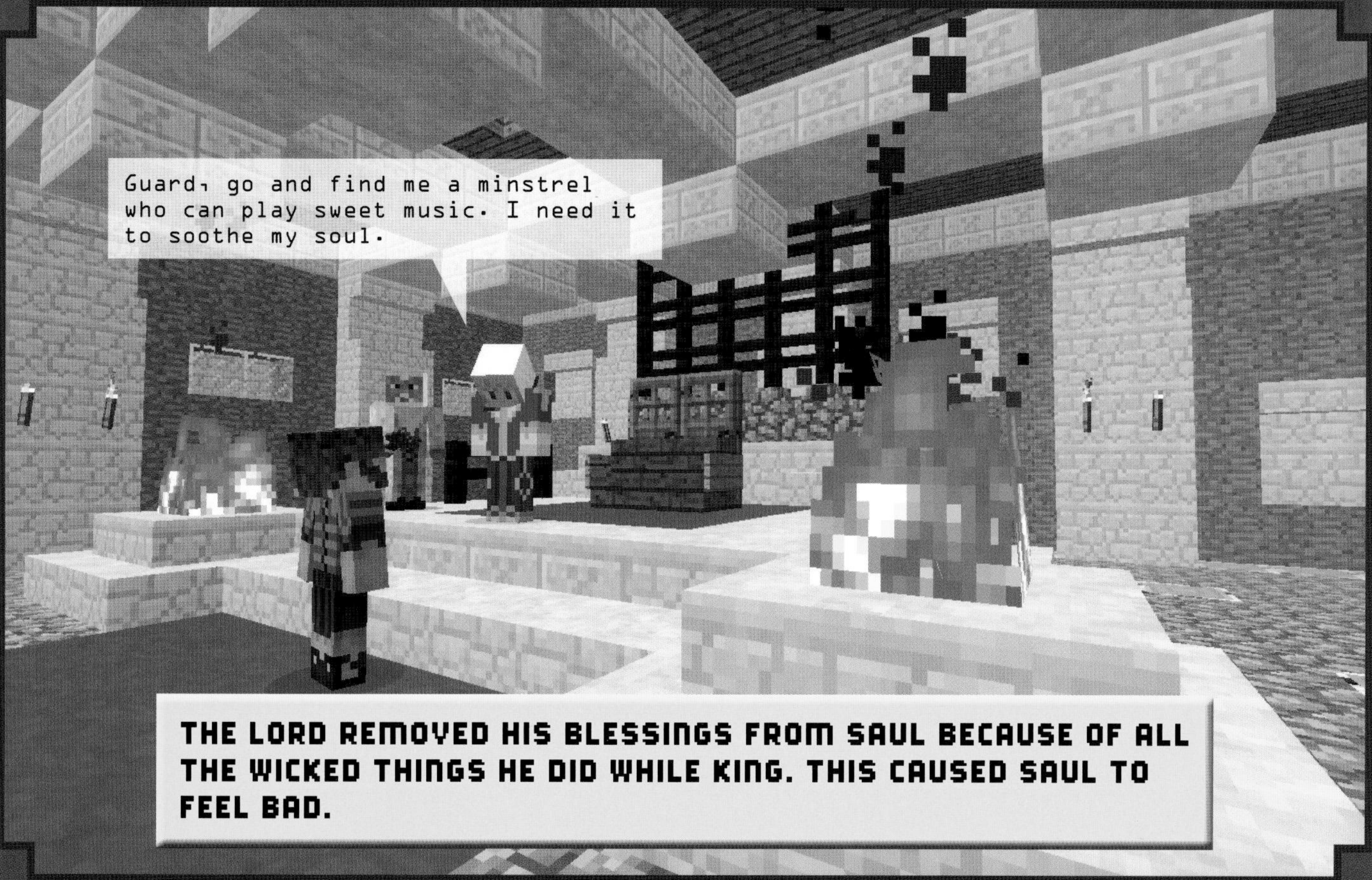
Guard, go and find me a minstrel who can play sweet music. I need it to soothe my soul.
THE LORD REMOVED HIS BLESSINGS FROM SAUL BECAUSE OF ALL THE WICKED THINGS HE DID WHILE KING. THIS CAUSED SAUL TO FEEL BAD.

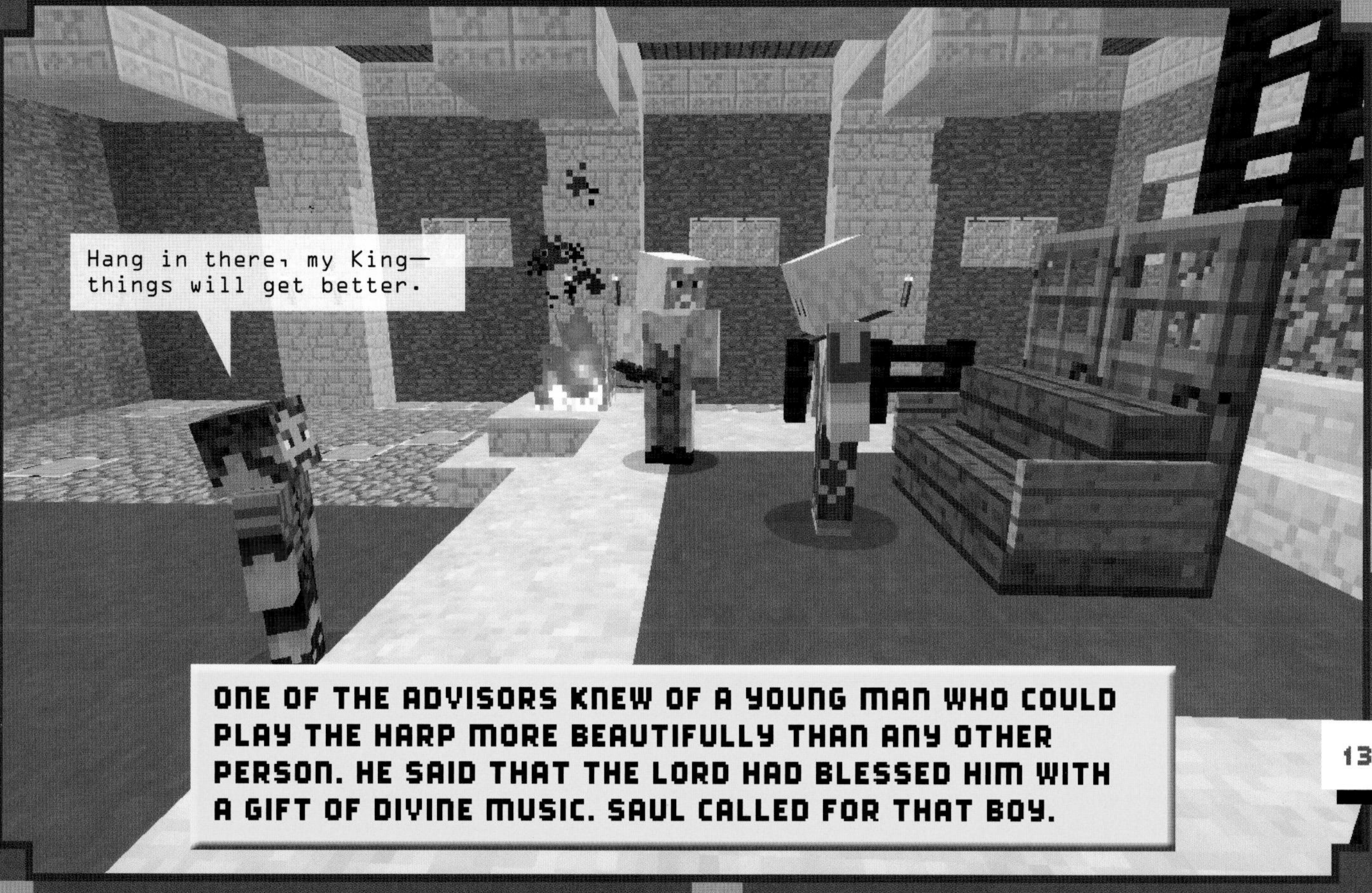
Hang in there, my King—things will get better.
ONE OF THE ADVISORS KNEW OF A YOUNG MAN WHO COULD PLAY THE HARP MORE BEAUTIFULLY THAN ANY OTHER PERSON. HE SAID THAT THE LORD HAD BLESSED HIM WITH A GIFT OF DIVINE MUSIC. SAUL CALLED FOR THAT BOY.

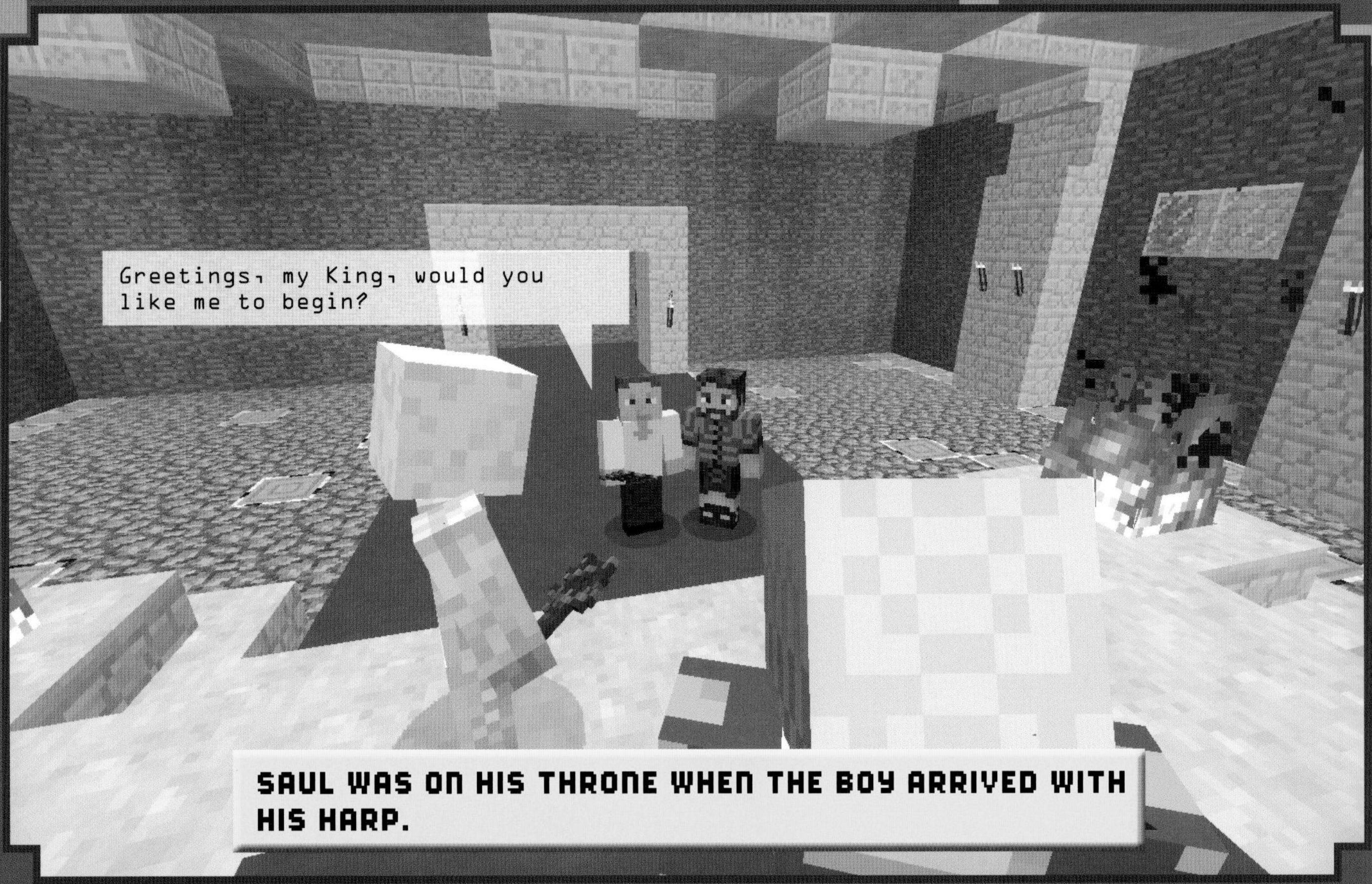
Greetings, my King, would you like me to begin?
SAUL WAS ON HIS THRONE WHEN THE BOY ARRIVED WITH HIS HARP.

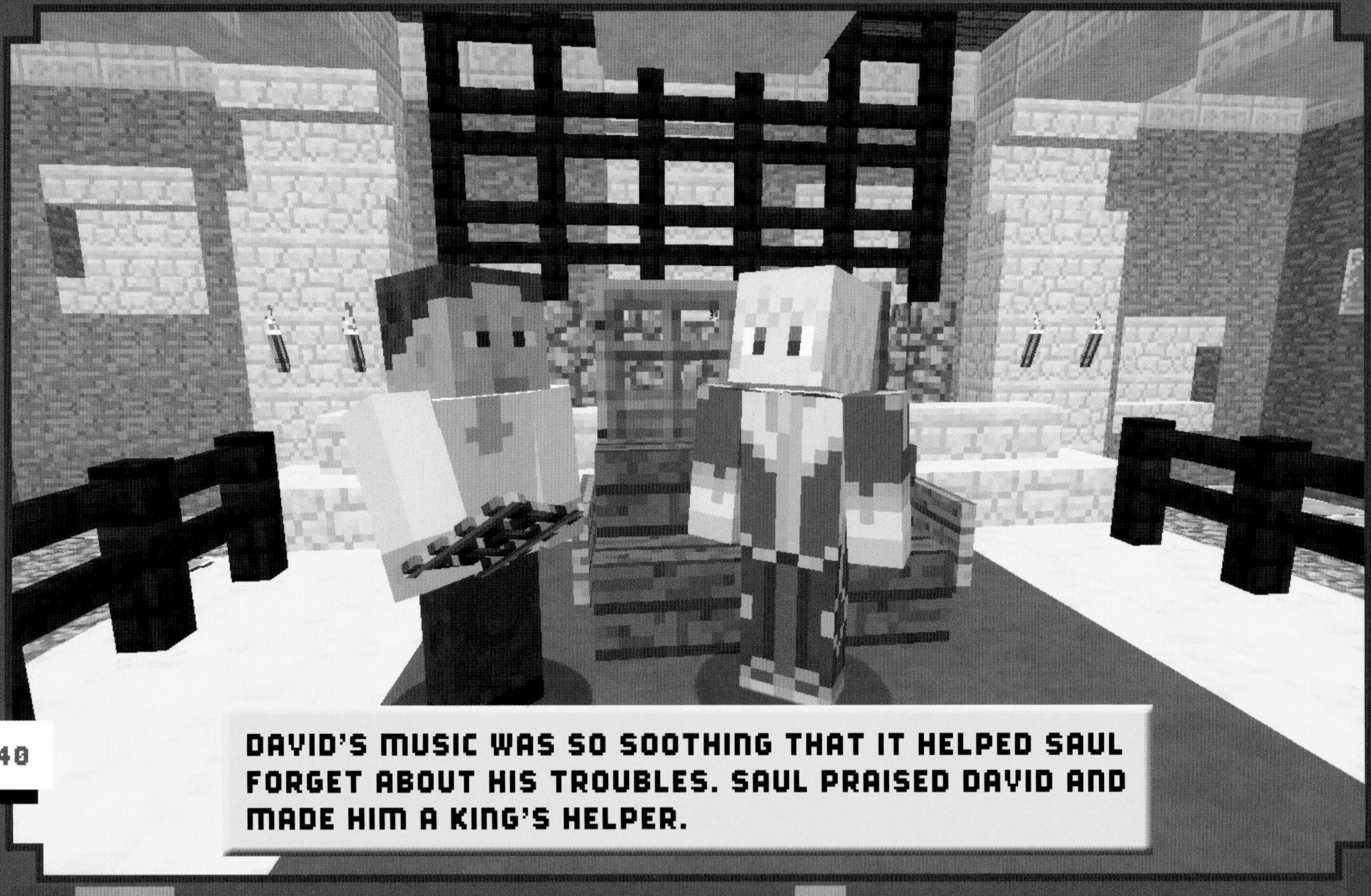
DAVID'S MUSIC WAS SO SOOTHING THAT IT HELPED SAUL FORGET ABOUT HIS TROUBLES. SAUL PRAISED DAVID AND MADE HIM A KING'S HELPER.

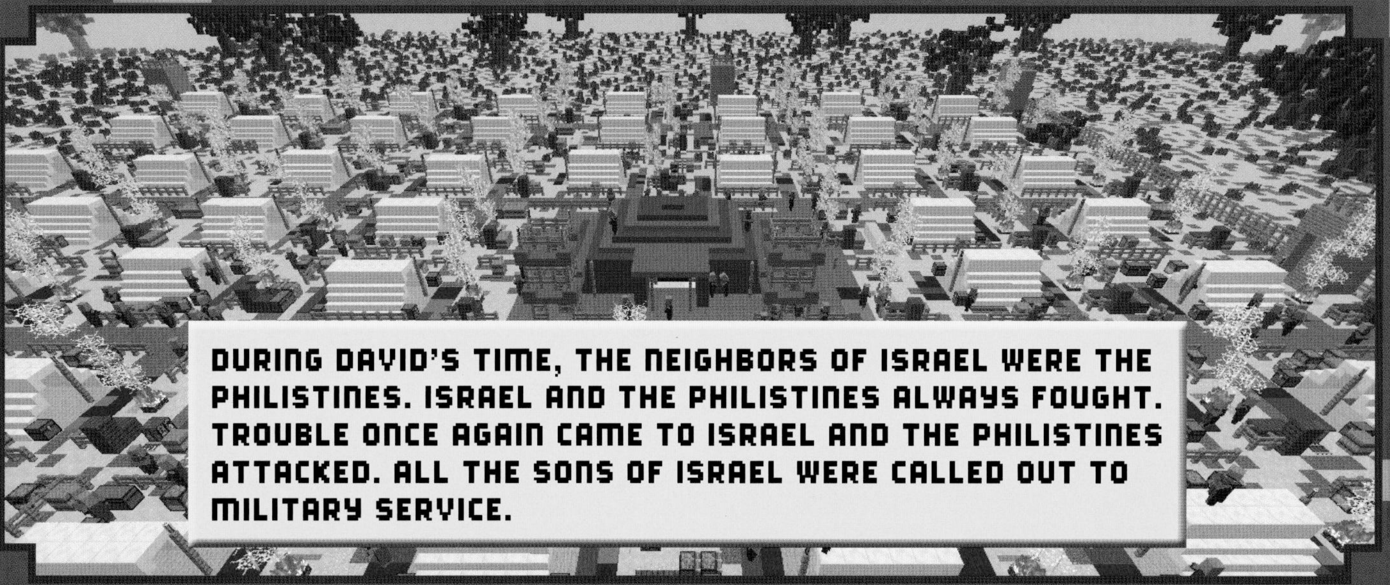
DURING DAVID'S TIME, THE NEIGHBORS OF ISRAEL WERE THE PHILISTINES. ISRAEL AND THE PHILISTINES ALWAYS FOUGHT. TROUBLE ONCE AGAIN CAME TO ISRAEL AND THE PHILISTINES ATTACKED. ALL THE SONS OF ISRAEL WERE CALLED OUT TO MILITARY SERVICE.

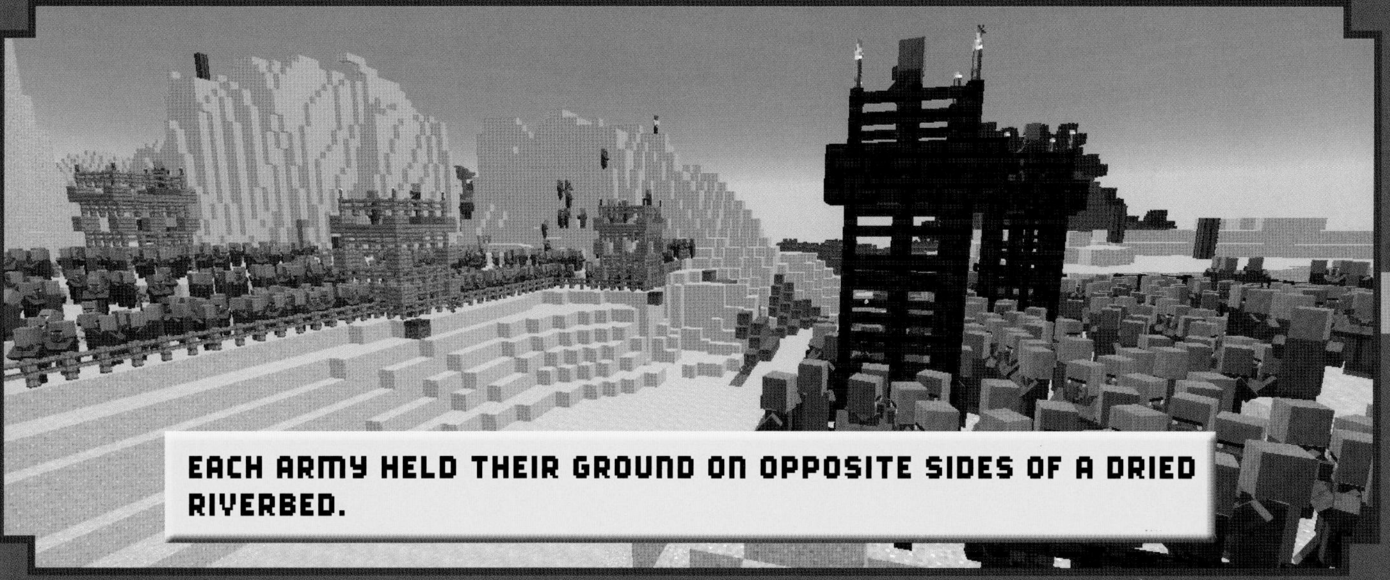
EACH ARMY HELD THEIR GROUND ON OPPOSITE SIDES OF A DRIED RIVERBED.

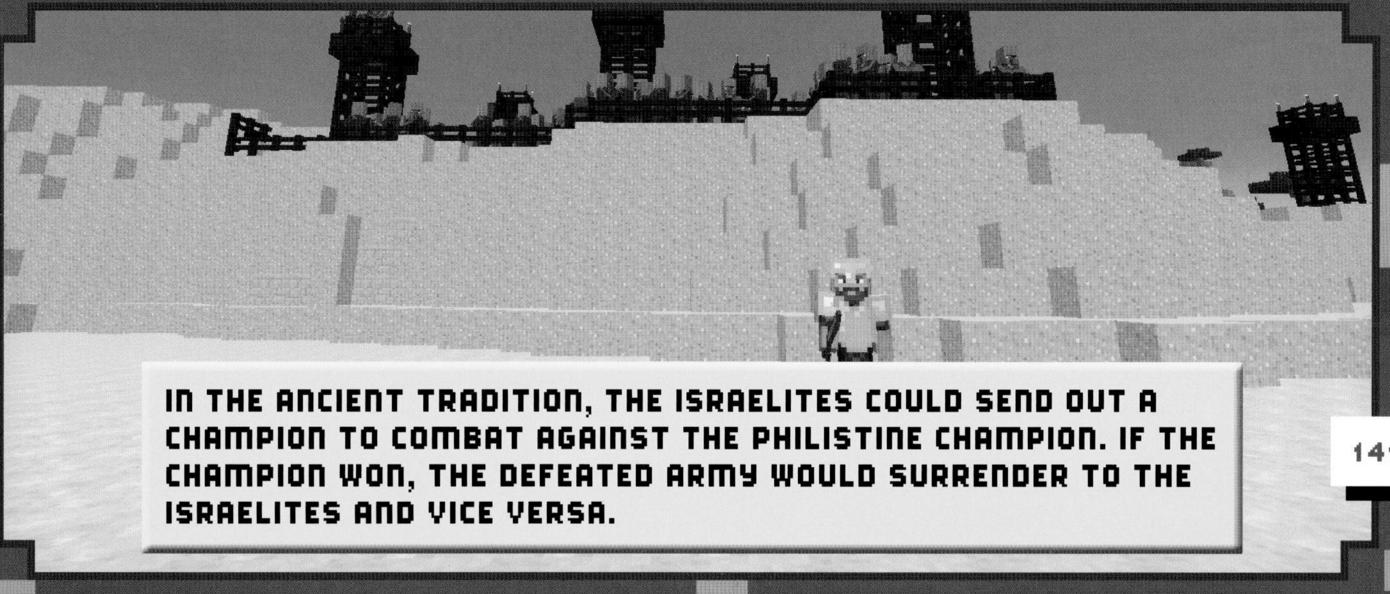
IN THE ANCIENT TRADITION, THE ISRAELITES COULD SEND OUT A CHAMPION TO COMBAT AGAINST THE PHILISTINE CHAMPION. IF THE CHAMPION WON, THE DEFEATED ARMY WOULD SURRENDER TO THE ISRAELITES AND VICE VERSA.

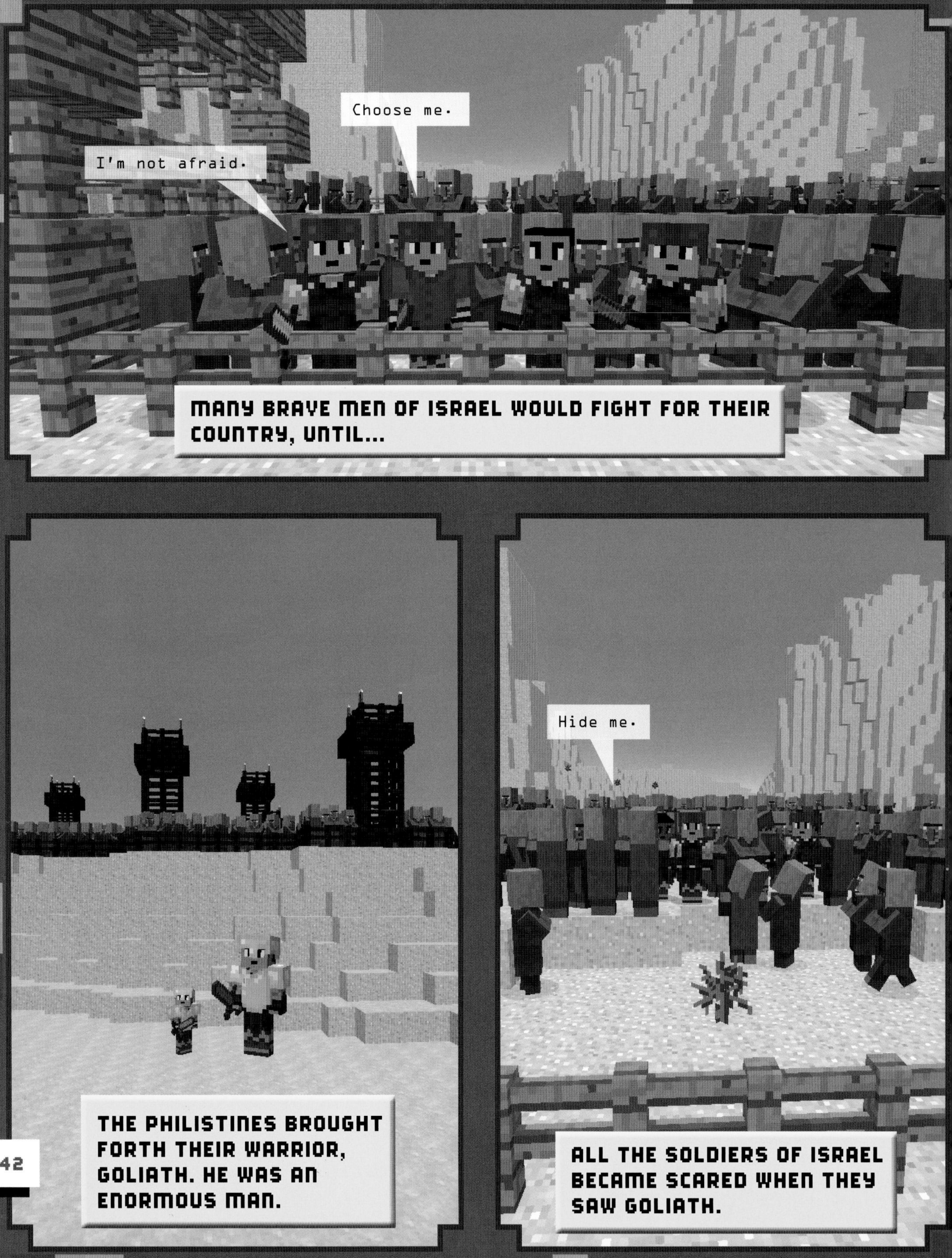
I'm not afraid.
Choose me.
MANY BRAVE MEN OF ISRAEL WOULD FIGHT FOR THEIR COUNTRY, UNTIL...
THE PHILISTINES BROUGHT FORTH THEIR WARRIOR, GOLIATH. HE WAS AN ENORMOUS MAN.
Hide me.
ALL THE SOLDIERS OF ISRAEL BECAME SCARED WHEN THEY SAW GOLIATH.

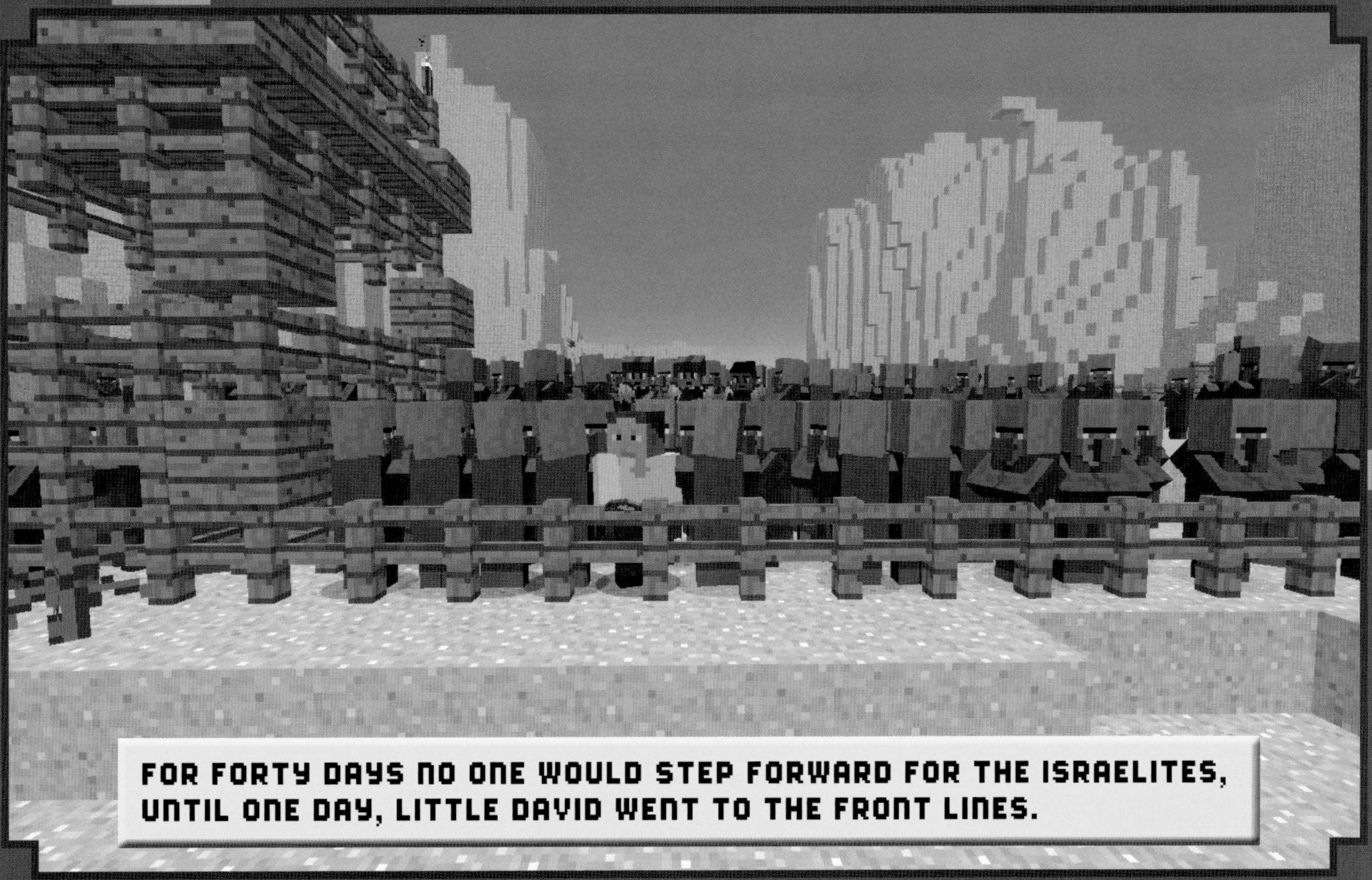
FOR FORTY DAYS NO ONE WOULD STEP FORWARD FOR THE ISRAELITES, UNTIL ONE DAY, LITTLE DAVID WENT TO THE FRONT LINES.

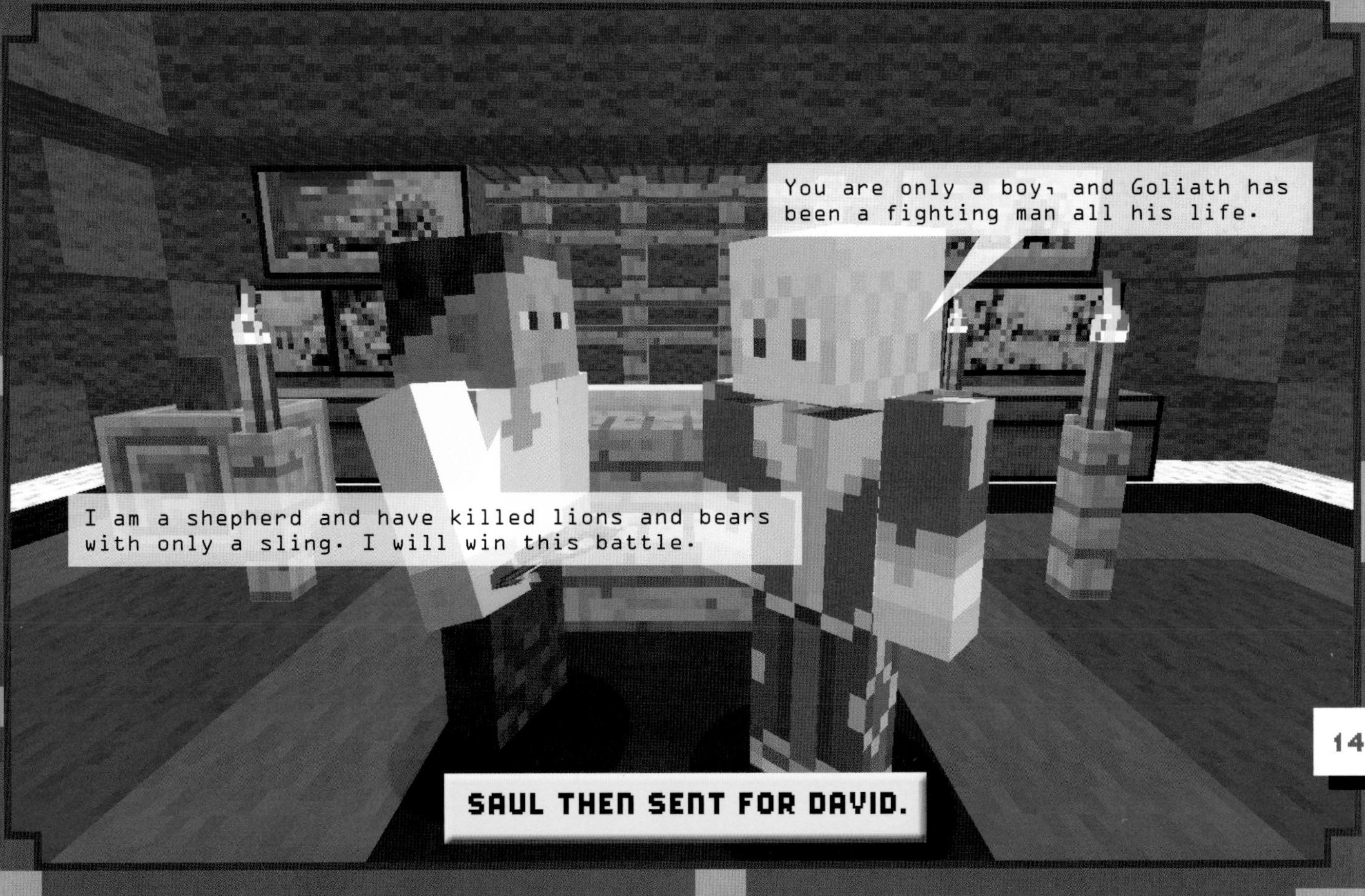
You are only a boy, and Goliath has been a fighting man all his life.
I am a shepherd and have killed lions and bears with only a sling. I will win this battle.
SAUL THEN SENT FOR DAVID.

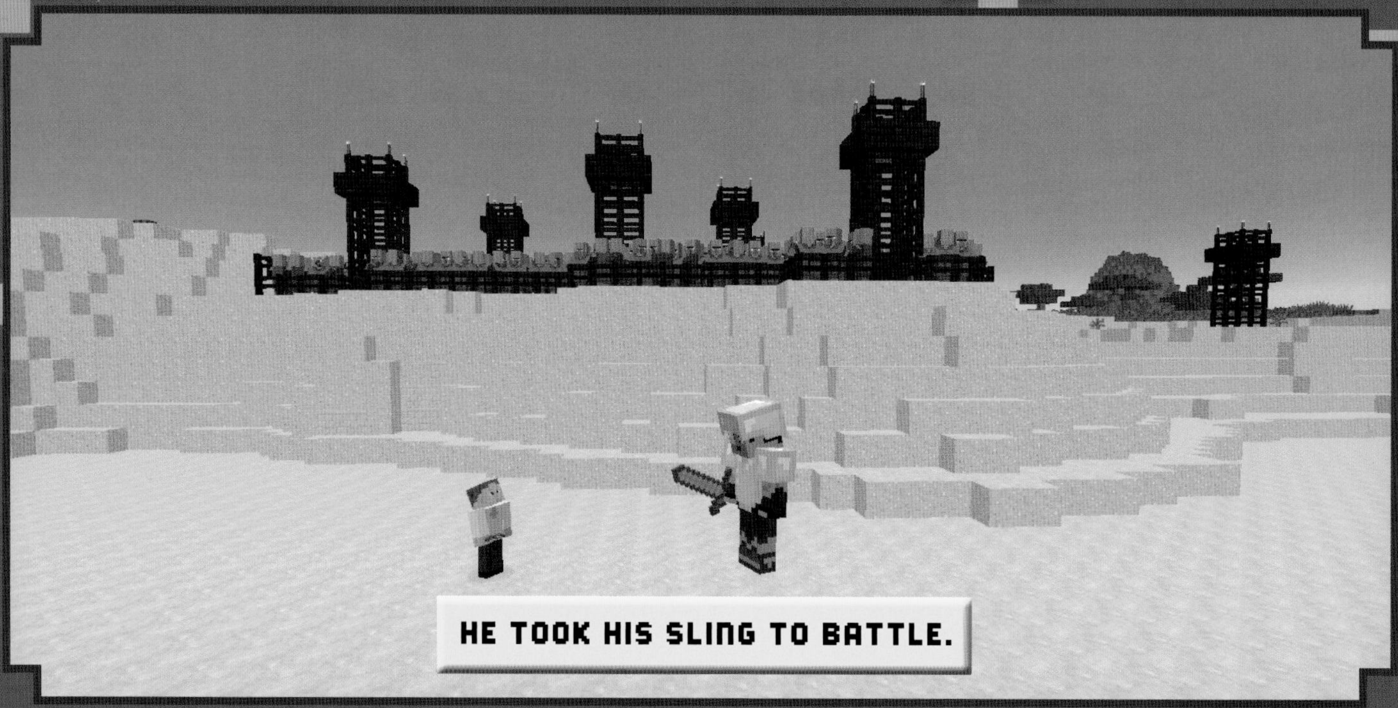
HE TOOK HIS SLING TO BATTLE.

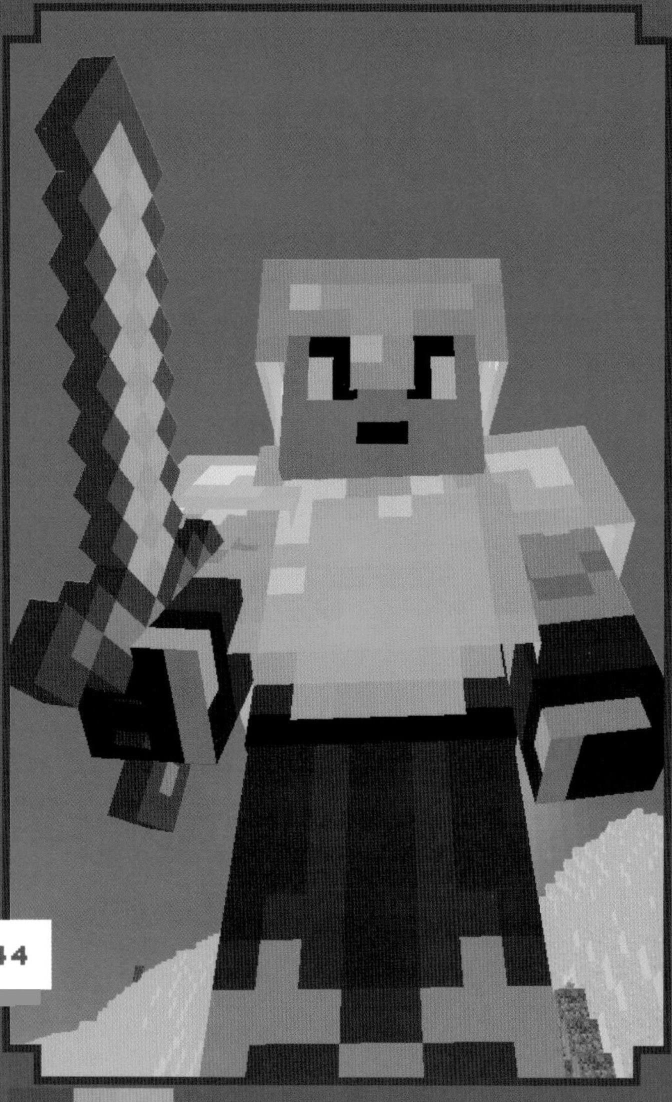

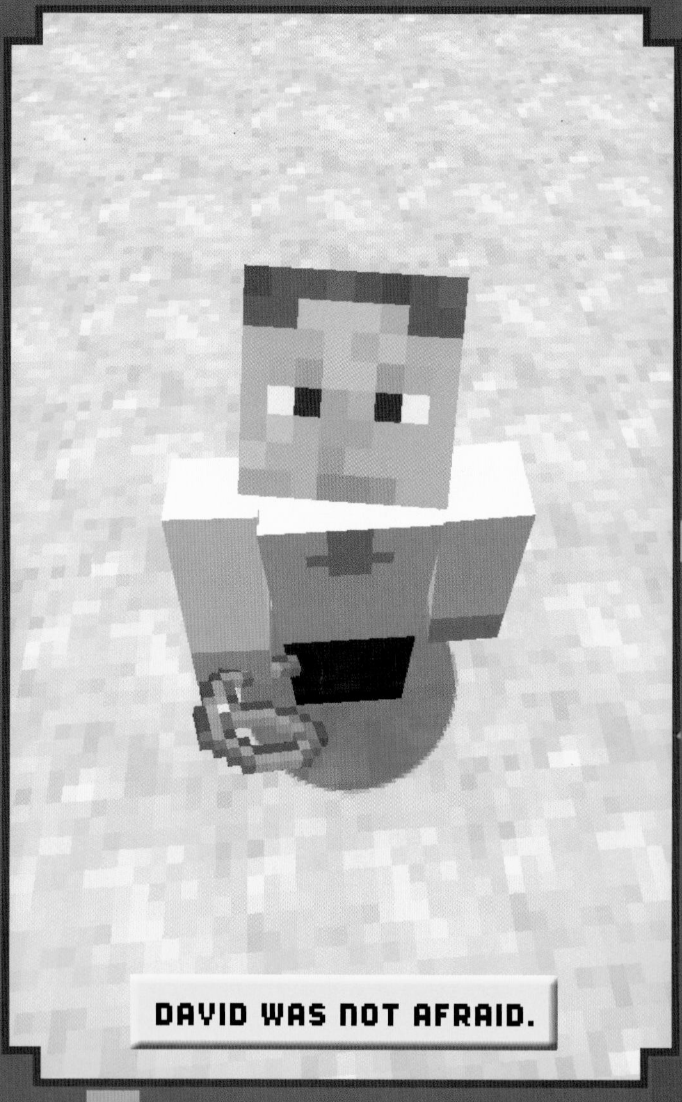
DAVID WAS NOT AFRAID.

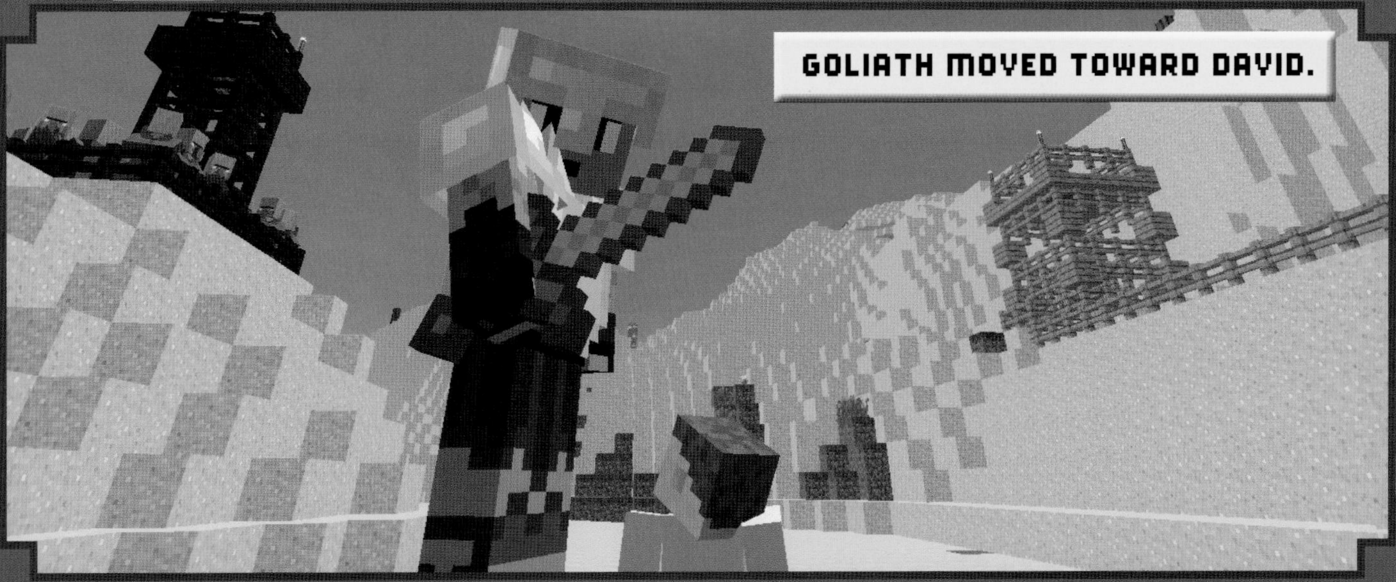
GOLIATH MOVED TOWARD DAVID.

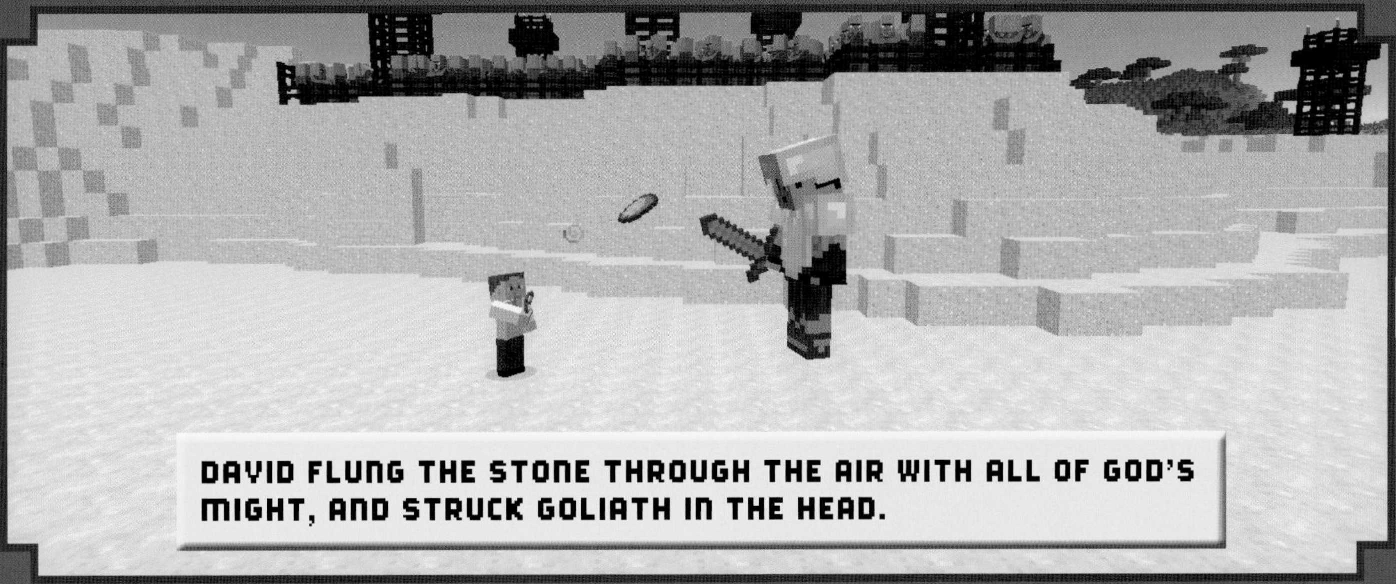
DAVID FLUNG THE STONE THROUGH THE AIR WITH ALL OF GOD'S MIGHT, AND STRUCK GOLIATH IN THE HEAD.

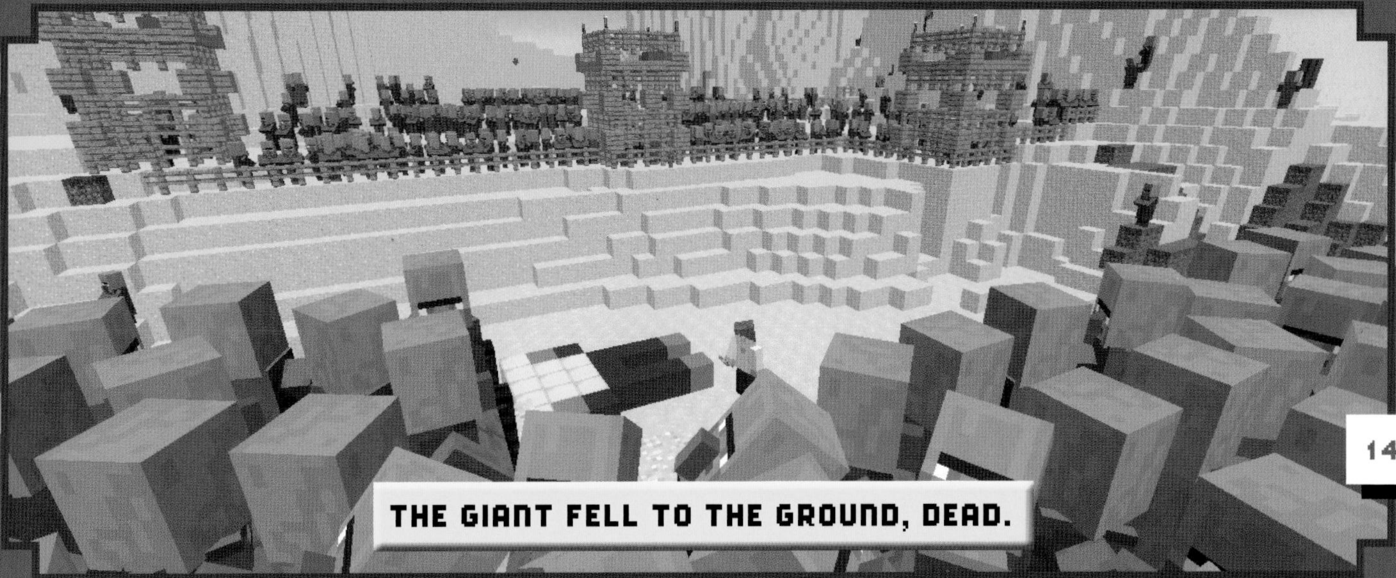
THE GIANT FELL TO THE GROUND, DEAD.

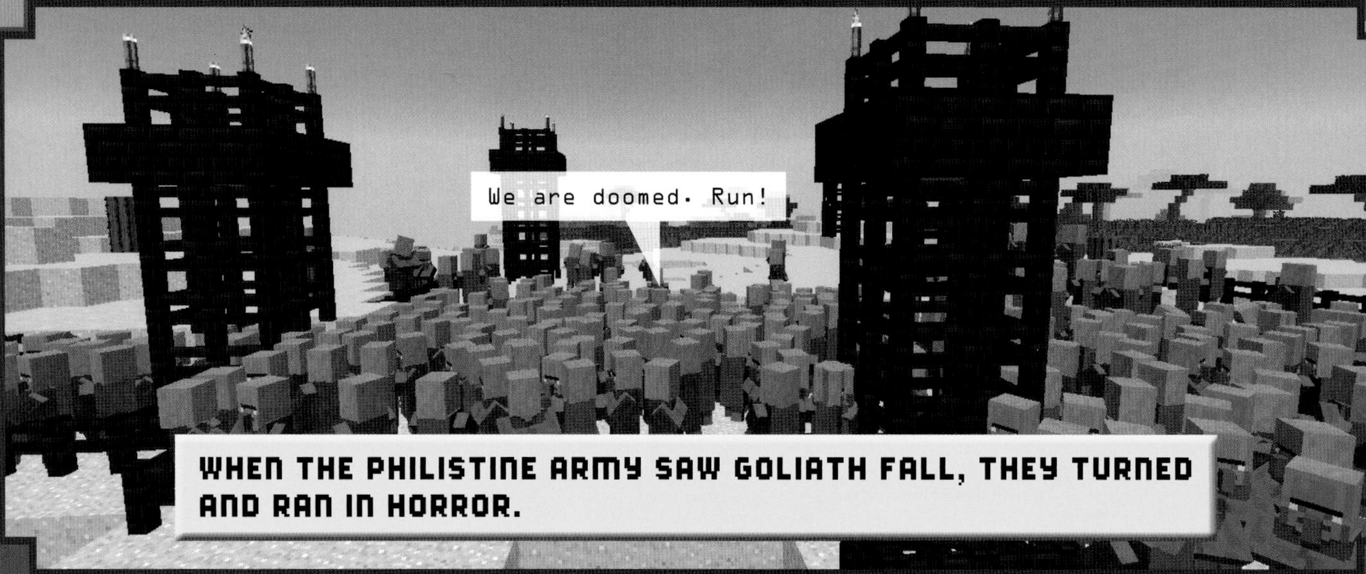
We are doomed. Run!
WHEN THE PHILISTINE ARMY SAW GOLIATH FALL, THEY TURNED AND RAN IN HORROR.

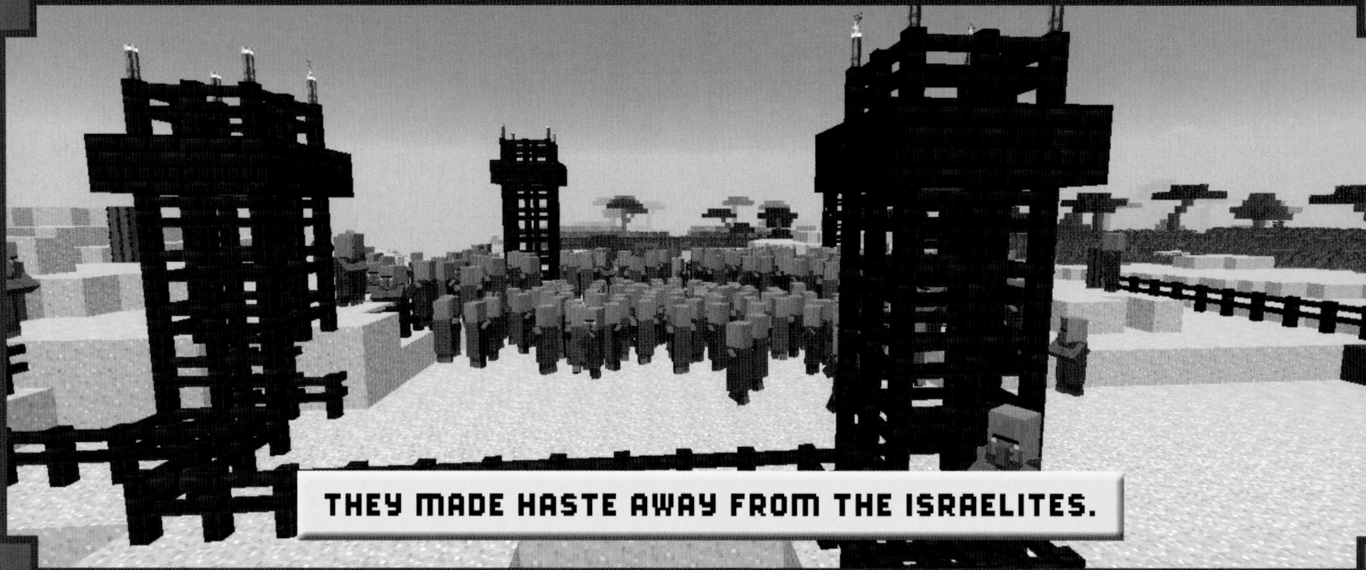
THEY MADE HASTE AWAY FROM THE ISRAELITES.

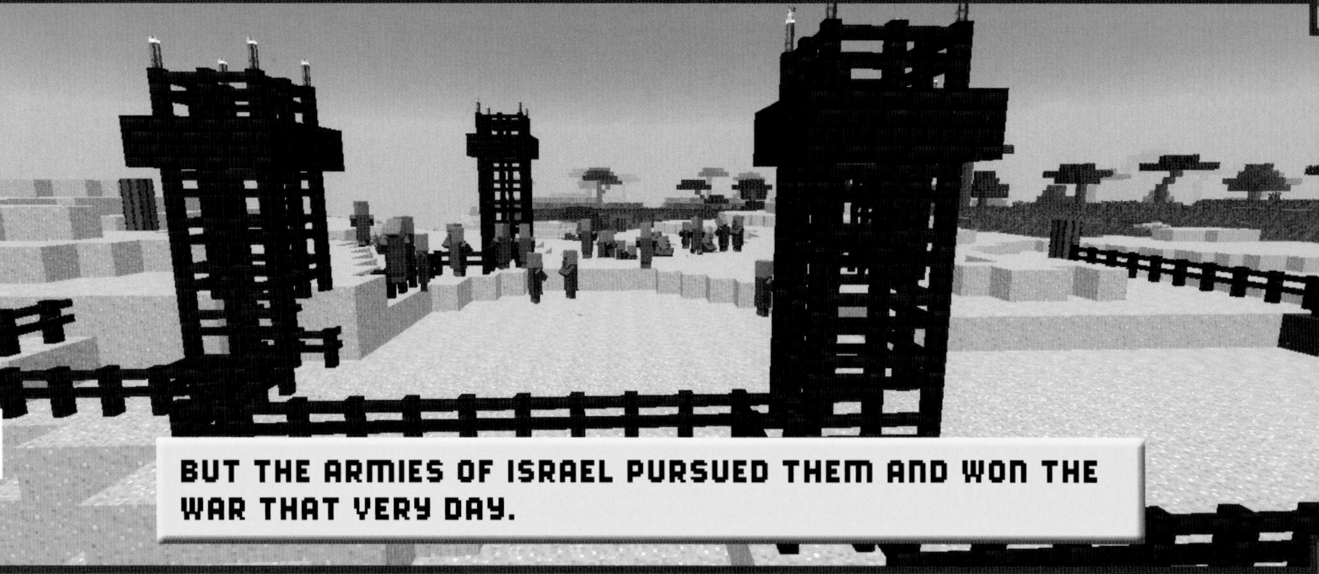
BUT THE ARMIES OF ISRAEL PURSUED THEM AND WON THE WAR THAT VERY DAY.

DAVID BECOMES KING

That was an epic takedown for someone so small!

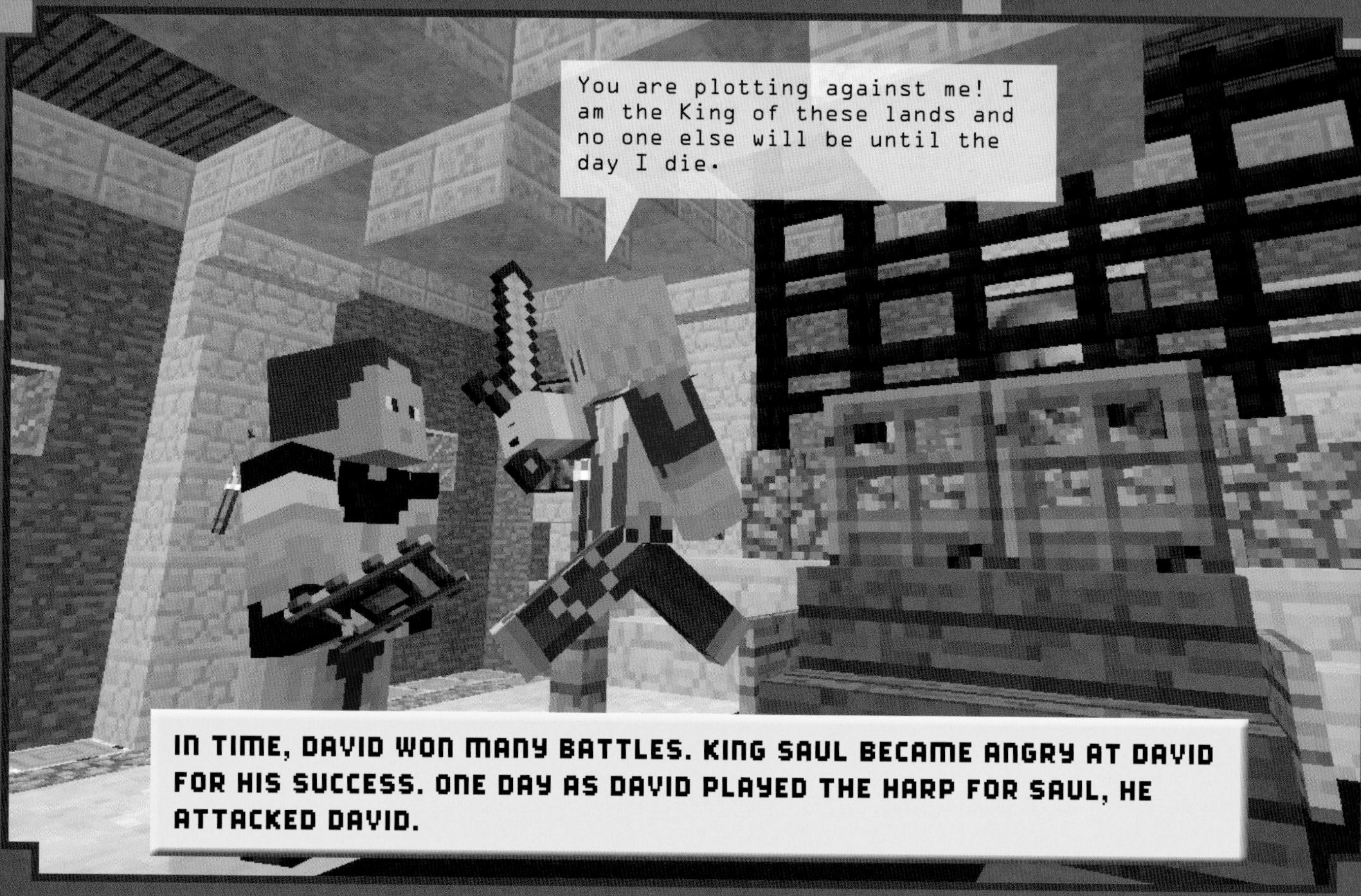
You are plotting against me! I am the King of these lands and no one else will be until the day I die.
IN TIME, DAVID WON MANY BATTLES. KING SAUL BECAME ANGRY AT DAVID FOR HIS SUCCESS. ONE DAY AS DAVID PLAYED THE HARP FOR SAUL, HE ATTACKED DAVID.

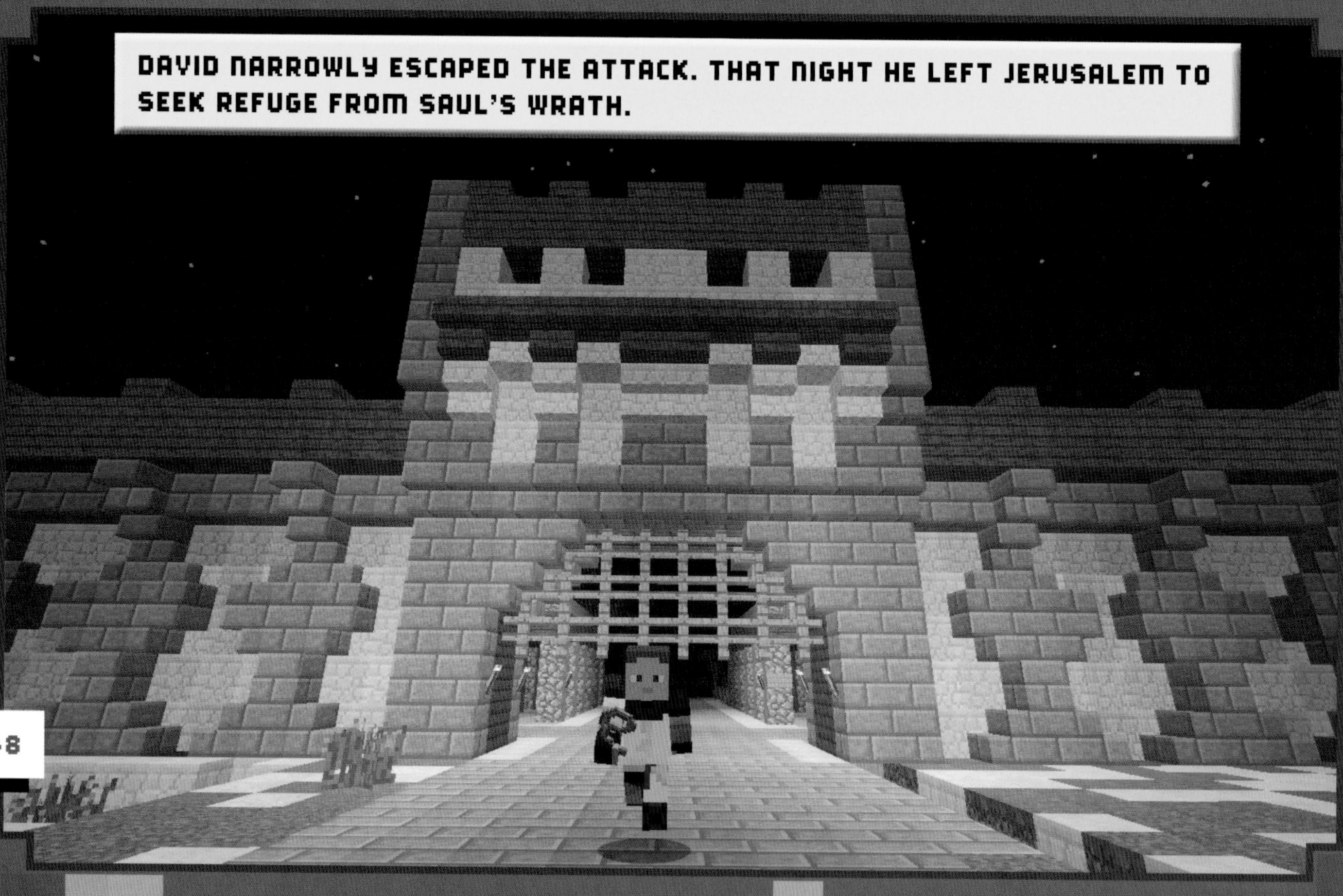
DAVID NARROWLY ESCAPED THE ATTACK. THAT NIGHT HE LEFT JERUSALEM TO SEEK REFUGE FROM SAUL'S WRATH.

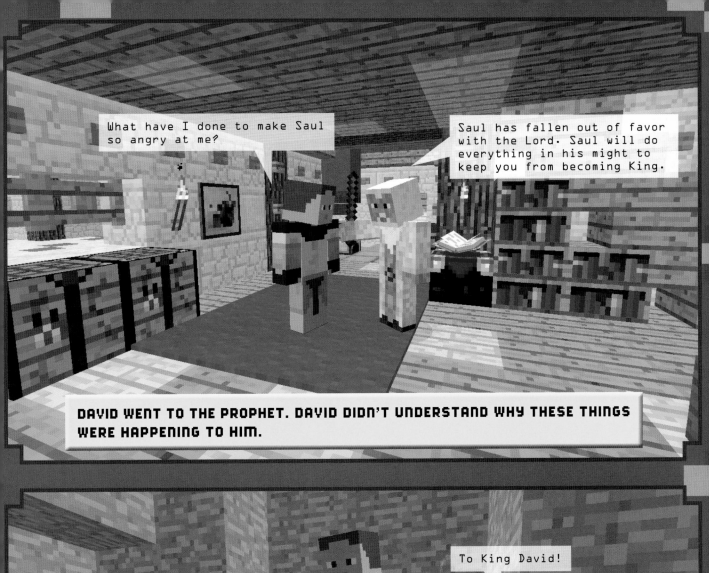

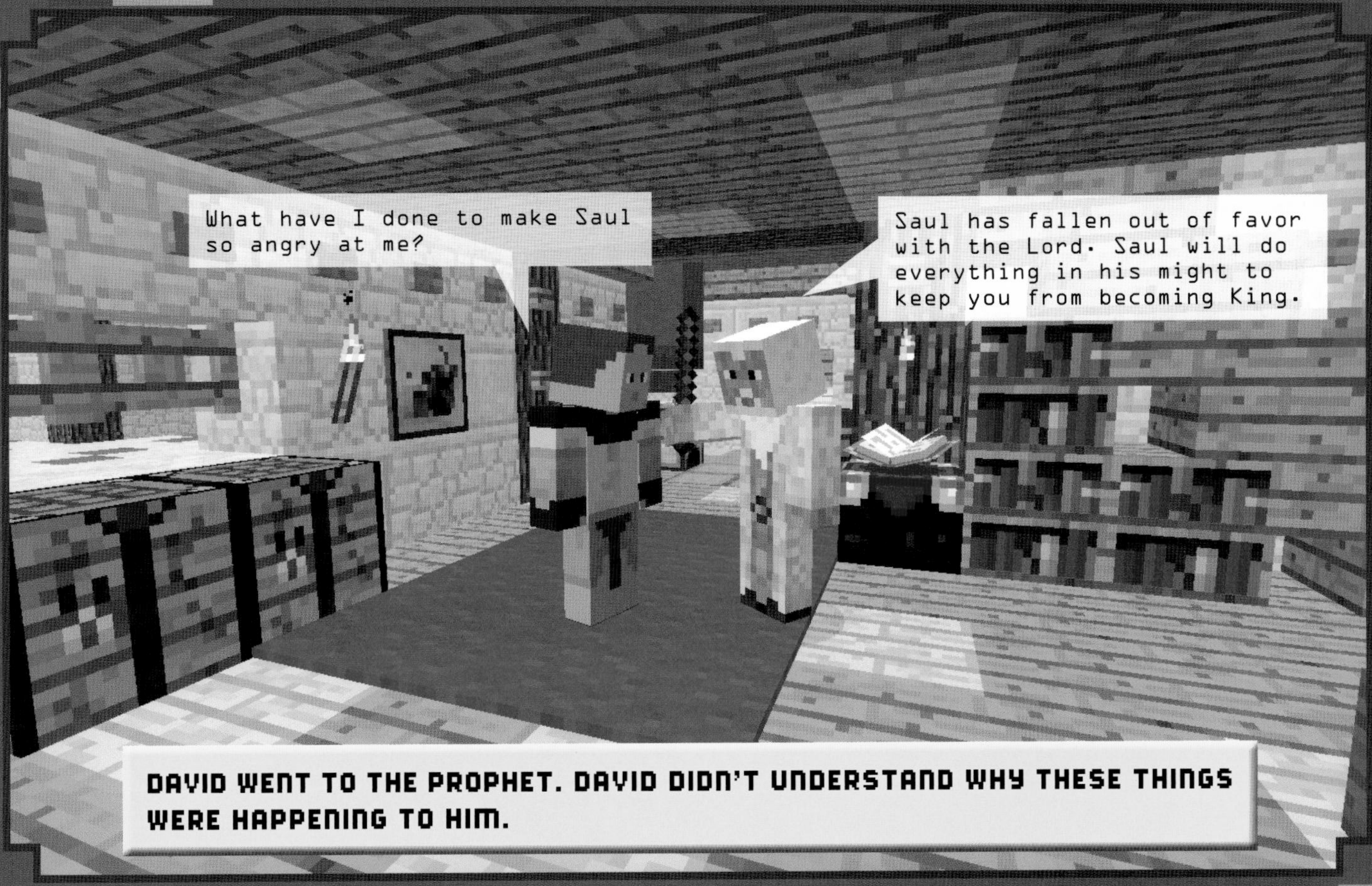
What have I done to make Saul so angry at me?
Saul has fallen out of favor with the Lord. Saul will do everything in his might to keep you from becoming King.
DAVID WENT TO THE PROPHET. DAVID DIDN'T UNDERSTAND WHY THESE THINGS WERE HAPPENING TO HIM.

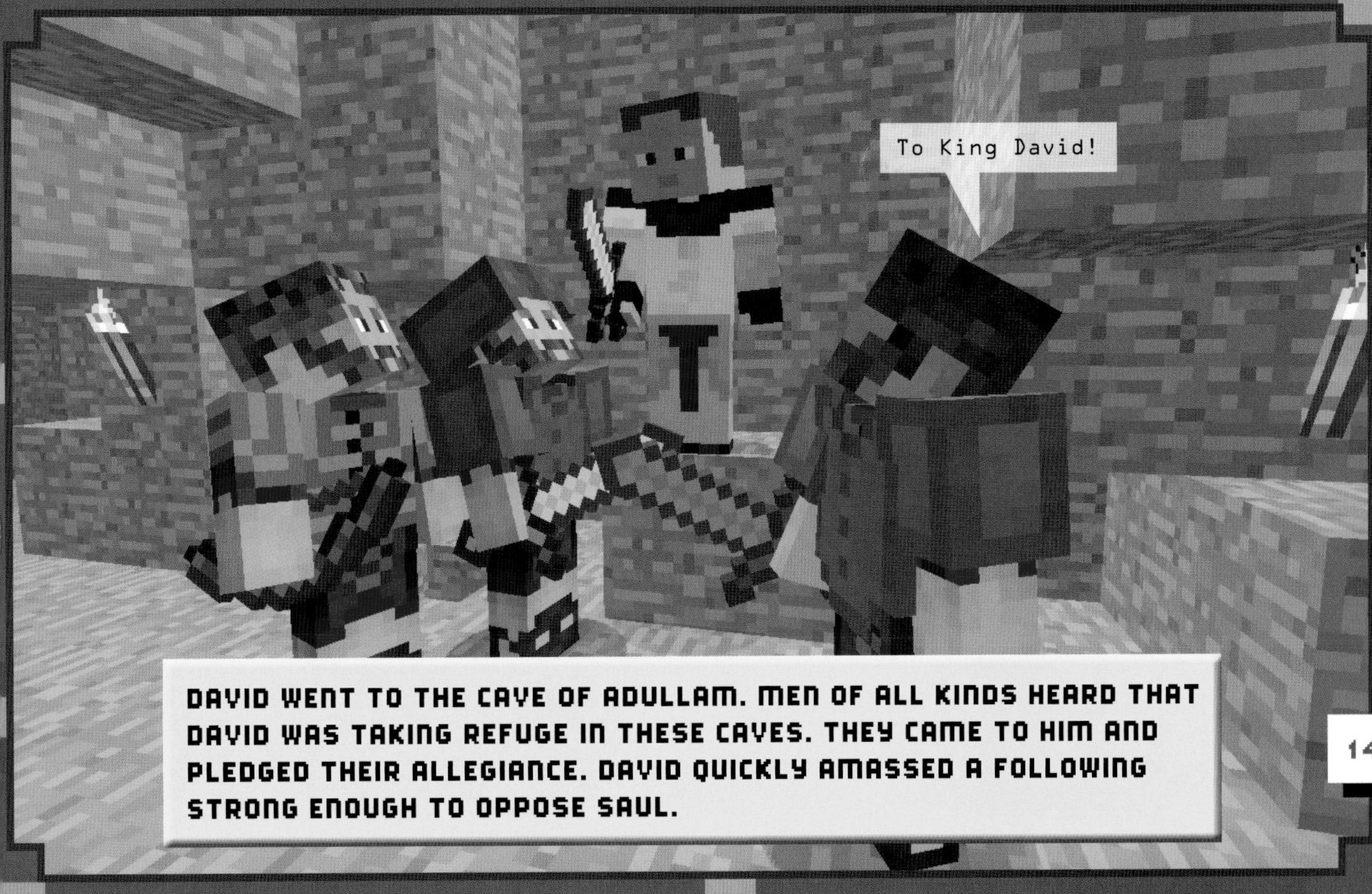
To King David!
DAVID WENT TO THE CAVE OF ADULLAM. MEN OF ALL KINDS HEARD THAT DAVID WAS TAKING REFUGE IN THESE CAVES. THEY CAME TO HIM AND PLEDGED THEIR ALLEGIANCE. DAVID QUICKLY AMASSED A FOLLOWING STRONG ENOUGH TO OPPOSE SAUL.

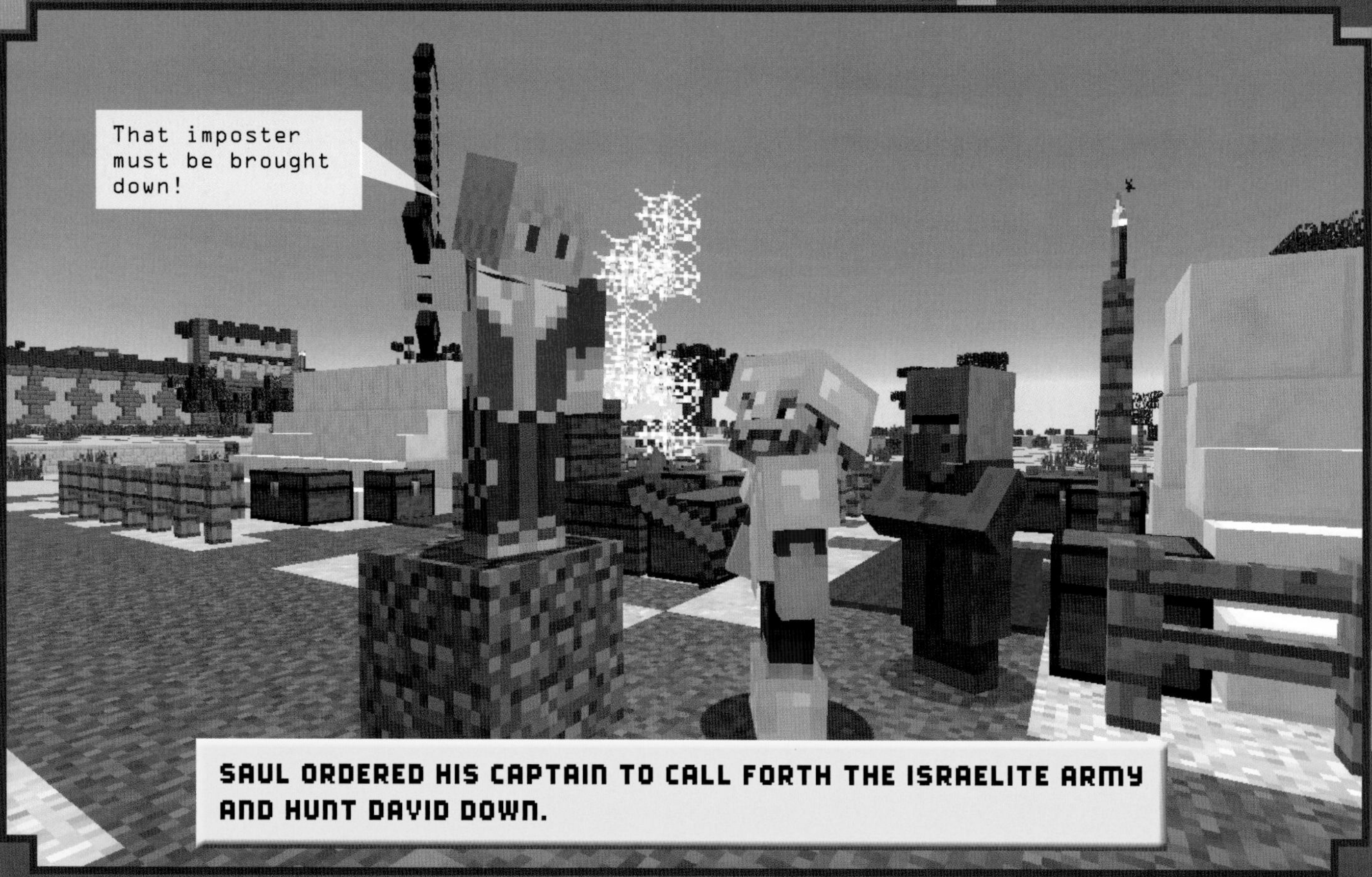
That imposter must be brought down!
SAUL ORDERED HIS CAPTAIN TO CALL FORTH THE ISRAELITE ARMY AND HUNT DAVID DOWN.

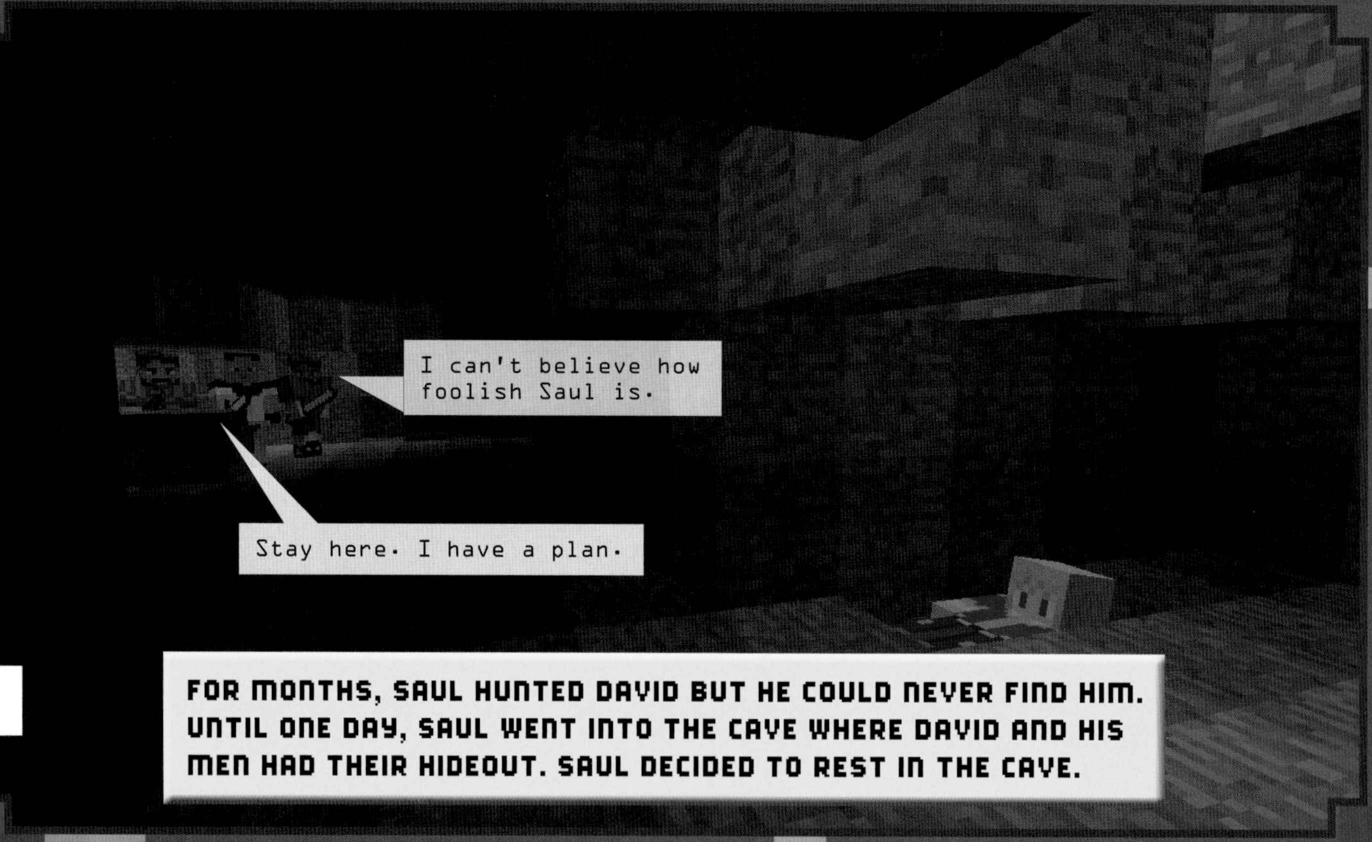
I can't believe how foolish Saul is.
Stay here. I have a plan.
FOR MONTHS, SAUL HUNTED DAVID BUT HE COULD NEVER FIND HIM. UNTIL ONE DAY, SAUL WENT INTO THE CAVE WHERE DAVID AND HIS MEN HAD THEIR HIDEOUT. SAUL DECIDED TO REST IN THE CAVE.

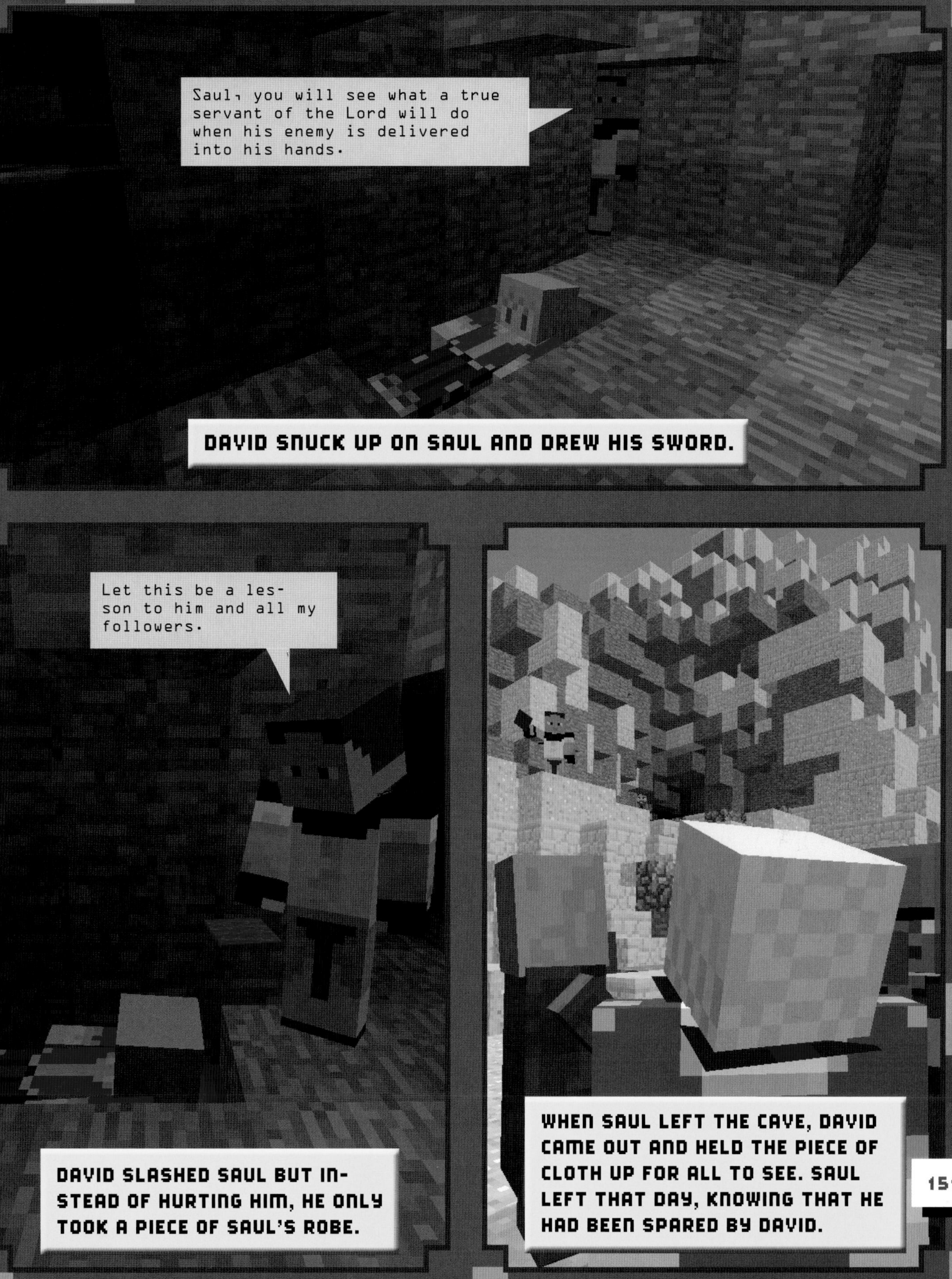
Saul, you will see what a true servant of the Lord will do when his enemy is delivered into his hands.
DAVID SNUCK UP ON SAUL AND DREW HIS SWORD.
Let this be a lesson to him and all my followers.
DAVID SLASHED SAUL BUT INSTEAD OF HURTING HIM, HE ONLY TOOK A PIECE OF SAUL'S ROBE.
WHEN SAUL LEFT THE CAVE, DAVID CAME OUT AND HELD THE PIECE OF CLOTH UP FOR ALL TO SEE. SAUL LEFT THAT DAY, KNOWING THAT HE HAD BEEN SPARED BY DAVID.

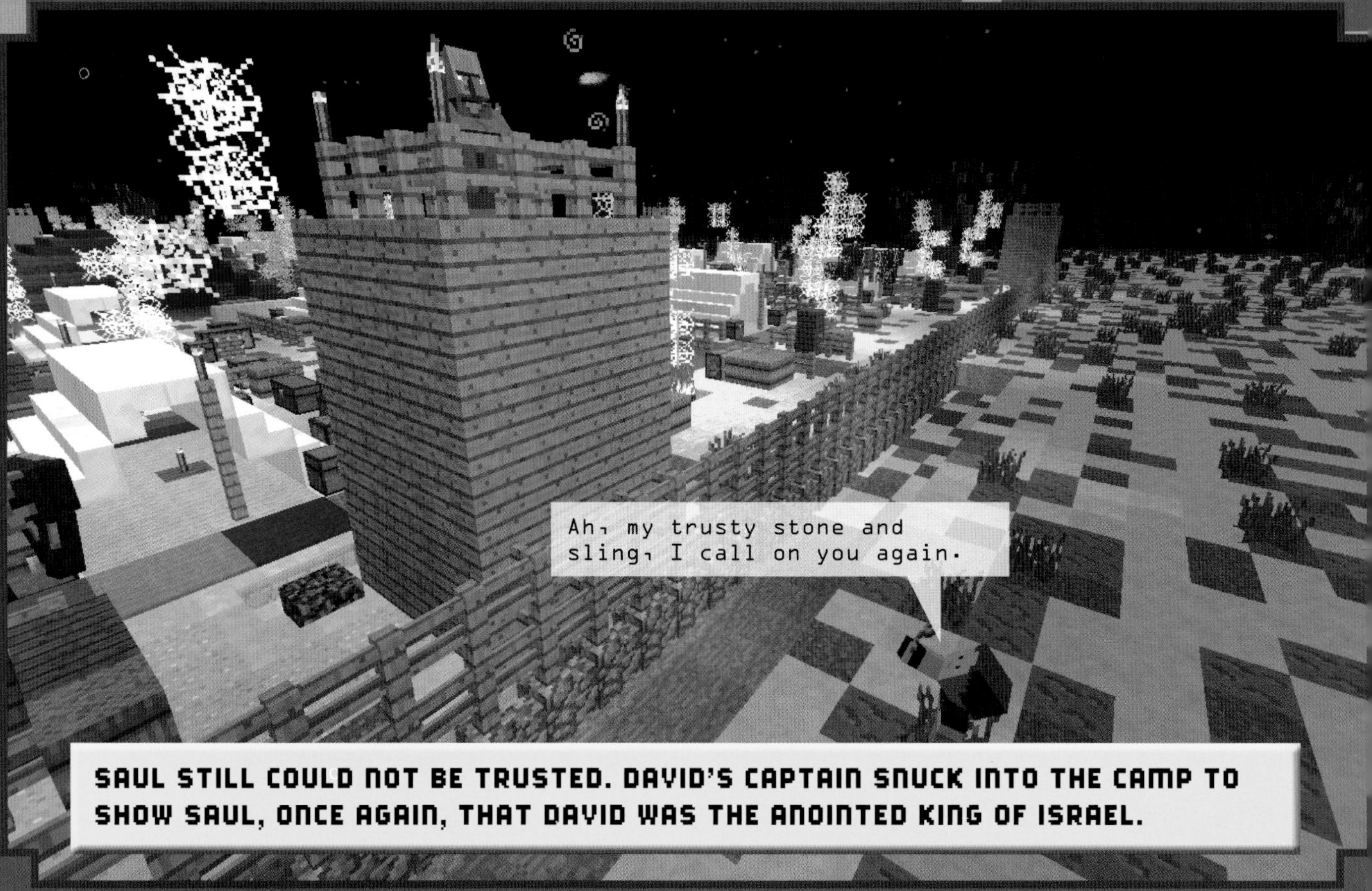
Ah, my trusty stone and sling, I call on you again.
SAUL STILL COULD NOT BE TRUSTED. DAVID'S CAPTAIN SNUCK INTO THE CAMP TO SHOW SAUL, ONCE AGAIN, THAT DAVID WAS THE ANOINTED KING OF ISRAEL.

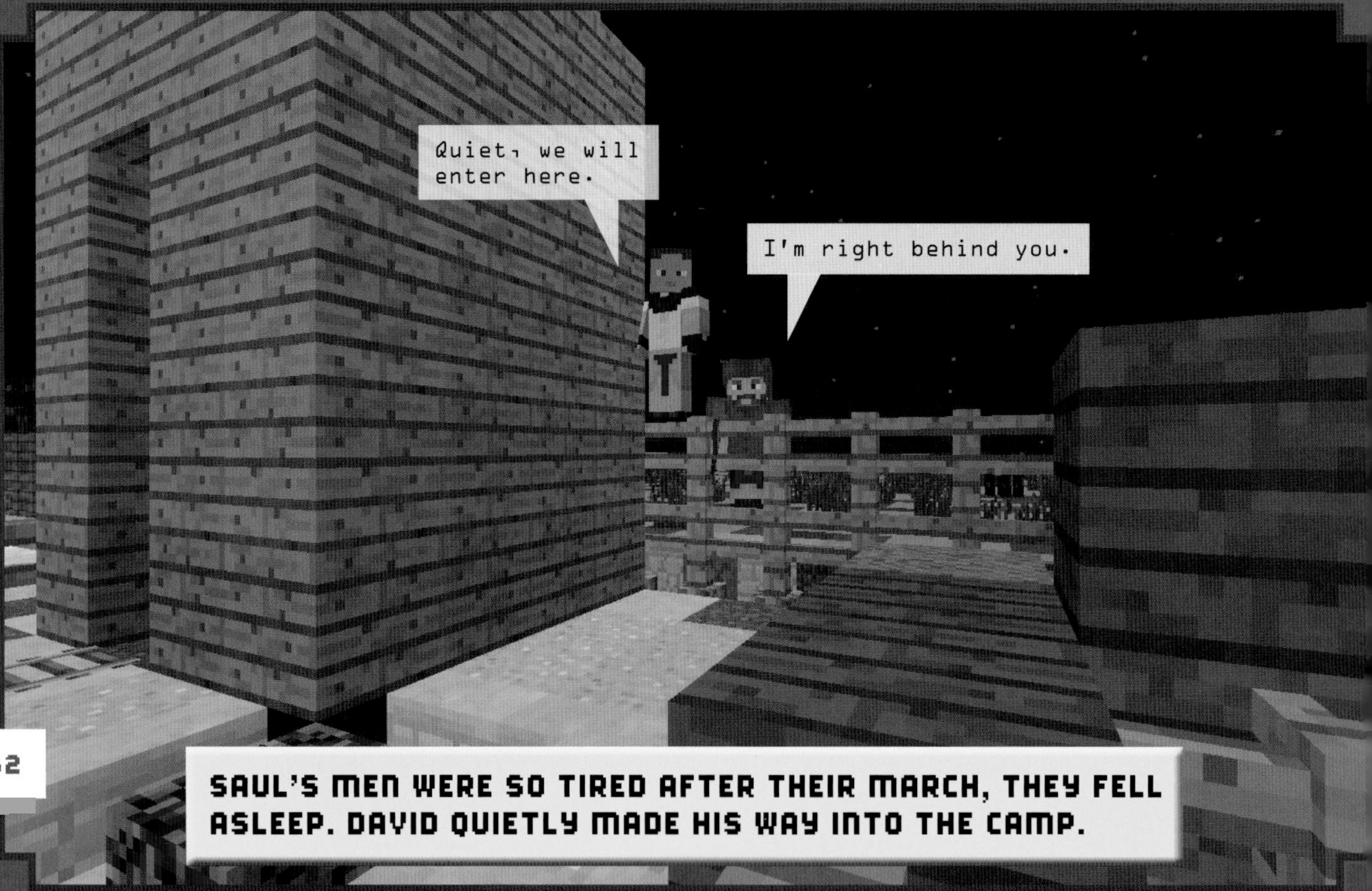
Quiet, we will enter here.
I'm right behind you.
SAUL'S MEN WERE SO TIRED AFTER THEIR MARCH, THEY FELL ASLEEP. DAVID QUIETLY MADE HIS WAY INTO THE CAMP.

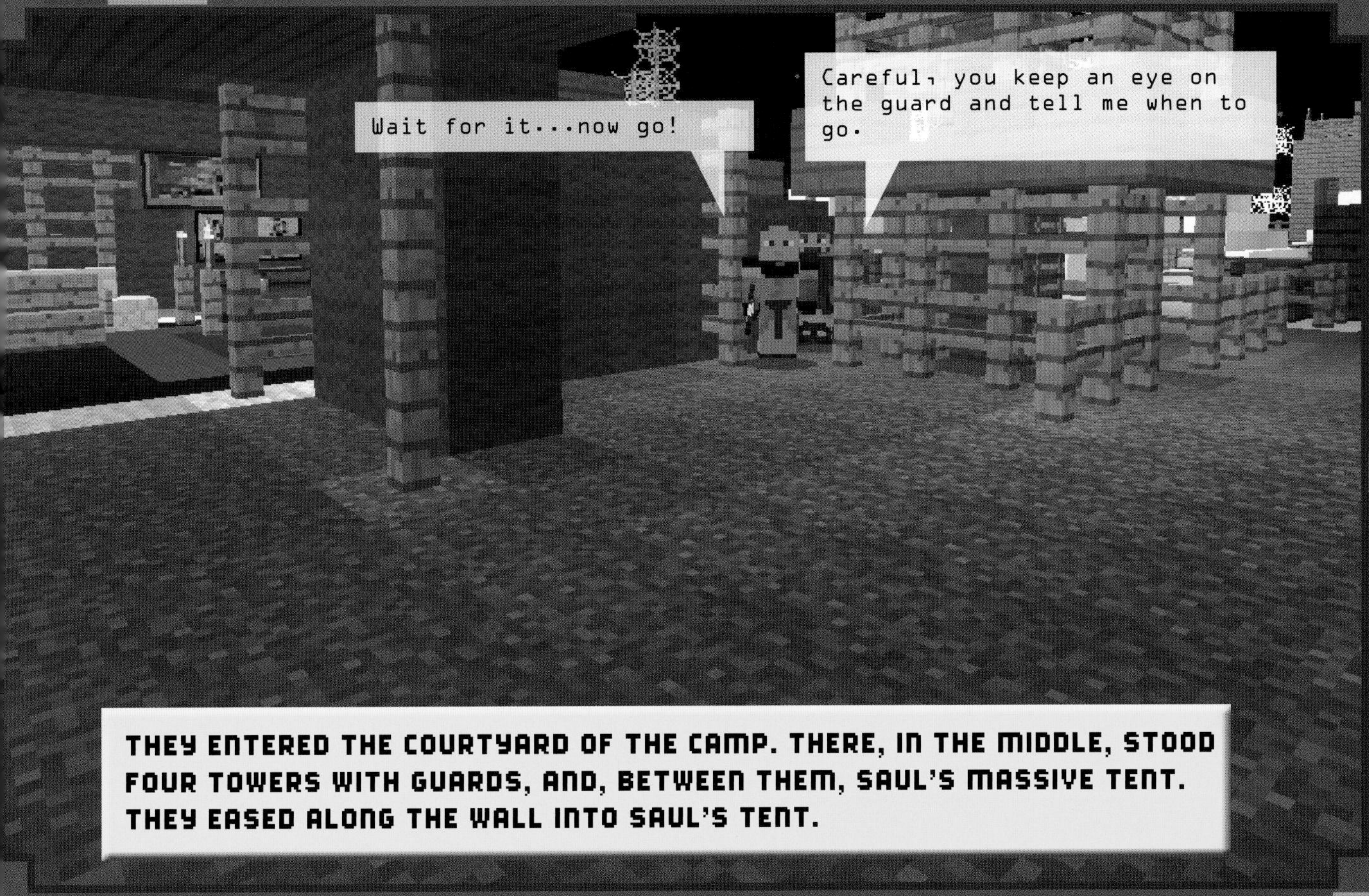
Wait for it...now go!
Careful, you keep an eye on the guard and tell me when to go.
THEY ENTERED THE COURTYARD OF THE CAMP. THERE, IN THE MIDDLE, STOOD FOUR TOWERS WITH GUARDS, AND, BETWEEN THEM, SAUL'S MASSIVE TENT. THEY EASED ALONG THE WALL INTO SAUL'S TENT.

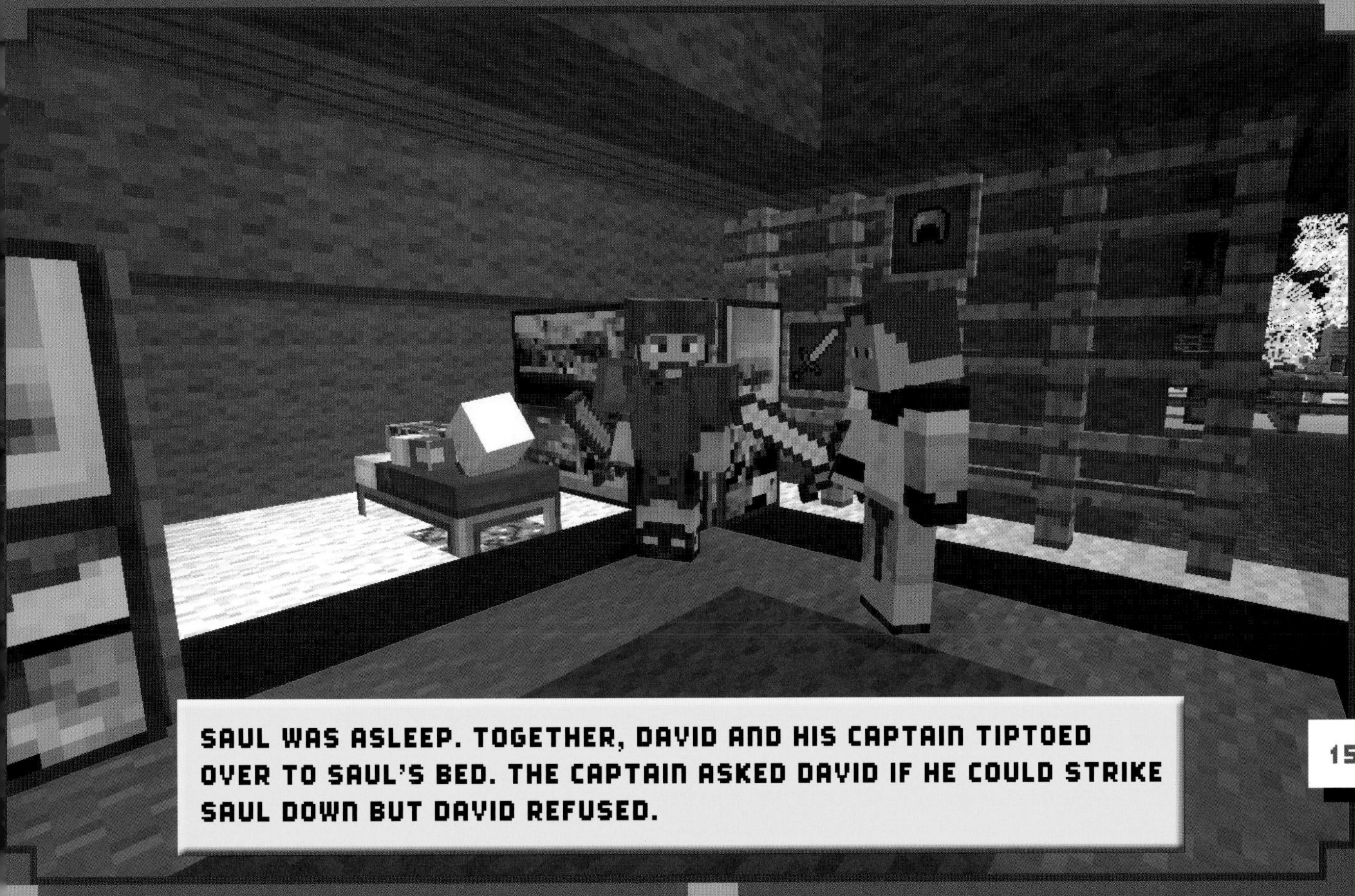
SAUL WAS ASLEEP. TOGETHER, DAVID AND HIS CAPTAIN TIPTOED OVER TO SAUL'S BED. THE CAPTAIN ASKED DAVID IF HE COULD STRIKE SAUL DOWN BUT DAVID REFUSED.

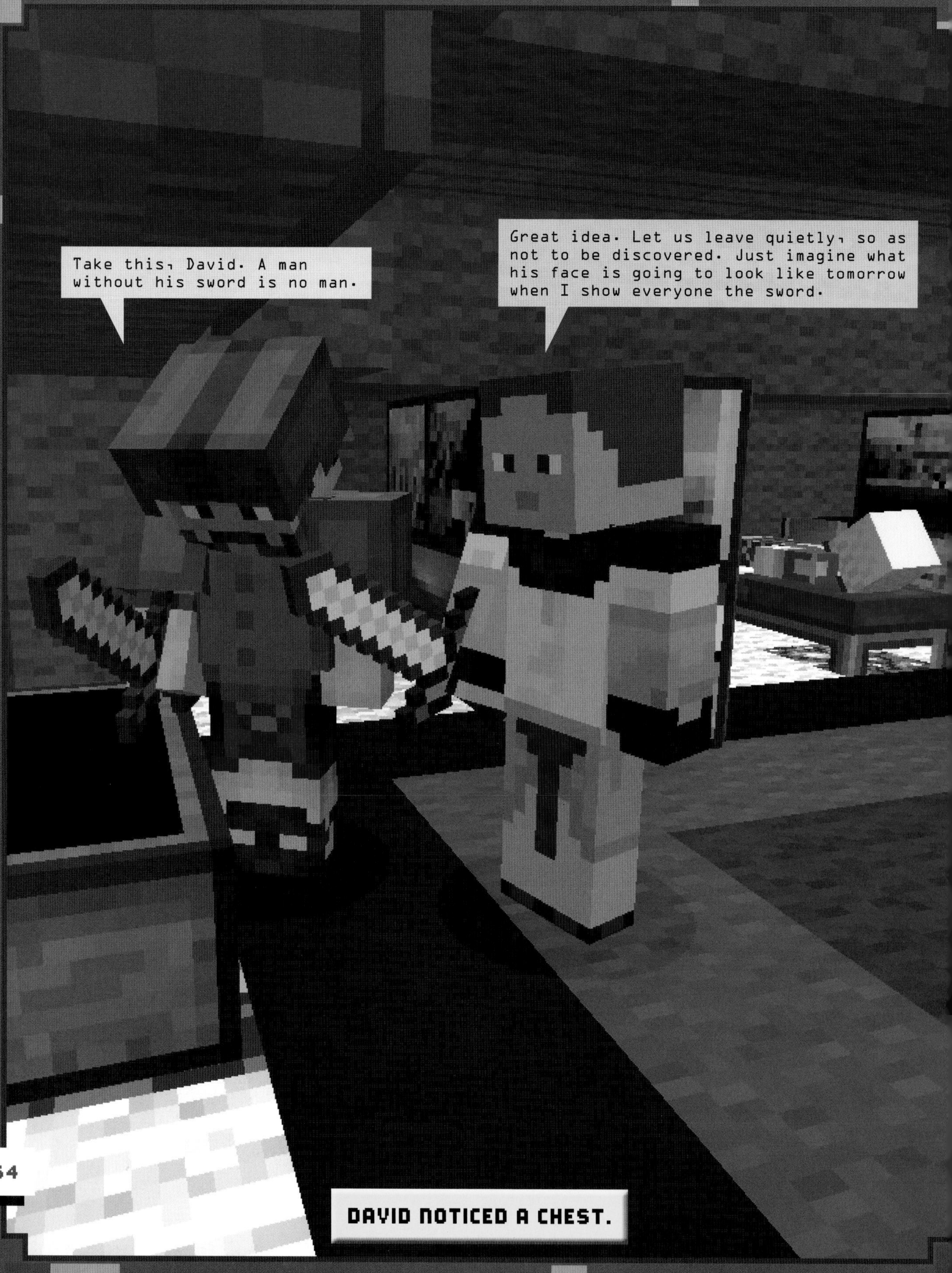
Take this, David. A man without his sword is no man.
Great idea. Let us leave quietly, so as not to be discovered. Just imagine what his face is going to look like tomorrow when I show everyone the sword.
DAVID NOTICED A CHEST.

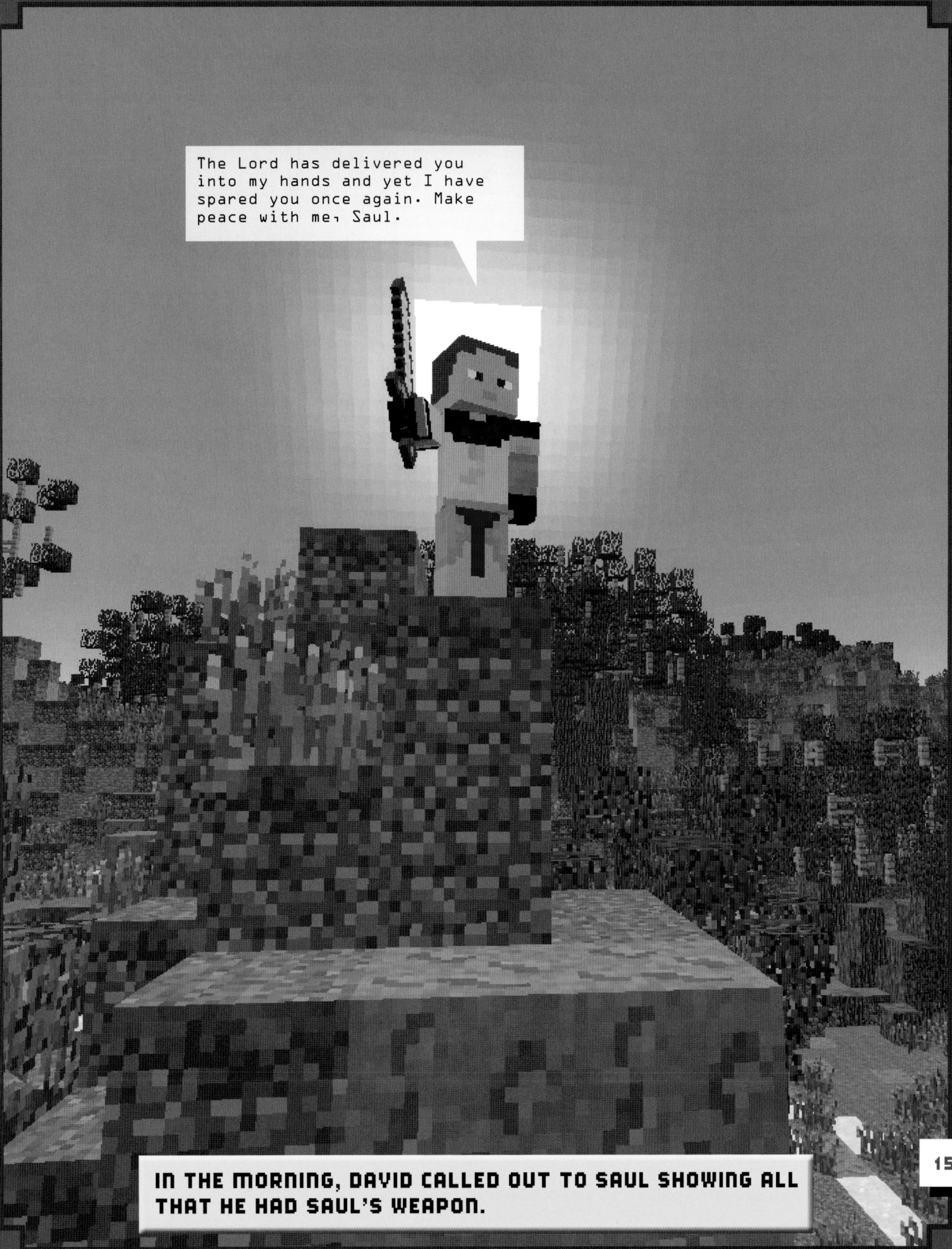
The Lord has delivered you into my hands and yet I have spared you once again. Make peace with me, Saul.
IN THE MORNING, DAVID CALLED OUT TO SAUL SHOWING ALL THAT HE HAD SAUL'S WEAPON.

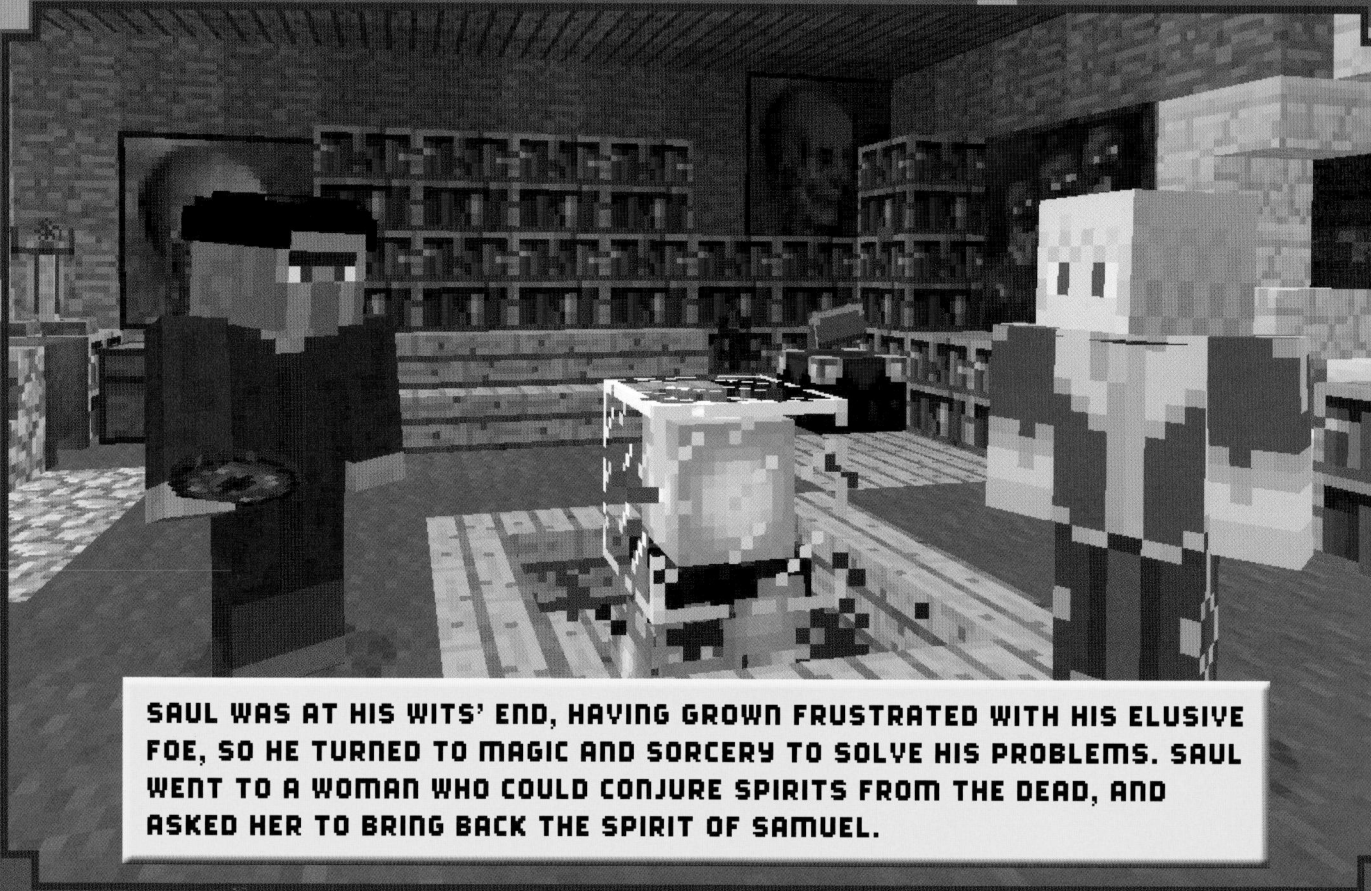
SAUL WAS AT HIS WITS' END, HAVING GROWN FRUSTRATED WITH HIS ELUSIVE FOE, SO HE TURNED TO MAGIC AND SORCERY TO SOLVE HIS PROBLEMS. SAUL WENT TO A WOMAN WHO COULD CONJURE SPIRITS FROM THE DEAD, AND ASKED HER TO BRING BACK THE SPIRIT OF SAMUEL.

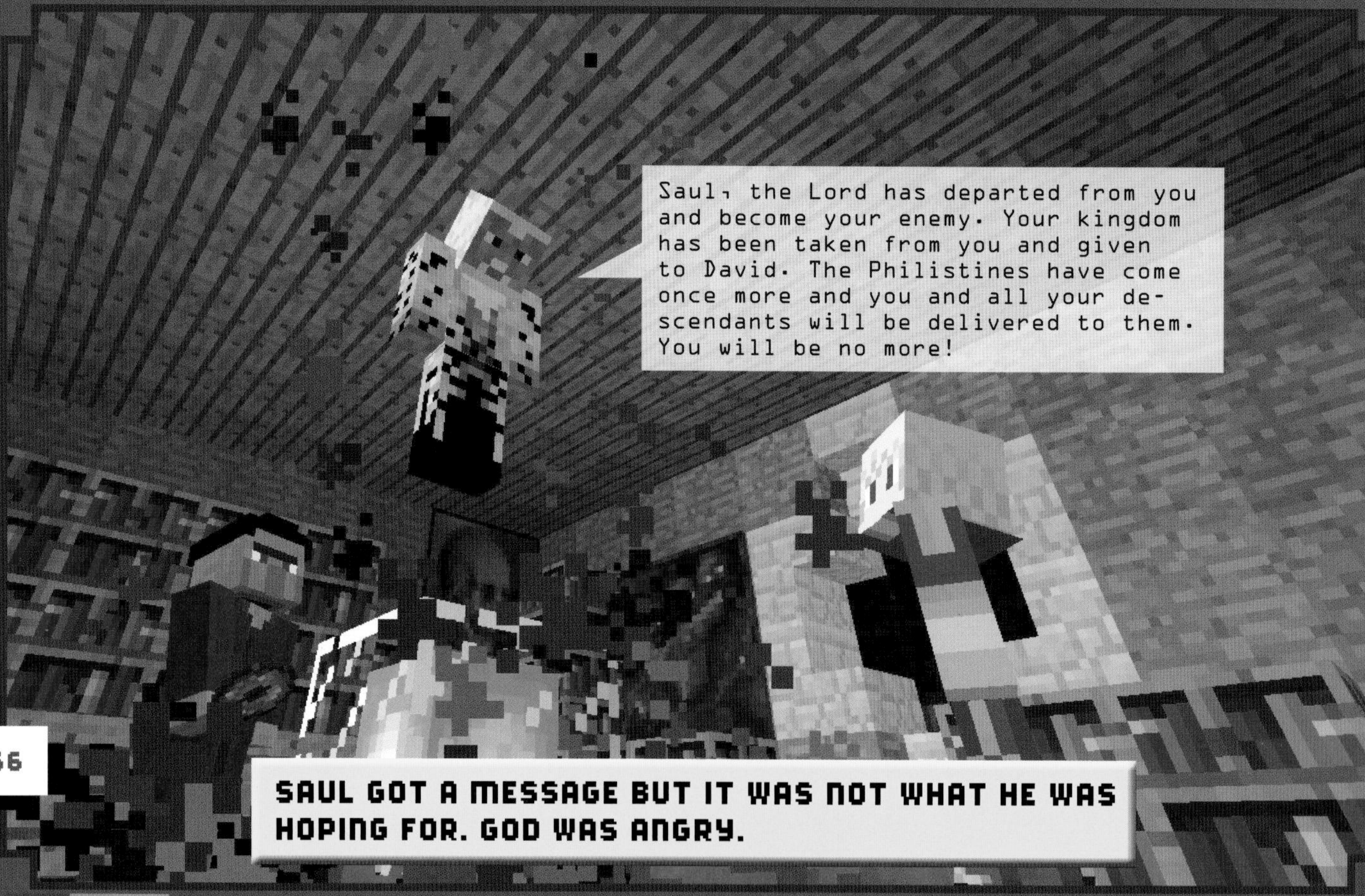
Saul, the Lord has departed from you and become your enemy. Your kingdom has been taken from you and given to David. The Philistines have come once more and you and all your descendants will be delivered to them. You will be no more!
SAUL GOT A MESSAGE BUT IT WAS NOT WHAT HE WAS HOPING FOR. GOD WAS ANGRY.

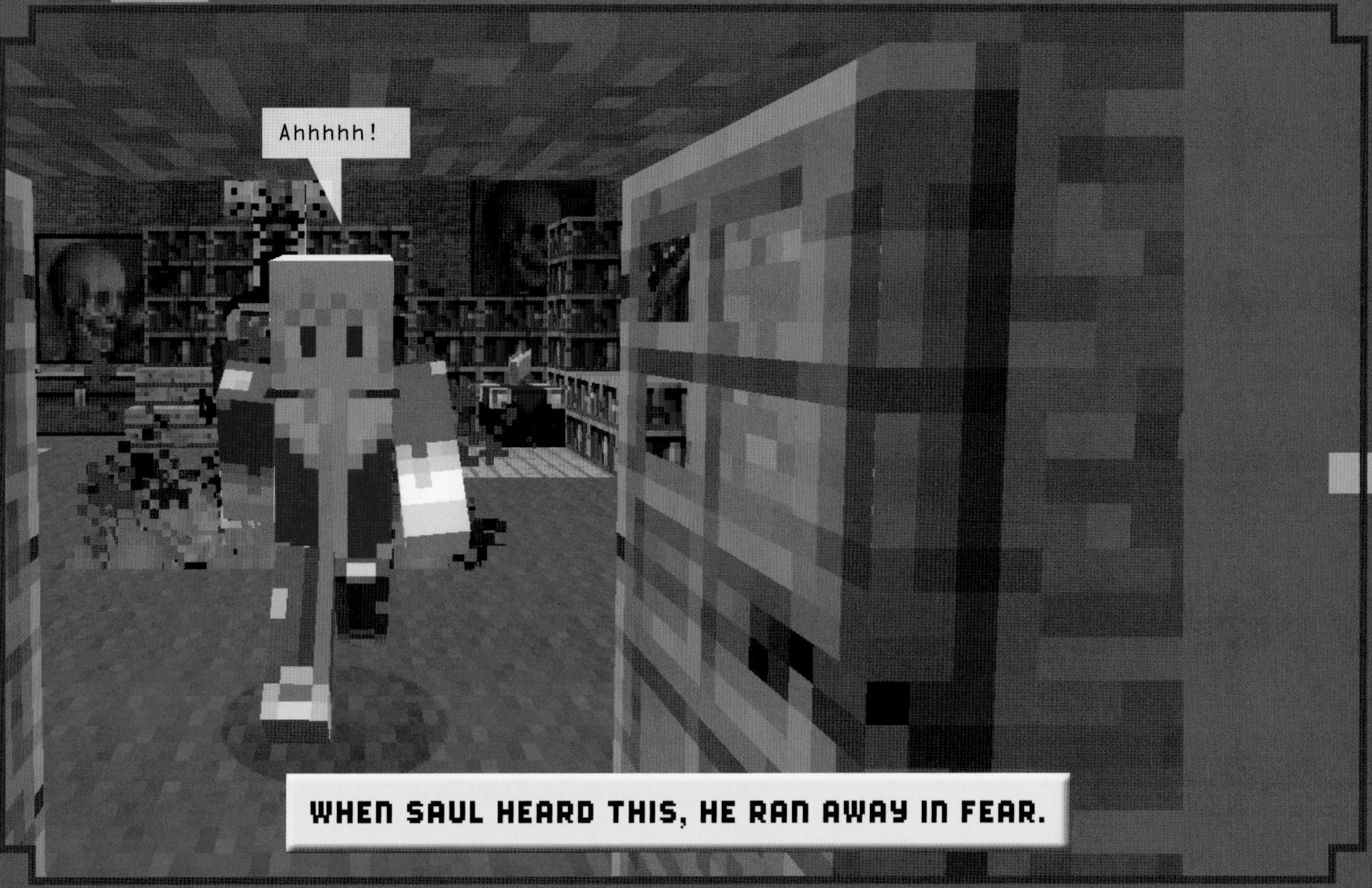
Ahhhhh!
WHEN SAUL HEARD THIS, HE RAN AWAY IN FEAR.

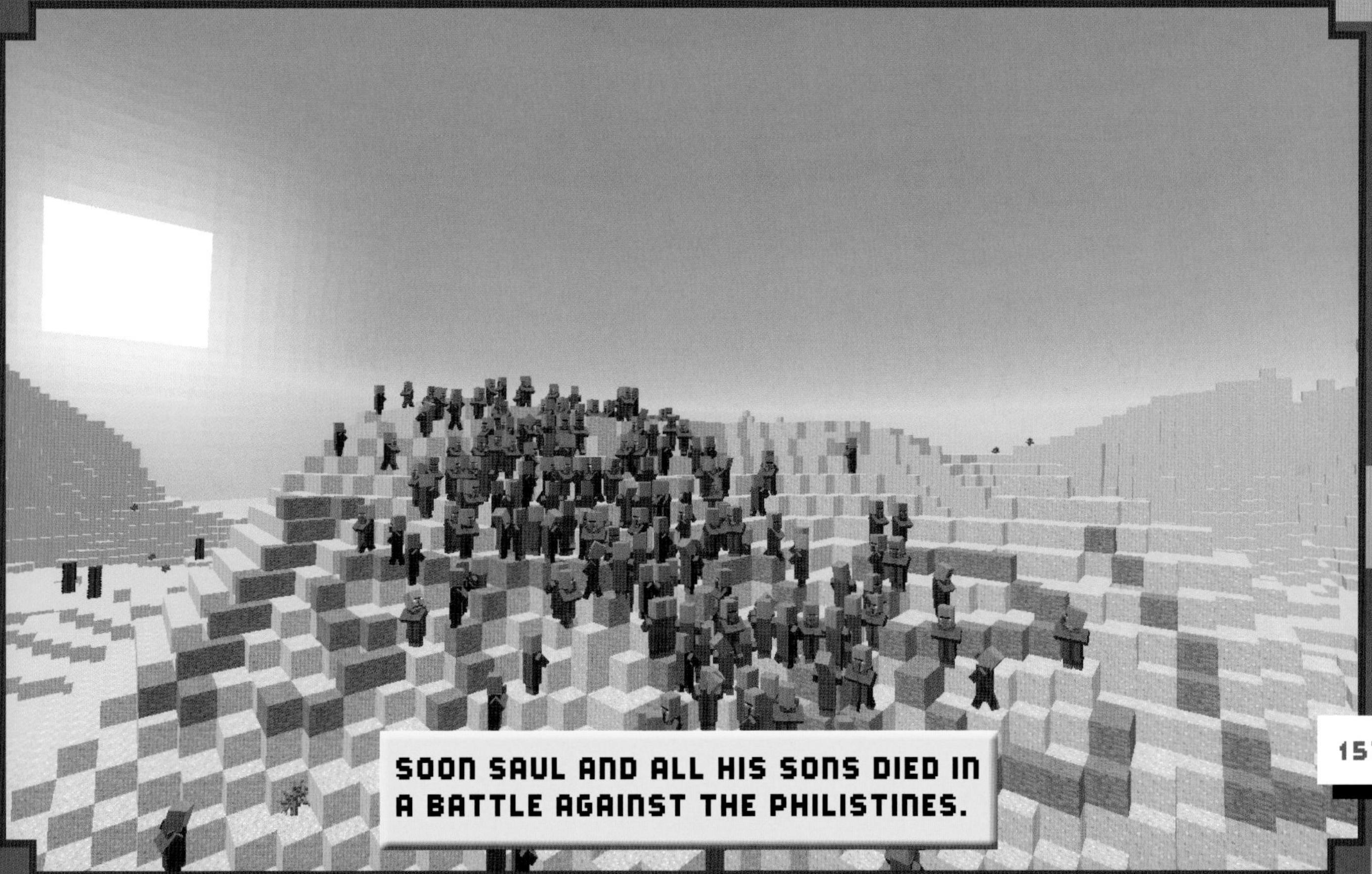
SOON SAUL AND ALL HIS SONS DIED IN A BATTLE AGAINST THE PHILISTINES.

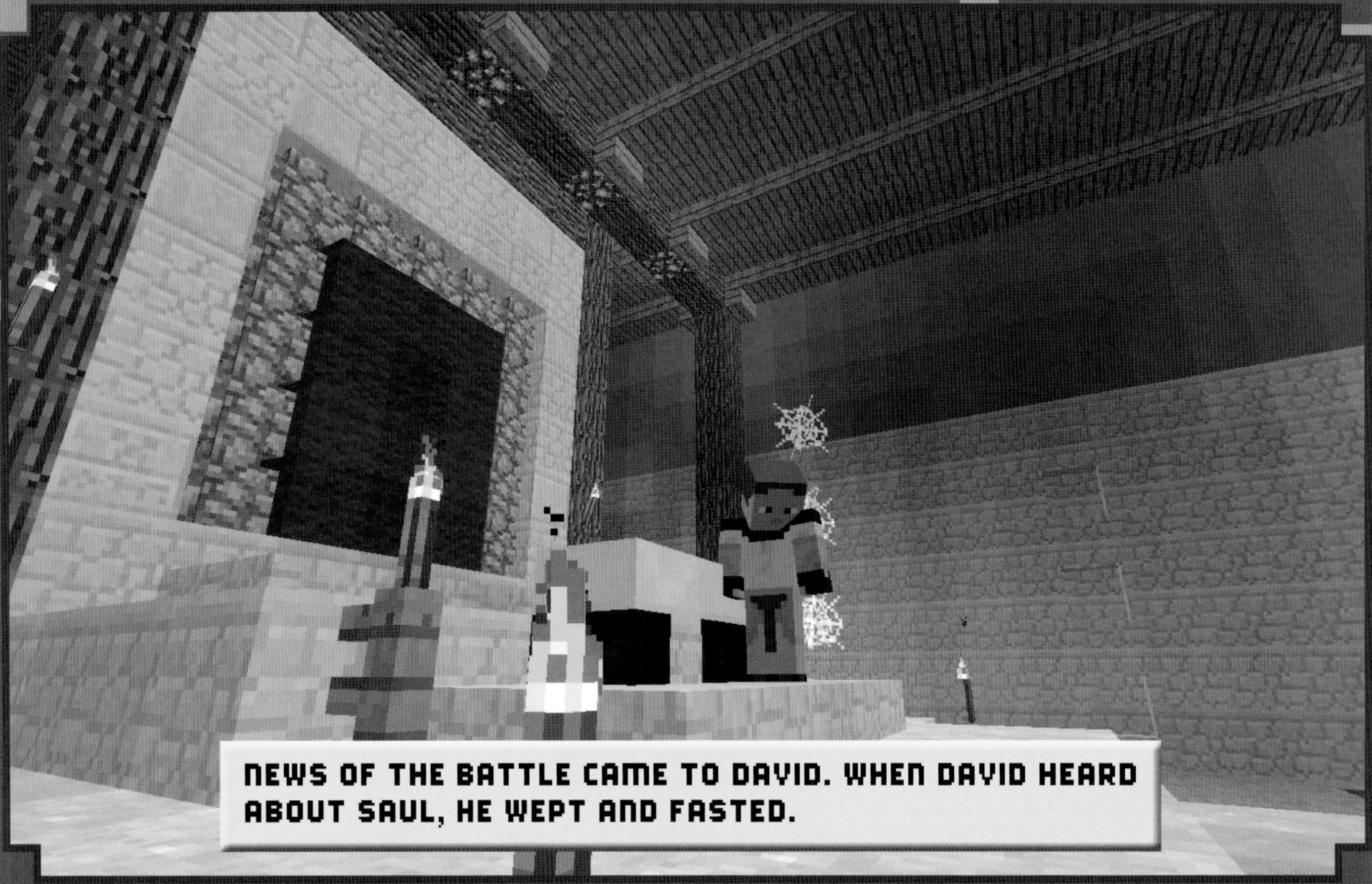
NEWS OF THE BATTLE CAME TO DAVID. WHEN DAVID HEARD ABOUT SAUL, HE WEPT AND FASTED.

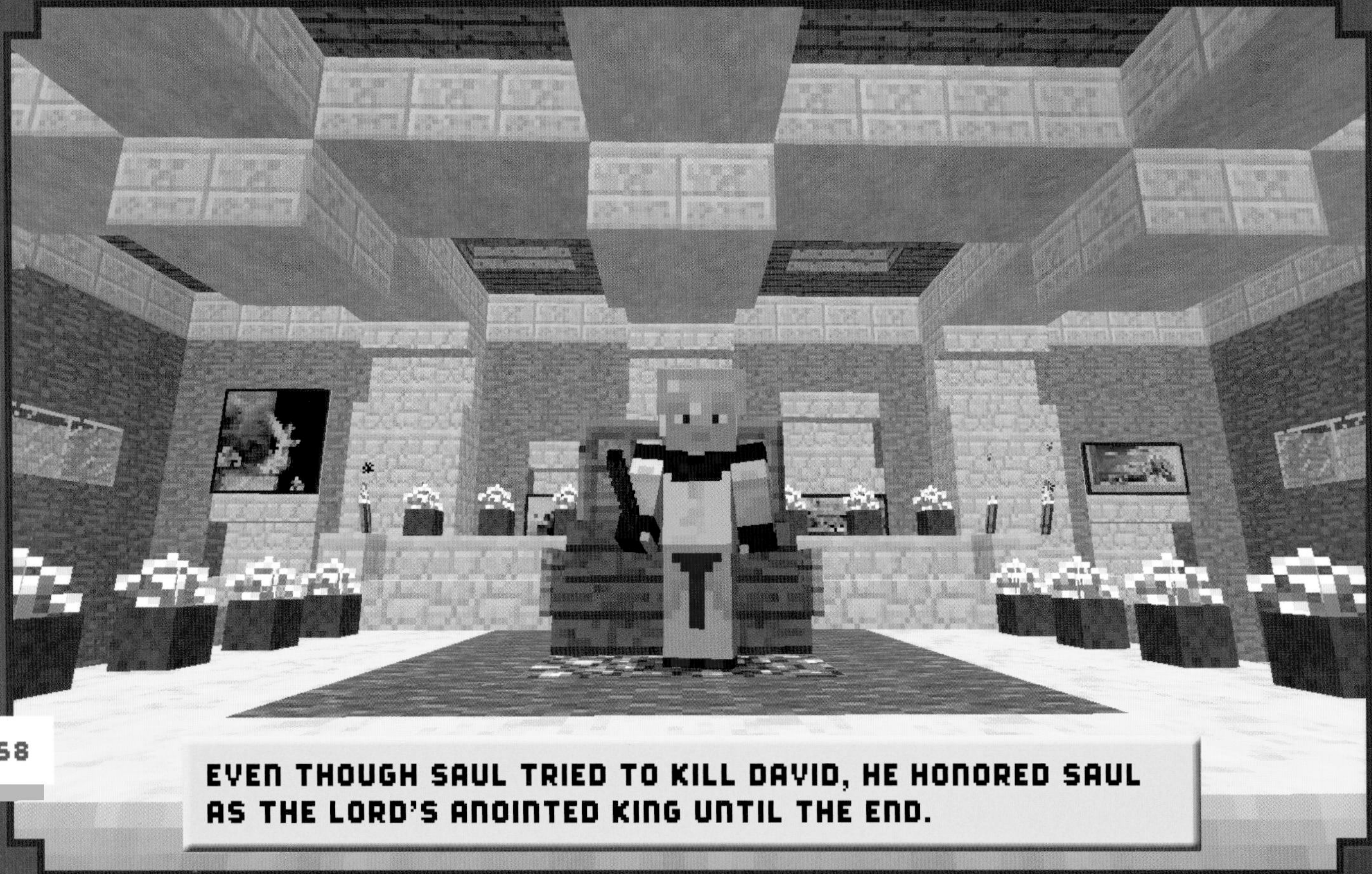
EVEN THOUGH SAUL TRIED TO KILL DAVID, HE HONORED SAUL AS THE LORD'S ANOINTED KING UNTIL THE END.

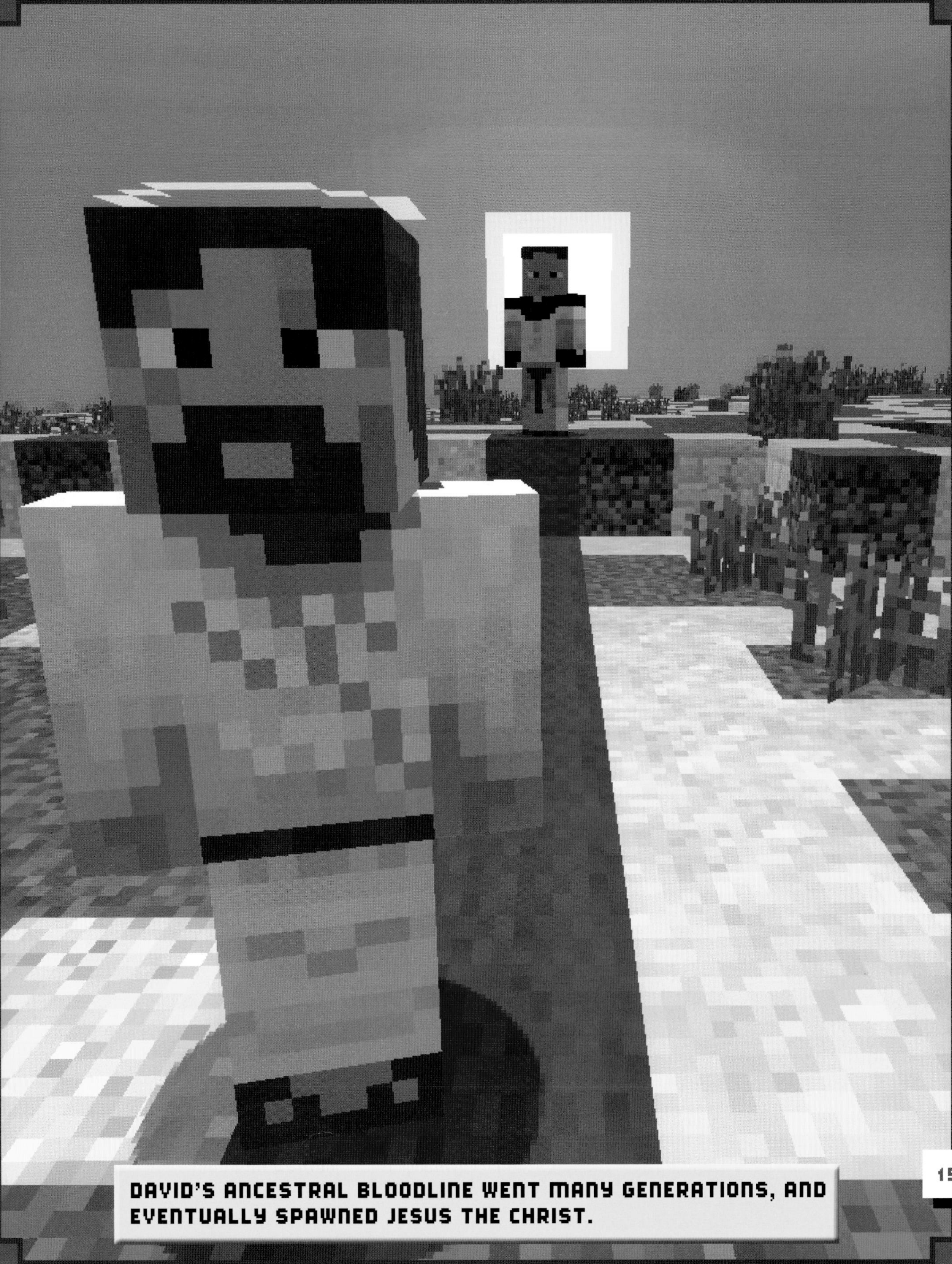

DAVID'S ANCESTRAL BLOODLINE WENT MANY GENERATIONS, AND EVENTUALLY SPAWNED JESUS THE CHRIST.

JONAH AND THE WHALE

Boy, that David is quite a star!

After David will come a series of prophets who continue to illuminate the masses with my message. One in particular, however, is quite stubborn.

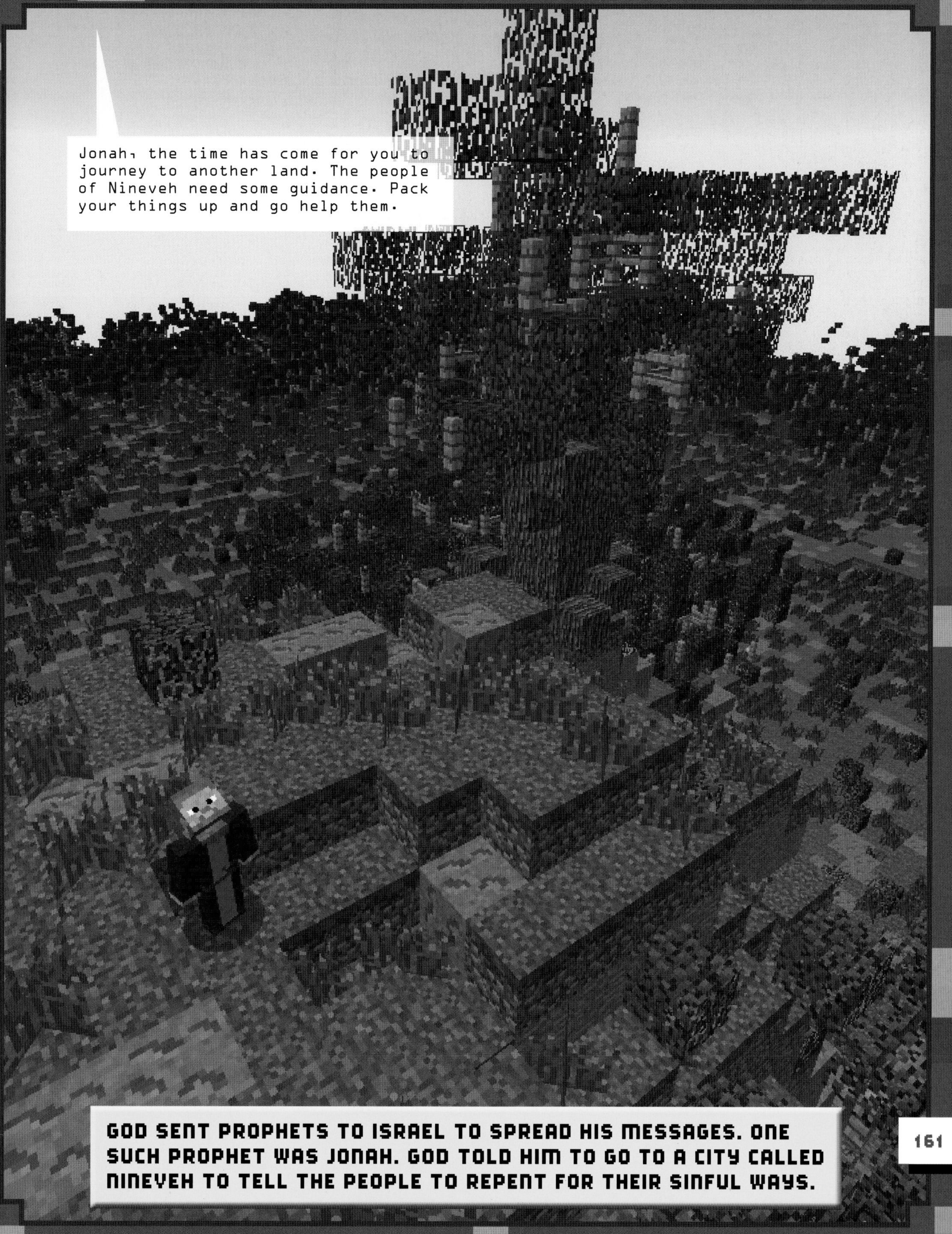
Jonah, the time has come for you to journey to another land. The people of Nineveh need some guidance. Pack your things up and go help them.
GOD SENT PROPHETS TO ISRAEL TO SPREAD HIS MESSAGES. ONE SUCH PROPHET WAS JONAH. GOD TOLD HIM TO GO TO A CITY CALLED NINEVEH TO TELL THE PEOPLE TO REPENT FOR THEIR SINFUL WAYS.

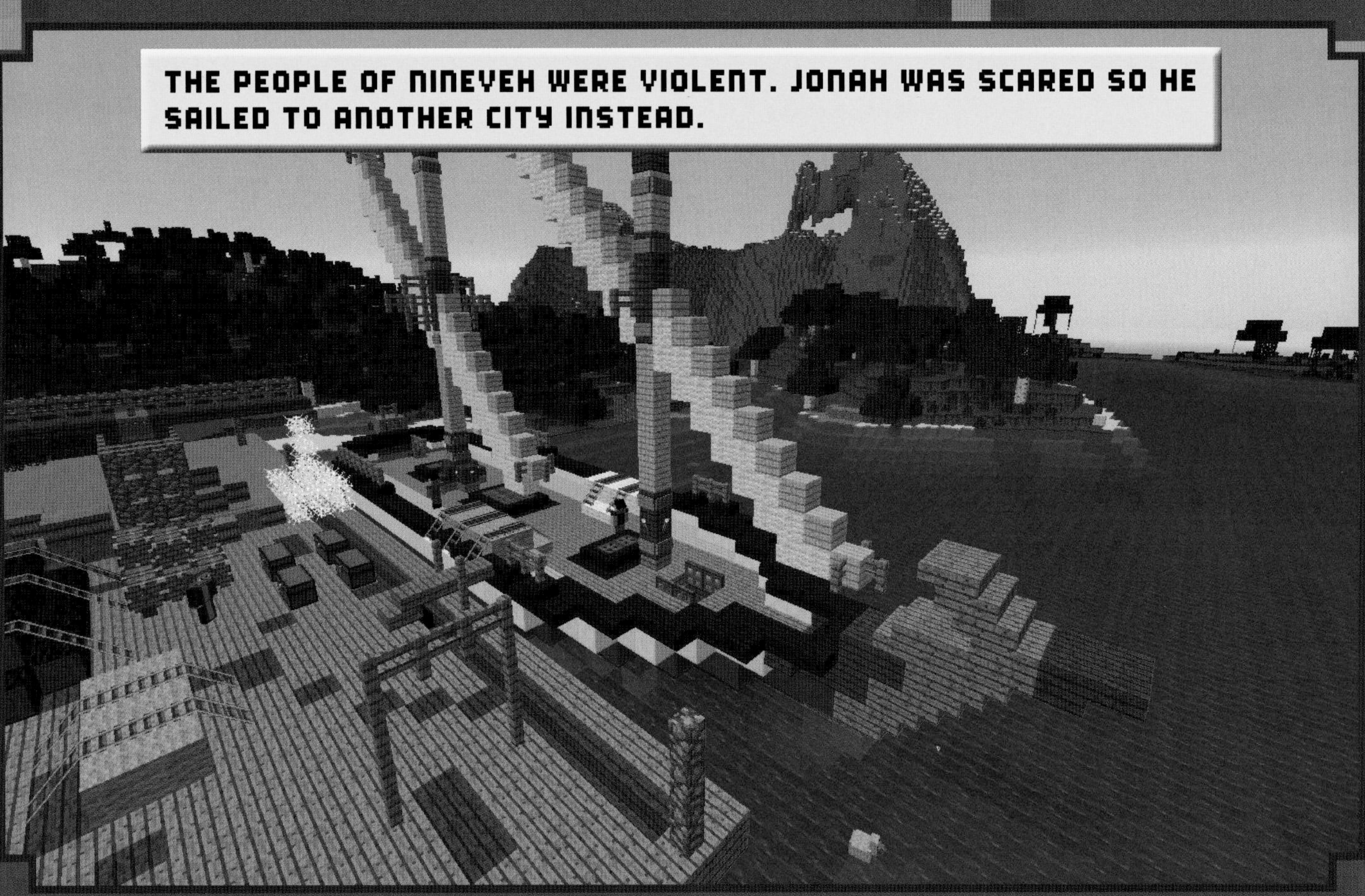
THE PEOPLE OF NINEVEH WERE VIOLENT. JONAH WAS SCARED SO HE SAILED TO ANOTHER CITY INSTEAD.

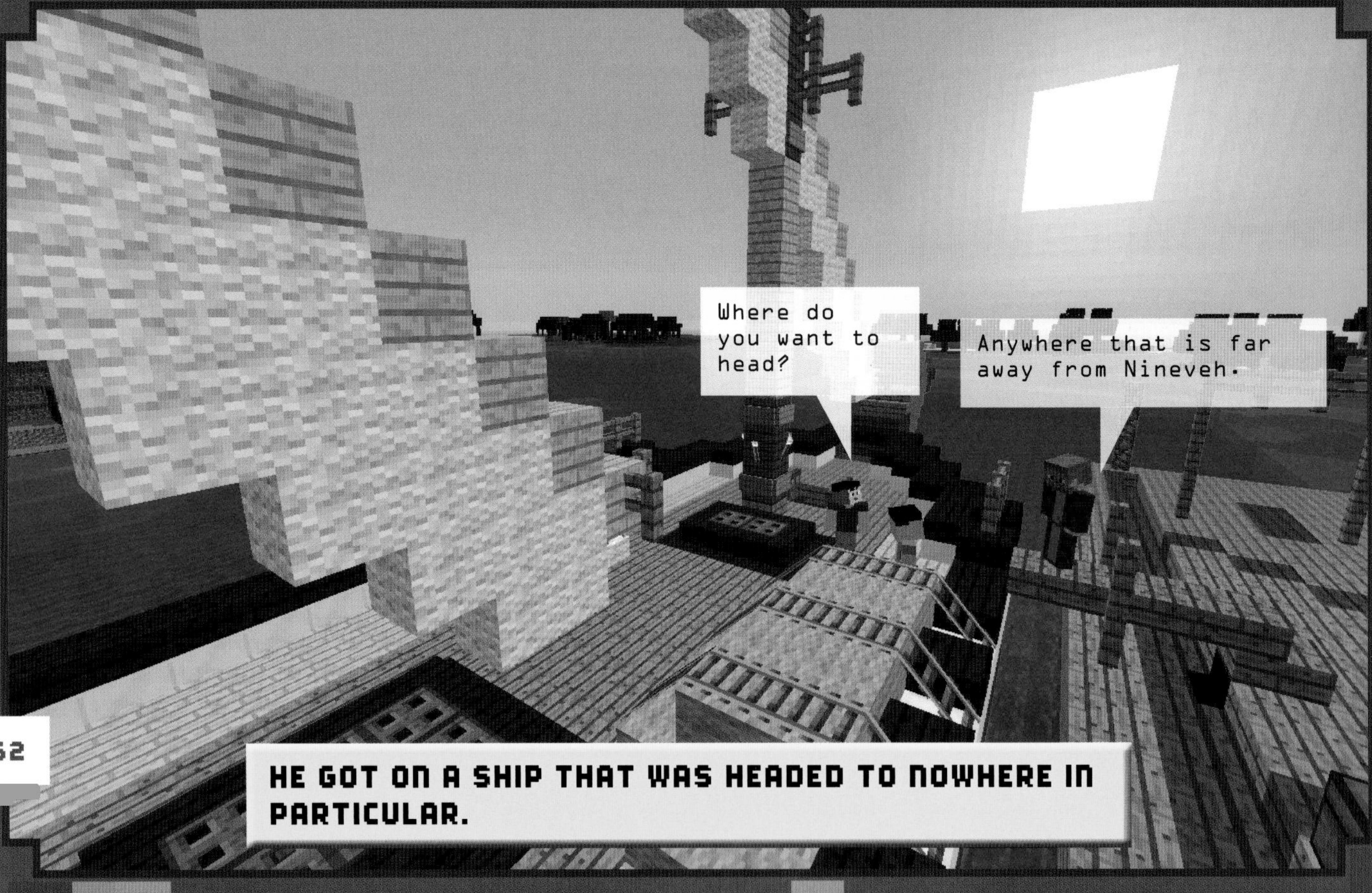
Where do you want to head?
Anywhere that is far away from Nineveh.
HE GOT ON A SHIP THAT WAS HEADED TO NOWHERE IN PARTICULAR.

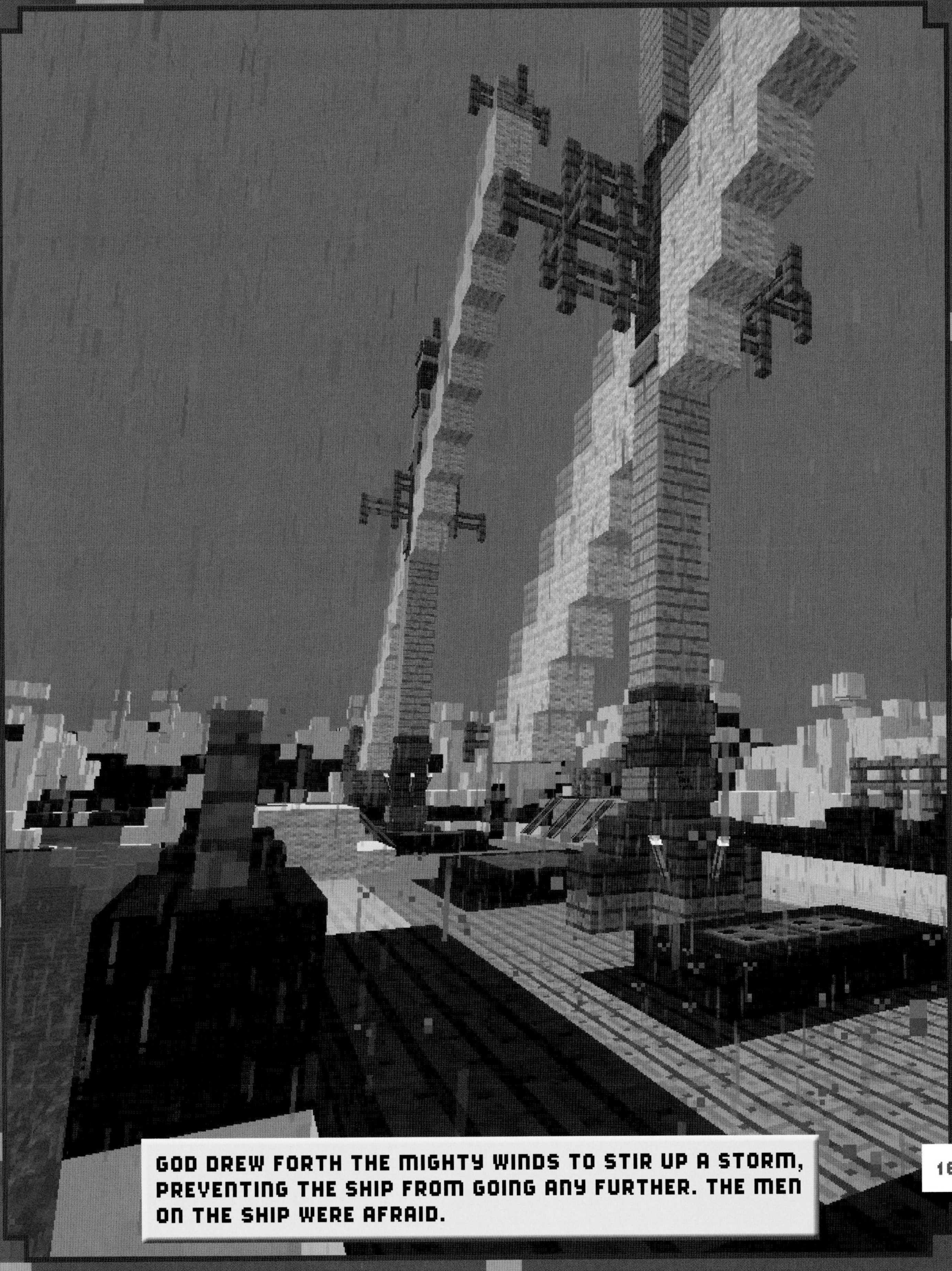

GOD DREW FORTH THE MIGHTY WINDS TO STIR UP A STORM, PREVENTING THE SHIP FROM GOING ANY FURTHER. THE MEN ON THE SHIP WERE AFRAID.

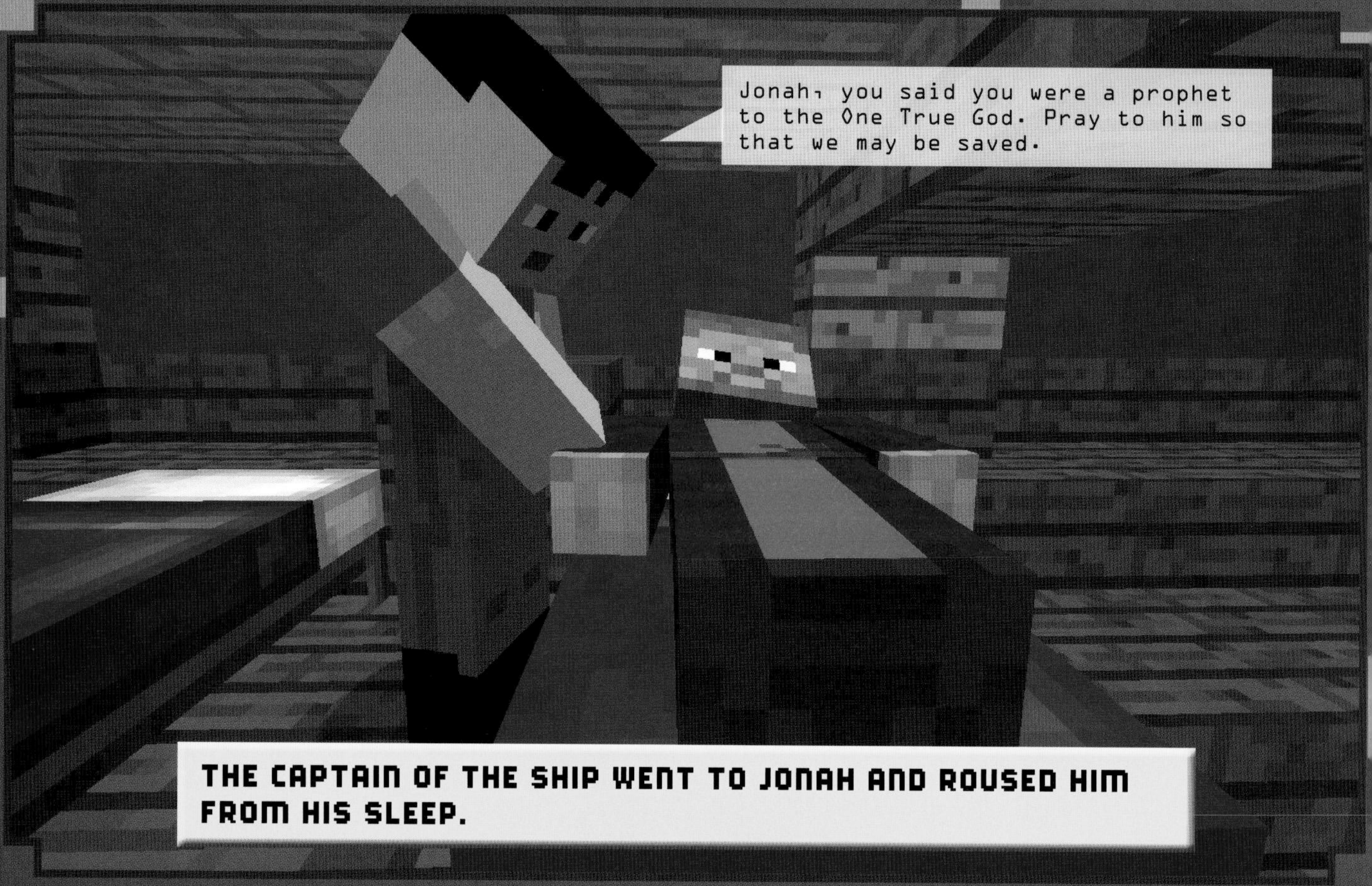
Jonah, you said you were a prophet to the One True God. Pray to him so that we may be saved.
THE CAPTAIN OF THE SHIP WENT TO JONAH AND ROUSED HIM FROM HIS SLEEP.

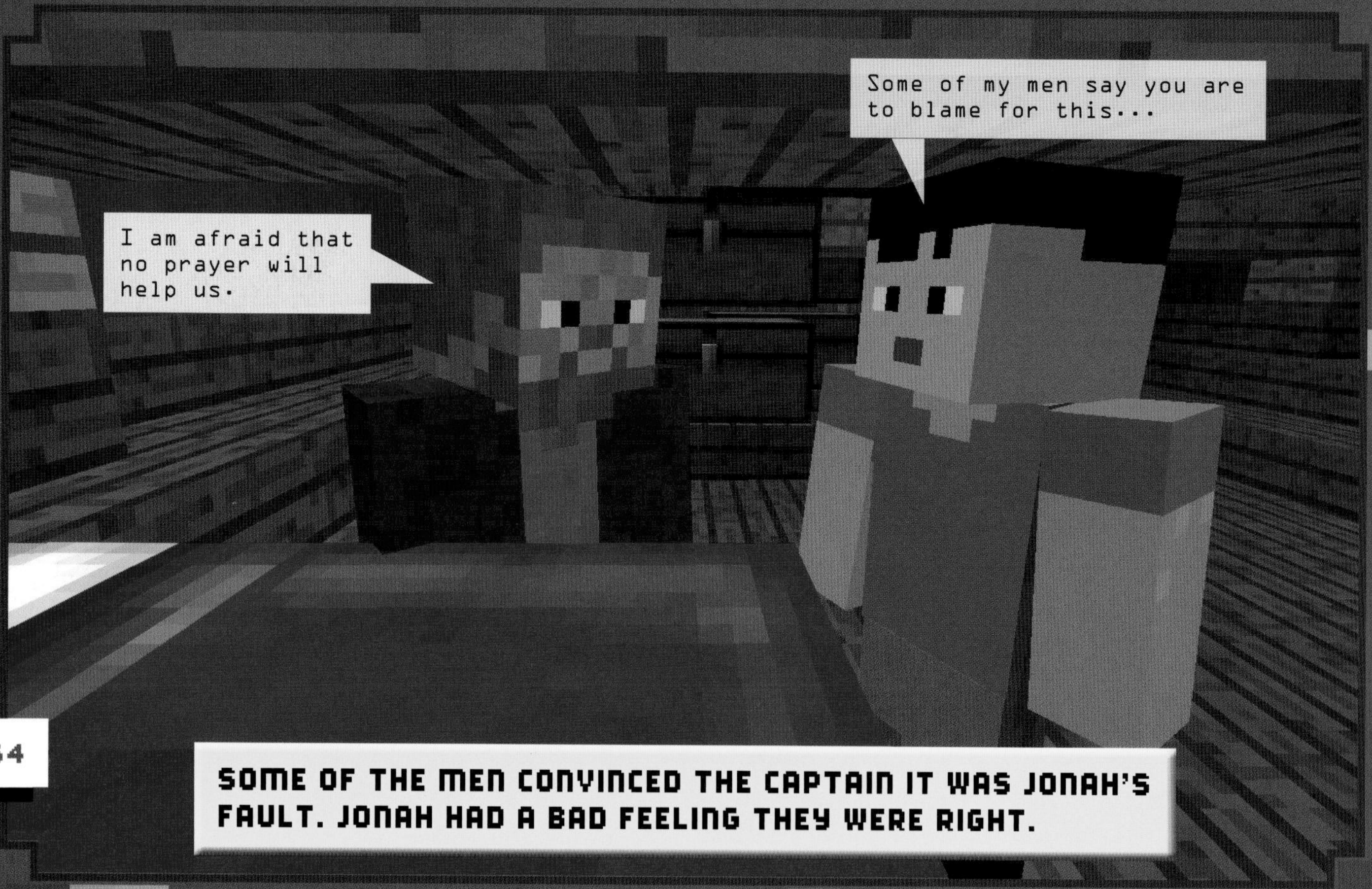
Some of my men say you are to blame for this...
I am afraid that no prayer will help us.
SOME OF THE MEN CONVINCED THE CAPTAIN IT WAS JONAH'S FAULT. JONAH HAD A BAD FEELING THEY WERE RIGHT.

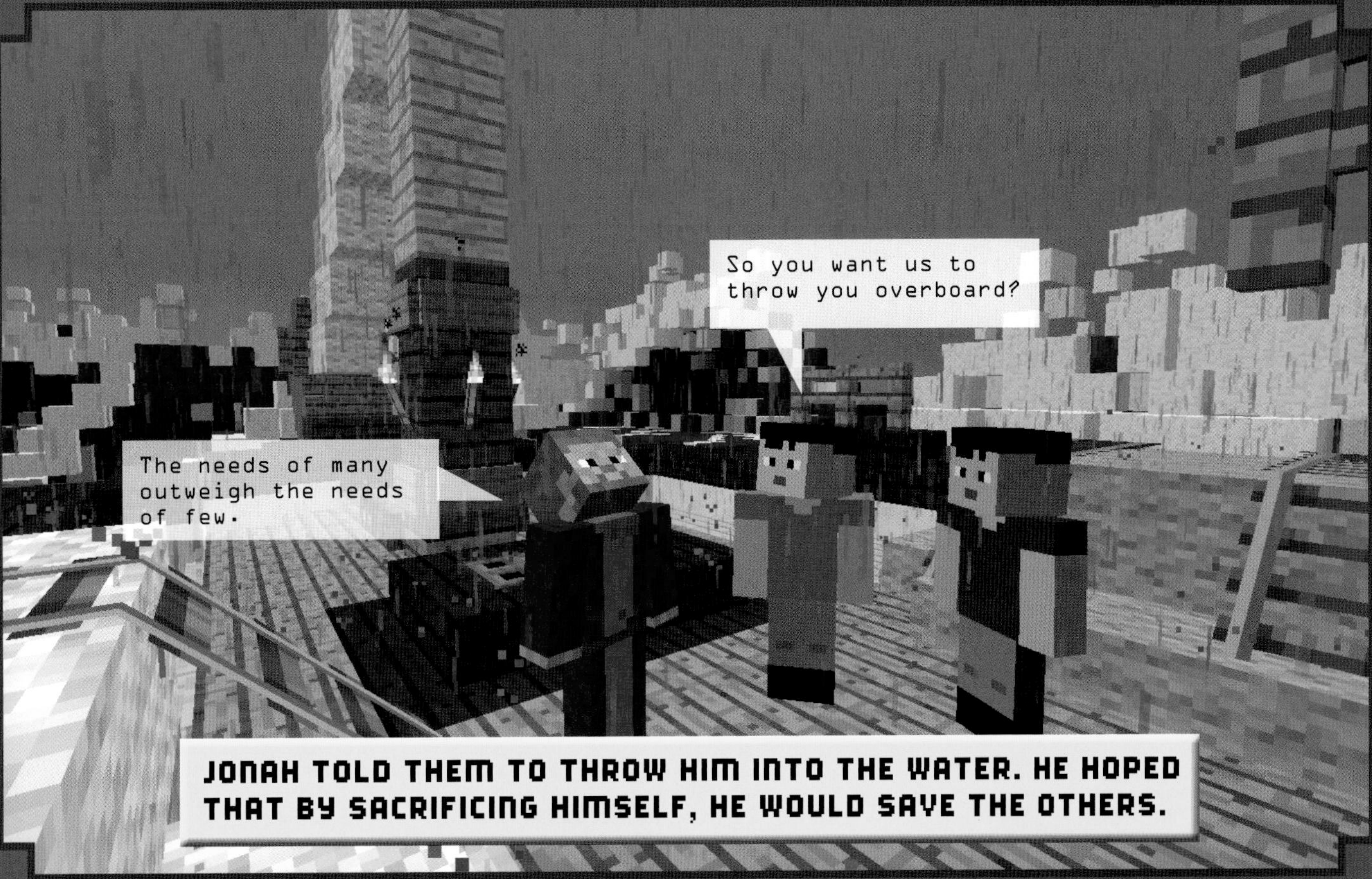
The needs of many outweigh the needs of few.
So you want us to throw you overboard?
JONAH TOLD THEM TO THROW HIM INTO THE WATER. HE HOPED THAT BY SACRIFICING HIMSELF, HE WOULD SAVE THE OTHERS.

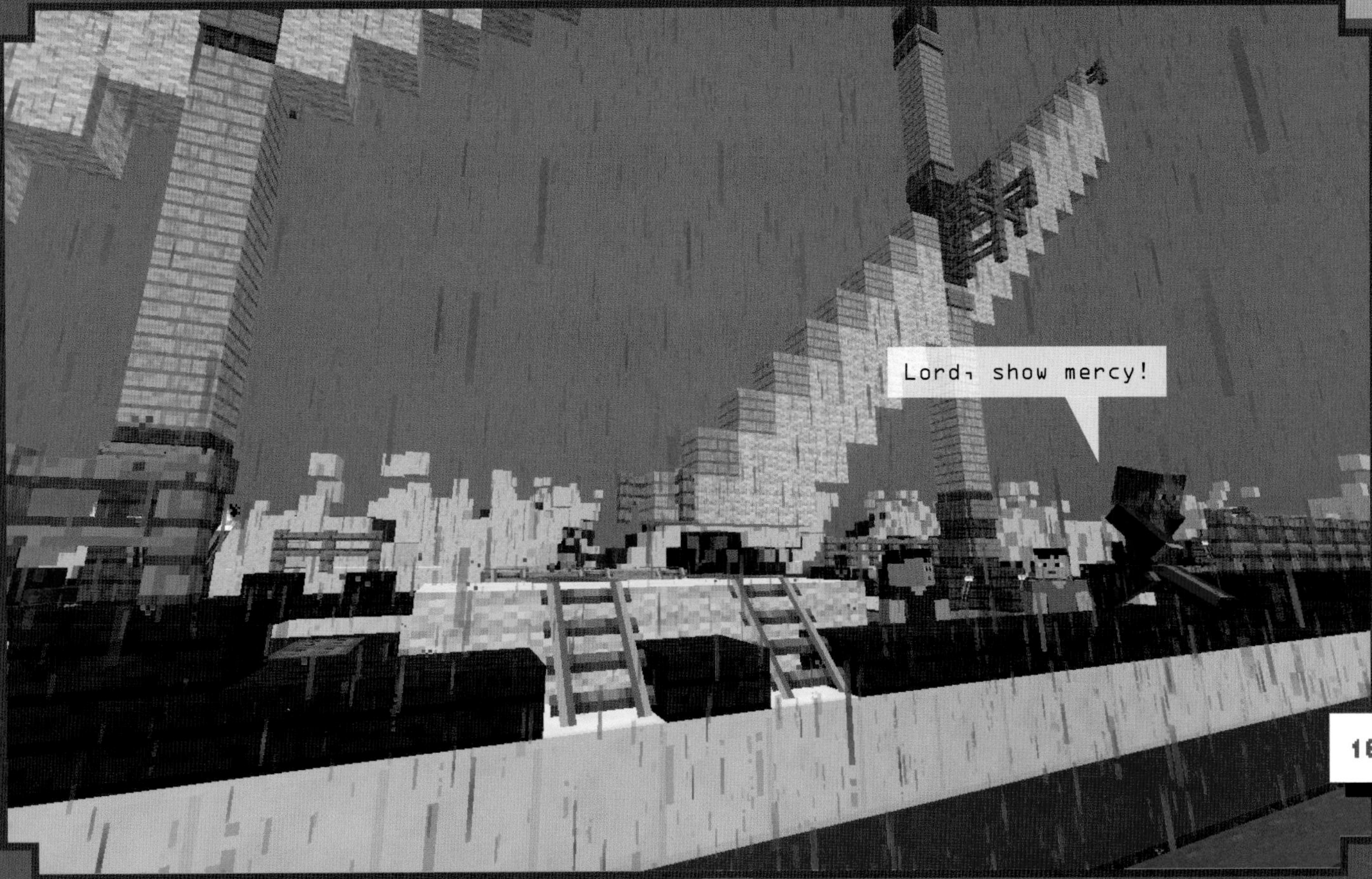
Lord, show mercy!

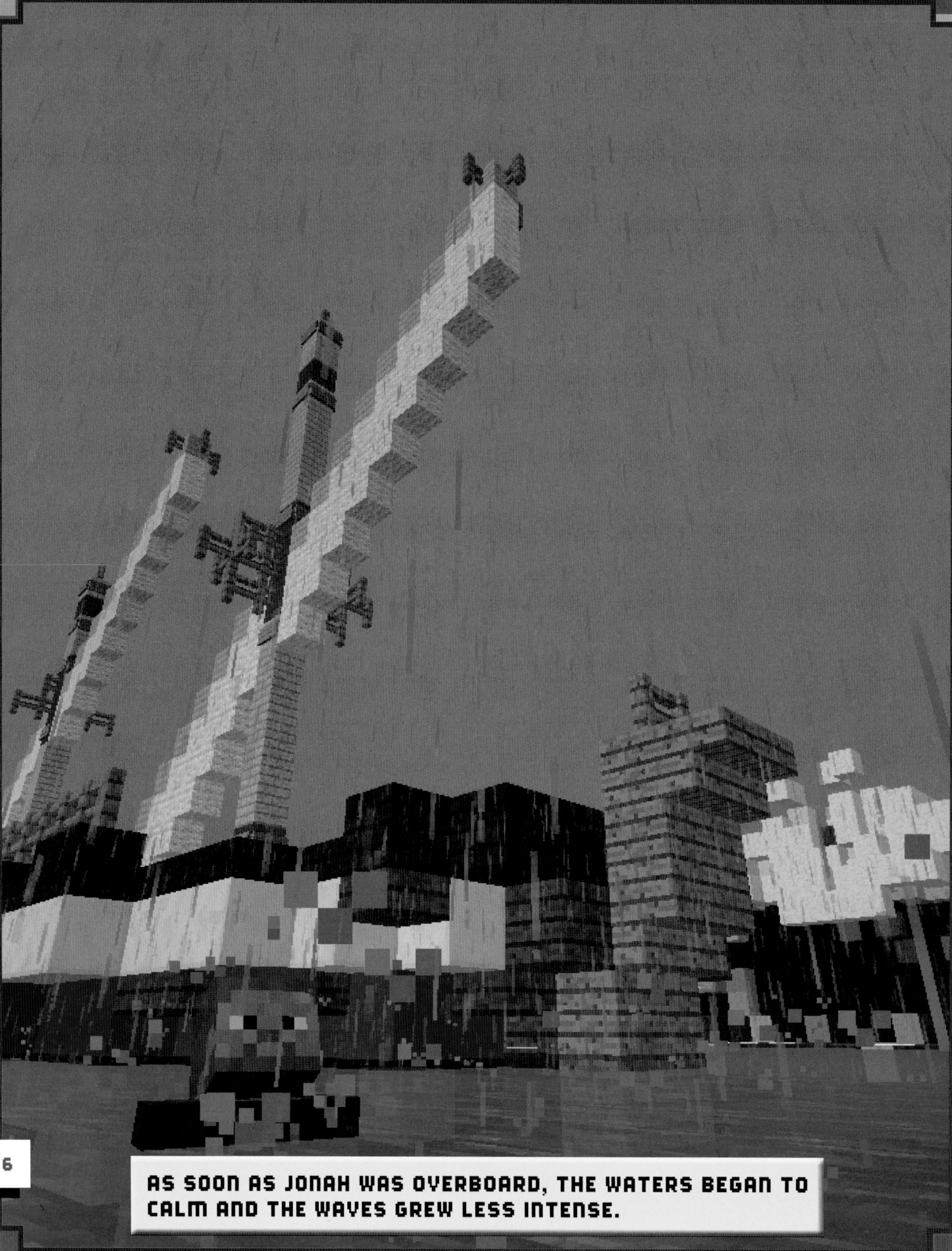

AS SOON AS JONAH WAS OVERBOARD, THE WATERS BEGAN TO CALM AND THE WAVES GREW LESS INTENSE.

AS THE SHIP MOVED FURTHER AWAY FROM JONAH, A MASSIVE CREATURE EMERGED FROM THE DEEP. WITH ONE BIG GULP, JONAH WAS SWALLOWED UP BY THE WHALE.

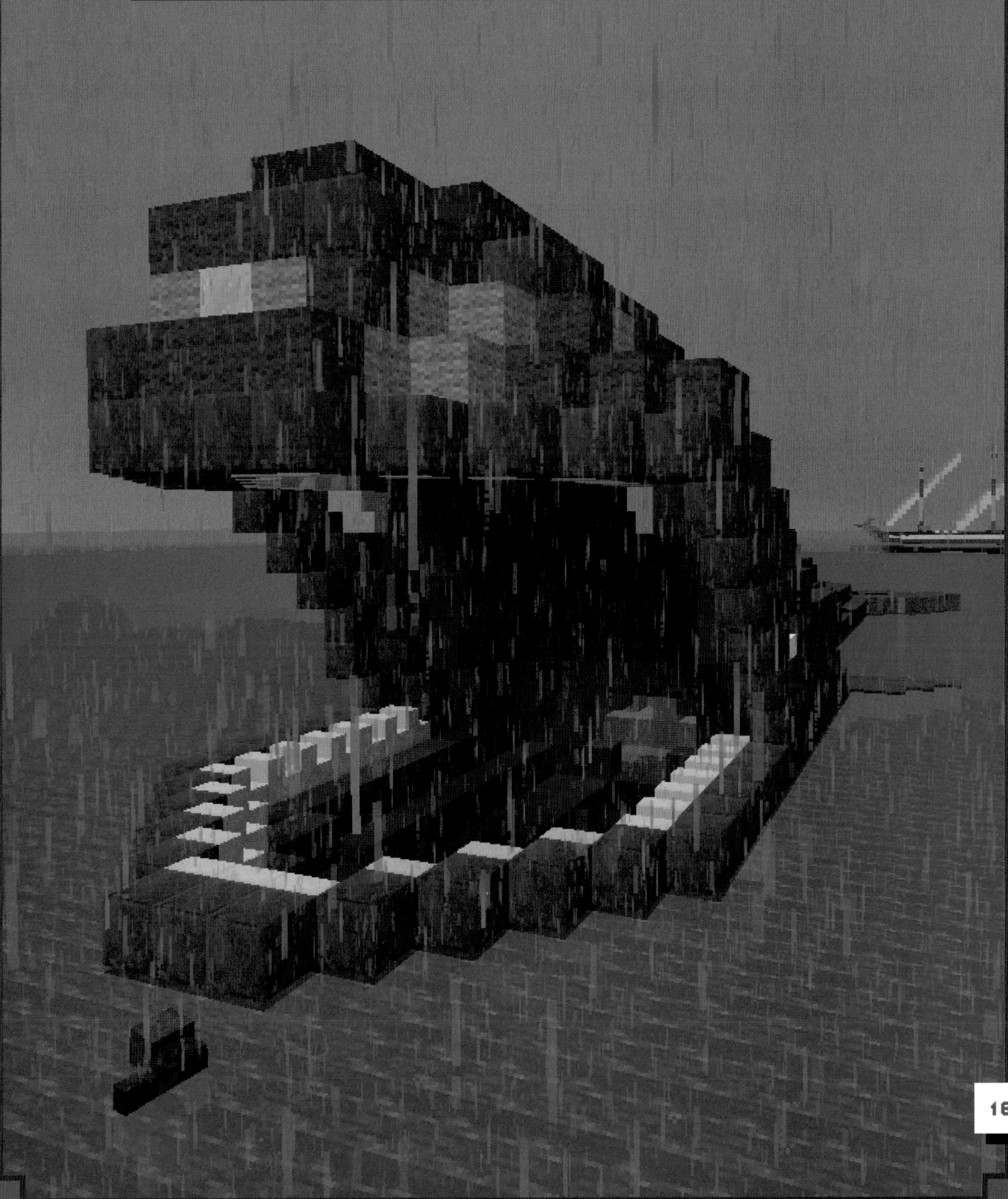

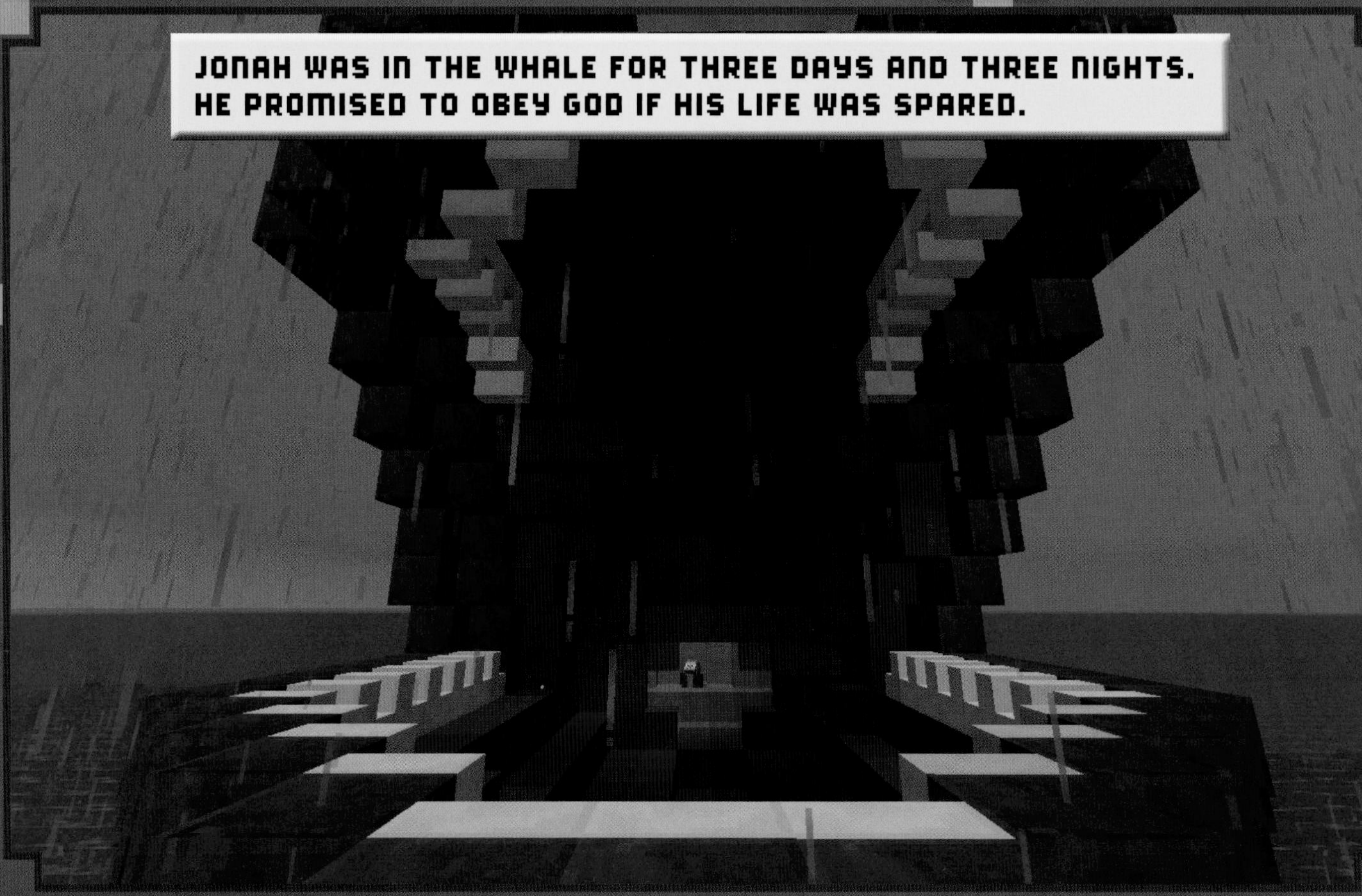
JONAH WAS IN THE WHALE FOR THREE DAYS AND THREE NIGHTS. HE PROMISED TO OBEY GOD IF HIS LIFE WAS SPARED.

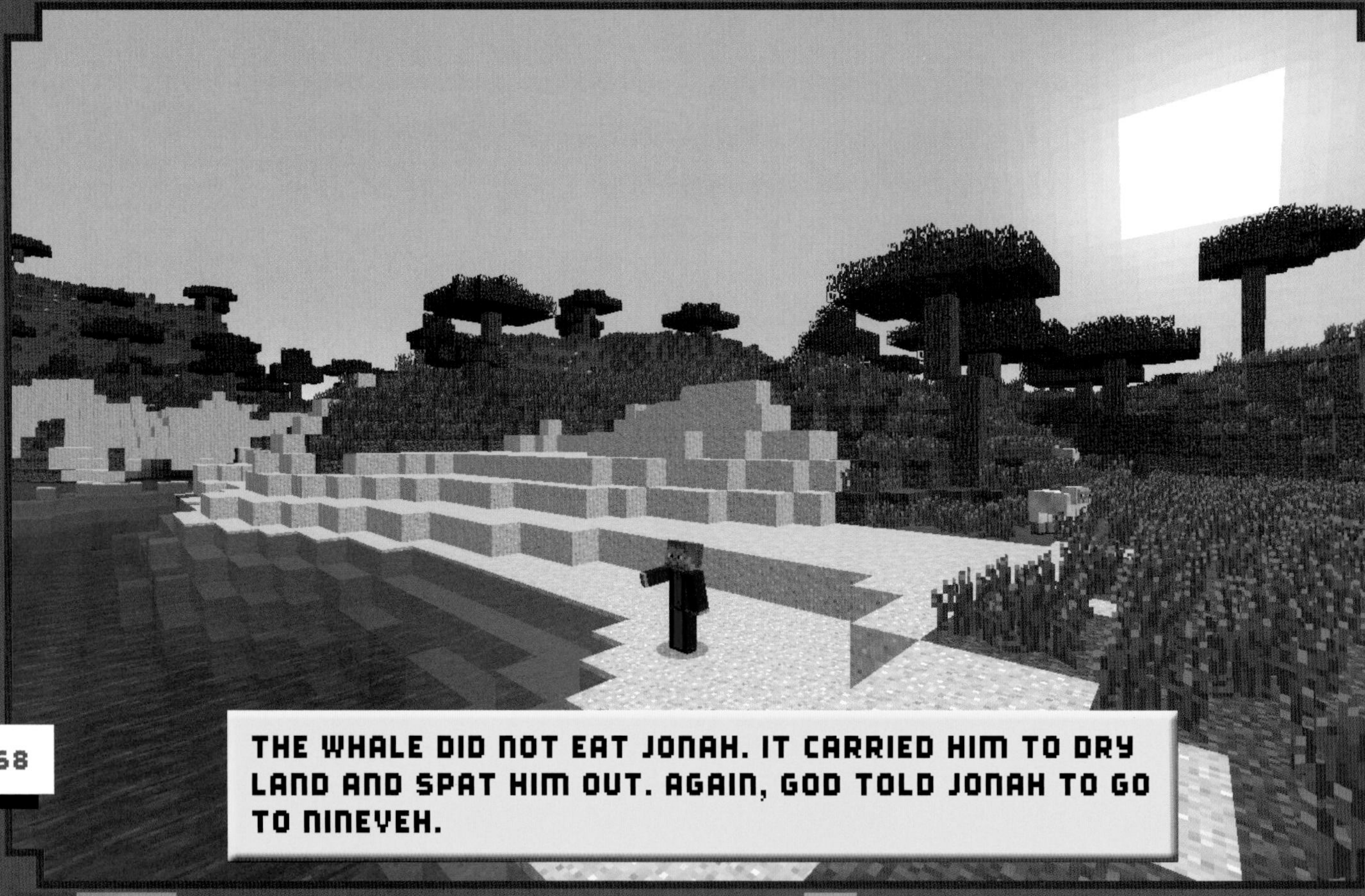
THE WHALE DID NOT EAT JONAH. IT CARRIED HIM TO DRY LAND AND SPAT HIM OUT. AGAIN, GOD TOLD JONAH TO GO TO NINEVEH.

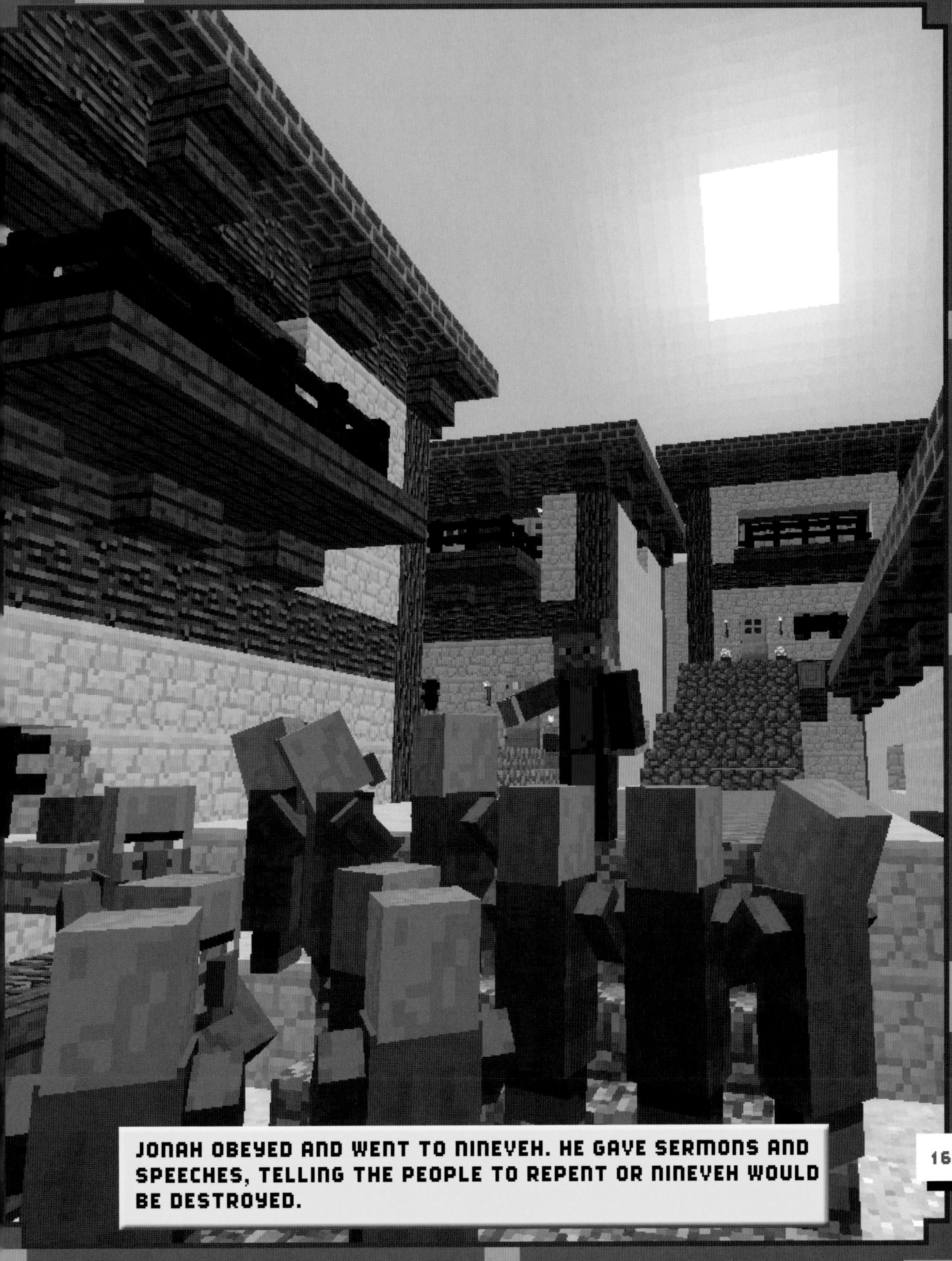
JONAH OBEYED AND WENT TO NINEVEH. HE GAVE SERMONS AND SPEECHES, TELLING THE PEOPLE TO REPENT OR NINEVEH WOULD BE DESTROYED.

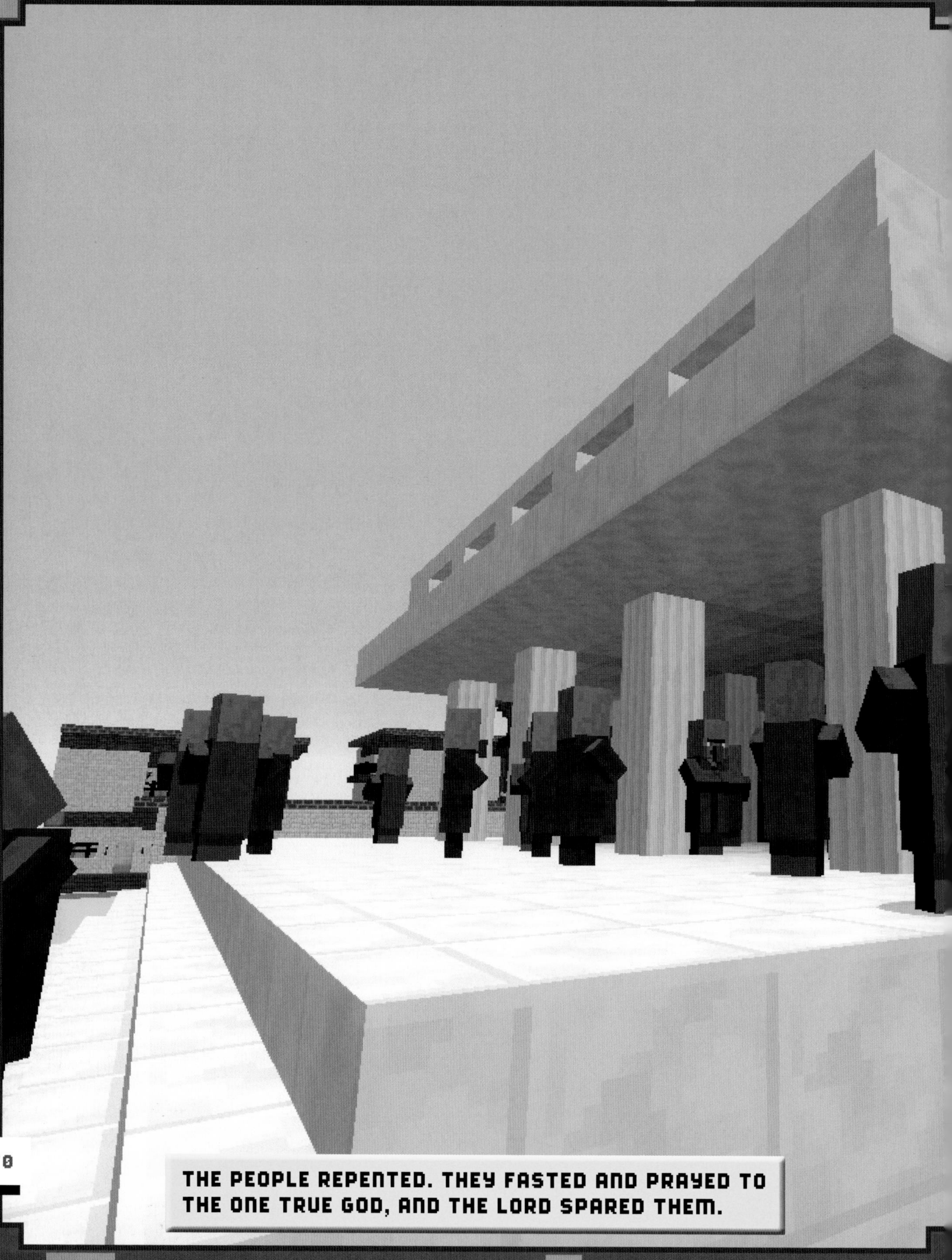

THE PEOPLE REPENTED. THEY FASTED AND PRAYED TO THE ONE TRUE GOD, AND THE LORD SPARED THEM.

THE BIRTH OF CHRIST

Woo-hoo, the New Testament!

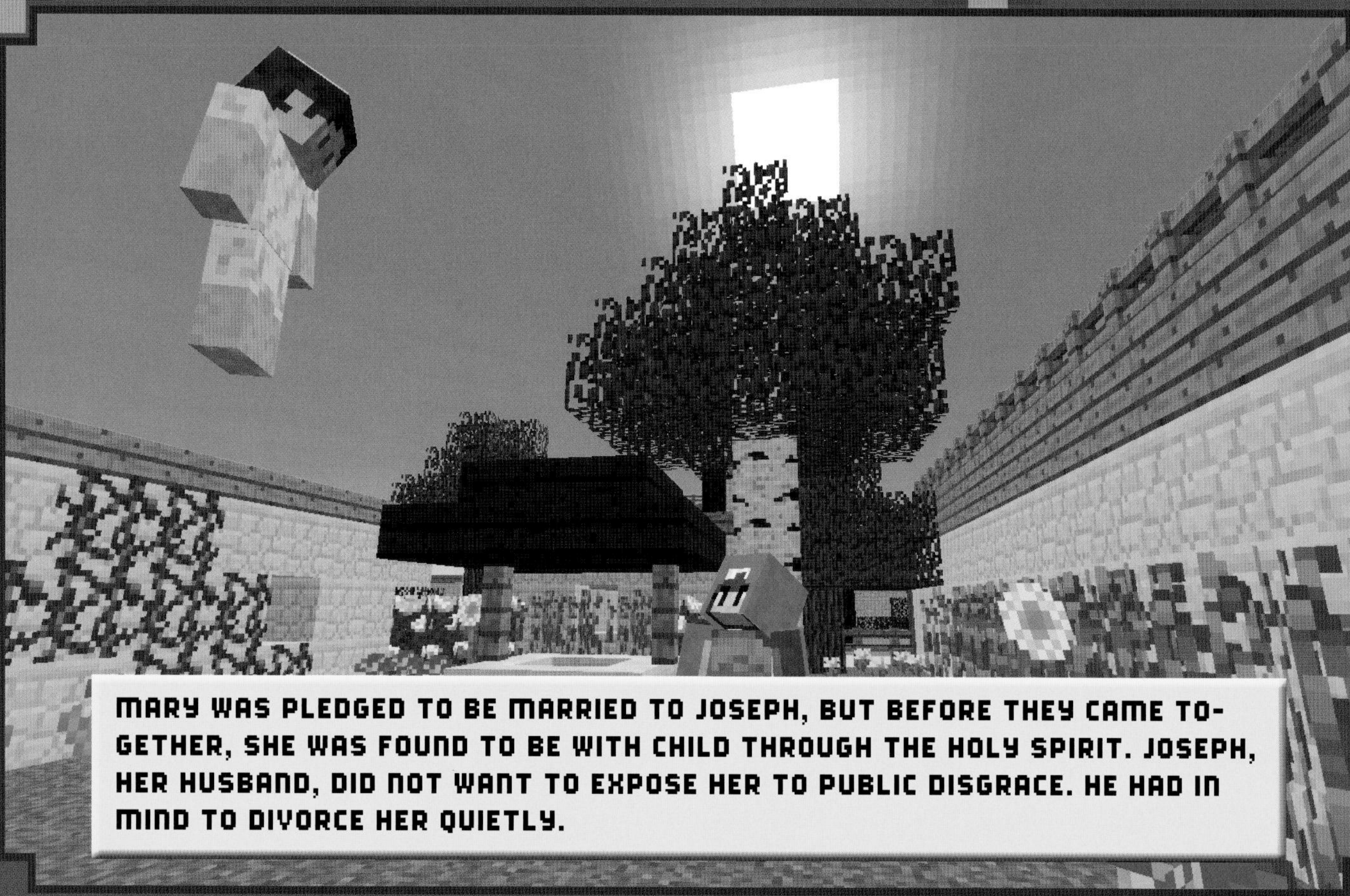
MARY WAS PLEDGED TO BE MARRIED TO JOSEPH, BUT BEFORE THEY CAME TOGETHER, SHE WAS FOUND TO BE WITH CHILD THROUGH THE HOLY SPIRIT. JOSEPH, HER HUSBAND, DID NOT WANT TO EXPOSE HER TO PUBLIC DISGRACE. HE HAD IN MIND TO DIVORCE HER QUIETLY.

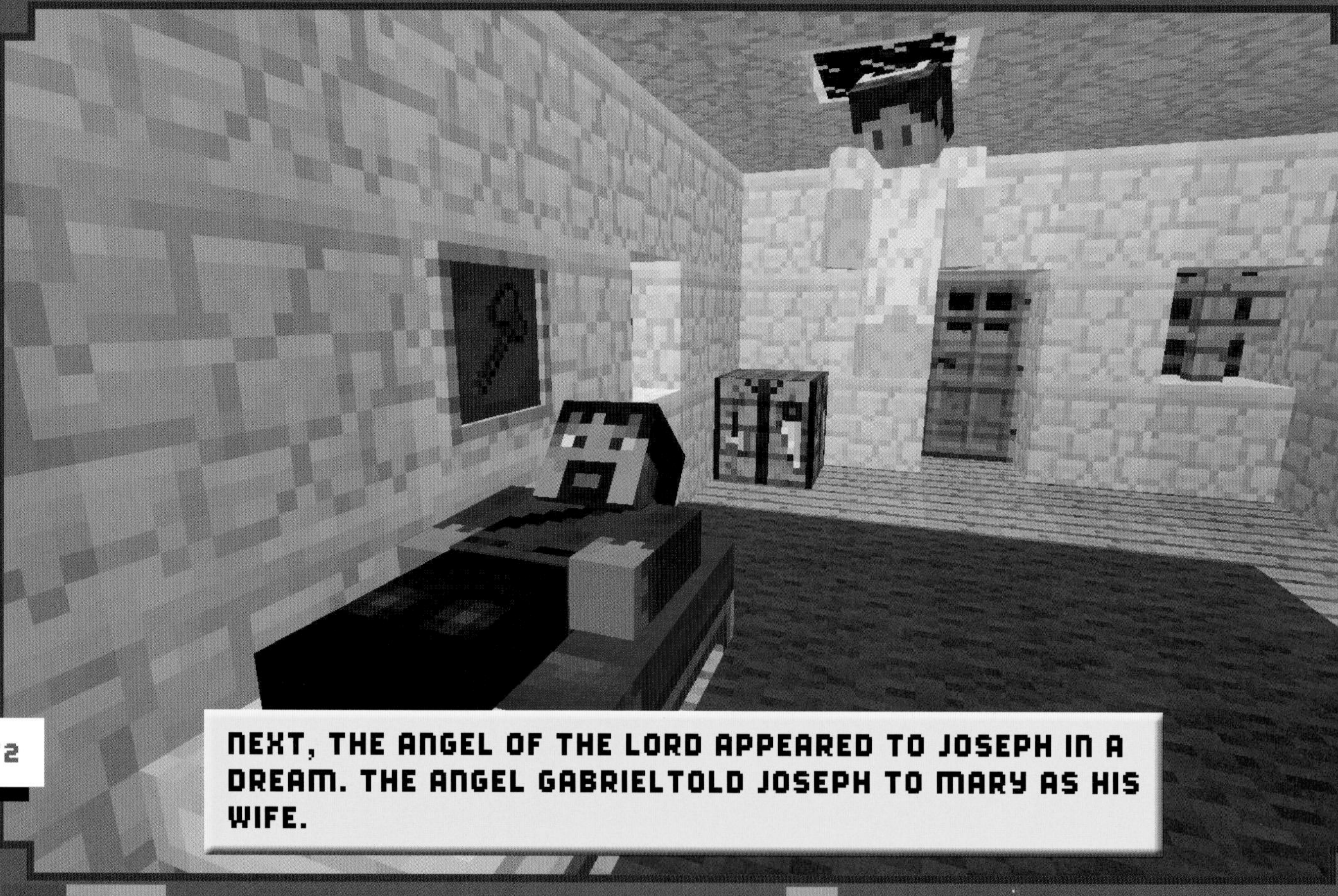
NEXT, THE ANGEL OF THE LORD APPEARED TO JOSEPH IN A DREAM. THE ANGEL GABRIELTOLD JOSEPH TO MARY AS HIS WIFE.

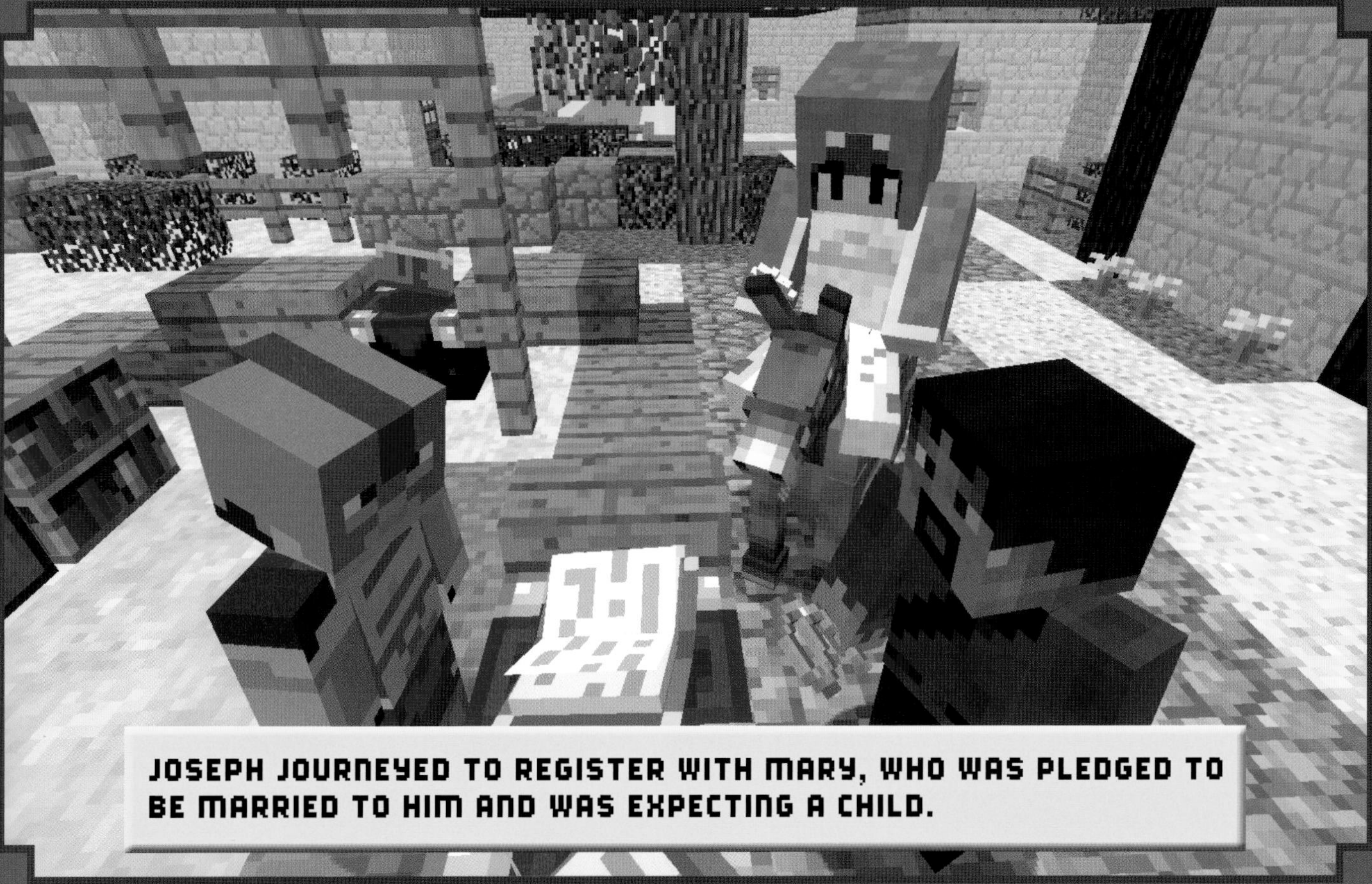
JOSEPH JOURNEYED TO REGISTER WITH MARY, WHO WAS PLEDGED TO BE MARRIED TO HIM AND WAS EXPECTING A CHILD.

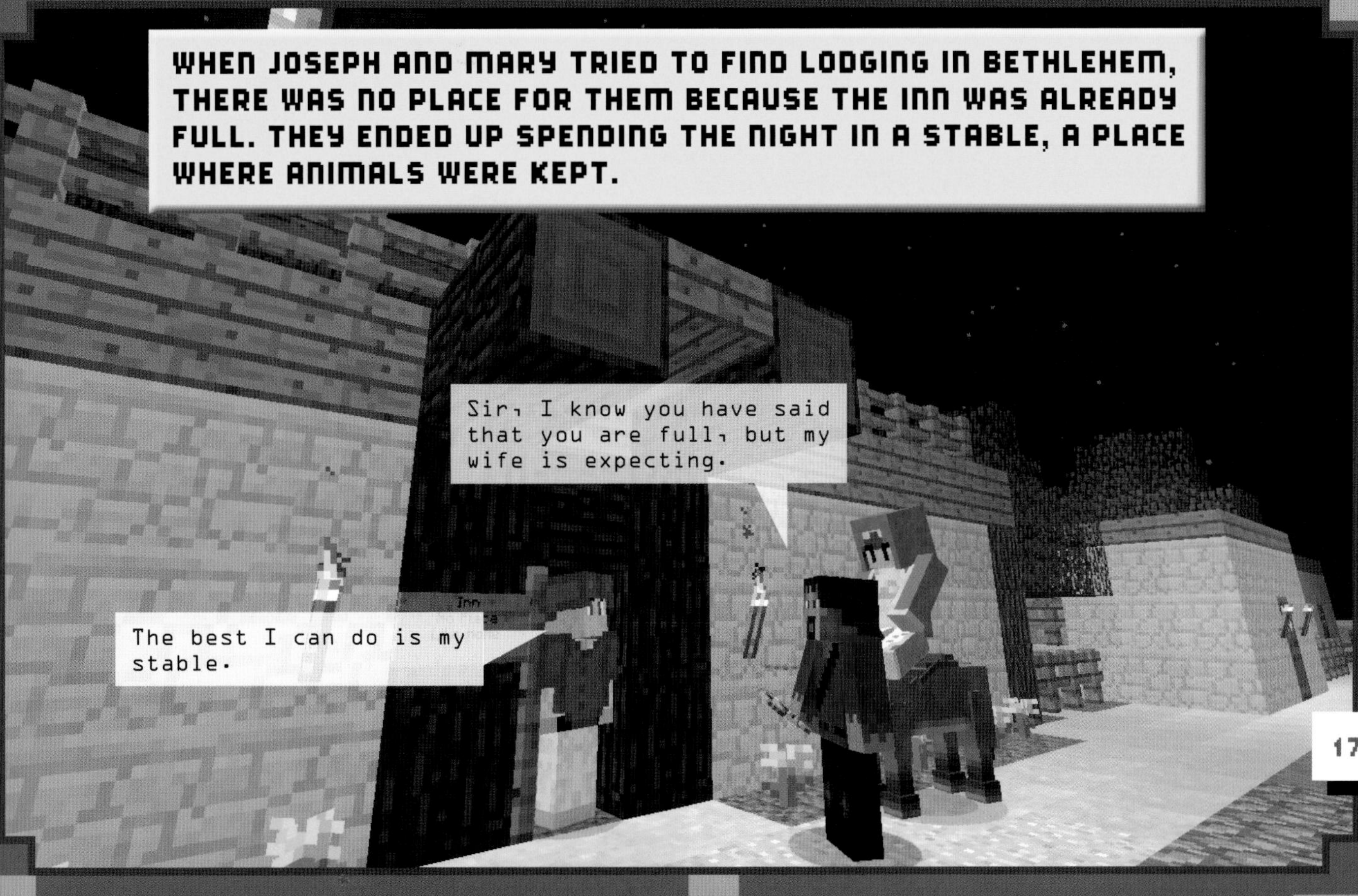
WHEN JOSEPH AND MARY TRIED TO FIND LODGING IN BETHLEHEM, THERE WAS NO PLACE FOR THEM BECAUSE THE INN WAS ALREADY FULL. THEY ENDED UP SPENDING THE NIGHT IN A STABLE, A PLACE WHERE ANIMALS WERE KEPT.
Sir, I know you have said that you are full, but my wife is expecting.
The best I can do is my stable.

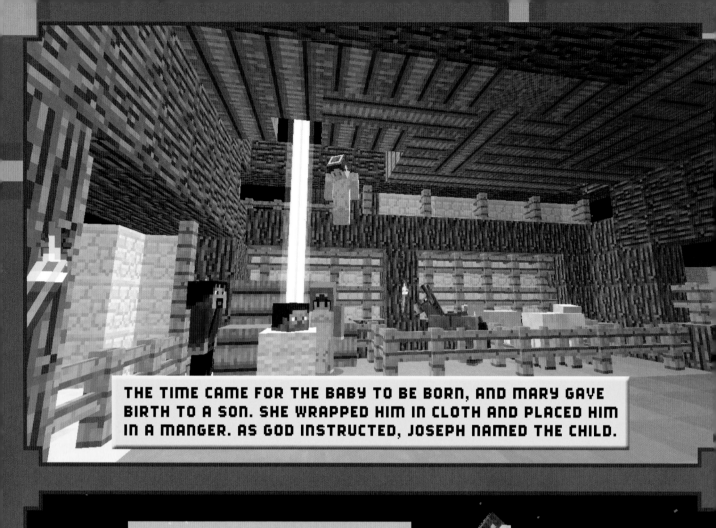

THE TIME CAME FOR THE BABY TO BE BORN, AND MARY GAVE BIRTH TO A SON. SHE WRAPPED HIM IN CLOTH AND PLACED HIM IN A MANGER. AS GOD INSTRUCTED, JOSEPH NAMED THE CHILD.

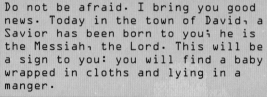

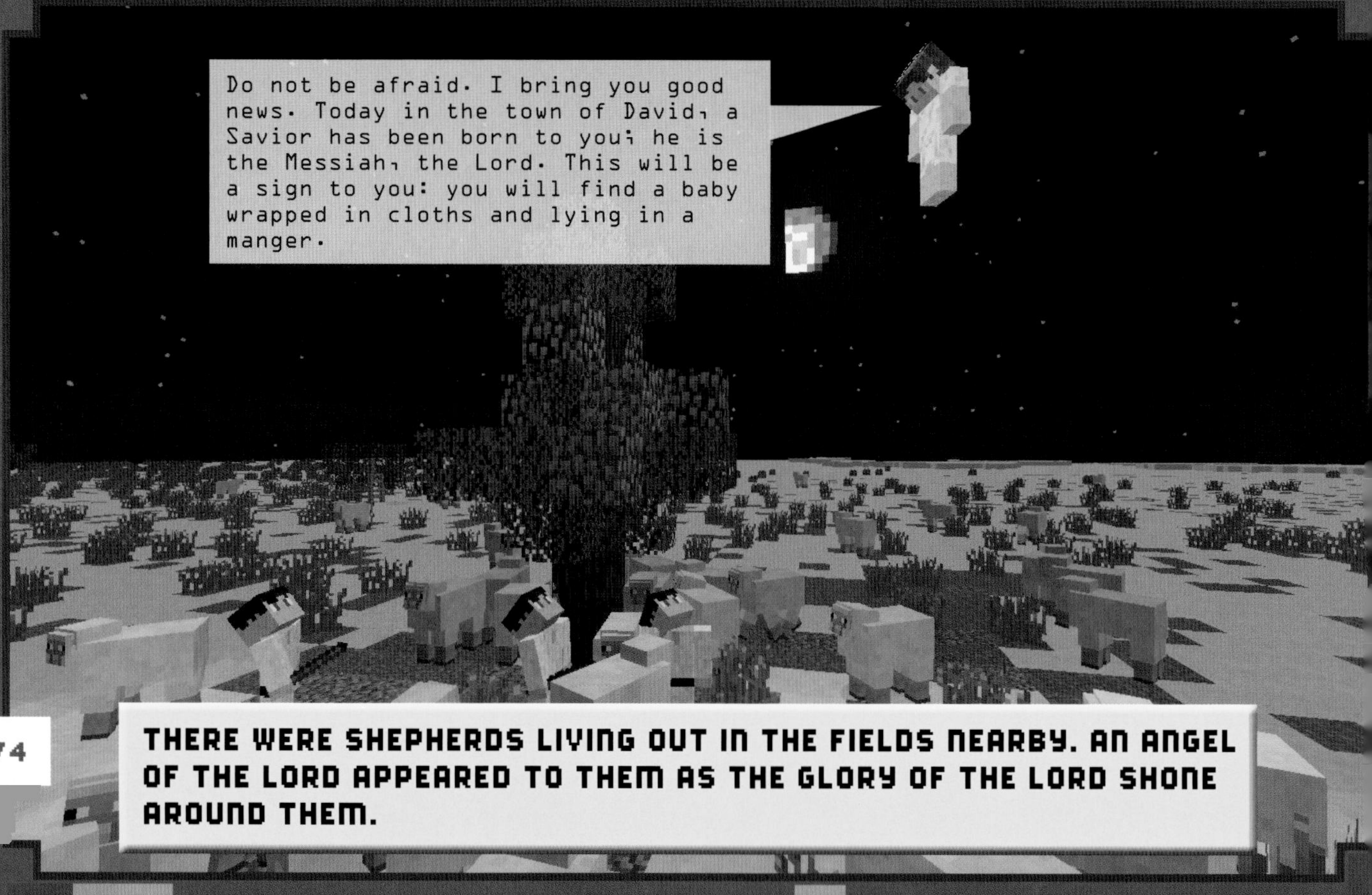

Do not be afraid. I bring you good news. Today in the town of David, a Savior has been born to you; he is the Messiah, the Lord. This will be a sign to you: you will find a baby wrapped in cloths and lying in a manger.

THERE WERE SHEPHERDS LIVING OUT IN THE FIELDS NEARBY. AN ANGEL OF THE LORD APPEARED TO THEM AS THE GLORY OF THE LORD SHONE AROUND THEM.

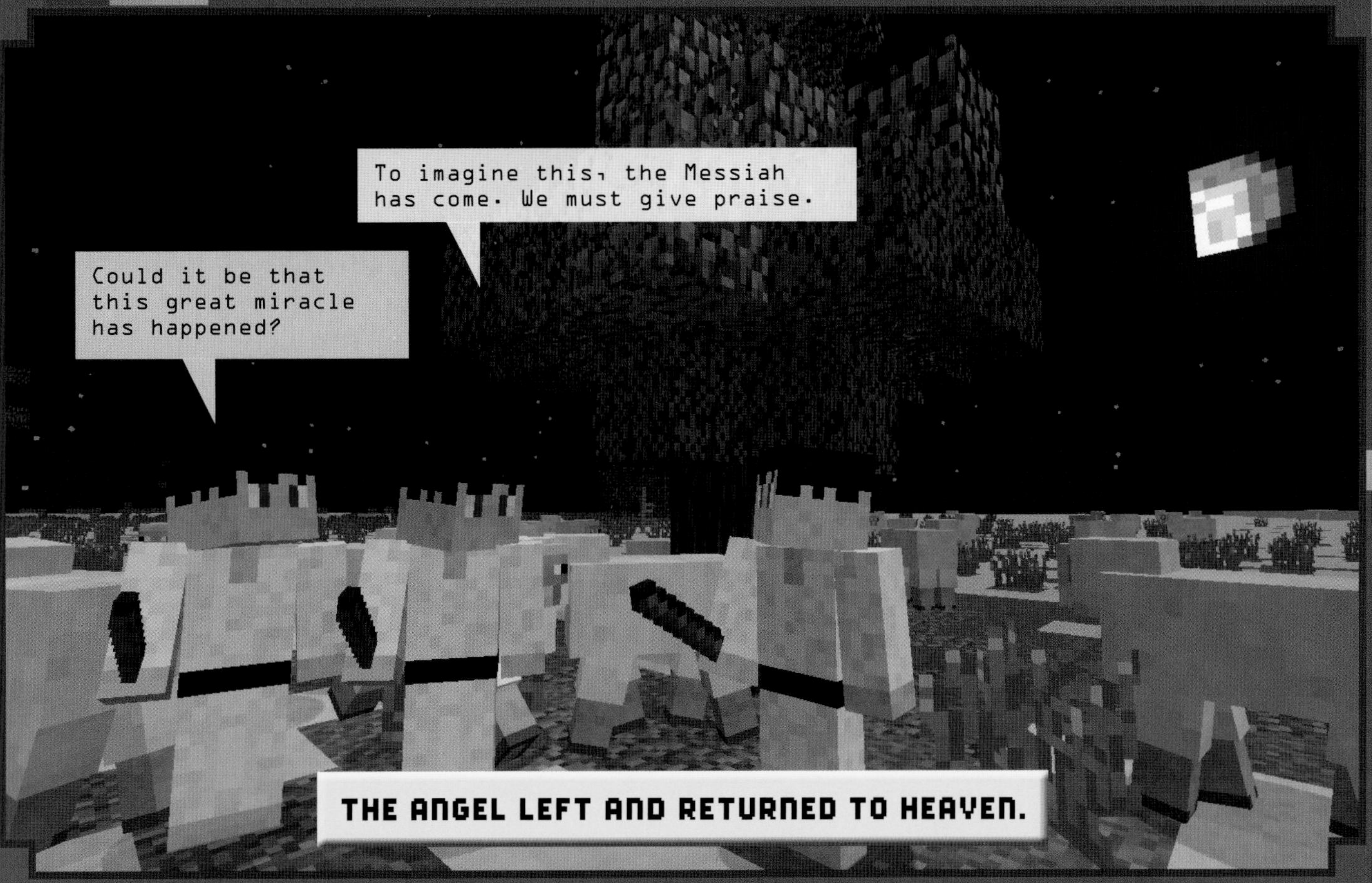
Could it be that this great miracle has happened?
To imagine this, the Messiah has come. We must give praise.
THE ANGEL LEFT AND RETURNED TO HEAVEN.

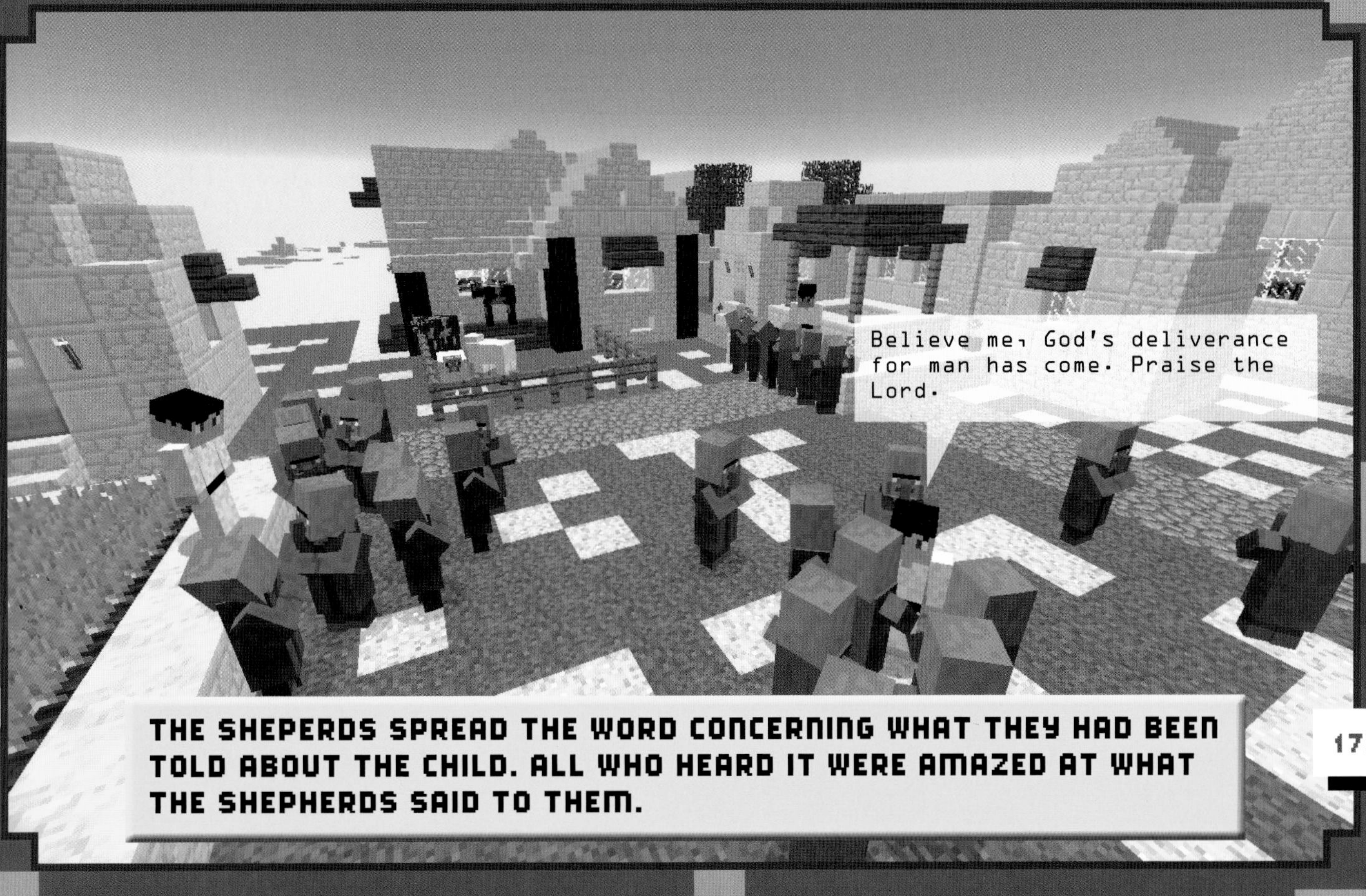
Believe me, God's deliverance for man has come. Praise the Lord.
THE SHEPERDS SPREAD THE WORD CONCERNING WHAT THEY HAD BEEN TOLD ABOUT THE CHILD. ALL WHO HEARD IT WERE AMAZED AT WHAT THE SHEPHERDS SAID TO THEM.

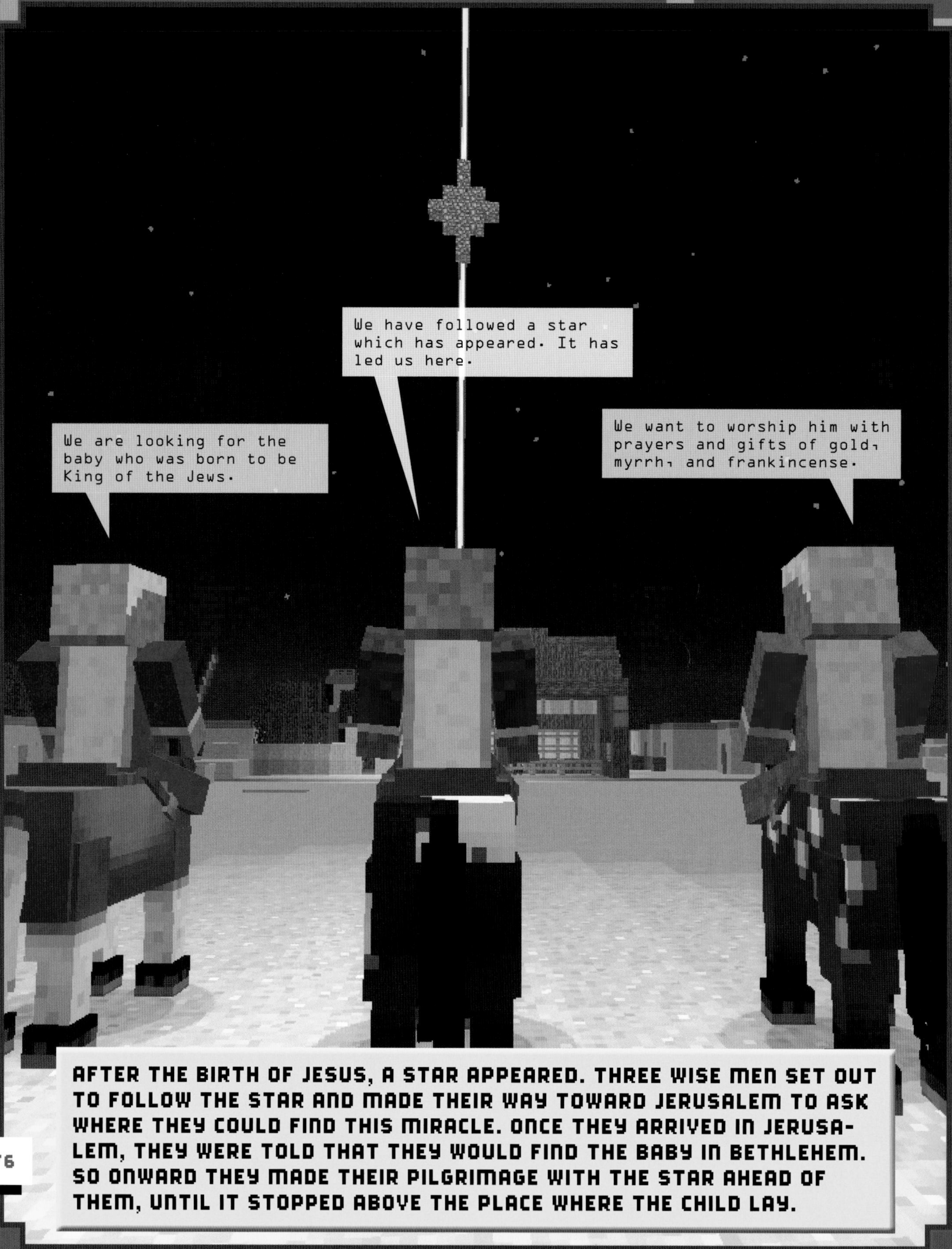
We are looking for the baby who was born to be King of the Jews.
We have followed a star which has appeared. It has led us here.
We want to worship him with prayers and gifts of gold, myrrh, and frankincense.
AFTER THE BIRTH OF JESUS, A STAR APPEARED. THREE WISE MEN SET OUT TO FOLLOW THE STAR AND MADE THEIR WAY TOWARD JERUSALEM TO ASK WHERE THEY COULD FIND THIS MIRACLE. ONCE THEY ARRIVED IN JERUSALEM, THEY WERE TOLD THAT THEY WOULD FIND THE BABY IN BETHLEHEM. SO ONWARD THEY MADE THEIR PILGRIMAGE WITH THE STAR AHEAD OF THEM, UNTIL IT STOPPED ABOVE THE PLACE WHERE THE CHILD LAY.

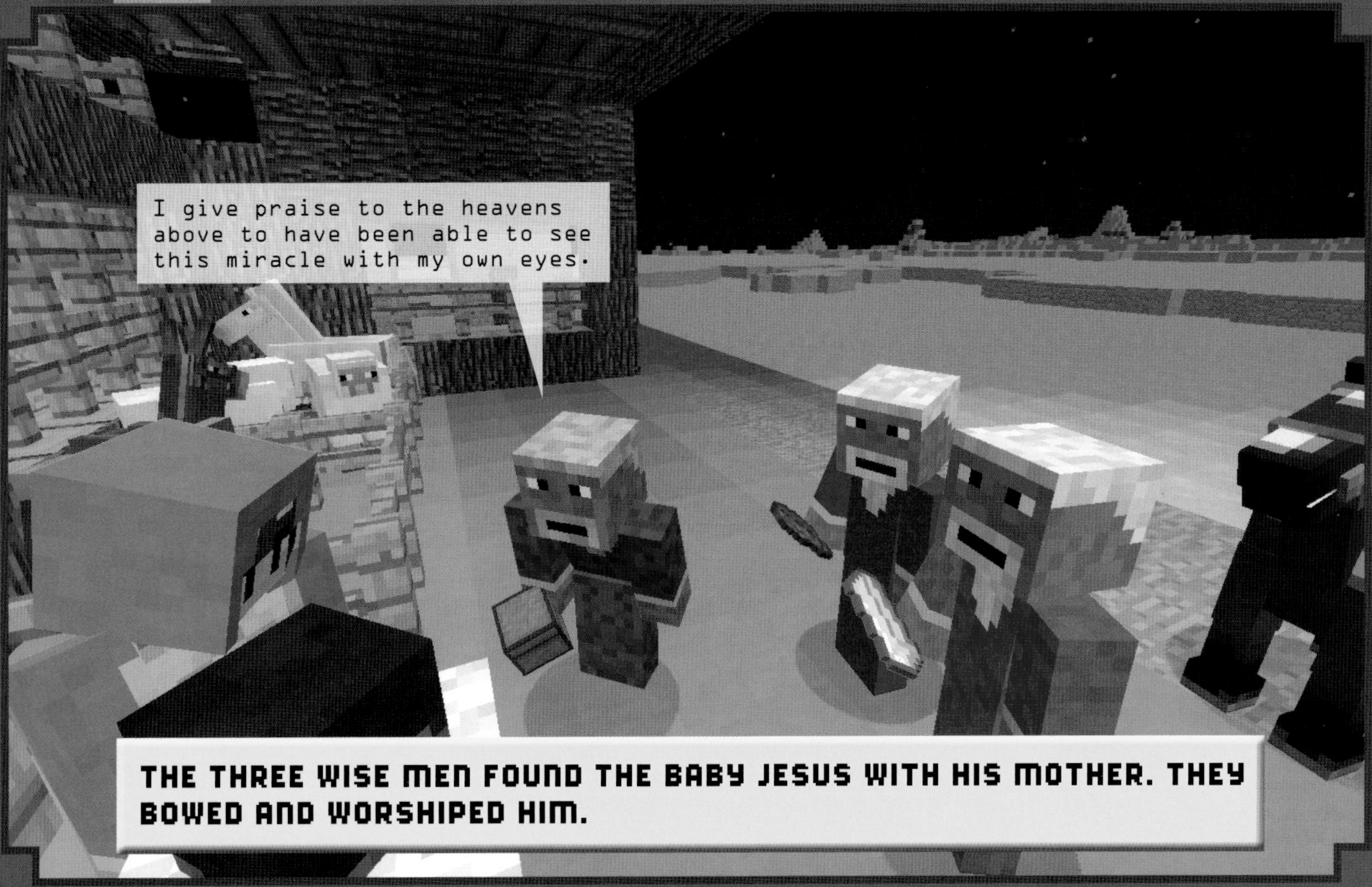
I give praise to the heavens above to have been able to see this miracle with my own eyes.
THE THREE WISE MEN FOUND THE BABY JESUS WITH HIS MOTHER. THEY BOWED AND WORSHIPED HIM.

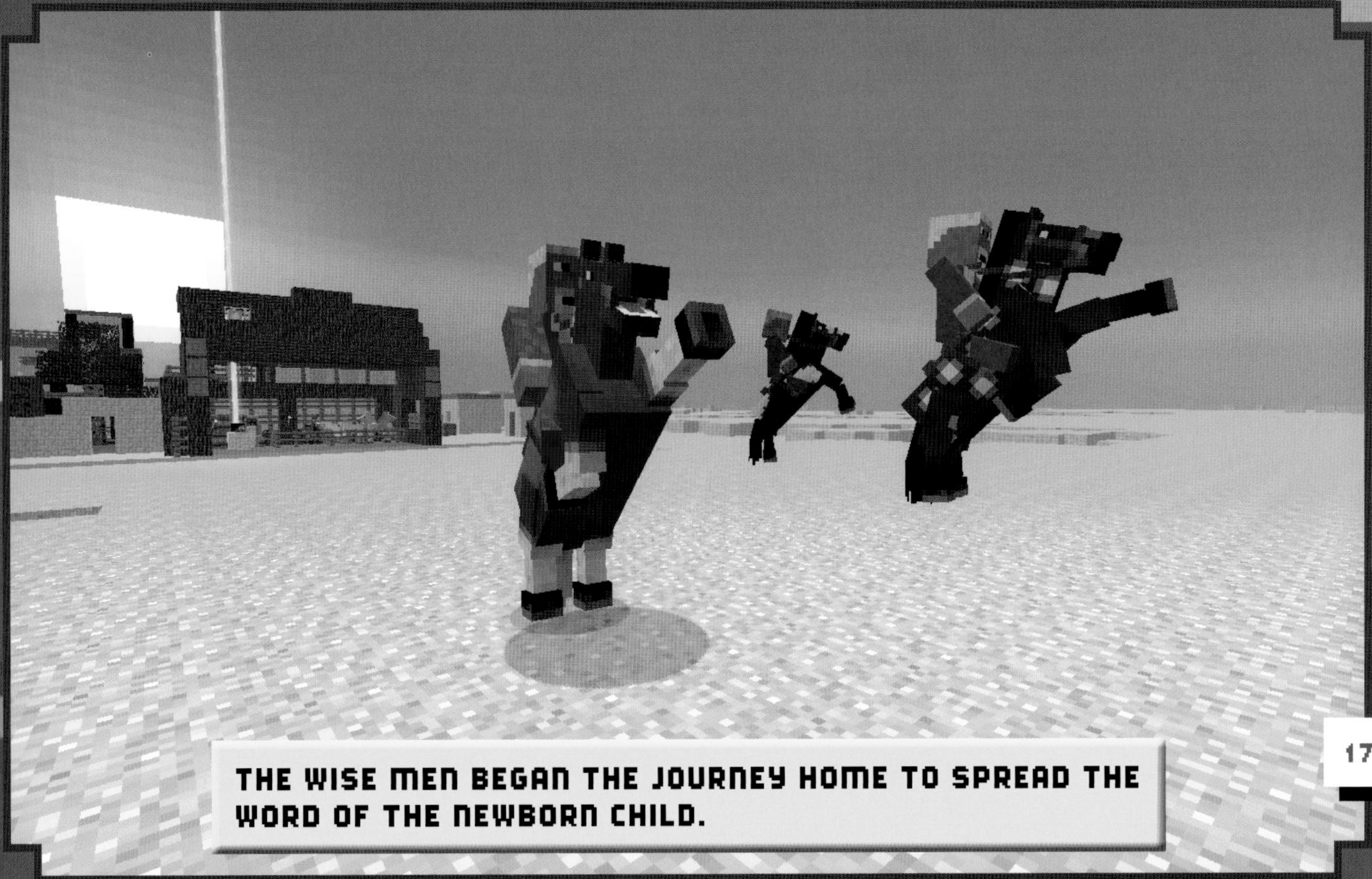
THE WISE MEN BEGAN THE JOURNEY HOME TO SPREAD THE WORD OF THE NEWBORN CHILD.

JESUS GOES ABOUT HIS FATHER'S WORK

Jesus has grown. He is now a man.

Yes, he is a great man in my likeness.

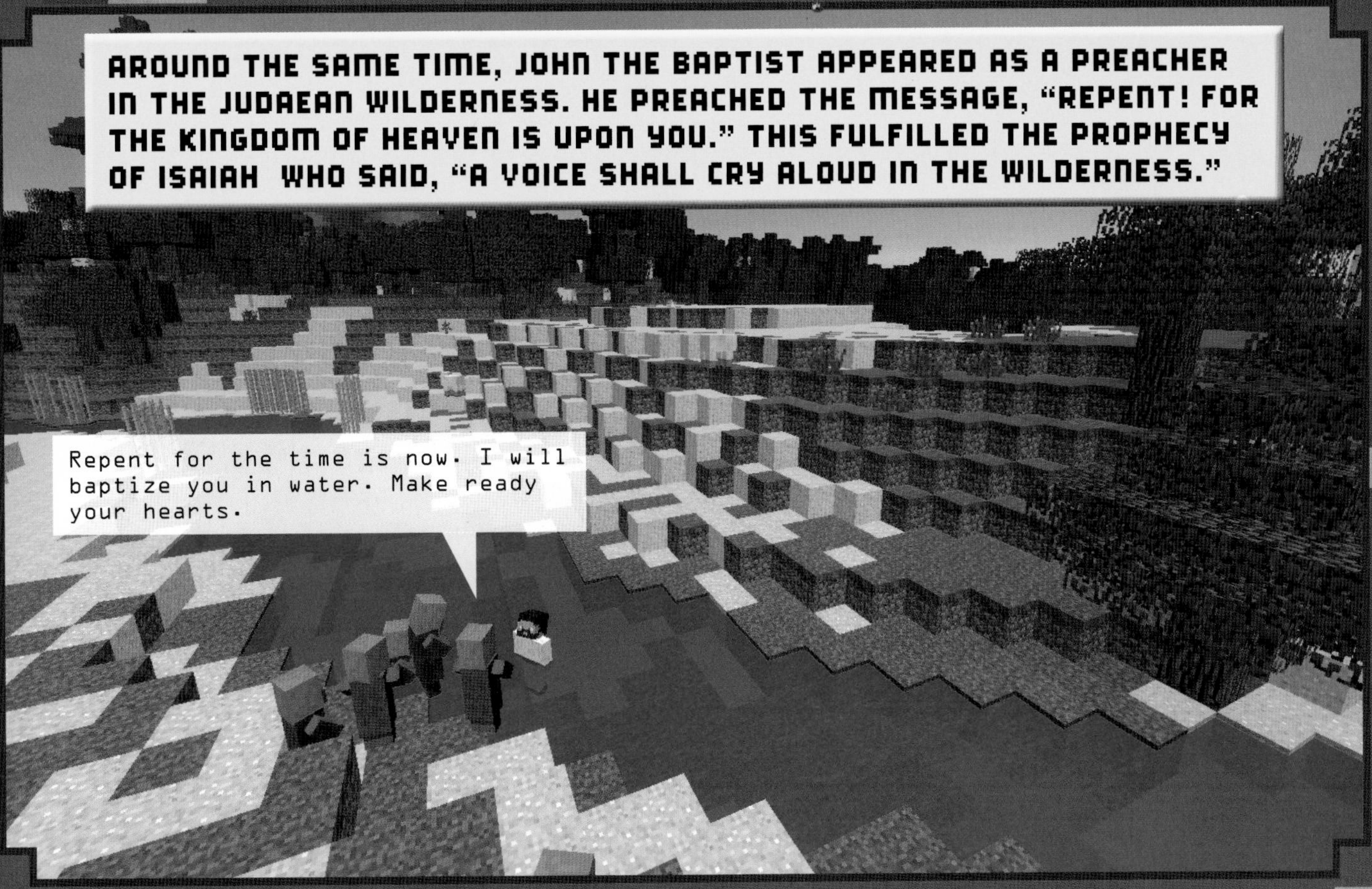
AROUND THE SAME TIME, JOHN THE BAPTIST APPEARED AS A PREACHER IN THE JUDAEAN WILDERNESS. HE PREACHED THE MESSAGE, "REPENT! FOR THE KINGDOM OF HEAVEN IS UPON YOU." THIS FULFILLED THE PROPHECY OF ISAIAH WHO SAID, "A VOICE SHALL CRY ALOUD IN THE WILDERNESS."
Repent for the time is now. I will baptize you in water. Make ready your hearts.

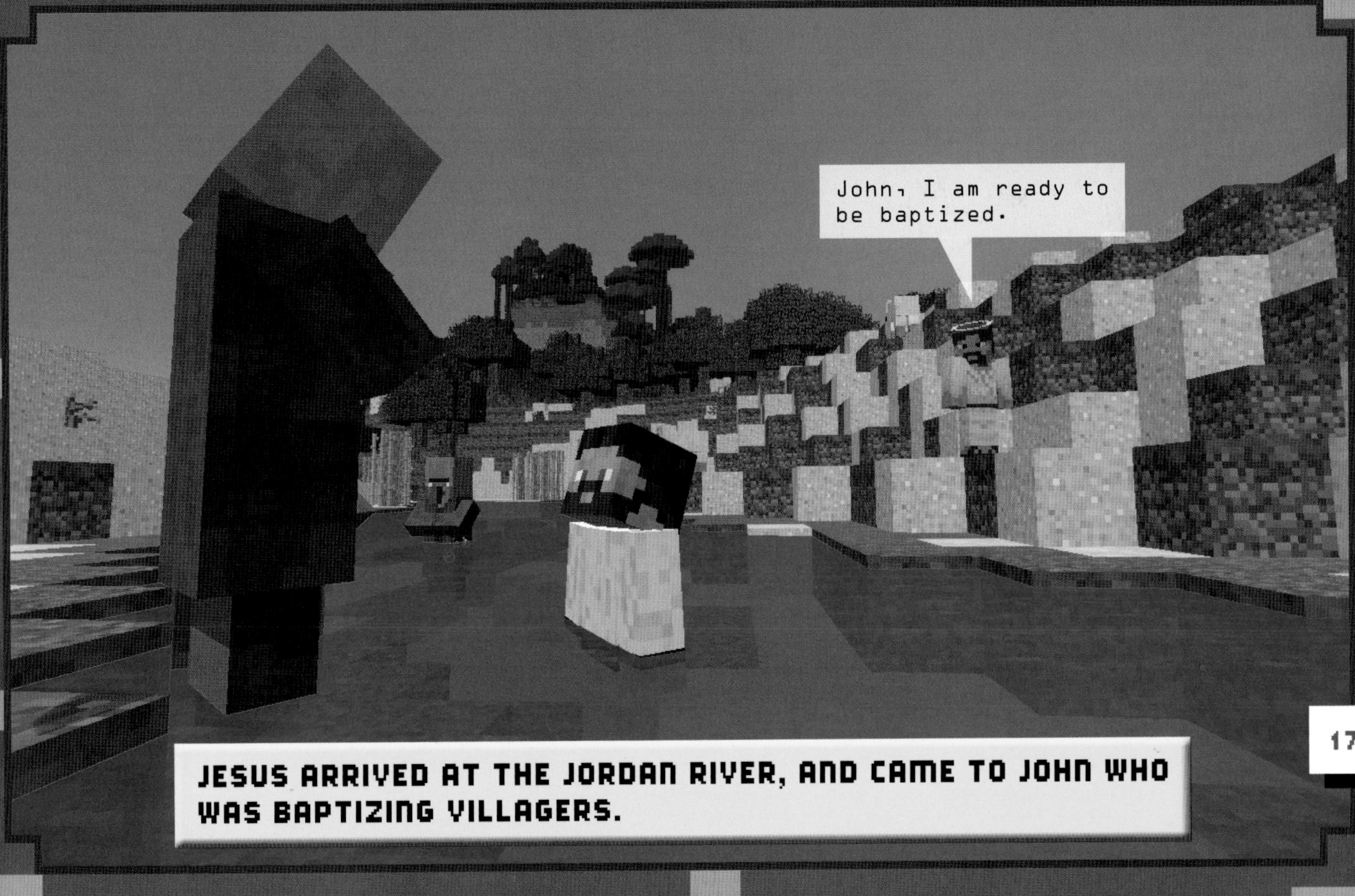
John, I am ready to be baptized.
JESUS ARRIVED AT THE JORDAN RIVER, AND CAME TO JOHN WHO WAS BAPTIZING VILLAGERS.

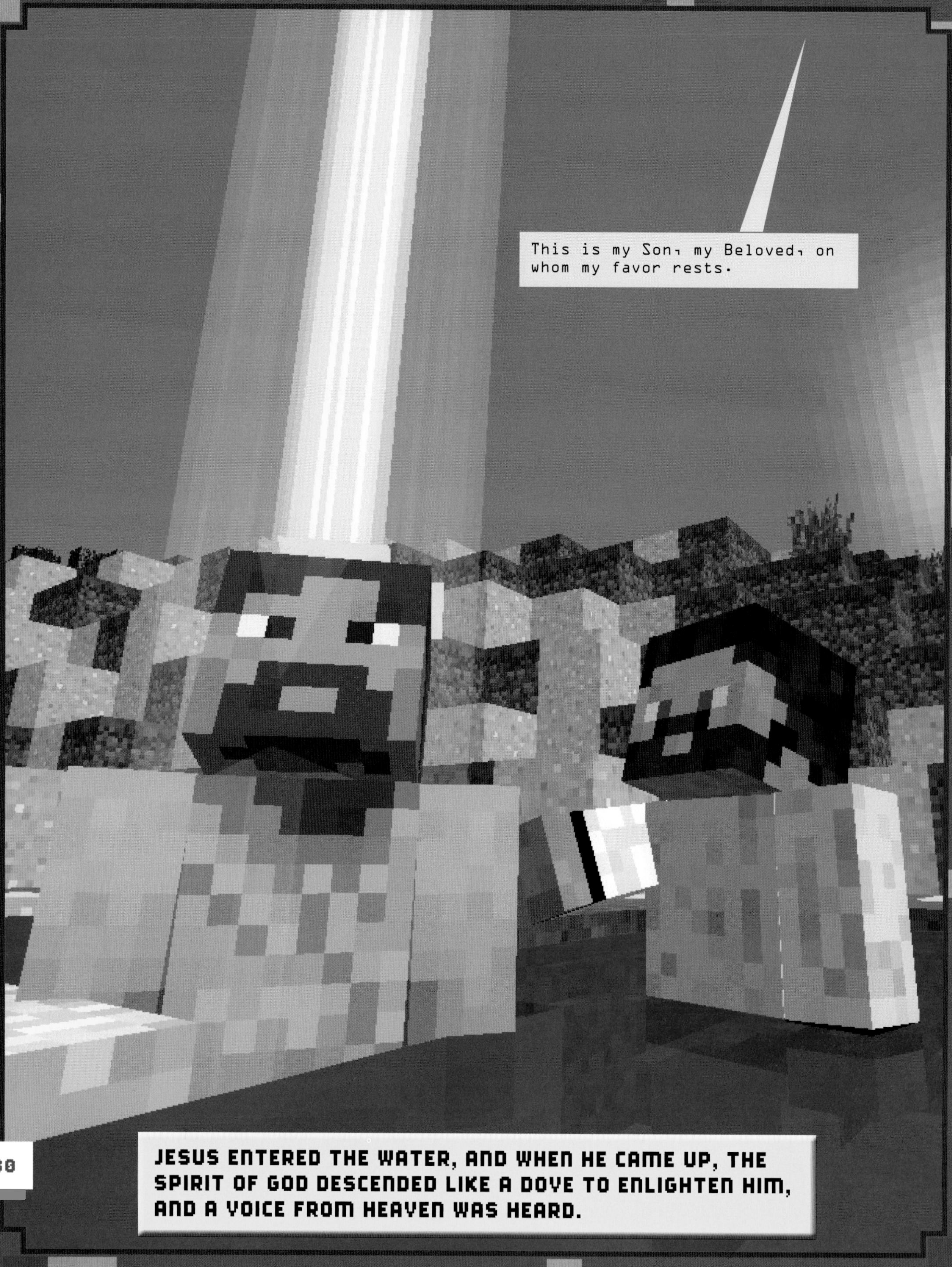
This is my Son, my Beloved, on whom my favor rests.
JESUS ENTERED THE WATER, AND WHEN HE CAME UP, THE SPIRIT OF GOD DESCENDED LIKE A DOVE TO ENLIGHTEN HIM, AND A VOICE FROM HEAVEN WAS HEARD.

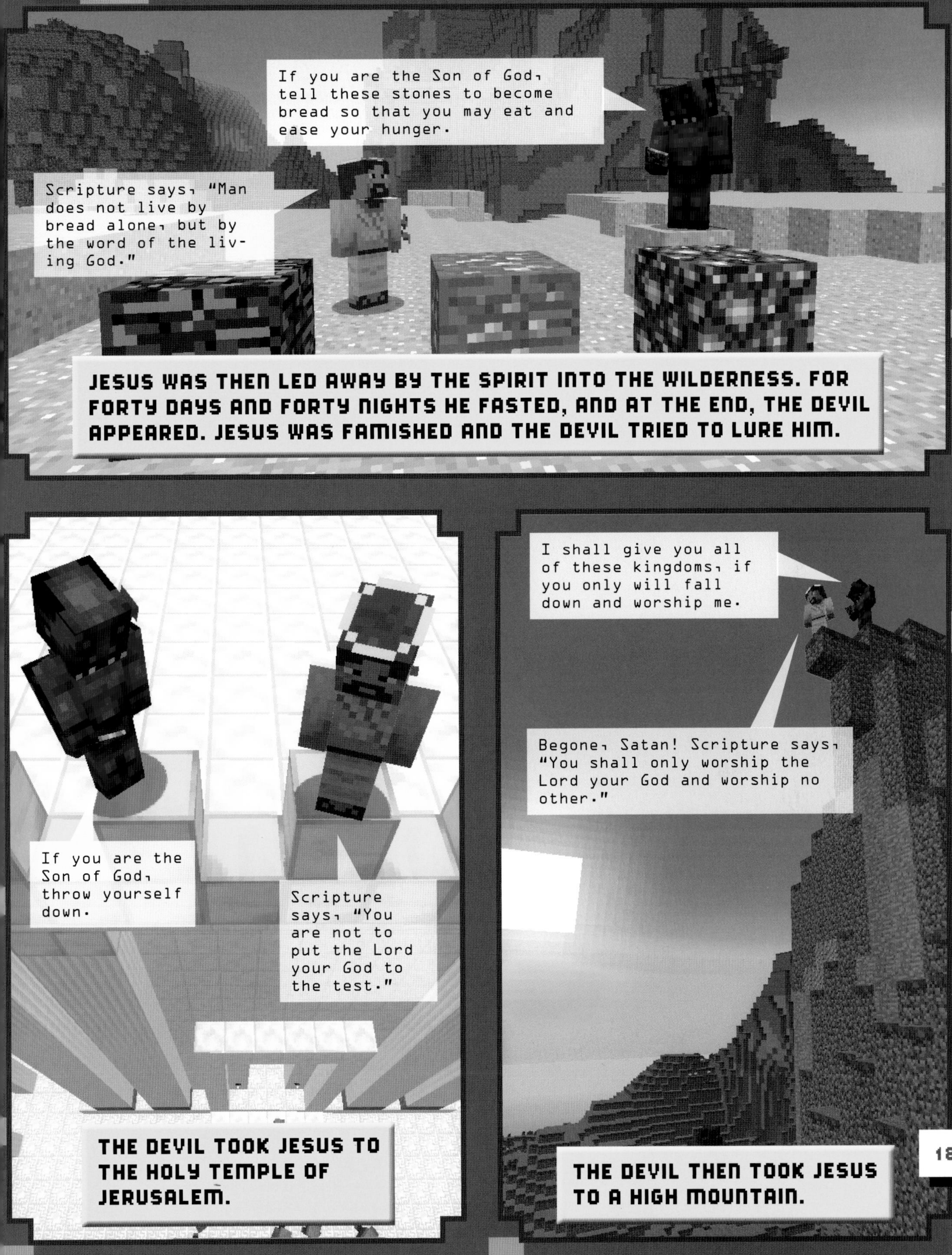

If you are the Son of God, tell these stones to become bread so that you may eat and ease your hunger.

Scripture says, "Man does not live by bread alone, but by the word of the living God."

JESUS WAS THEN LED AWAY BY THE SPIRIT INTO THE WILDERNESS. FOR FORTY DAYS AND FORTY NIGHTS HE FASTED, AND AT THE END, THE DEVIL APPEARED. JESUS WAS FAMISHED AND THE DEVIL TRIED TO LURE HIM.

If you are the Son of God, throw yourself down.

Scripture says, "You are not to put the Lord your God to the test."

THE DEVIL TOOK JESUS TO THE HOLY TEMPLE OF JERUSALEM.

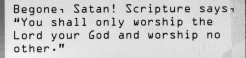

I shall give you all of these kingdoms, if you only will fall down and worship me.

Begone, Satan! Scripture says, "You shall only worship the Lord your God and worship no other."

181

THE DEVIL THEN TOOK JESUS TO A HIGH MOUNTAIN.

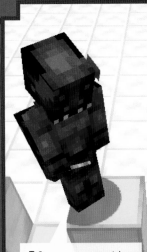

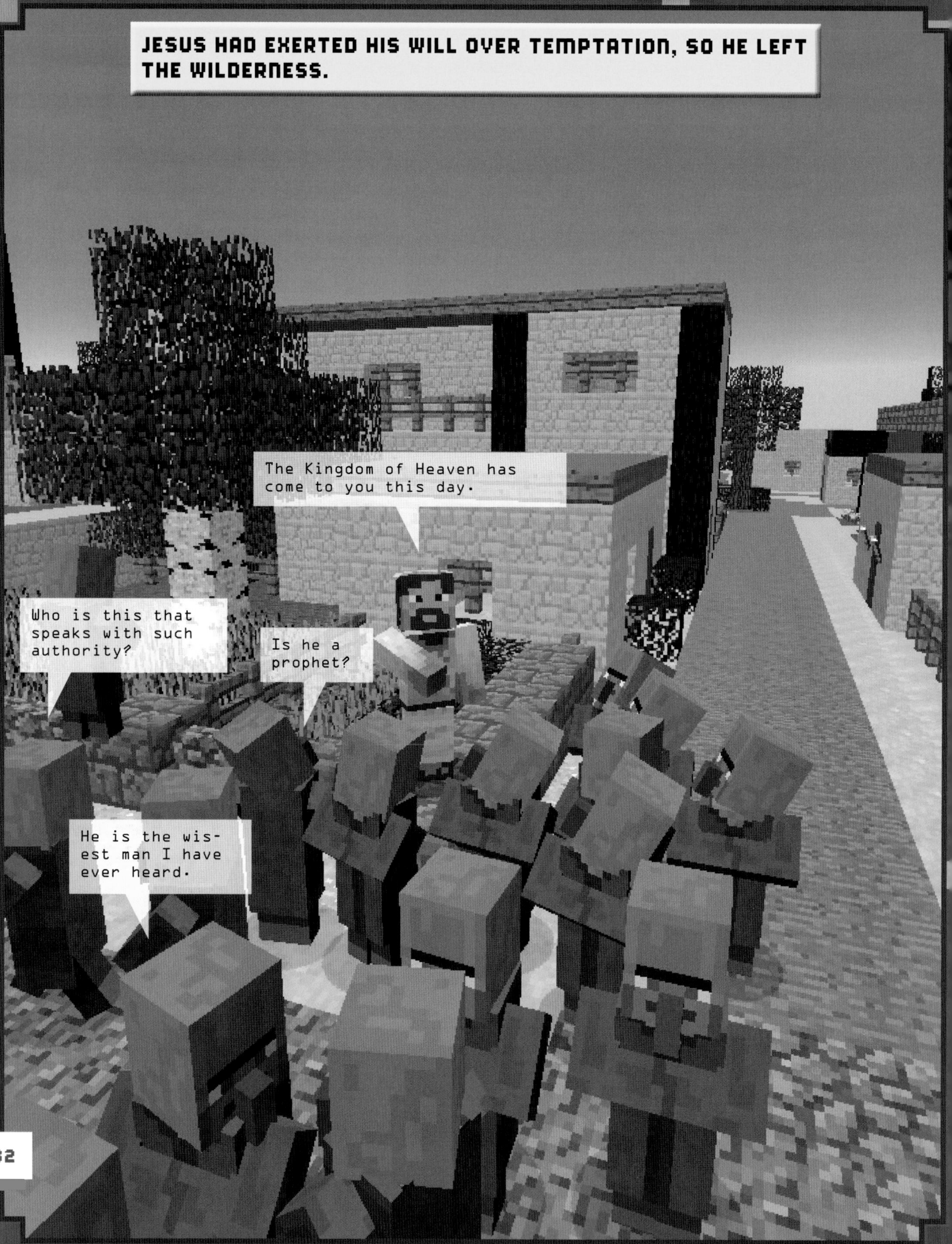
JESUS HAD EXERTED HIS WILL OVER TEMPTATION, SO HE LEFT THE WILDERNESS.
The Kingdom of Heaven has come to you this day.
Who is this that speaks with such authority?
Is he a prophet?
He is the wis-est man I have ever heard.

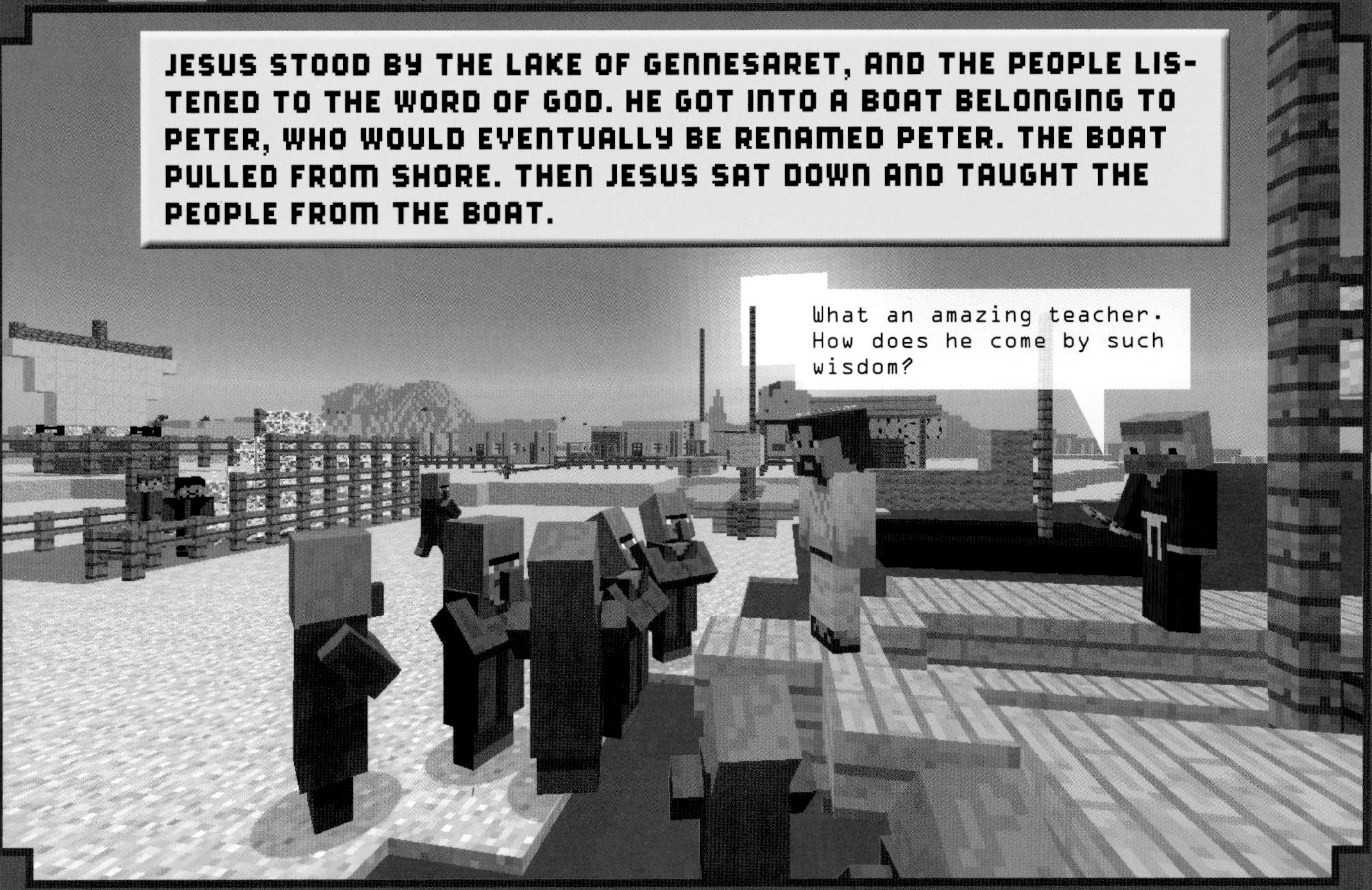
JESUS STOOD BY THE LAKE OF GENNESARET, AND THE PEOPLE LISTENED TO THE WORD OF GOD. HE GOT INTO A BOAT BELONGING TO PETER, WHO WOULD EVENTUALLY BE RENAMED PETER. THE BOAT PULLED FROM SHORE. THEN JESUS SAT DOWN AND TAUGHT THE PEOPLE FROM THE BOAT.
What an amazing teacher. How does he come by such wisdom?

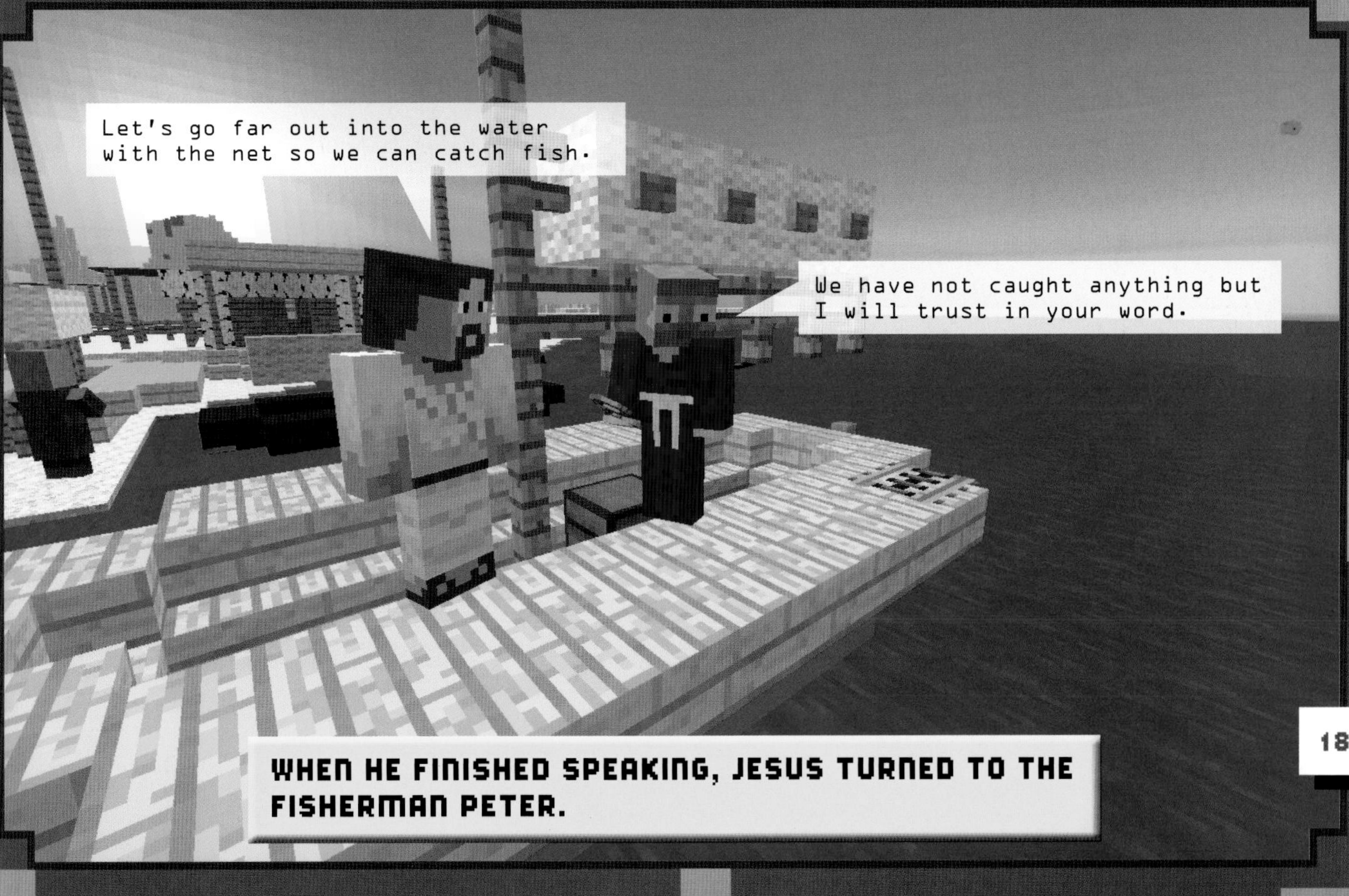
Let's go far out into the water with the net so we can catch fish.
We have not caught anything but I will trust in your word.
WHEN HE FINISHED SPEAKING, JESUS TURNED TO THE FISHERMAN PETER.

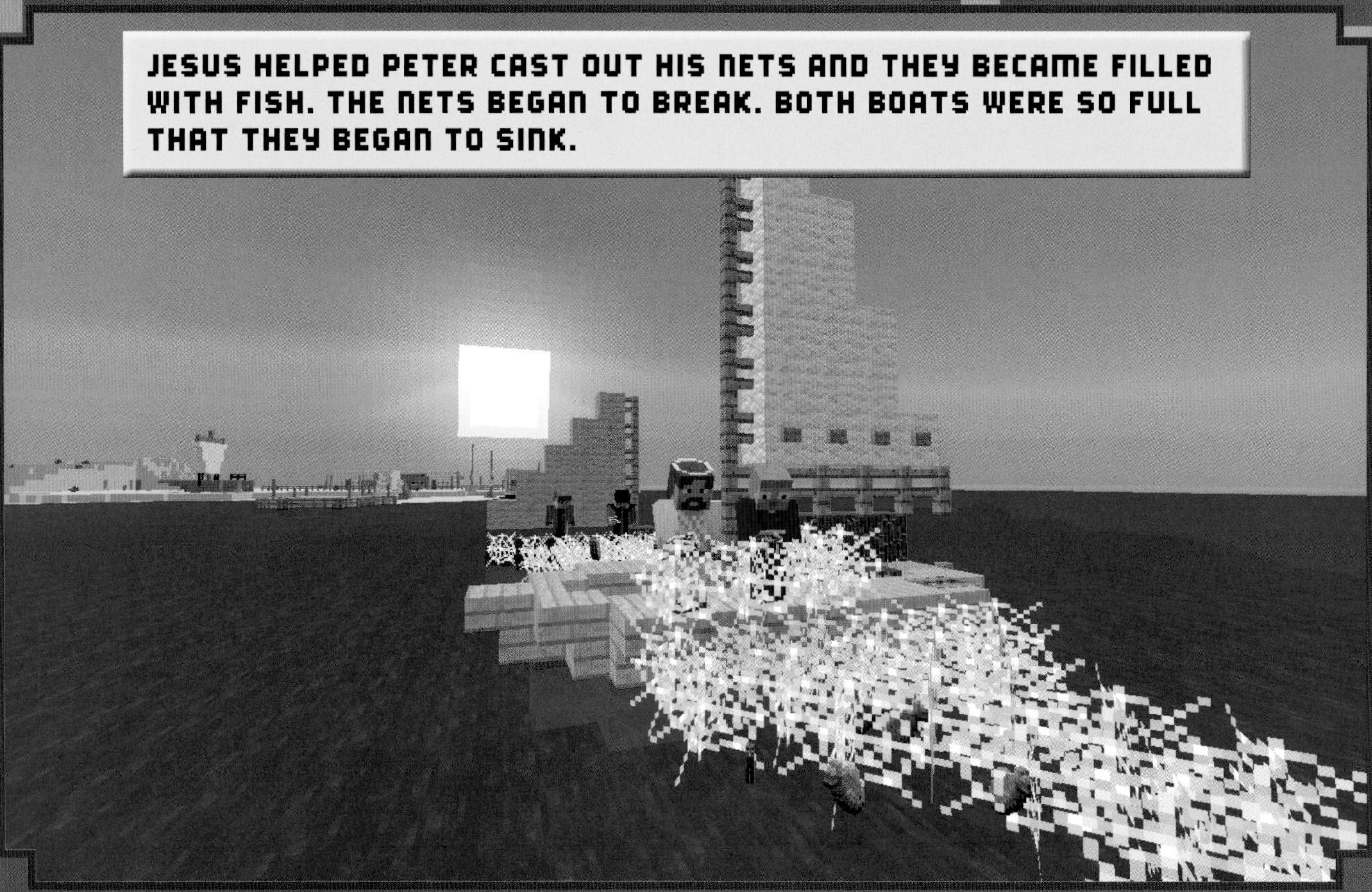
JESUS HELPED PETER CAST OUT HIS NETS AND THEY BECAME FILLED WITH FISH. THE NETS BEGAN TO BREAK. BOTH BOATS WERE SO FULL THAT THEY BEGAN TO SINK.

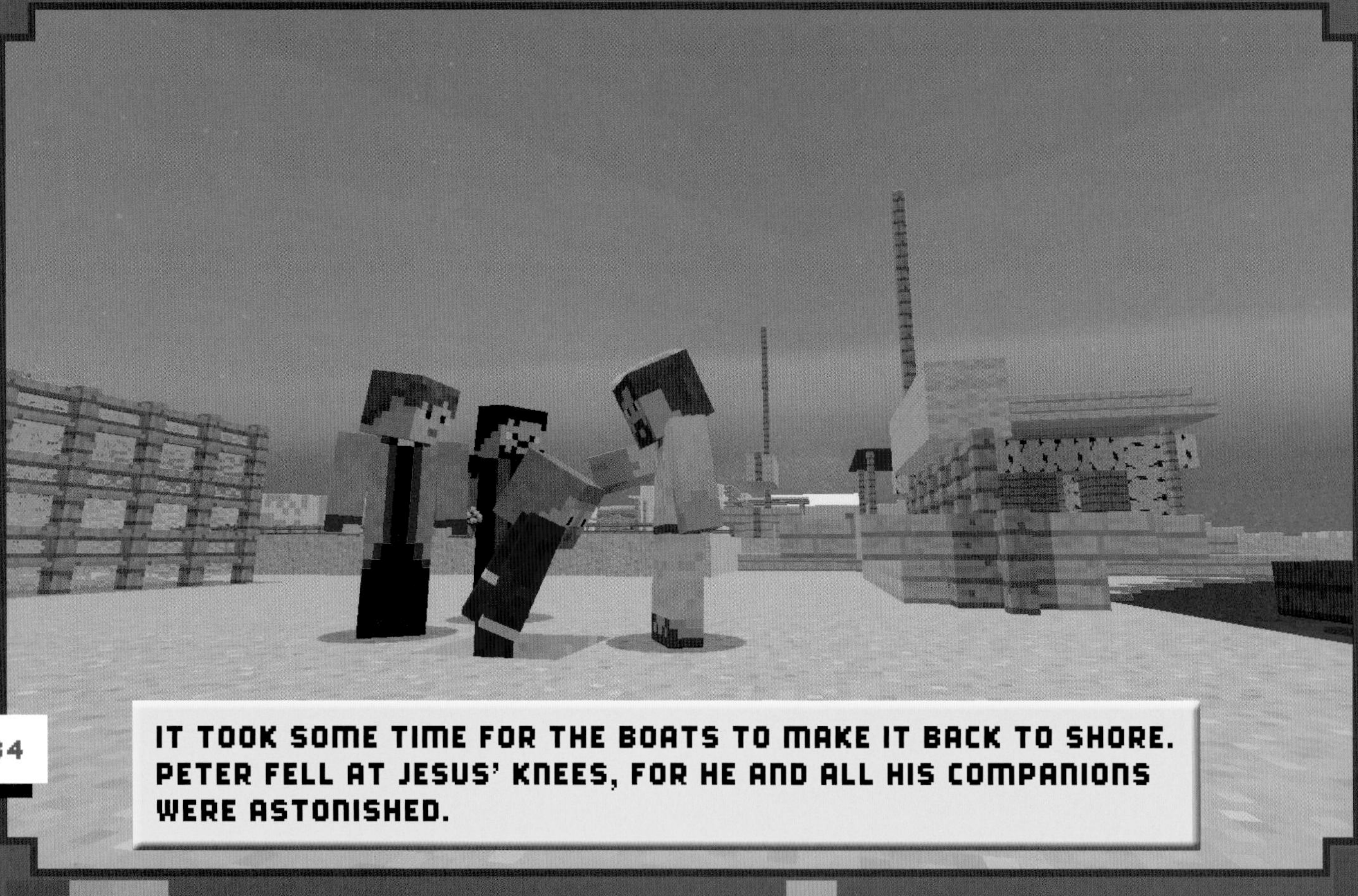
IT TOOK SOME TIME FOR THE BOATS TO MAKE IT BACK TO SHORE. PETER FELL AT JESUS' KNEES, FOR HE AND ALL HIS COMPANIONS WERE ASTONISHED.

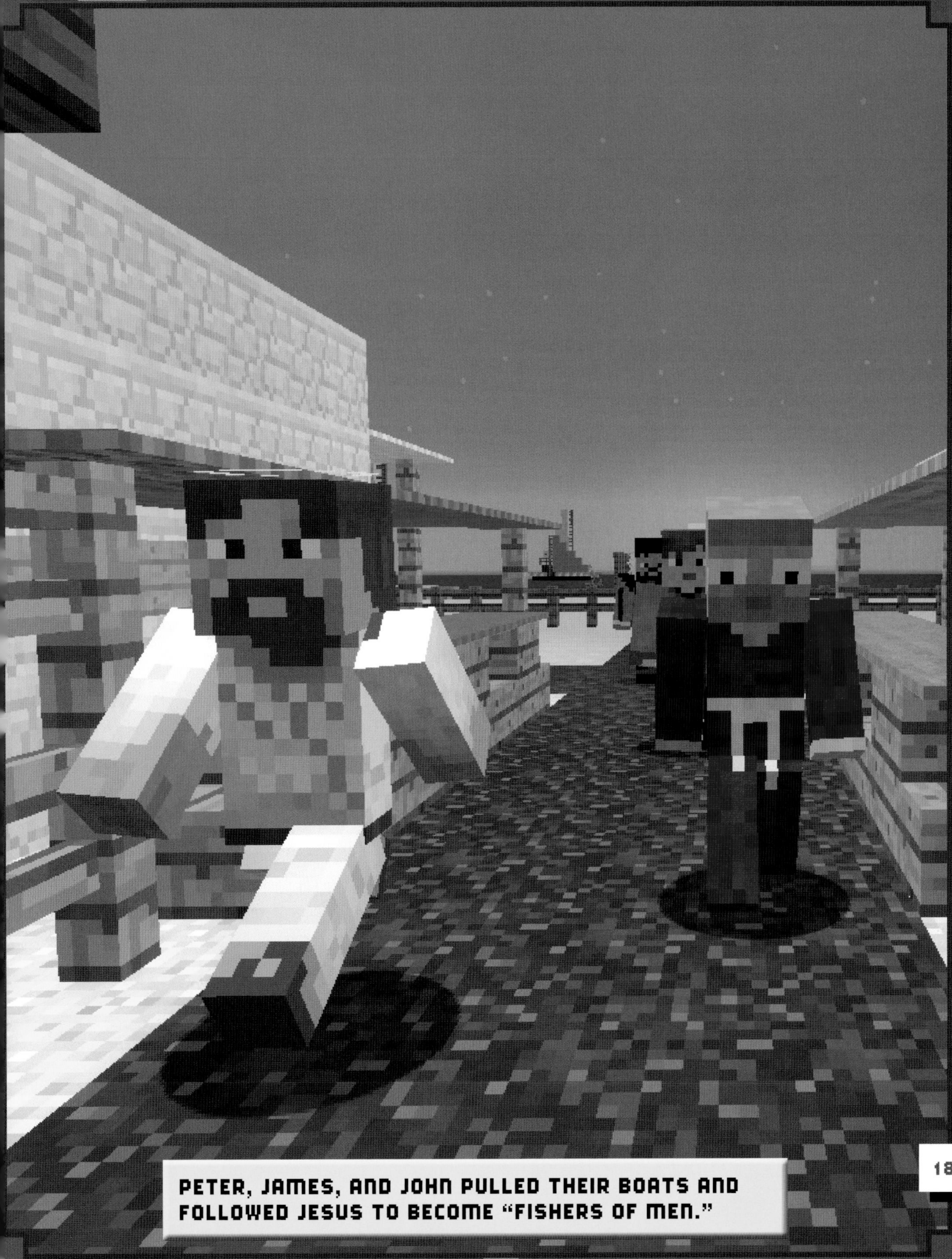

PETER, JAMES, AND JOHN PULLED THEIR BOATS AND FOLLOWED JESUS TO BECOME "FISHERS OF MEN."

JESUS HEALS THE SICK

Wow, it didn't take long for Jesus to develop a following.

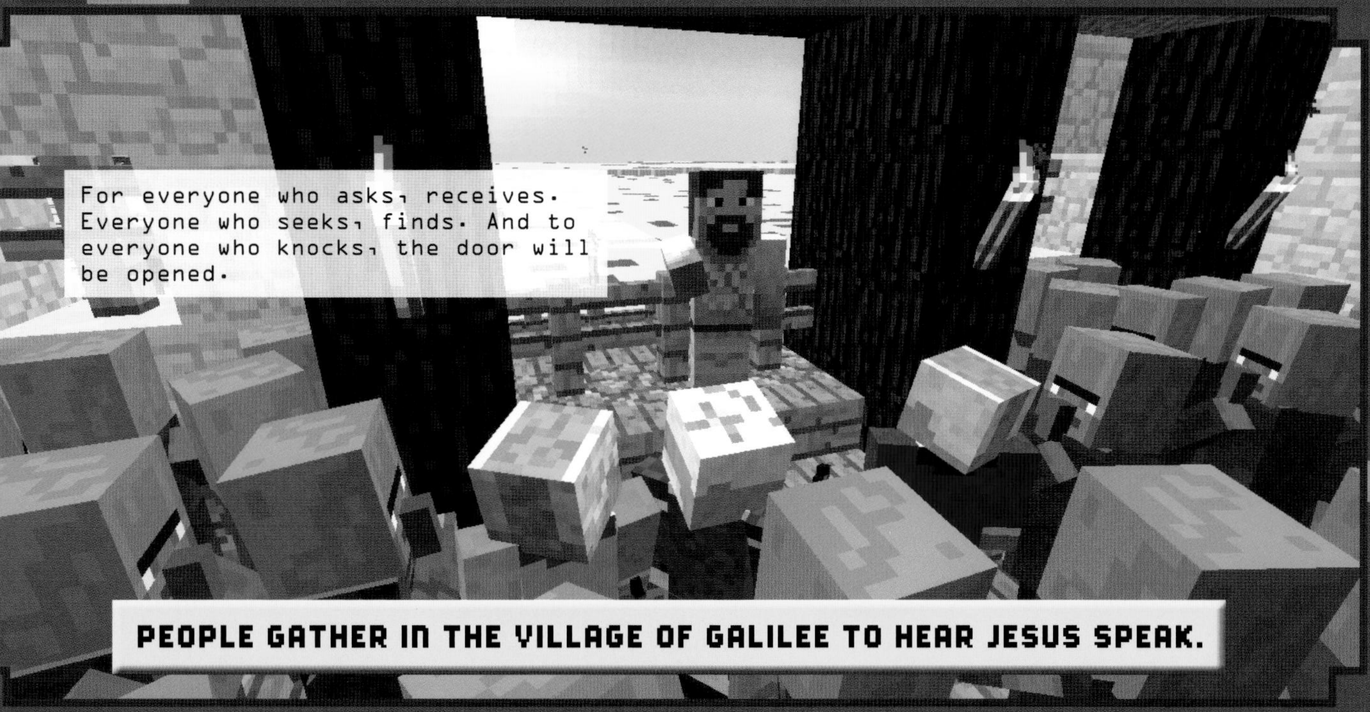
For everyone who asks, receives. Everyone who seeks, finds. And to everyone who knocks, the door will be opened.
PEOPLE GATHER IN THE VILLAGE OF GALILEE TO HEAR JESUS SPEAK.

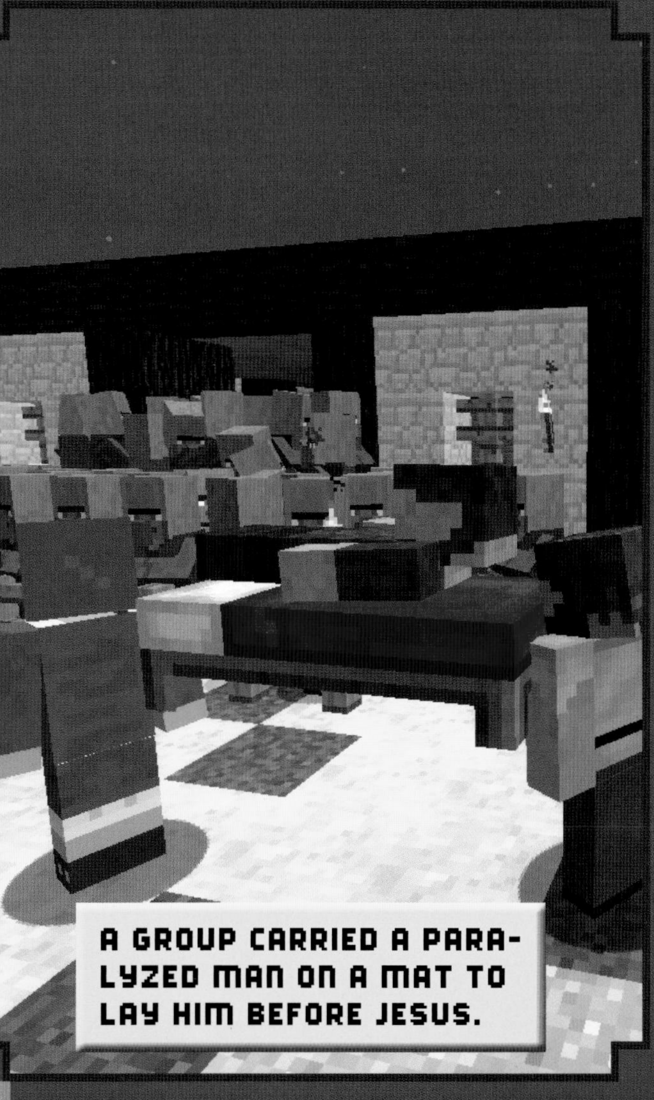
A GROUP CARRIED A PARALYZED MAN ON A MAT TO LAY HIM BEFORE JESUS.

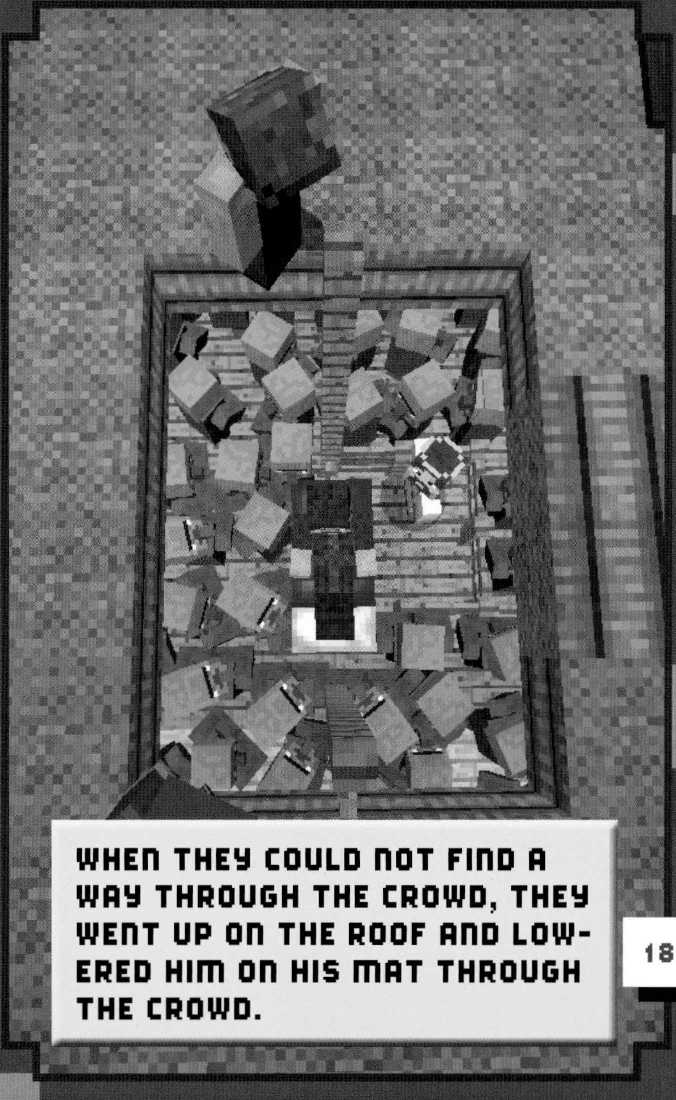
WHEN THEY COULD NOT FIND A WAY THROUGH THE CROWD, THEY WENT UP ON THE ROOF AND LOWERED HIM ON HIS MAT THROUGH THE CROWD.

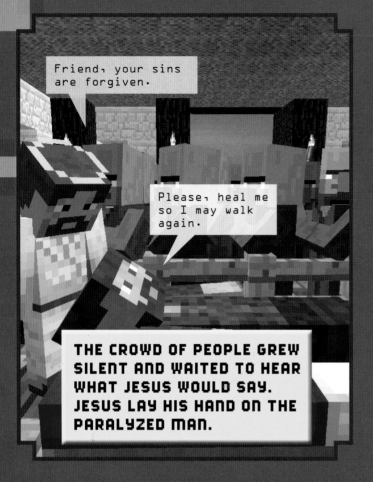

Friend, your sins are forgiven.

Please, heal me so I may walk again.

THE CROWD OF PEOPLE GREW SILENT AND WAITED TO HEAR WHAT JESUS WOULD SAY. JESUS LAY HIS HAND ON THE PARALYZED MAN.

He is no longer just teaching, he is now forgiving sins.

THE PHARISEES AND THE TEACHERS OF THE LAW GATHERED.

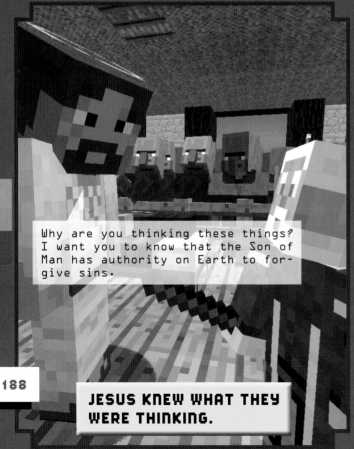

Why are you thinking these things? I want you to know that the Son of Man has authority on Earth to forgive sins.

JESUS KNEW WHAT THEY WERE THINKING.

Get up, take your mat, and go home.

HE THEN SPOKE TO THE PARALYZED MAN.

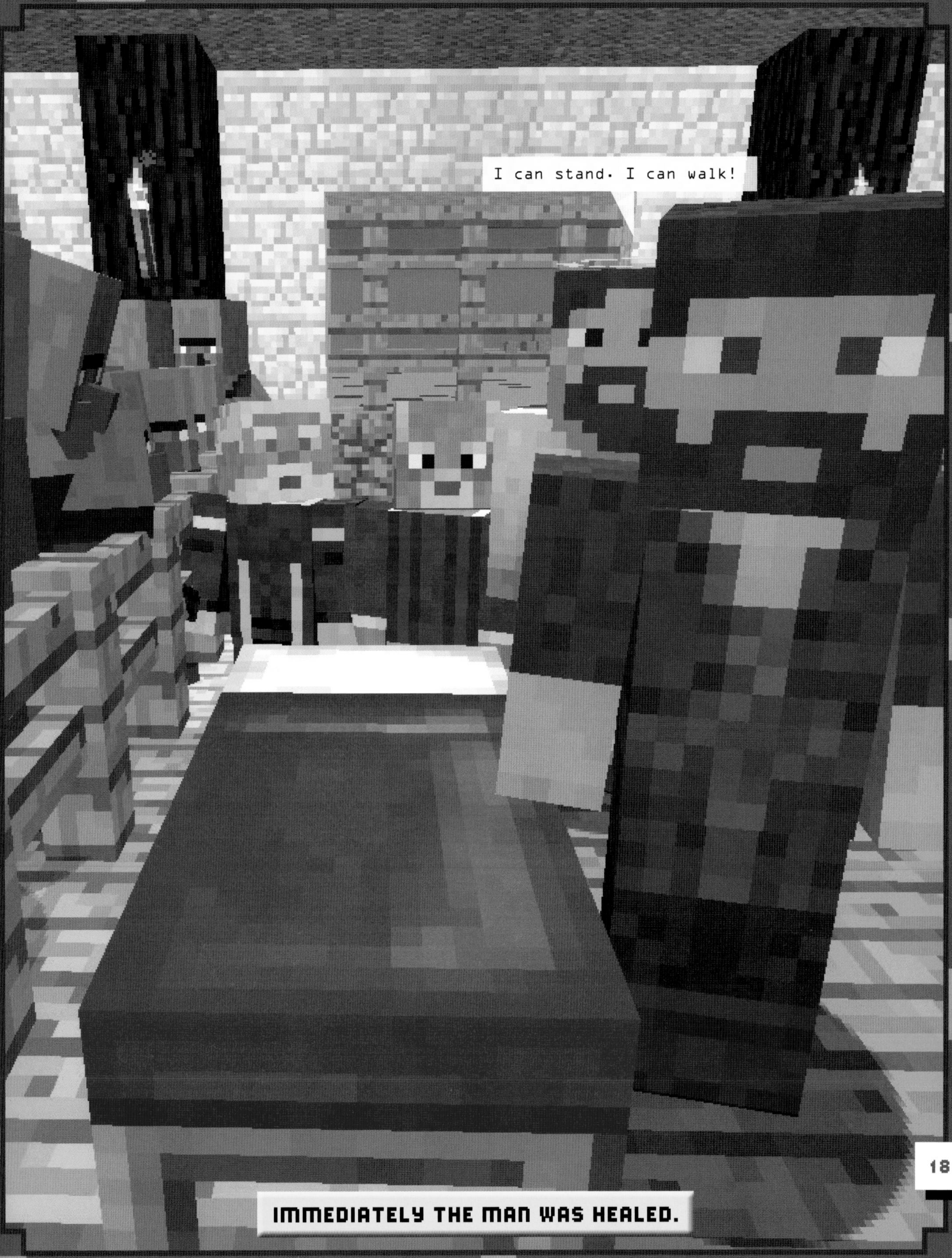
I can stand. I can walk!
IMMEDIATELY THE MAN WAS HEALED.

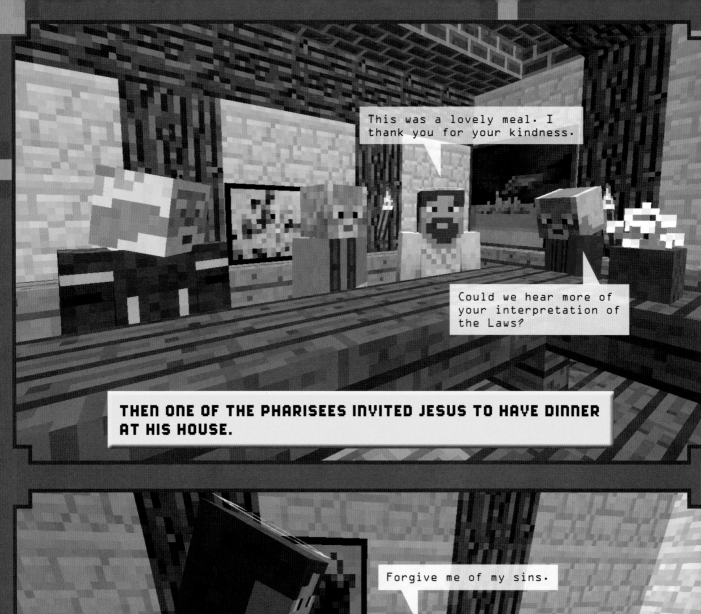

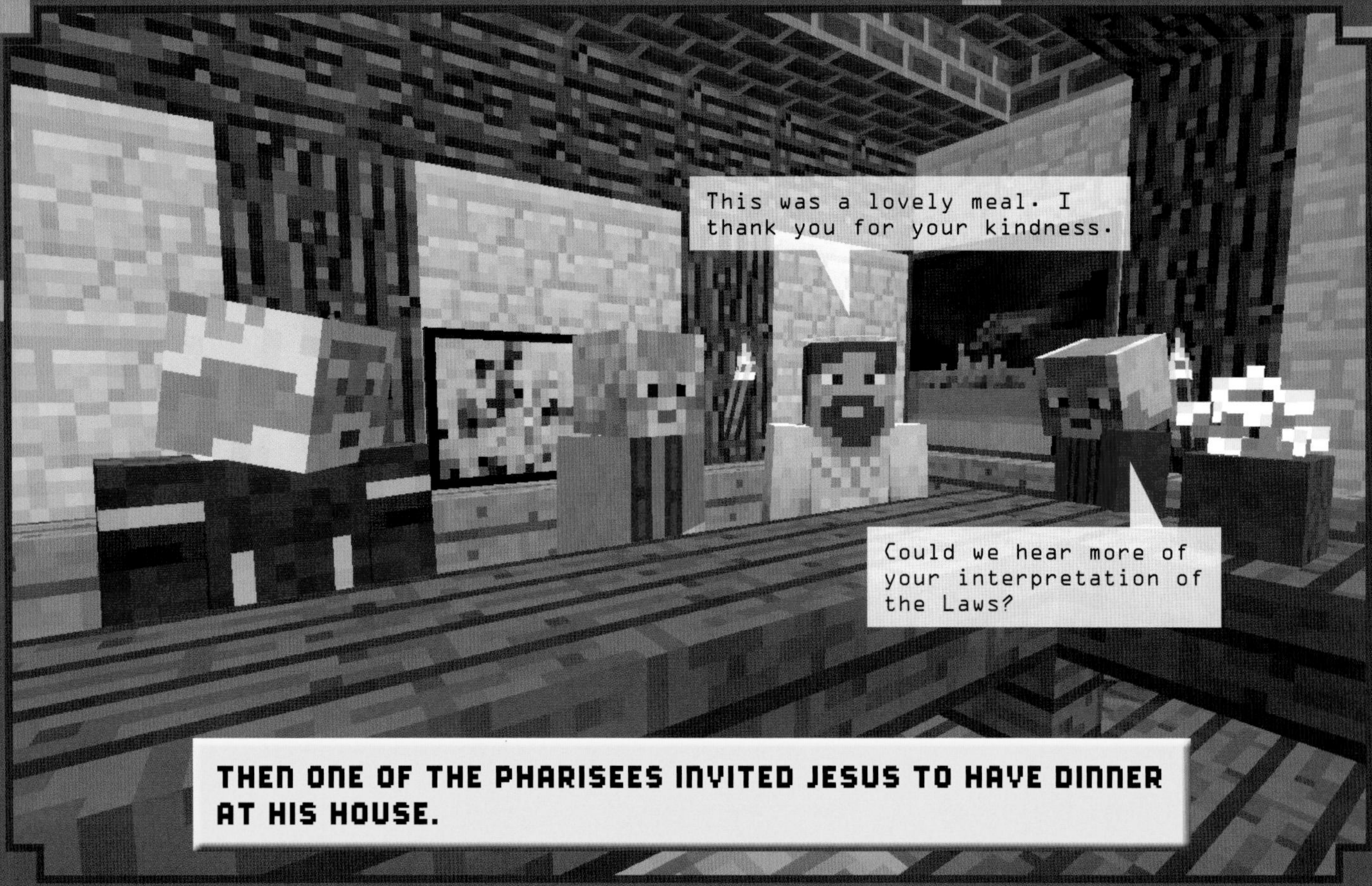
This was a lovely meal. I thank you for your kindness.
Could we hear more of your interpretation of the Laws?
THEN ONE OF THE PHARISEES INVITED JESUS TO HAVE DINNER AT HIS HOUSE.

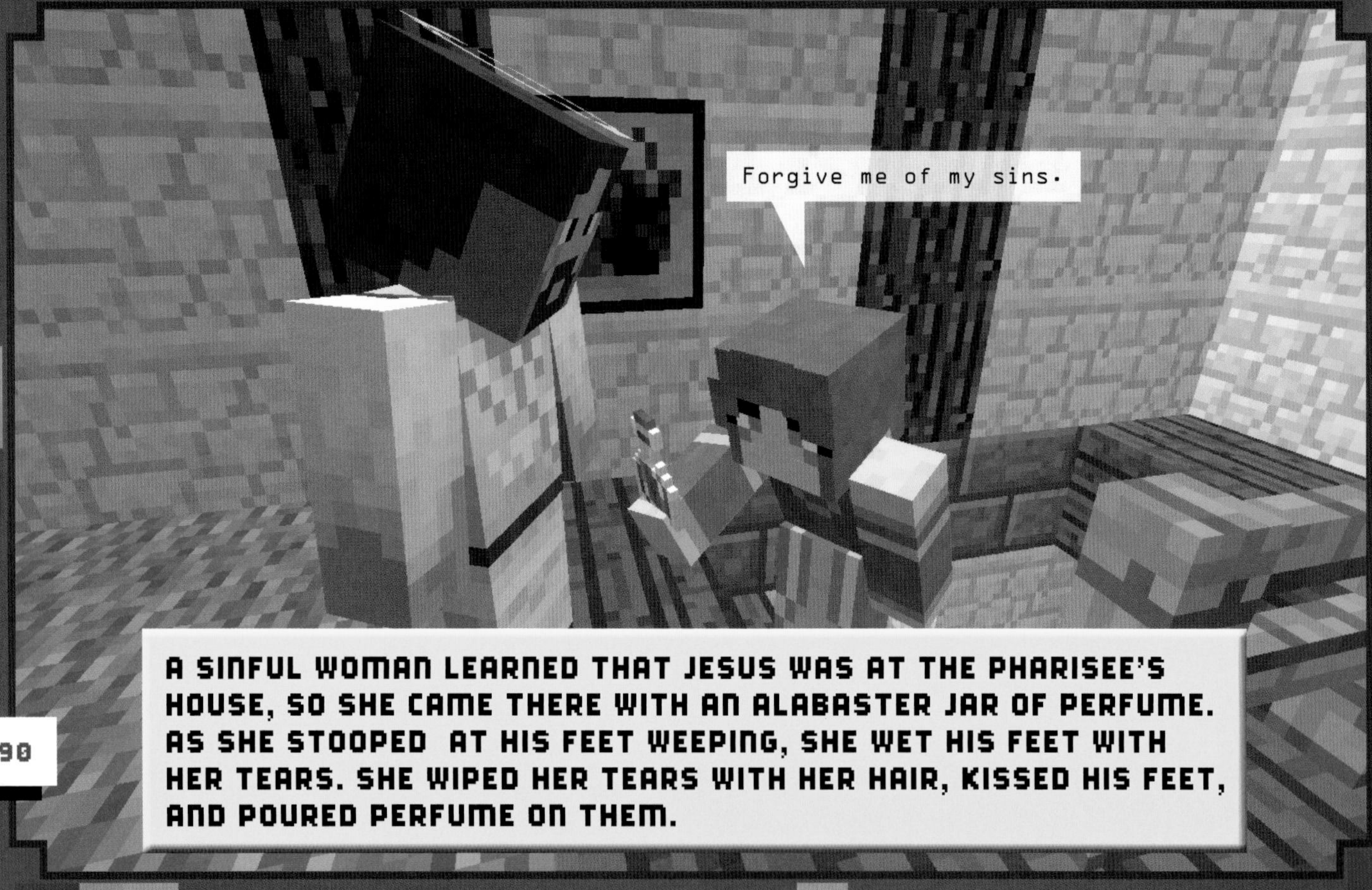
Forgive me of my sins.
A SINFUL WOMAN LEARNED THAT JESUS WAS AT THE PHARISEE'S HOUSE, SO SHE CAME THERE WITH AN ALABASTER JAR OF PERFUME. AS SHE STOOPED AT HIS FEET WEEPING, SHE WET HIS FEET WITH HER TEARS. SHE WIPED HER TEARS WITH HER HAIR, KISSED HIS FEET, AND POURED PERFUME ON THEM.

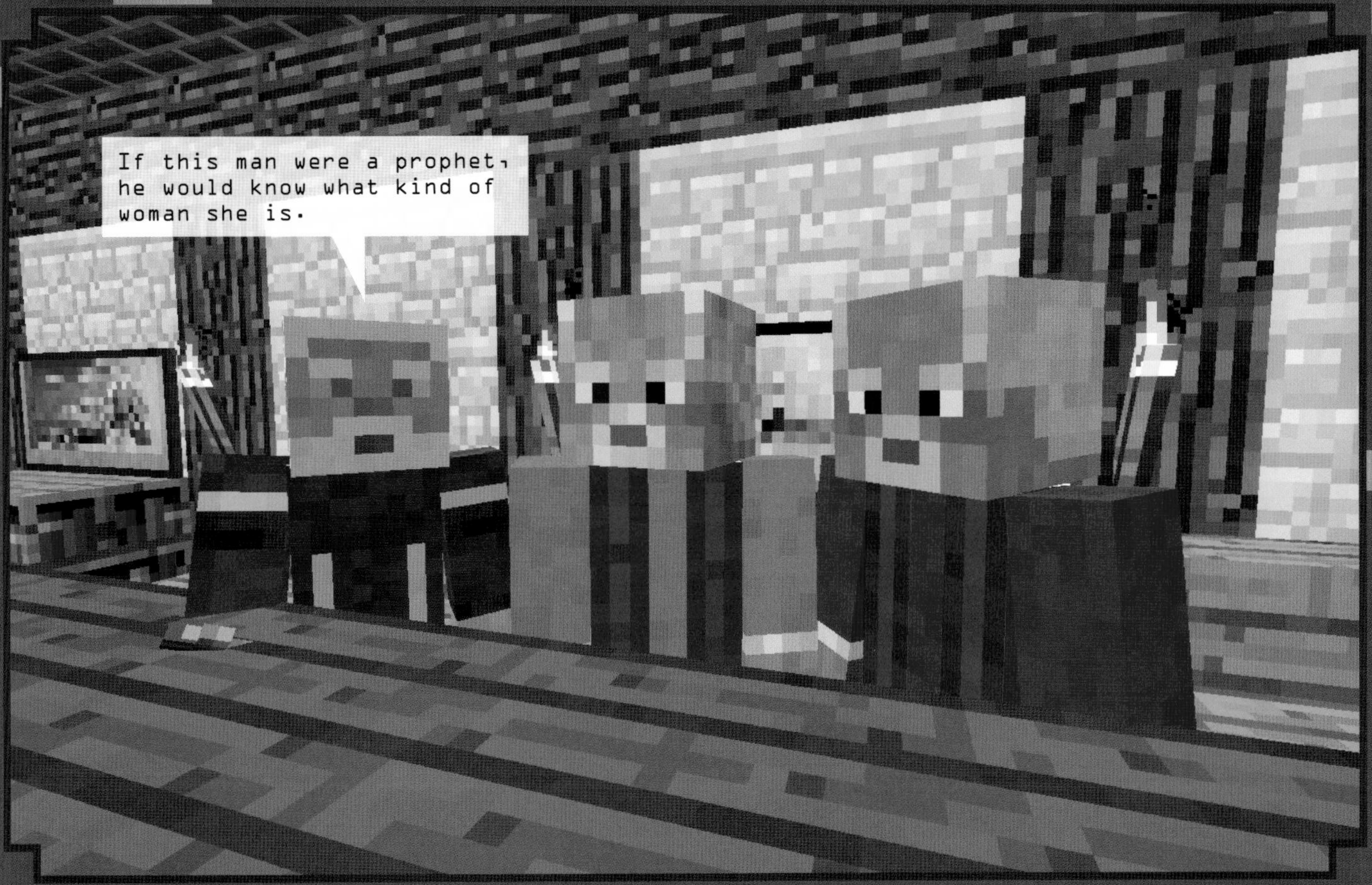
If this man were a prophet, he would know what kind of woman she is.

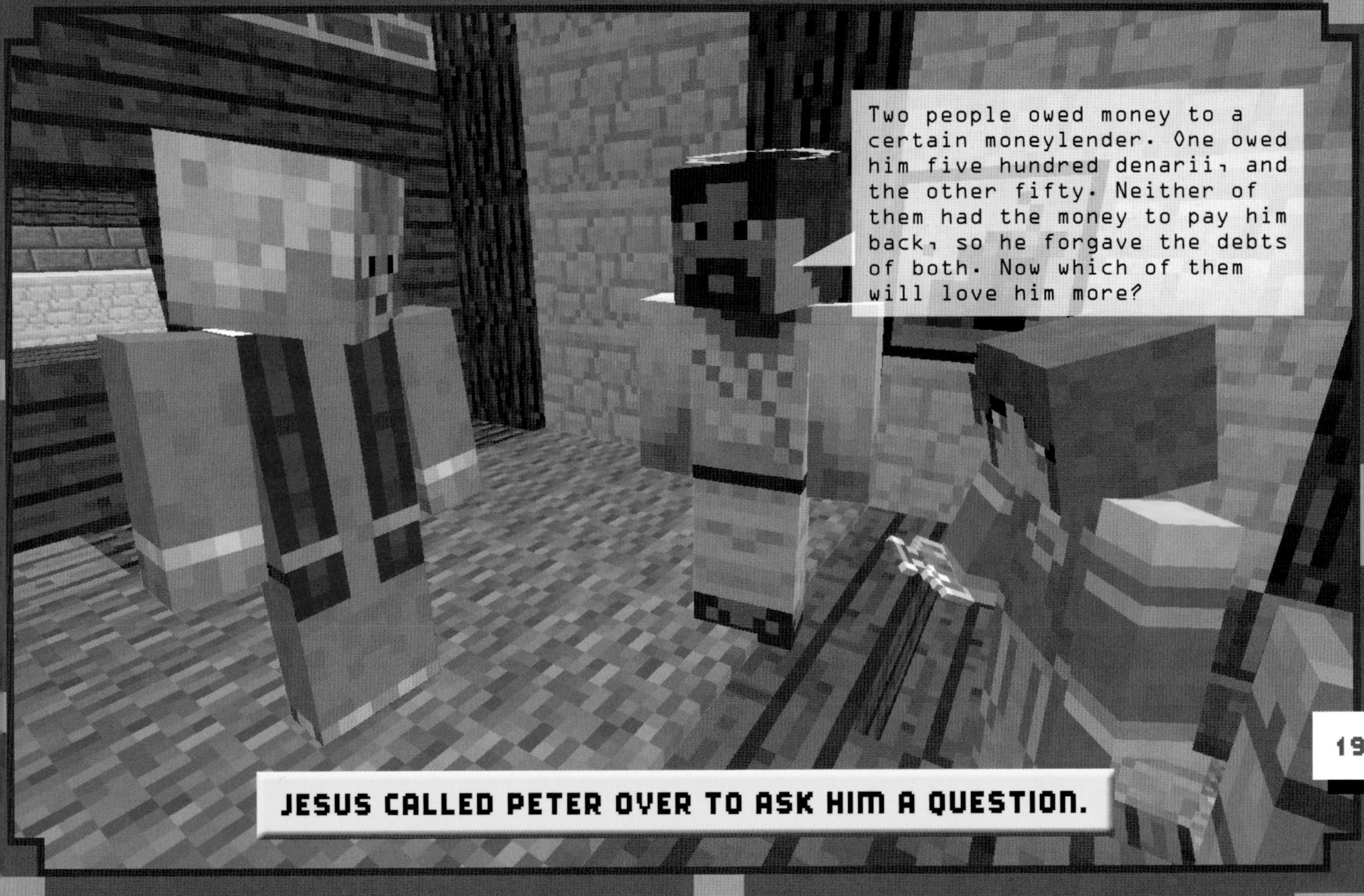
Two people owed money to a certain moneylender. One owed him five hundred denarii, and the other fifty. Neither of them had the money to pay him back, so he forgave the debts of both. Now which of them will love him more?
JESUS CALLED PETER OVER TO ASK HIM A QUESTION.

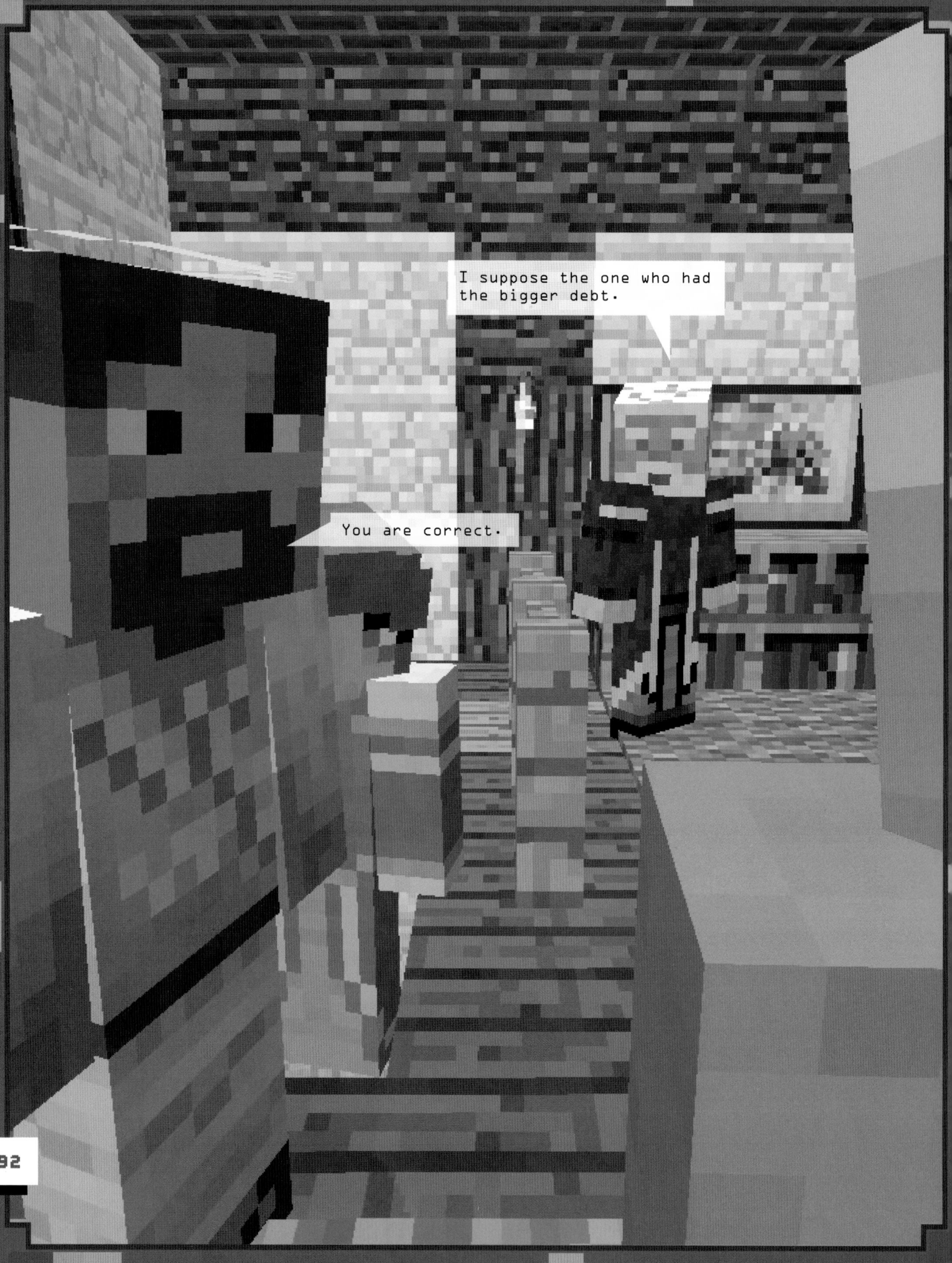
I suppose the one who had the bigger debt.
You are correct.

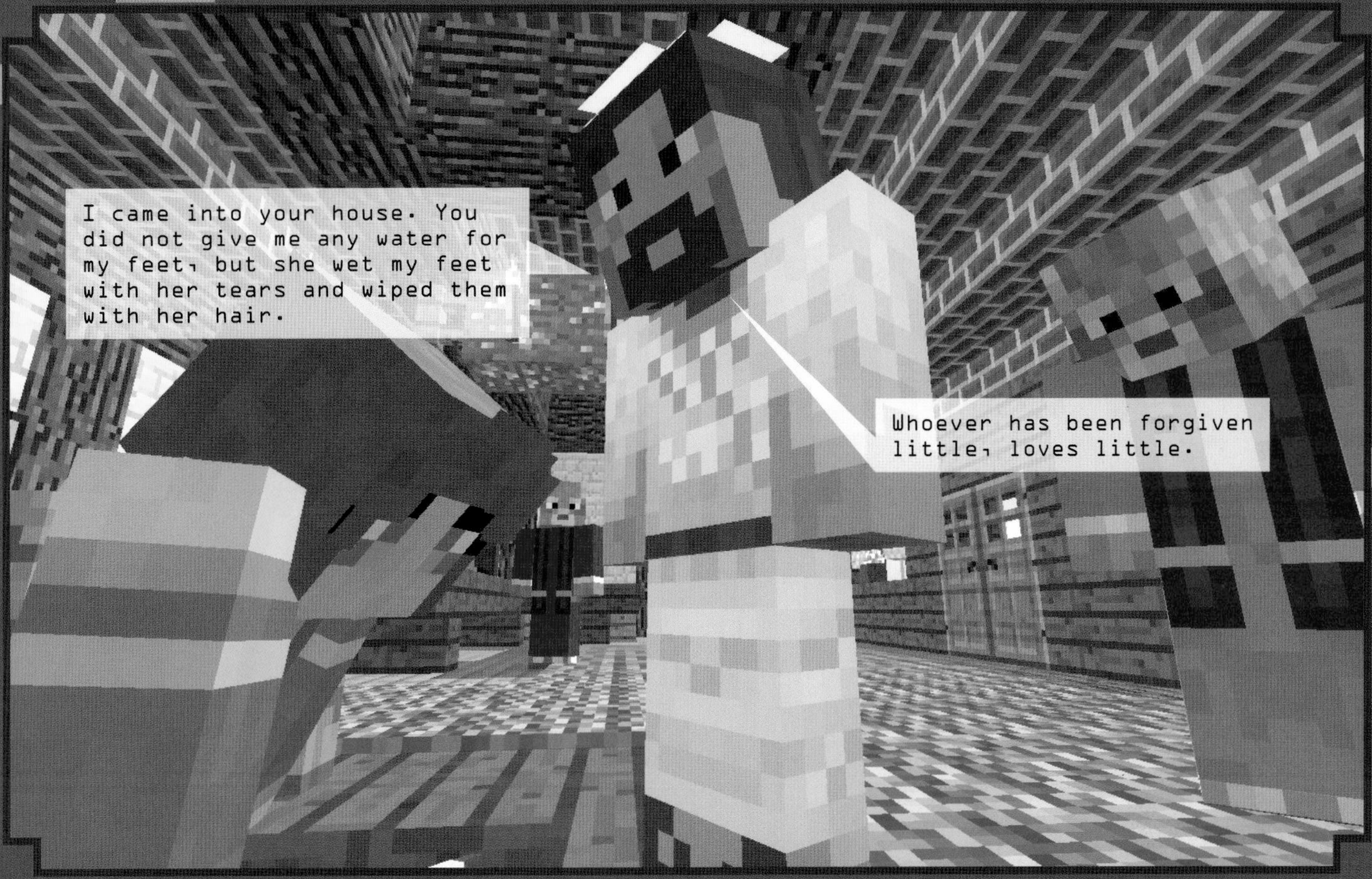
I came into your house. You did not give me any water for my feet, but she wet my feet with her tears and wiped them with her hair.
Whoever has been forgiven little, loves little.

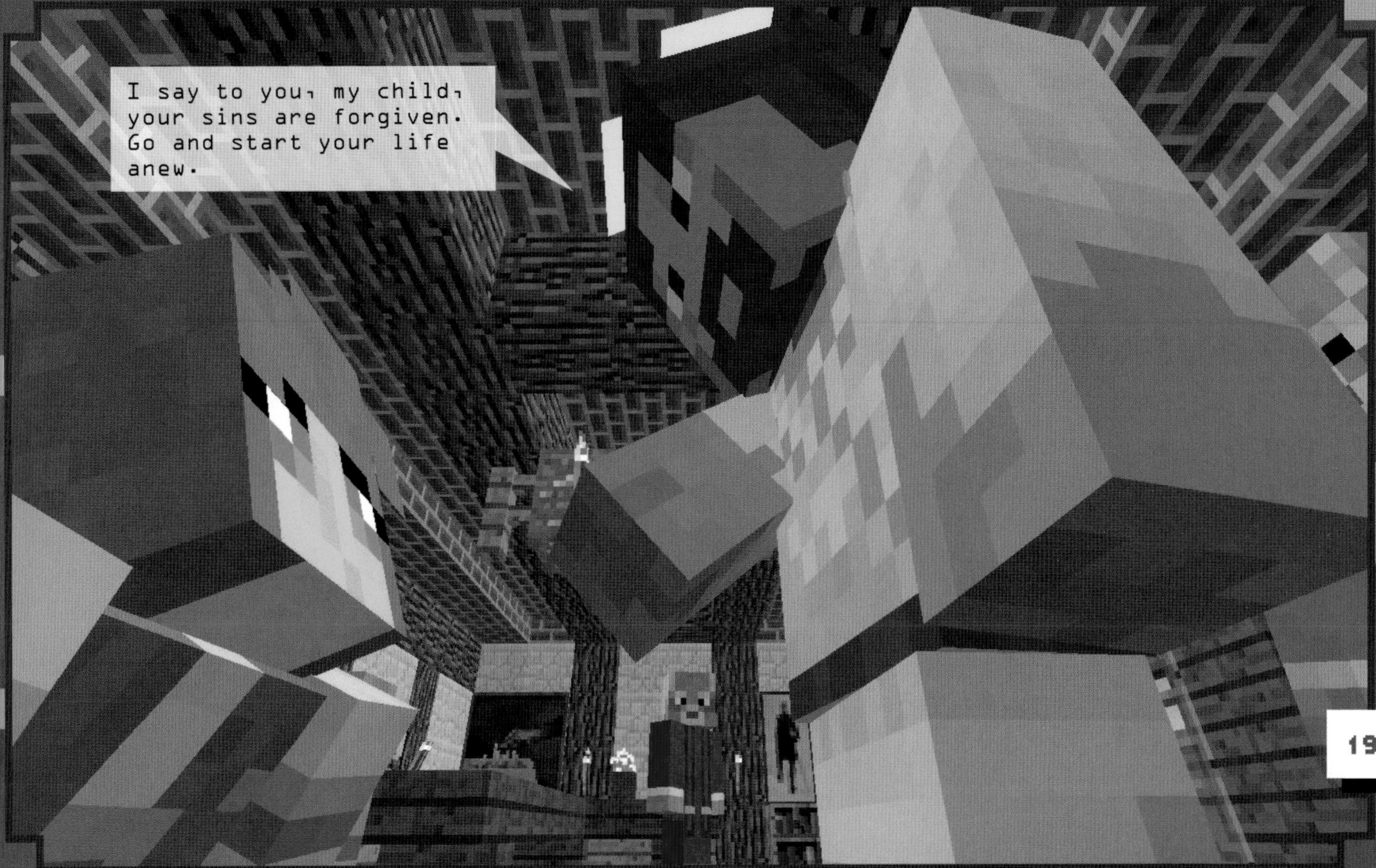
I say to you, my child, your sins are forgiven. Go and start your life anew.

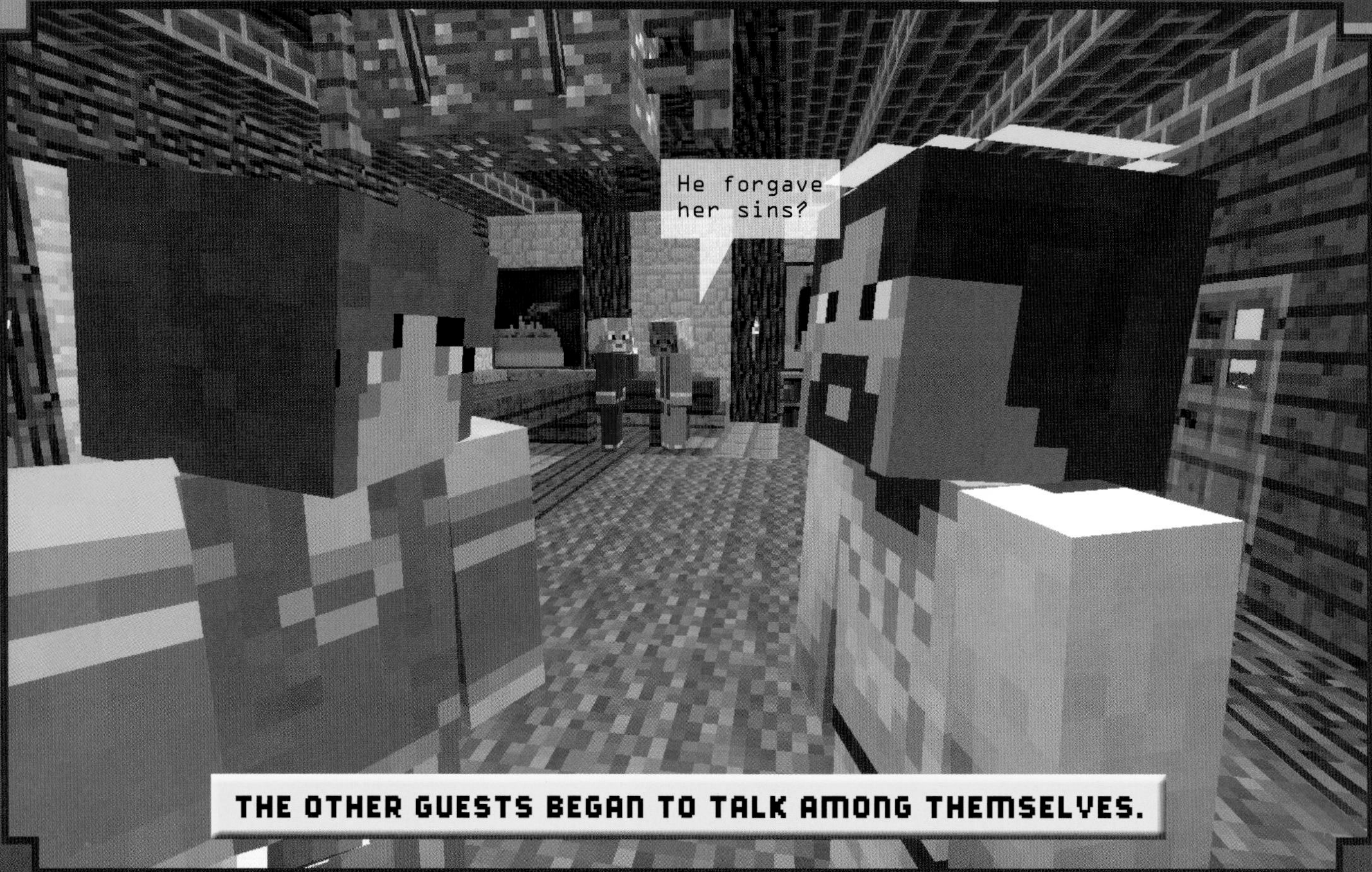
He forgave her sins?
THE OTHER GUESTS BEGAN TO TALK AMONG THEMSELVES.

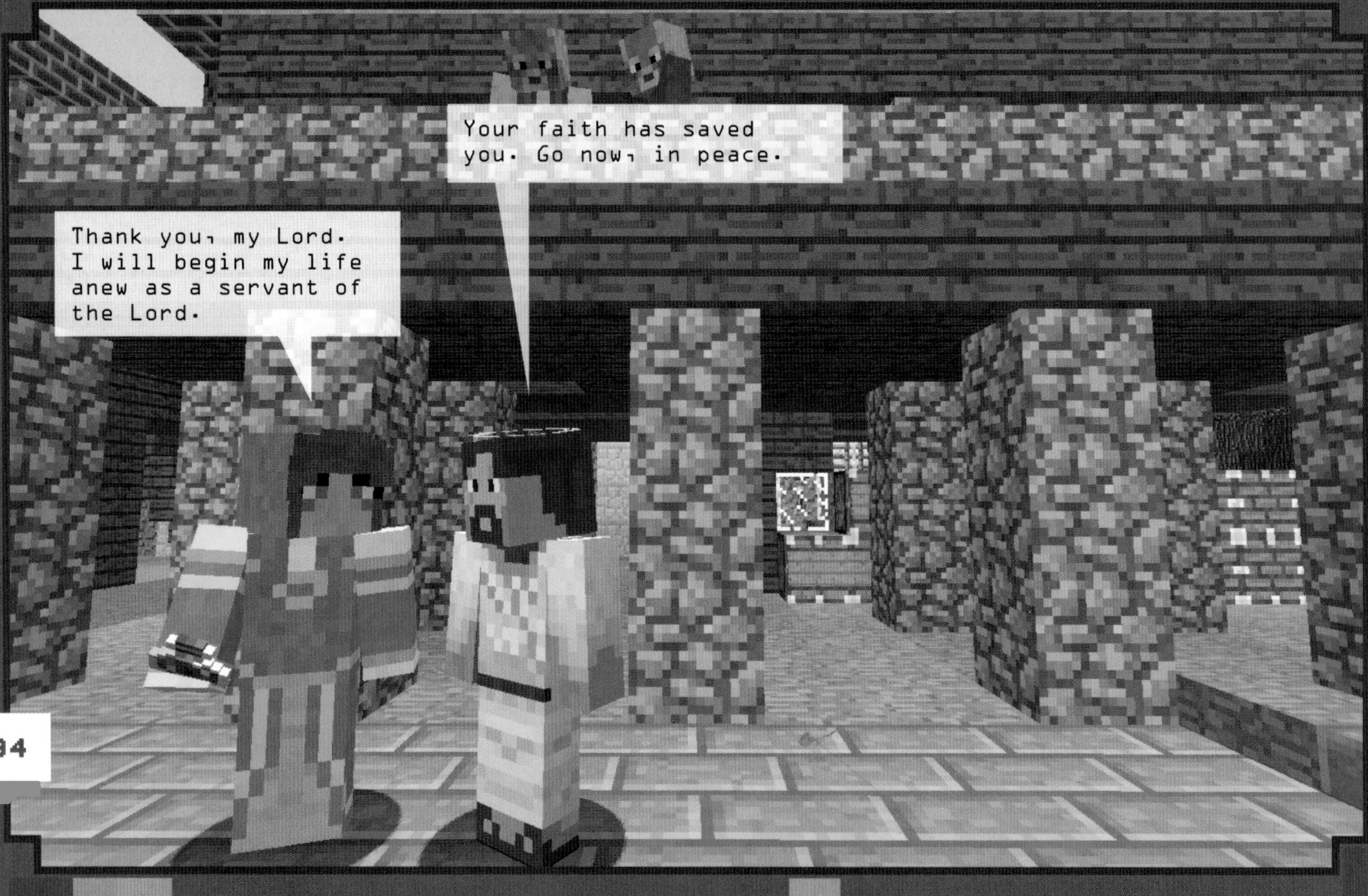
Your faith has saved you. Go now, in peace.
Thank you, my Lord. I will begin my life anew as a servant of the Lord.

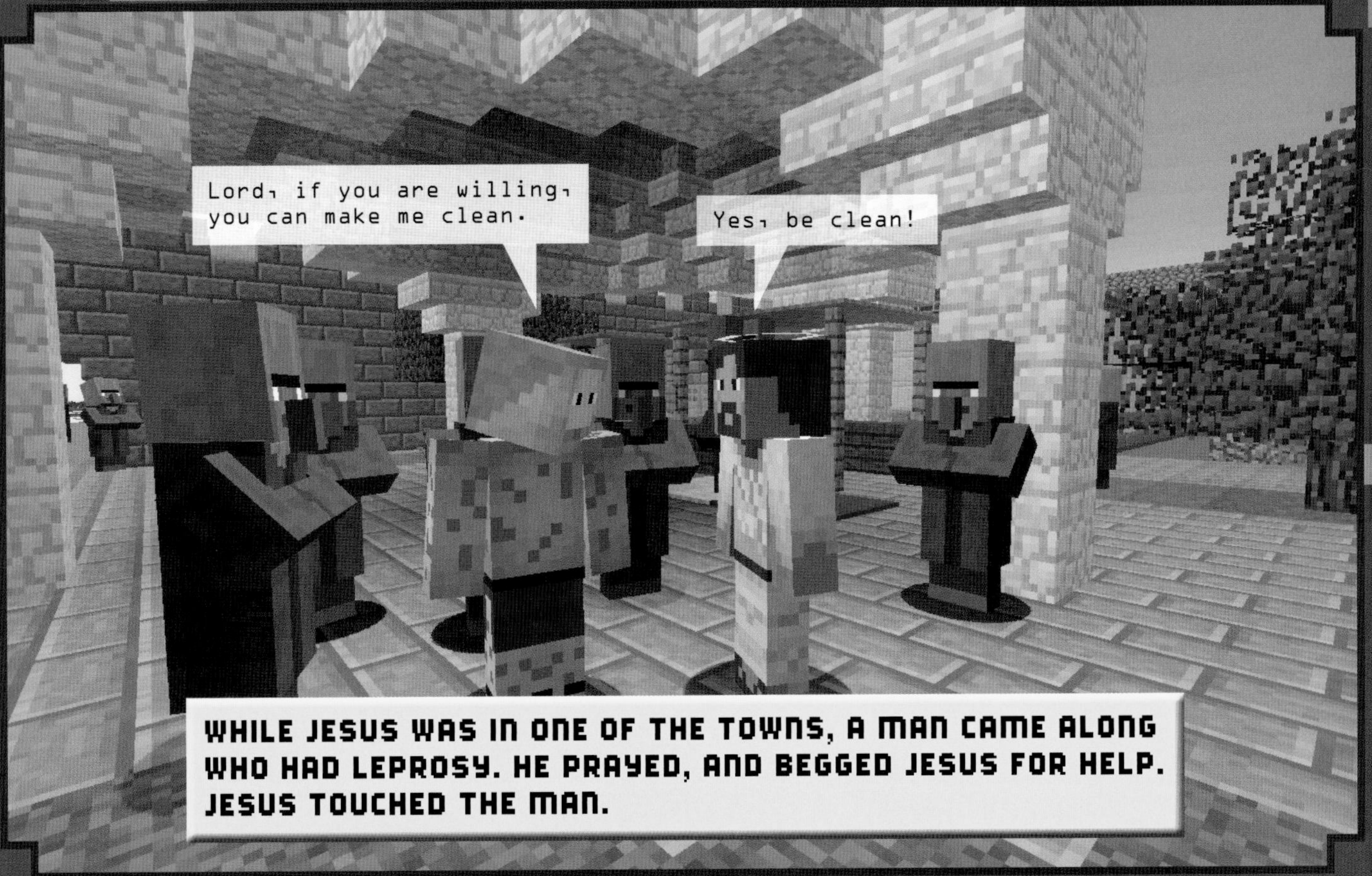
Lord, if you are willing, you can make me clean.
Yes, be clean!
WHILE JESUS WAS IN ONE OF THE TOWNS, A MAN CAME ALONG WHO HAD LEPROSY. HE PRAYED, AND BEGGED JESUS FOR HELP. JESUS TOUCHED THE MAN.

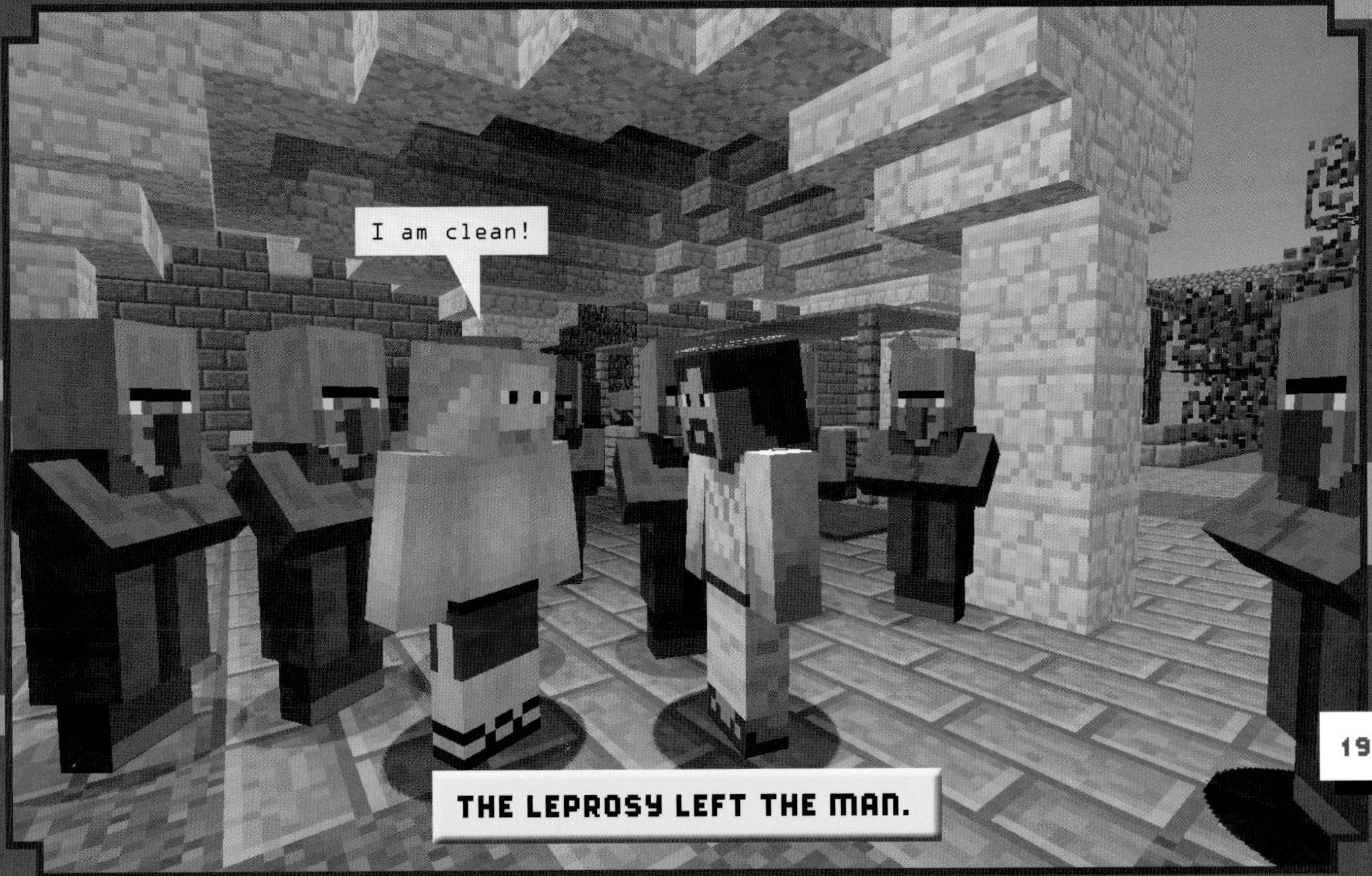
I am clean!
THE LEPROSY LEFT THE MAN.

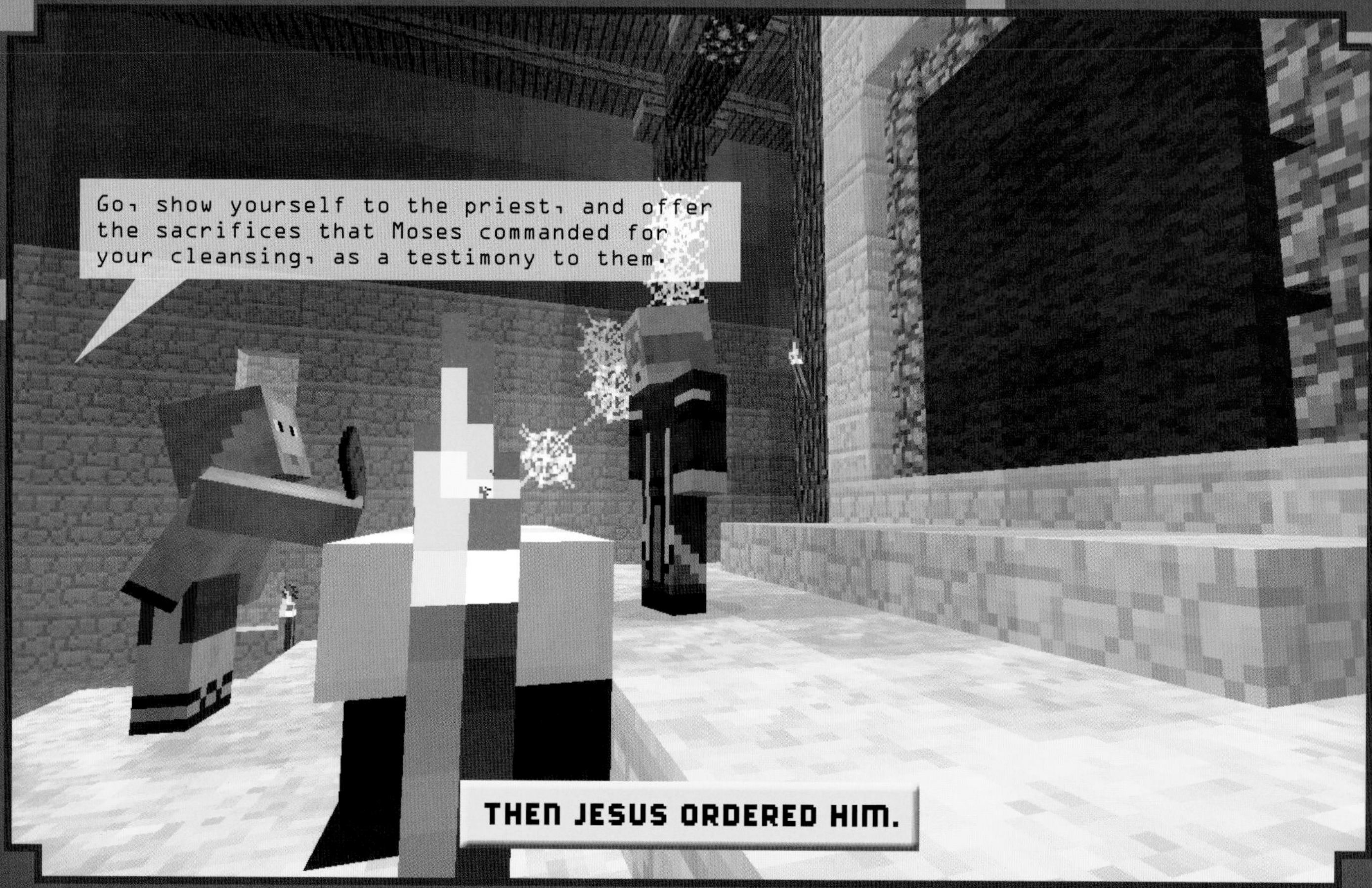
Go, show yourself to the priest, and offer the sacrifices that Moses commanded for your cleansing, as a testimony to them.
THEN JESUS ORDERED HIM.

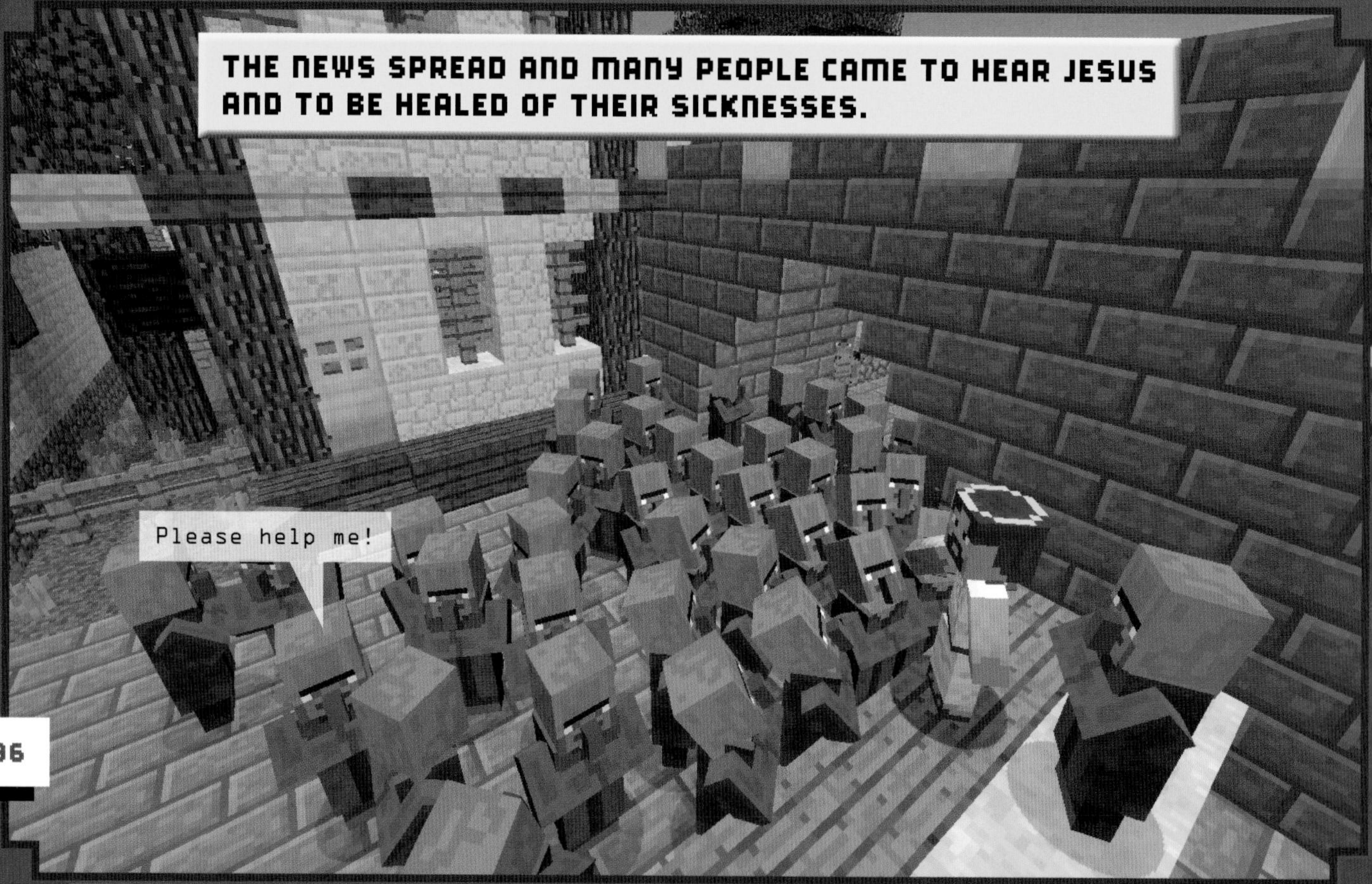
THE NEWS SPREAD AND MANY PEOPLE CAME TO HEAR JESUS AND TO BE HEALED OF THEIR SICKNESSES.
Please help me!

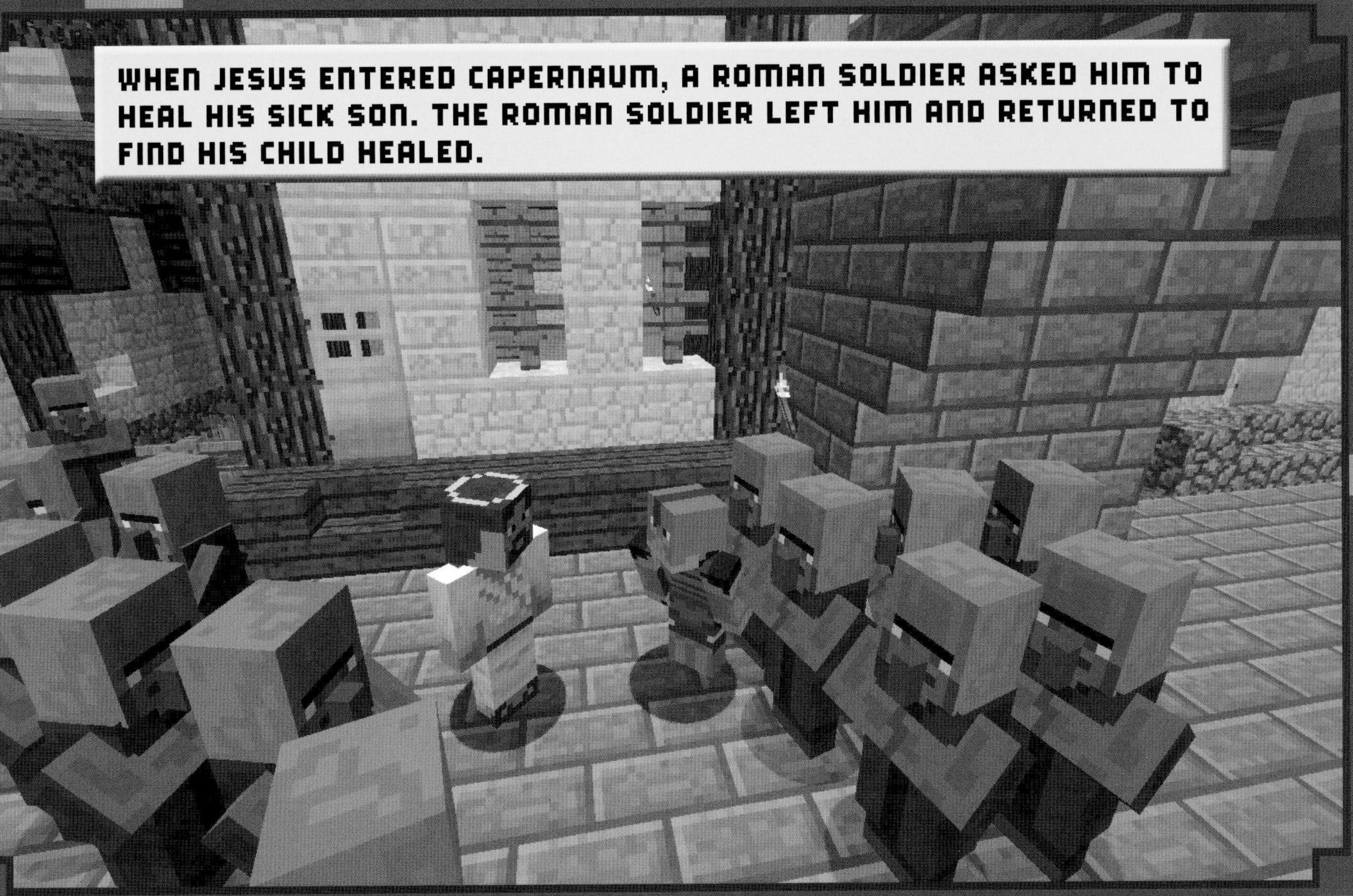
WHEN JESUS ENTERED CAPERNAUM, A ROMAN SOLDIER ASKED HIM TO HEAL HIS SICK SON. THE ROMAN SOLDIER LEFT HIM AND RETURNED TO FIND HIS CHILD HEALED.

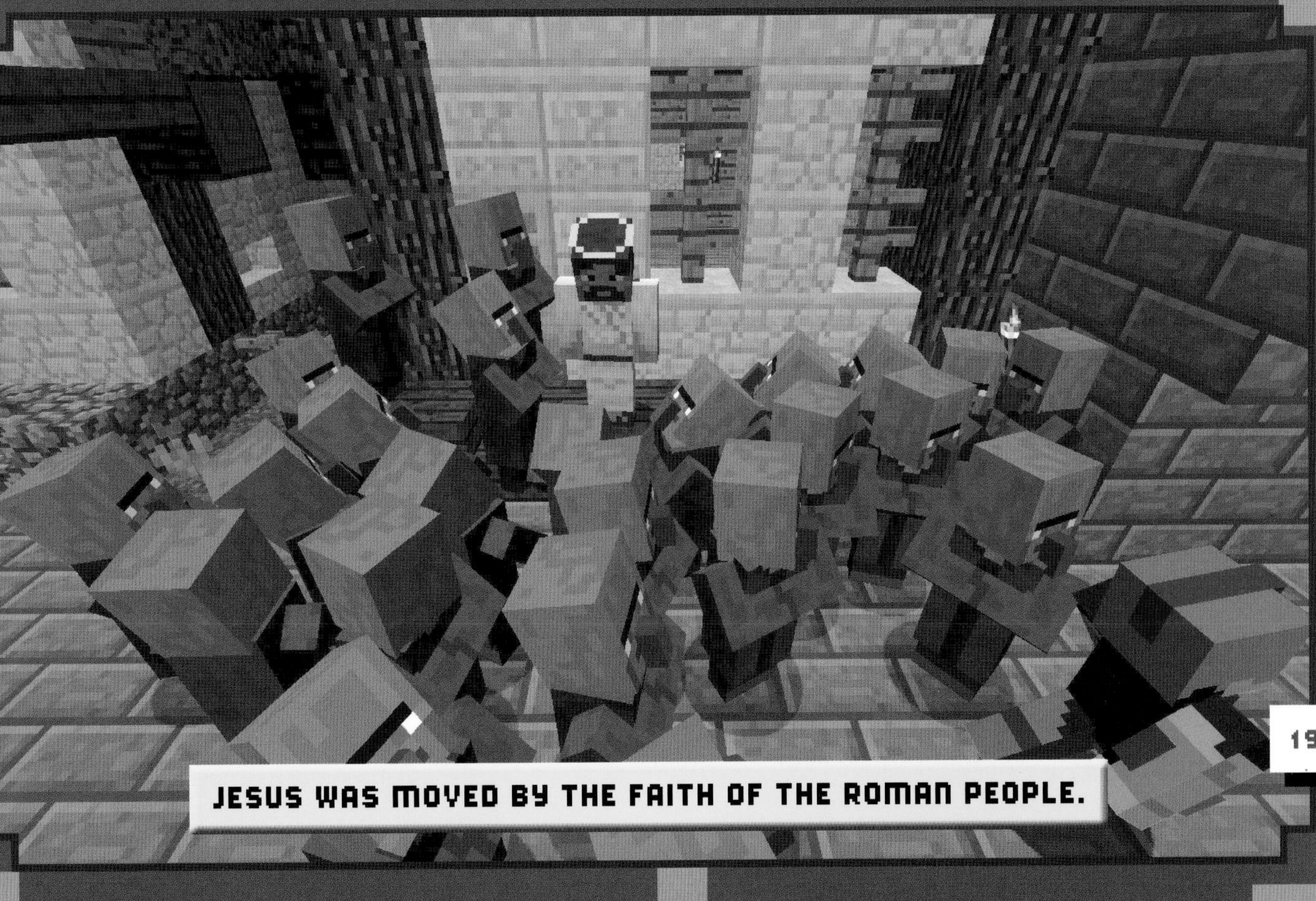
JESUS WAS MOVED BY THE FAITH OF THE ROMAN PEOPLE.

SERMON ON THE MOUNT

Is Jesus going to go to Jerusalem?

He still has work to do.

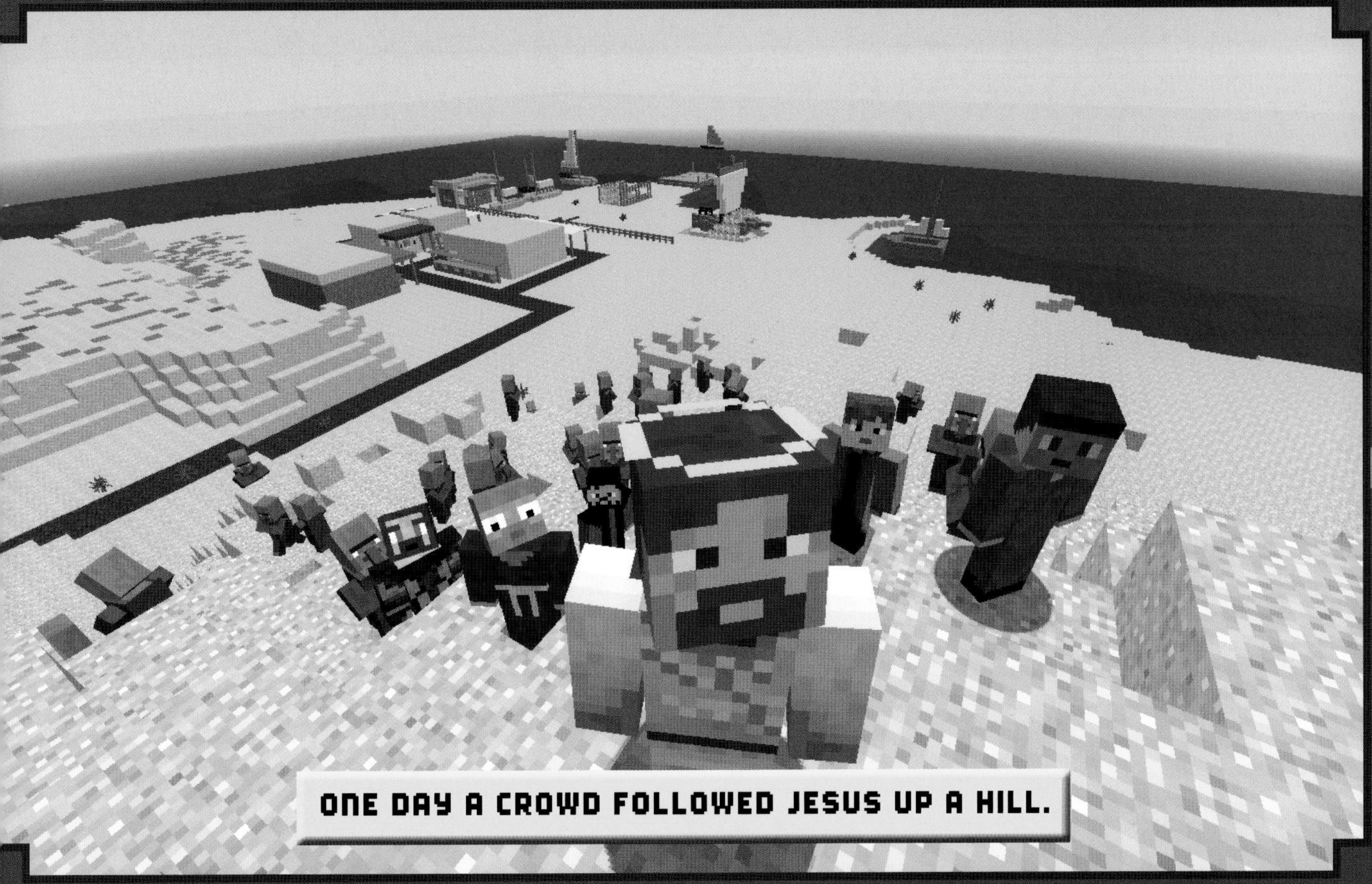
ONE DAY A CROWD FOLLOWED JESUS UP A HILL.

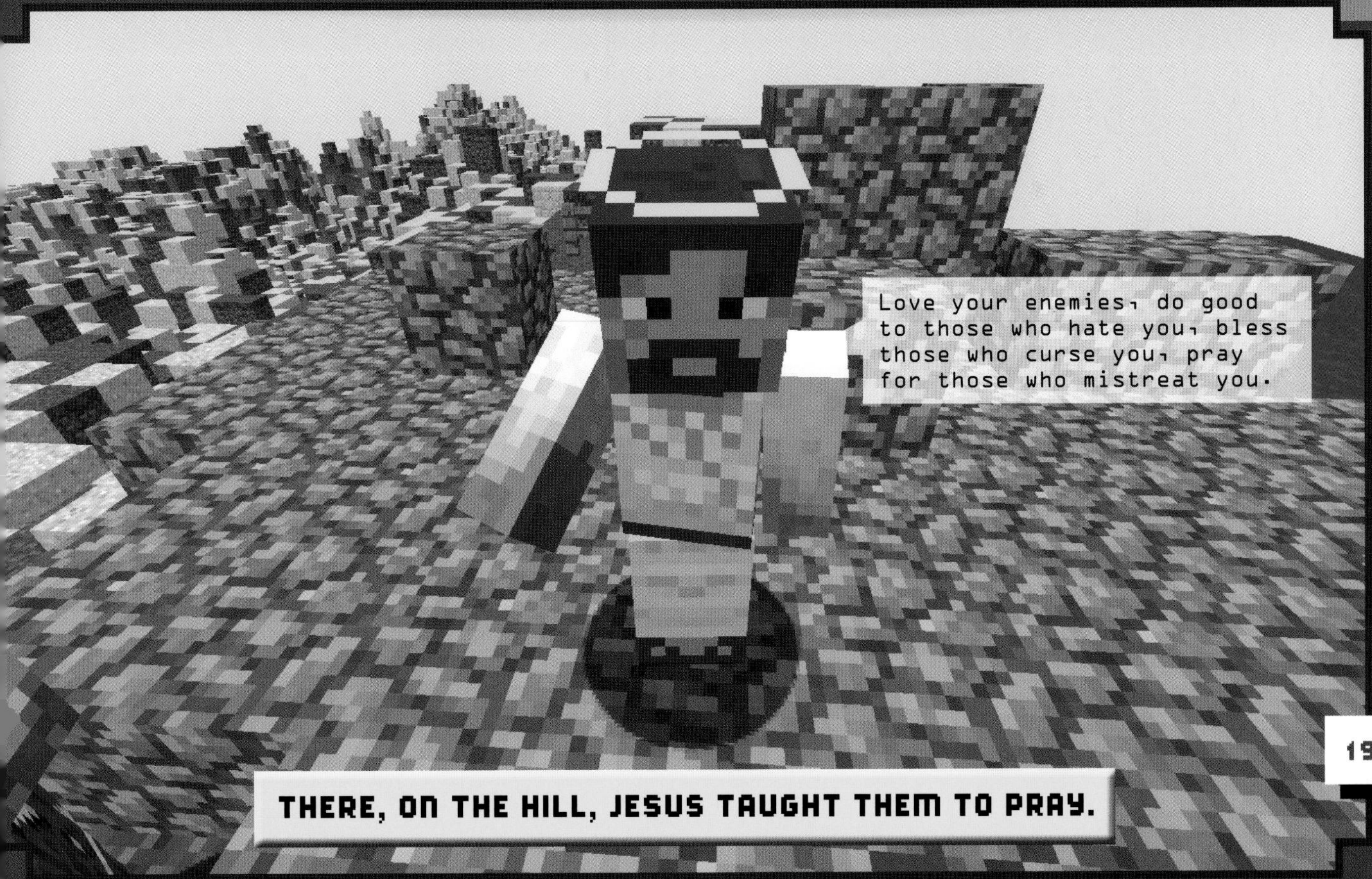
Love your enemies, do good to those who hate you, bless those who curse you, pray for those who mistreat you.
THERE, ON THE HILL, JESUS TAUGHT THEM TO PRAY.

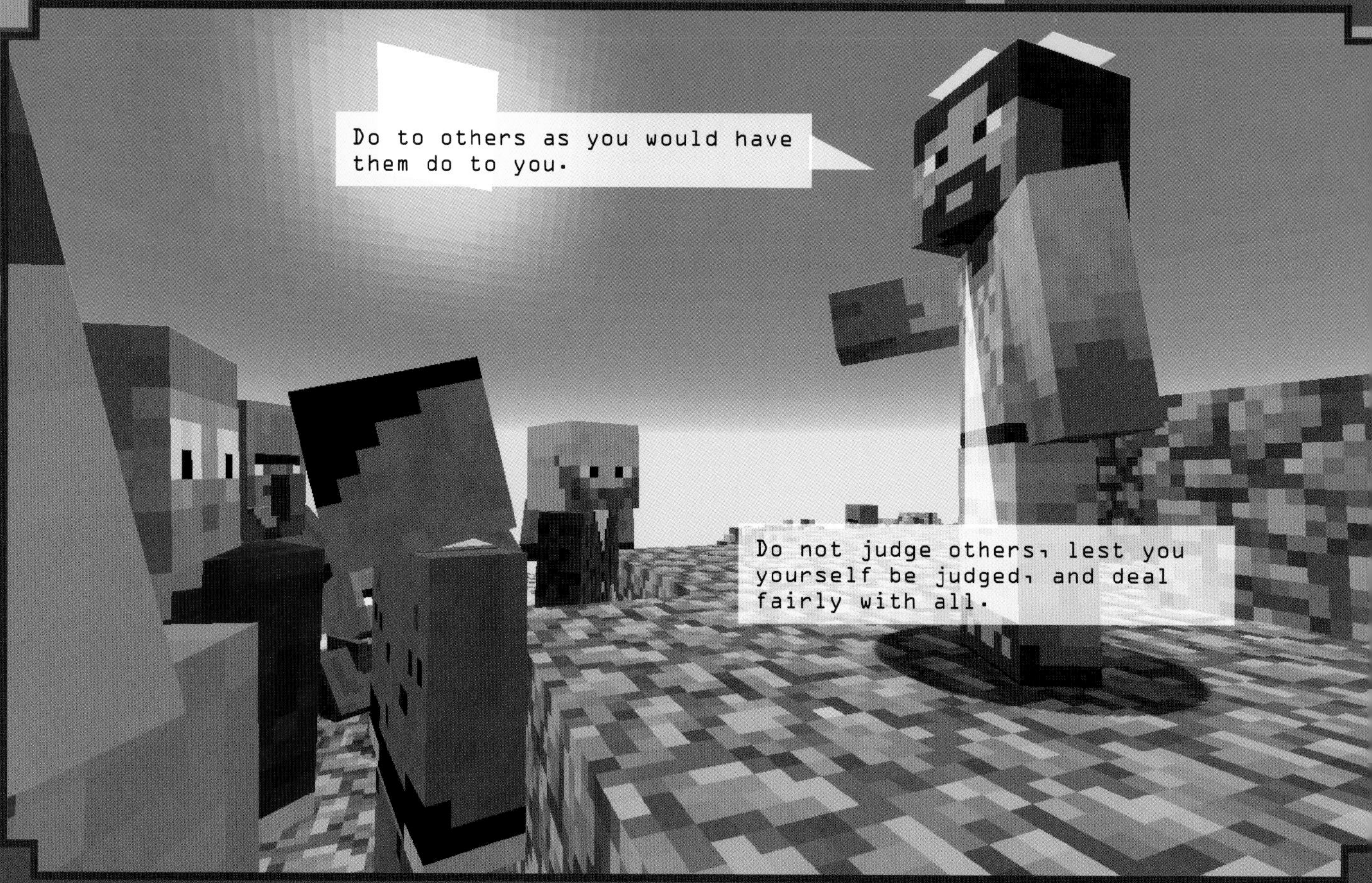
Do to others as you would have them do to you.
Do not judge others, lest you yourself be judged, and deal fairly with all.

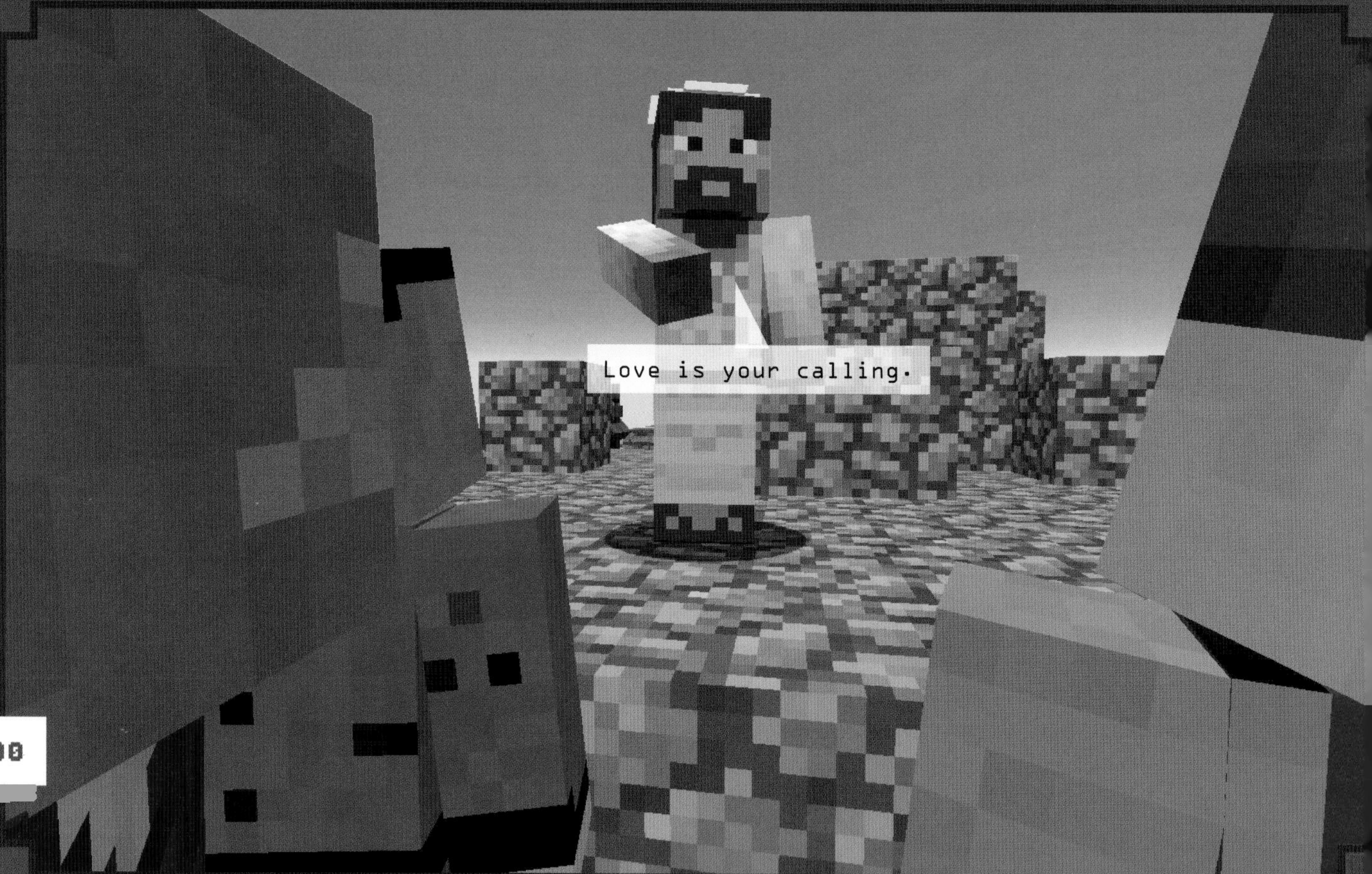
Love is your calling.

JESUS HEADED TO THE LAKE WITH HIS DISCIPLES AND THE CROWD. HE GAVE THE WORD TO CROSS THE LAKE TO THE OTHER SHORE.

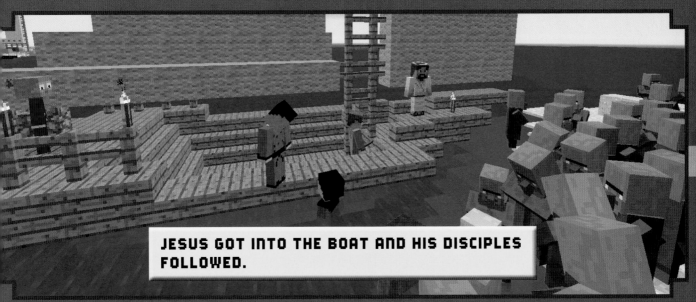

JESUS GOT INTO THE BOAT AND HIS DISCIPLES FOLLOWED.

THE BOAT SAILED A GREAT DISTANCE FROM SHORE WHEN ALL AT ONCE A GREAT STORM AROSE. JESUS WAS EXHAUSTED AND WENT TO TAKE A NAP.

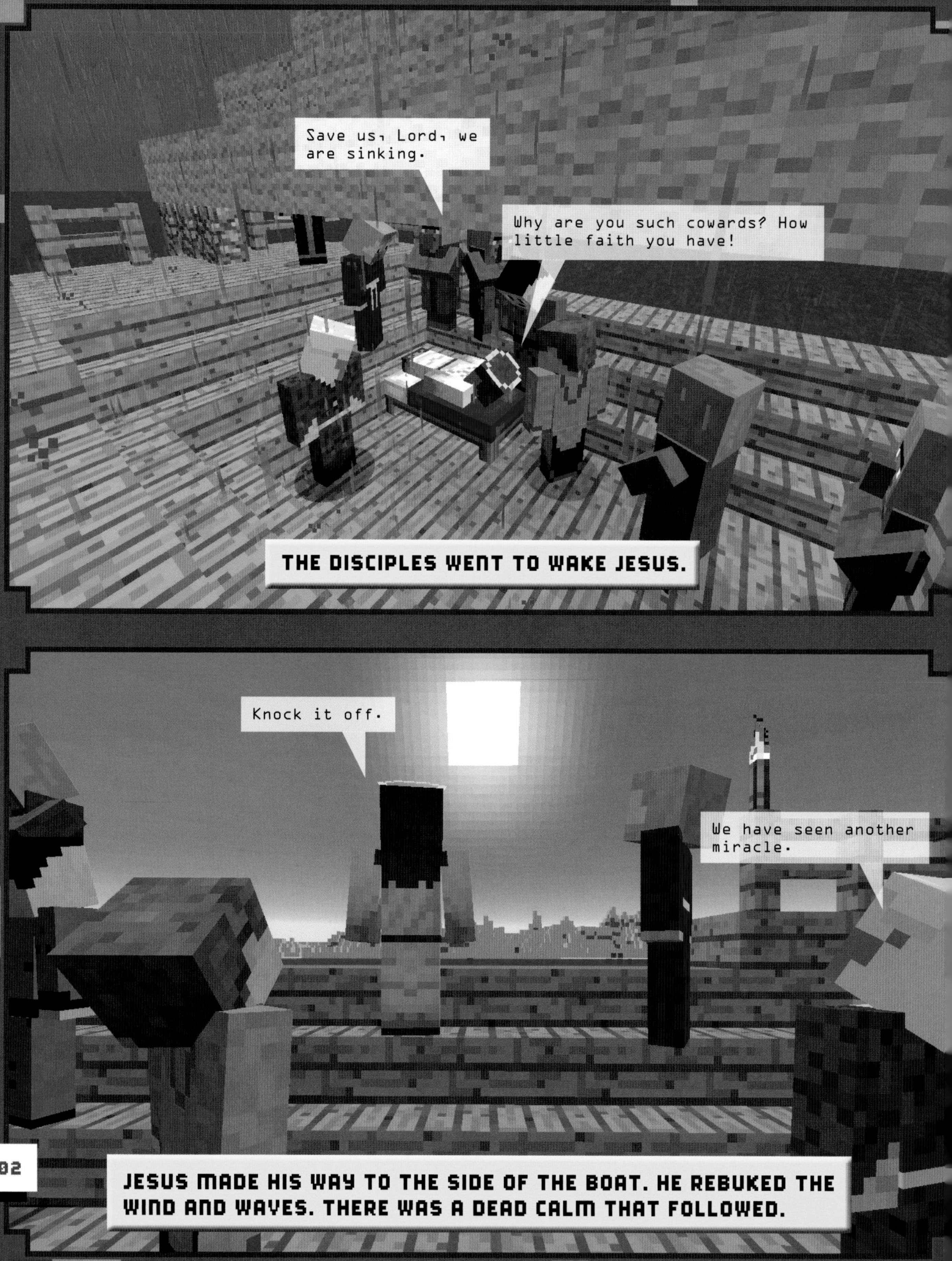
Save us, Lord, we are sinking.
Why are you such cowards? How little faith you have!
THE DISCIPLES WENT TO WAKE JESUS.
Knock it off.
We have seen another miracle.
JESUS MADE HIS WAY TO THE SIDE OF THE BOAT. HE REBUKED THE WIND AND WAVES. THERE WAS A DEAD CALM THAT FOLLOWED.

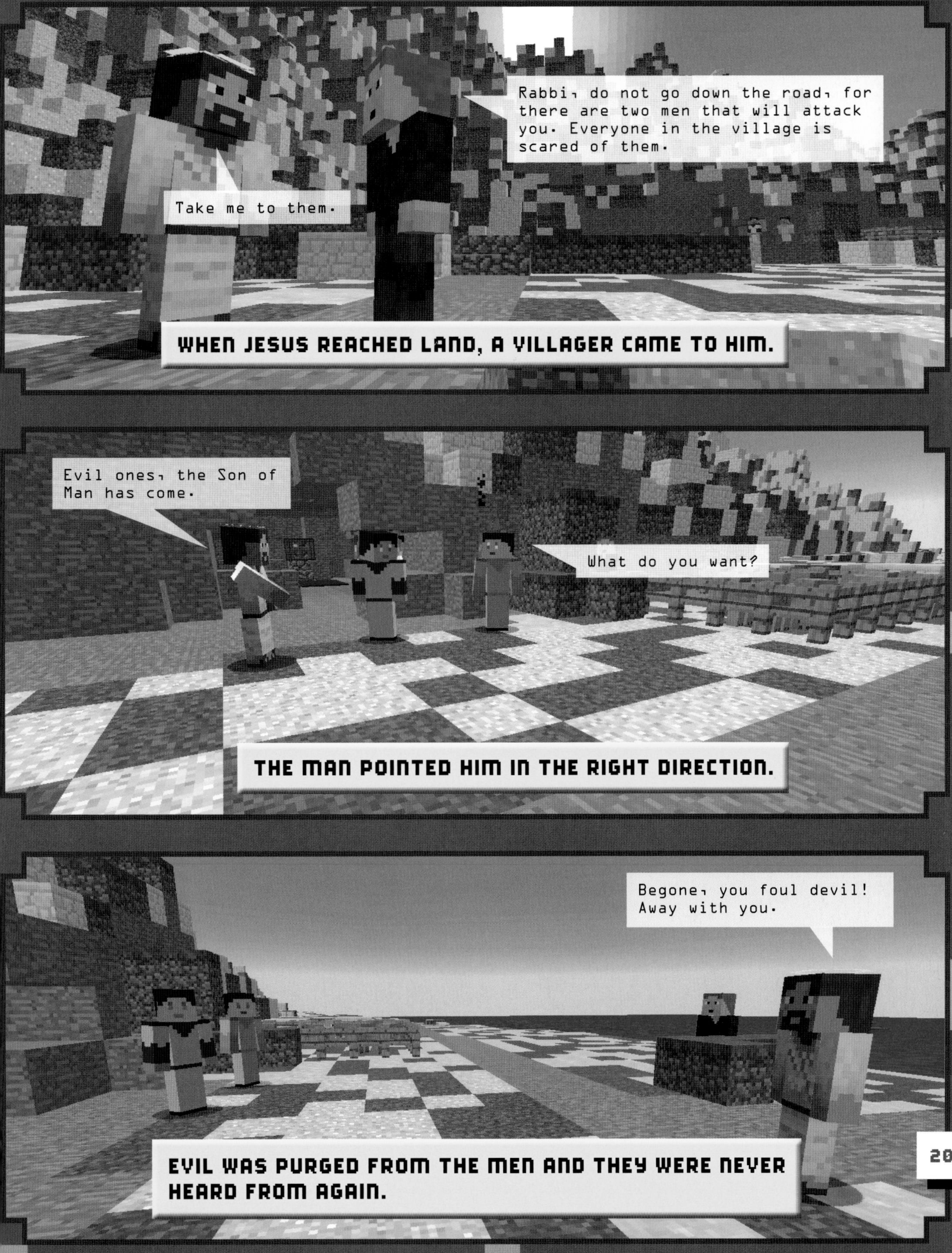
Rabbi, do not go down the road, for there are two men that will attack you. Everyone in the village is scared of them.
Take me to them.
WHEN JESUS REACHED LAND, A VILLAGER CAME TO HIM.
Evil ones, the Son of Man has come.
What do you want?
THE MAN POINTED HIM IN THE RIGHT DIRECTION.
Begone, you foul devil! Away with you.
EVIL WAS PURGED FROM THE MEN AND THEY WERE NEVER HEARD FROM AGAIN.

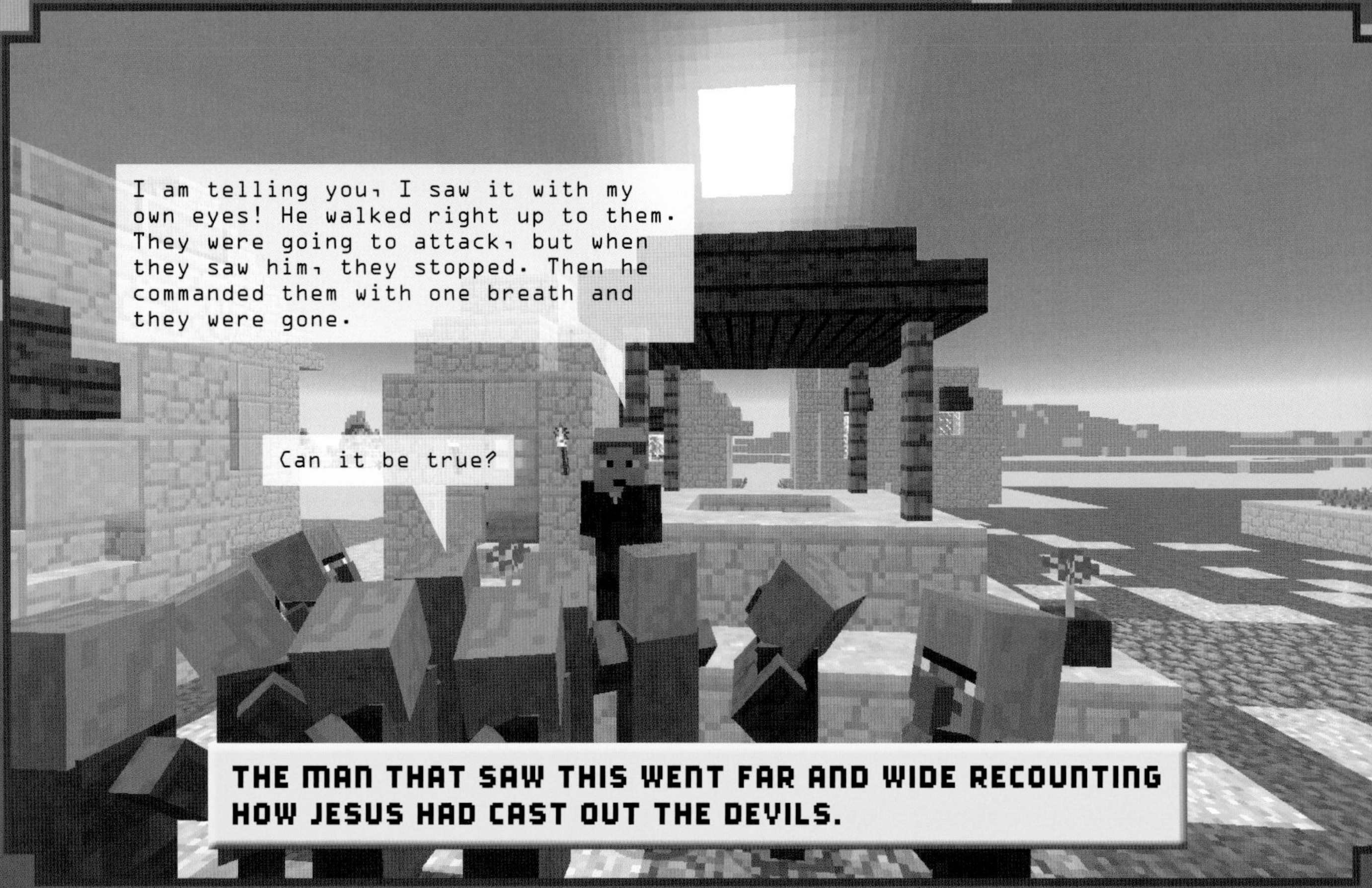
I am telling you, I saw it with my own eyes! He walked right up to them. They were going to attack, but when they saw him, they stopped. Then he commanded them with one breath and they were gone.
Can it be true?
THE MAN THAT SAW THIS WENT FAR AND WIDE RECOUNTING HOW JESUS HAD CAST OUT THE DEVILS.

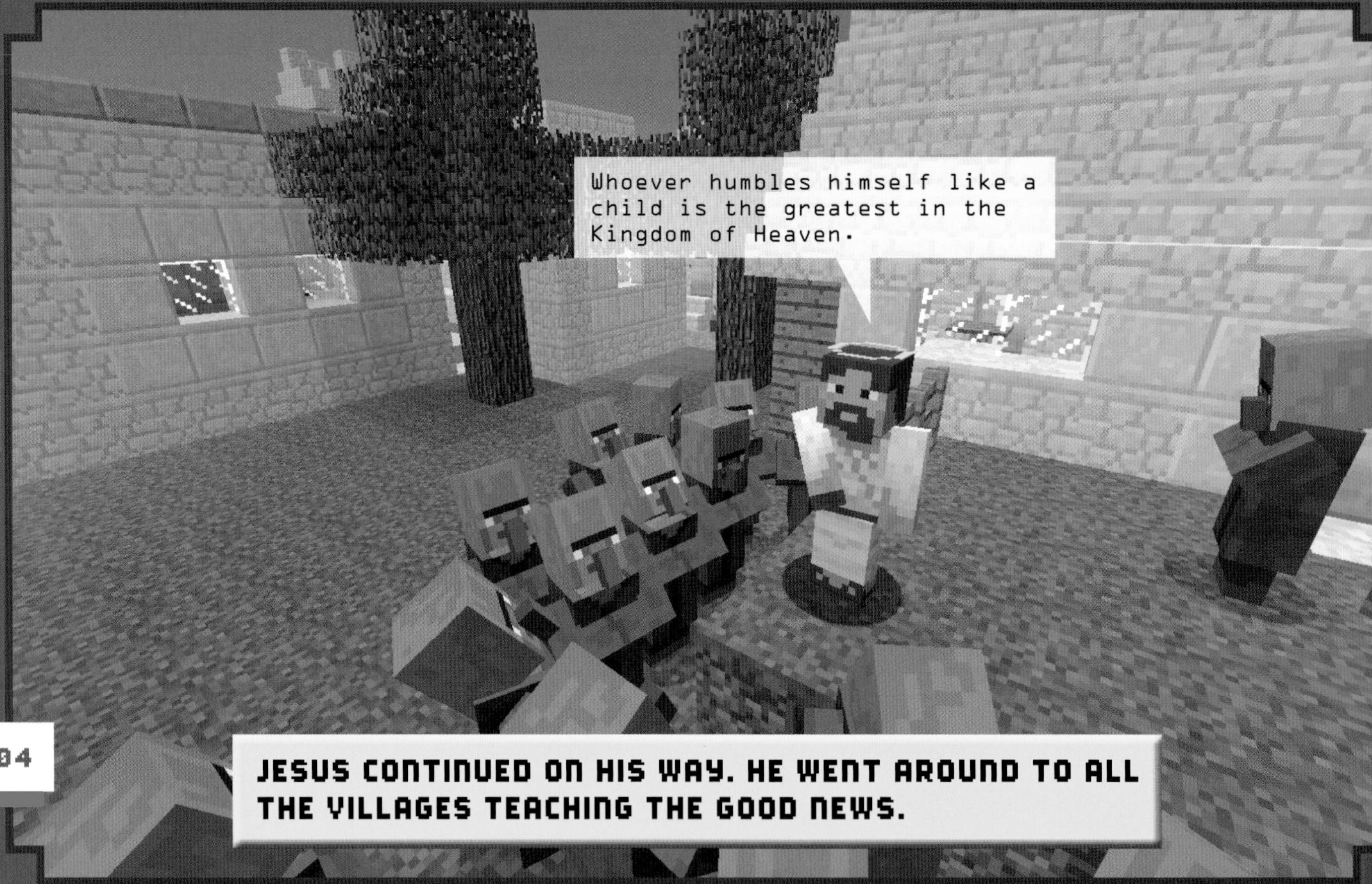
Whoever humbles himself like a child is the greatest in the Kingdom of Heaven.
JESUS CONTINUED ON HIS WAY. HE WENT AROUND TO ALL THE VILLAGES TEACHING THE GOOD NEWS.

JESUS GAVE HIS TWELVE DISCIPLES AUTHORITY TO CAST OUT UN-CLEAN SPIRITS AND TO CURE EVERY KIND OF AILMENT AND DISEASE.

THE CHOSEN FEW TO CONTINUE THE WORK OF JESUS AS HIS APOSTLES WERE JOHN, JAMES, THE SON OF ZEBEDEE, PETER, MATTHEW, LEVI, BARTHOLOMEW, JUDAS, JAMES, THE SON OF ALPHAEUS, PHILIP, PETER, THOMAS, ANDREW

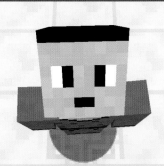

JESUS' PARABLES

Jesus has a lot of followers now. How will he teach them all?

Jesus teaches through the telling of parables, and the asking of questions.

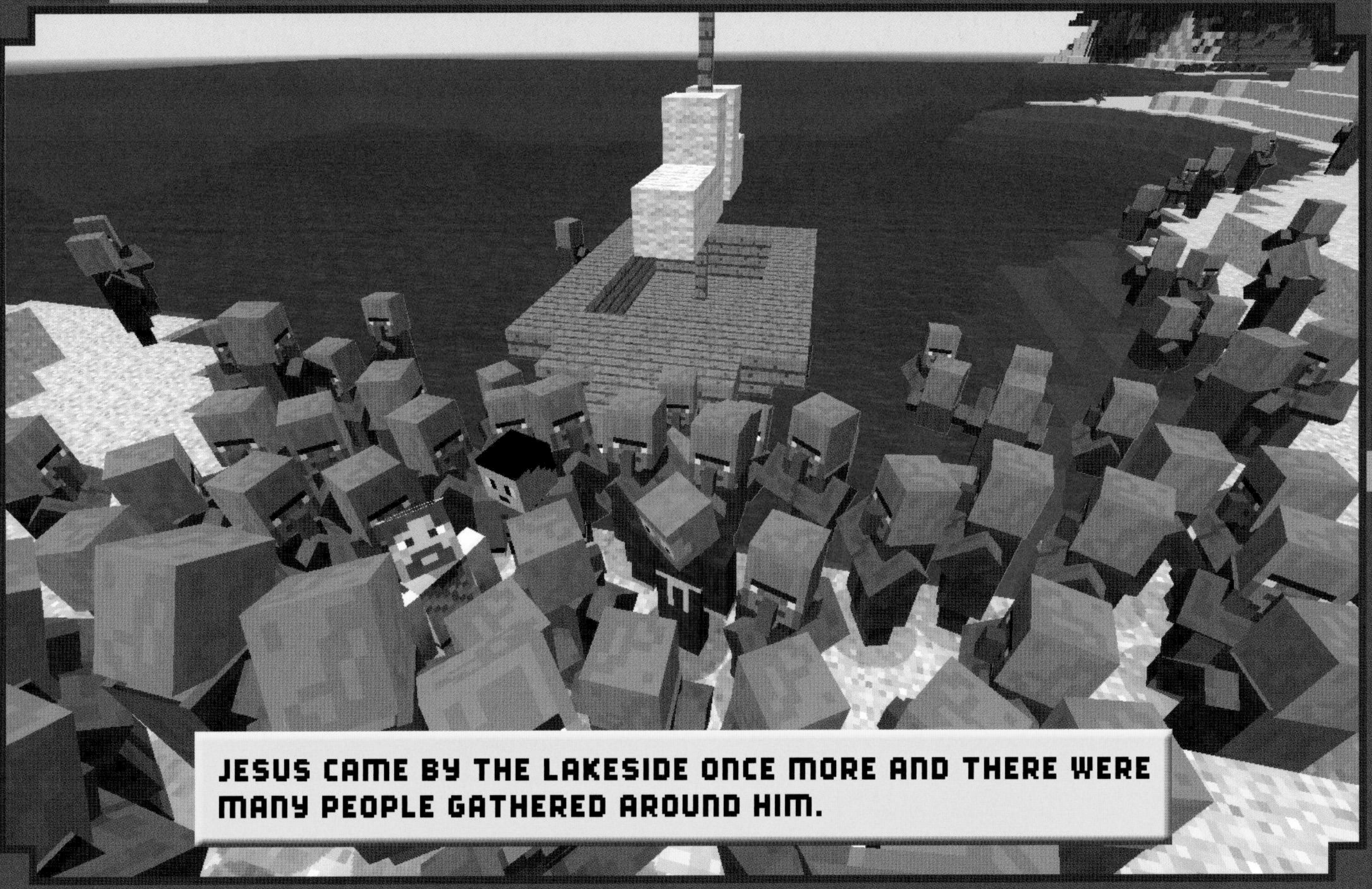
JESUS CAME BY THE LAKESIDE ONCE MORE AND THERE WERE MANY PEOPLE GATHERED AROUND HIM.

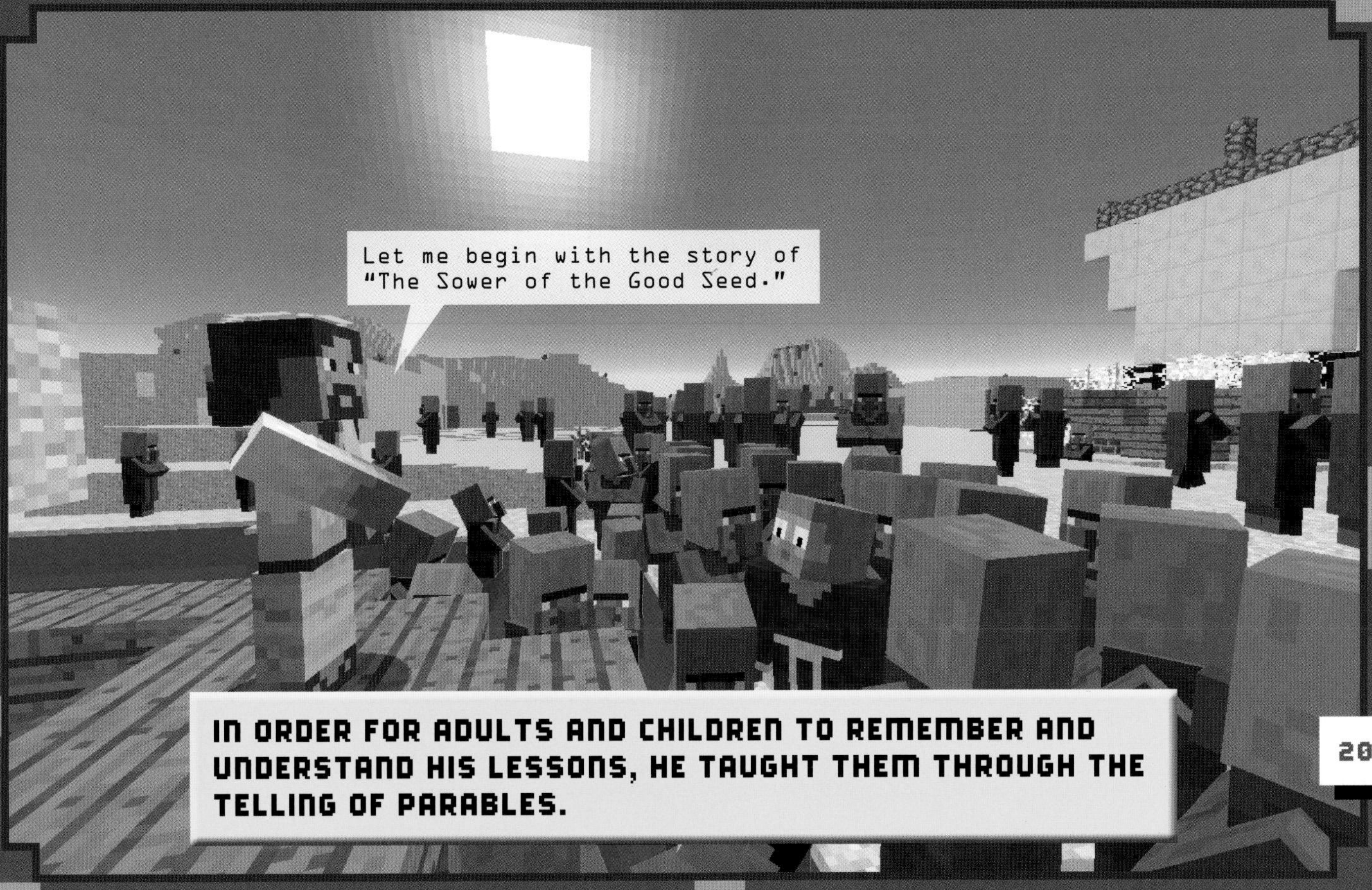
Let me begin with the story of "The Sower of the Good Seed."
IN ORDER FOR ADULTS AND CHILDREN TO REMEMBER AND UNDERSTAND HIS LESSONS, HE TAUGHT THEM THROUGH THE TELLING OF PARABLES.

A SOWER WENT OUT TO SOW HIS FIELDS, AS IT HAD BECOME THE TIME FOR PLANTING. WITH BAG AND SEED HE WALKED ALONG HIS FIELD SCATTERING THE SEEDS, AND SOME SEEDS FELL ALONG THE FOOTPATH.

THESE SEEDS COULD NOT FIND GOOD SOIL, SO THE BIRDS CAME AND ATE THEM UP.

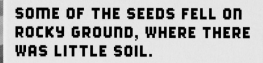

SOME OF THE SEEDS FELL ON ROCKY GROUND, WHERE THERE WAS LITTLE SOIL.

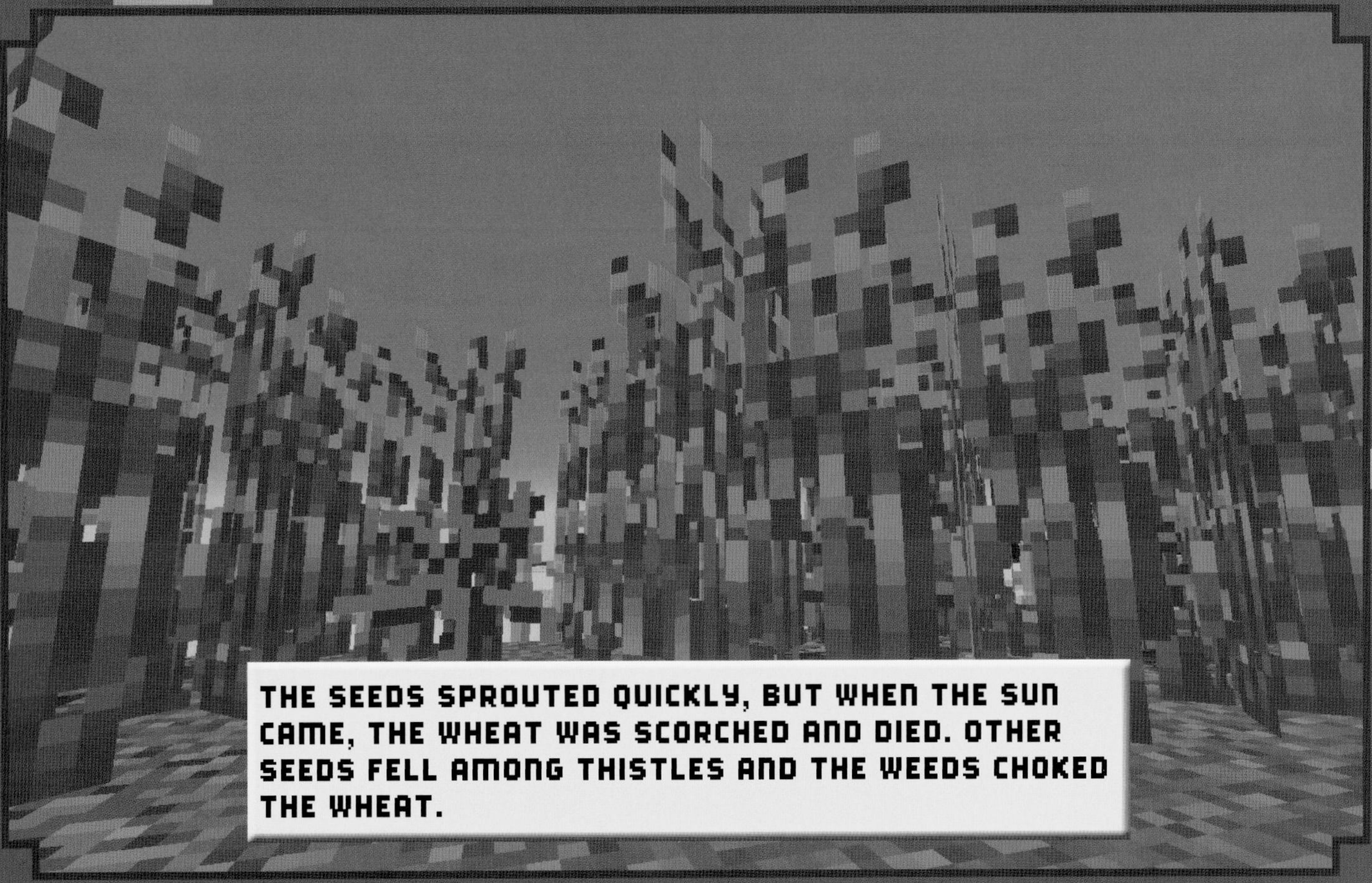
THE SEEDS SPROUTED QUICKLY, BUT WHEN THE SUN CAME, THE WHEAT WAS SCORCHED AND DIED. OTHER SEEDS FELL AMONG THISTLES AND THE WEEDS CHOKED THE WHEAT.

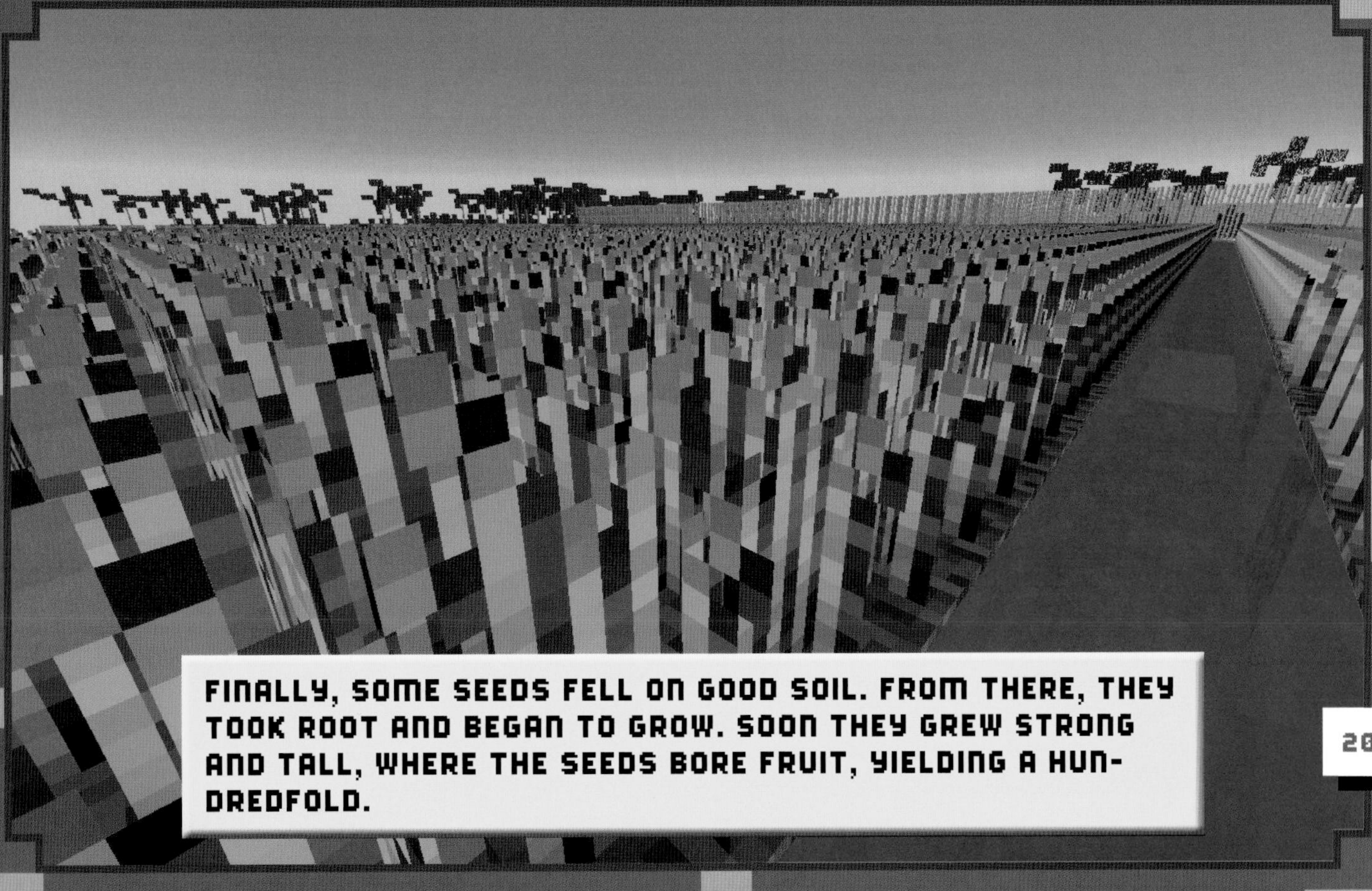
FINALLY, SOME SEEDS FELL ON GOOD SOIL. FROM THERE, THEY TOOK ROOT AND BEGAN TO GROW. SOON THEY GREW STRONG AND TALL, WHERE THE SEEDS BORE FRUIT, YIELDING A HUN-DREDFOLD.

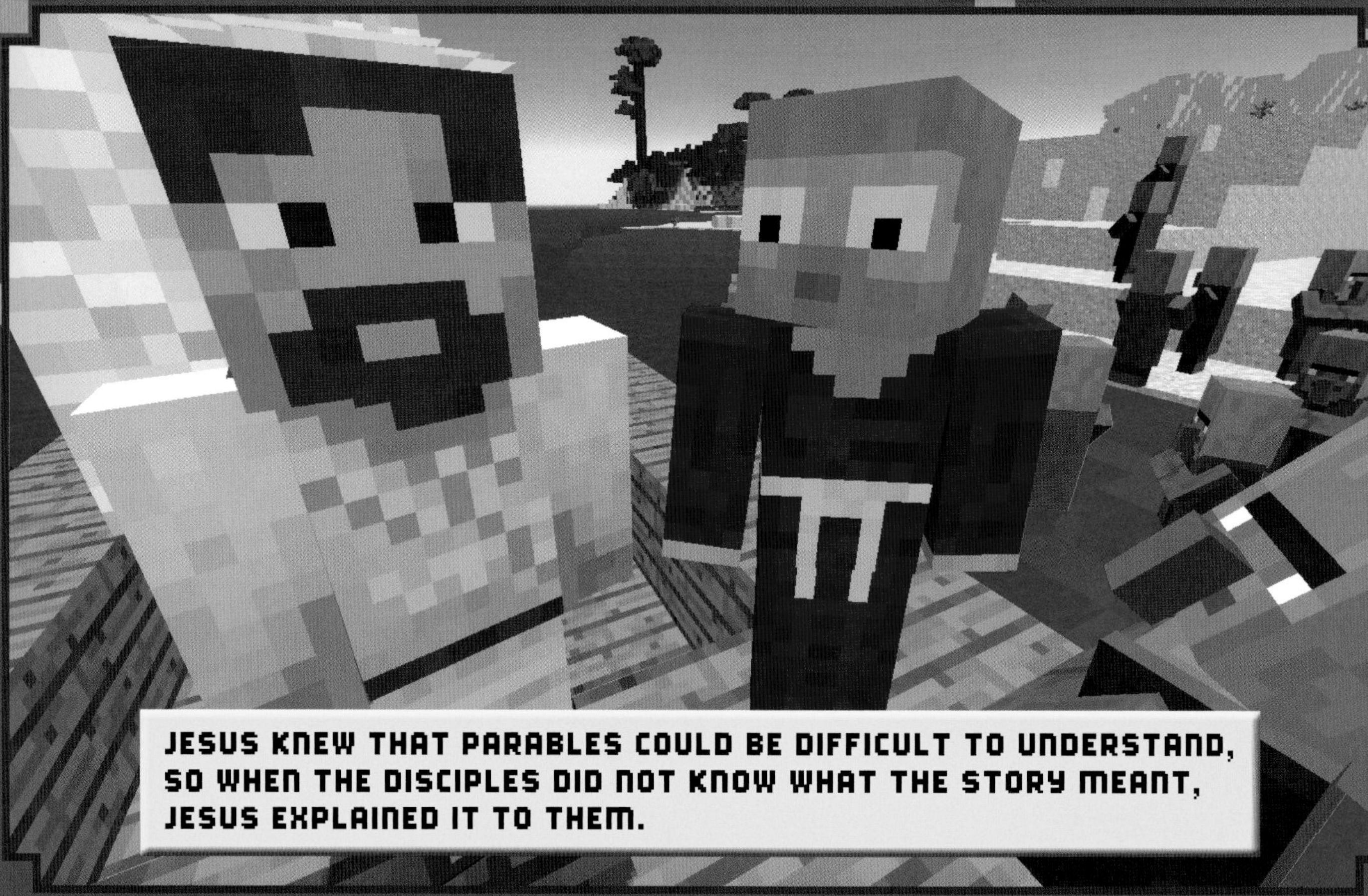
JESUS KNEW THAT PARABLES COULD BE DIFFICULT TO UNDERSTAND, SO WHEN THE DISCIPLES DID NOT KNOW WHAT THE STORY MEANT, JESUS EXPLAINED IT TO THEM.

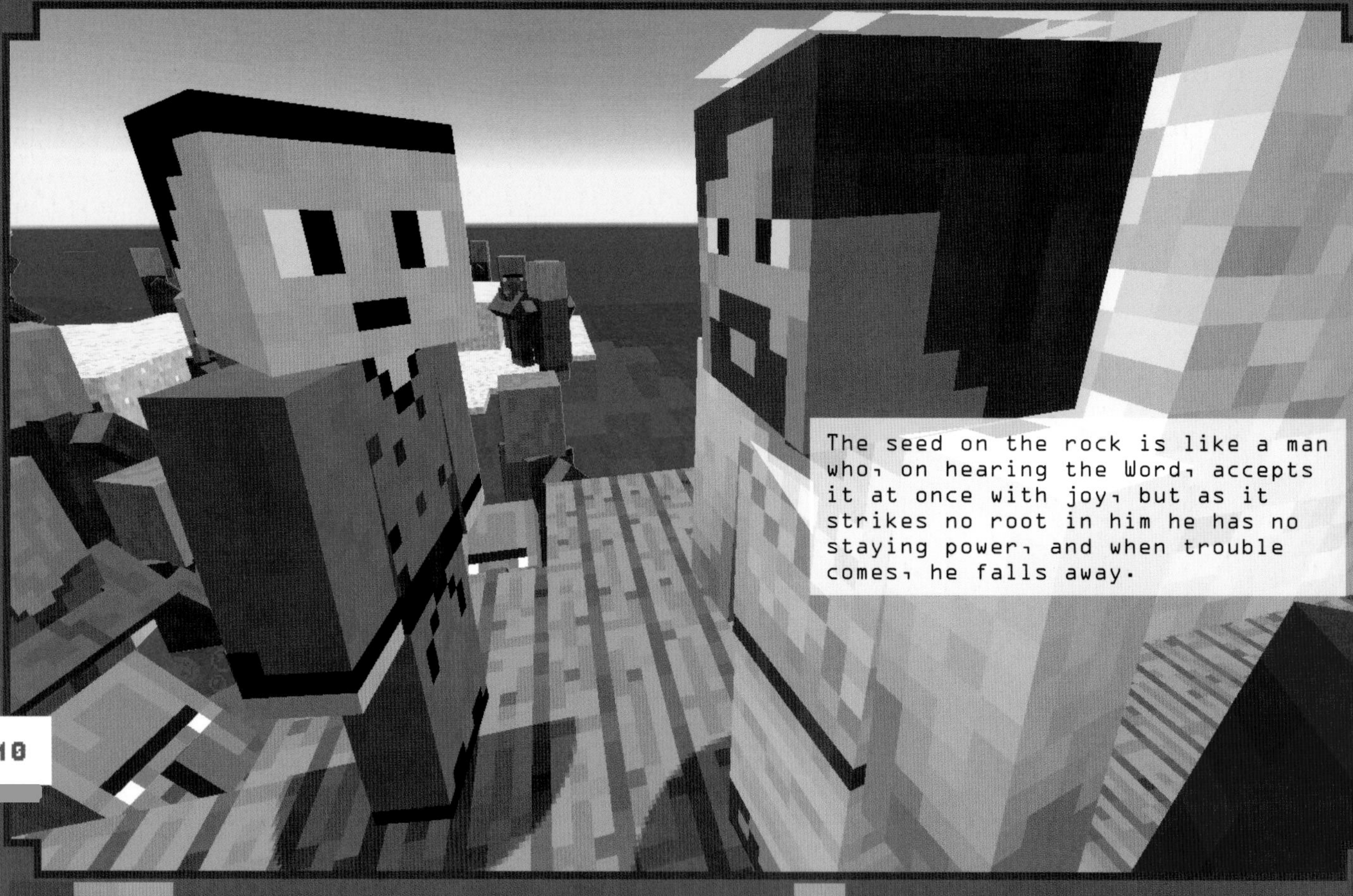
The seed on the rock is like a man who, on hearing the Word, accepts it at once with joy, but as it strikes no root in him he has no staying power, and when trouble comes, he falls away.

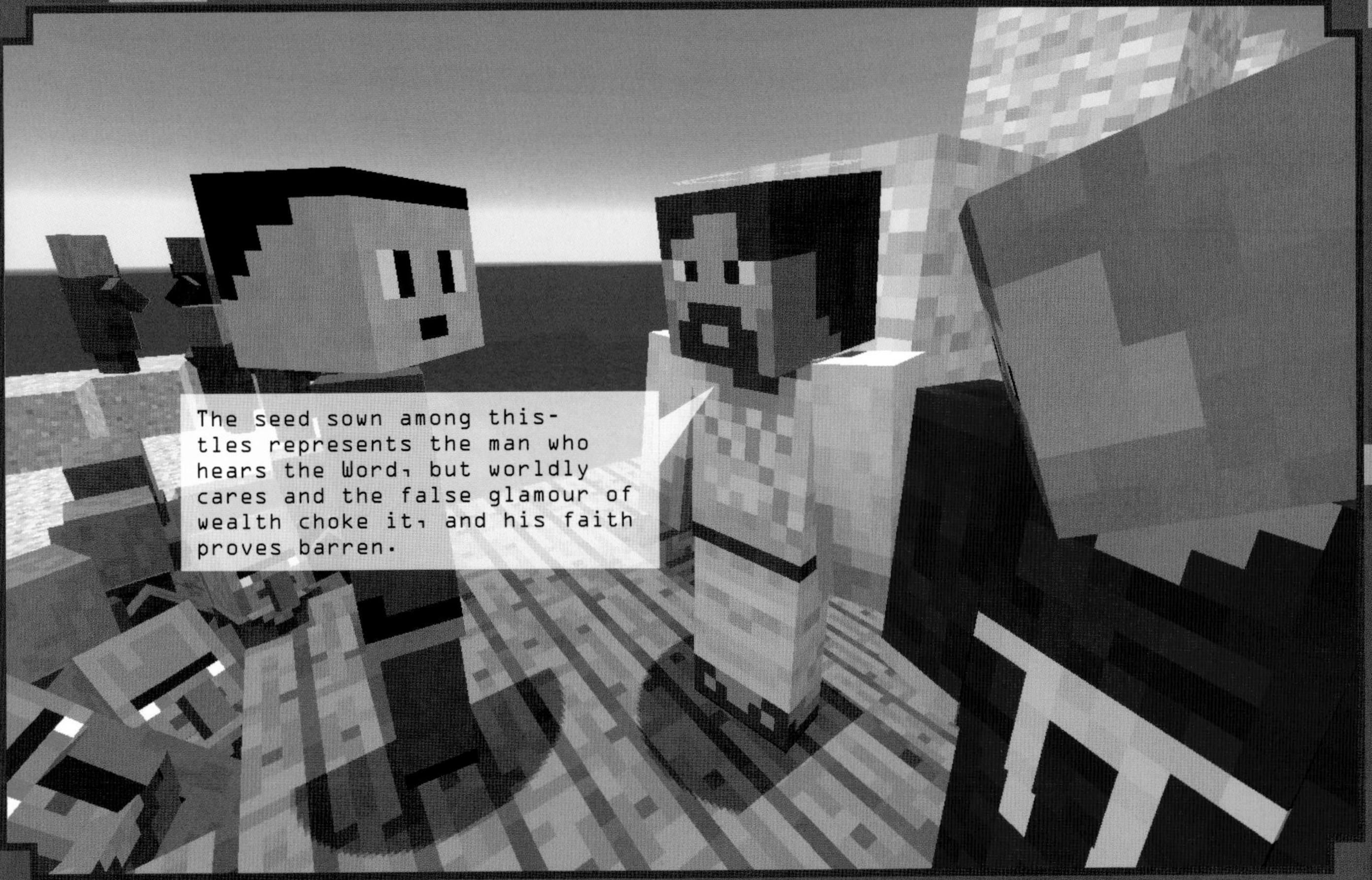
The seed sown among this-
tles represents the man who
hears the Word, but worldly
cares and the false glamour of
wealth choke it, and his faith
proves barren.

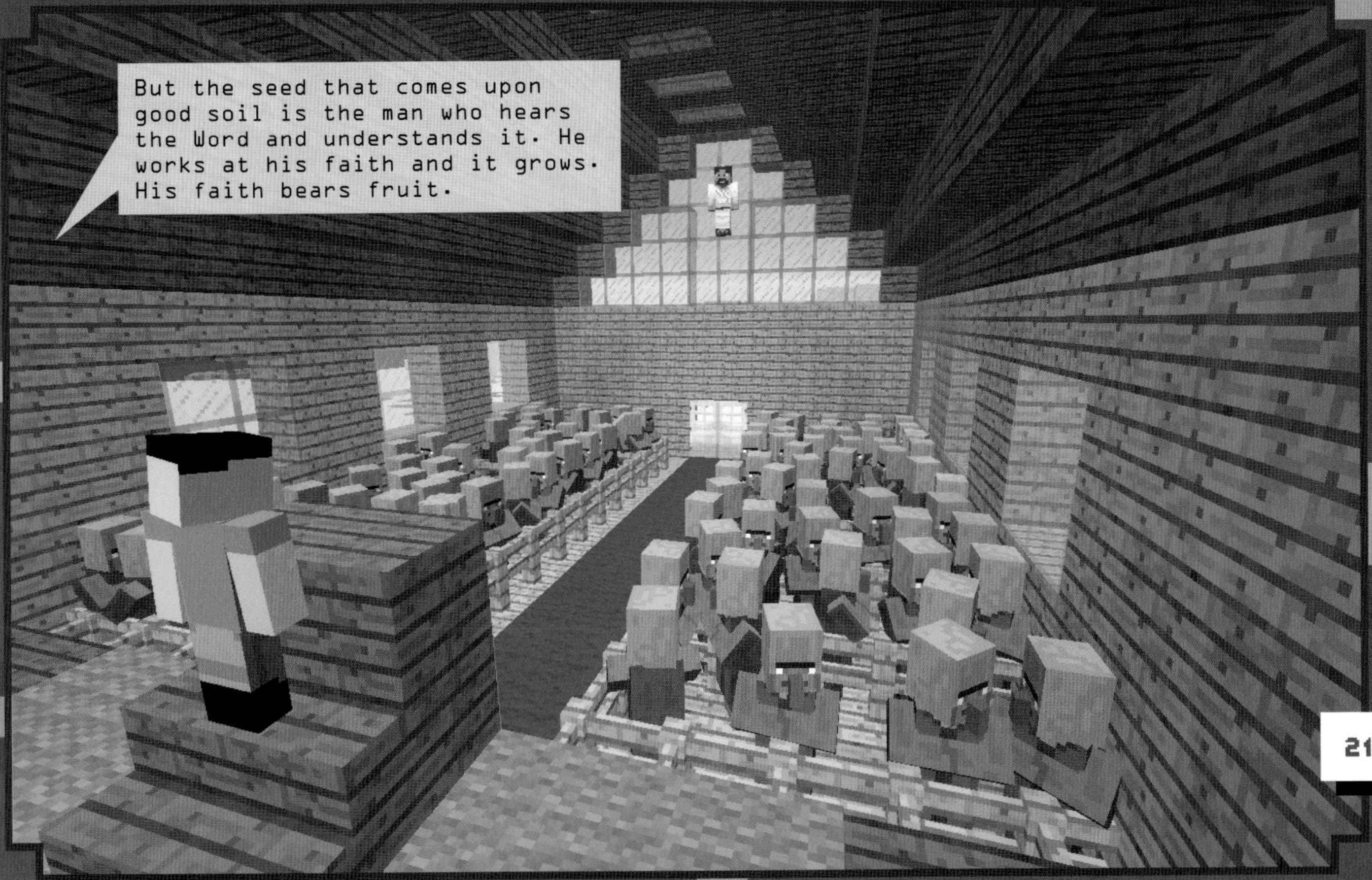
But the seed that comes upon
good soil is the man who hears
the Word and understands it. He
works at his faith and it grows.
His faith bears fruit.

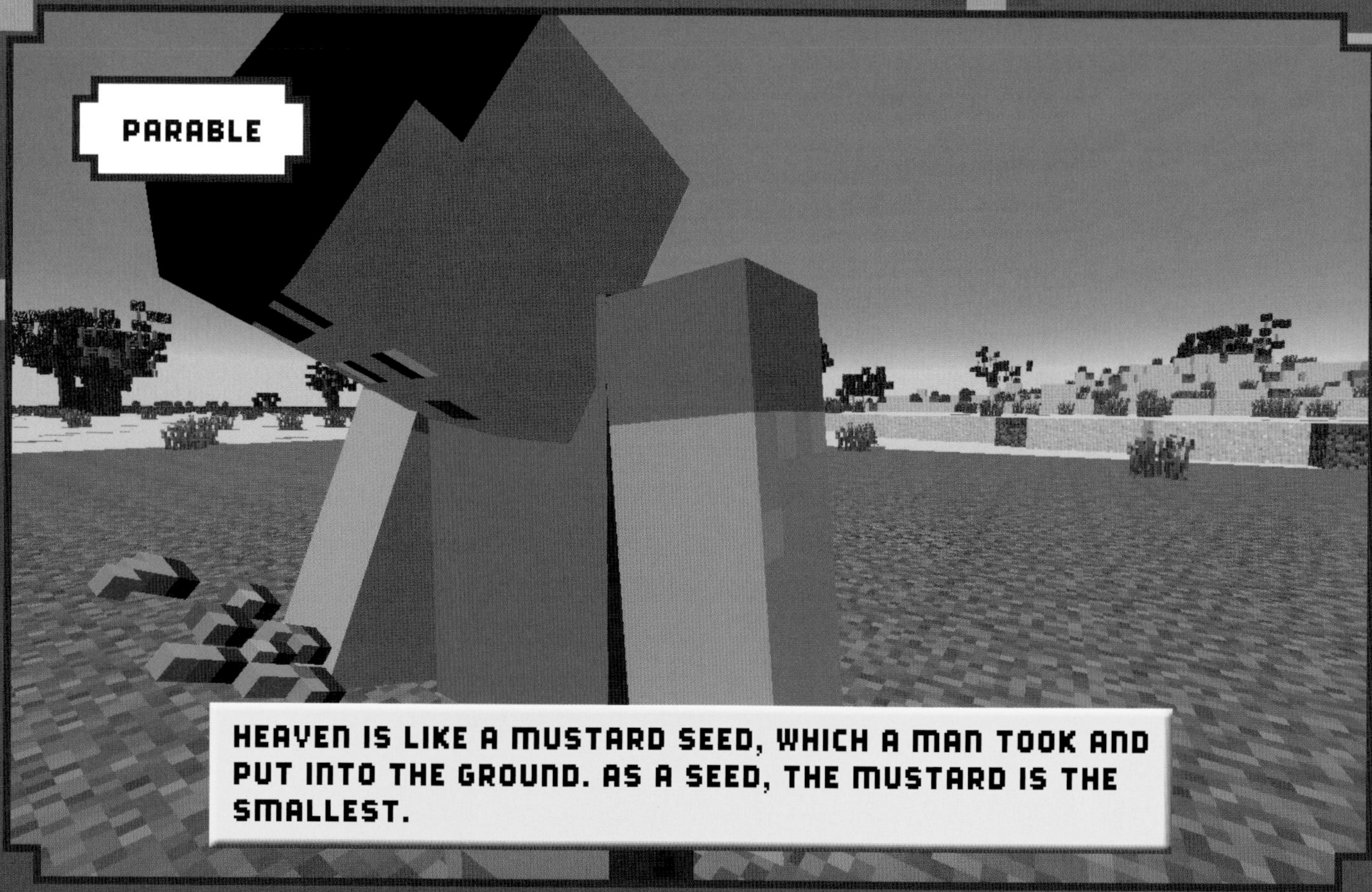
PARABLE
HEAVEN IS LIKE A MUSTARD SEED, WHICH A MAN TOOK AND PUT INTO THE GROUND. AS A SEED, THE MUSTARD IS THE SMALLEST.

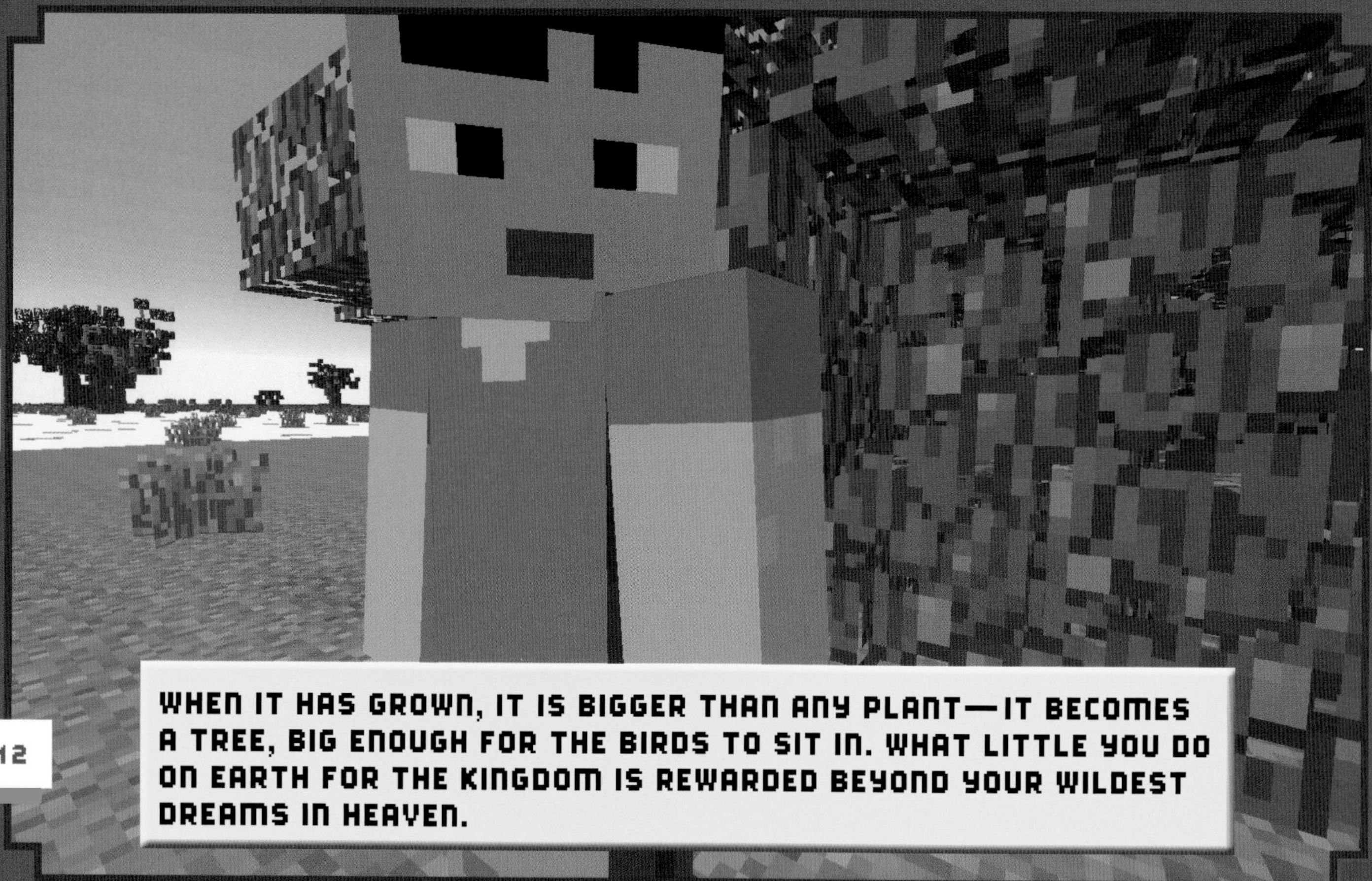
WHEN IT HAS GROWN, IT IS BIGGER THAN ANY PLANT—IT BECOMES A TREE, BIG ENOUGH FOR THE BIRDS TO SIT IN. WHAT LITTLE YOU DO ON EARTH FOR THE KINGDOM IS REWARDED BEYOND YOUR WILDEST DREAMS IN HEAVEN.

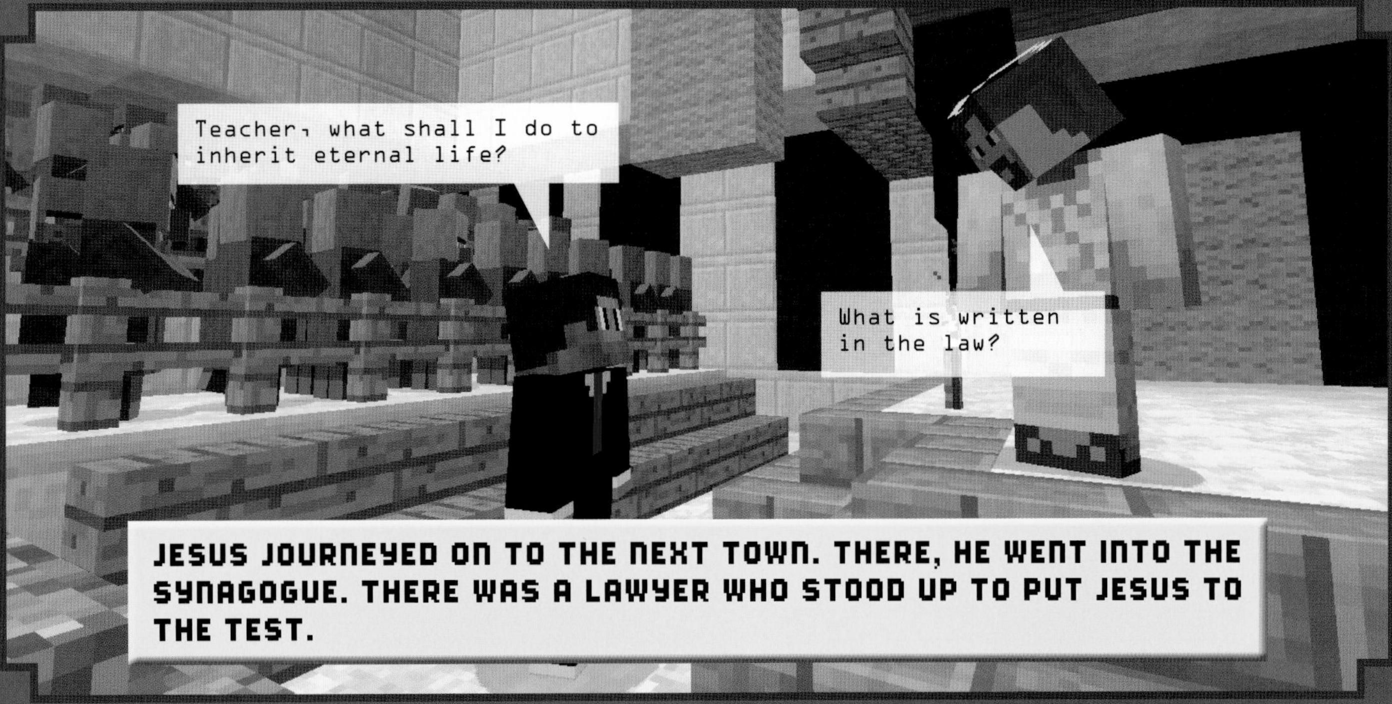
Teacher, what shall I do to inherit eternal life?
What is written in the law?
JESUS JOURNEYED ON TO THE NEXT TOWN. THERE, HE WENT INTO THE SYNAGOGUE. THERE WAS A LAWYER WHO STOOD UP TO PUT JESUS TO THE TEST.

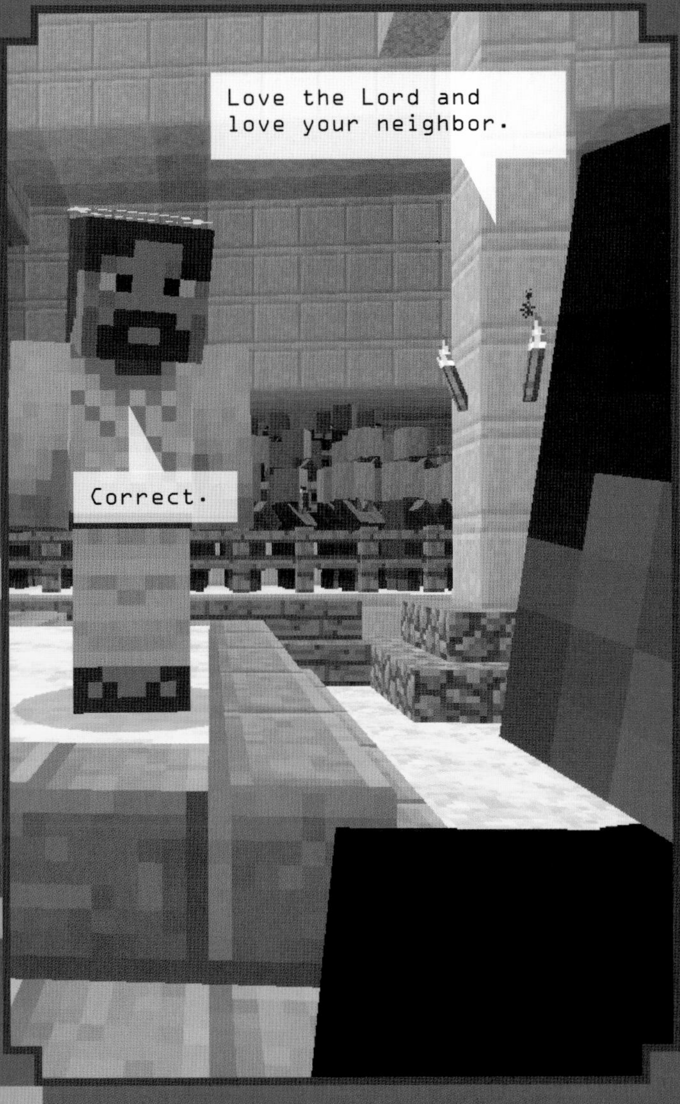
Love the Lord and love your neighbor.
Correct.

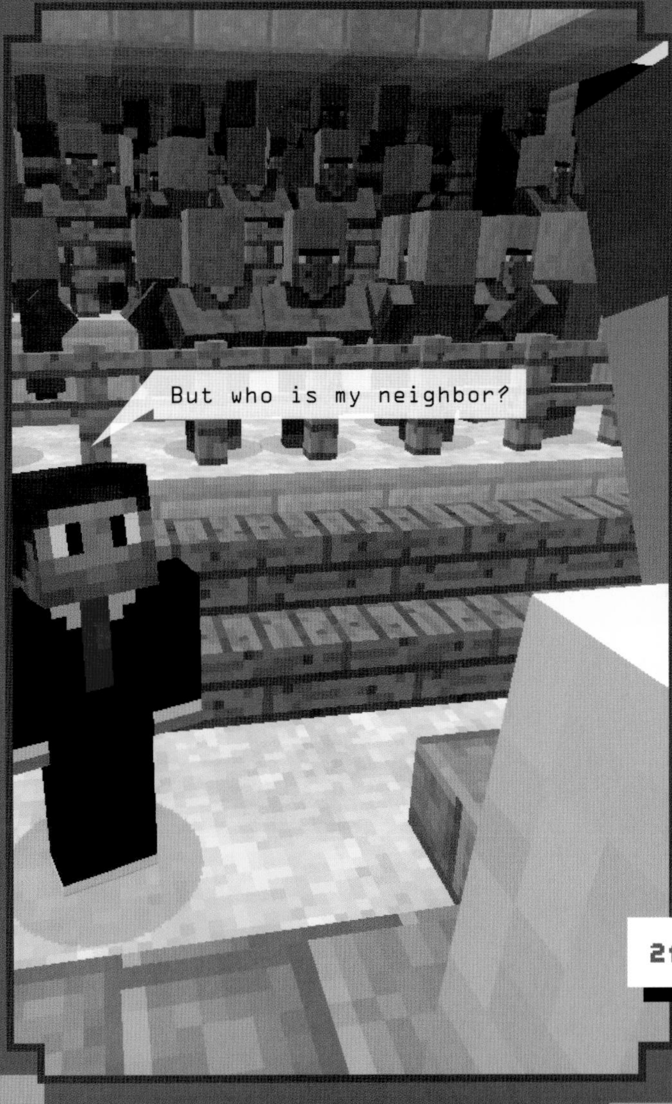
But who is my neighbor?

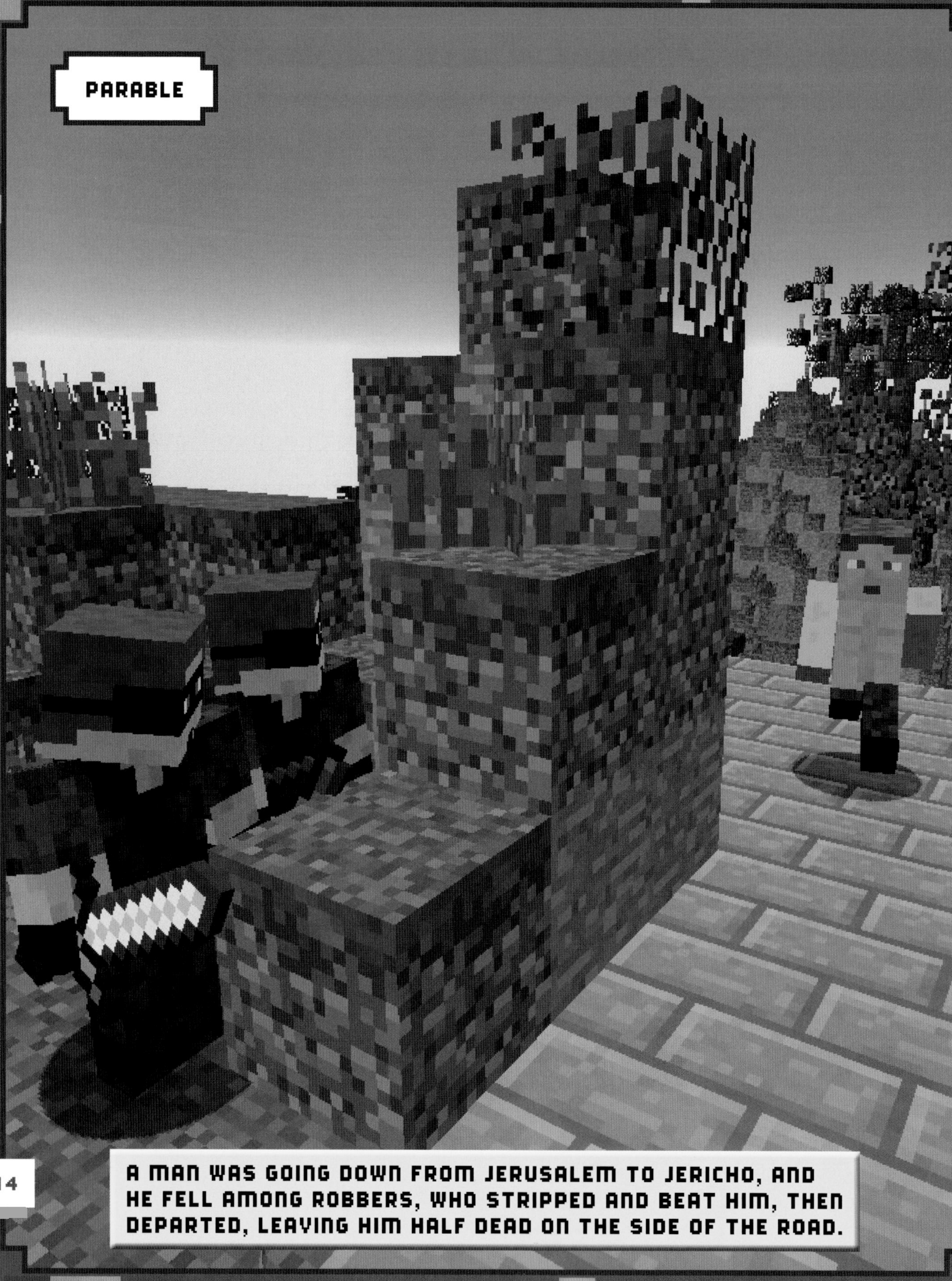
PARABLE
A MAN WAS GOING DOWN FROM JERUSALEM TO JERICHO, AND HE FELL AMONG ROBBERS, WHO STRIPPED AND BEAT HIM, THEN DEPARTED, LEAVING HIM HALF DEAD ON THE SIDE OF THE ROAD.

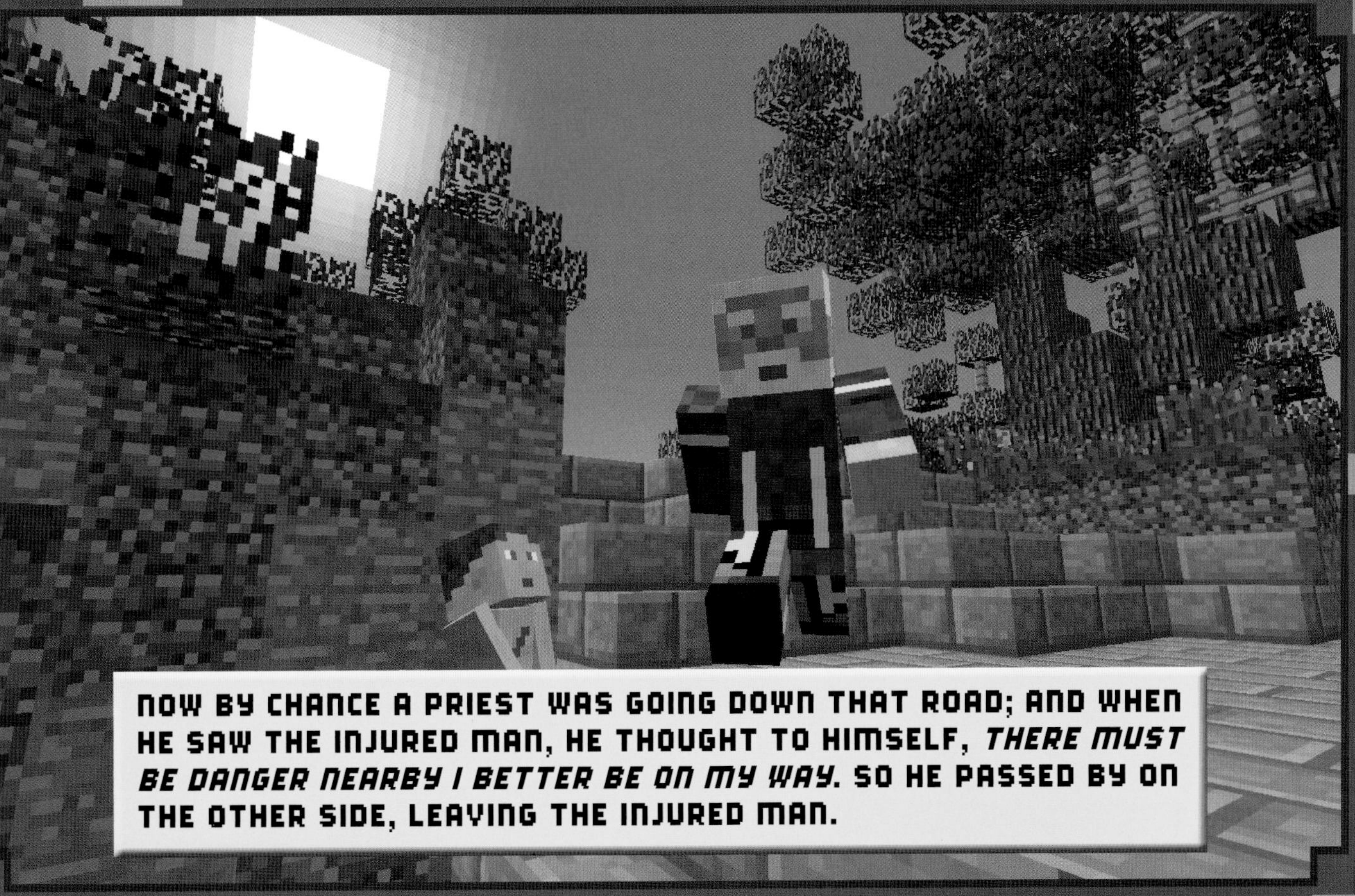
NOW BY CHANCE A PRIEST WAS GOING DOWN THAT ROAD; AND WHEN HE SAW THE INJURED MAN, HE THOUGHT TO HIMSELF, *THERE MUST BE DANGER NEARBY I BETTER BE ON MY WAY*. SO HE PASSED BY ON THE OTHER SIDE, LEAVING THE INJURED MAN.

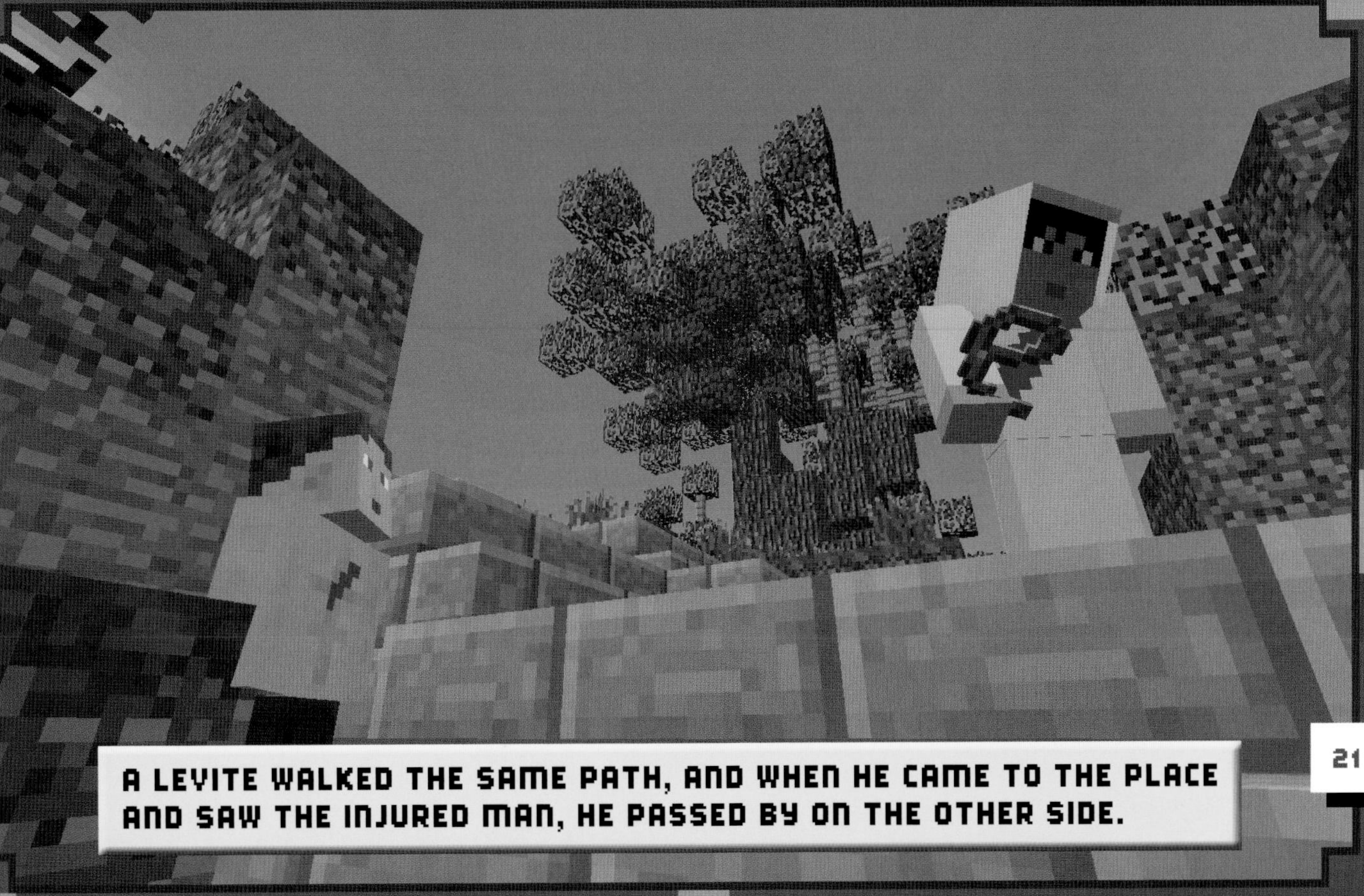
A LEVITE WALKED THE SAME PATH, AND WHEN HE CAME TO THE PLACE AND SAW THE INJURED MAN, HE PASSED BY ON THE OTHER SIDE.

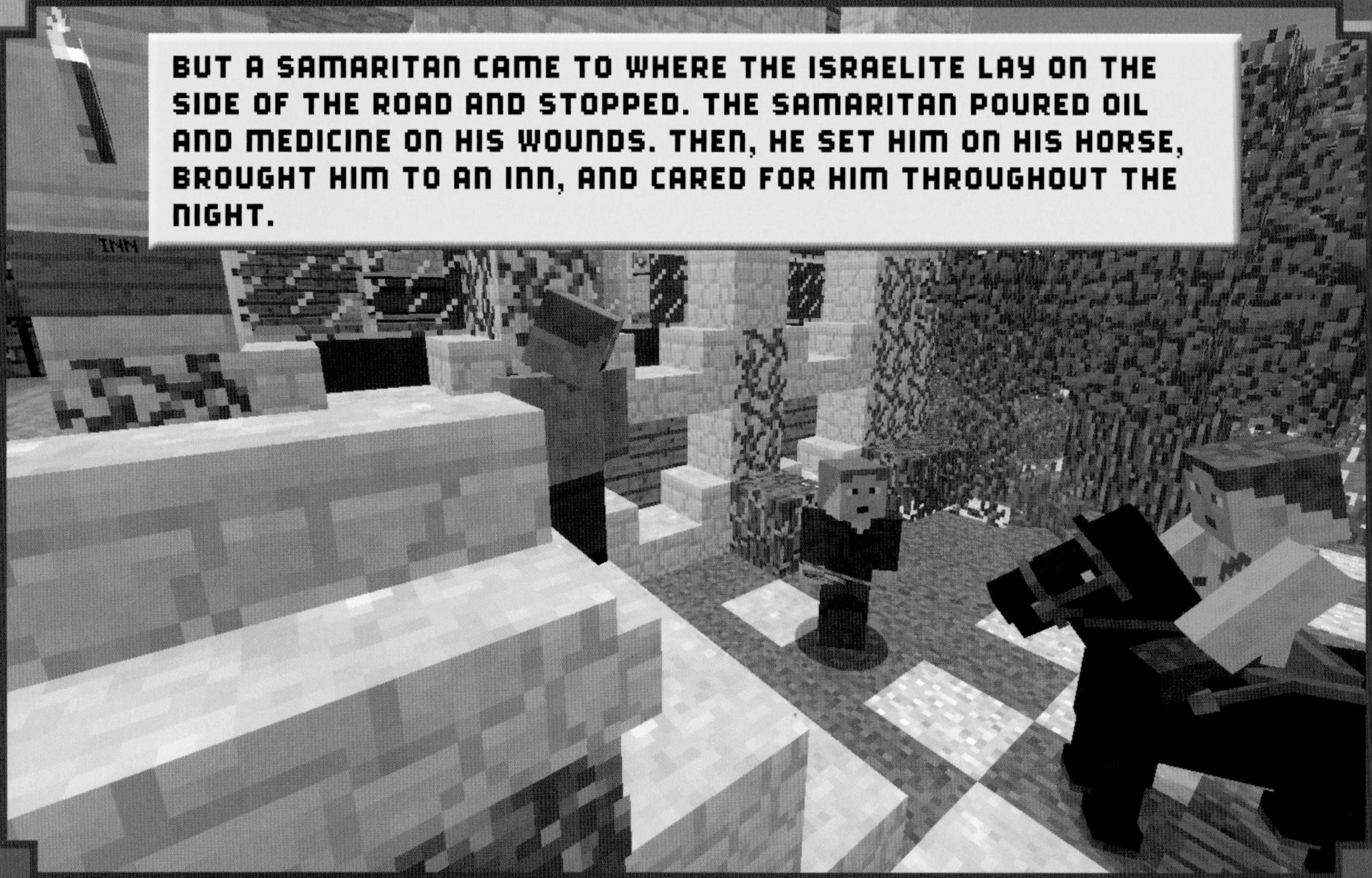
BUT A SAMARITAN CAME TO WHERE THE ISRAELITE LAY ON THE SIDE OF THE ROAD AND STOPPED. THE SAMARITAN POURED OIL AND MEDICINE ON HIS WOUNDS. THEN, HE SET HIM ON HIS HORSE, BROUGHT HIM TO AN INN, AND CARED FOR HIM THROUGHOUT THE NIGHT.

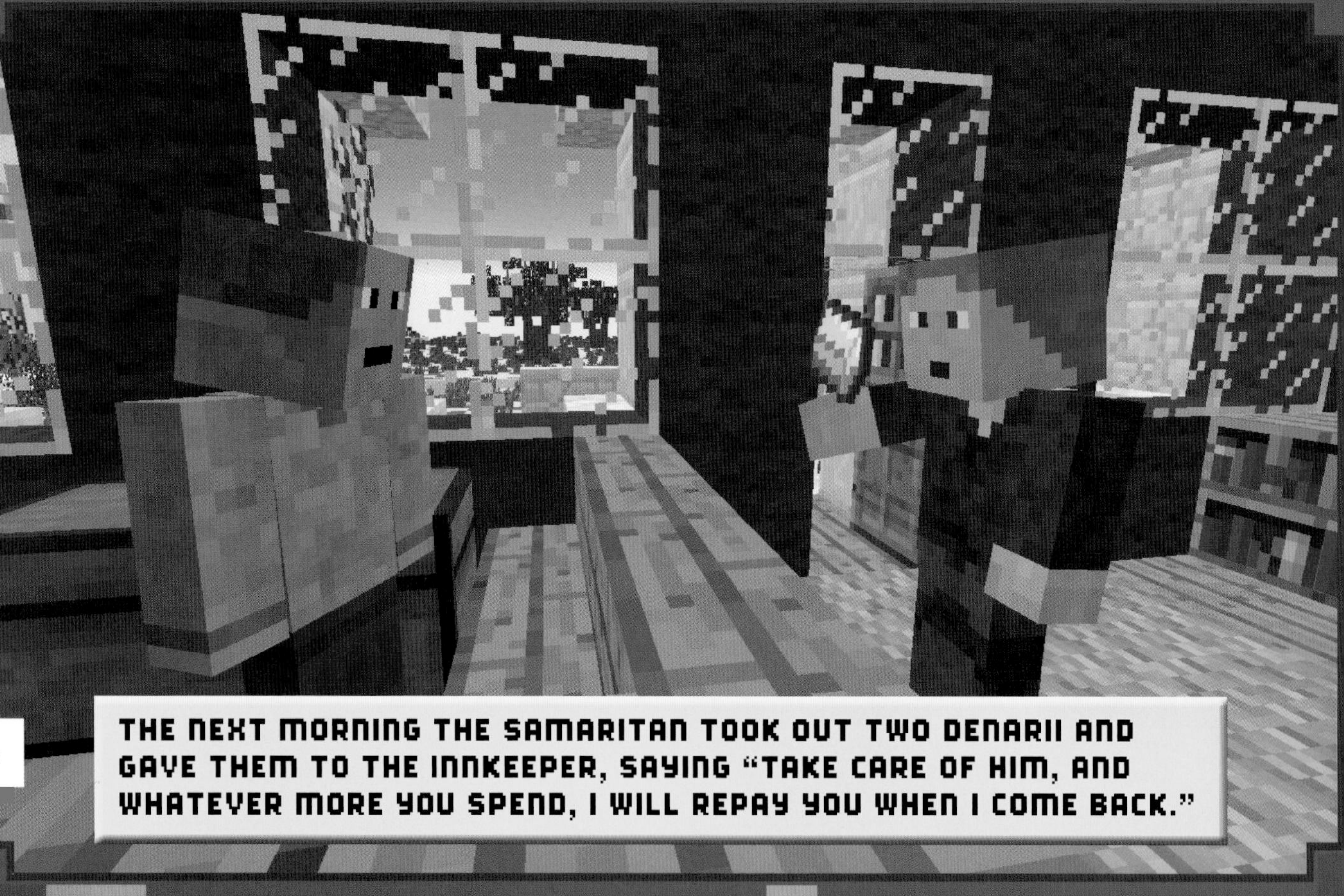
THE NEXT MORNING THE SAMARITAN TOOK OUT TWO DENARII AND GAVE THEM TO THE INNKEEPER, SAYING “TAKE CARE OF HIM, AND WHATEVER MORE YOU SPEND, I WILL REPAY YOU WHEN I COME BACK.”

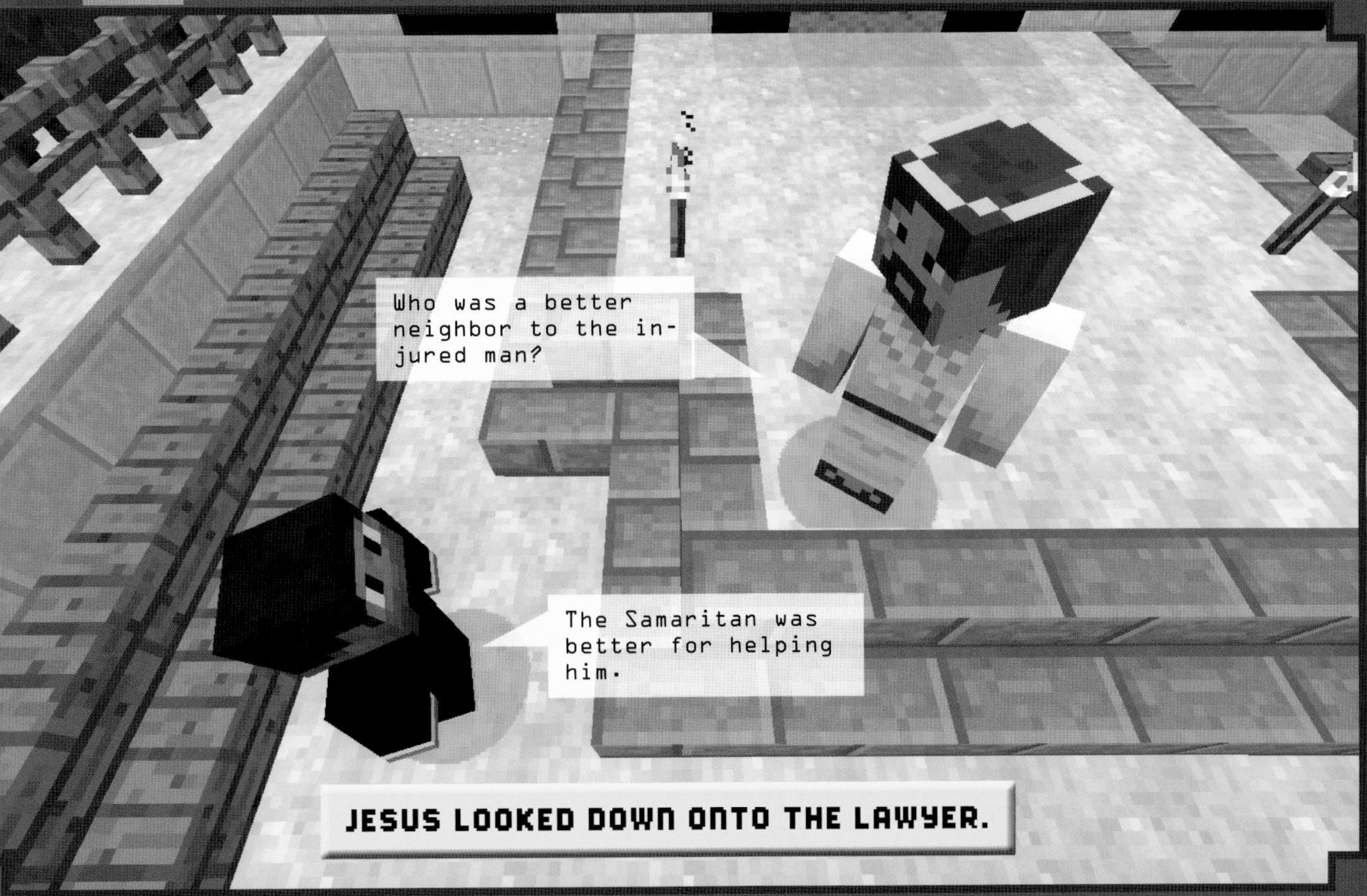
Who was a better neighbor to the in-jured man?
The Samaritan was better for helping him.
JESUS LOOKED DOWN ONTO THE LAWYER.

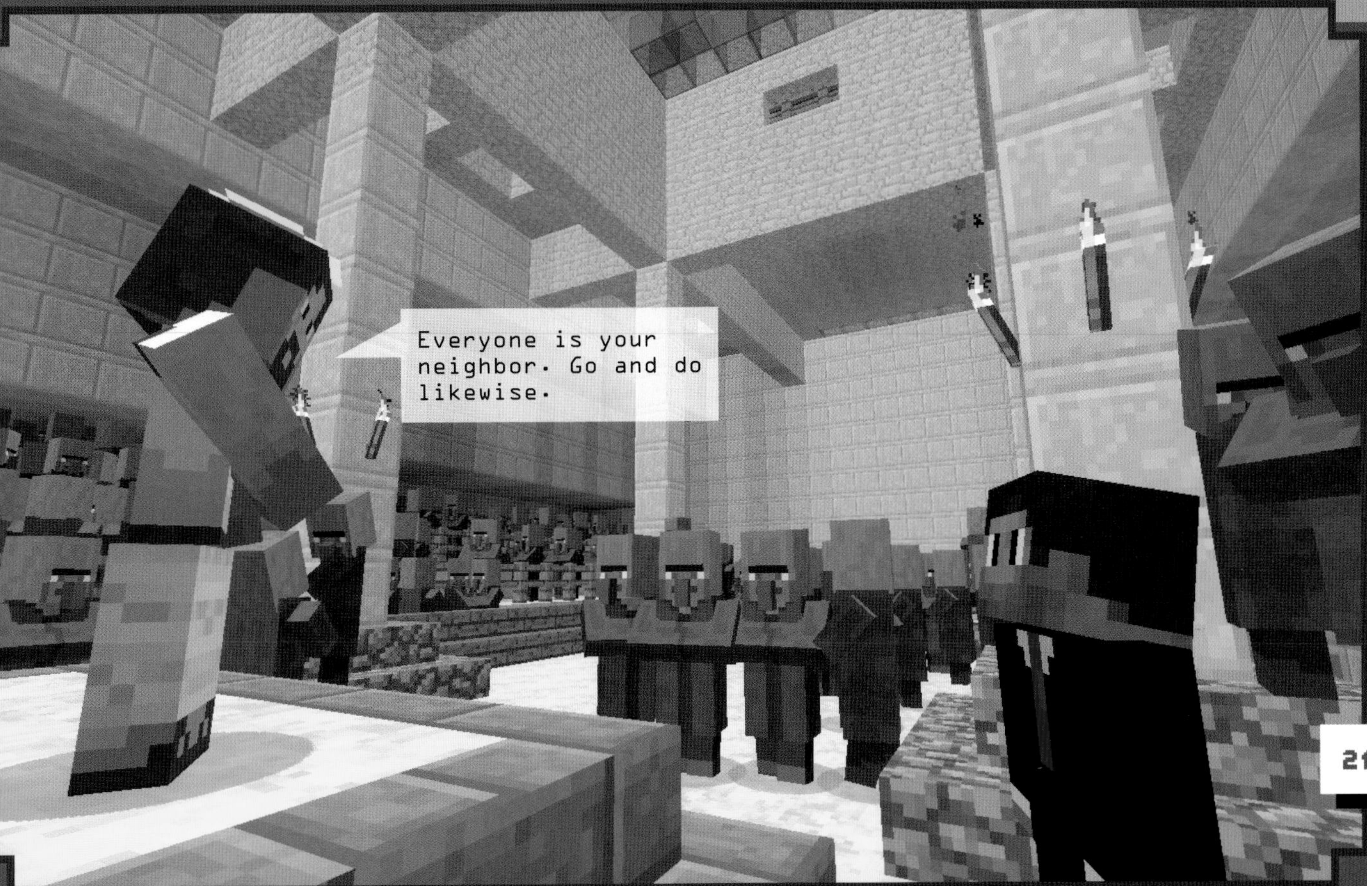
Everyone is your neighbor. Go and do likewise.

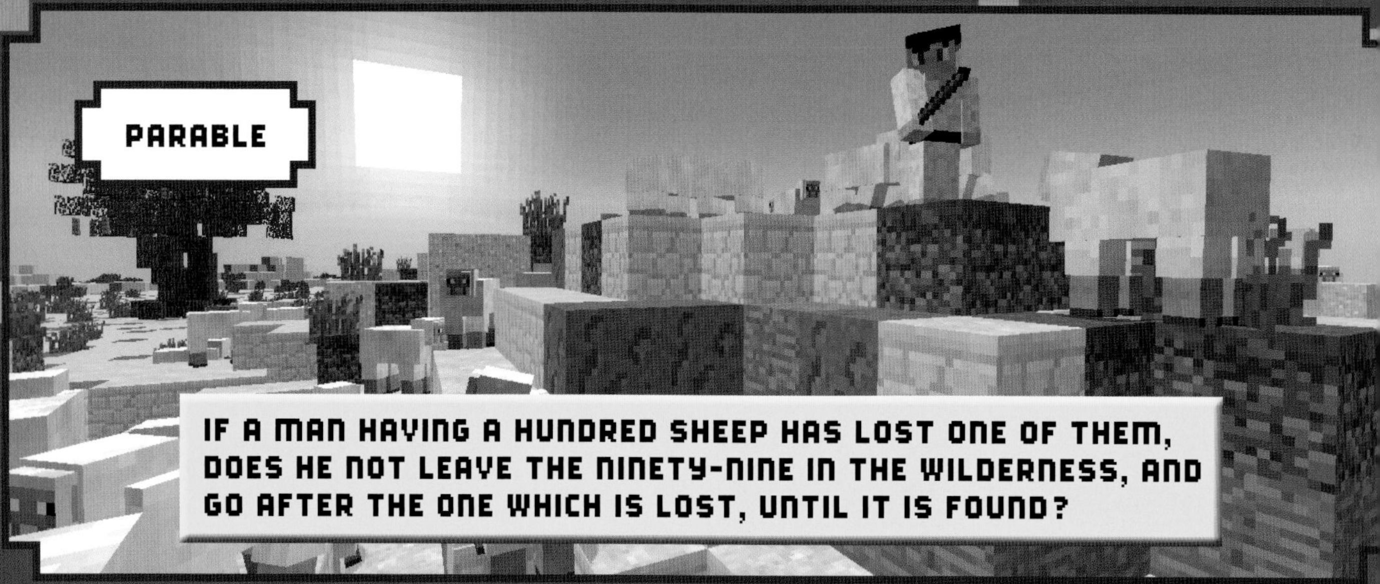
PARABLE
IF A MAN HAVING A HUNDRED SHEEP HAS LOST ONE OF THEM, DOES HE NOT LEAVE THE NINETY-NINE IN THE WILDERNESS, AND GO AFTER THE ONE WHICH IS LOST, UNTIL IT IS FOUND?

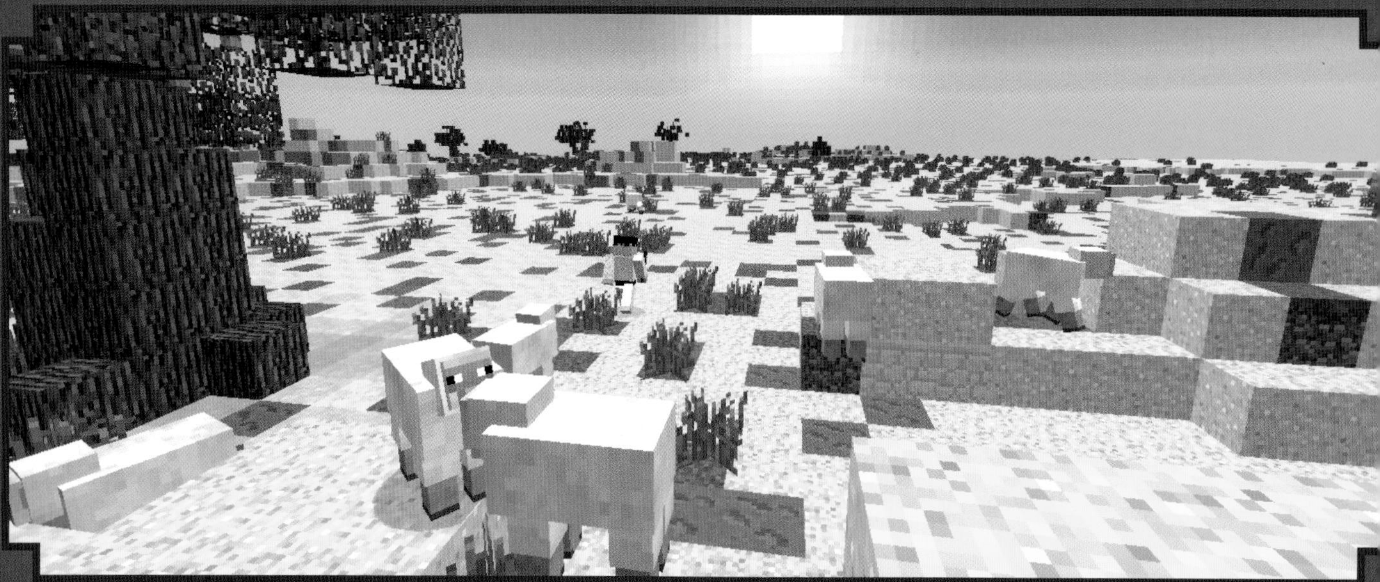

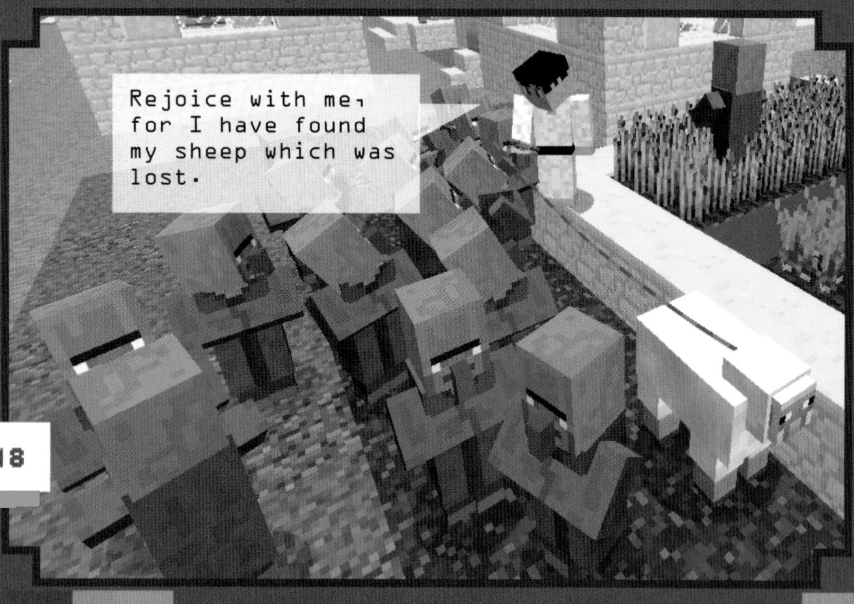
Rejoice with me, for I have found my sheep which was lost.

WHEN HE HAS FOUND IT, HE LAYS IT ON HIS SHOULDERS, REJOICING. AND WHEN HE COMES HOME, HE CALLS TOGETHER HIS FRIENDS AND HIS NEIGHBORS ASKING THEM TO SHARE IN HIS JOY. JUST SO, THERE WILL BE MORE JOY IN HEAVEN OVER ONE SINNER WHO REPENTS THAN OVER NINETY-NINE RIGHTEOUS PERSONS WHO NEED NO REPENTANCE.

JESUS FEEDS 5,000 PEOPLE

I think I'm beginning to understand how these parables work.

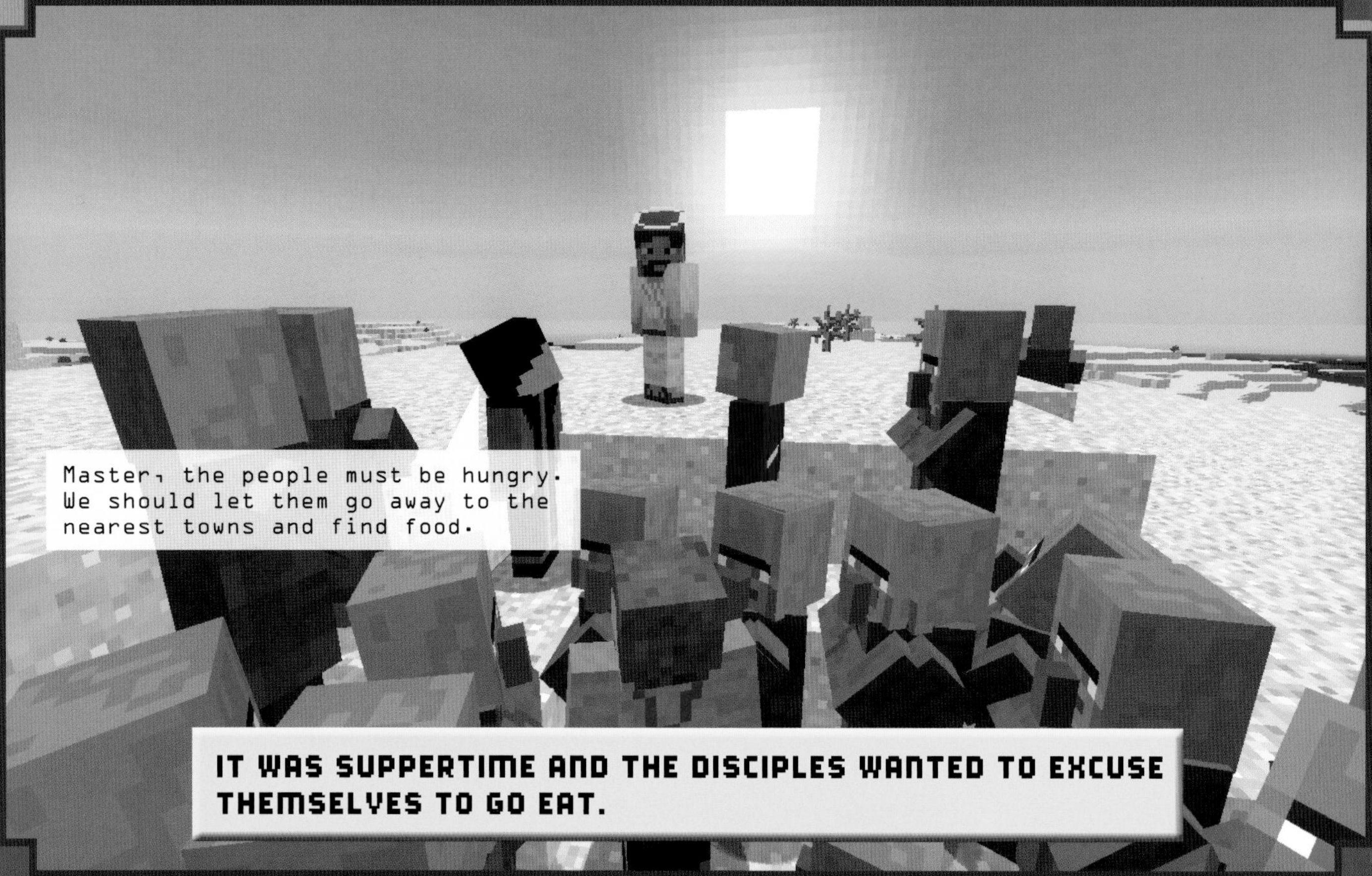
Master, the people must be hungry. We should let them go away to the nearest towns and find food.
IT WAS SUPPERTIME AND THE DISCIPLES WANTED TO EXCUSE THEMSELVES TO GO EAT.

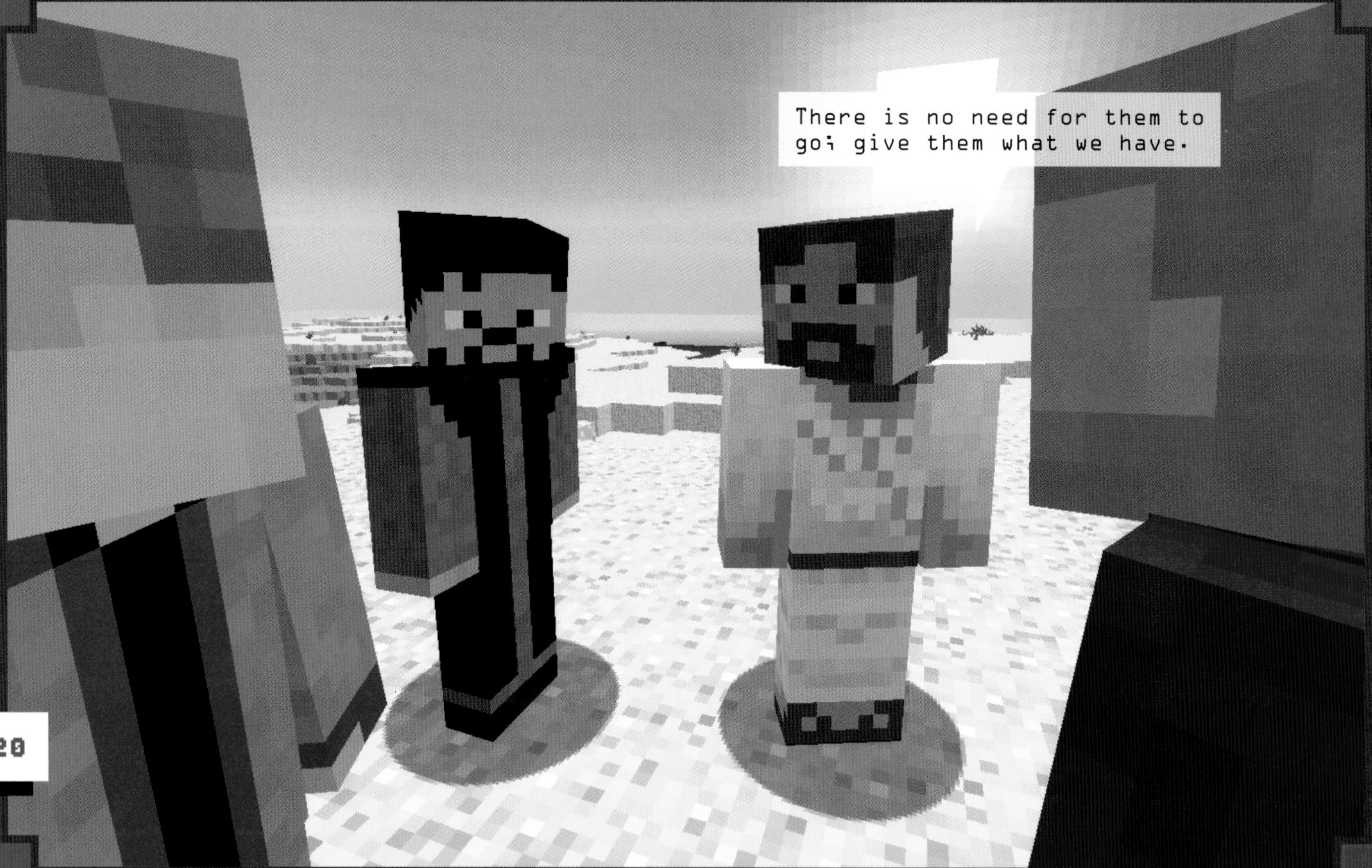
There is no need for them to go; give them what we have.

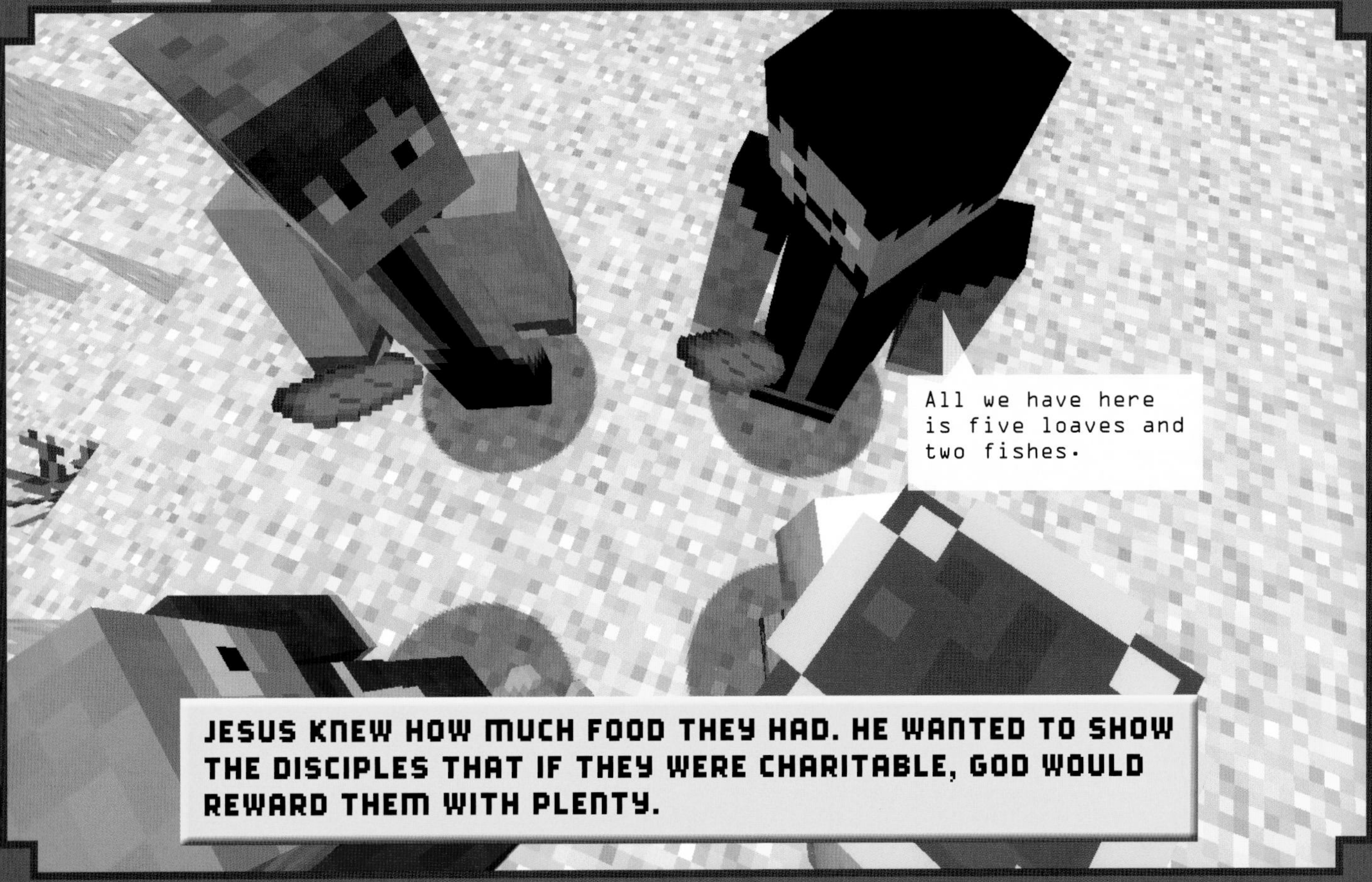
All we have here is five loaves and two fishes.
JESUS KNEW HOW MUCH FOOD THEY HAD. HE WANTED TO SHOW THE DISCIPLES THAT IF THEY WERE CHARITABLE, GOD WOULD REWARD THEM WITH PLENTY.

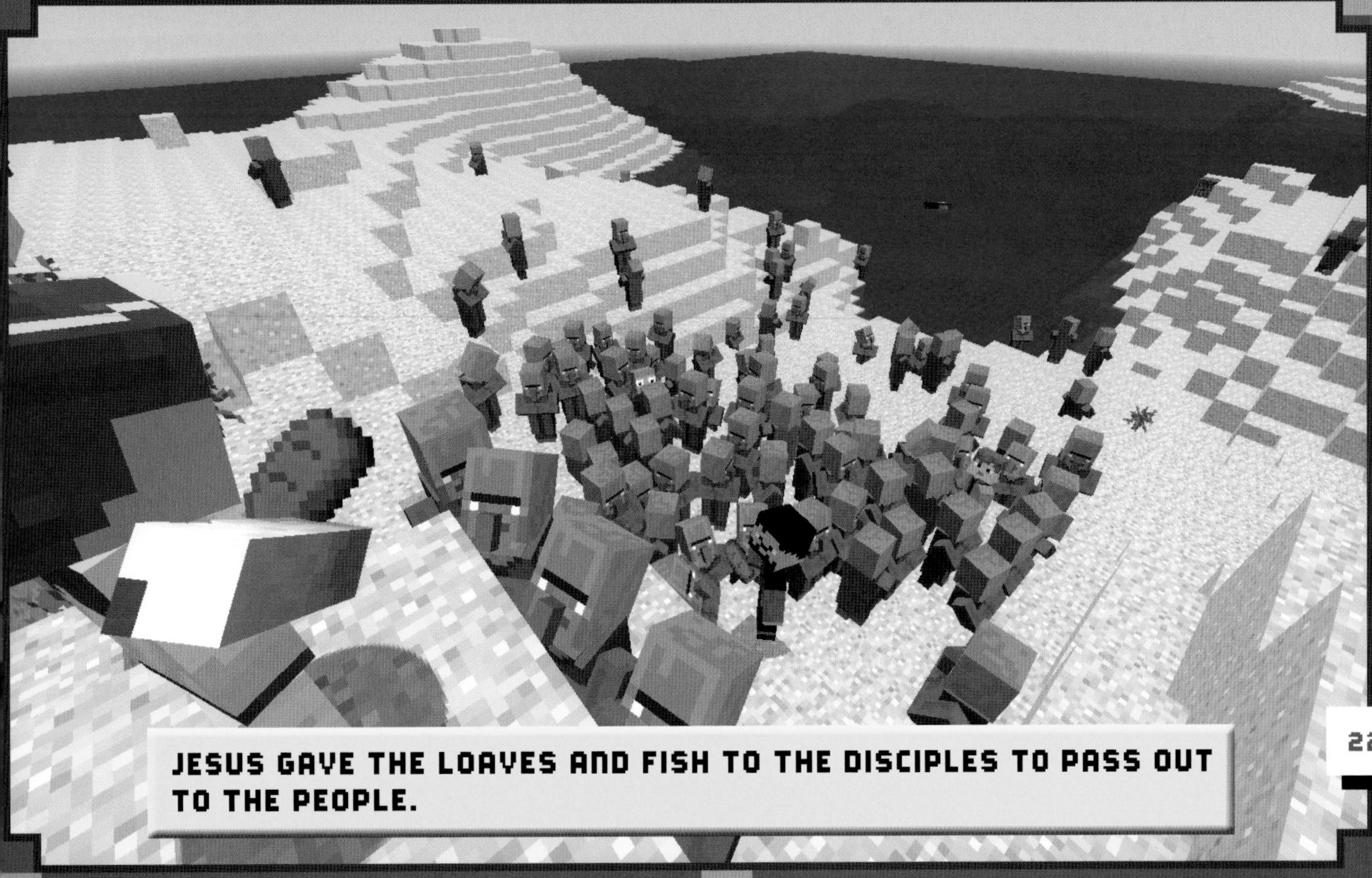
JESUS GAVE THE LOAVES AND FISH TO THE DISCIPLES TO PASS OUT TO THE PEOPLE.

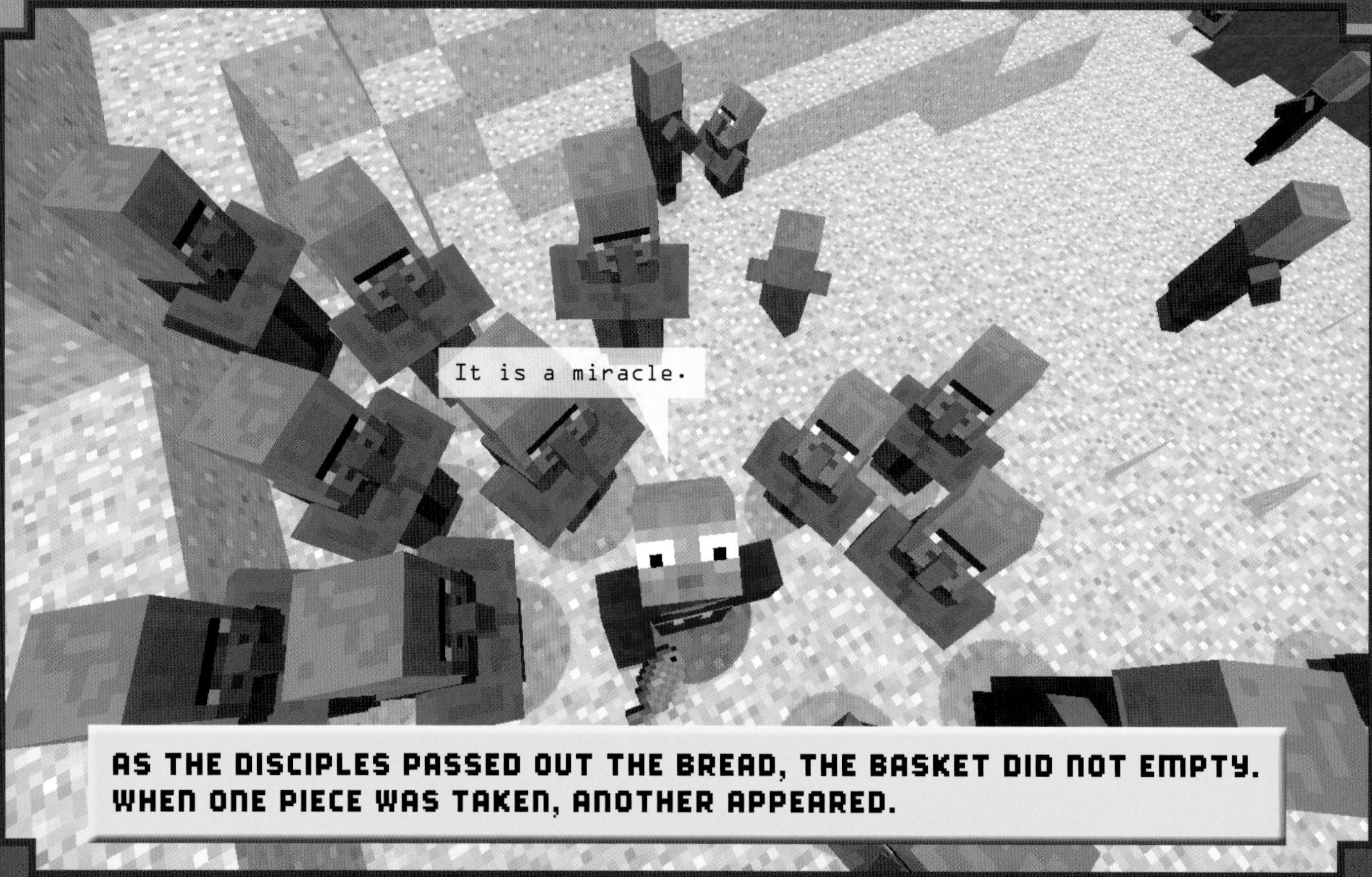
It is a miracle.
AS THE DISCIPLES PASSED OUT THE BREAD, THE BASKET DID NOT EMPTY. WHEN ONE PIECE WAS TAKEN, ANOTHER APPEARED.

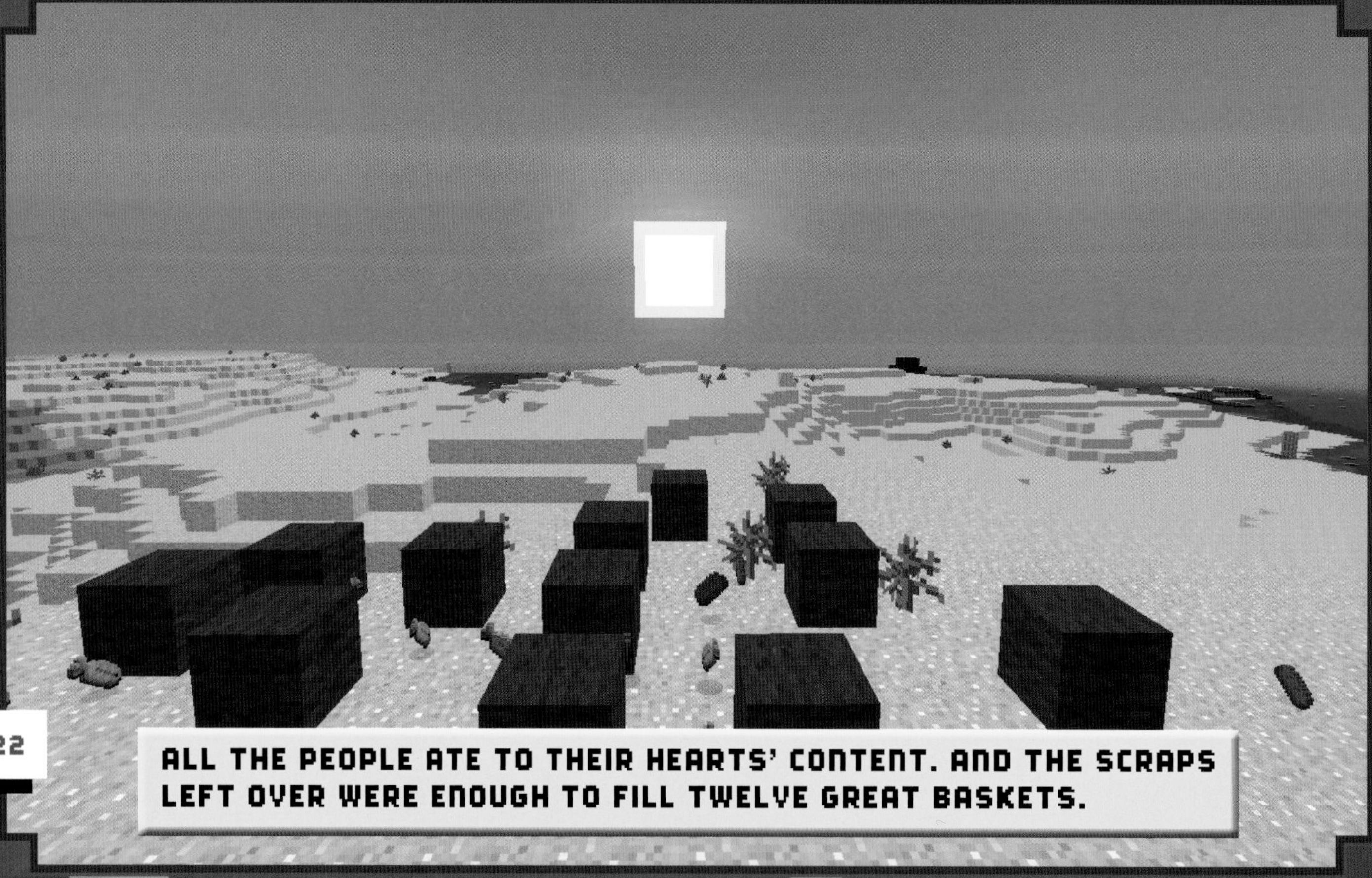
ALL THE PEOPLE ATE TO THEIR HEARTS' CONTENT. AND THE SCRAPS LEFT OVER WERE ENOUGH TO FILL TWELVE GREAT BASKETS.

JESUS WALKS ON WATER

Is there no end to the amazing acts of Jesus? He's got quite an array of talents.

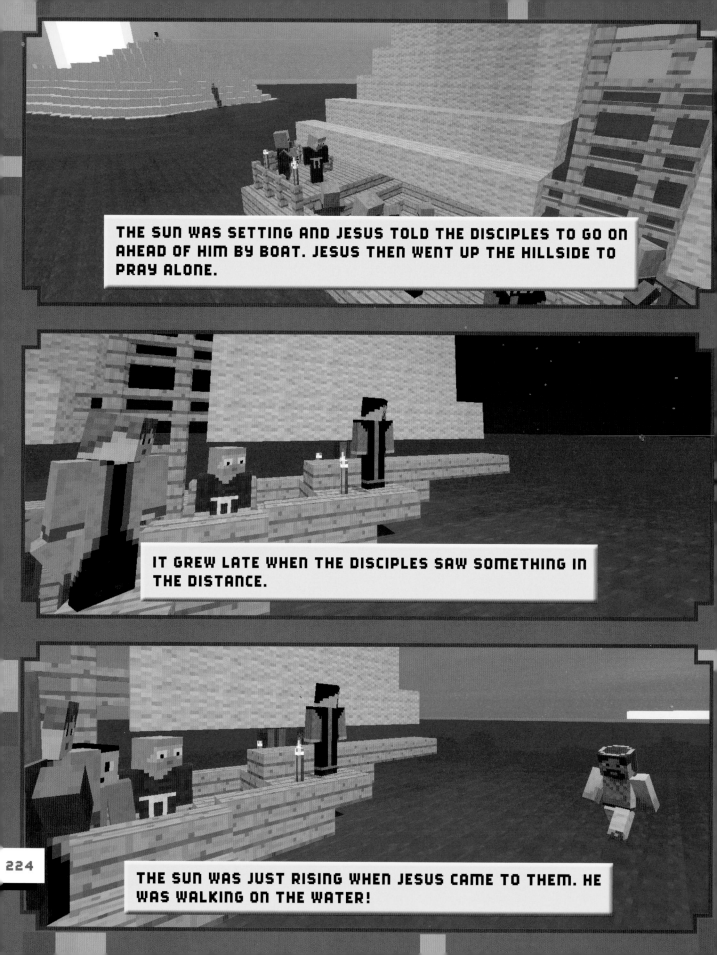

THE SUN WAS SETTING AND JESUS TOLD THE DISCIPLES TO GO ON AHEAD OF HIM BY BOAT. JESUS THEN WENT UP THE HILLSIDE TO PRAY ALONE.

IT GREW LATE WHEN THE DISCIPLES SAW SOMETHING IN THE DISTANCE.

THE SUN WAS JUST RISING WHEN JESUS CAME TO THEM. HE WAS WALKING ON THE WATER!

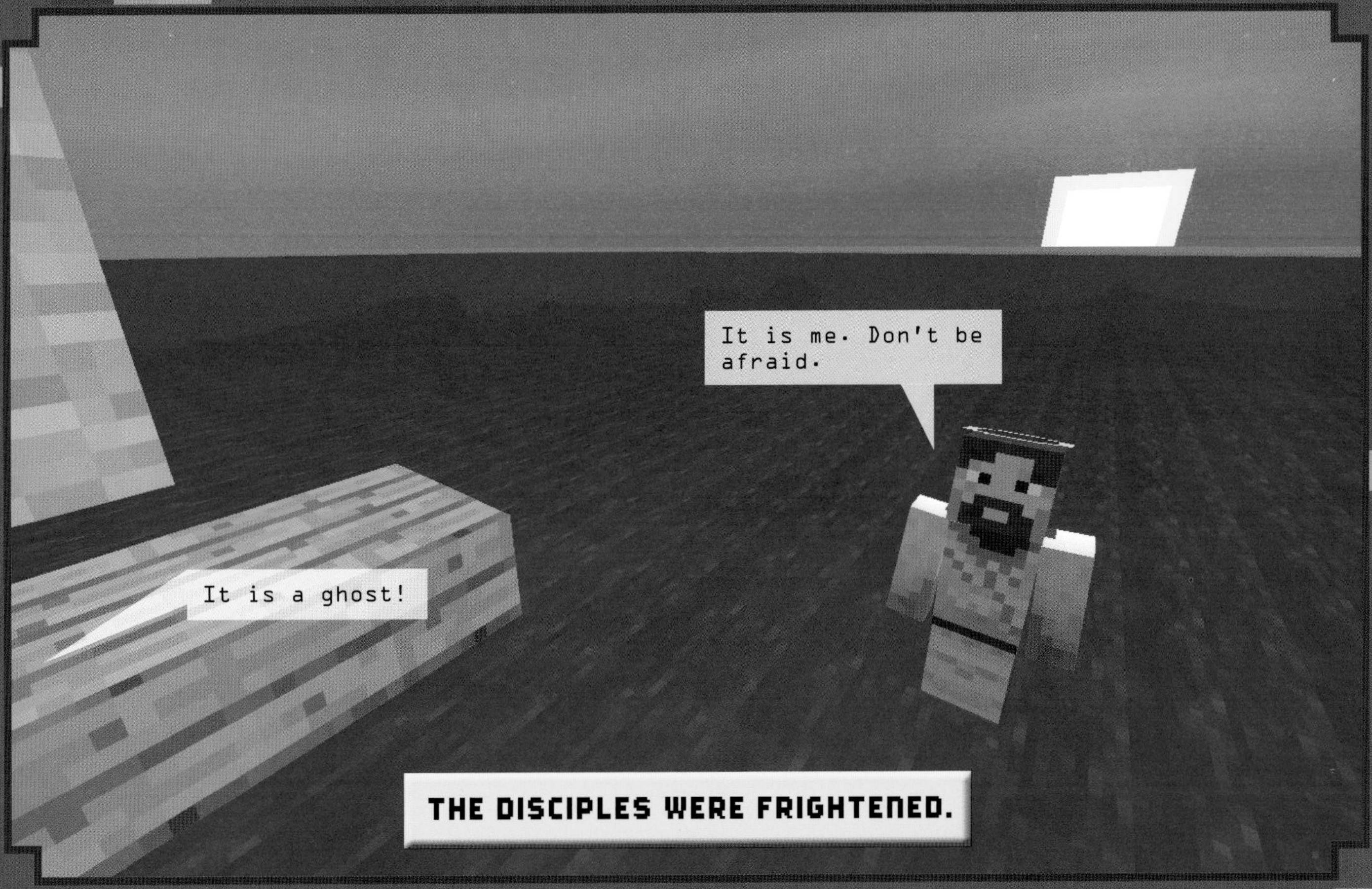
It is me. Don't be afraid.
It is a ghost!
THE DISCIPLES WERE FRIGHTENED.

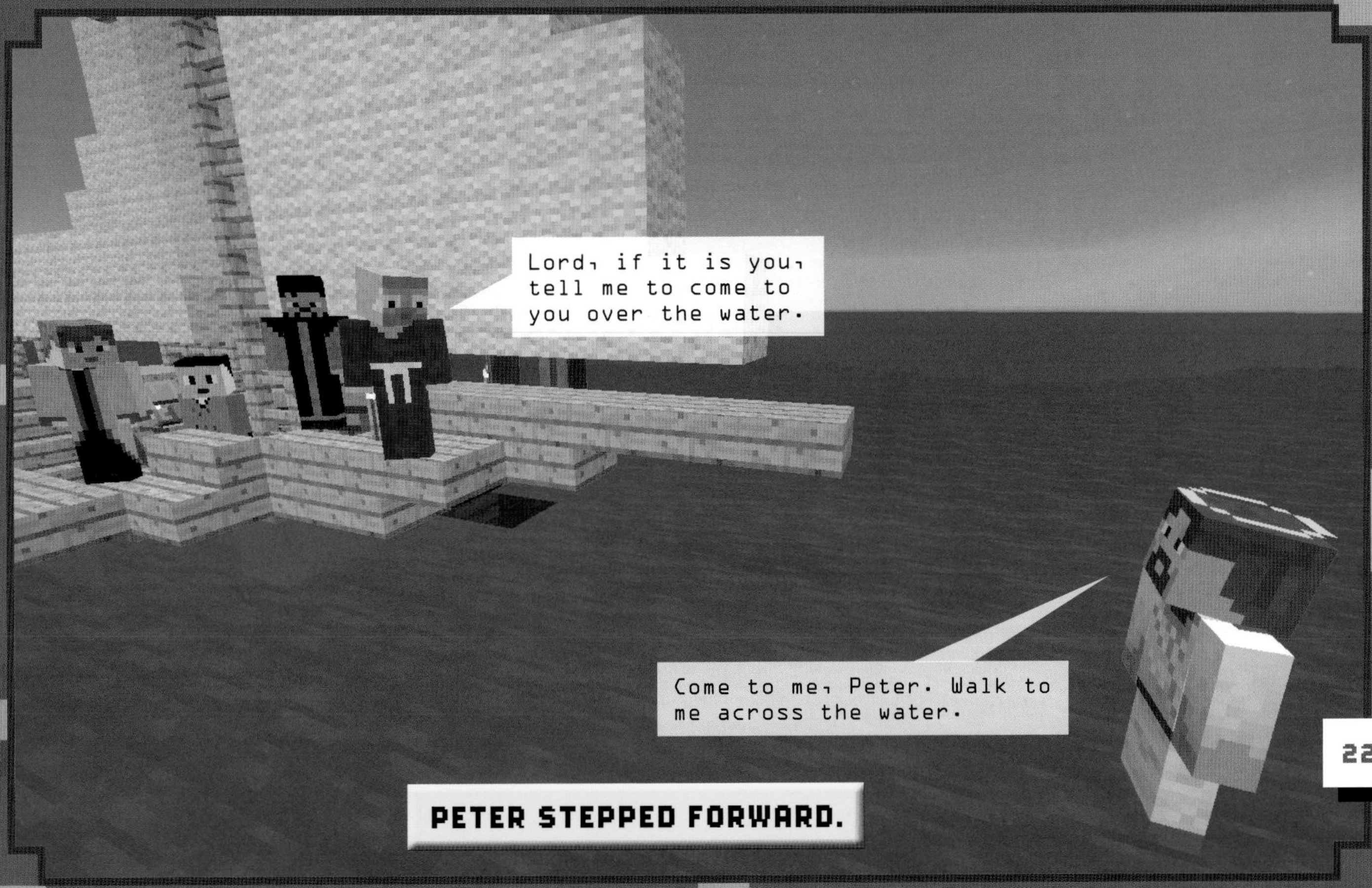
Lord, if it is you, tell me to come to you over the water.
Come to me, Peter. Walk to me across the water.
PETER STEPPED FORWARD.

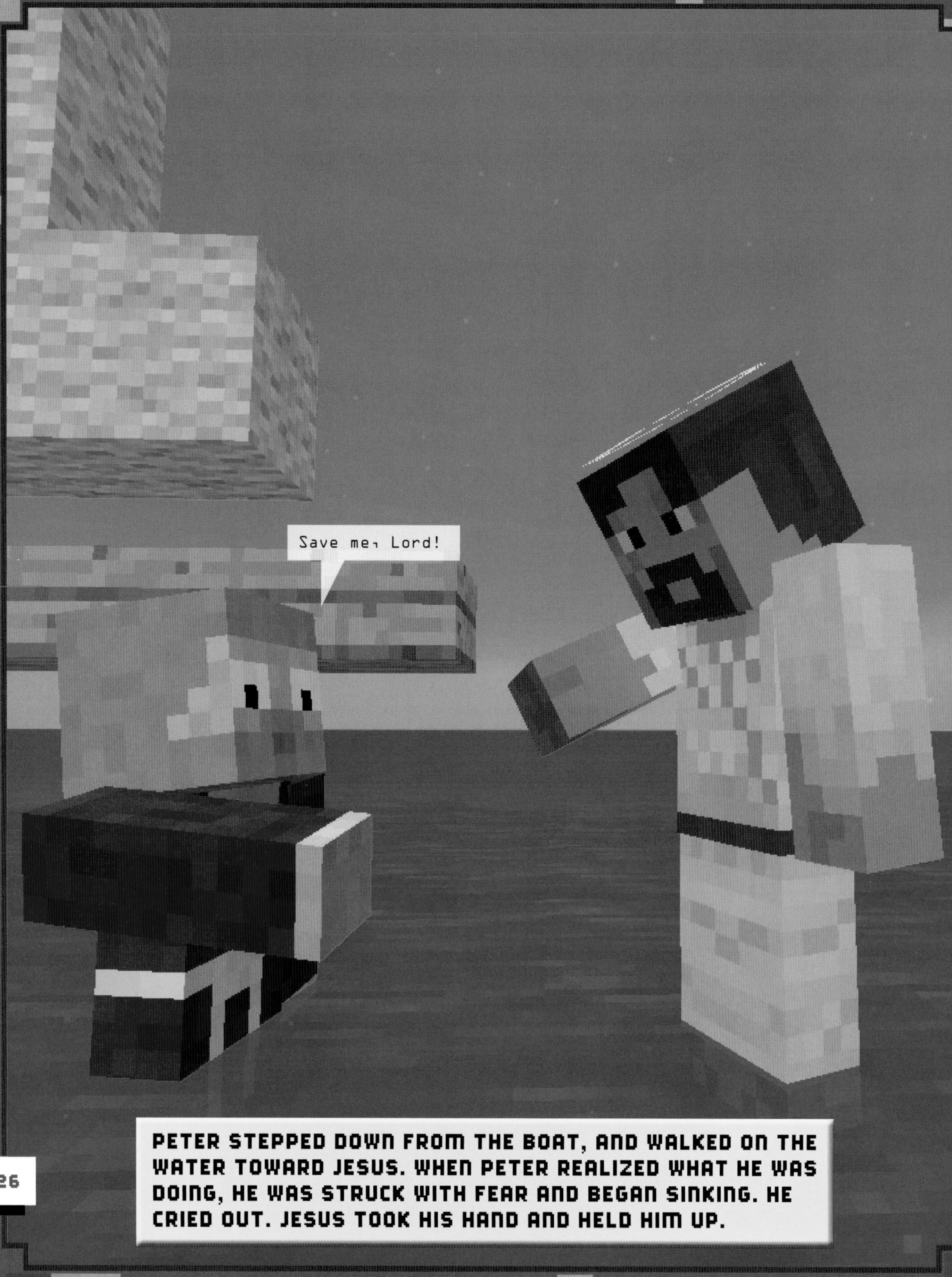
Save me, Lord!
PETER STEPPED DOWN FROM THE BOAT, AND WALKED ON THE WATER TOWARD JESUS. WHEN PETER REALIZED WHAT HE WAS DOING, HE WAS STRUCK WITH FEAR AND BEGAN SINKING. HE CRIED OUT. JESUS TOOK HIS HAND AND HELD HIM UP.

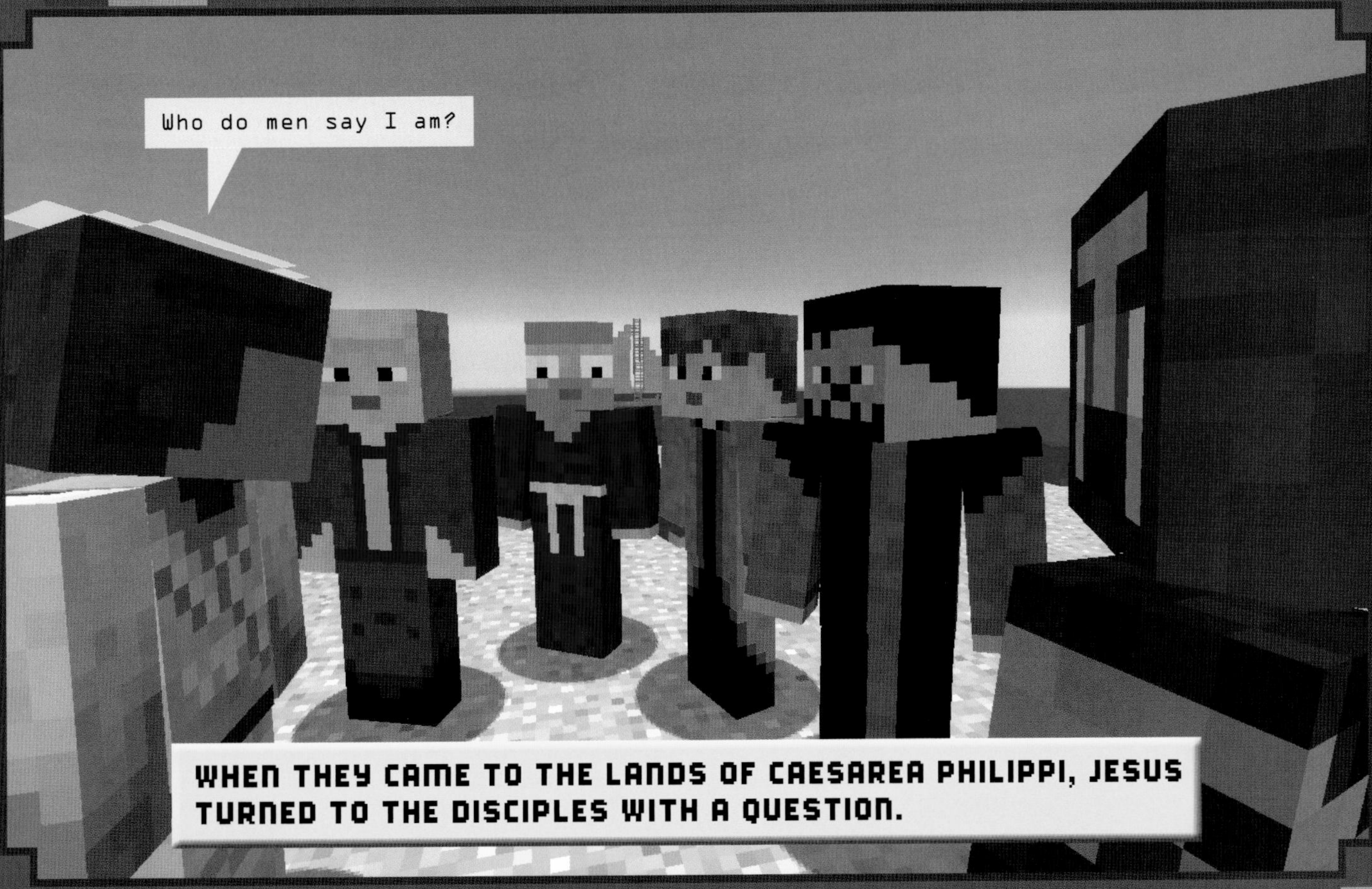
Who do men say I am?
WHEN THEY CAME TO THE LANDS OF CAESAREA PHILIPPI, JESUS TURNED TO THE DISCIPLES WITH A QUESTION.

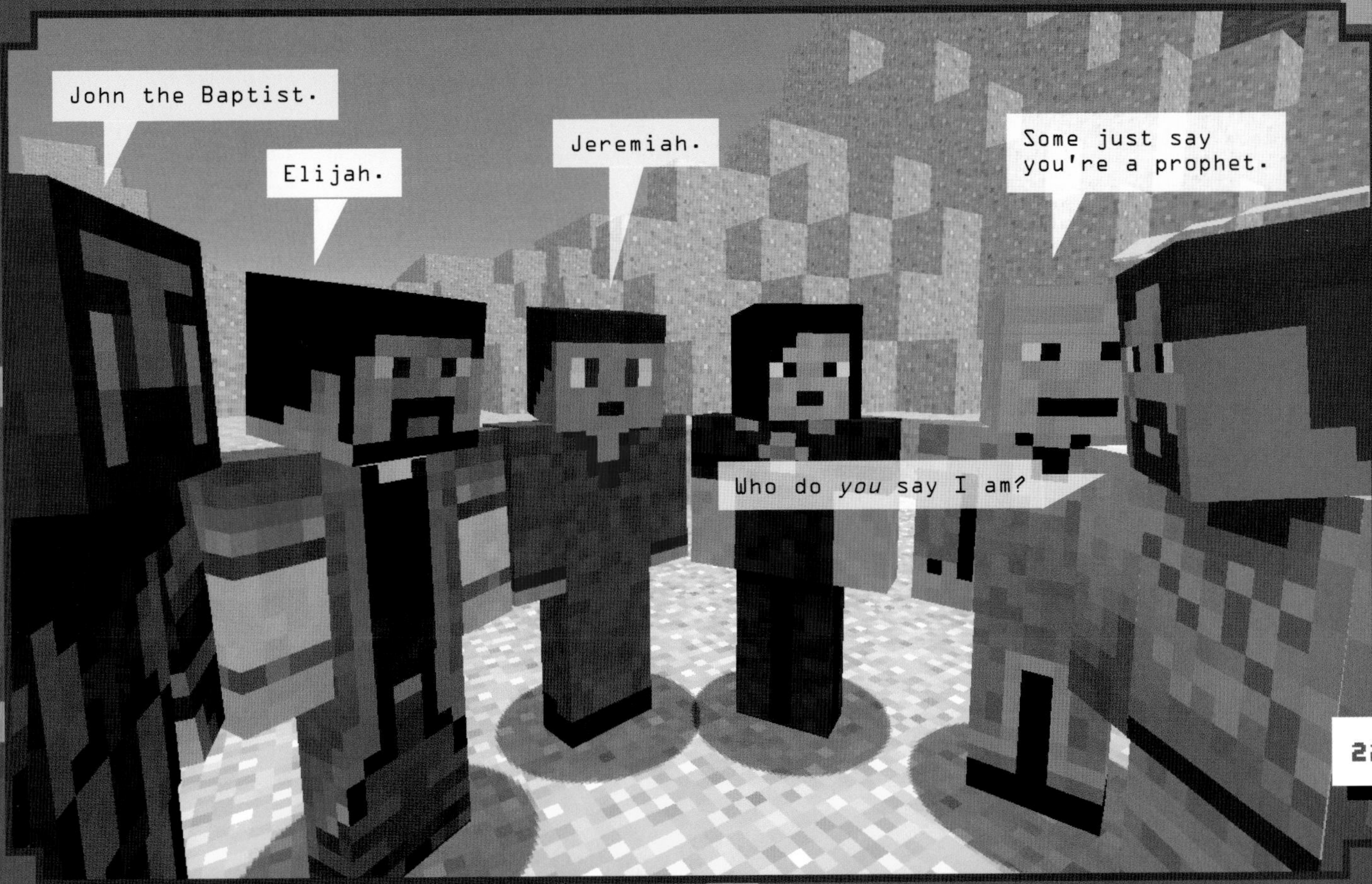
John the Baptist.
Elijah.
Jeremiah.
Some just say you're a prophet.
Who do *you* say I am?

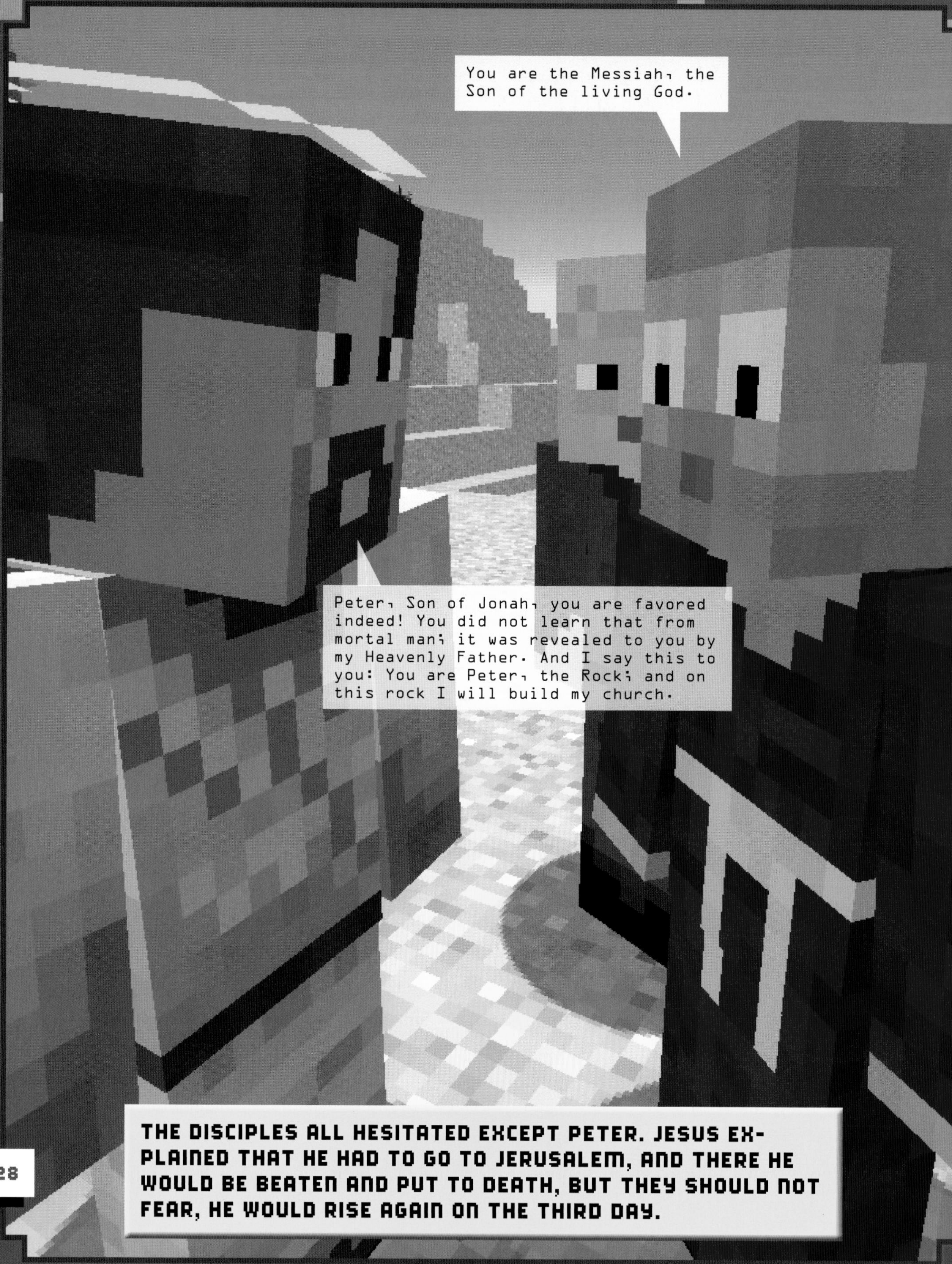
You are the Messiah, the Son of the living God.
Peter, Son of Jonah, you are favored indeed! You did not learn that from mortal man; it was revealed to you by my Heavenly Father. And I say this to you: You are Peter, the Rock; and on this rock I will build my church.
THE DISCIPLES ALL HESITATED EXCEPT PETER. JESUS EXPLAINED THAT HE HAD TO GO TO JERUSALEM, AND THERE HE WOULD BE BEATEN AND PUT TO DEATH, BUT THEY SHOULD NOT FEAR, HE WOULD RISE AGAIN ON THE THIRD DAY.

JESUS RAISES LAZARUS

Wow! He's like that one kind of lizard...

The Jesus Lizard is named after him.

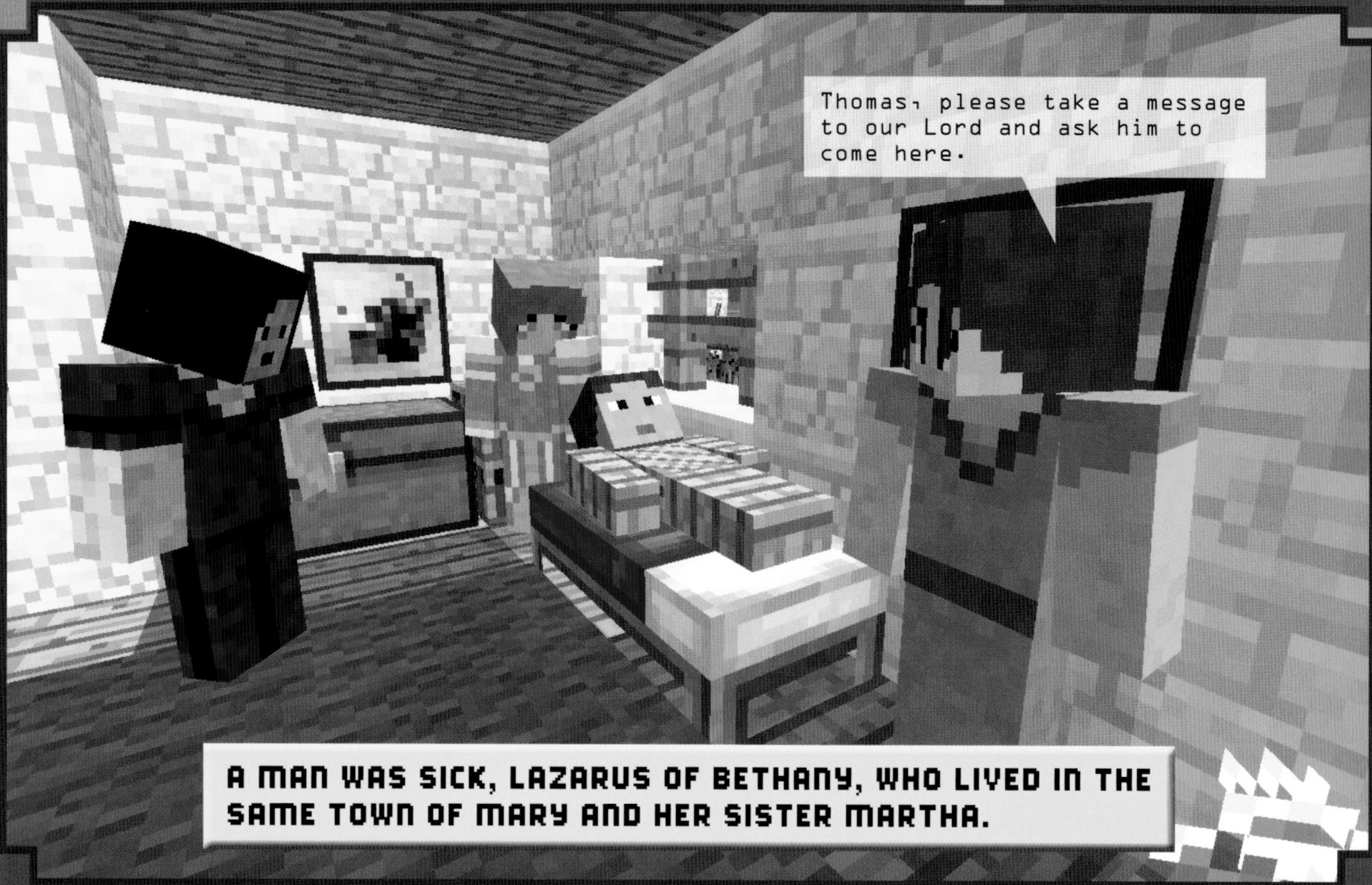
Thomas, please take a message to our Lord and ask him to come here.
A MAN WAS SICK, LAZARUS OF BETHANY, WHO LIVED IN THE SAME TOWN OF MARY AND HER SISTER MARTHA.

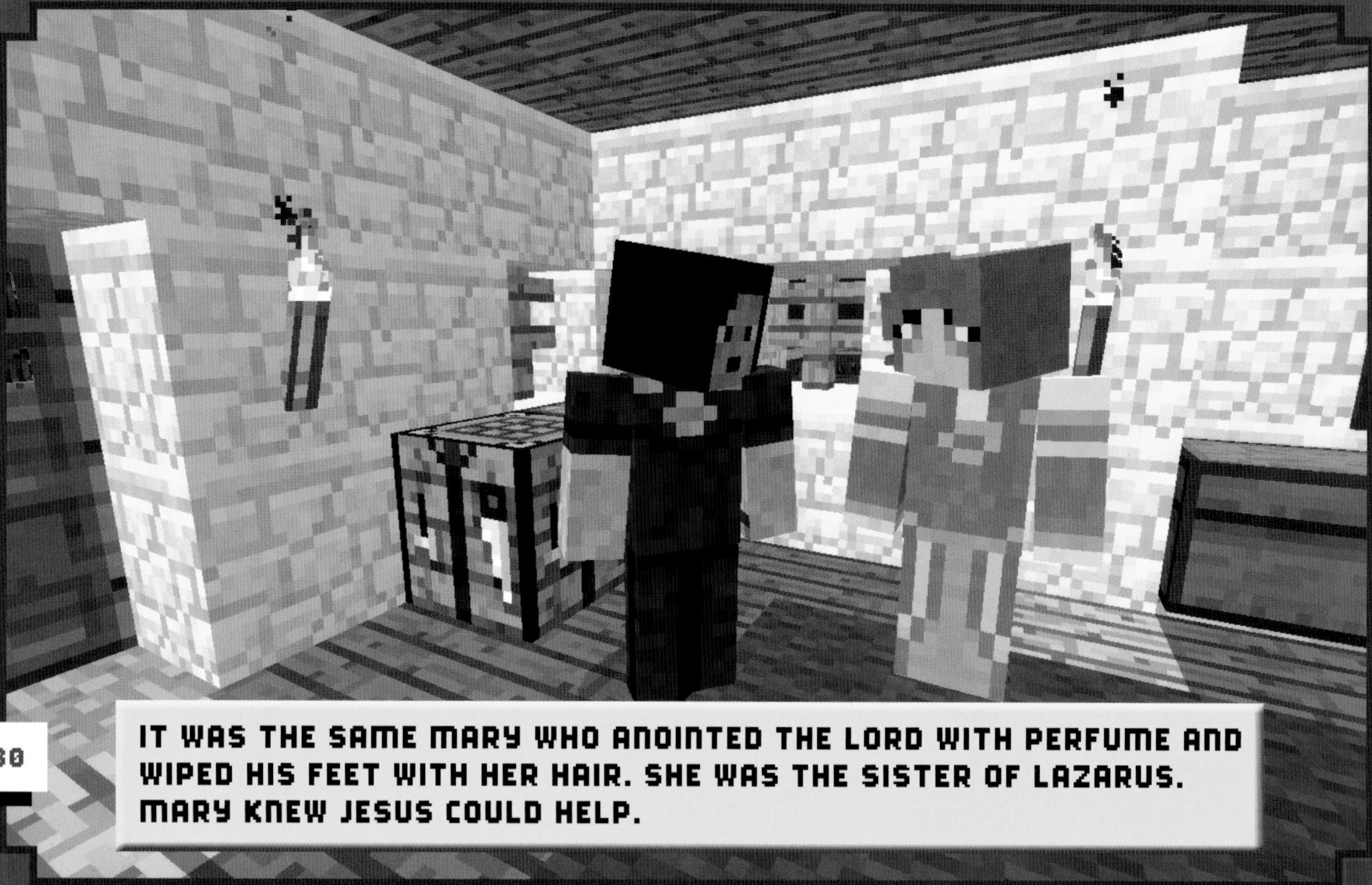
IT WAS THE SAME MARY WHO ANOINTED THE LORD WITH PERFUME AND WIPED HIS FEET WITH HER HAIR. SHE WAS THE SISTER OF LAZARUS. MARY KNEW JESUS COULD HELP.

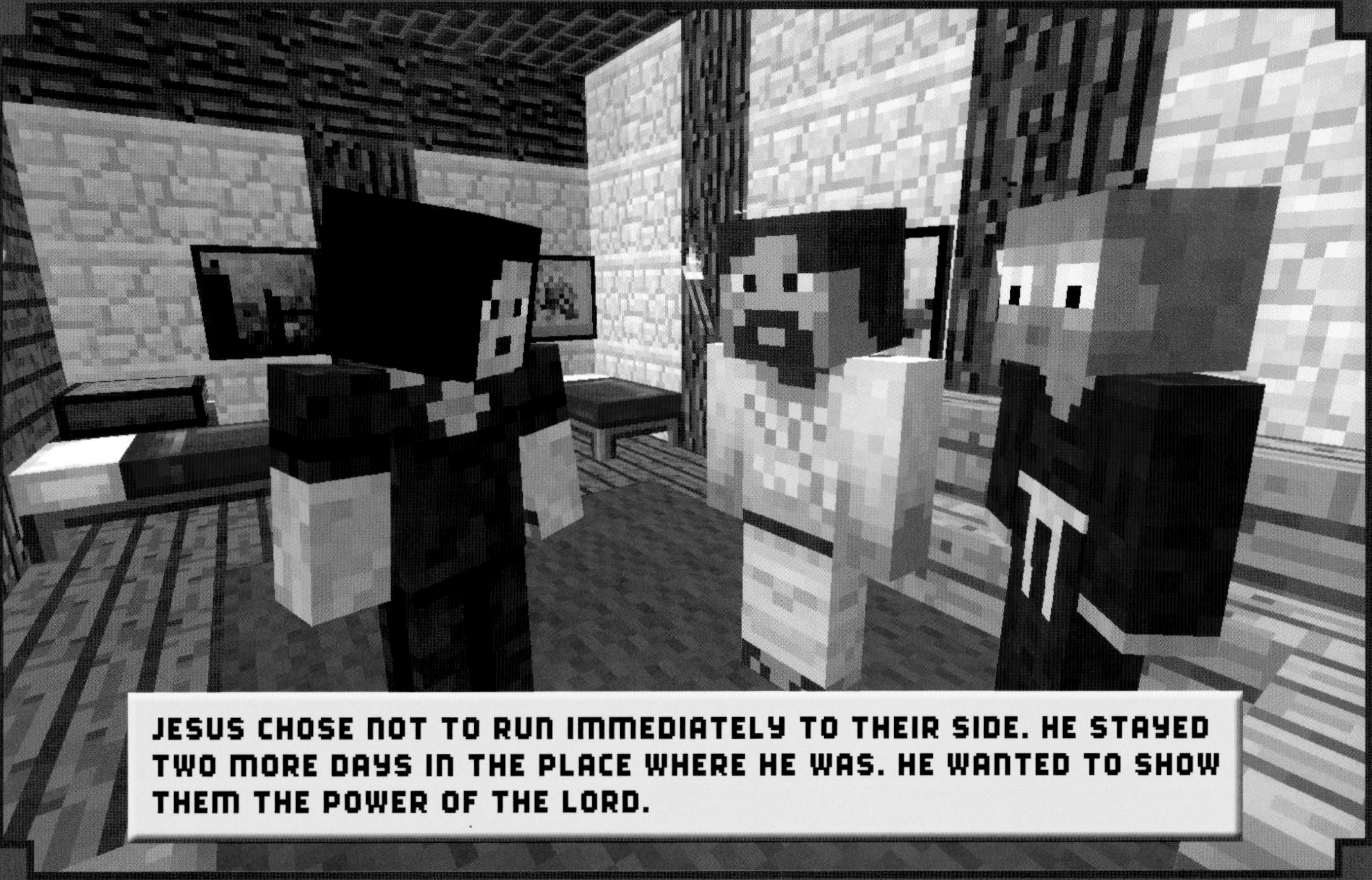
JESUS CHOSE NOT TO RUN IMMEDIATELY TO THEIR SIDE. HE STAYED TWO MORE DAYS IN THE PLACE WHERE HE WAS. HE WANTED TO SHOW THEM THE POWER OF THE LORD.

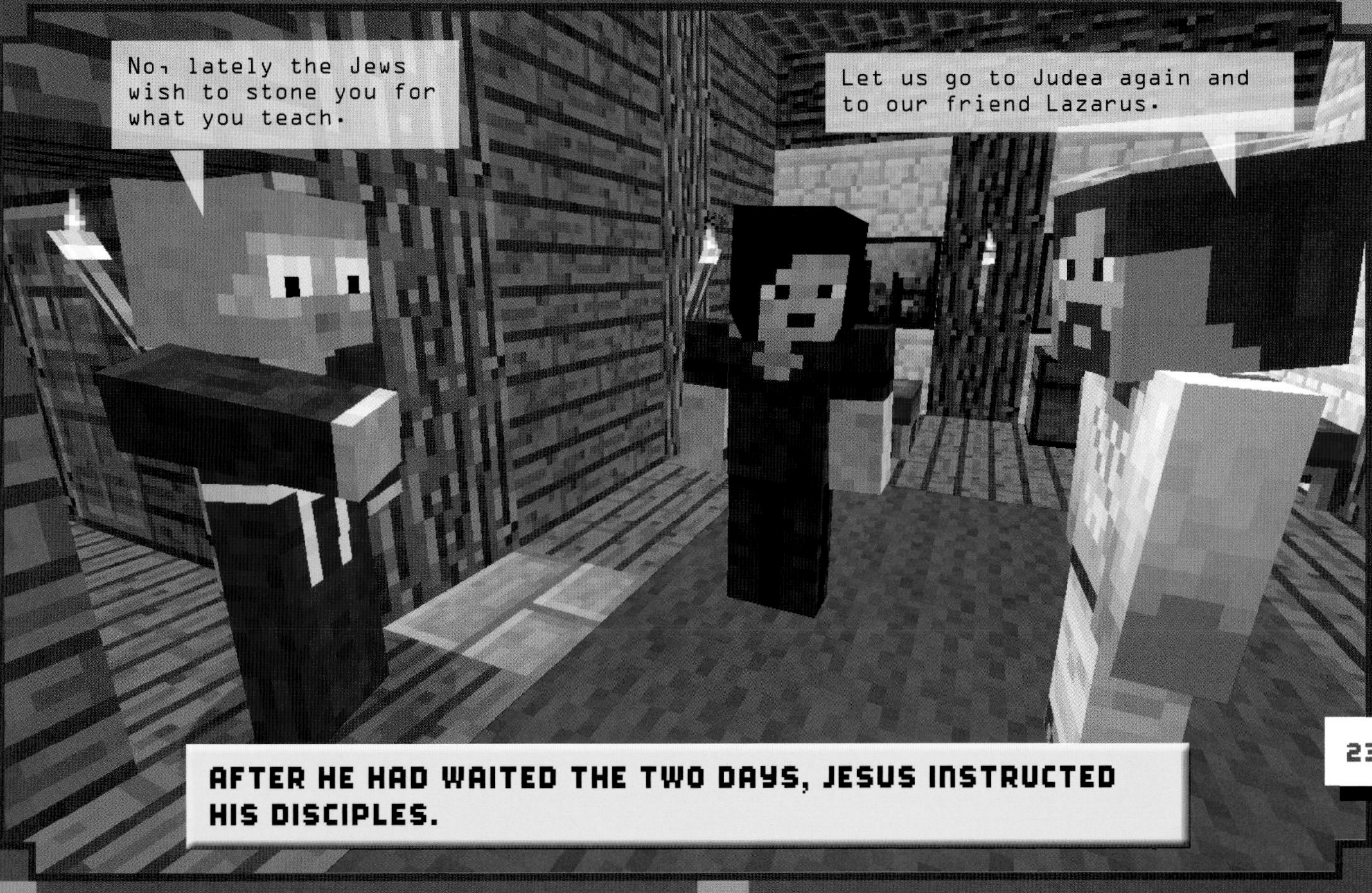
No, lately the Jews wish to stone you for what you teach.
Let us go to Judea again and to our friend Lazarus.
AFTER HE HAD WAITED THE TWO DAYS, JESUS INSTRUCTED HIS DISCIPLES.

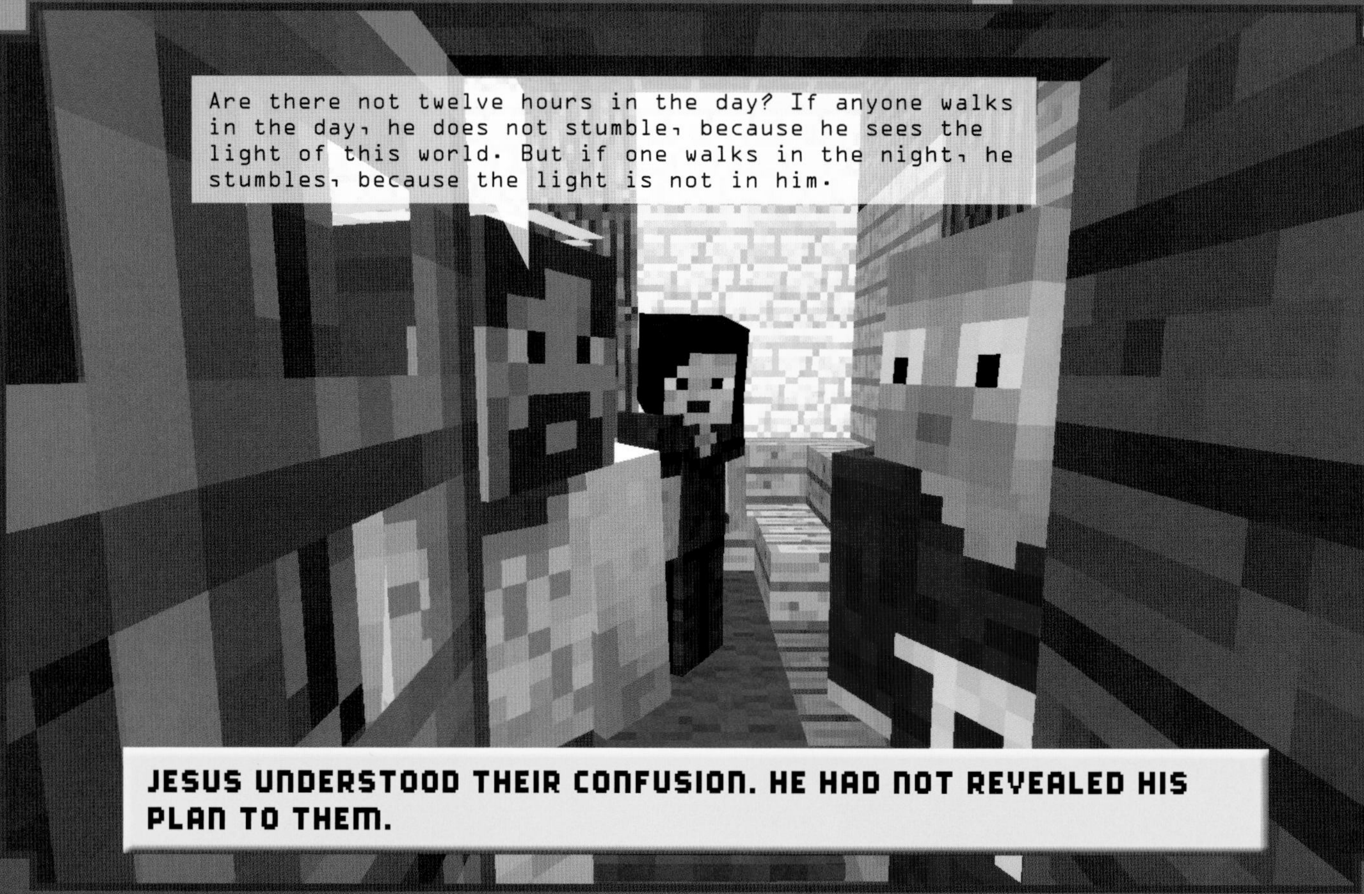
Are there not twelve hours in the day? If anyone walks in the day, he does not stumble, because he sees the light of this world. But if one walks in the night, he stumbles, because the light is not in him.
JESUS UNDERSTOOD THEIR CONFUSION. HE HAD NOT REVEALED HIS PLAN TO THEM.

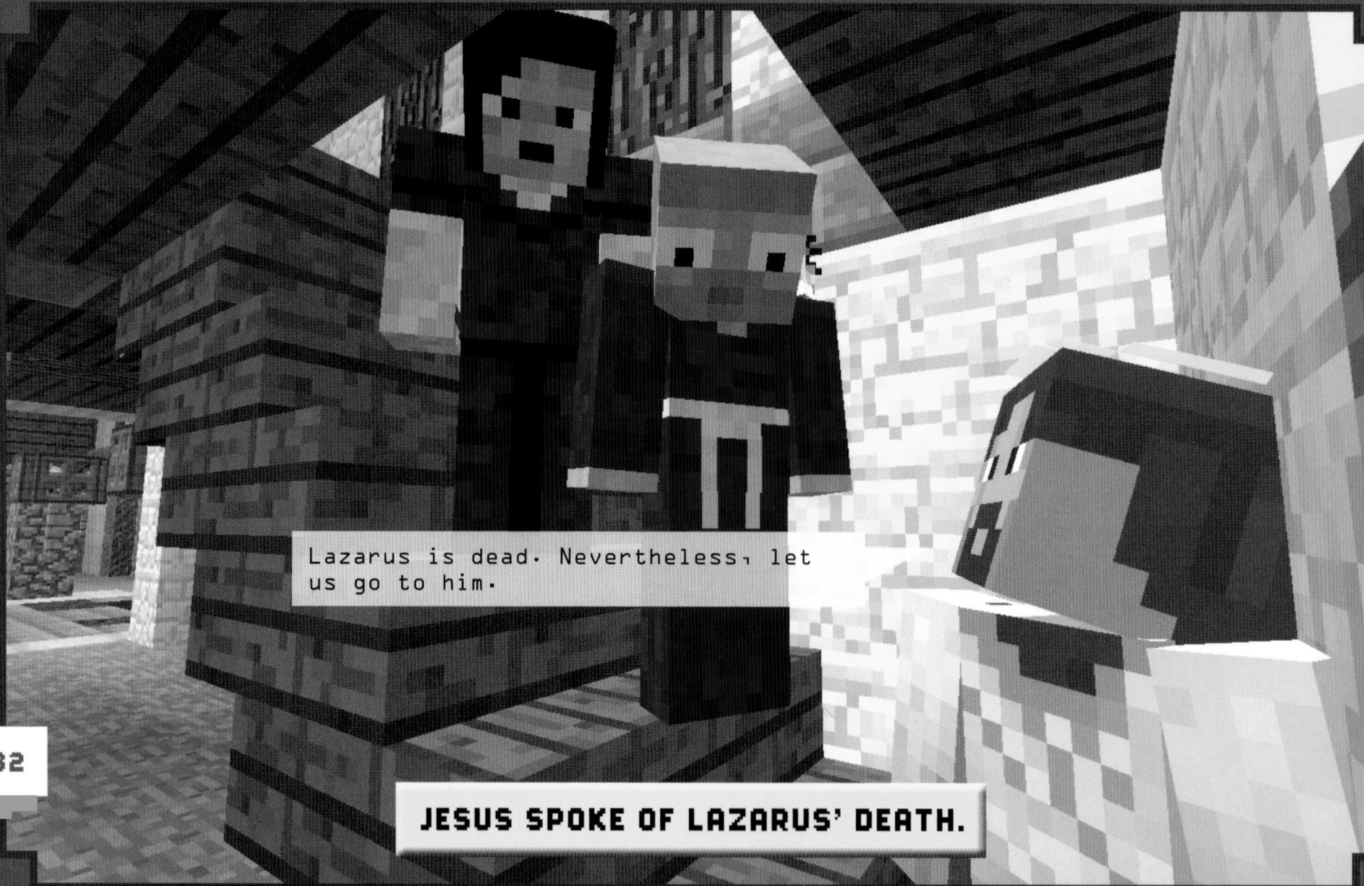
Lazarus is dead. Nevertheless, let us go to him.
JESUS SPOKE OF LAZARUS' DEATH.

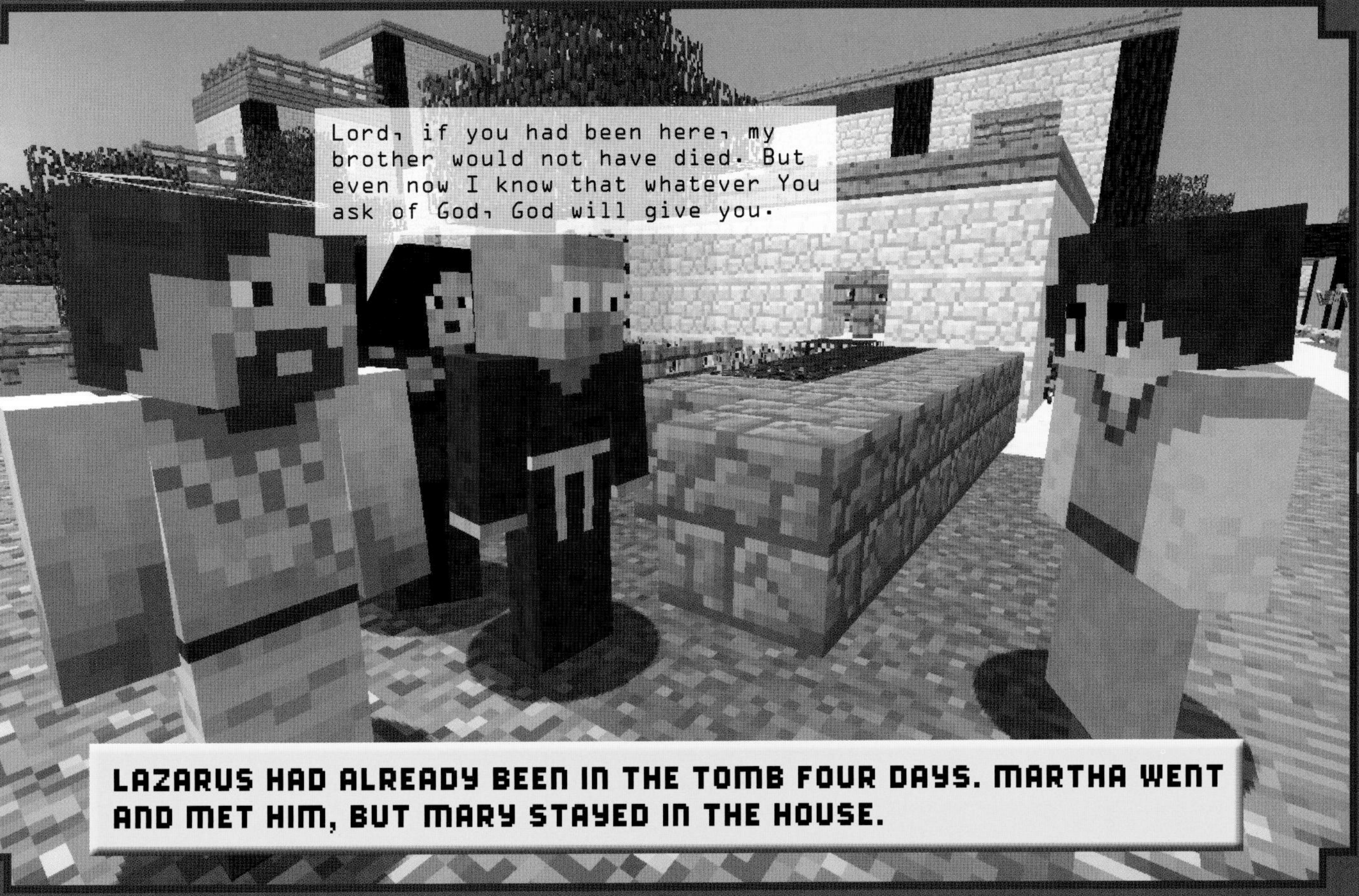
Lord, if you had been here, my brother would not have died. But even now I know that whatever You ask of God, God will give you.
LAZARUS HAD ALREADY BEEN IN THE TOMB FOUR DAYS. MARTHA WENT AND MET HIM, BUT MARY STAYED IN THE HOUSE.

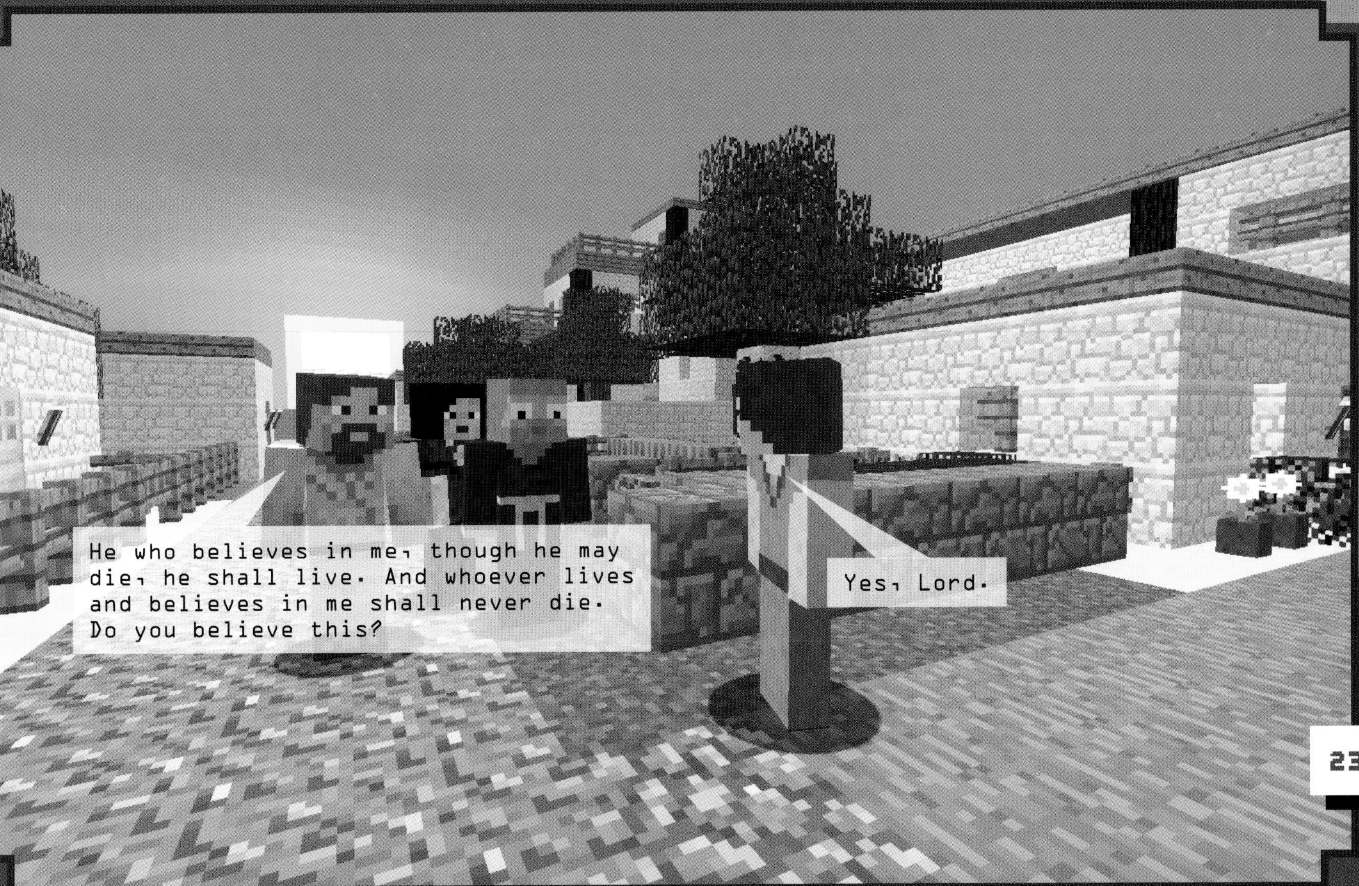
He who believes in me, though he may die, he shall live. And whoever lives and believes in me shall never die. Do you believe this?
Yes, Lord.

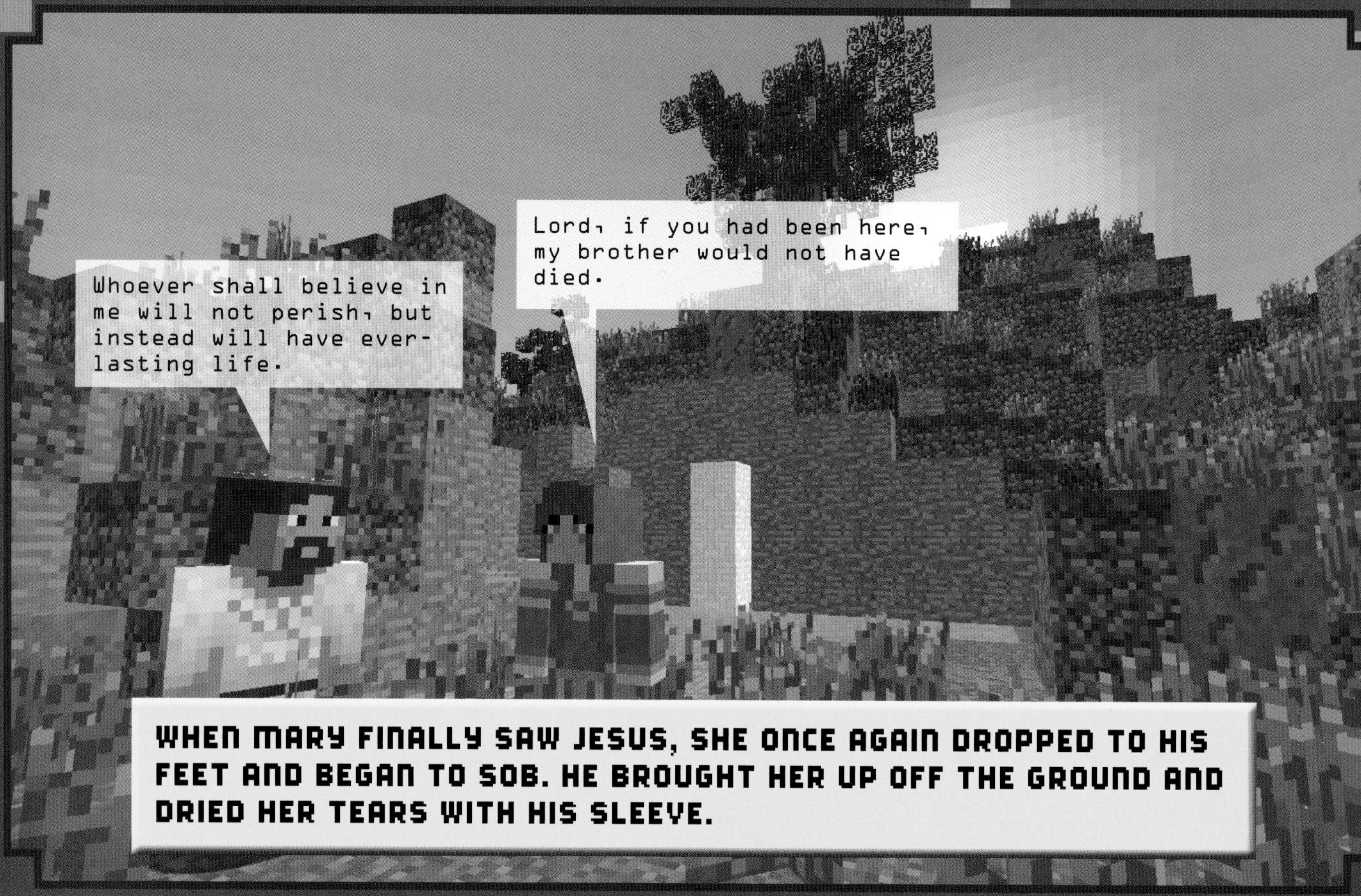
Whoever shall believe in me will not perish, but instead will have ever-lasting life.
Lord, if you had been here, my brother would not have died.
WHEN MARY FINALLY SAW JESUS, SHE ONCE AGAIN DROPPED TO HIS FEET AND BEGAN TO SOB. HE BROUGHT HER UP OFF THE GROUND AND DRIED HER TEARS WITH HIS SLEEVE.

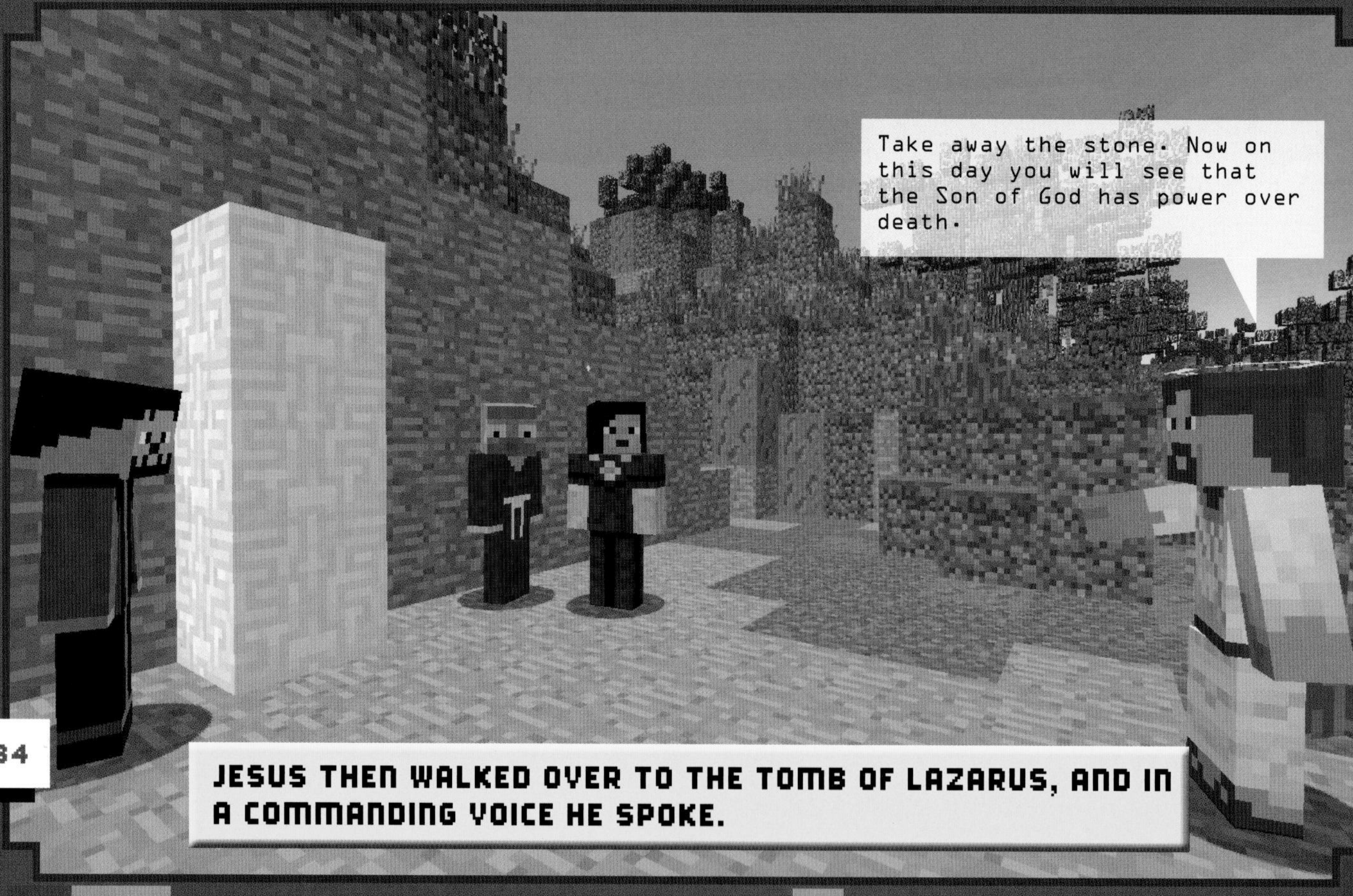
Take away the stone. Now on this day you will see that the Son of God has power over death.
JESUS THEN WALKED OVER TO THE TOMB OF LAZARUS, AND IN A COMMANDING VOICE HE SPOKE.

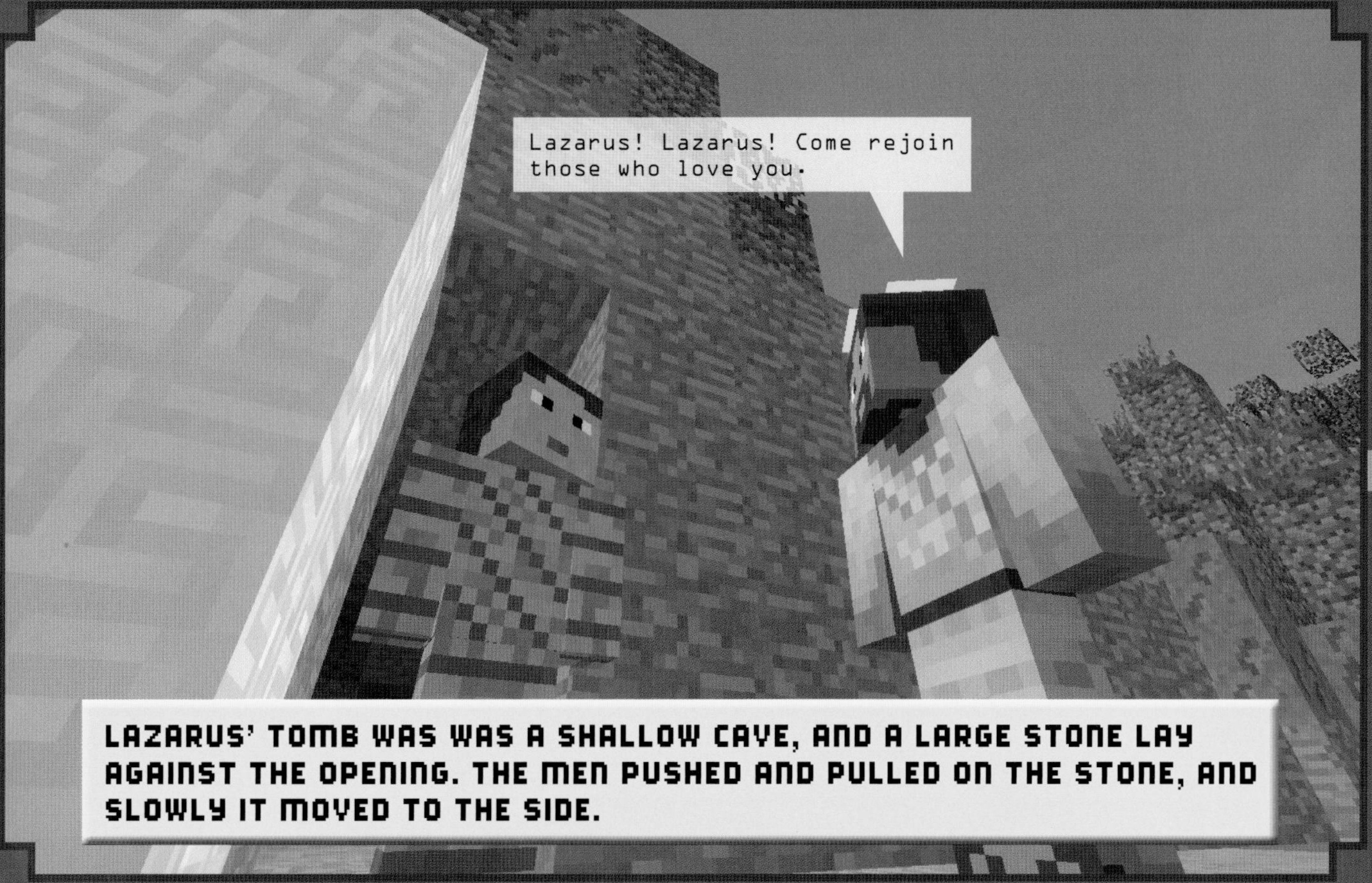
Lazarus! Lazarus! Come rejoin those who love you.
LAZARUS' TOMB WAS WAS A SHALLOW CAVE, AND A LARGE STONE LAY AGAINST THE OPENING. THE MEN PUSHED AND PULLED ON THE STONE, AND SLOWLY IT MOVED TO THE SIDE.

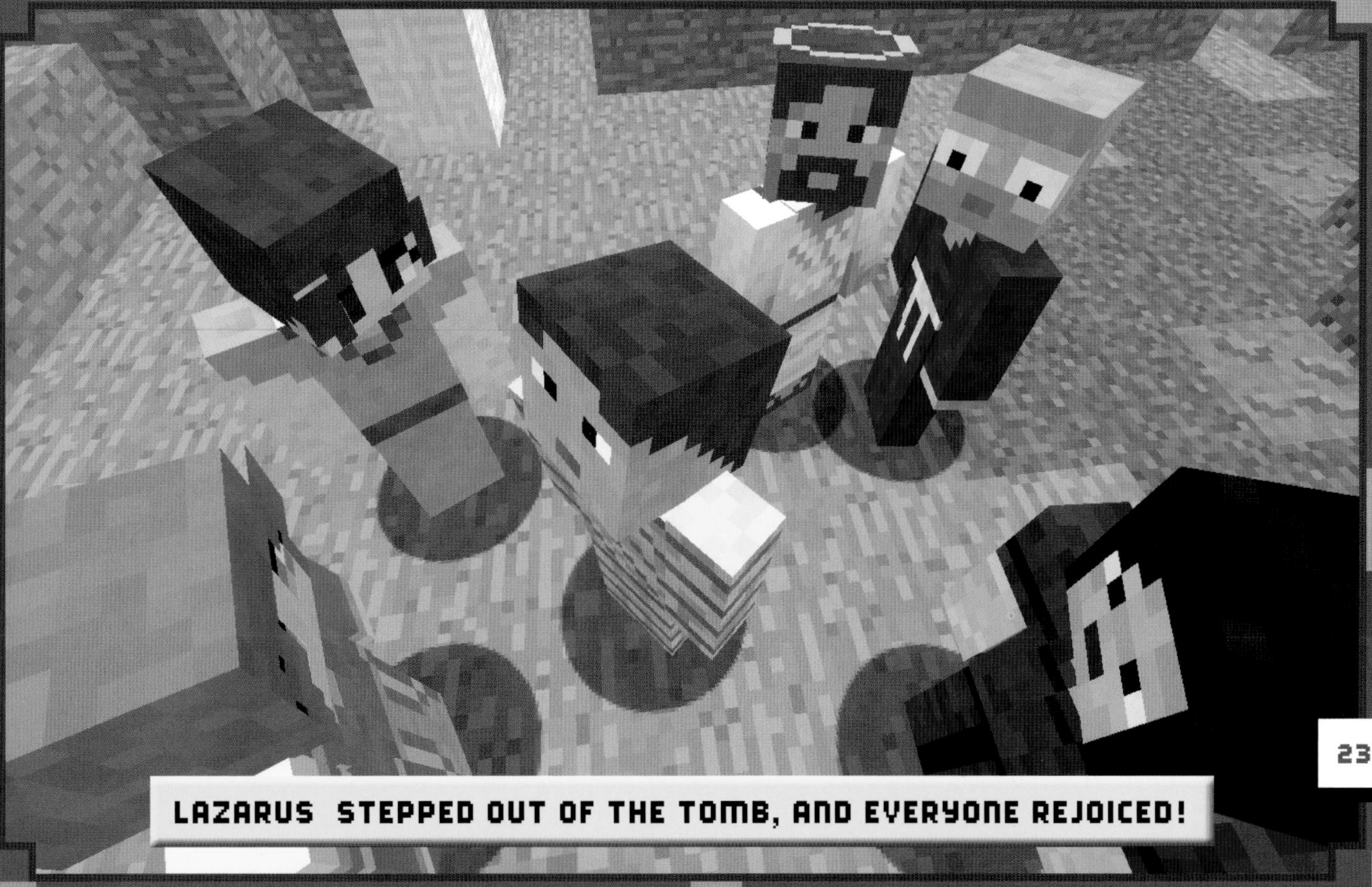
LAZARUS STEPPED OUT OF THE TOMB, AND EVERYONE REJOICED!

JESUS' ENTRY INTO JERUSALEM

On to Jerusalem!

You got it! Enough groundwork has been laid. Jesus is ready to begin the end.

The end?

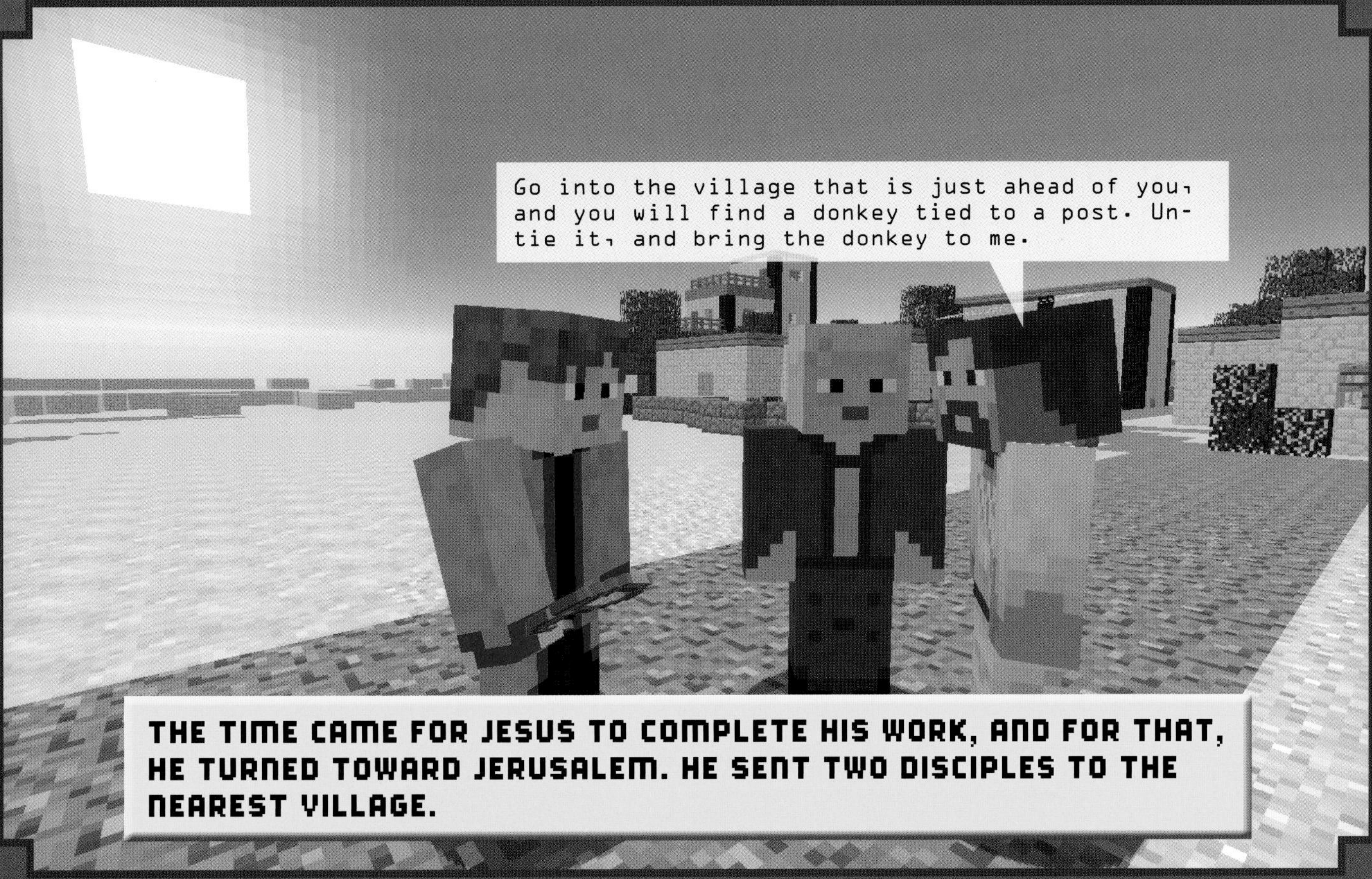
Go into the village that is just ahead of you, and you will find a donkey tied to a post. Untie it, and bring the donkey to me.
THE TIME CAME FOR JESUS TO COMPLETE HIS WORK, AND FOR THAT, HE TURNED TOWARD JERUSALEM. HE SENT TWO DISCIPLES TO THE NEAREST VILLAGE.

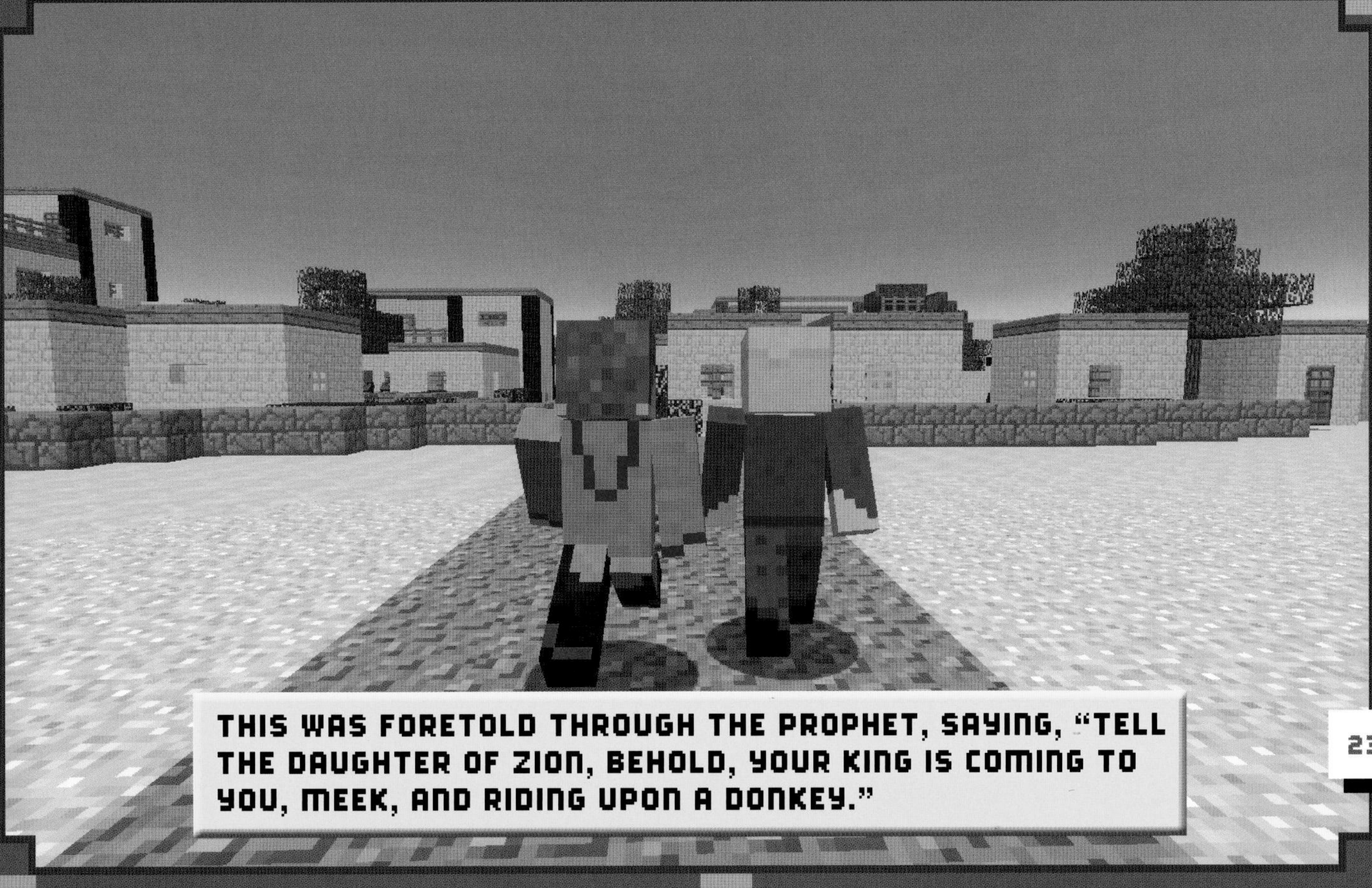
THIS WAS FORETOLD THROUGH THE PROPHET, SAYING, "TELL THE DAUGHTER OF ZION, BEHOLD, YOUR KING IS COMING TO YOU, MEEK, AND RIDING UPON A DONKEY."

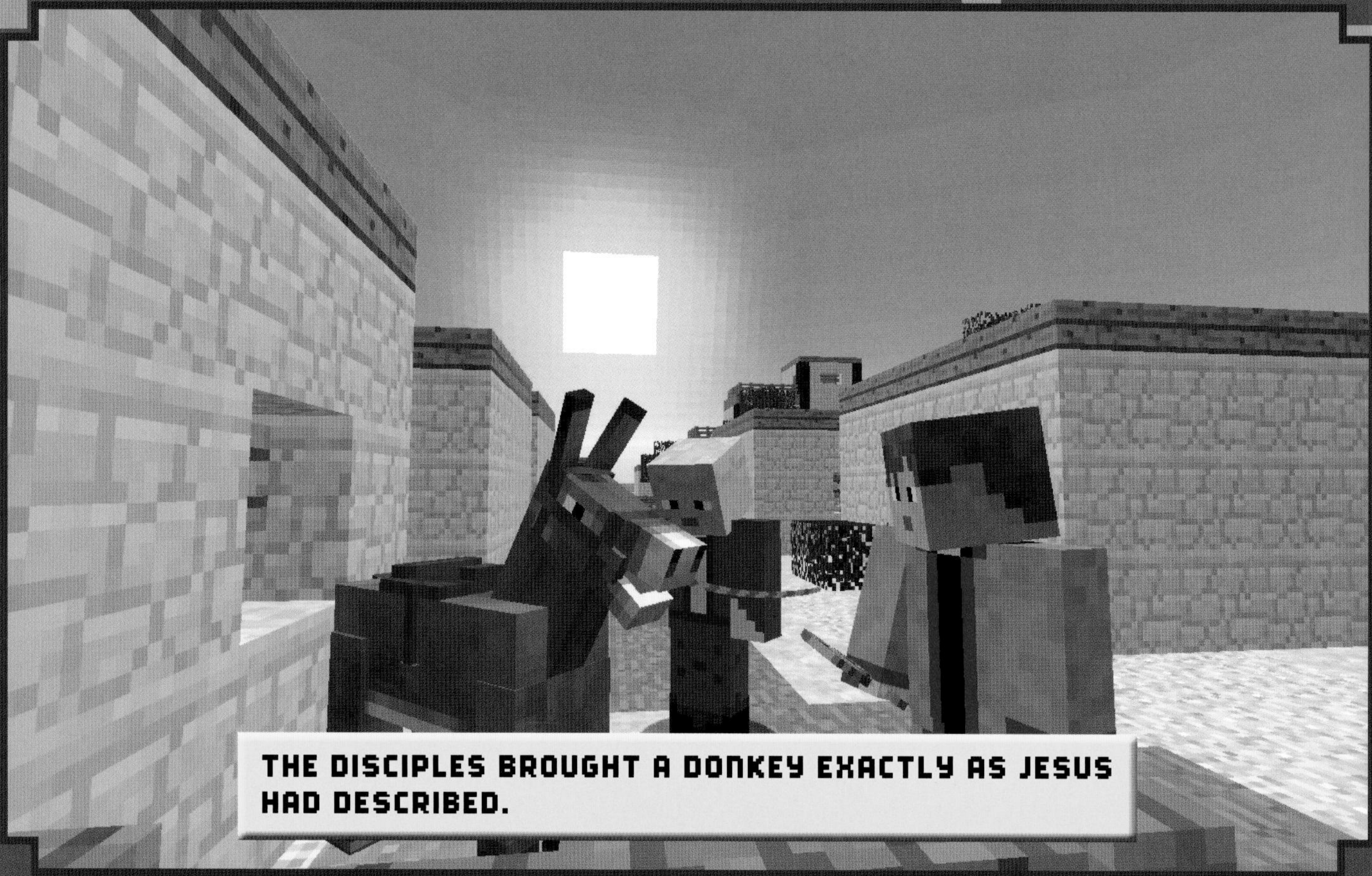
THE DISCIPLES BROUGHT A DONKEY EXACTLY AS JESUS HAD DESCRIBED.

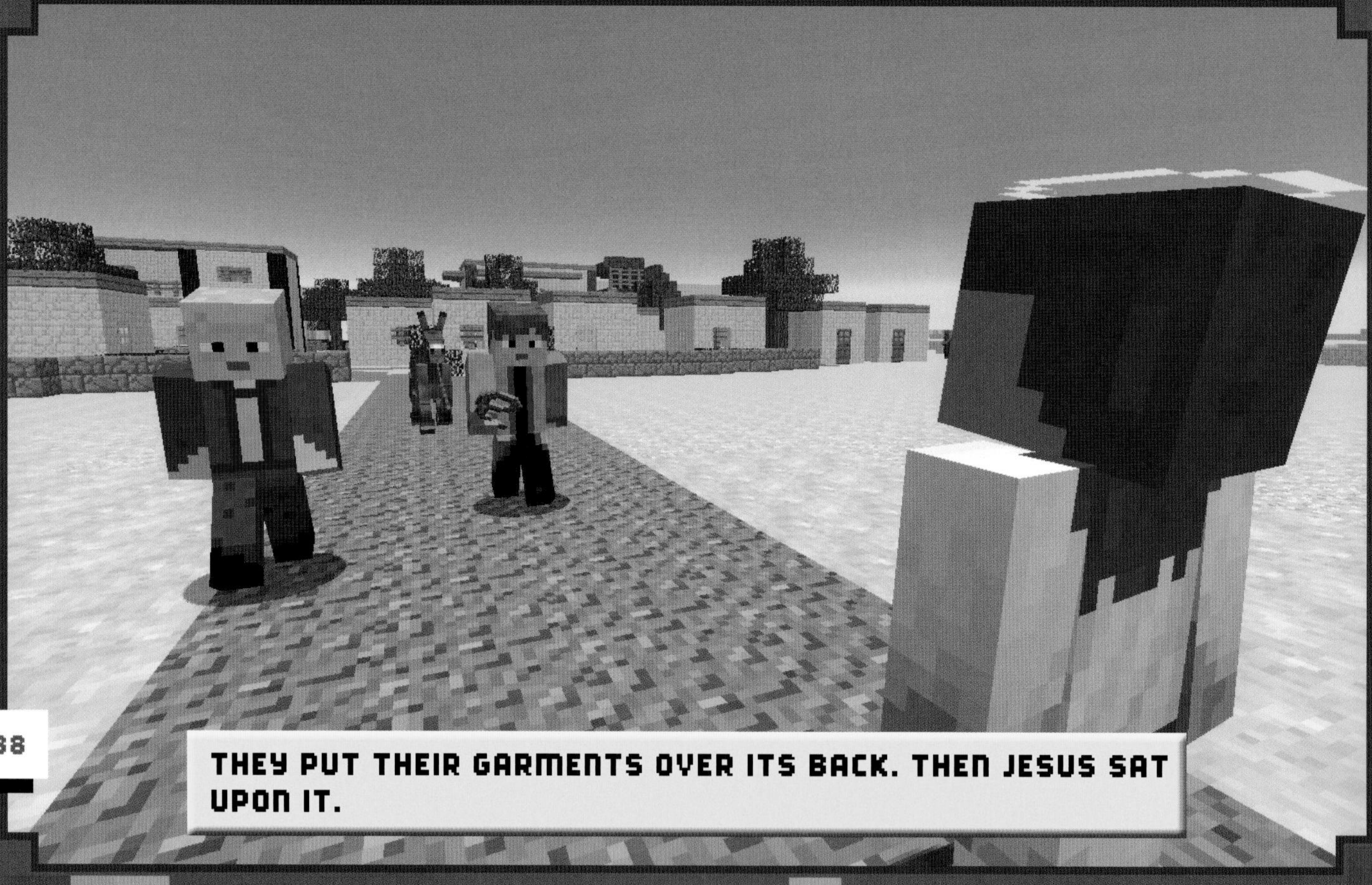
THEY PUT THEIR GARMENTS OVER ITS BACK. THEN JESUS SAT UPON IT.

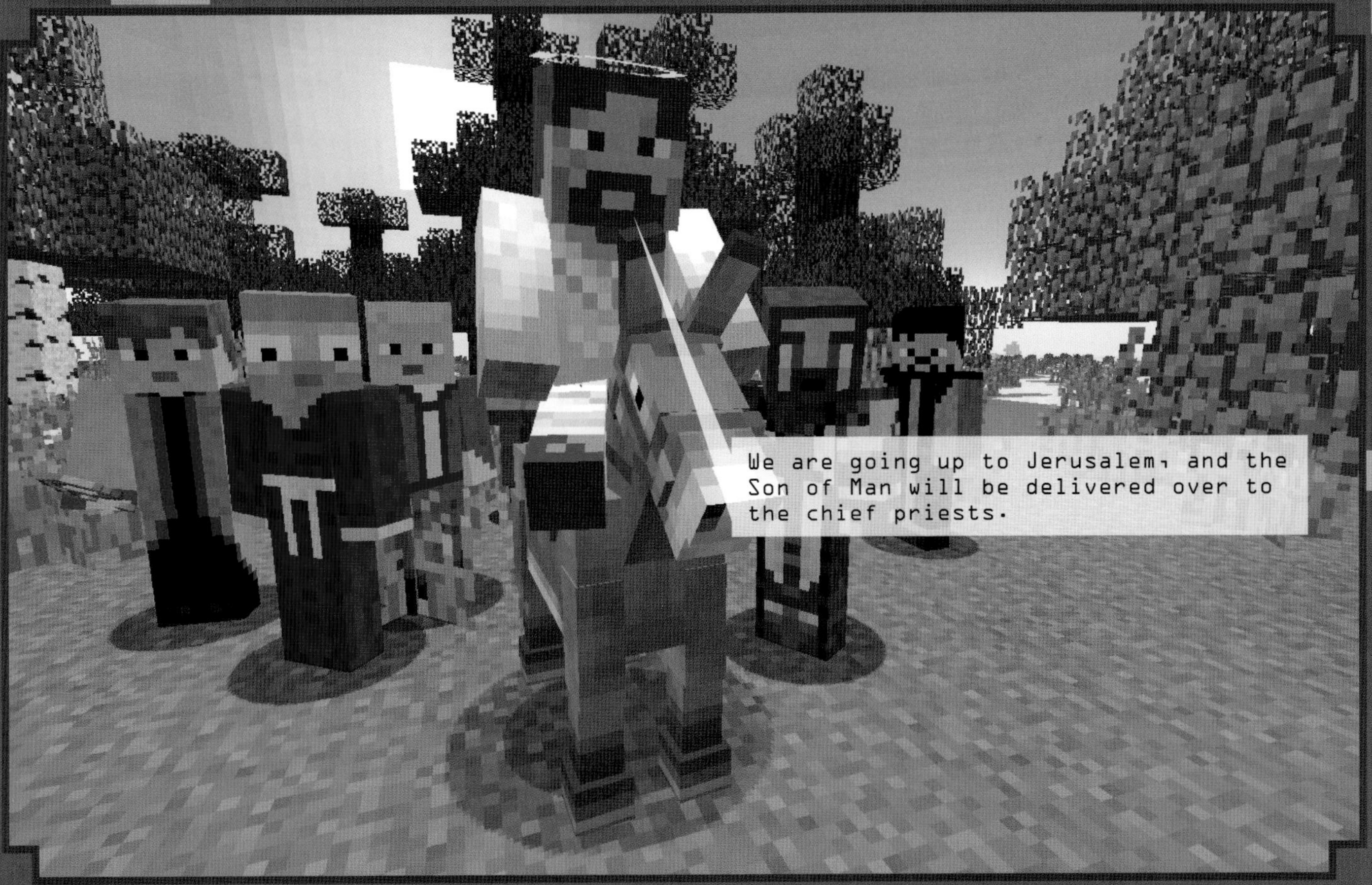
We are going up to Jerusalem, and the Son of Man will be delivered over to the chief priests.

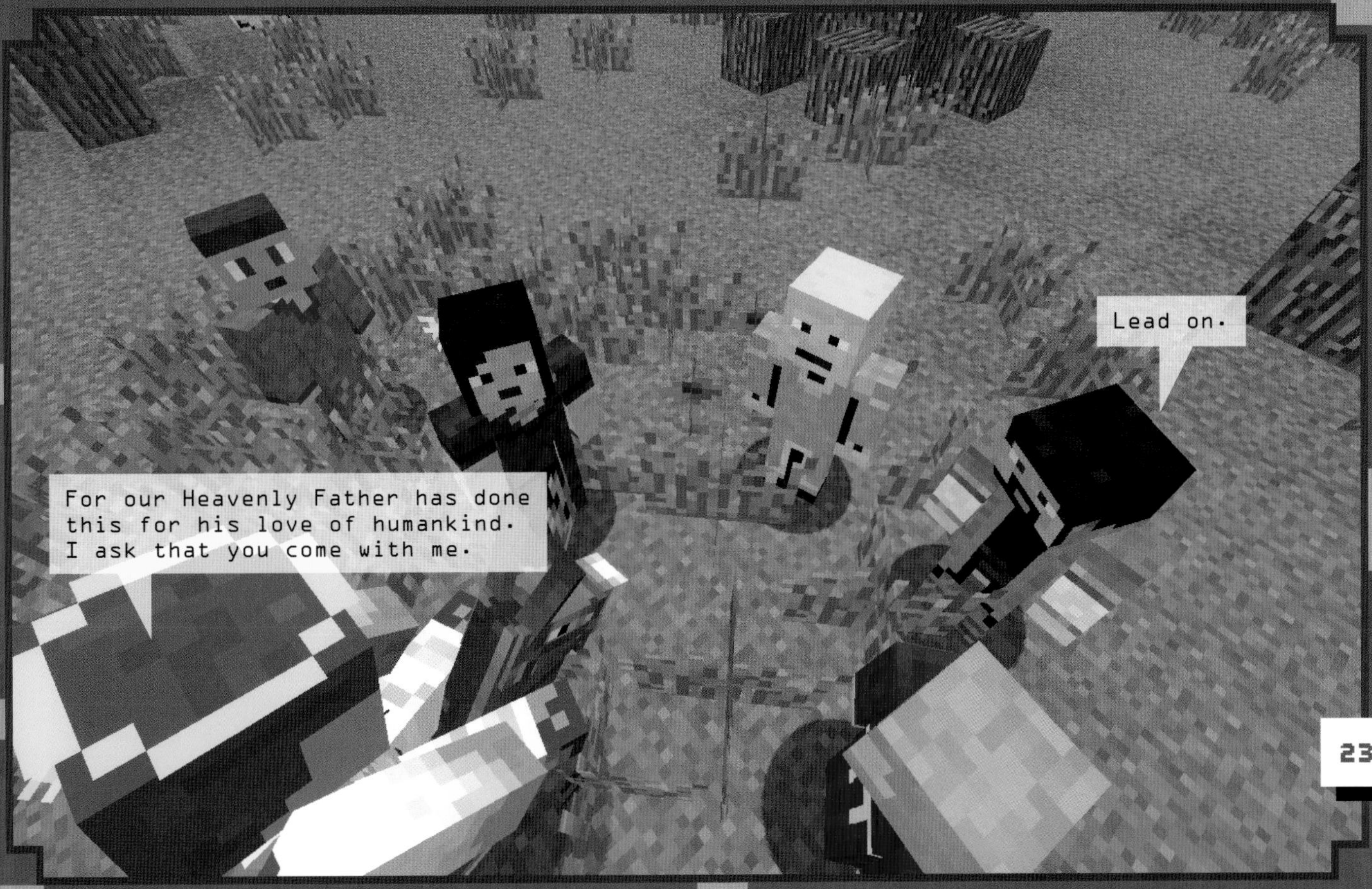
Lead on.
For our Heavenly Father has done this for his love of humankind. I ask that you come with me.

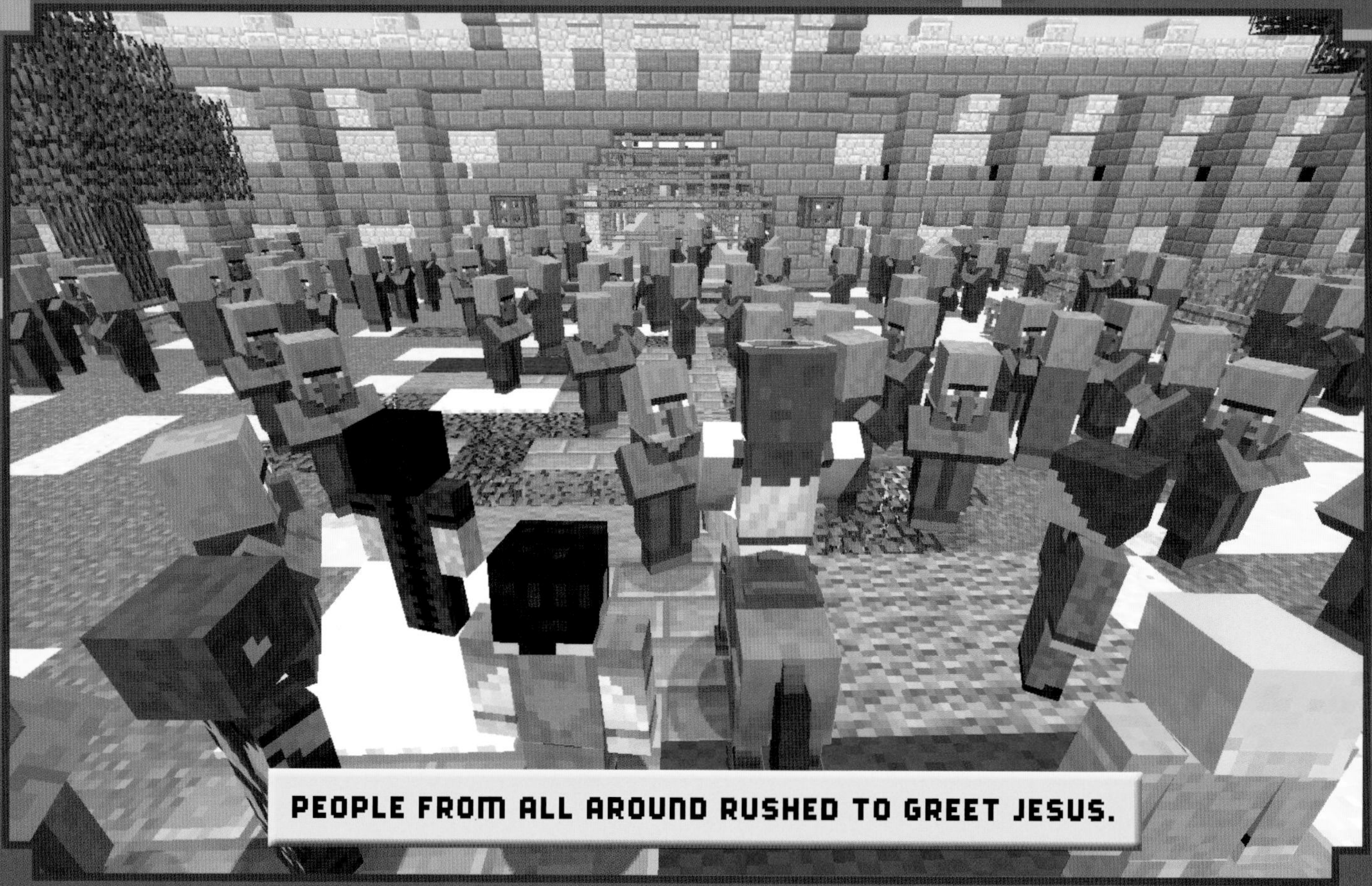
PEOPLE FROM ALL AROUND RUSHED TO GREET JESUS.

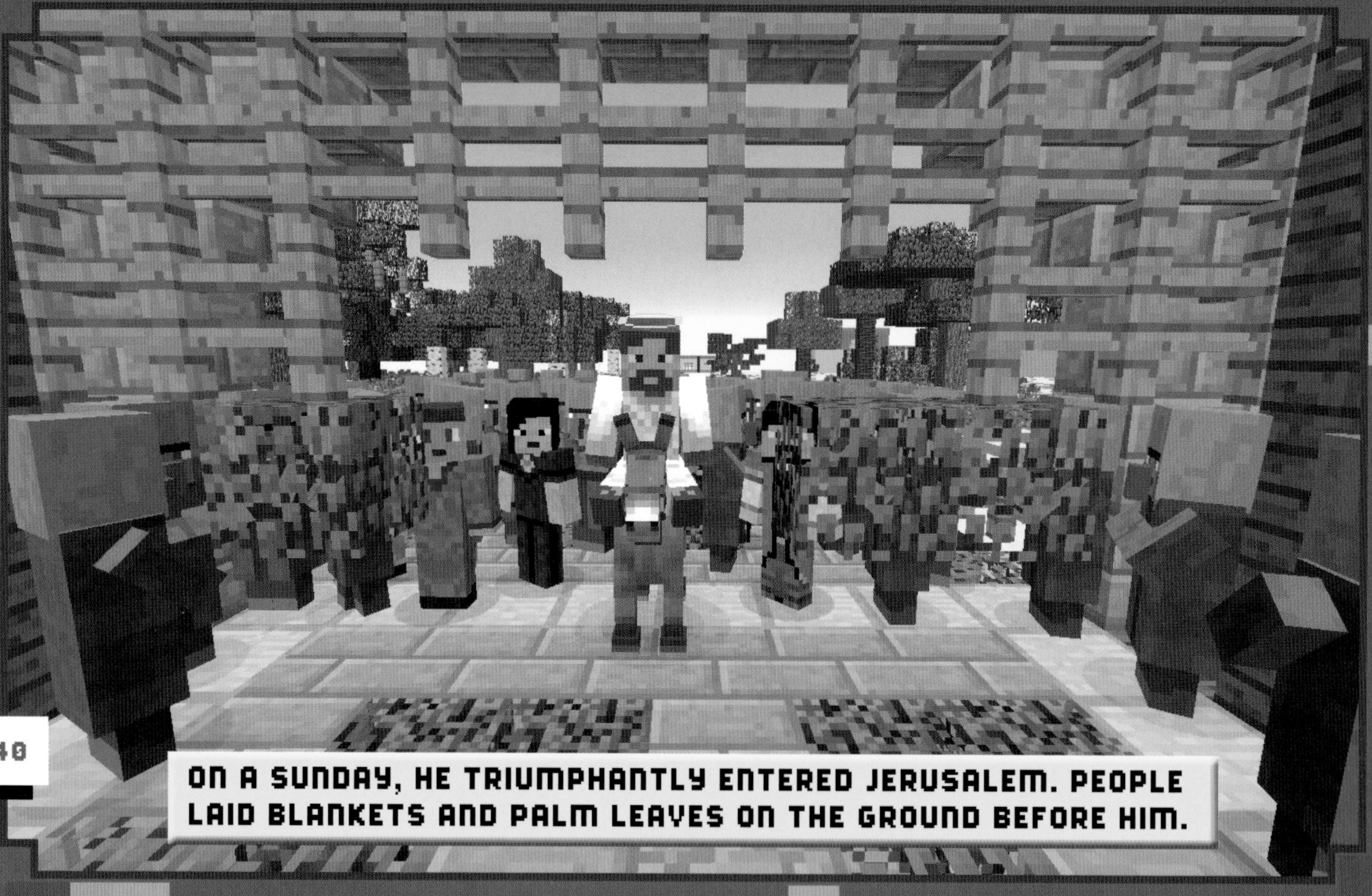
ON A SUNDAY, HE TRIUMPHANTLY ENTERED JERUSALEM. PEOPLE LAID BLANKETS AND PALM LEAVES ON THE GROUND BEFORE HIM.

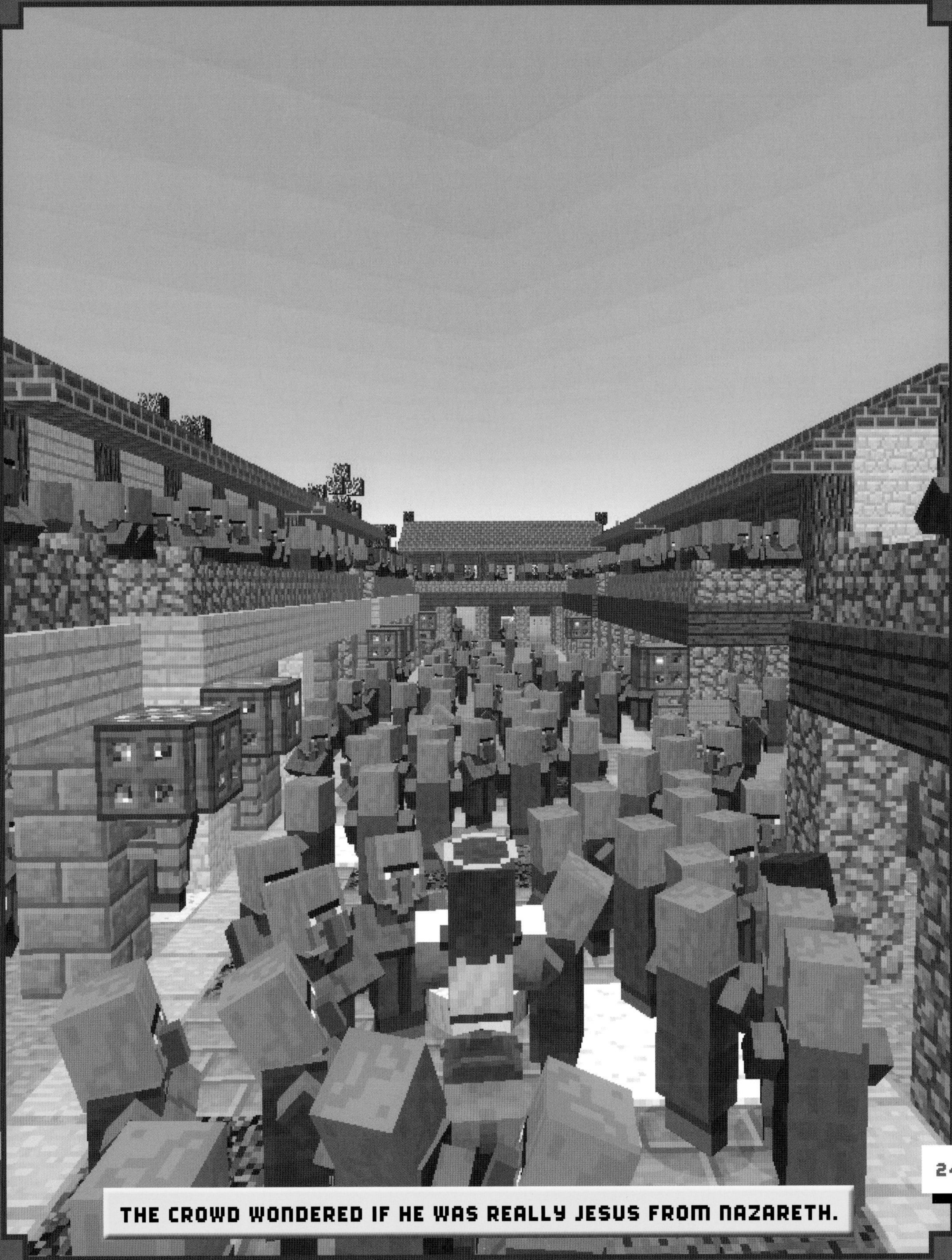

THE CROWD WONDERED IF HE WAS REALLY JESUS FROM NAZARETH.

JESUS CHALLENGES THE AUTHORITIES

Now my Son will challenge the authorities that have corrupted my house and my kingdom.

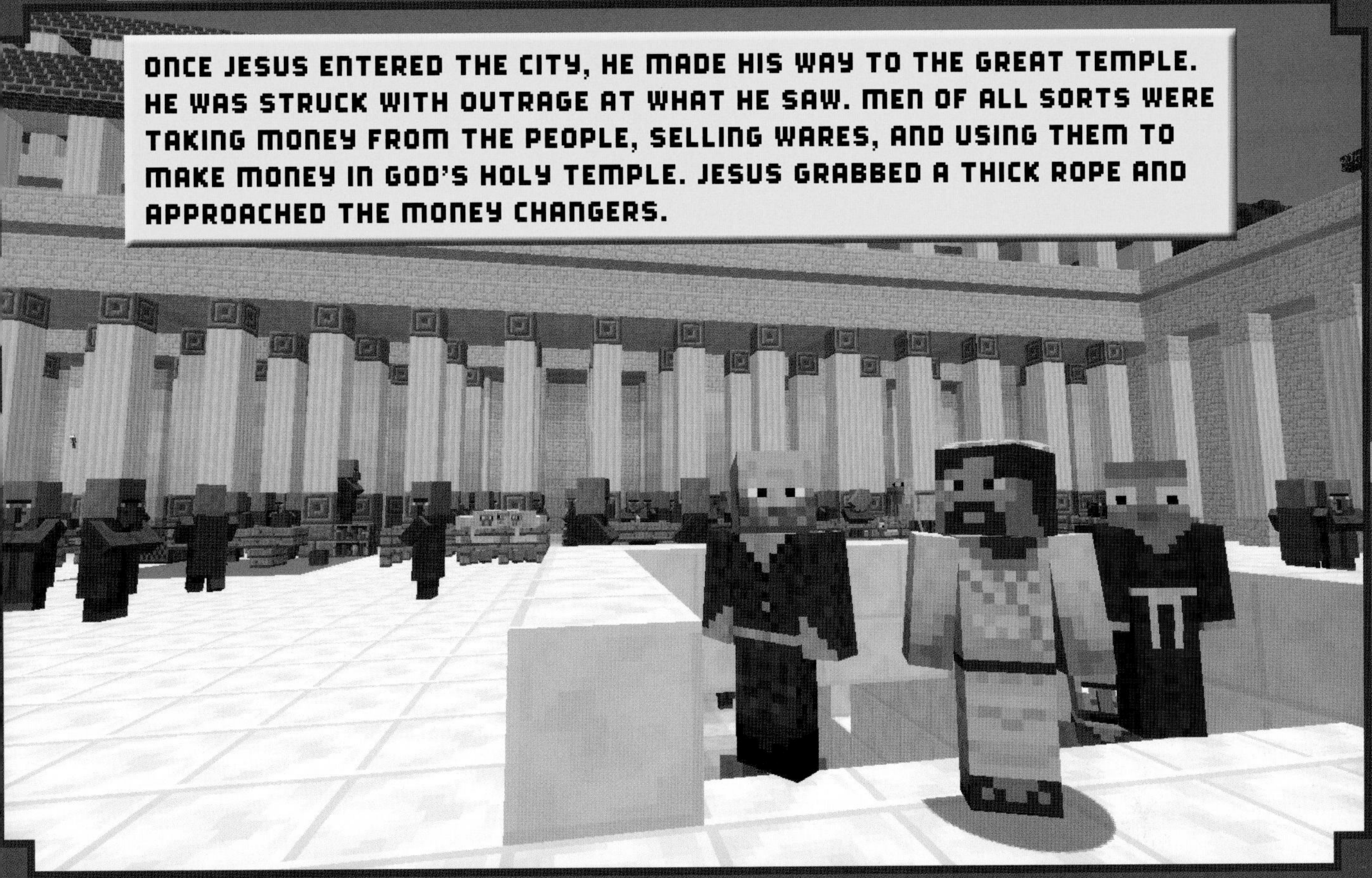
ONCE JESUS ENTERED THE CITY, HE MADE HIS WAY TO THE GREAT TEMPLE. HE WAS STRUCK WITH OUTRAGE AT WHAT HE SAW. MEN OF ALL SORTS WERE TAKING MONEY FROM THE PEOPLE, SELLING WARES, AND USING THEM TO MAKE MONEY IN GOD'S HOLY TEMPLE. JESUS GRABBED A THICK ROPE AND APPROACHED THE MONEY CHANGERS.

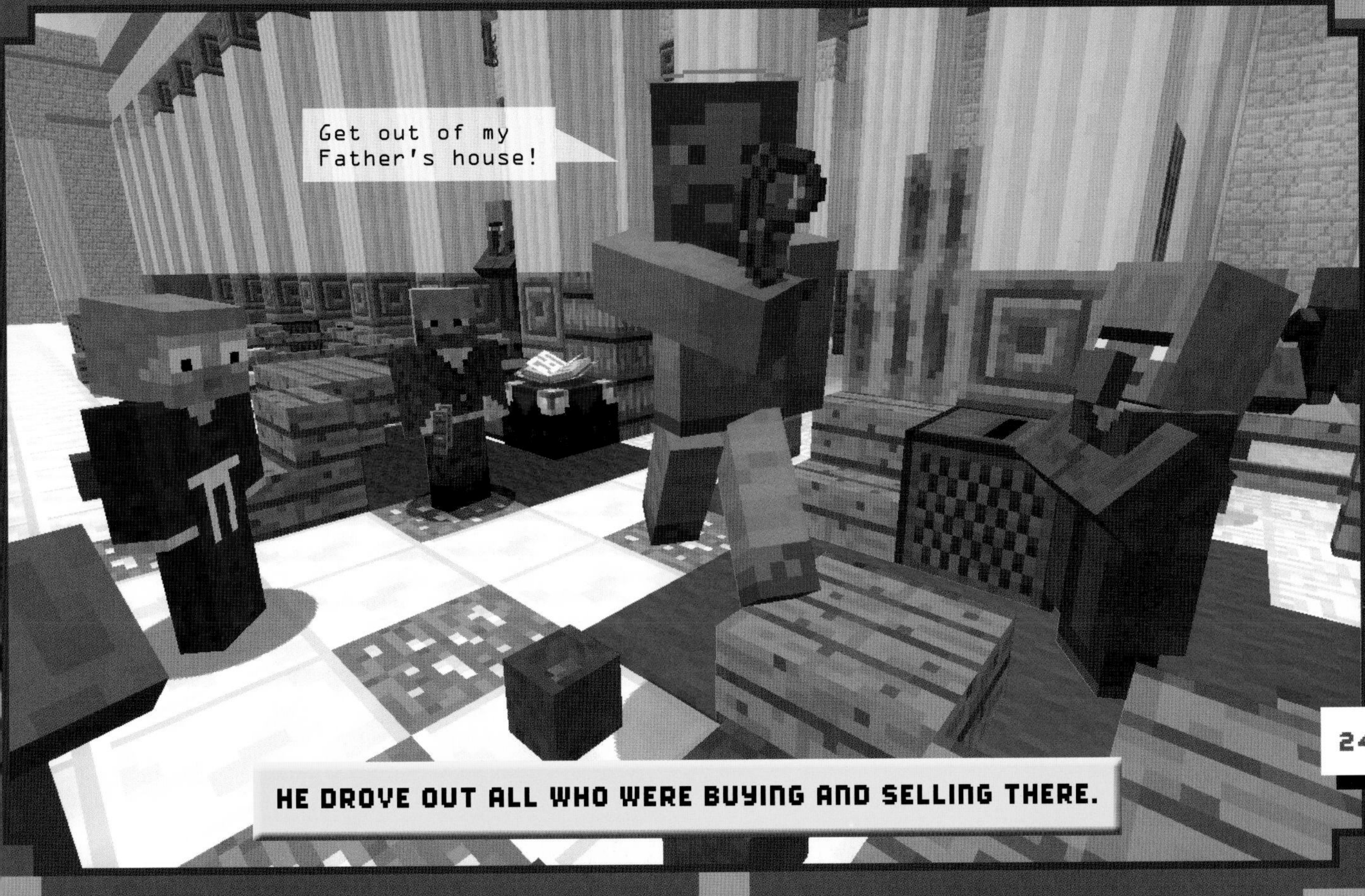
Get out of my Father's house!
HE DROVE OUT ALL WHO WERE BUYING AND SELLING THERE.

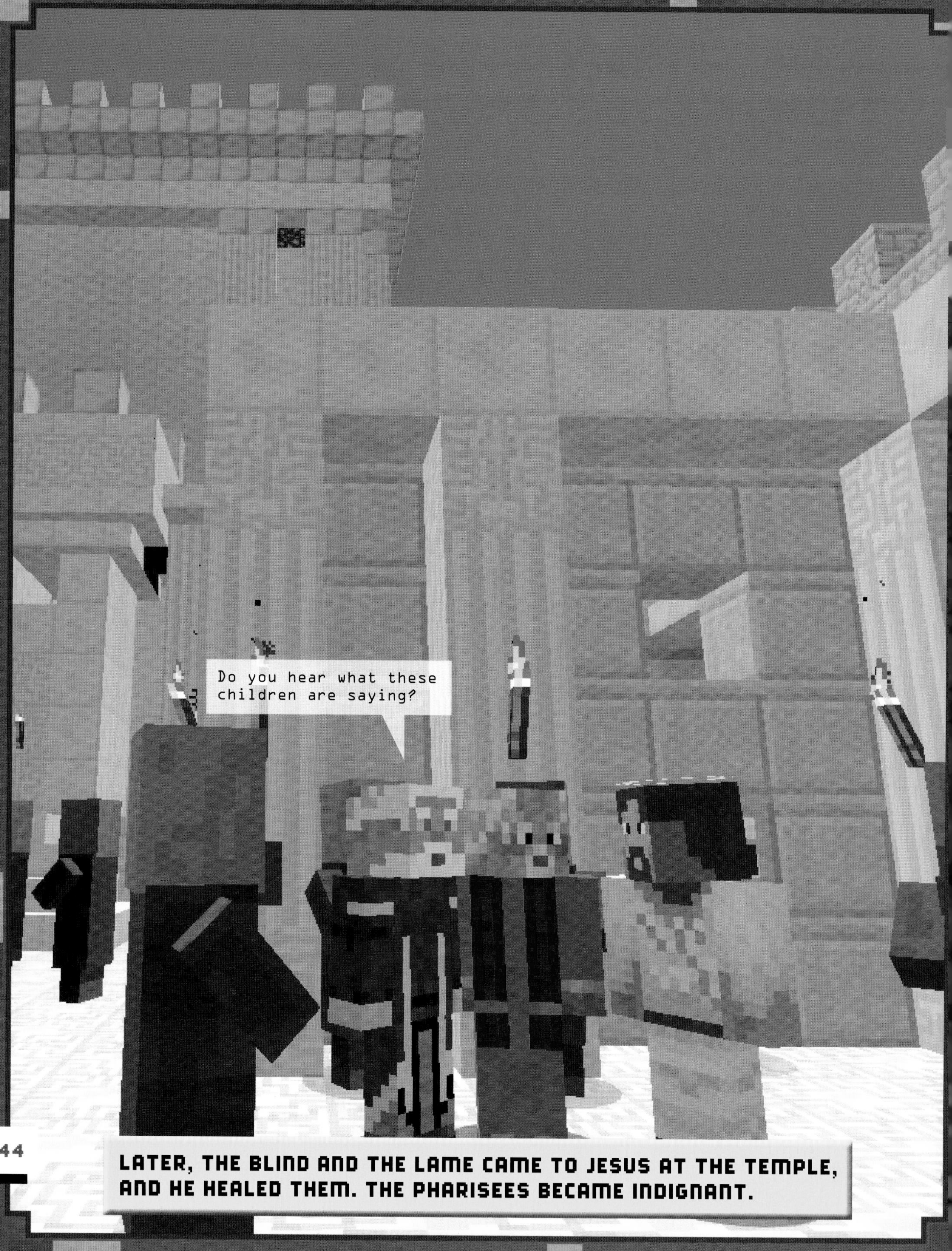
Do you hear what these children are saying?
LATER, THE BLIND AND THE LAME CAME TO JESUS AT THE TEMPLE, AND HE HEALED THEM. THE PHARISEES BECAME INDIGNANT.

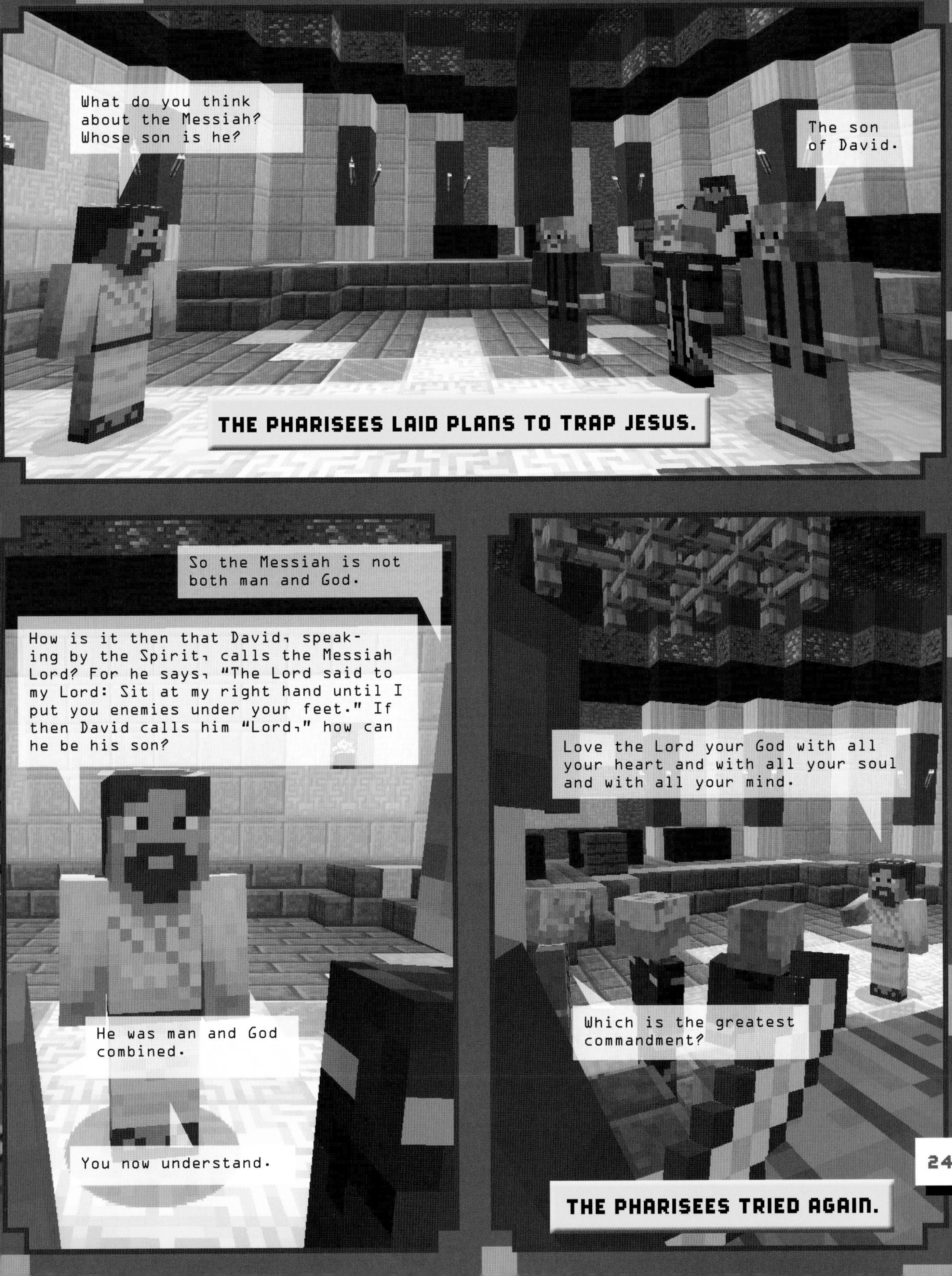
What do you think about the Messiah? Whose son is he?
The son of David.
THE PHARISEES LAID PLANS TO TRAP JESUS.
So the Messiah is not both man and God.
How is it then that David, speaking by the Spirit, calls the Messiah Lord? For he says, "The Lord said to my Lord: Sit at my right hand until I put you enemies under your feet." If then David calls him "Lord," how can he be his son?
He was man and God combined.
You now understand.
Love the Lord your God with all your heart and with all your soul and with all your mind.
Which is the greatest commandment?
THE PHARISEES TRIED AGAIN.

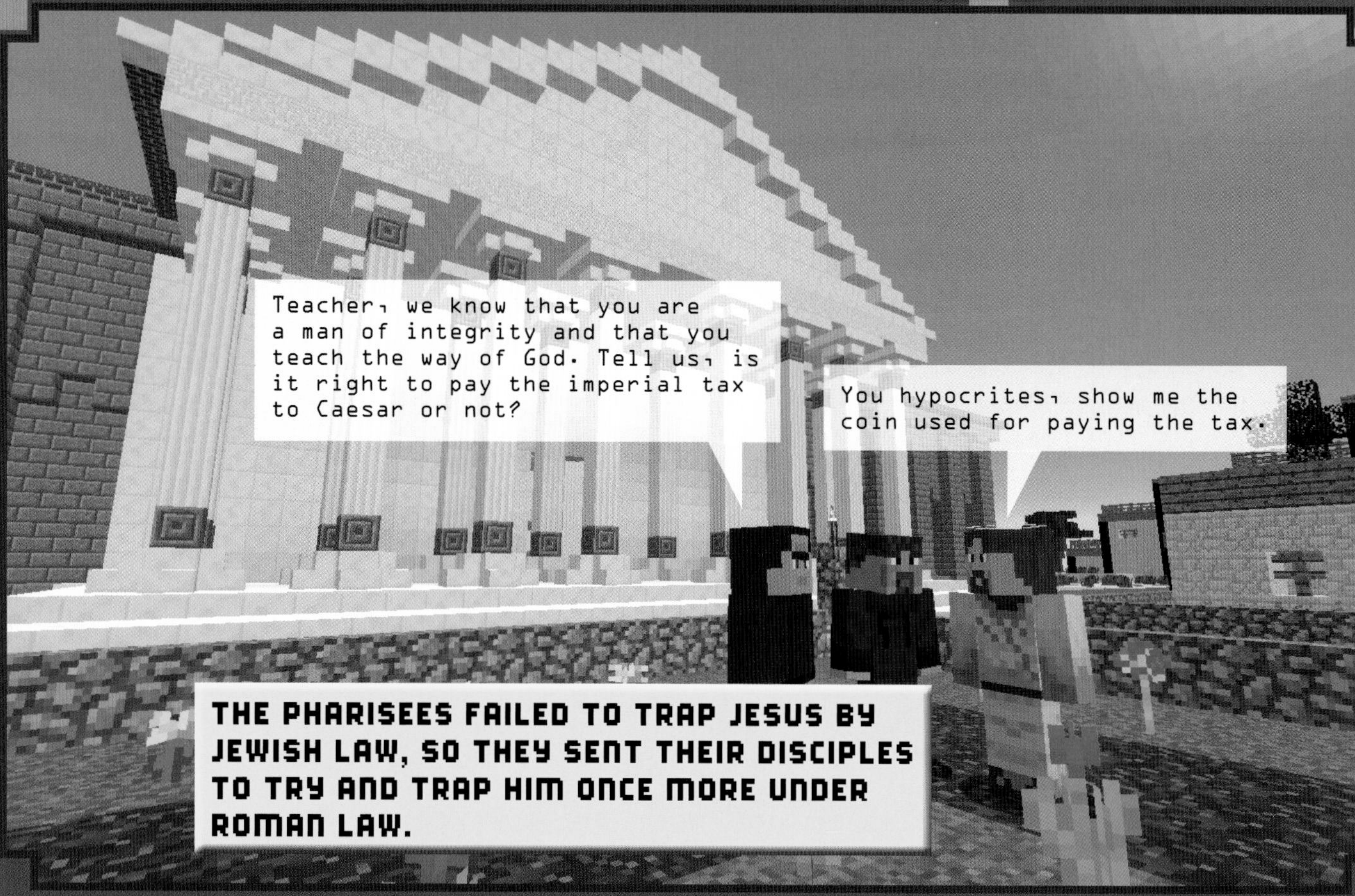
Teacher, we know that you are a man of integrity and that you teach the way of God. Tell us, is it right to pay the imperial tax to Caesar or not?
You hypocrites, show me the coin used for paying the tax.
THE PHARISEES FAILED TO TRAP JESUS BY JEWISH LAW, SO THEY SENT THEIR DISCIPLES TO TRY AND TRAP HIM ONCE MORE UNDER ROMAN LAW.

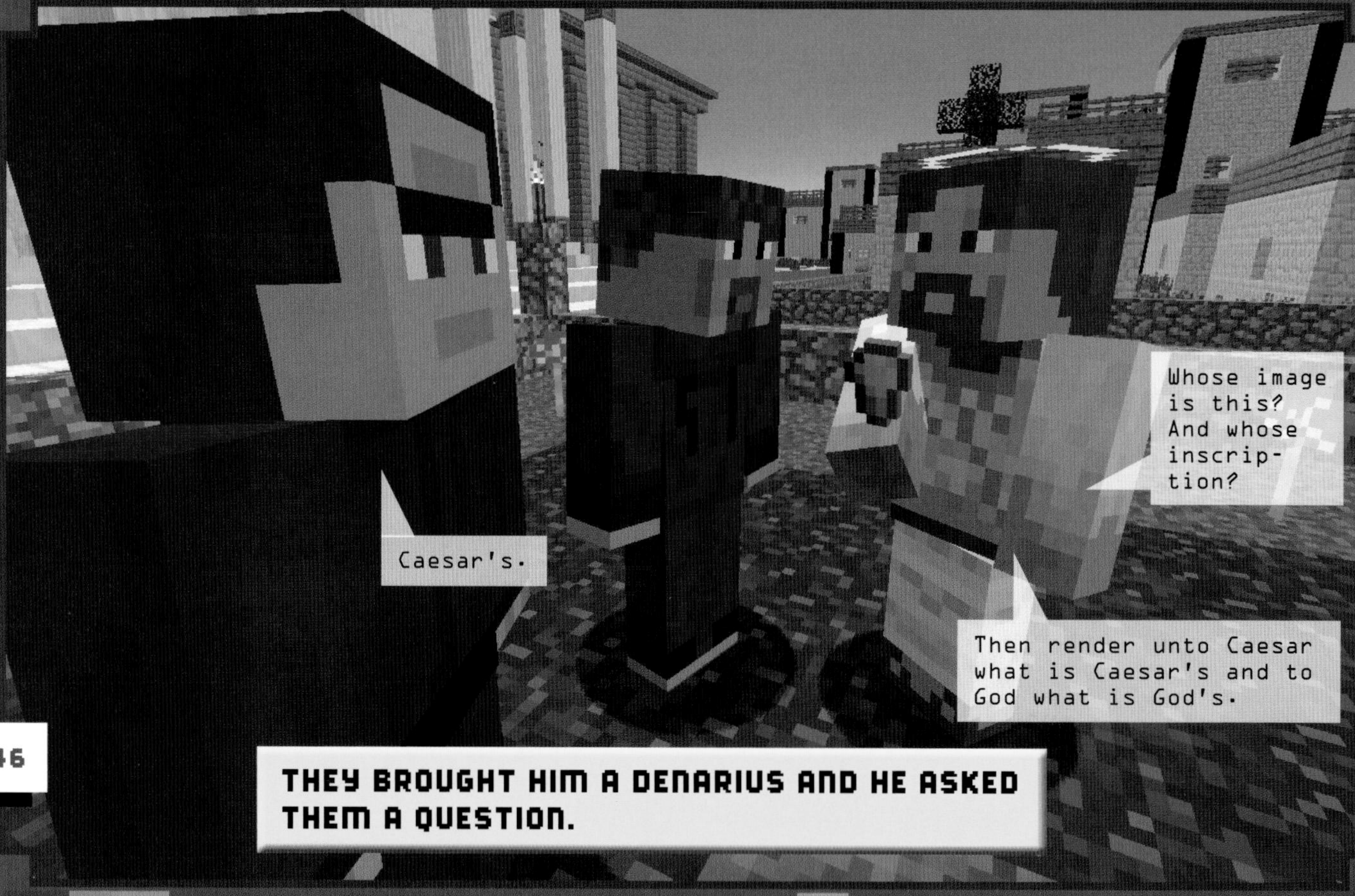
Whose image is this? And whose inscrip-tion?
Caesar's.
Then render unto Caesar what is Caesar's and to God what is God's.
THEY BROUGHT HIM A DENARIUS AND HE ASKED THEM A QUESTION.

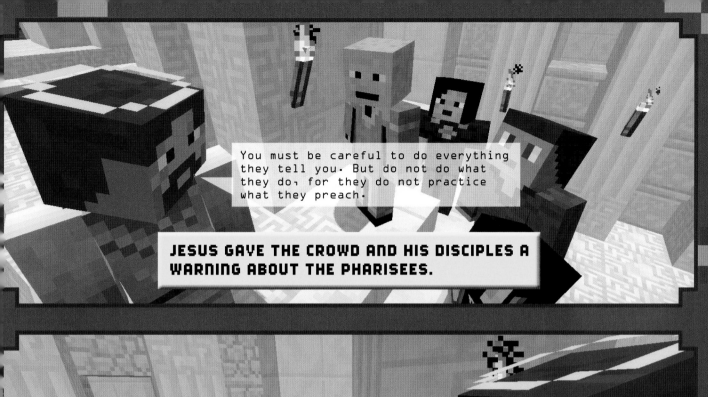

You must be careful to do everything they tell you. But do not do what they do, for they do not practice what they preach.

JESUS GAVE THE CROWD AND HIS DISCIPLES A WARNING ABOUT THE PHARISEES.

Everything they do is done for people to see: they love the place of honor at banquets and the most important seats in the synagogues; they love to be called Rabbi by others.

You are not to be called Rabbi, for you have one Teacher. And do not call anyone on Earth father, for you have one Father, and he is in heaven. For those who exalt themselves will be humbled, and those who humble themselves will be exalted.

JESUS' FINAL DAYS

The final moment has arrived. Salvation has come and my plan will be fulfilled.

It's not going to be easy, is it?

Yes, his greatest challenges are ahead of him, and his divine strength will be needed.

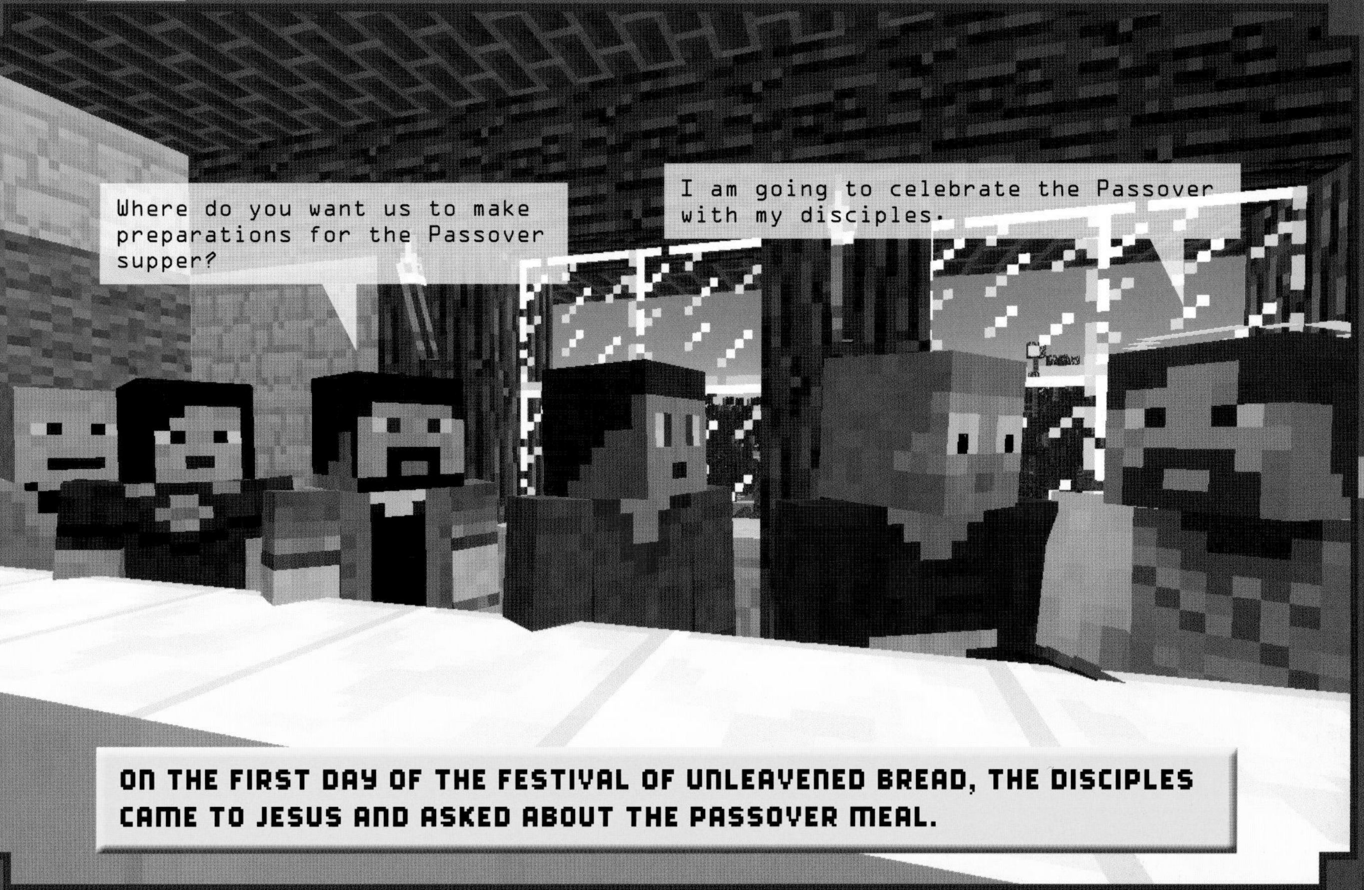
Where do you want us to make preparations for the Passover supper?
I am going to celebrate the Passover with my disciples.
ON THE FIRST DAY OF THE FESTIVAL OF UNLEAVENED BREAD, THE DISCIPLES CAME TO JESUS AND ASKED ABOUT THE PASSOVER MEAL.

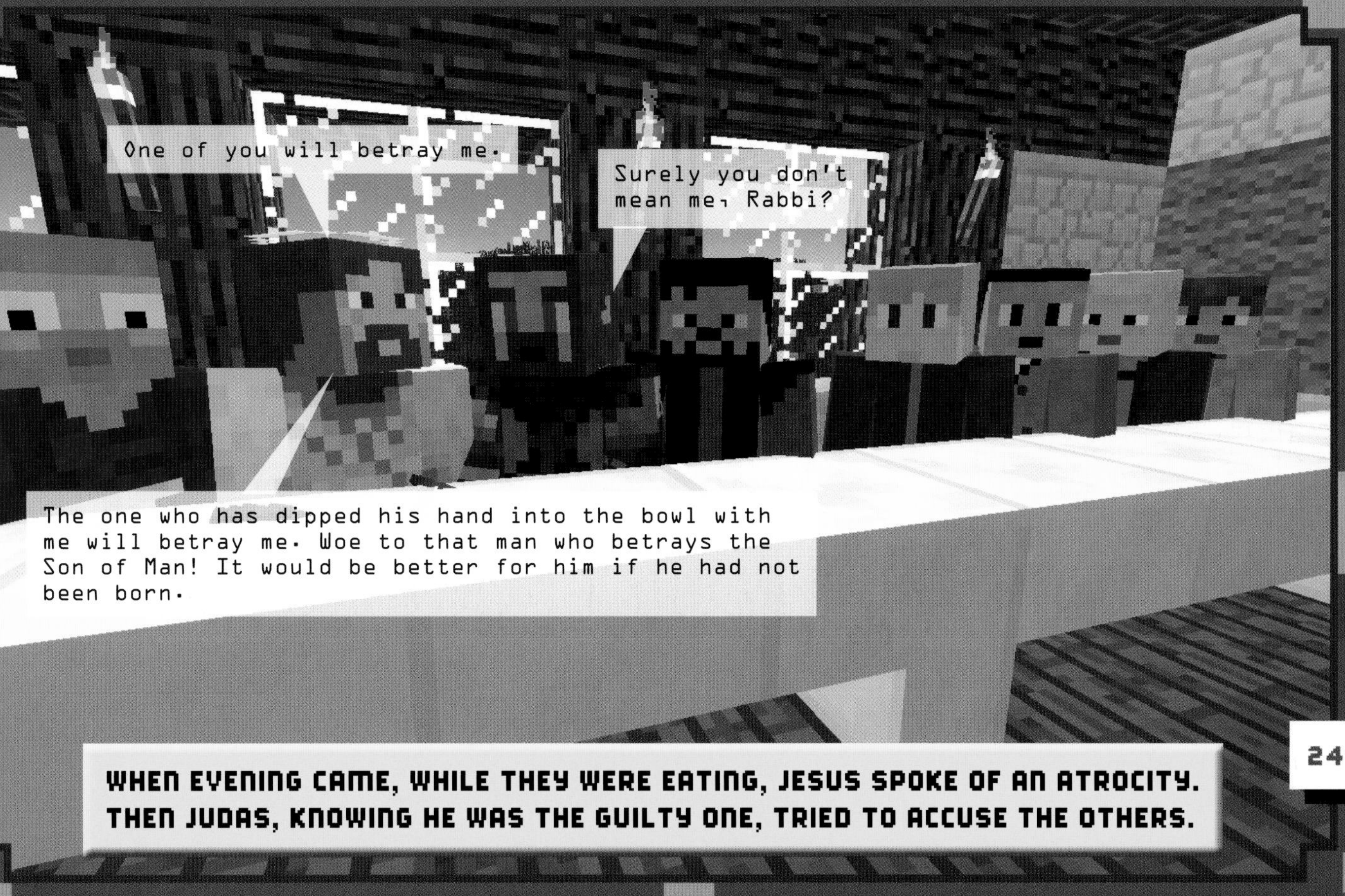
One of you will betray me.
Surely you don't mean me, Rabbi?
The one who has dipped his hand into the bowl with me will betray me. Woe to that man who betrays the Son of Man! It would be better for him if he had not been born.
WHEN EVENING CAME, WHILE THEY WERE EATING, JESUS SPOKE OF AN ATROCITY. THEN JUDAS, KNOWING HE WAS THE GUILTY ONE, TRIED TO ACCUSE THE OTHERS.

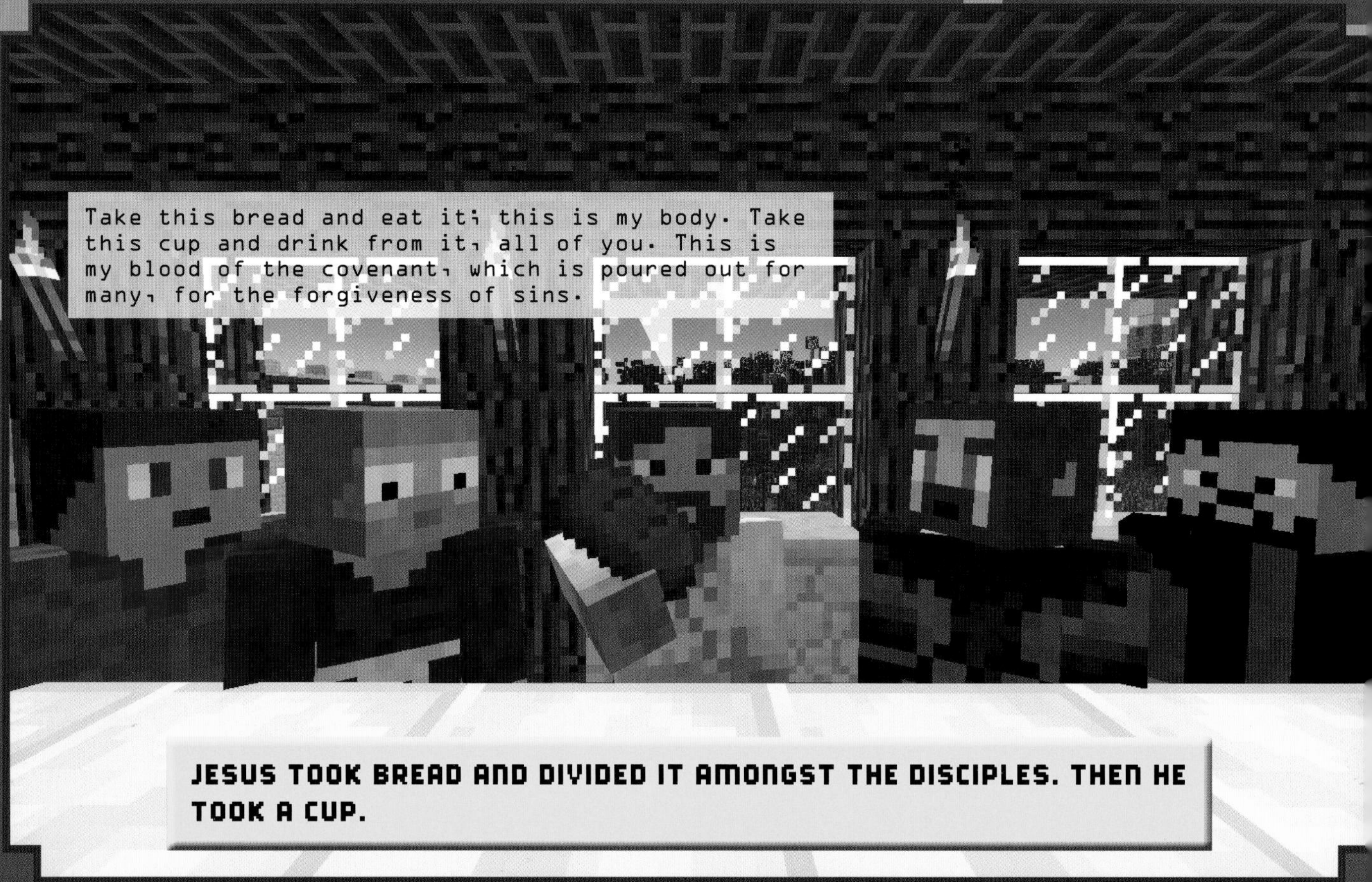
Take this bread and eat it; this is my body. Take this cup and drink from it, all of you. This is my blood of the covenant, which is poured out for many, for the forgiveness of sins.
JESUS TOOK BREAD AND DIVIDED IT AMONGST THE DISCIPLES. THEN HE TOOK A CUP.

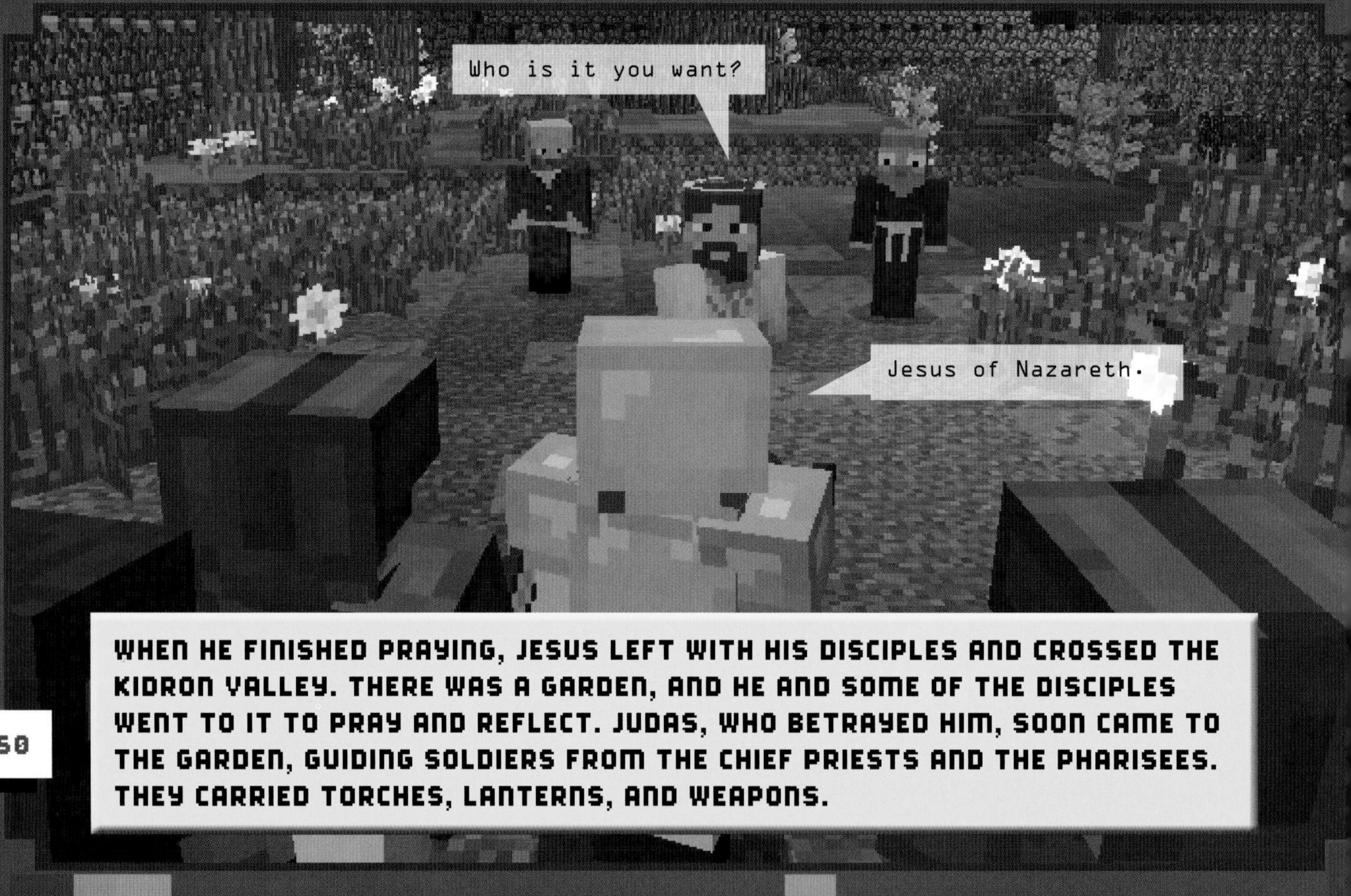
Who is it you want?
Jesus of Nazareth.
WHEN HE FINISHED PRAYING, JESUS LEFT WITH HIS DISCIPLES AND CROSSED THE KIDRON VALLEY. THERE WAS A GARDEN, AND HE AND SOME OF THE DISCIPLES WENT TO IT TO PRAY AND REFLECT. JUDAS, WHO BETRAYED HIM, SOON CAME TO THE GARDEN, GUIDING SOLDIERS FROM THE CHIEF PRIESTS AND THE PHARISEES. THEY CARRIED TORCHES, LANTERNS, AND WEAPONS.

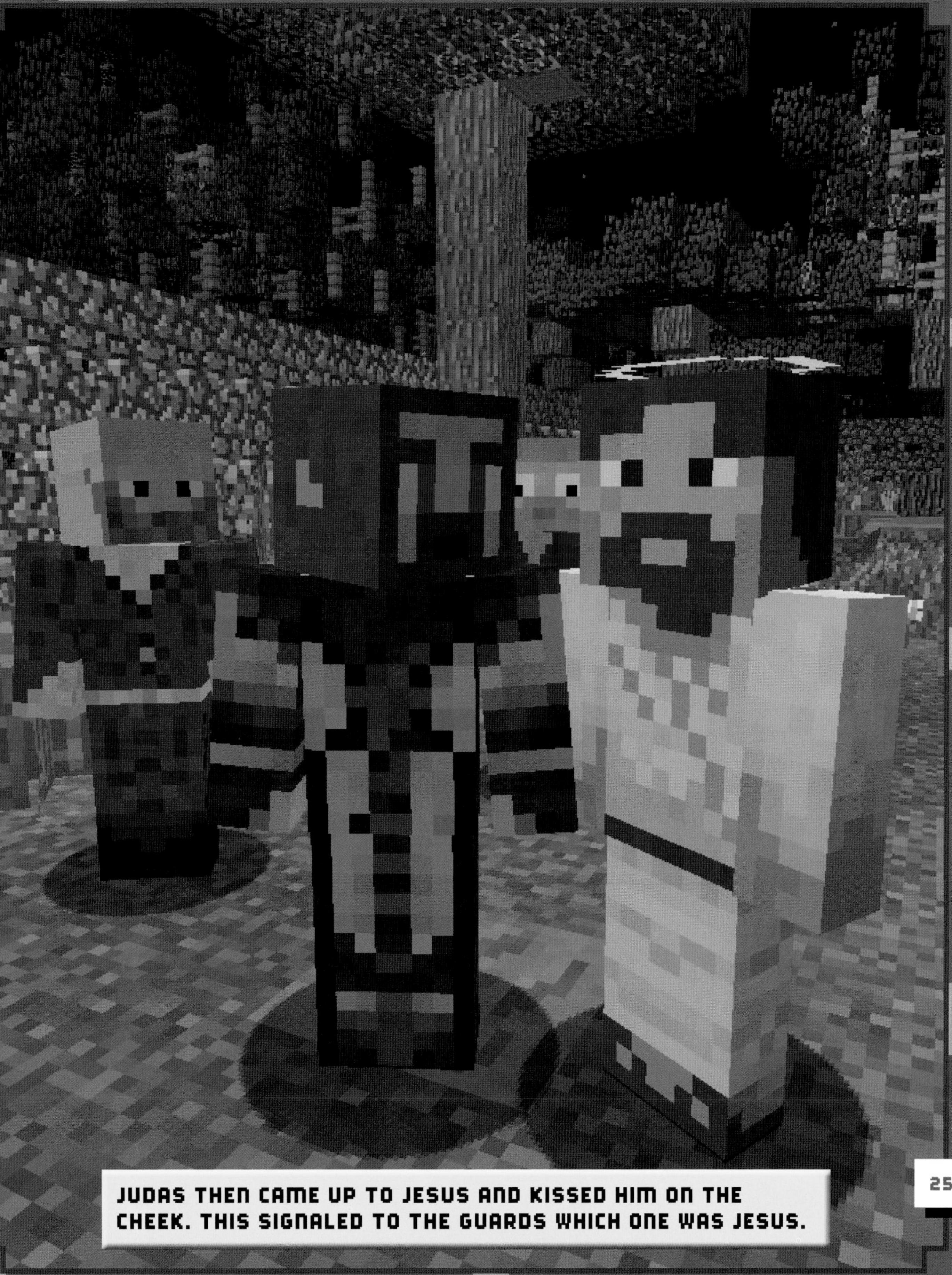

JUDAS THEN CAME UP TO JESUS AND KISSED HIM ON THE CHEEK. THIS SIGNALED TO THE GUARDS WHICH ONE WAS JESUS.

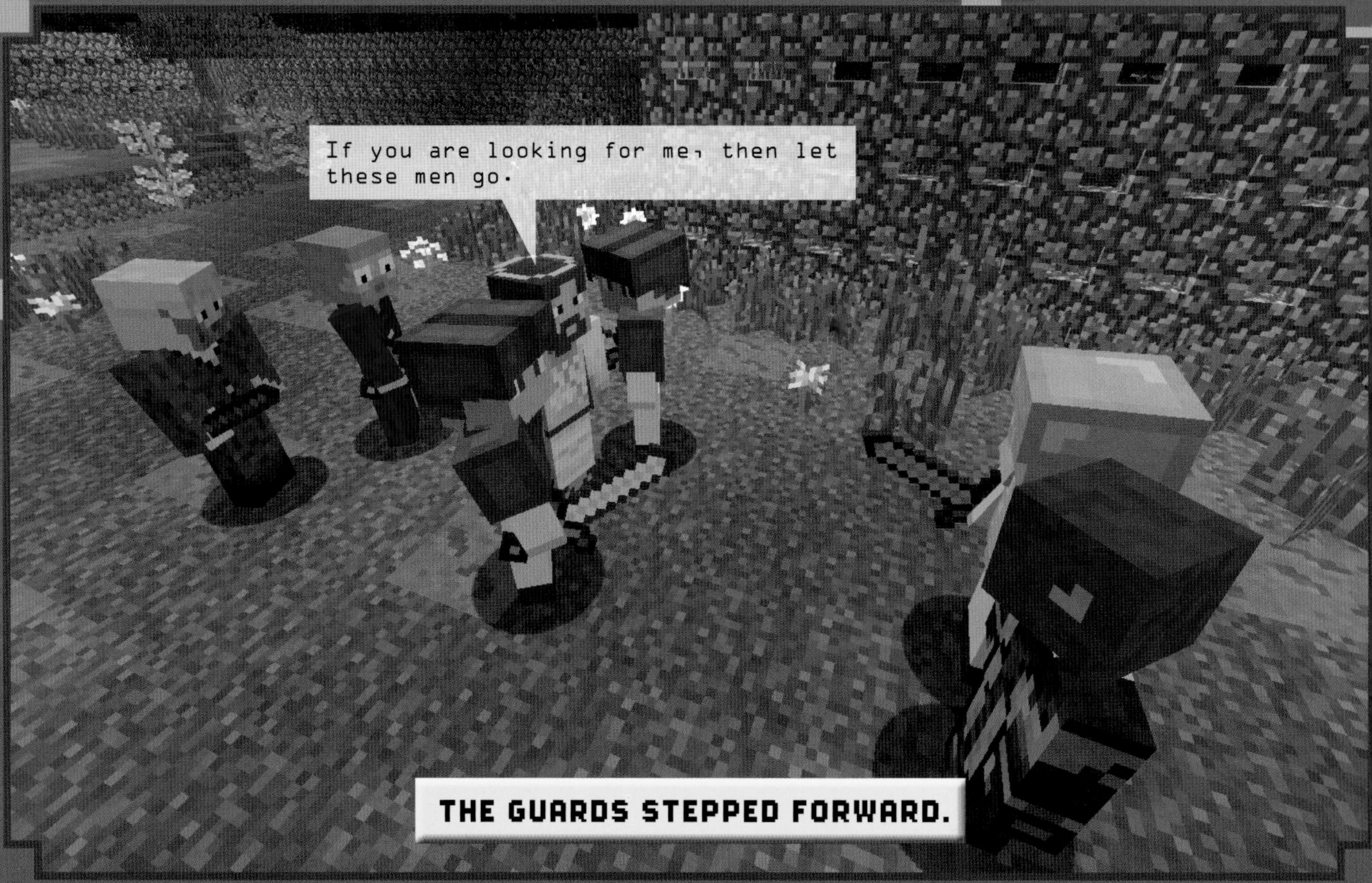

If you are looking for me, then let these men go.
THE GUARDS STEPPED FORWARD.

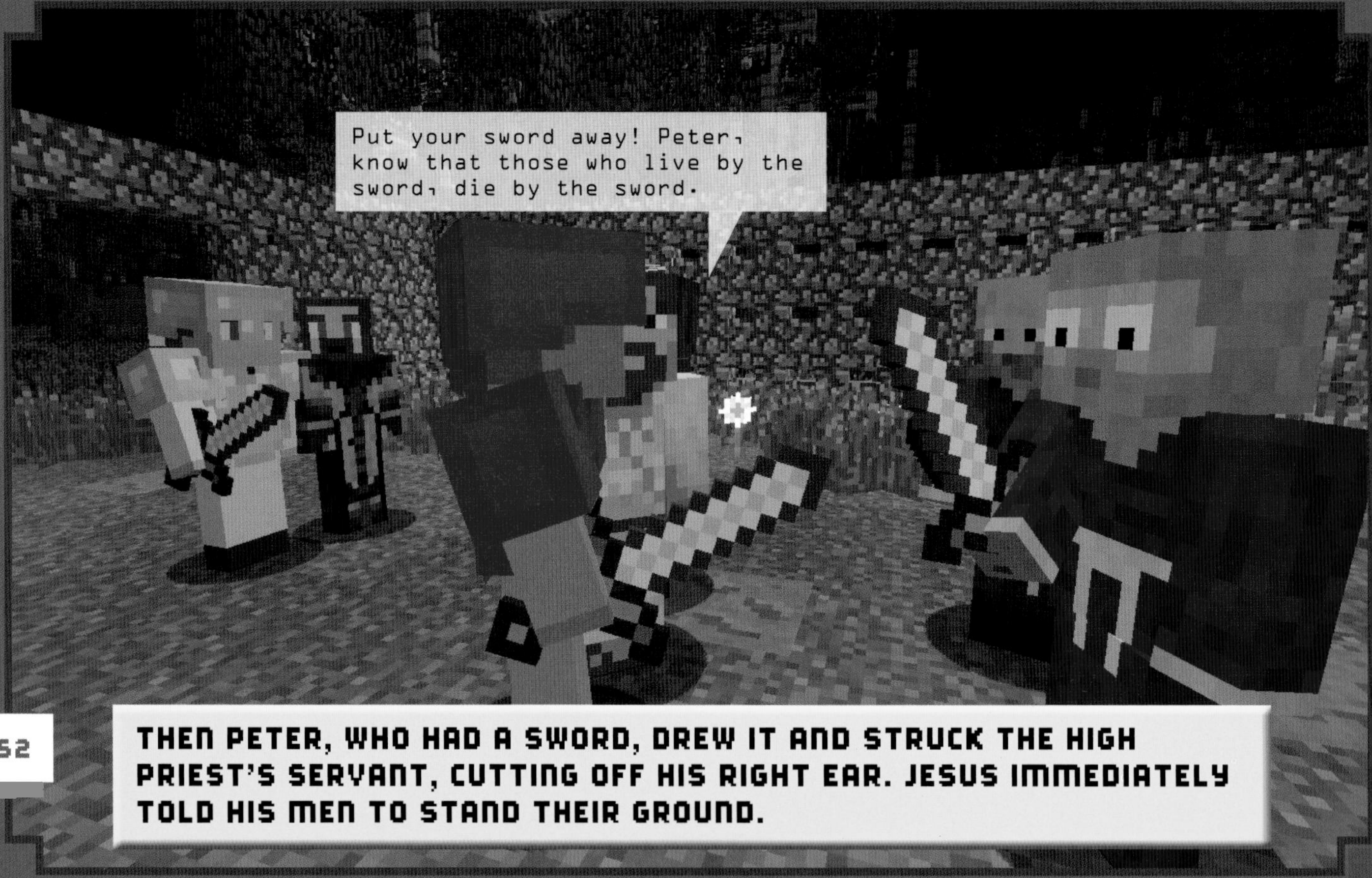

Put your sword away! Peter, know that those who live by the sword, die by the sword.
THEN PETER, WHO HAD A SWORD, DREW IT AND STRUCK THE HIGH PRIEST'S SERVANT, CUTTING OFF HIS RIGHT EAR. JESUS IMMEDIATELY TOLD HIS MEN TO STAND THEIR GROUND.

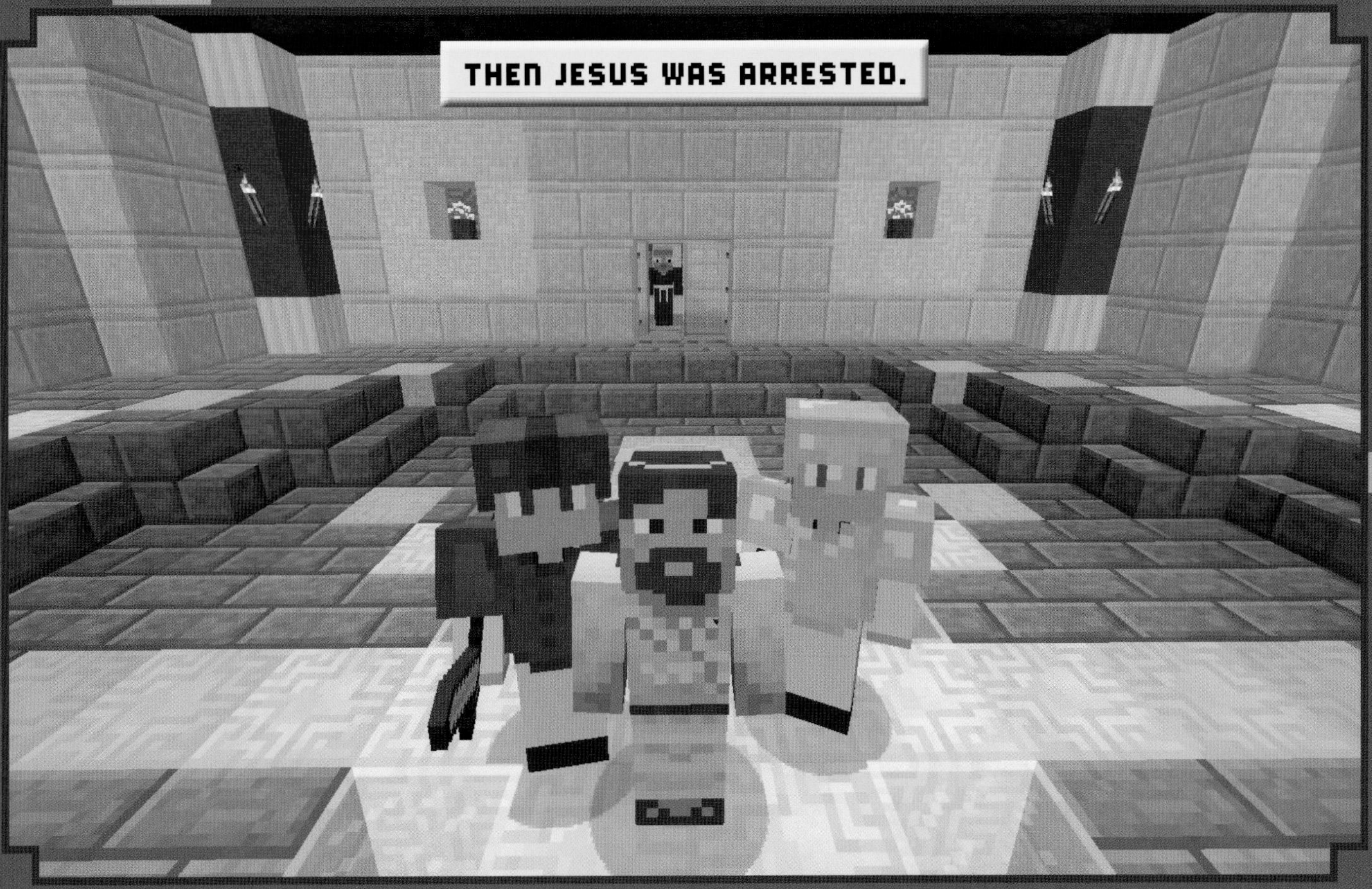
THEN JESUS WAS ARRESTED.

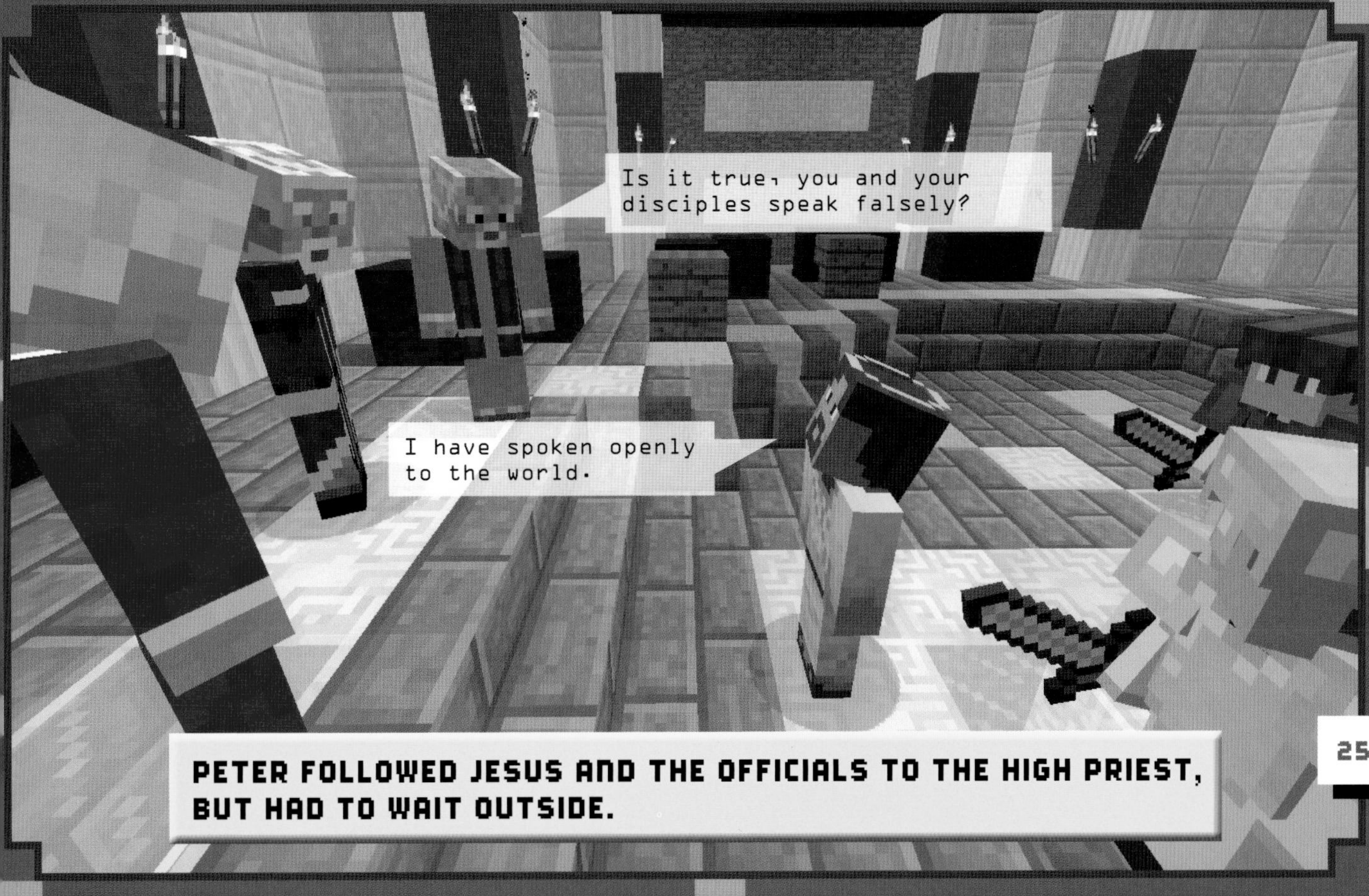
Is it true, you and your disciples speak falsely?
I have spoken openly to the world.
PETER FOLLOWED JESUS AND THE OFFICIALS TO THE HIGH PRIEST, BUT HAD TO WAIT OUTSIDE.

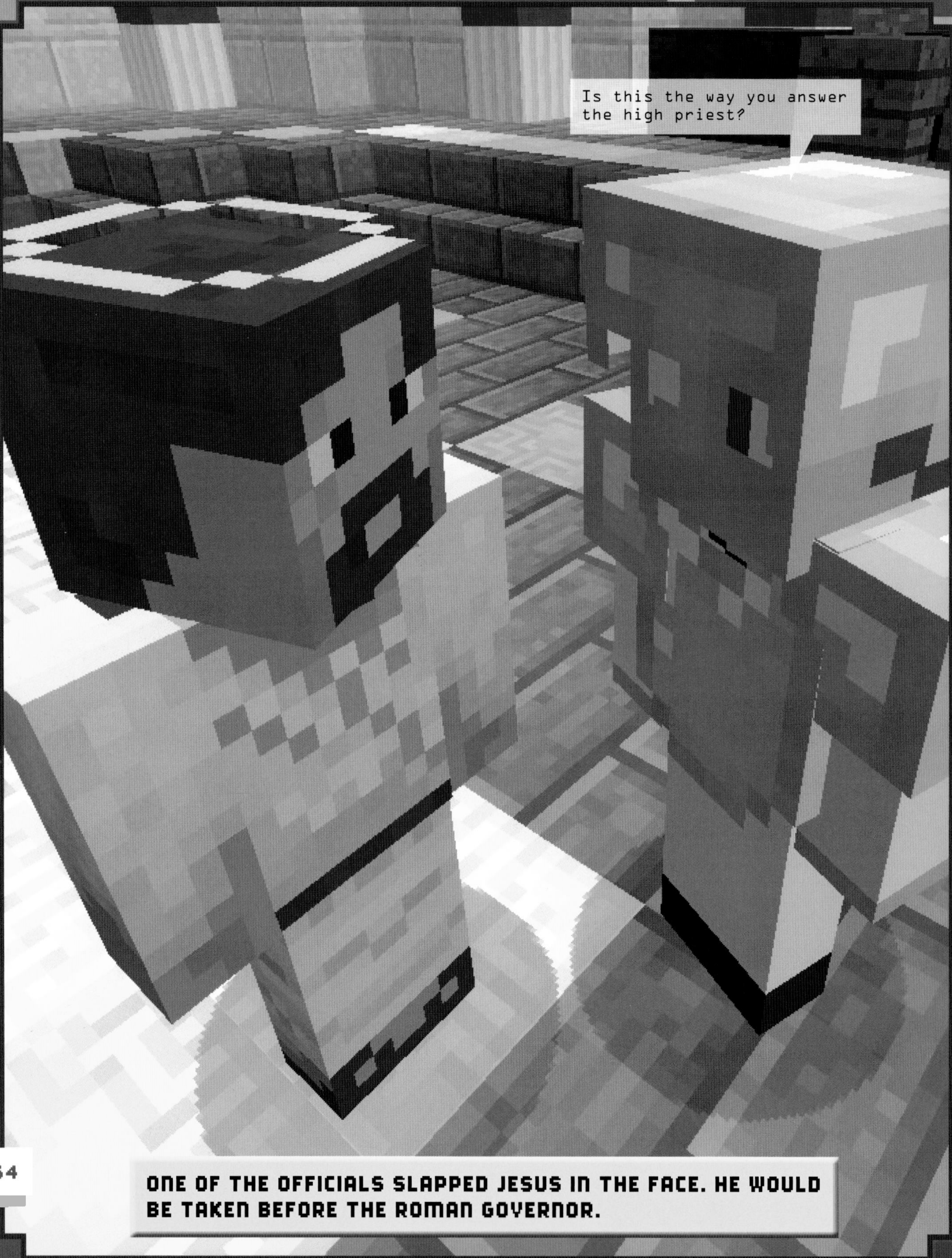
Is this the way you answer the high priest?
ONE OF THE OFFICIALS SLAPPED JESUS IN THE FACE. HE WOULD BE TAKEN BEFORE THE ROMAN GOVERNOR.

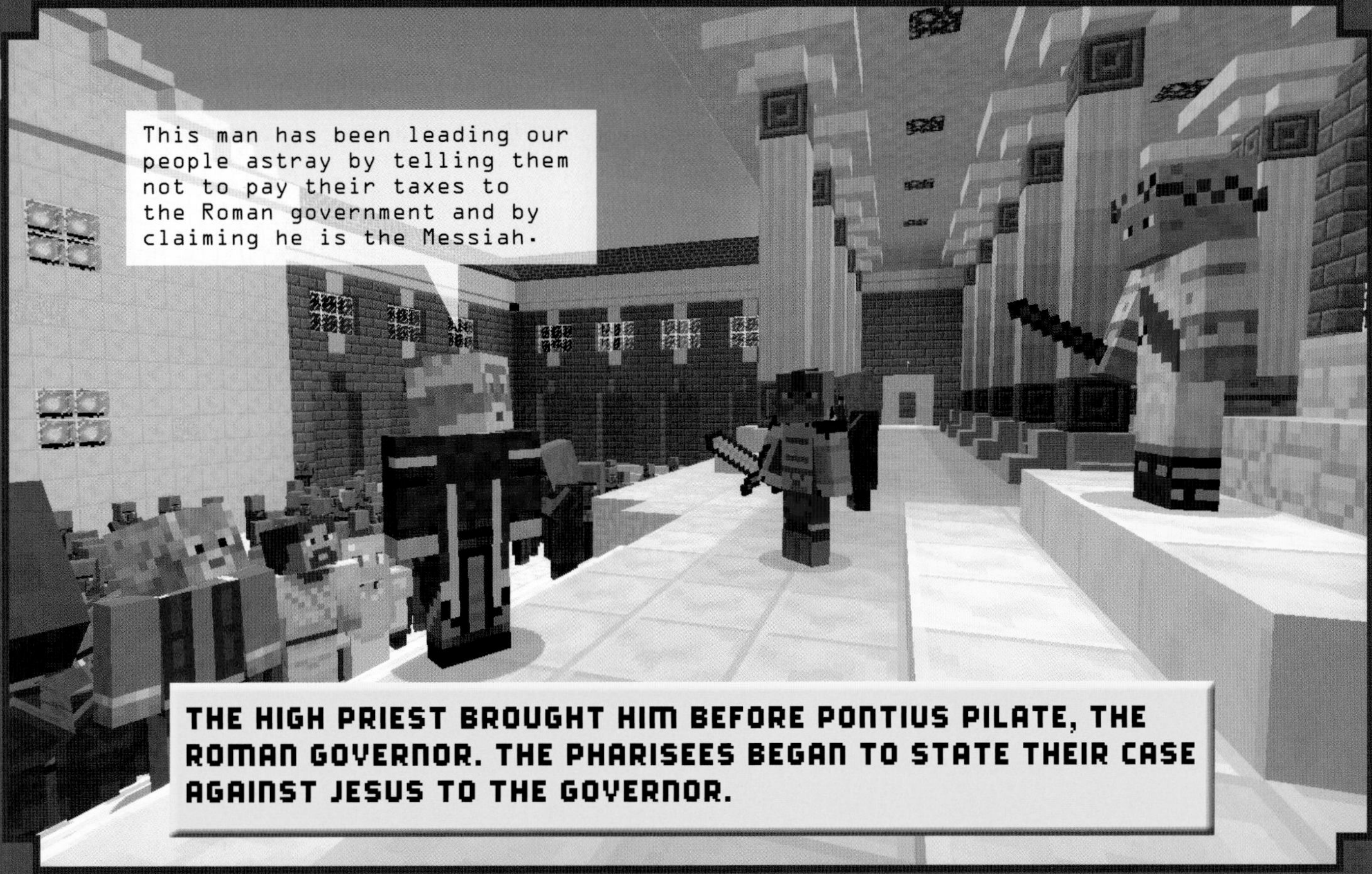
This man has been leading our people astray by telling them not to pay their taxes to the Roman government and by claiming he is the Messiah.
THE HIGH PRIEST BROUGHT HIM BEFORE PONTIUS PILATE, THE ROMAN GOVERNOR. THE PHARISEES BEGAN TO STATE THEIR CASE AGAINST JESUS TO THE GOVERNOR.

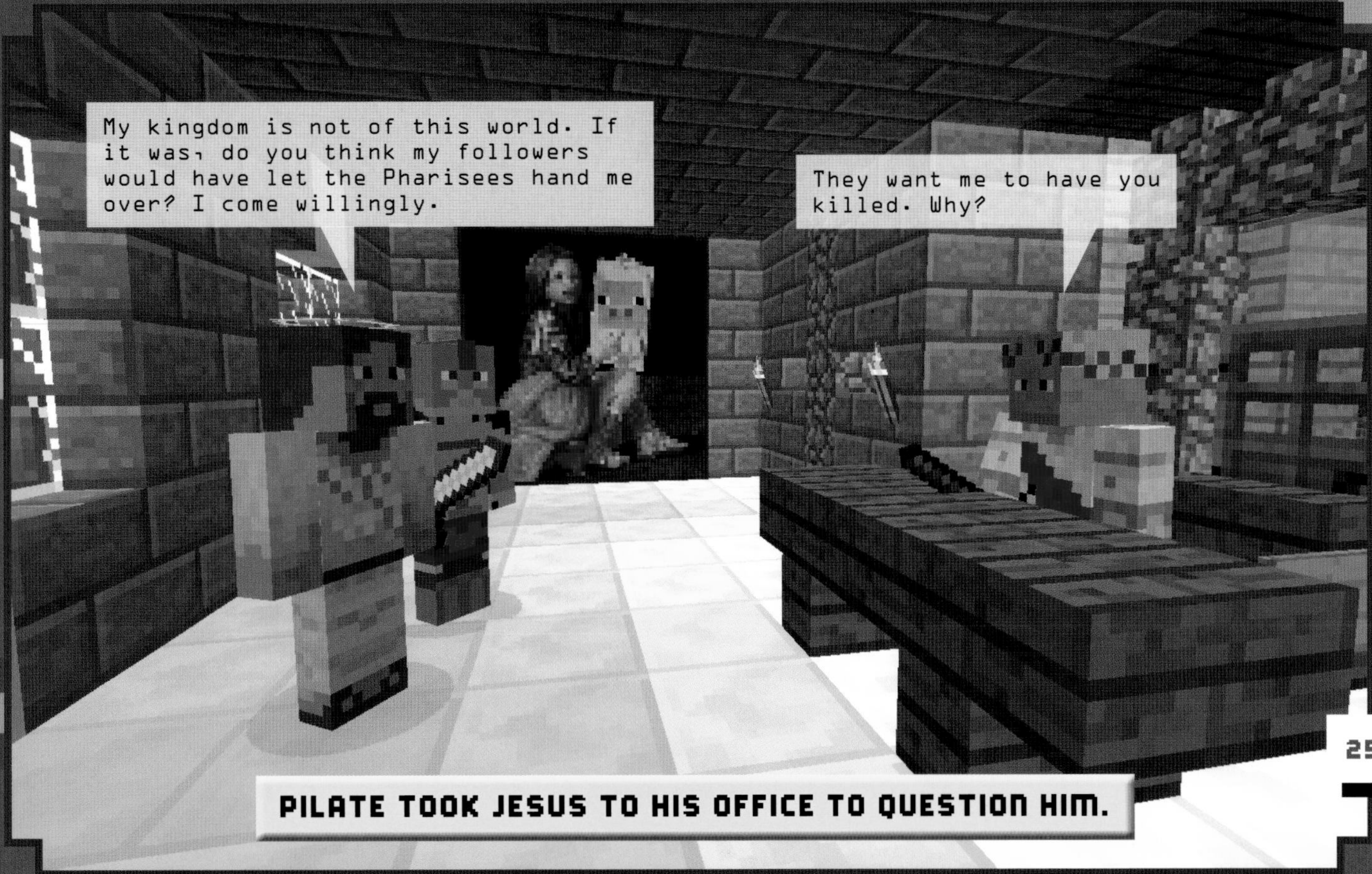
My kingdom is not of this world. If it was, do you think my followers would have let the Pharisees hand me over? I come willingly.
They want me to have you killed. Why?
PILATE TOOK JESUS TO HIS OFFICE TO QUESTION HIM.

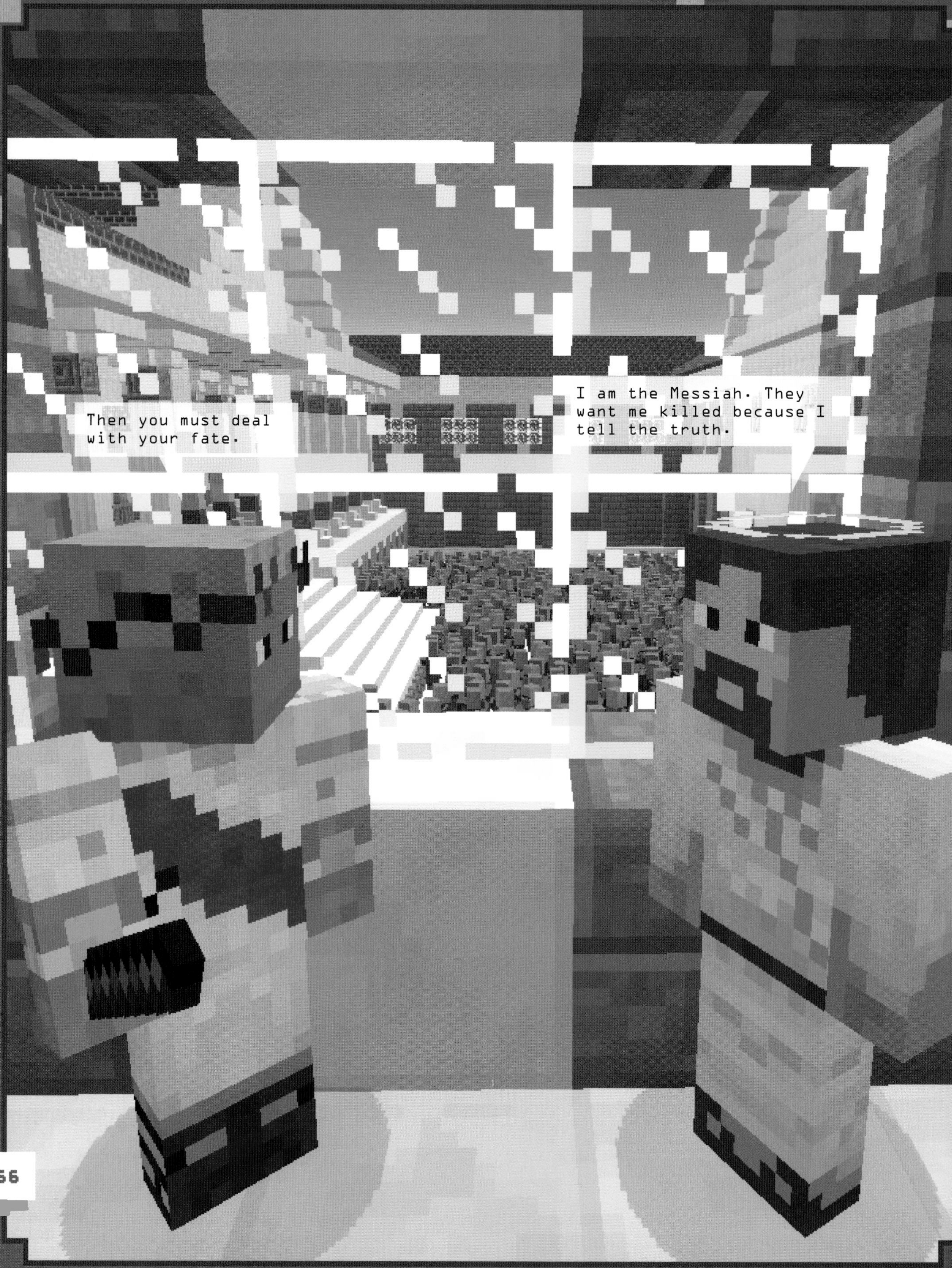
Then you must deal with your fate.
I am the Messiah. They want me killed because I tell the truth.

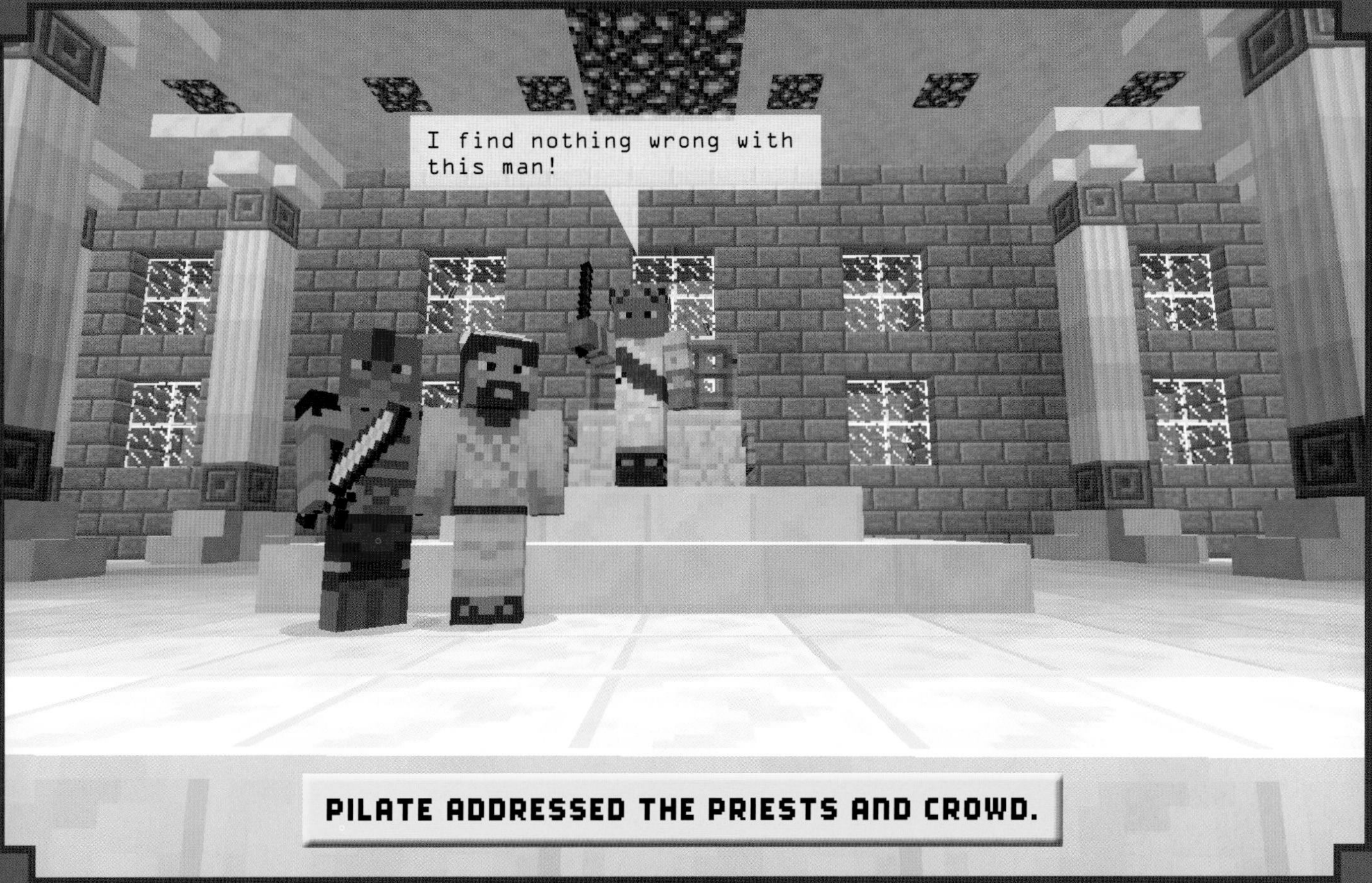
I find nothing wrong with this man!
PILATE ADDRESSED THE PRIESTS AND CROWD.

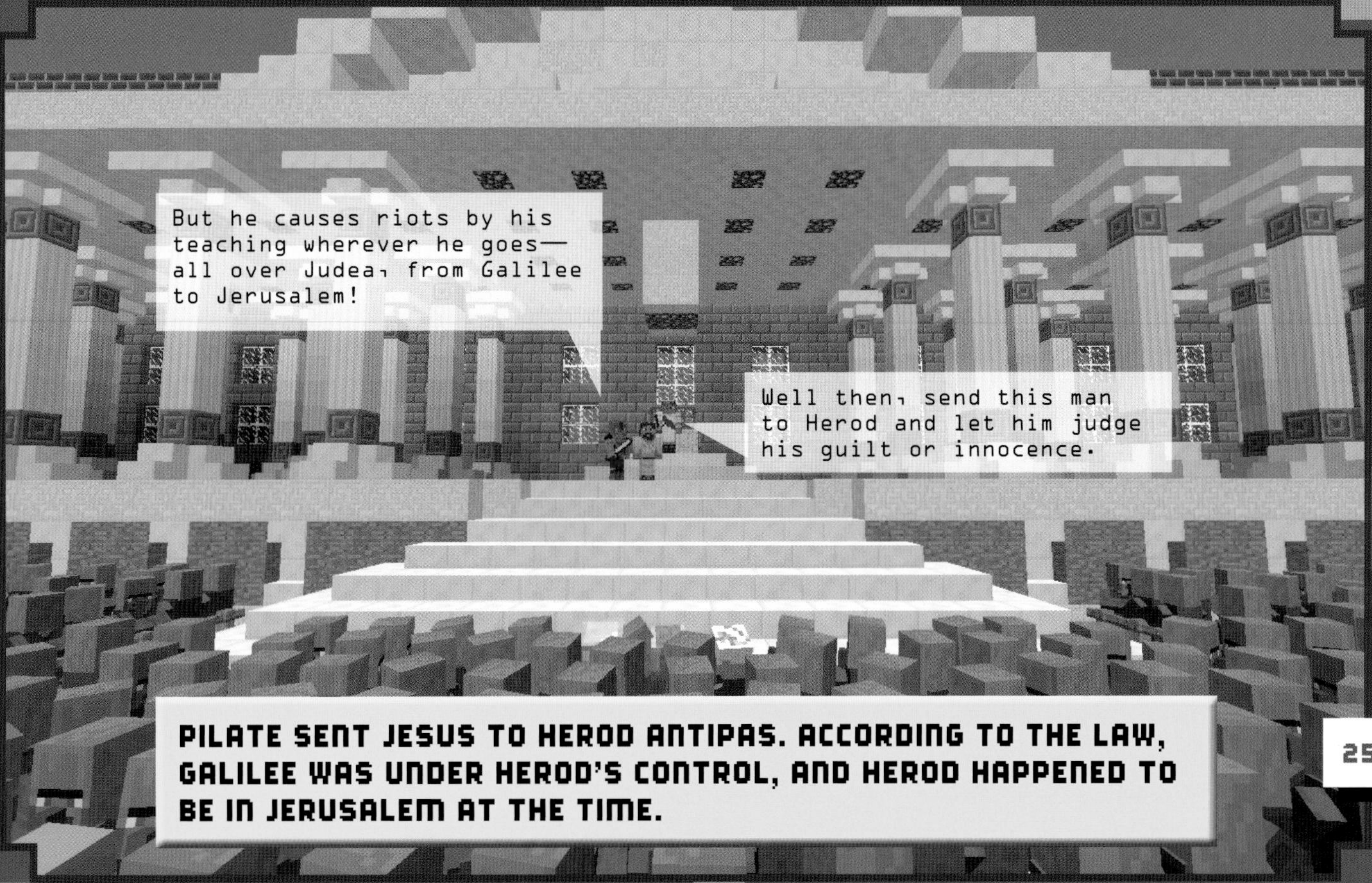
But he causes riots by his teaching wherever he goes—all over Judea, from Galilee to Jerusalem!
Well then, send this man to Herod and let him judge his guilt or innocence.
PILATE SENT JESUS TO HEROD ANTIPAS. ACCORDING TO THE LAW, GALILEE WAS UNDER HEROD'S CONTROL, AND HEROD HAPPENED TO BE IN JERUSALEM AT THE TIME.

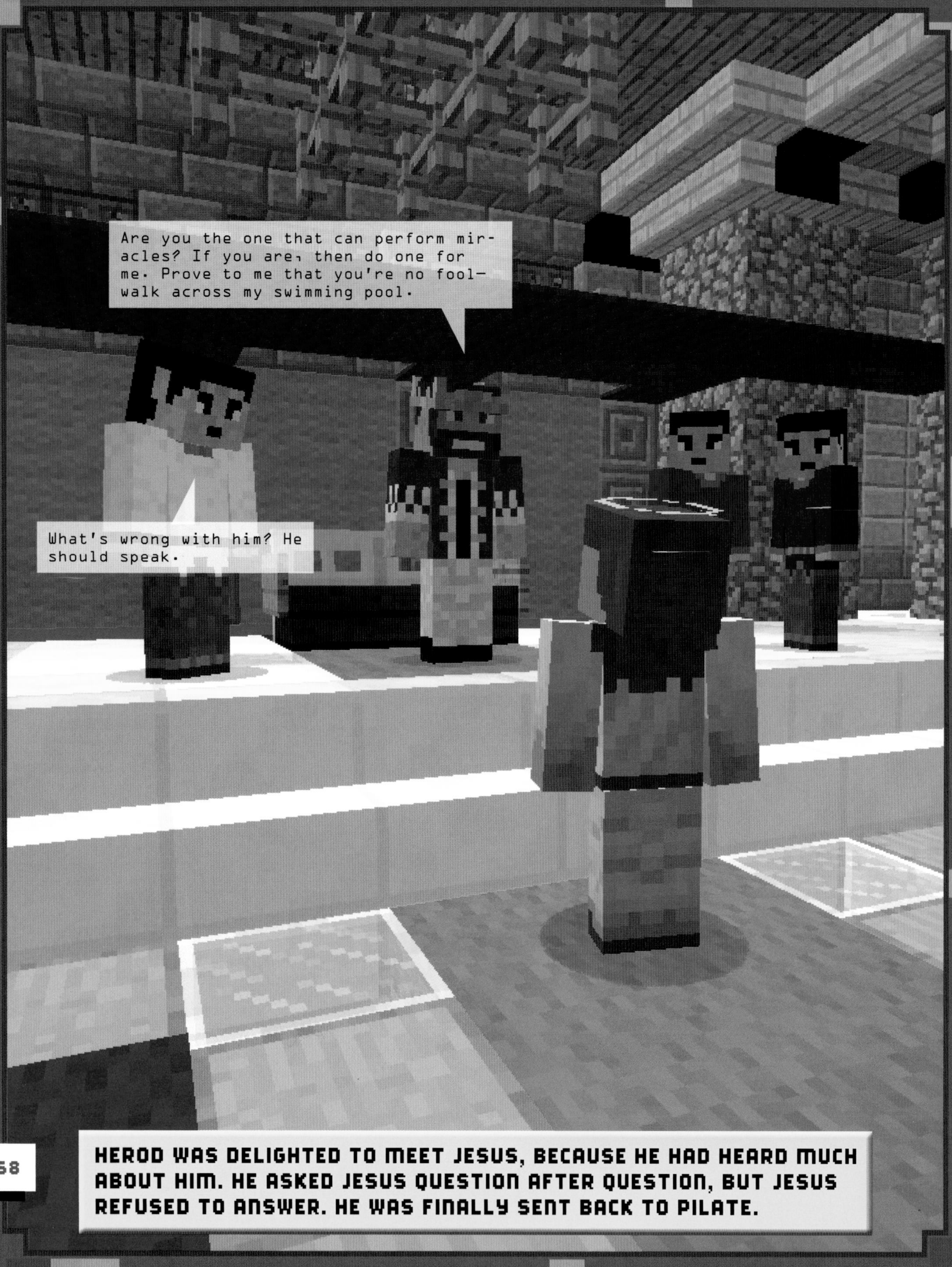
Are you the one that can perform miracles? If you are, then do one for me. Prove to me that you're no fool—walk across my swimming pool.
What's wrong with him? He should speak.
HEROD WAS DELIGHTED TO MEET JESUS, BECAUSE HE HAD HEARD MUCH ABOUT HIM. HE ASKED JESUS QUESTION AFTER QUESTION, BUT JESUS REFUSED TO ANSWER. HE WAS FINALLY SENT BACK TO PILATE.

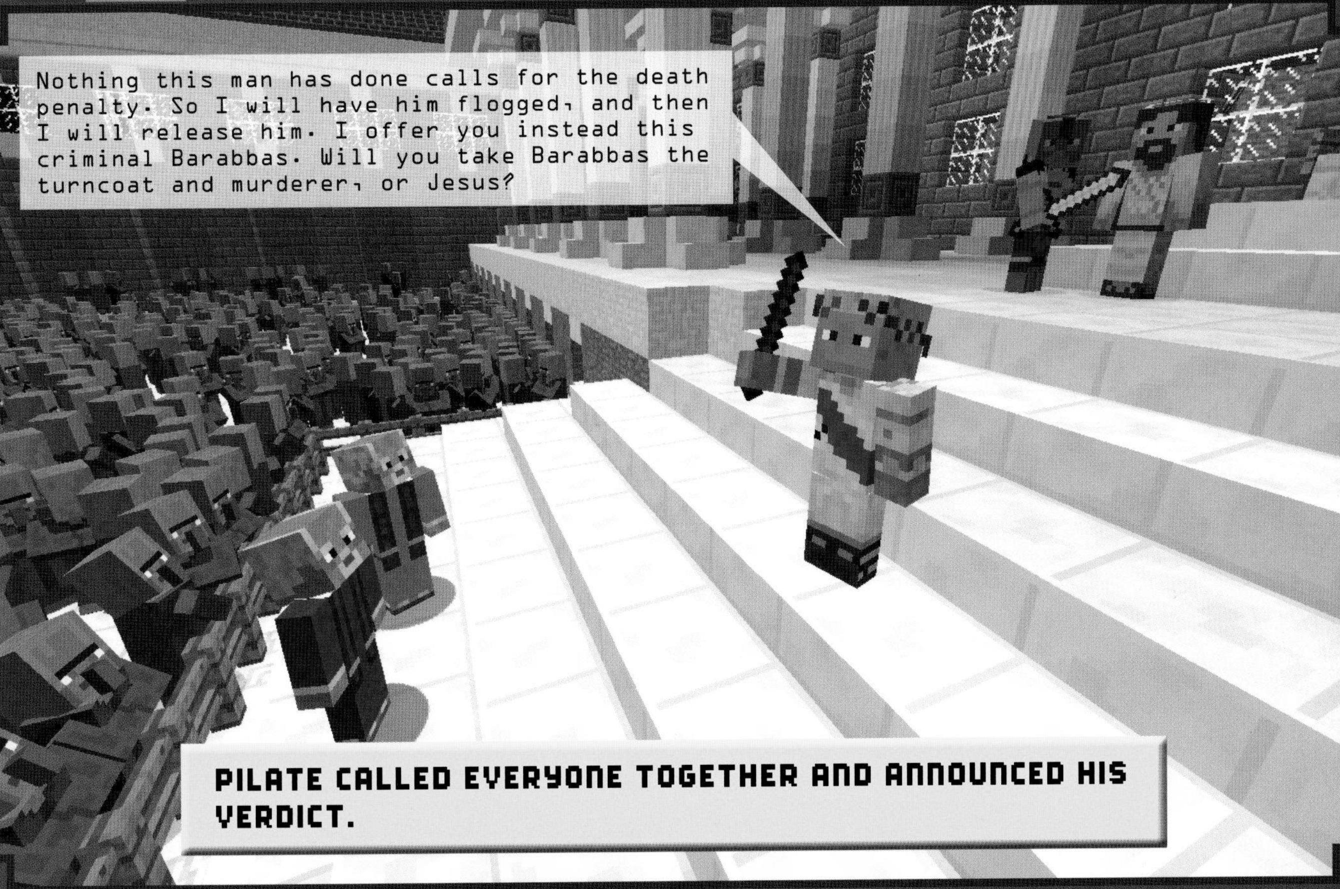
Nothing this man has done calls for the death penalty. So I will have him flogged, and then I will release him. I offer you instead this criminal Barabbas. Will you take Barabbas the turncoat and murderer, or Jesus?
PILATE CALLED EVERYONE TOGETHER AND ANNOUNCED HIS VERDICT.

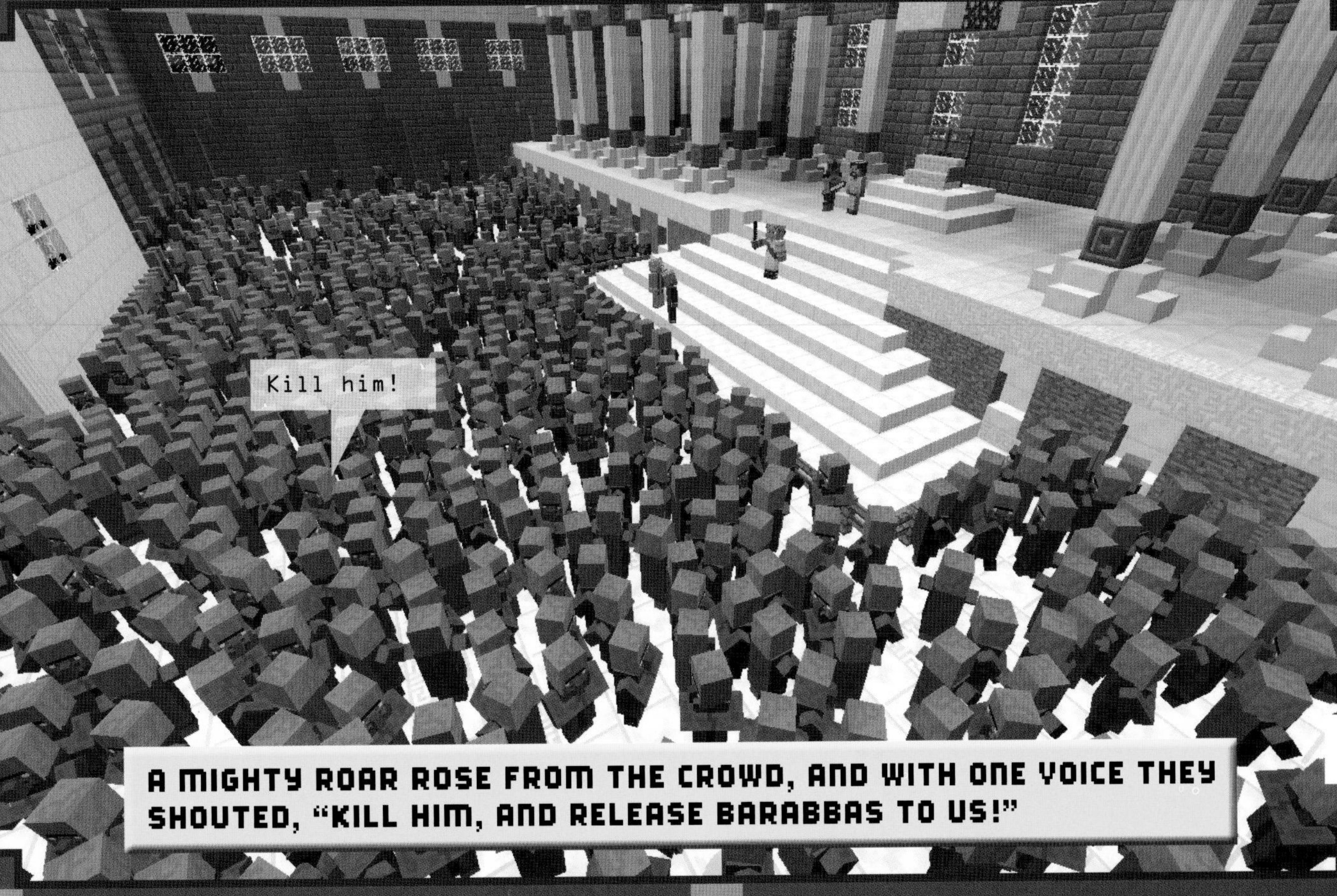
Kill him!
A MIGHTY ROAR ROSE FROM THE CROWD, AND WITH ONE VOICE THEY SHOUTED, "KILL HIM, AND RELEASE BARABBAS TO US!"

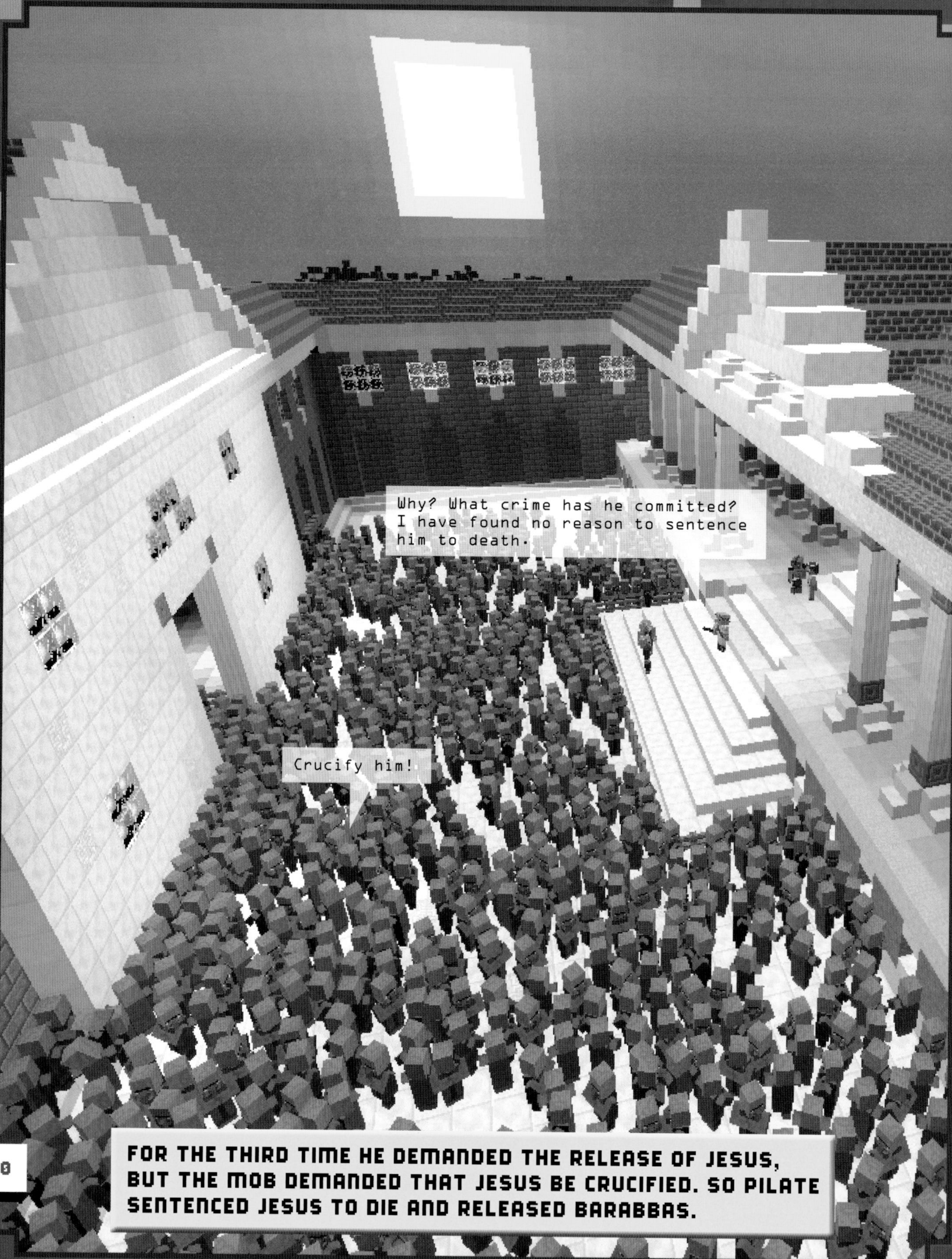
Why? What crime has he committed? I have found no reason to sentence him to death.
Crucify him!
FOR THE THIRD TIME HE DEMANDED THE RELEASE OF JESUS, BUT THE MOB DEMANDED THAT JESUS BE CRUCIFIED. SO PILATE SENTENCED JESUS TO DIE AND RELEASED BARABBAS.

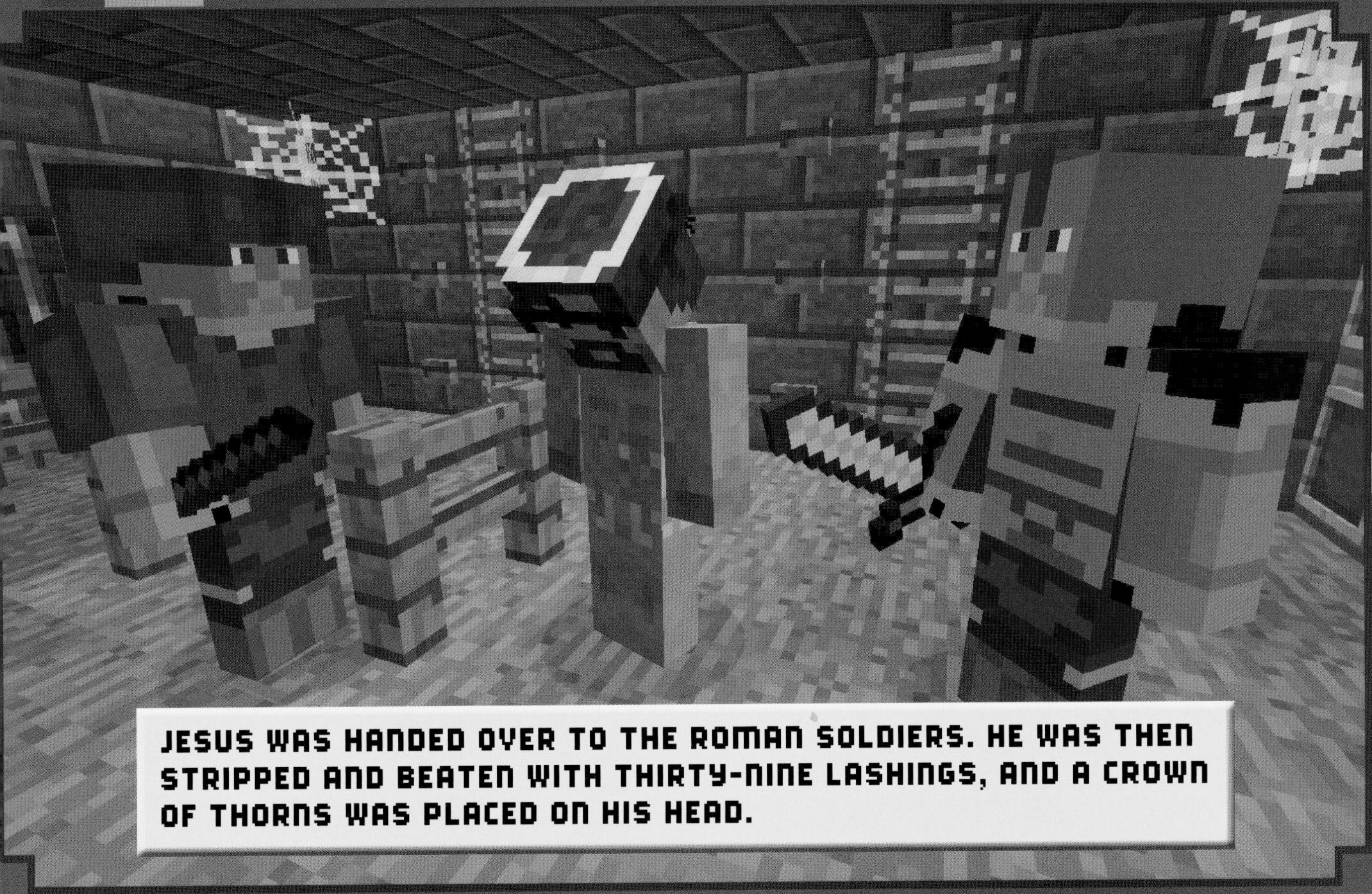
JESUS WAS HANDED OVER TO THE ROMAN SOLDIERS. HE WAS THEN STRIPPED AND BEATEN WITH THIRTY-NINE LASHINGS, AND A CROWN OF THORNS WAS PLACED ON HIS HEAD.

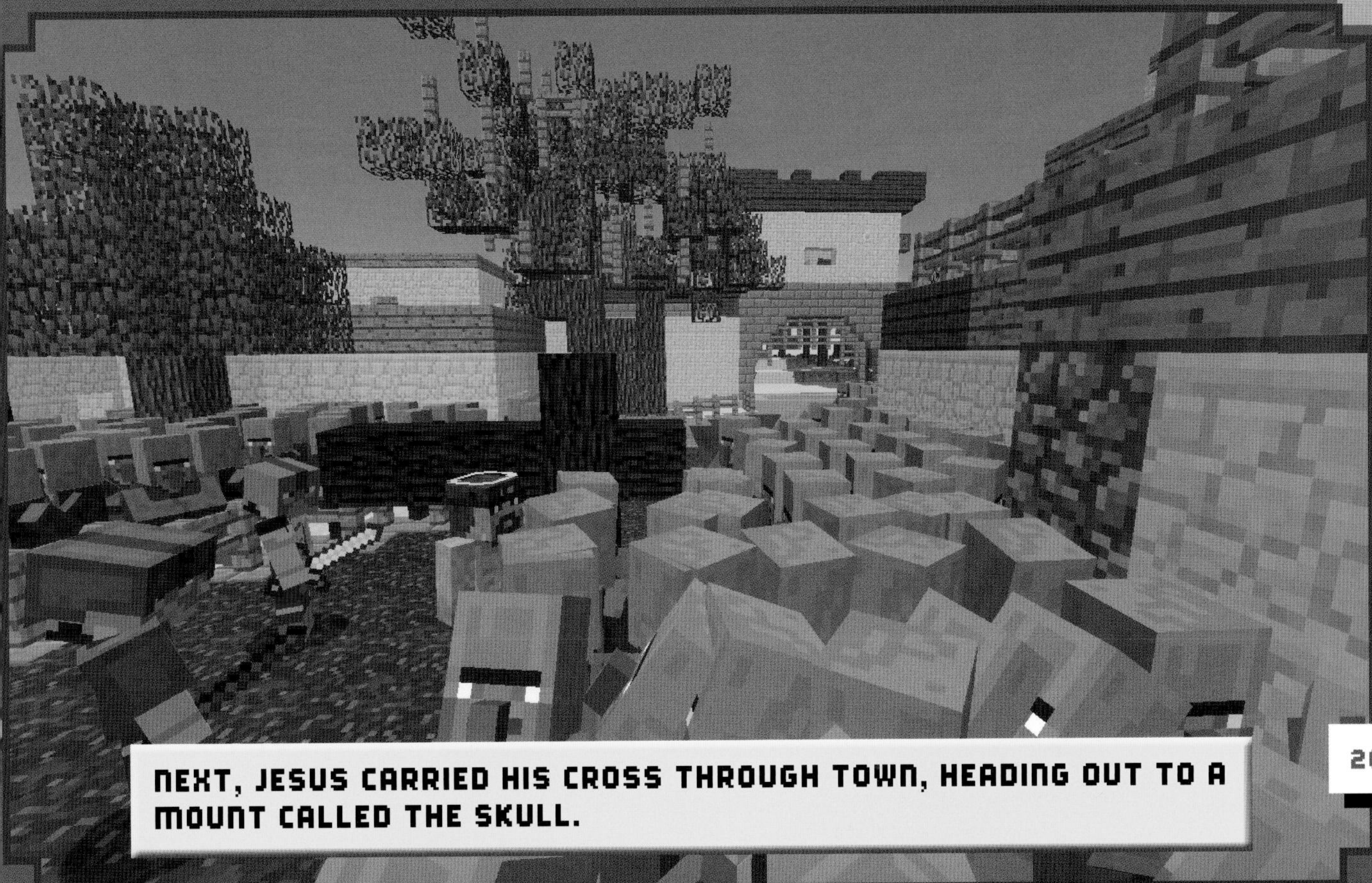
NEXT, JESUS CARRIED HIS CROSS THROUGH TOWN, HEADING OUT TO A MOUNT CALLED THE SKULL.

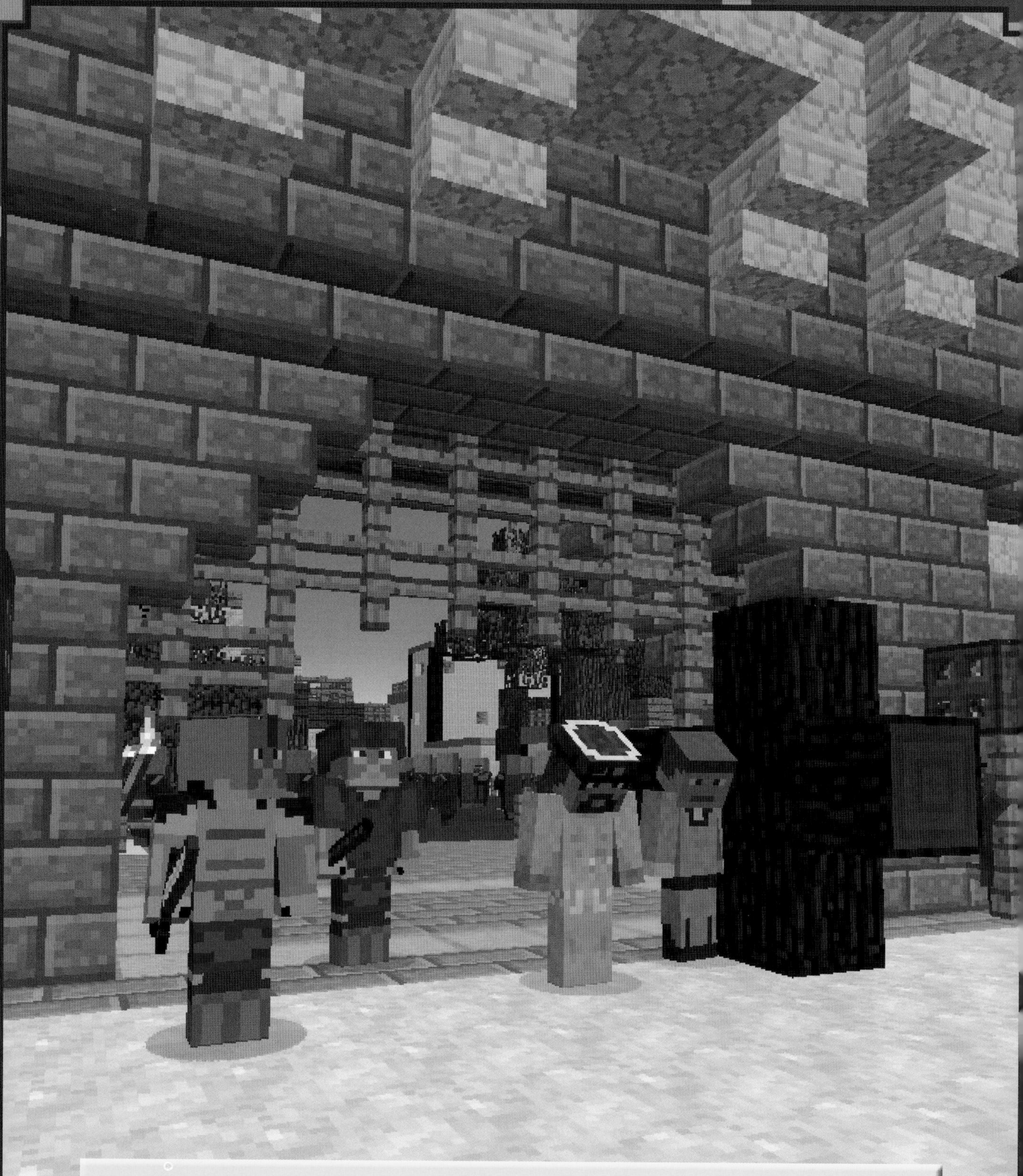

AT THE EDGE OF THE CITY, JESUS COULD NO LONGER BEAR THE WEIGHT OF THE CROSS AND COLLAPSED. A MAN NAMED PETER, WHO WAS FROM CYRENE, HAPPENED TO BE COMING IN FROM THE COUNTRYSIDE. THE SOLDIERS SEIZED HIM AND PUT THE CROSS ON HIM, MAKING HIM CARRY IT BEHIND JESUS.

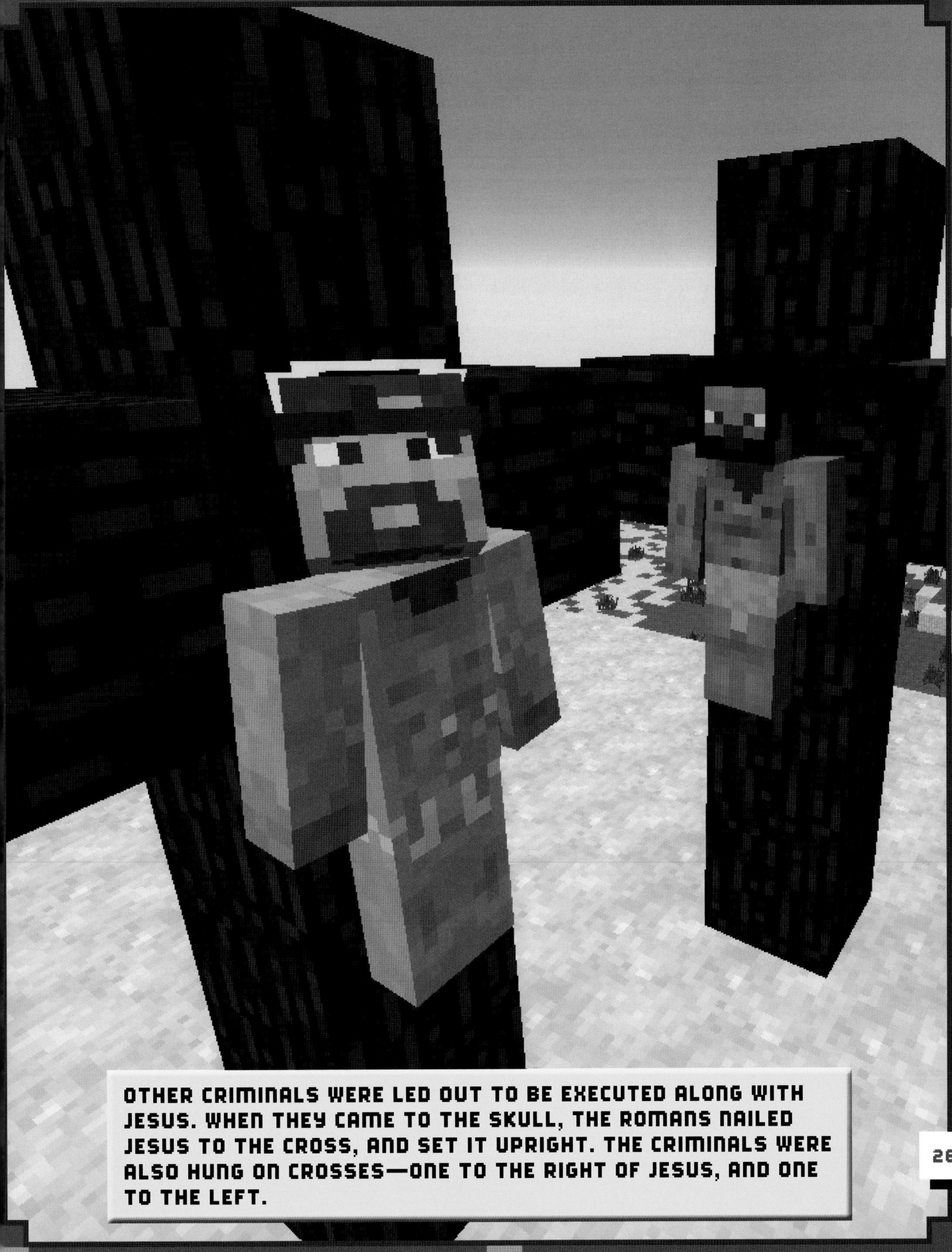

OTHER CRIMINALS WERE LED OUT TO BE EXECUTED ALONG WITH JESUS. WHEN THEY CAME TO THE SKULL, THE ROMANS NAILED JESUS TO THE CROSS, AND SET IT UPRIGHT. THE CRIMINALS WERE ALSO HUNG ON CROSSES—ONE TO THE RIGHT OF JESUS, AND ONE TO THE LEFT.

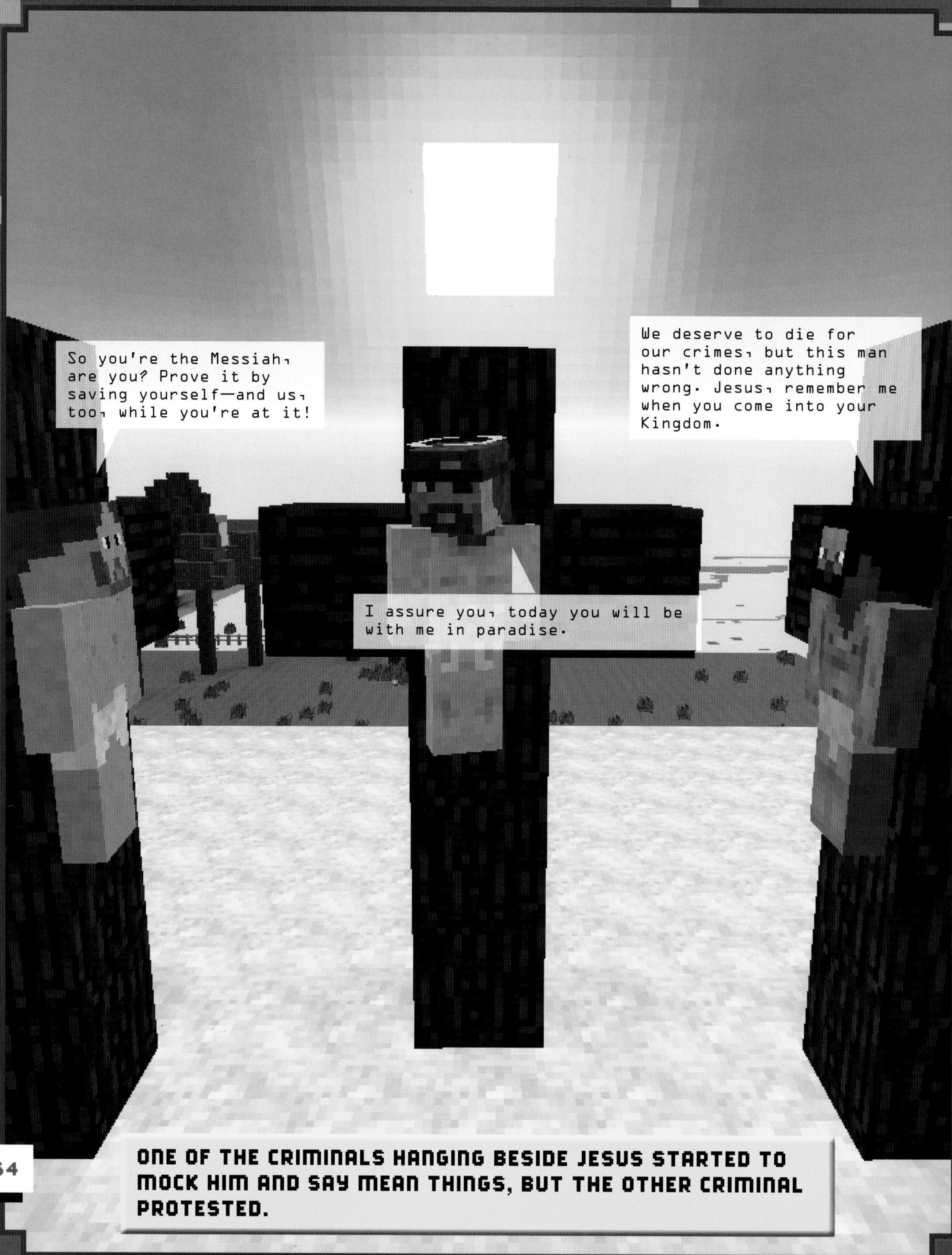
So you're the Messiah, are you? Prove it by saving yourself—and us, too, while you're at it!
We deserve to die for our crimes, but this man hasn't done anything wrong. Jesus, remember me when you come into your Kingdom.
I assure you, today you will be with me in paradise.

ONE OF THE CRIMINALS HANGING BESIDE JESUS STARTED TO MOCK HIM AND SAY MEAN THINGS, BUT THE OTHER CRIMINAL PROTESTED.

THE DEATH AND
RESURRECTION OF JESUS

I can't look, I have to turn away.

Don't worry. My Son's mission will be fulfilled.

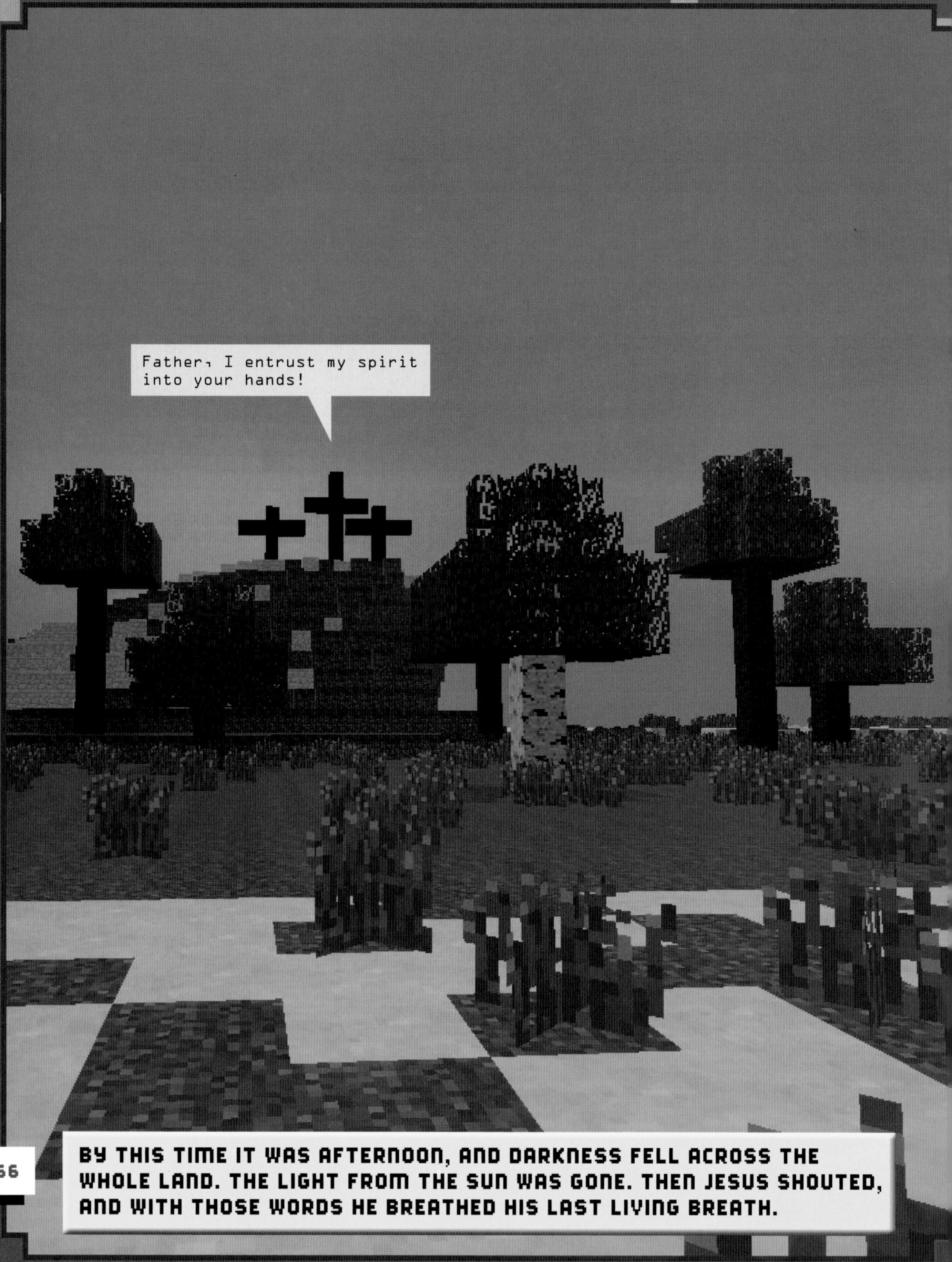
Father, I entrust my spirit into your hands!
BY THIS TIME IT WAS AFTERNOON, AND DARKNESS FELL ACROSS THE WHOLE LAND. THE LIGHT FROM THE SUN WAS GONE. THEN JESUS SHOUTED, AND WITH THOSE WORDS HE BREATHED HIS LAST LIVING BREATH.

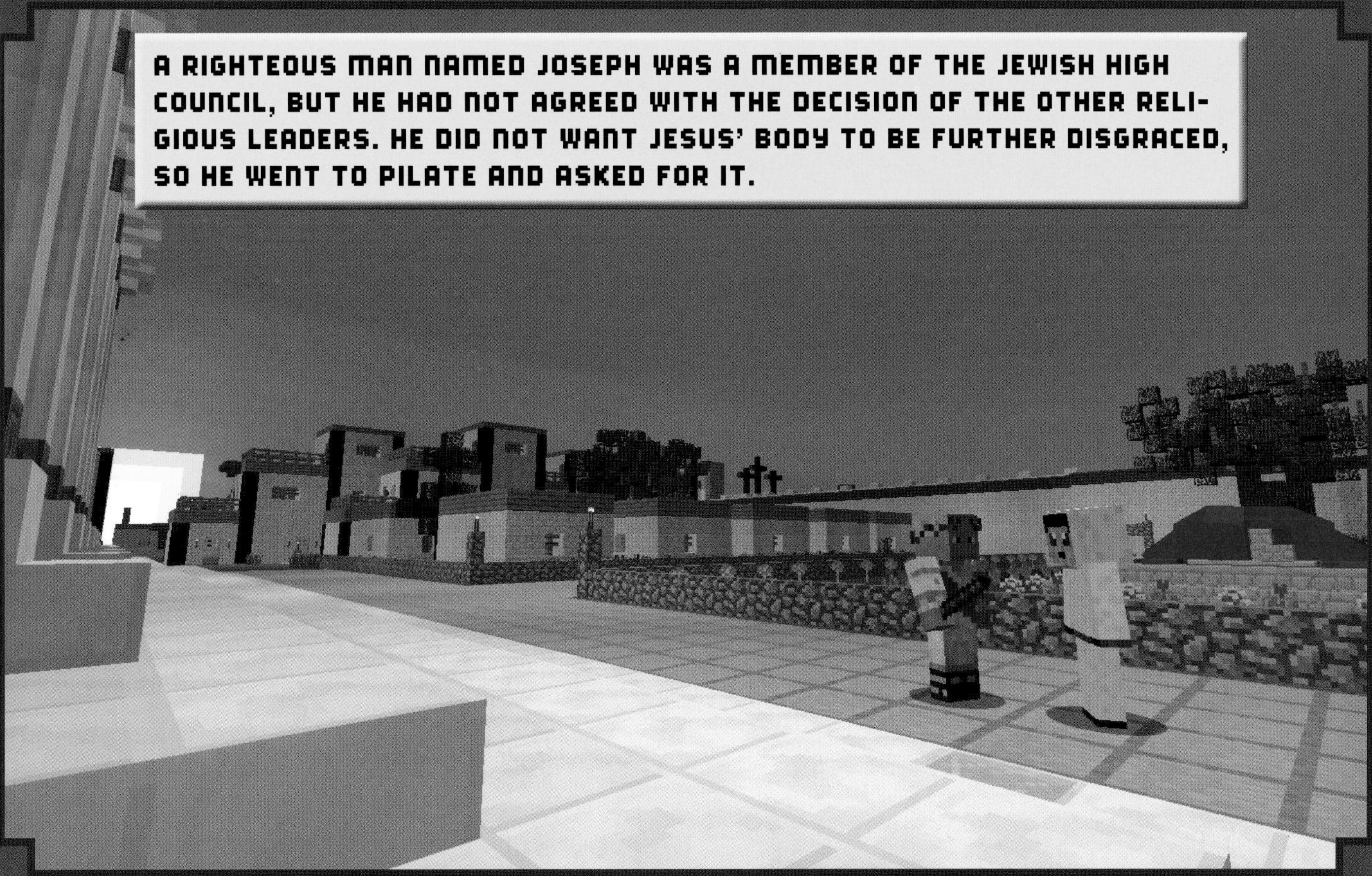
A RIGHTEOUS MAN NAMED JOSEPH WAS A MEMBER OF THE JEWISH HIGH COUNCIL, BUT HE HAD NOT AGREED WITH THE DECISION OF THE OTHER RELIGIOUS LEADERS. HE DID NOT WANT JESUS' BODY TO BE FURTHER DISGRACED, SO HE WENT TO PILATE AND ASKED FOR IT.

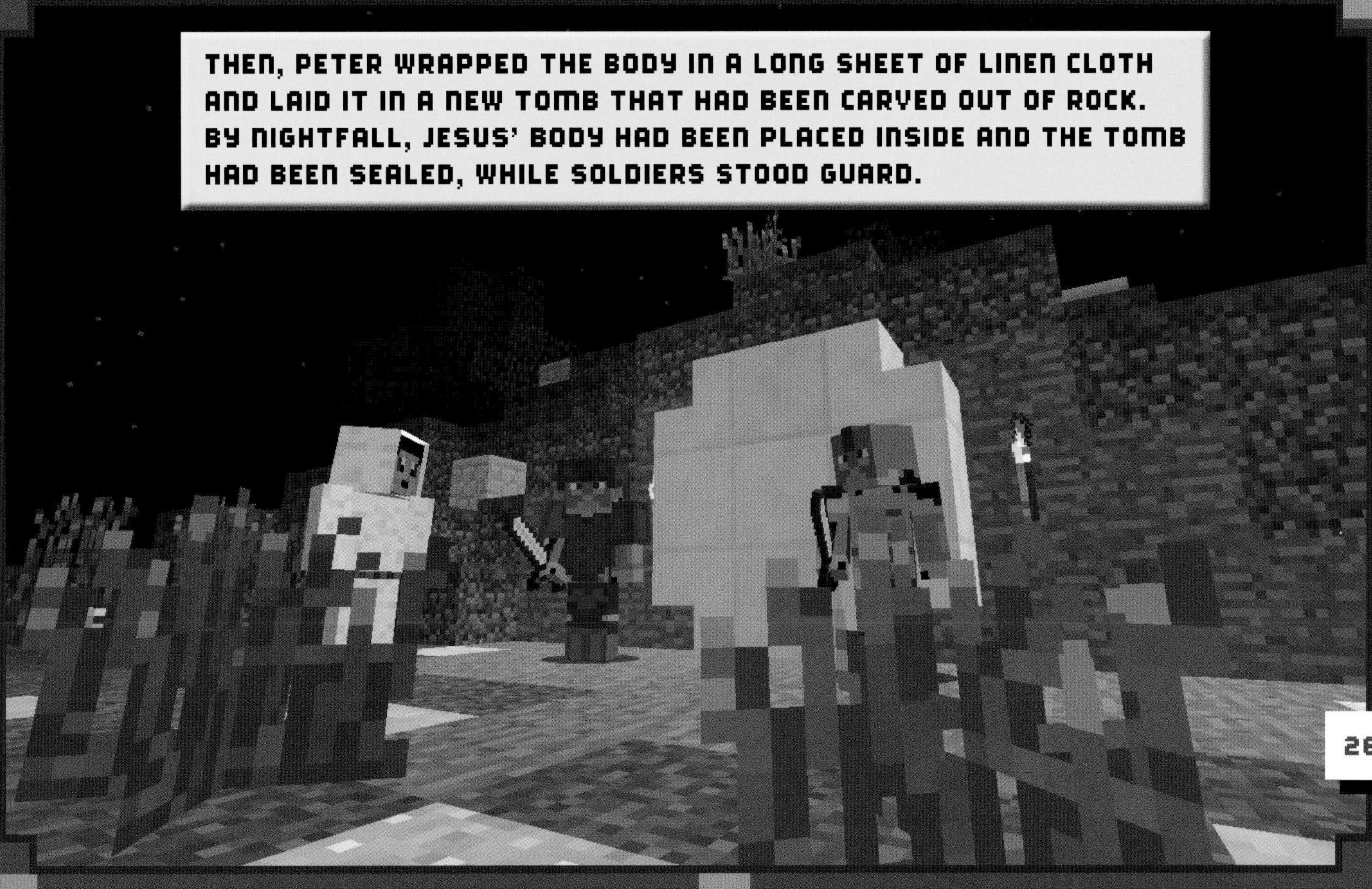
THEN, PETER WRAPPED THE BODY IN A LONG SHEET OF LINEN CLOTH AND LAID IT IN A NEW TOMB THAT HAD BEEN CARVED OUT OF ROCK. BY NIGHTFALL, JESUS' BODY HAD BEEN PLACED INSIDE AND THE TOMB HAD BEEN SEALED, WHILE SOLDIERS STOOD GUARD.

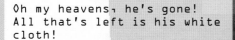

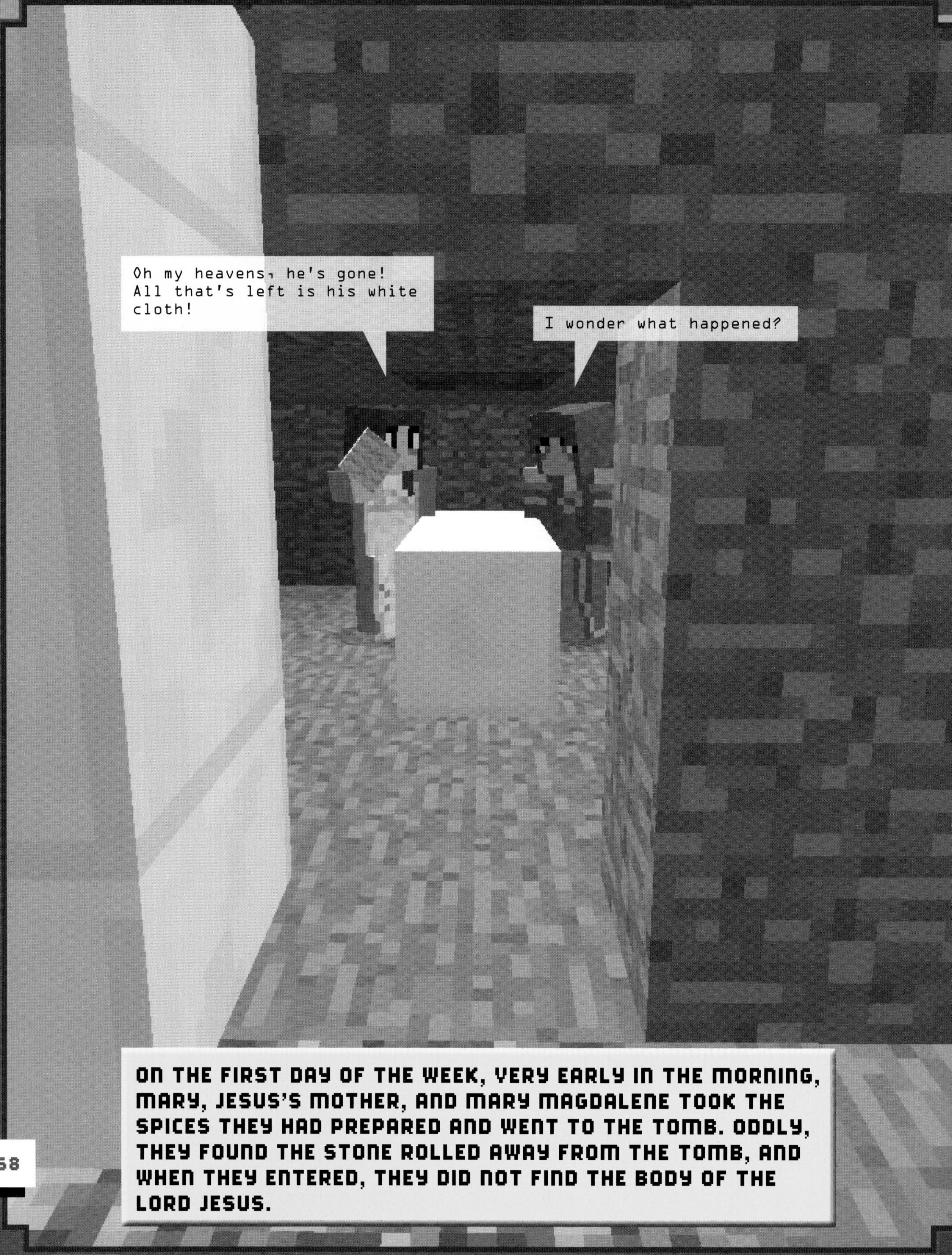

Oh my heavens, he's gone! All that's left is his white cloth!

I wonder what happened?

ON THE FIRST DAY OF THE WEEK, VERY EARLY IN THE MORNING, MARY, JESUS'S MOTHER, AND MARY MAGDALENE TOOK THE SPICES THEY HAD PREPARED AND WENT TO THE TOMB. ODDLY, THEY FOUND THE STONE ROLLED AWAY FROM THE TOMB, AND WHEN THEY ENTERED, THEY DID NOT FIND THE BODY OF THE LORD JESUS.

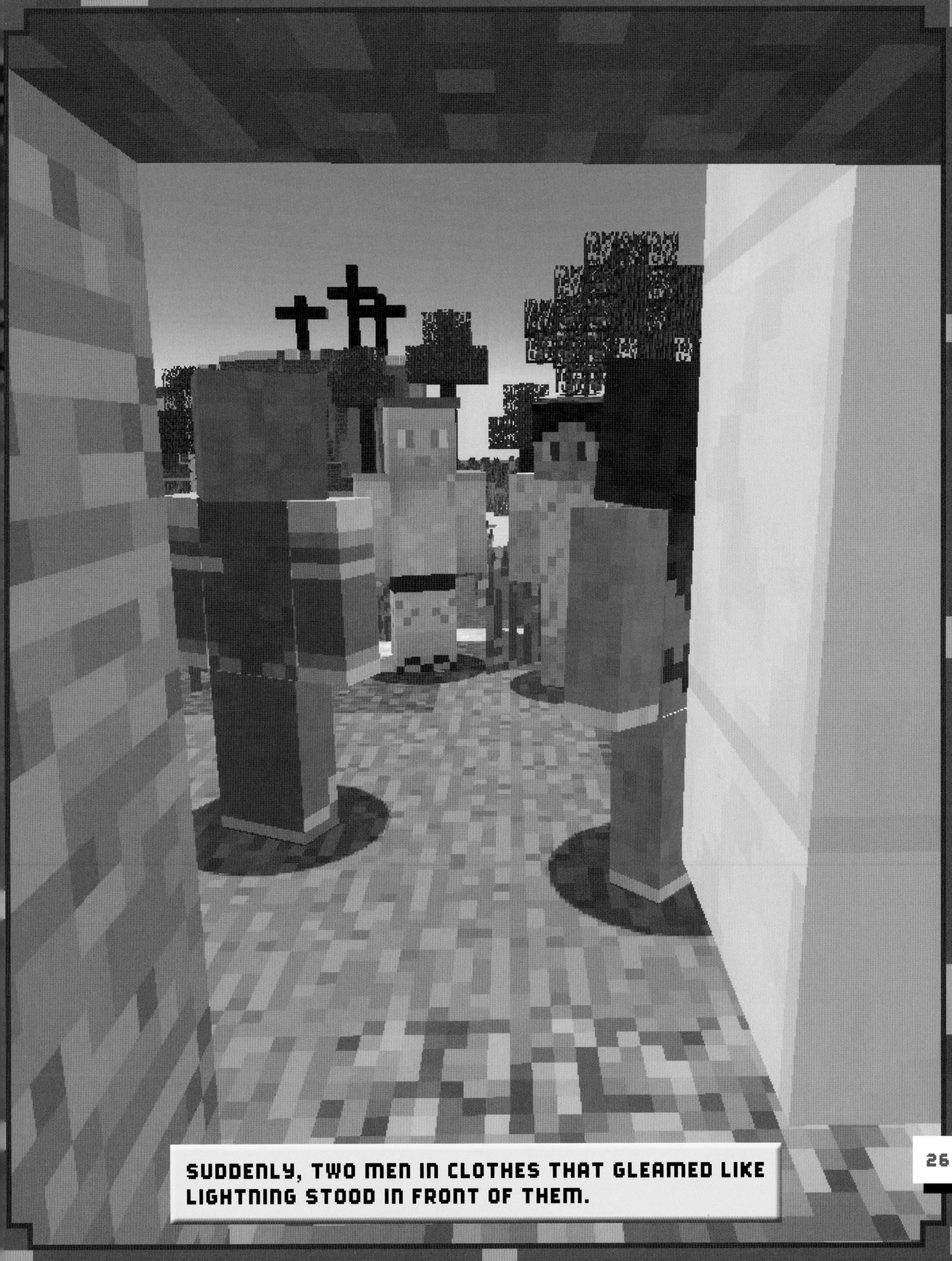
SUDDENLY, TWO MEN IN CLOTHES THAT GLEAMED LIKE LIGHTNING STOOD IN FRONT OF THEM.

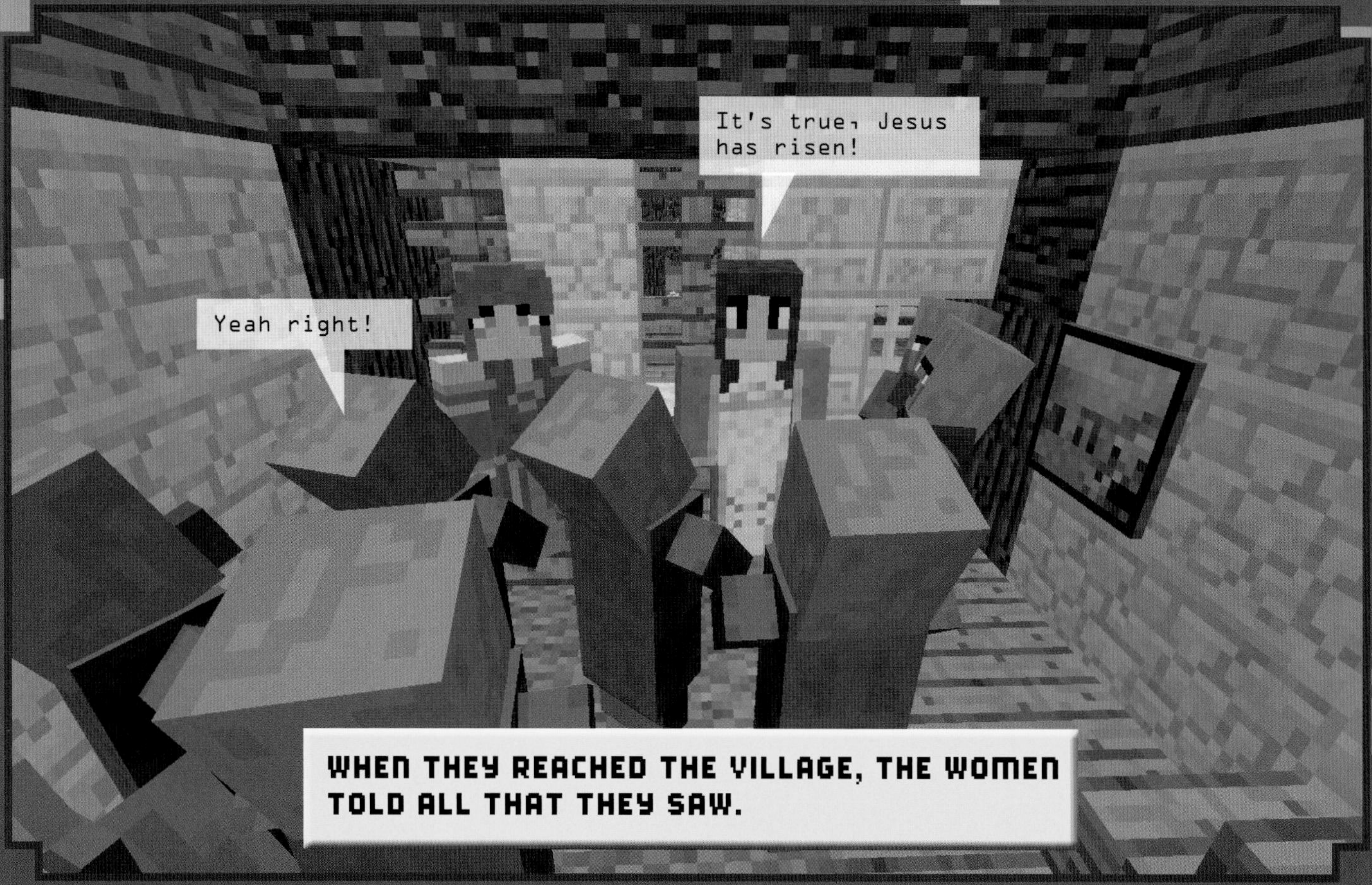

Yeah right!
It's true, Jesus has risen!
WHEN THEY REACHED THE VILLAGE, THE WOMEN TOLD ALL THAT THEY SAW.

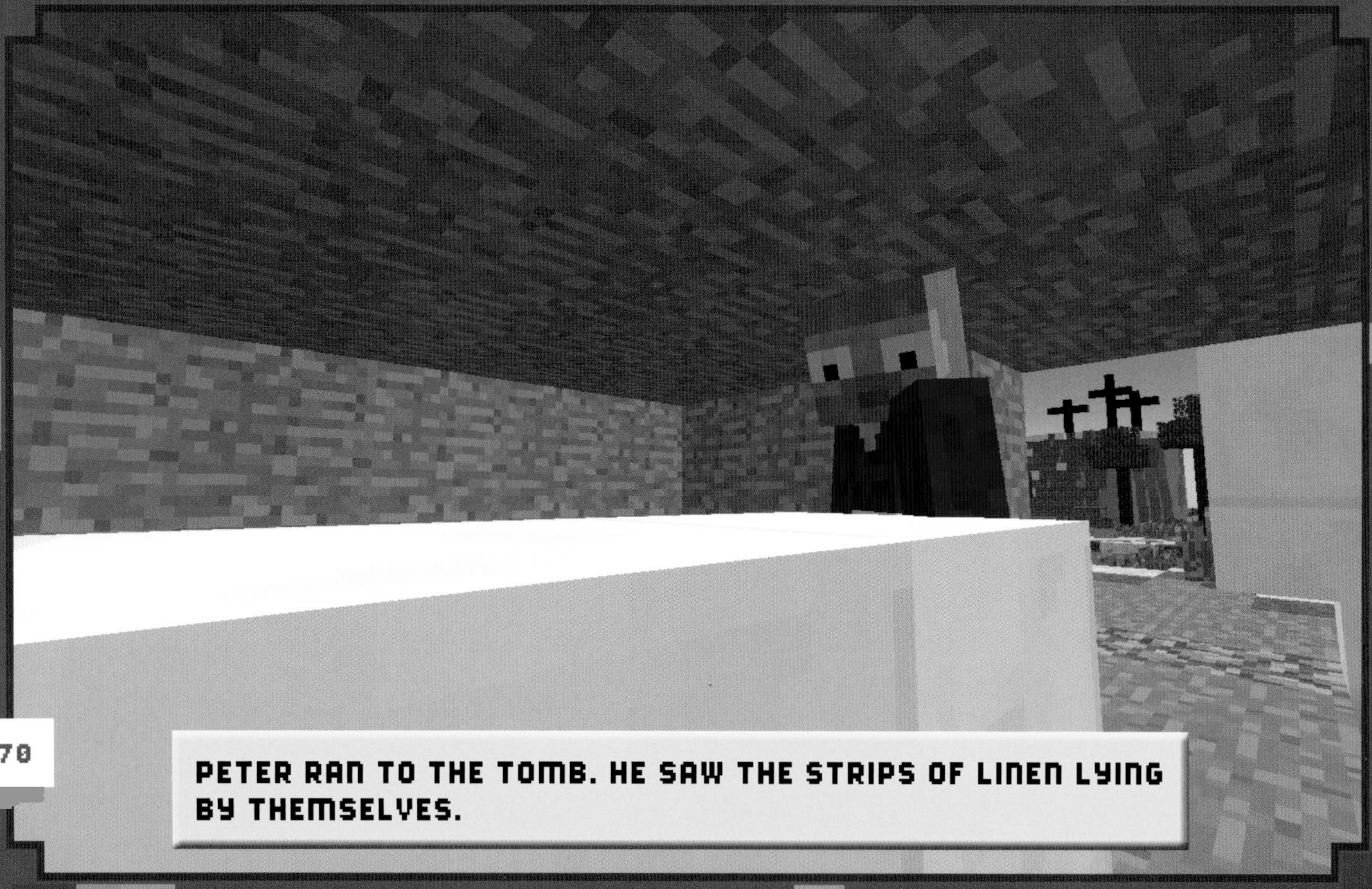

PETER RAN TO THE TOMB. HE SAW THE STRIPS OF LINEN LYING BY THEMSELVES.

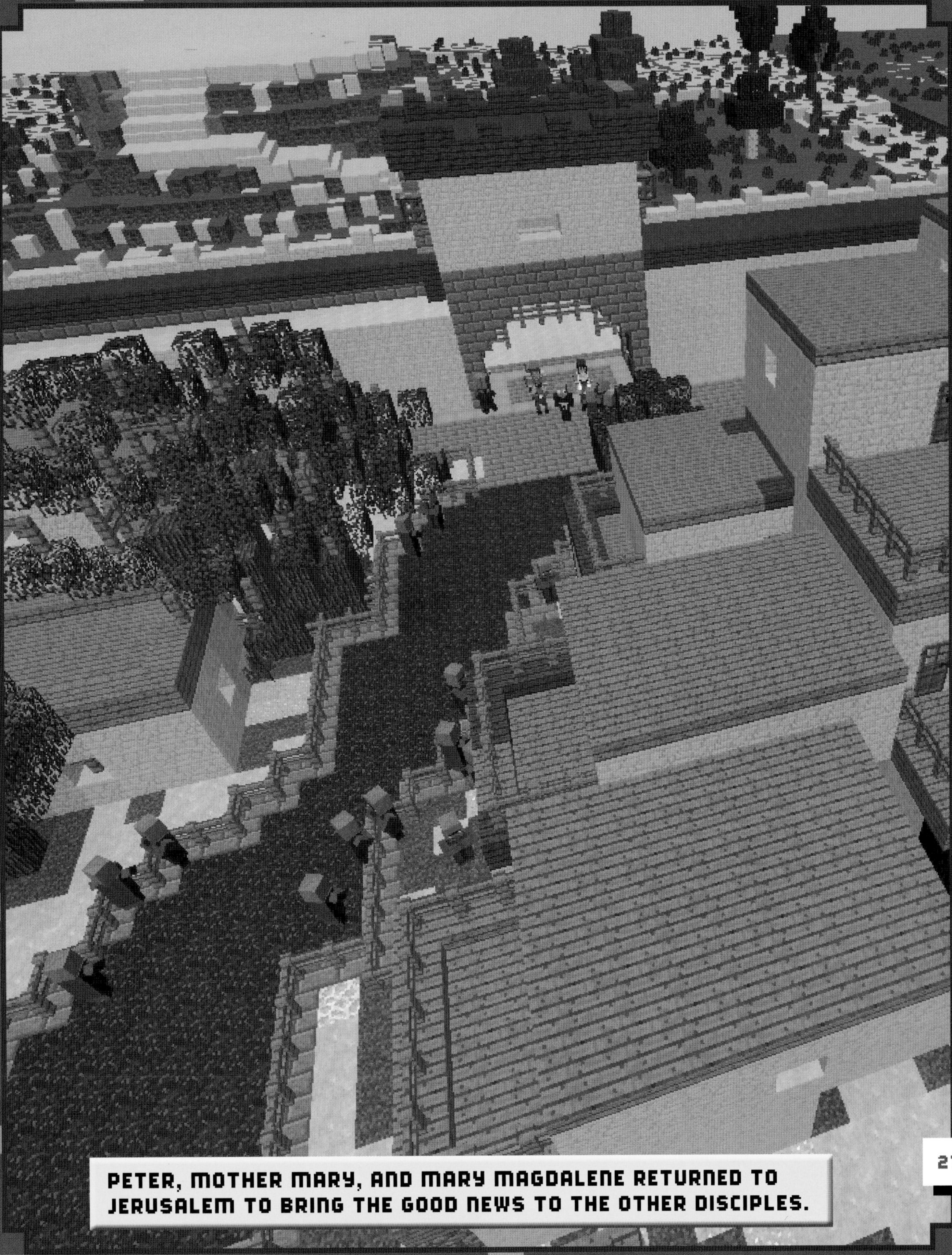
PETER, MOTHER MARY, AND MARY MAGDALENE RETURNED TO JERUSALEM TO BRING THE GOOD NEWS TO THE OTHER DISCIPLES.

JESUS ASCENDS TO HEAVEN

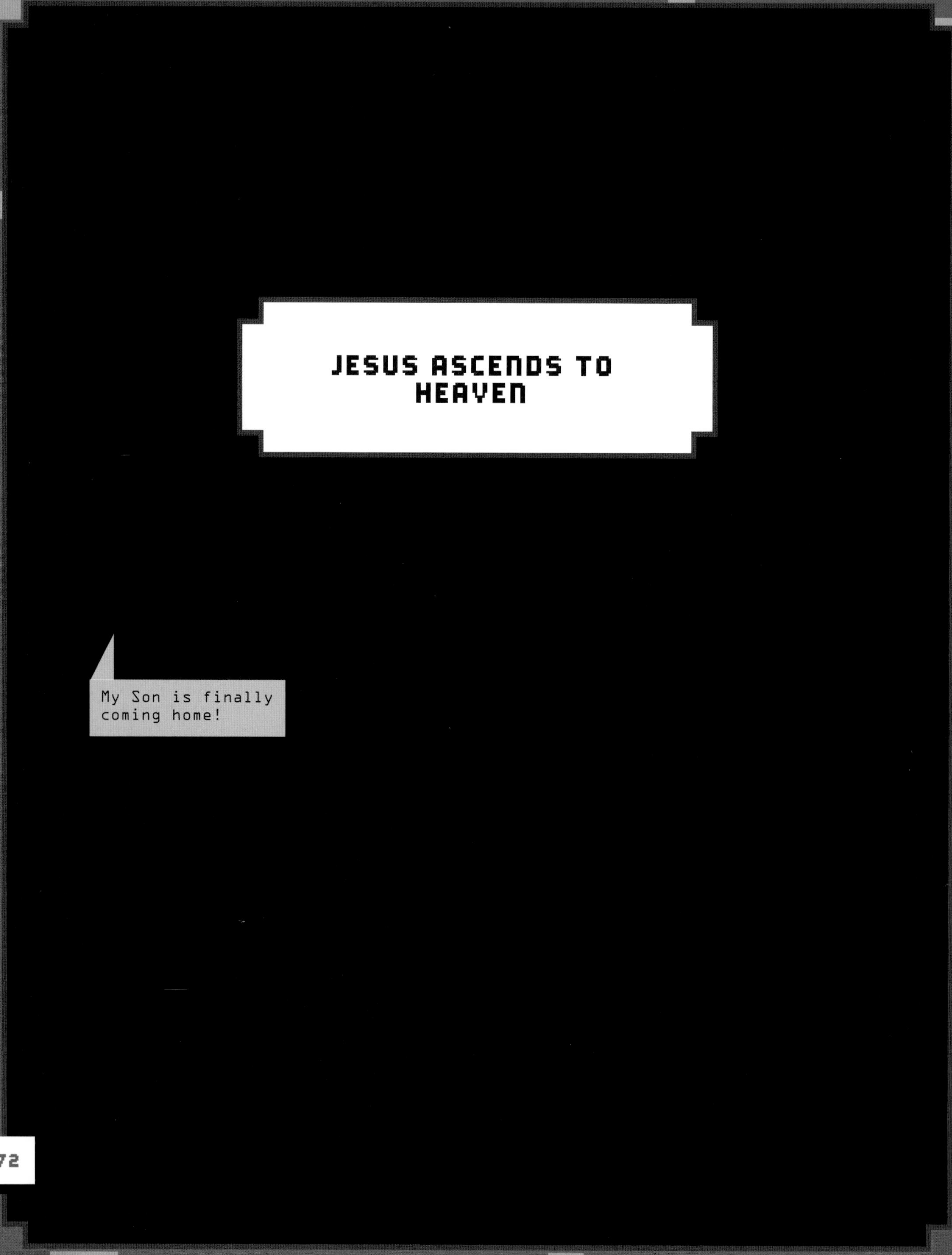
My Son is finally coming home!

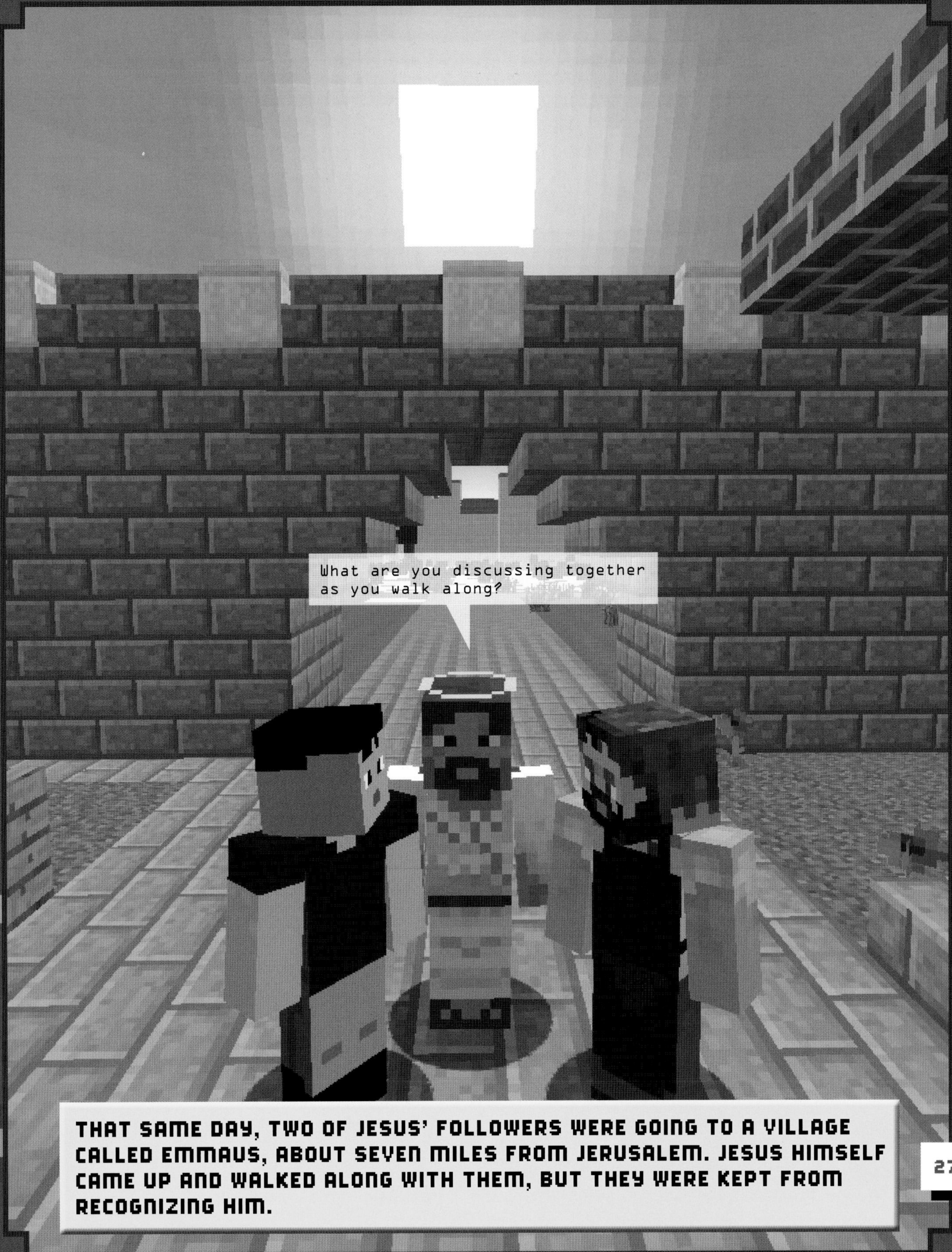
What are you discussing together as you walk along?
THAT SAME DAY, TWO OF JESUS' FOLLOWERS WERE GOING TO A VILLAGE CALLED EMMAUS, ABOUT SEVEN MILES FROM JERUSALEM. JESUS HIMSELF CAME UP AND WALKED ALONG WITH THEM, BUT THEY WERE KEPT FROM RECOGNIZING HIM.

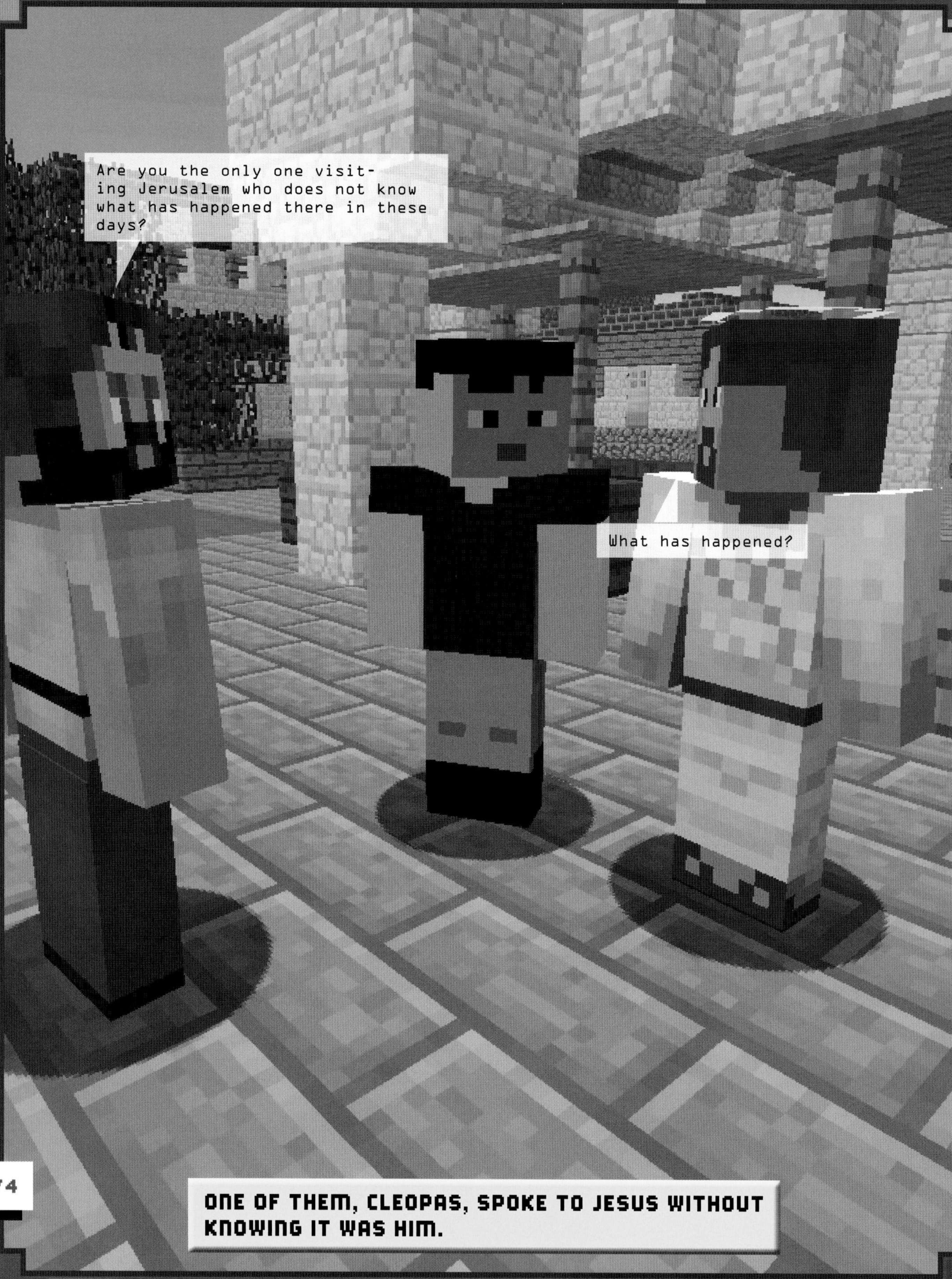
Are you the only one visit-
ing Jerusalem who does not know
what has happened there in these
days?
What has happened?
ONE OF THEM, CLEOPAS, SPOKE TO JESUS WITHOUT
KNOWING IT WAS HIM.

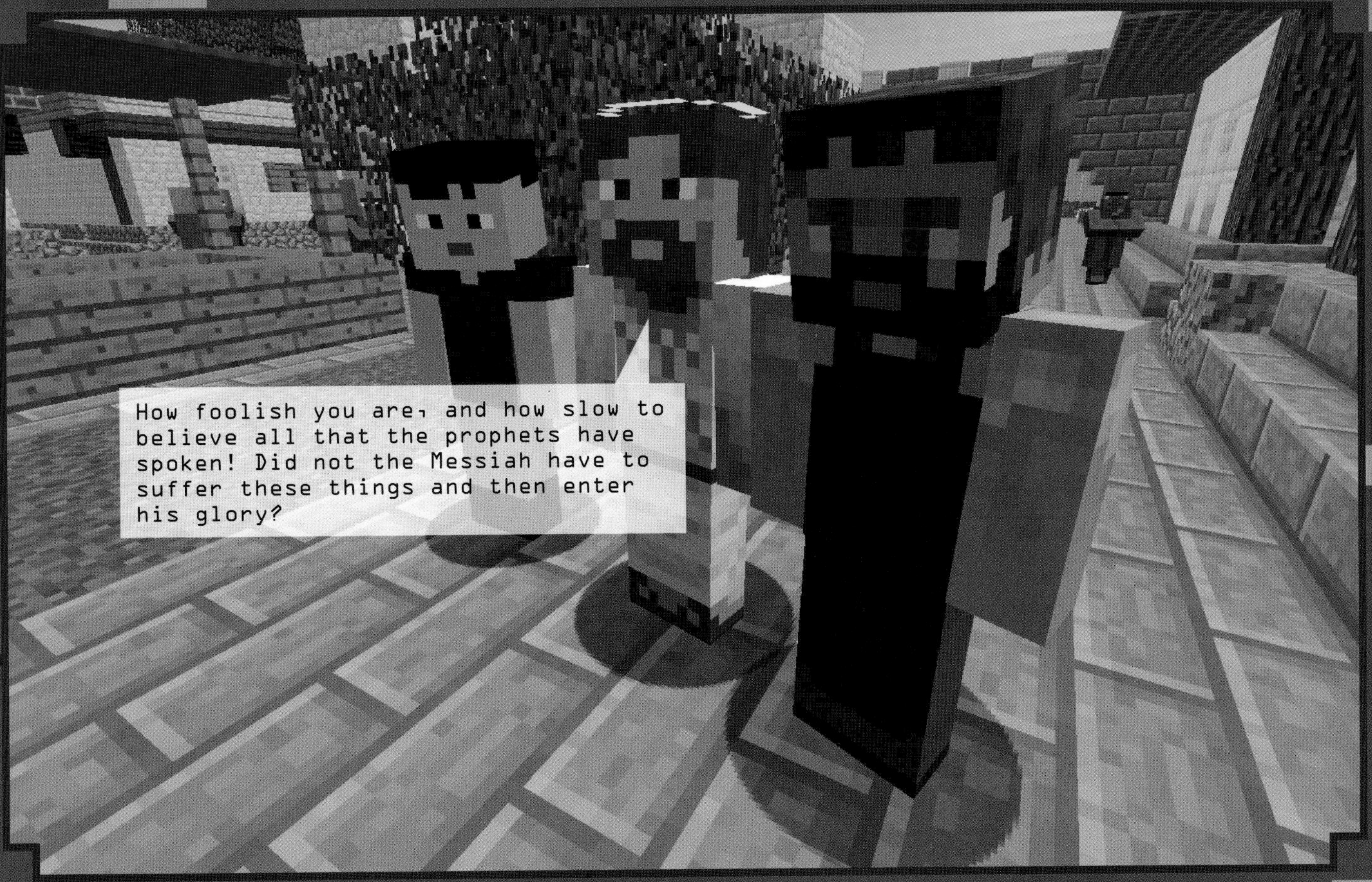
How foolish you are, and how slow to believe all that the prophets have spoken! Did not the Messiah have to suffer these things and then enter his glory?

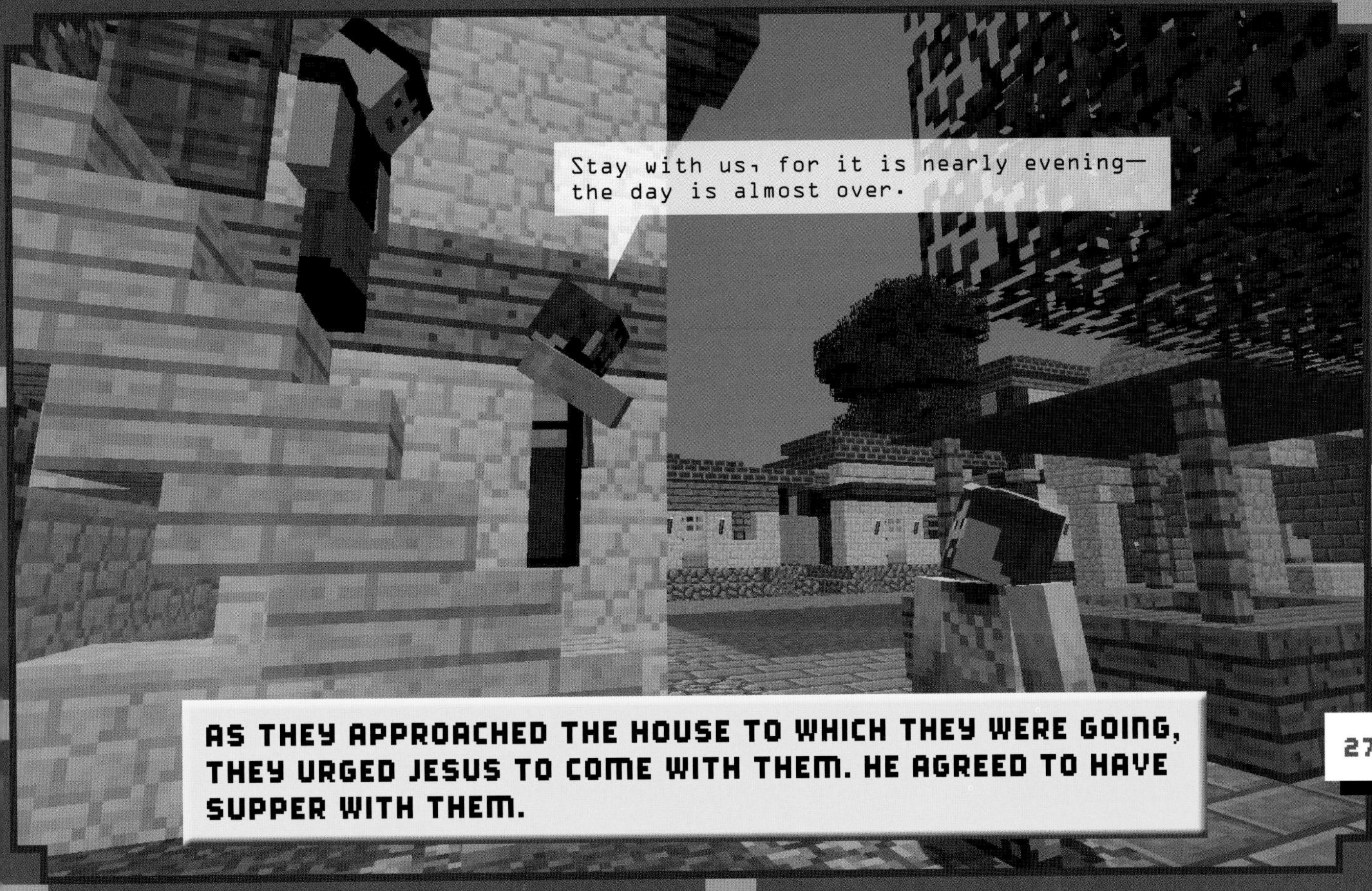
Stay with us, for it is nearly evening—the day is almost over.
AS THEY APPROACHED THE HOUSE TO WHICH THEY WERE GOING, THEY URGED JESUS TO COME WITH THEM. HE AGREED TO HAVE SUPPER WITH THEM.

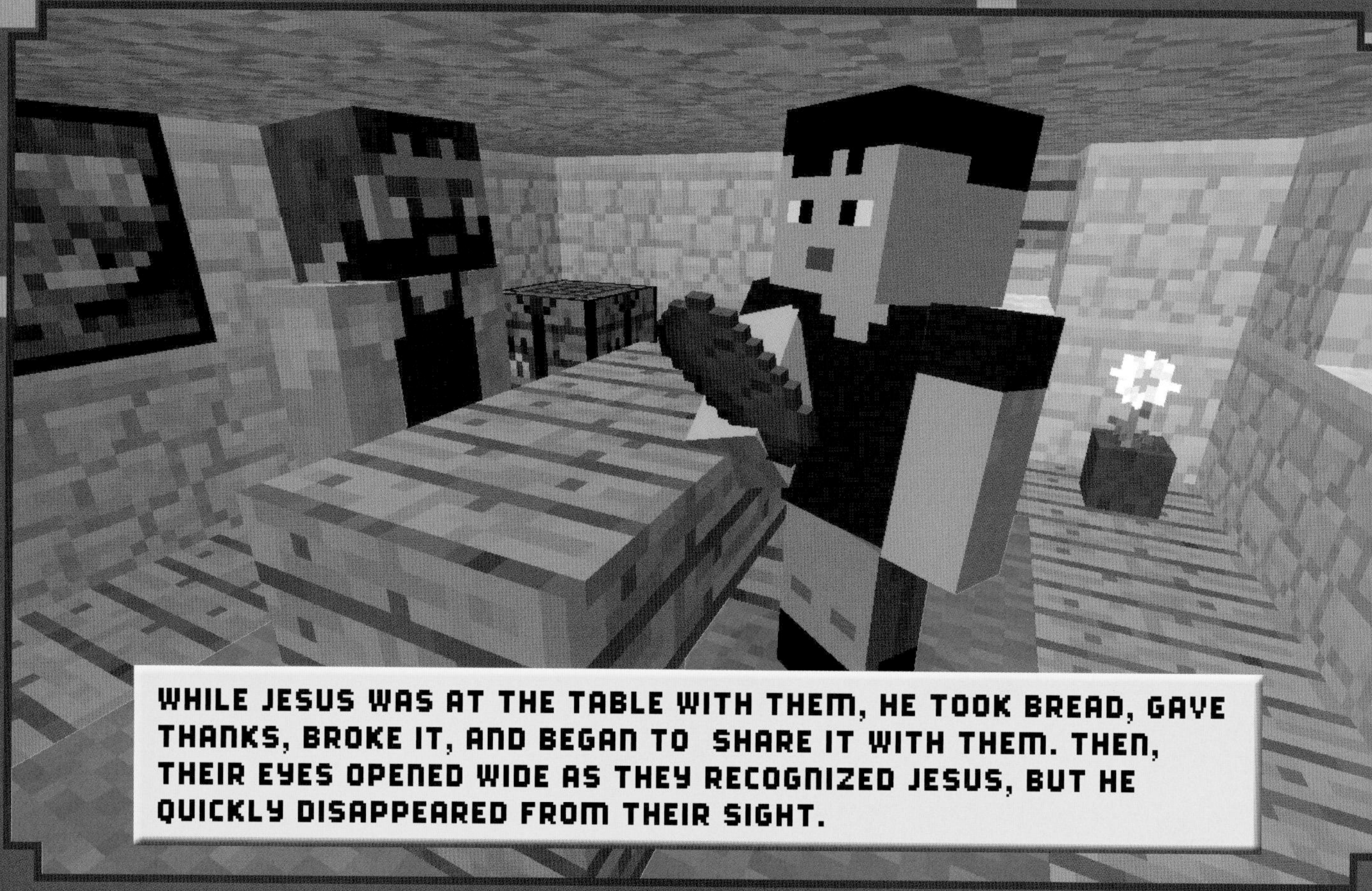
WHILE JESUS WAS AT THE TABLE WITH THEM, HE TOOK BREAD, GAVE THANKS, BROKE IT, AND BEGAN TO SHARE IT WITH THEM. THEN, THEIR EYES OPENED WIDE AS THEY RECOGNIZED JESUS, BUT HE QUICKLY DISAPPEARED FROM THEIR SIGHT.

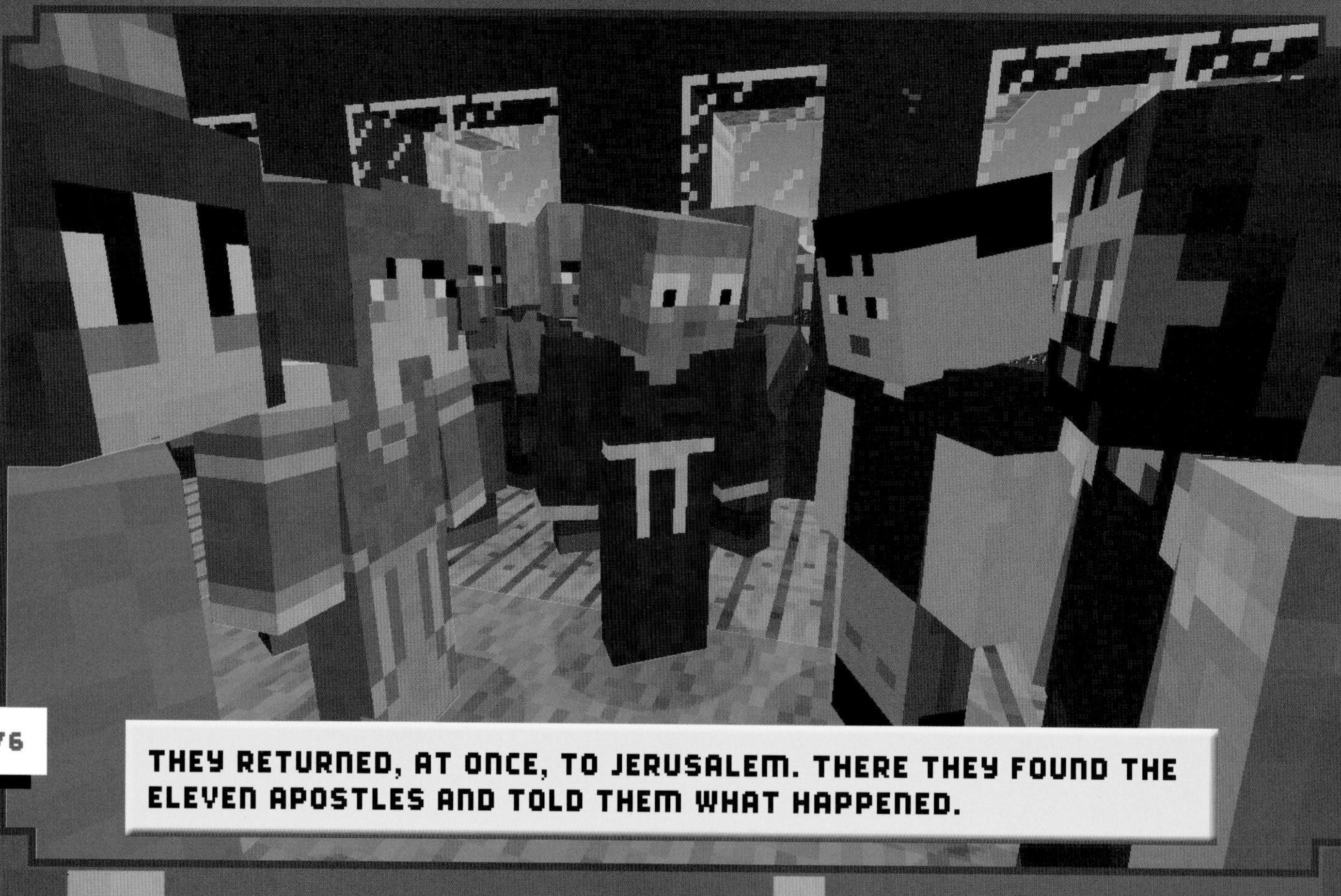
THEY RETURNED, AT ONCE, TO JERUSALEM. THERE THEY FOUND THE ELEVEN APOSTLES AND TOLD THEM WHAT HAPPENED.

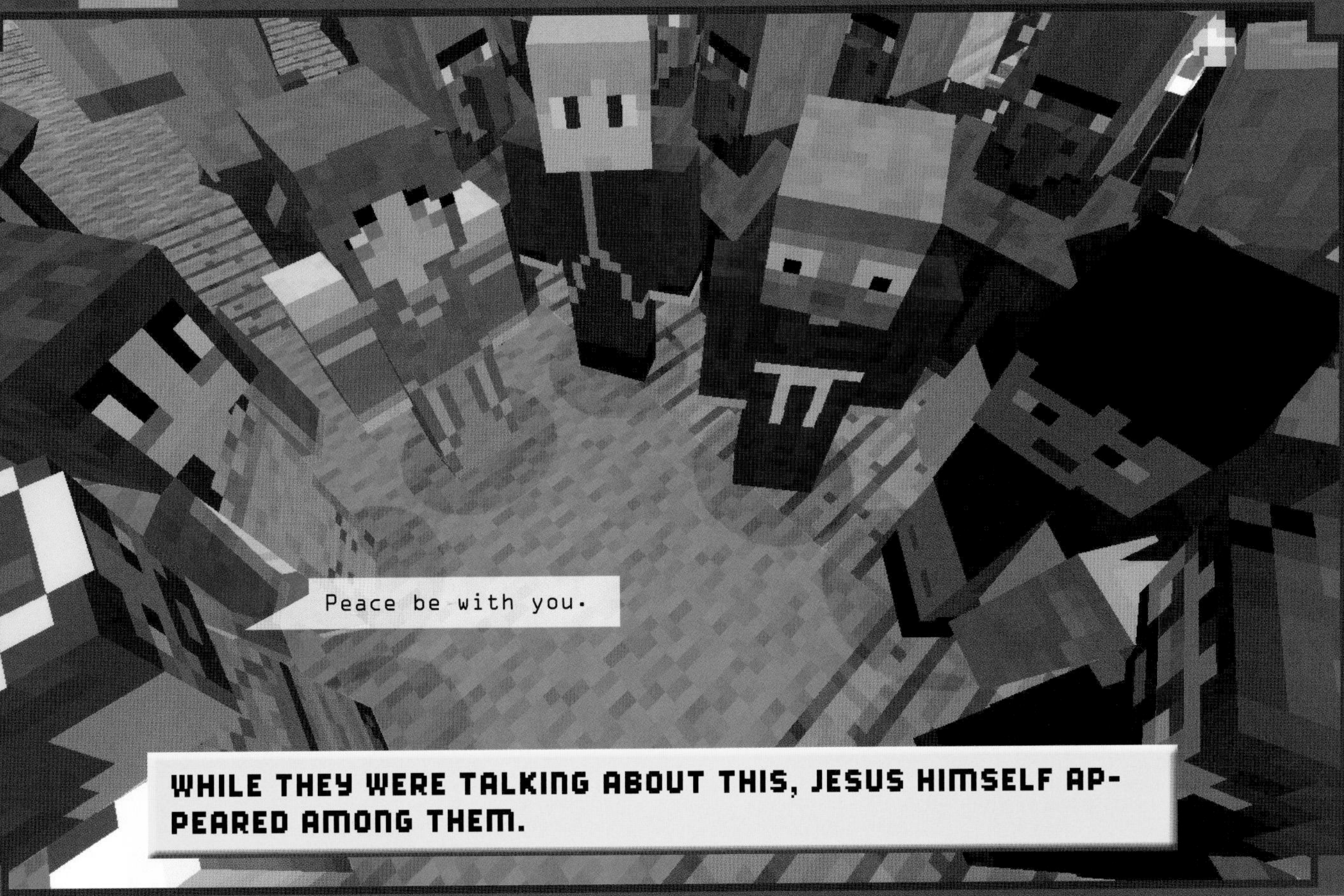
Peace be with you.
WHILE THEY WERE TALKING ABOUT THIS, JESUS HIMSELF APPEARED AMONG THEM.

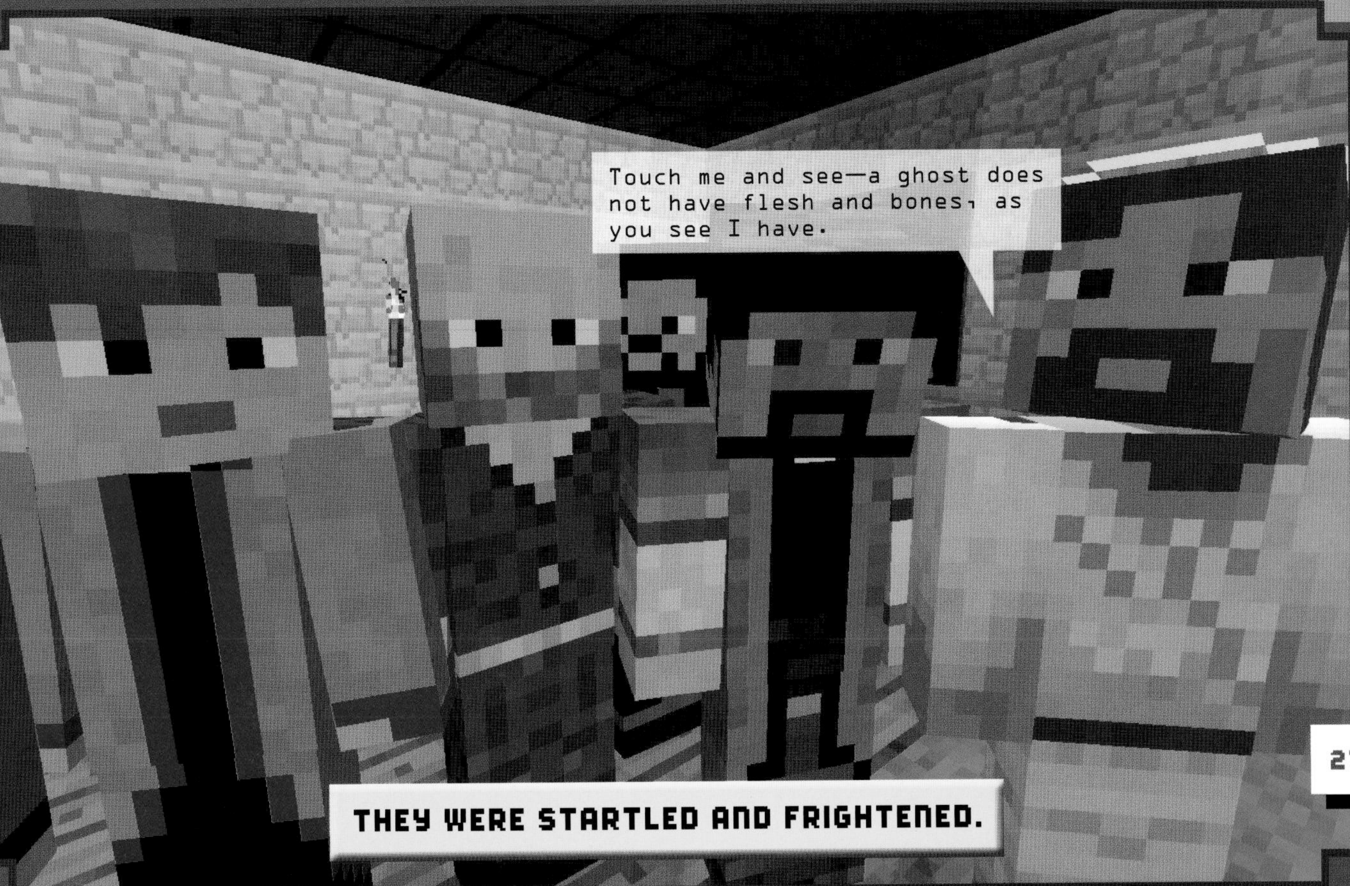
Touch me and see—a ghost does not have flesh and bones, as you see I have.
THEY WERE STARTLED AND FRIGHTENED.

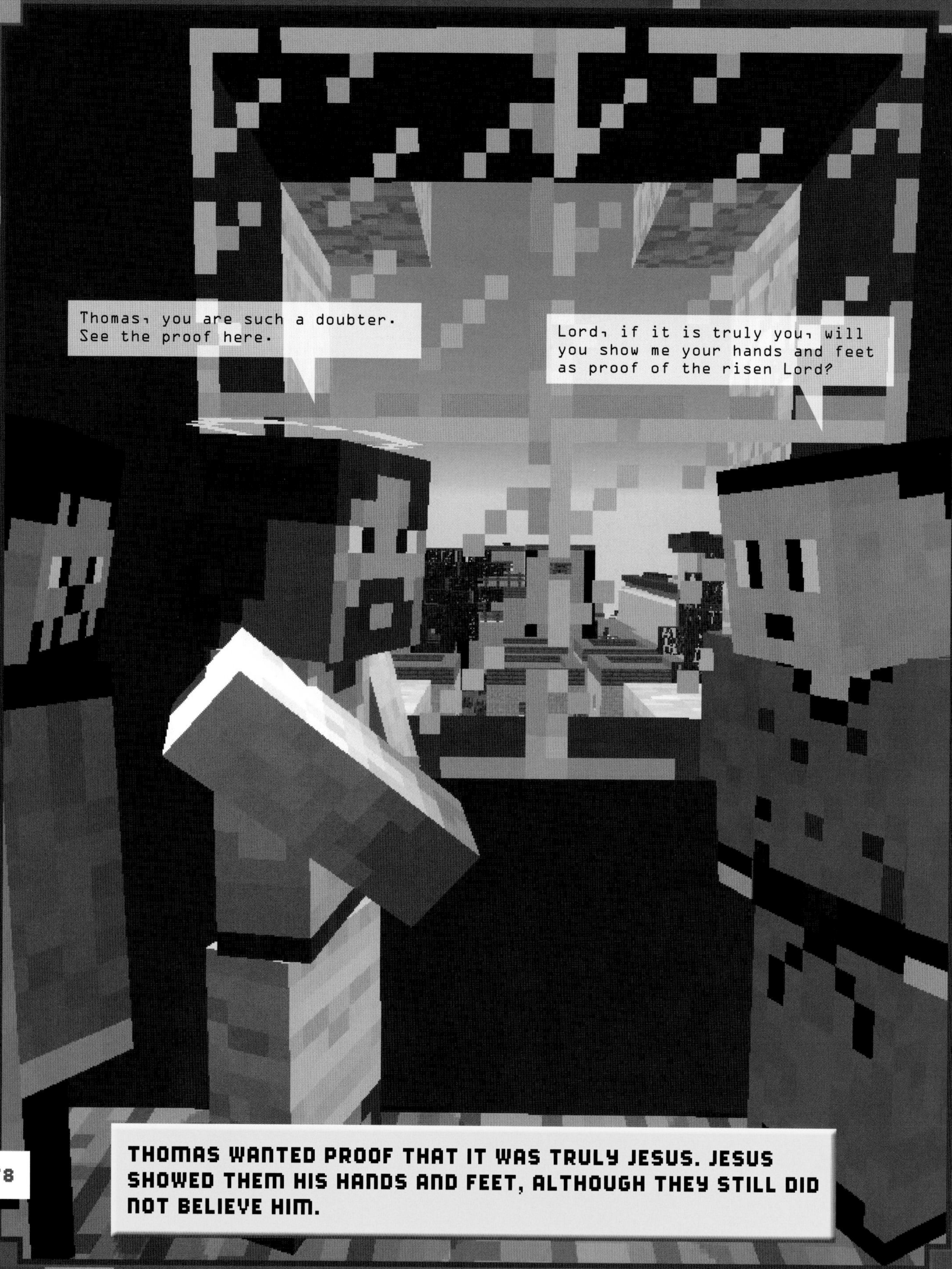
Thomas, you are such a doubter. See the proof here.
Lord, if it is truly you, will you show me your hands and feet as proof of the risen Lord?
THOMAS WANTED PROOF THAT IT WAS TRULY JESUS. JESUS SHOWED THEM HIS HANDS AND FEET, ALTHOUGH THEY STILL DID NOT BELIEVE HIM.

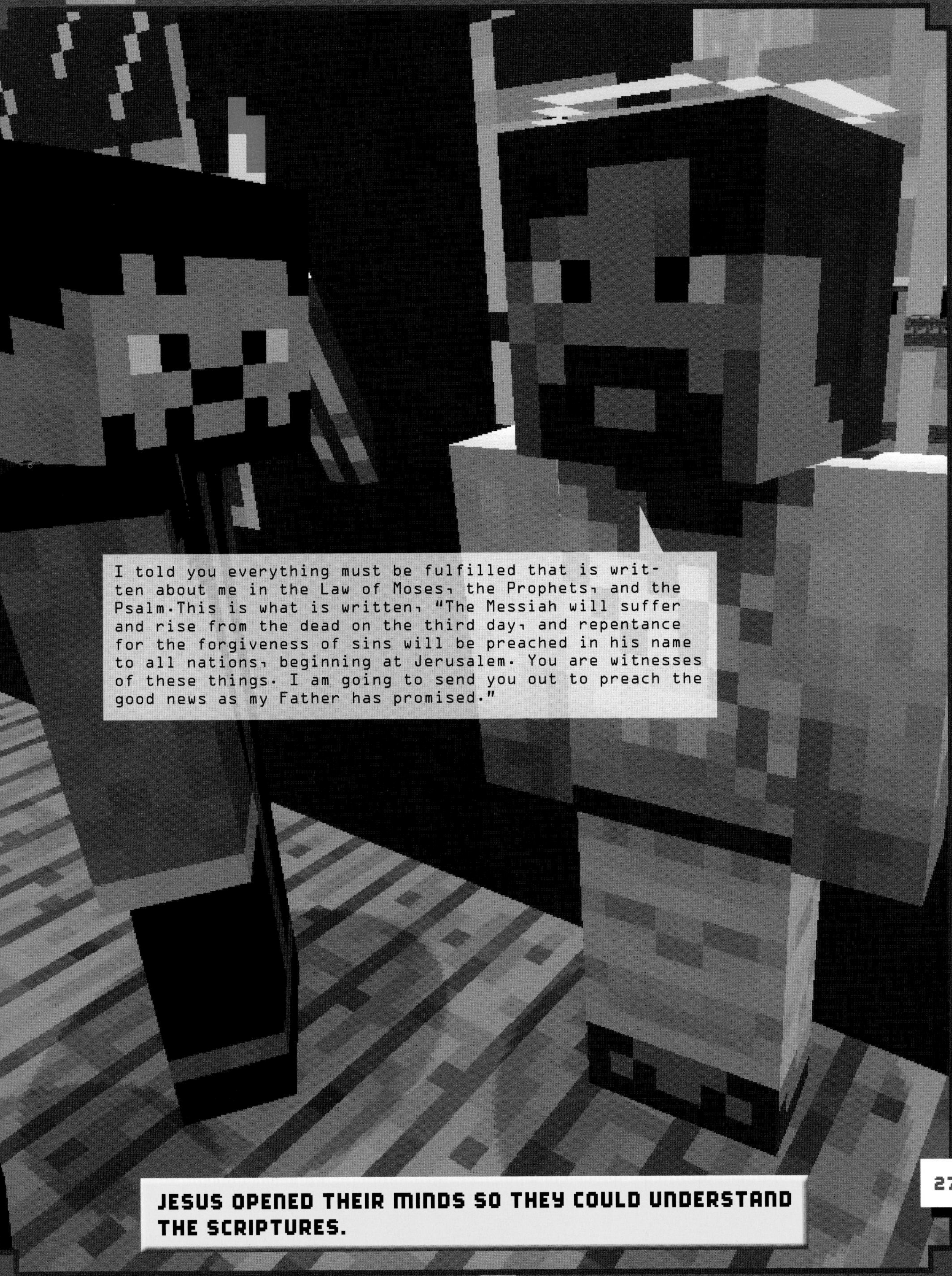
I told you everything must be fulfilled that is written about me in the Law of Moses, the Prophets, and the Psalm.This is what is written, "The Messiah will suffer and rise from the dead on the third day, and repentance for the forgiveness of sins will be preached in his name to all nations, beginning at Jerusalem. You are witnesses of these things. I am going to send you out to preach the good news as my Father has promised."
JESUS OPENED THEIR MINDS SO THEY COULD UNDERSTAND THE SCRIPTURES.

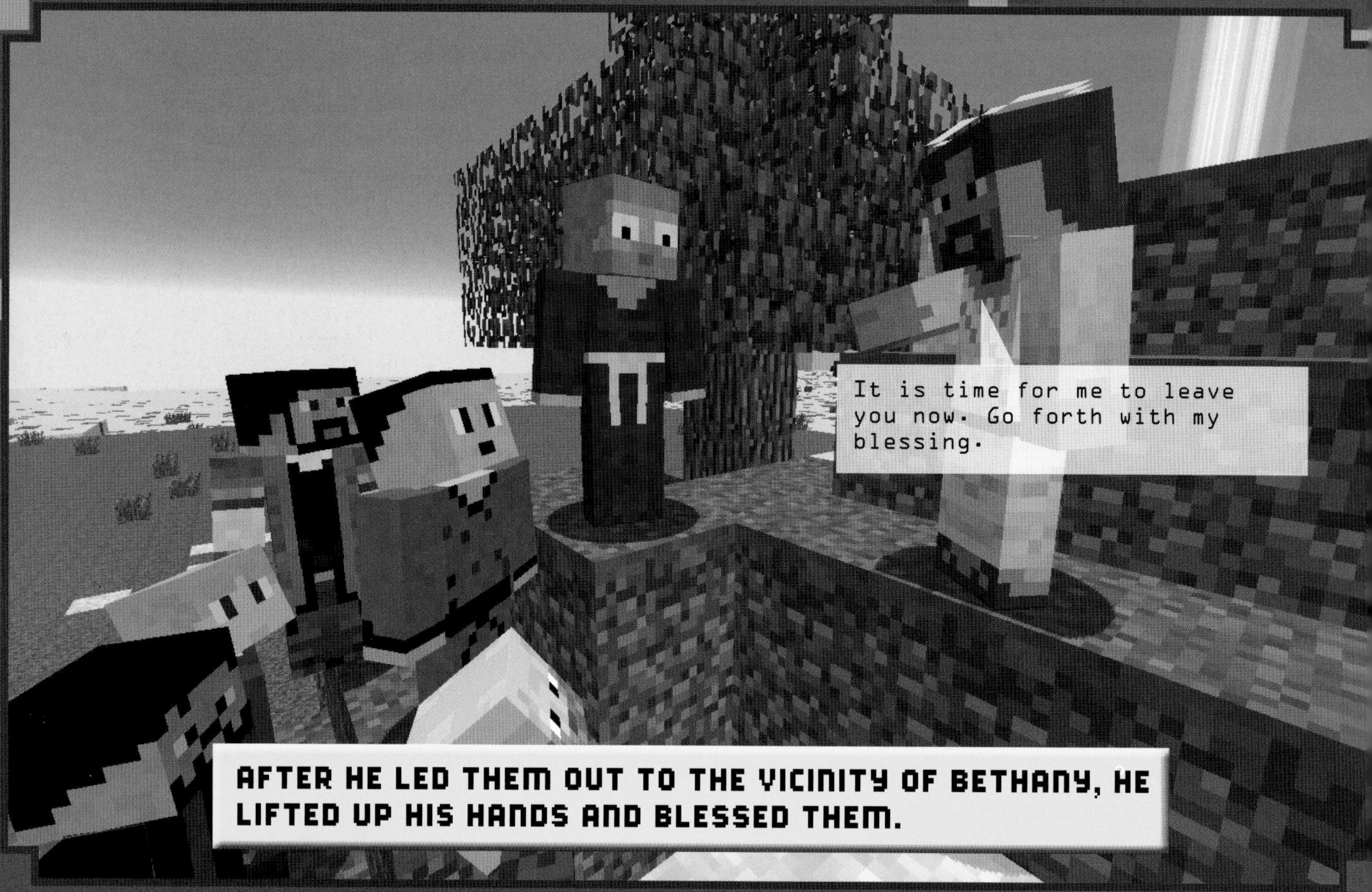
It is time for me to leave you now. Go forth with my blessing.
AFTER HE LED THEM OUT TO THE VICINITY OF BETHANY, HE LIFTED UP HIS HANDS AND BLESSED THEM.

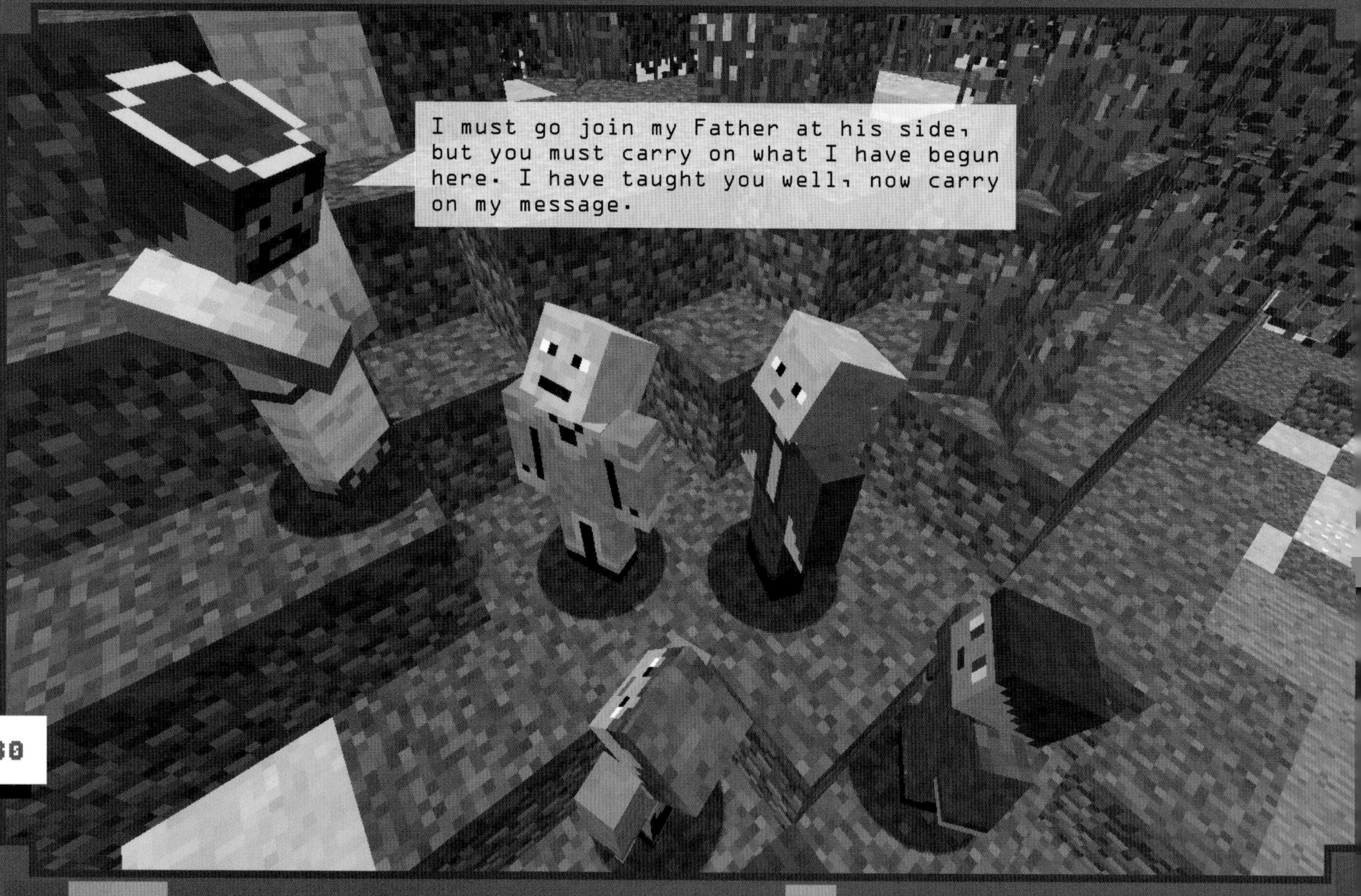
I must go join my Father at his side, but you must carry on what I have begun here. I have taught you well, now carry on my message.

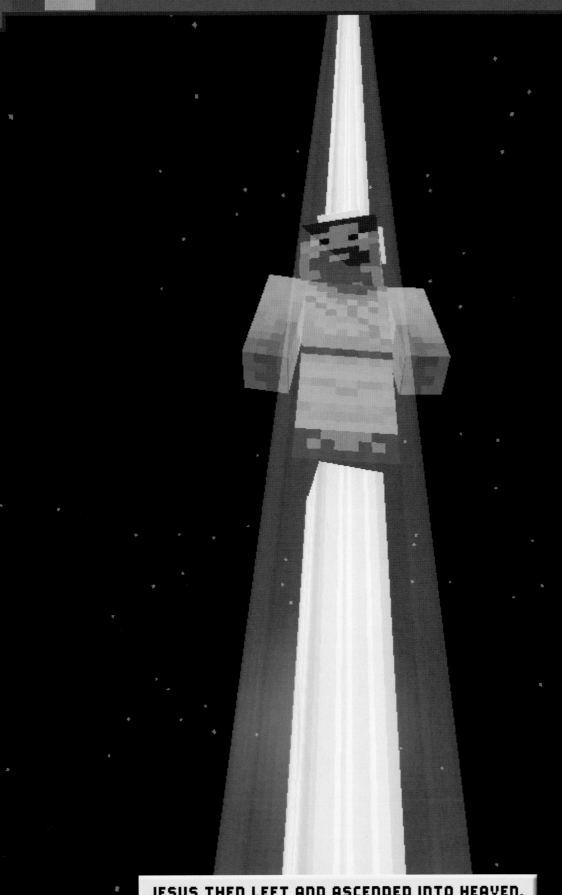

JESUS THEN LEFT AND ASCENDED INTO HEAVEN.

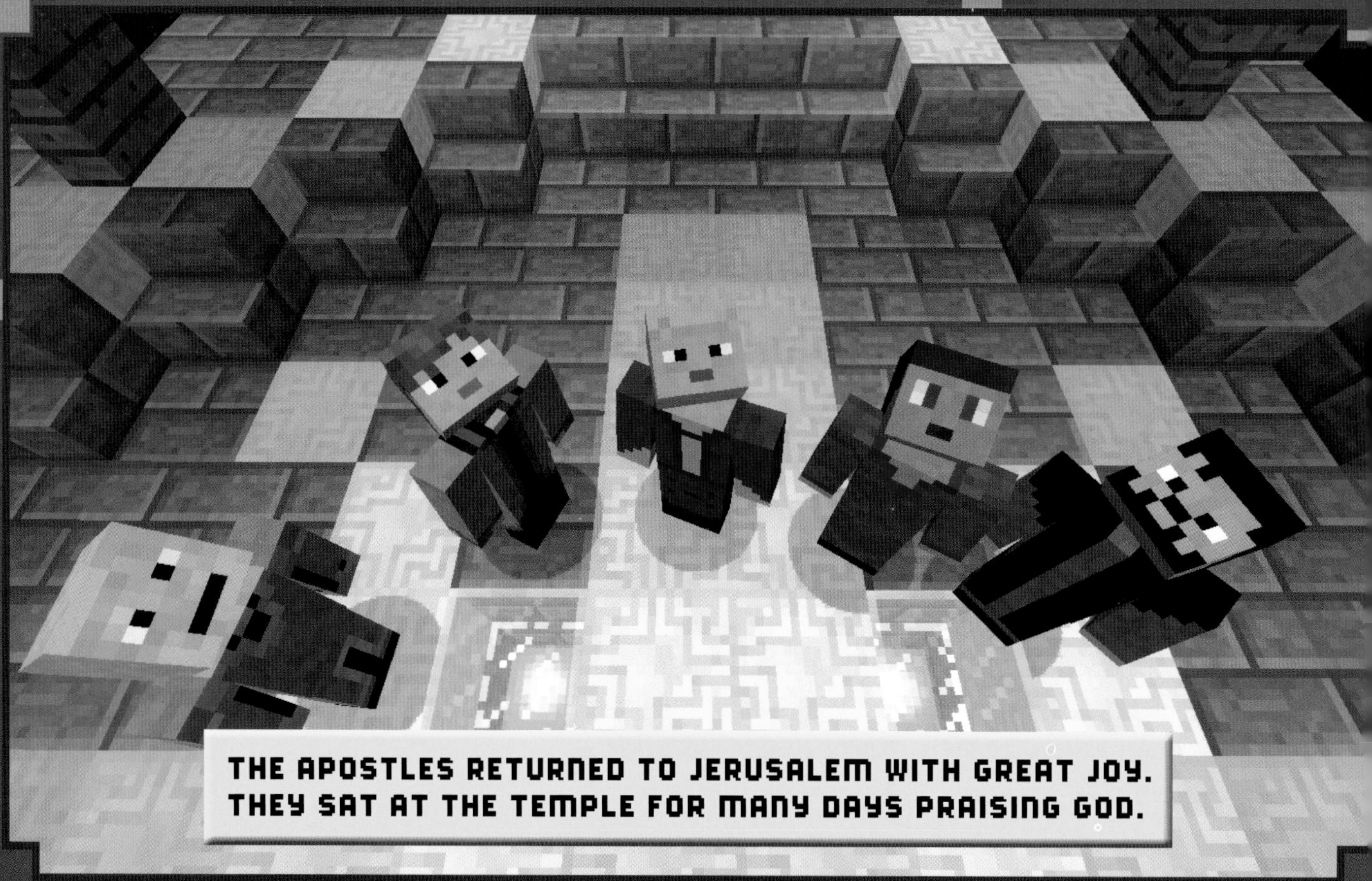
THE APOSTLES RETURNED TO JERUSALEM WITH GREAT JOY. THEY SAT AT THE TEMPLE FOR MANY DAYS PRAISING GOD.

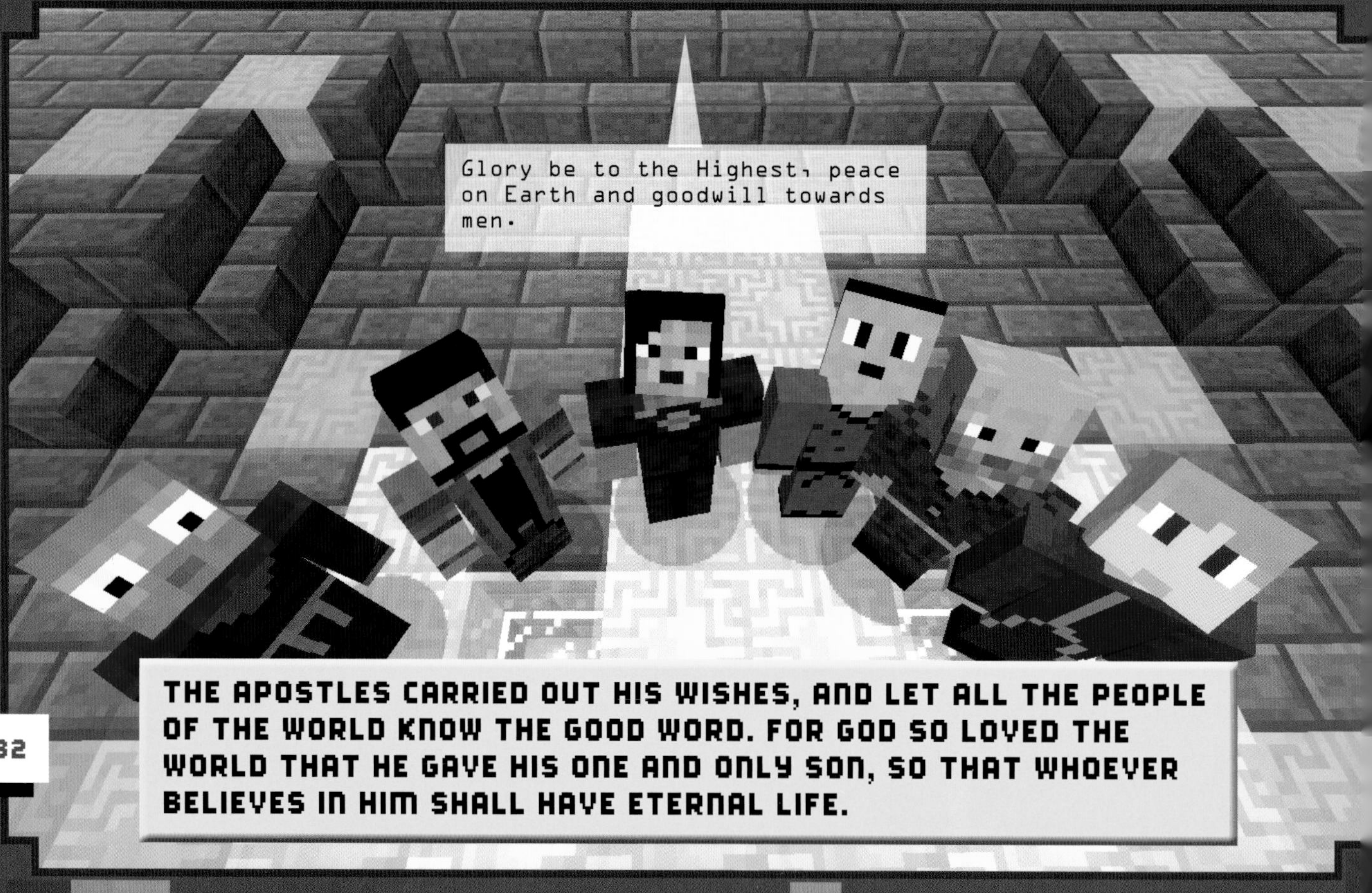
Glory be to the Highest, peace on Earth and goodwill towards men.
THE APOSTLES CARRIED OUT HIS WISHES, AND LET ALL THE PEOPLE OF THE WORLD KNOW THE GOOD WORD. FOR GOD SO LOVED THE WORLD THAT HE GAVE HIS ONE AND ONLY SON, SO THAT WHOEVER BELIEVES IN HIM SHALL HAVE ETERNAL LIFE.